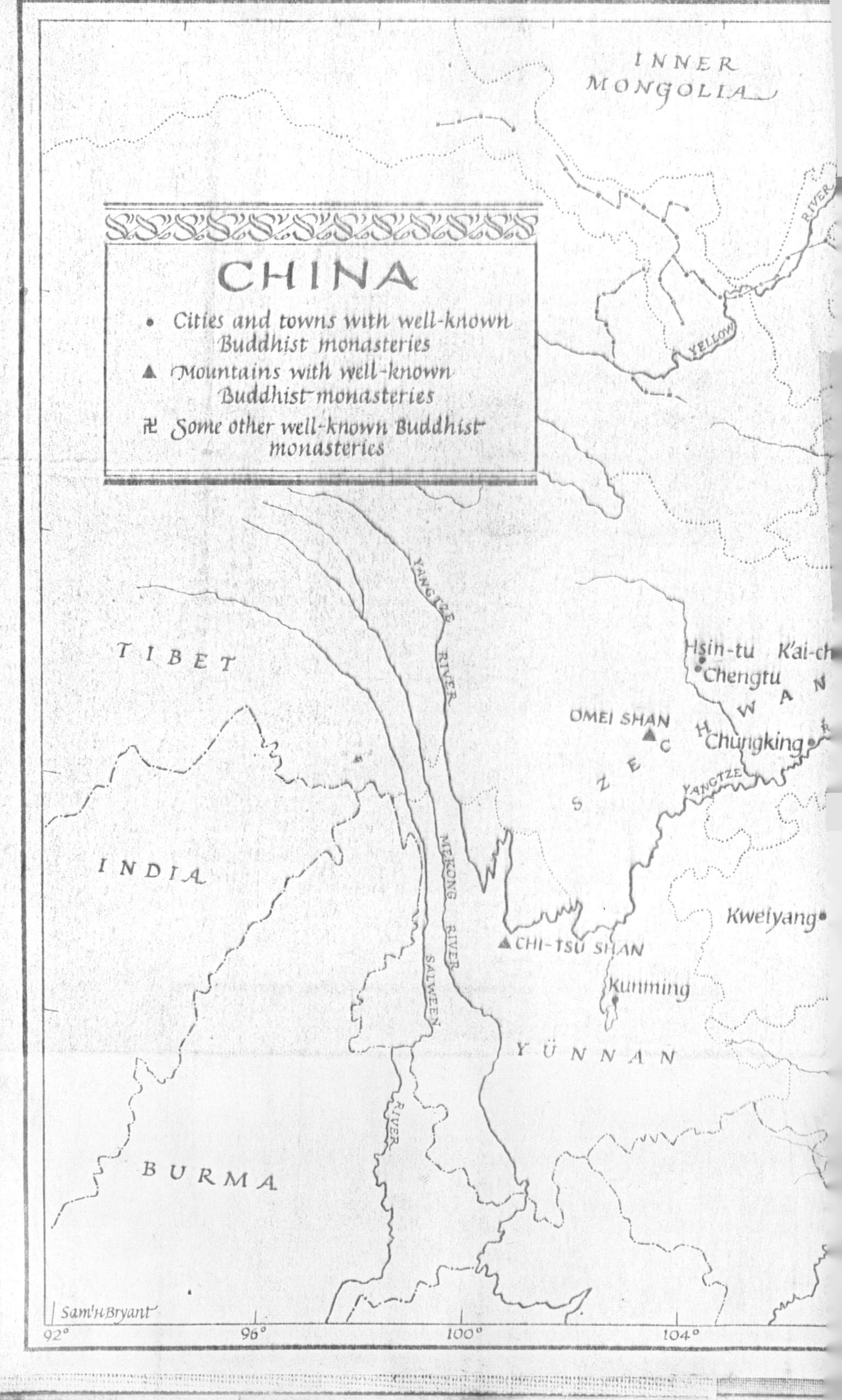
CHINA
• Cities and towns with well-known Buddhist monasteries
▲ Mountains with well-known Buddhist monasteries
卍 Some other well-known Buddhist monasteries
INNER MONGOLIA
YELLOW
RIVER
TIBET
INDIA
BURMA
YANGTZE RIVER
MEKONG RIVER
SALWEEN
RIVER
YANGTZE
SZECHWAN
YÜNNAN
Hsin-tu
Chengtu
OMEI SHAN
Chungking
Kweiyang
CHI-TSU SHAN
Kunming
Sam'l H Bryant
92°
96°
100°
104°

POCKET ON NEXT PAGE

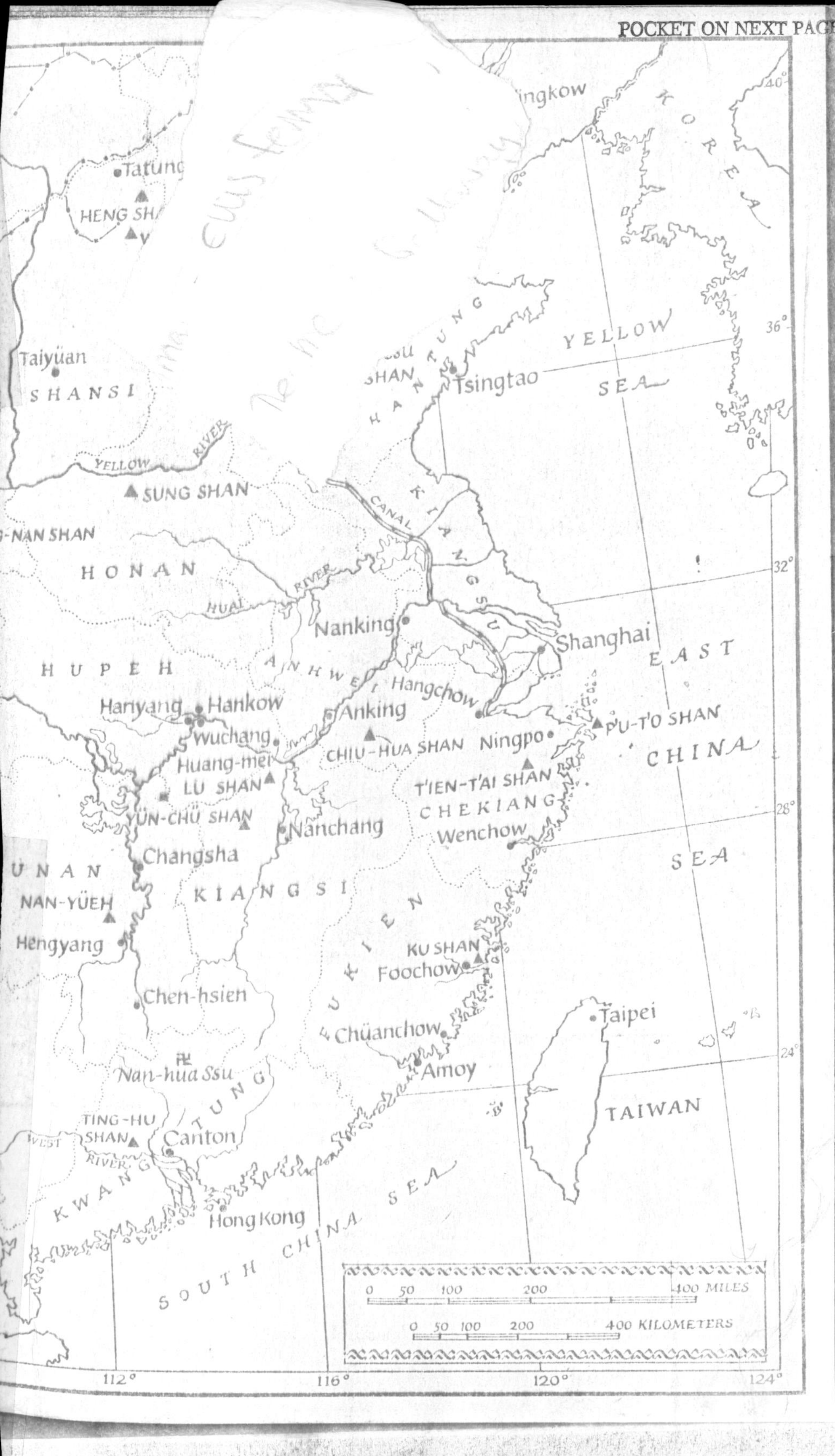

HARVARD EAST ASIAN SERIES 69

Buddhism under Mao

The East Asian Research Center at Harvard University administers research projects designed to further scholarly understanding of China, Japan, Korea, Vietnam, and adjacent areas.

HOLMES WELCH

Buddhism under Mao

HARVARD UNIVERSITY PRESS
CAMBRIDGE, MASSACHUSETTS
1972

Preparation of this volume has been aided by a grant from the Ford Foundation.

Library of Congress Catalog Card Number 72-78428

SBN 674-08565-5

Printed in the United States of America

Preface

This is the last in a series of three books on Buddhism in modern China.* It attempts to give the fullest answer so far to the question: What happens to religion in a Communist state? Implicit in this is the more poignant question: What happens to the men of religion who try to accommodate to Communism or even to find in it a chance for religious renewal?

Although the book is only about Buddhism, I believe it will be useful to those who study broader Chinese problems. First is the problem of Chinese culture, which has been a heavy burden for a nation trying to make rapid progress. How has Mao Tse-tung gone about keeping the grain while discarding the chaff or turning it into useful fuel? The fate of Buddhism provides a good illustration. Second is the problem of the "average man." We know a lot about political and intellectual leaders in China today; about heroes and models; but much less about the majority of the population, whose political awareness is low, who are poor, cautious, and backward. How have they reacted to coöperativization, political study, and mass movements? Again, Buddhists provide a good illustration. Third is a problem of cognition. People who are interested in Mao's China have very different pictures of it; indeed it is sometimes hard to believe that they are talking about the same

*The preceding volumes were *The Practice of Chinese Buddhism 1900-1950* (Cambridge, Mass.: Harvard University Press, 1967) and *The Buddhist Revival in China* (Cambridge, Mass.: Harvard University Press, 1968), which dealt respectively with the institutions and history of Buddhism in China in the decades before 1949.

country. The way Chinese have presented Buddhism to foreign Buddhists illustrates how this can happen.

The present volume has been more difficult to write than its predecessors, first of all because sources of information have been scant and have grown steadily scanter. Far fewer Buddhist books and journals have been published since 1949 than in the Republican period. Even in what has been published, government control of the press (far more efficient than under the Nationalists) has eliminated much of the news and comment that are needed to write a balanced account. Oral information has also been poorer. Since the mass exodus of 1949-50, very few Buddhist monks and nuns have managed to come abroad. Whereas in the case of the first two volumes a statement by one witness could often be confirmed by another or, if not, by a documentary source, that has seldom been possible in the present case.

Second, the first two volumes were noncontroversial: they had no implications for the political issues that divide people today. When it comes to Communist China, on the other hand, almost any statement is controversial, since it can be interpreted as praise or blame of Maoism. This book should be welcomed by authentic Maoists as a tribute to the dexterity and resourcefulness with which Mao Tse-tung has tried to cure the Chinese people of their addiction to religion. It should also be welcomed by professional anti-Maoists, for whose various mills it should provide considerable grist. But those who are simply friendly towards Communist China will, I am afraid, see it as a slanted, hostile attack. Because it is a dreary tale, unenlivened by suspense or success, they will find it tiresome to read; and they will demand proof of many of its assertions. It is most of all the need for proof that has made it such a difficult book to write.

The history of Chinese Buddhism since 1949 involves millions of people diffused over a vast area with many regional differences. I have tried to find out how many of their institutions and practices have changed and how much. This is the kind of information that the new regime, with its apparatus extending for the first time to the local level, has collected but not chosen to release. Until 1958 it was releasing fairly accurate figures on national production of grain and steel; but it has never revealed, for example, how many monks were ordained and disrobed in any year, either throughout the nation or in any locality. All I have been able to cull from the Mainland press are individual cases, not only of fluctuations in the clergy, but of every other significant change affecting Buddhists–land reform, coöperativization, political study, movements, struggle, and so on. Sometimes I have collected five cases, sometimes twenty, almost never more than fifty. To generalize about the activities of millions of people from twenty cases involving a few hundred people, especially when the cases do not reflect a representative sampling of areas and population groups, is methodological folly. But I have had to do it, as have many other writers on social change in Communist China since 1949.

What has particularly troubled me, since I care about making books readable, is the necessity for citing a good many of these cases, for giving a substantial part of the evidence I have collected. I have tried to relegate as much as possible to notes and appendices and to include in the text only the most important or interesting material. This has made the notes unusually numerous and long. I hope that most readers will ignore them and simply read ahead without interruption by superscript numbers.

Some readers will wonder whether I have used the evidence fairly. Have I cited only those cases that support my argument and omitted the rest? No, I have not done this, but I have tried to correct for imbalances that are inevitable when news detrimental to government aims is being systematically suppressed and news that serves them is being systematically inflated. For example, I have not cited all the reports of political study by monks, since all concerned, cadres as well as monks, were under pressure to submit such reports. When study campaigns were underway, the rise in the number of reports has (in my opinion) been disproportionately higher than the rise in the actual amount of study. Conversely, I have picked up almost every mention of monks' *failure* to study, since only a minority of such cases would have been made public, either to fulfill a quota of self-criticism or as a contribution to attacking an officially sanctioned target. This methodology will not be acceptable to those who believe that political pressures have not existed in China and that the press has been free.

Another method I have used to correct imbalances has been to draw on the reports of foreign visitors and refuges. Of course, they too have seen only a minute fraction of Chinese reality; and among them too each has his own selective bias. In addition, refugees often want to ingratiate themselves with the person who is interviewing them (although I have encountered this less often with Buddhist monks than with other refugees); and they may feel the need to paint a dark picture of the motherland in order to justify their having abandoned it. Many critics of China-watching would therefore discount whatever refugees say (just as they would, I presume, discount any statement about Nazi Germany made by the Jews who fled in the 1930's). This seems to me a little theoretical. In practice one learns to detect and correct for much of the distortion in oral as in documentary sources. What is more important, perhaps, is that by patient collation, particularly of details too trivial for people to think of distorting, one can learn a great deal. Ultimately a book like this has to depend on using odds and ends of inadequate data to make judgments, rather intuitively, about what *probably* happened.

Intuitive judgment is peculiarly liable to bias. What then are my biases? Only one is relevant, perhaps. Having studied Chinese Buddhism for some years, I have come to feel an affinity for it and to believe that it made life in China a little more tolerable for a majority of the people. So I am biased against its liquidation and occasionally express this in indignant asides—though never, I believe, in deliberate distortion.

For the chance to carry on my work over the past ten years I am indebted to Professor John K. Fairbank. His readiness to extend it has indicated a confidence in its value that has encouraged me more than any other factor. During the first three years I was largely supported by the Joint Committee on Contemporary China; and during three other years I was partly supported by the Center for the Study of World Religions, Harvard University. During the entire period I have been associated with Harvard's

East Asian Research Center and have benefited repeatedly from the suggestions and advice of fellow members.

I want to thank Vincent S. C. Shui for his great help in 1963 culling material from some Mainland periodicals; Edward C. M. Chan for information on Canton; Richard Gard for a microfilm of early copies of *Hsien-tai fo-hsüeh*; P'ei Yu-ming for the loan of copies of *Chüeh yu-ch'ing*; and the staff of the Union Research Institute for their courteous assistance on many occasions. I have also received valuable help from Marianne Bastid, Hubert Durt, Anna K. Seidel, N. Aramaki, H. Nagasaki, K. Tachibana, Zunvair Yue, Yen Chih-shih, and Mrs. John Quirk. I owe a particular debt to Makita Tairyo of the Jimbun Kagaku Kenkyūsho, who has shown me boundless generosity with his time and with rare materials in his possession.

This volume would not be what it is were it not for the kindness of D. du Boulay, who photographed many Chinese monasteries in 1962 and then made prints available to me—over three hundred in all. They are a precious supplement to the collection of Johannes Prip-Møller.

My family and friends have given me valuable suggestions and criticism of the manuscript. I thank them every one. Finally I want to thank Mrs. S. C. Chiu who has, as always, provided final copy of sparkling excellence.

Acknowledgments

Permission has kindly been granted by the *Far Eastern Economic Review* for the reprinting of the two articles in Appendices E and F.

Permission has kindly been granted by *The China Quarterly* and *Asian Survey* for the use of parts of other articles by the author that first appeared in their pages.

Permission has kindly been granted by the following to publish photographs supplied by them: Henri Cartier-Bresson, Fernand Gigon, Neale Hunter, Kyodo Photo Service, Makita Tairyo, Mibu Shojun, United Press International, and Yanagi Ryoken.

Contents

Appendices

Illustrations

Buddhism under Mao

Chapter I

A Policy Emerges

Until the Cultural Revolution began in 1966, it was the policy of the Chinese Communist Party to protect Buddhism, while at the same time keeping it under control and utilizing it in foreign policy. Yet in the first years after Liberation there were places in China where monasteries were destroyed, monks were beaten or killed, copies of the Buddhist canon were burned, and sacred images were melted down for their metal. In these places the sangha or Buddhist clergy, already worried about the effects of land reform, was reduced to "a state of terror."[1]

How could such things happen if the policy was one of protection? The answer is that the leadership was preoccupied with matters more important than religion. The policy had not yet emerged. Over the preceding decades many cadres had been inculcated with doctrinaire Marxist hostility towards anything religious, the momentum of which took time to reverse. The Party's treatment of monks and monasteries during these decades had itself been ambiguous, and hostile cadres could find ample precedents for regarding them as "symbols of feudal superstition."[2] Even the writings of Mao Tse-tung contained ambiguities.

Mao's first reference to the question was in his report "An Investigation into the Peasant Movement in Hunan," originally written in March 1927. In several passages he praised the anti-religious activities of the peasant associations: "Everywhere religious authority totters as the peasant movement develops. In many places the peasant associations have taken over the temples of the gods as their offices. Everywhere they advocate the appropriation of temple property in order to start peasant schools and to defray the expenses of the associations, calling it 'public revenue from superstition.' In Liling county prohibiting superstitious practices and smashing idols have become quite the vogue."[3] This last sentence is explained in a later reference to the "Liling prohibitions on incense burning . . . burning ritual paper garments during the Festival of Spirits [the Hungry Ghosts Festival] and pasting up good luck posters at the New Year . . . Religious rites for the dead are prohibited in the Seventh and Twentieth Districts. In the Eighteenth District, it is forbidden to make funeral gifts of money . . . [These developments] represent a revolt against bad social customs."[4]

One can imagine that to a young cadre in 1949, intoxicated with the success of the revolution, these passages would have sounded like a call to follow the example of the peasants of Hunan twenty years earlier, to smash idols, confiscate temples, and put a stop to Buddhist rites. It would have been easy for his eye to slip over another passage, in which Mao said that if the effort to abolish superstition was premature, "the local tyrants and evil gentry will seize the pretext to put about such counter-revolutionary propaganda as . . . 'the peasant association is blasphemous and is destroying religion' . . . It is the peasants who put up the idols and, when the time comes, they will throw the idols out with their own hands . . . It is wrong for anybody else to do it for them."[5]

Similarly, some young cadres in 1949 may have learned that, in the Kiangsi Soviet Republic of 1931, Buddhist monks were disenfranchised and deprived of political freedom and all their land was confiscated;[6] and not have learned that from 1937 to 1947 religious believers were included in the united front and the landholdings of Buddhist monasteries were specifically exempted from confiscation.[7] Even the old and experienced cadres who knew about both policies could not be certain which was now to be applied. It was true that in 1945 Mao had called for the protection of religious believers: "All religions are permitted in China's Liberated Areas in accordance with the principle of freedom of religious belief. All believers in Protestantism, Catholicism, Islam, Buddhism, and other faiths enjoy the protection of the People's Government so long as they are abiding by its laws. Every one is free to believe or not to believe; neither compulsion nor discrimination is permitted."[8] Yet two years later in northern Kiangsu and some other "liberated areas," monks had been executed as landlords and as representatives of feudal superstition.

The first indication that religion might now be protected came in the Common Program, passed by the CPPCC* on September 29, 1949. Article 5 provided for freedom of religious belief along with freedom of thought, speech, assembly, and so on.[9] It did not explain, however, what freedom of religious belief meant in practice, and cadres knew that none of the freedoms provided for in the Common Program were to be enjoyed by undesirable elements of the population, among which Buddhist monks and nuns might well be included. Cadres hostile to Buddhism saw no reason to exempt it from the campaign against feudal remnants.

The Buddhists themselves were being told that protection was on its way. For example, on May 5, 1950, Chou En-lai sent word to a symposium of Buddhist leaders in Peking that "the government in its cooperation with religion is after political, not ideological conformity. Every religion should stay within its proper confines. Christianity should resolutely oppose imperialism, principally American imperialism. *Occurrences in various localities that impair freedom of religious belief have to be censured and corrected with the utmost vigor.*"[10] In October 1950 this summary was published in *Modern Buddhism (Hsien-tai fo-hsüeh),* Peking's new Buddhist journal, and monks in various provinces were in a position to show it to hostile cadres, but of course it would scarcely have had the same effect on them as an official statement, published through regular channels.

Yet even official statements did not have an immediate effect. The first that I know of came in an editorial on the Christian patriotic movement, printed in the *People's Daily (Jen-min jih-pao)* on September 23, 1950.

*That is, the Chinese People's Political Consultative Conference. The full forms of acronyms used in this book, as well as brief definitions of terms like *sangha, bhiksu, Three Refuges,* will be found in the index.

> The religious policy of the Chinese Communist Party and the People's Government is consistent and correct. Article 5 of the Common Program of the CPPCC provides that the people have freedom of religious belief, that is, freedom to believe in a religion and freedom to refuse to believe in a religion. Both aspects of this freedom receive the protection of the law . . . Some people ask, since Communists are thorough-going atheists, then why do they advocate permitting freedom of religious belief? This is because religion came into being and has continued to exist during the time when mankind has been faced with natural and social forces that it felt it could not contend with and so looked to the mystical for help. Therefore only when man has adequate means to put nature at his disposal and thoroughly destroy the exploitative class system and its remnants—only then will religion go to its destruction. Until that time, so long as a part of mankind is technologically backward and hence continues to be dependent on natural forces and so long as a part of mankind has been unable to win its release from capitalist and feudal slavery, it will be impossible to bring about the universal elimination of religious phenomena from human society. Therefore with regard to the problem of religious belief as such, any idea about taking coercive action is useless and positively harmful. This is the reason why we advocate protecting freedom of religious belief, just as we advocate protecting freedom to reject religious belief.[11]

The reasons for tolerating the continued existence of religion were presented still more fully and persuasively in the March 1951 issue of *Study (Hsüeh-hsi),* a journal that was read by almost as many cadres as the *People's Daily*. Since religious concepts reflected the social and economic structure, then why, asked the author, did some people in the Soviet Union still have religious belief? The answer was that the traces of the old Russian society could not be destroyed at one stroke. "As to China, the people's democratic dictatorship has just been established for a little over a year. Our economic system is still that of the New Democracy and is not a socialist one. Therefore it will be quite a long time before our society achieves the basic prerequisites for eliminating religion that were pointed out by Marx. If in the Soviet Union, more than thirty years after the Socialist Revolution, the remnants of old thinking and consciousness have still not been overcome and religion has still not been eliminated, then the fact that here in China we cannot eliminate religion in the immediate future is entirely comprehensible."[12]

While statements of this kind were being published about policy, concrete laws and decrees were being handed down that provided for the physical protection of Buddhist monasteries. For example, the Agrarian Reform Law, promulgated on June 30, 1950, included a prohibition against damaging them.[13] Within the next month this was reinforced by a "very strict order" from the Government Administration Council holding local authorities responsible for the protection of Buddhist buildings and relics that had historical value. Several more such directives were issued in the years that followed.[14]

Yet despite these statements and directives, it is clear that monasteries and monks continued to suffer from deviations on the part of local cadres. Good evidence of this is the rather pathetic statement printed in *Modern Buddhism* for October 1950, explaining to Buddhists why freedom of religious belief could not be precisely defined. It said that at a recent meeting of the Religious Affairs Section of the CPPCC National Committee, the meaning of this guarantee in the Common Program had been given careful study and it had been decided that to define its scope would deprive it of "elasticity" (*ling-huo hsing*). It was true that article 124 of the Soviet Constitution included not only freedom of religious belief but freedom "to hold religious rites," but these provisions could not account for all the different freedoms that Soviet believers enjoyed in practice. They were free to study religion, to print books and conduct religious propoganda, to build temples, to preserve religious cultural objects–and the Soviet government facilitated this in every way. If the Soviet Constitution had defined–delimited–the scope of freedom of religious belief, then how could Soviet citizens enjoy such privileges? It was the same for Chinese citizens. If the scope of religious freedom were defined, they would not have the protection they now had. "As for some cadres' smashing Buddhist buildings and cultural objects [presumably meaning sacred images], prohibiting the propagation of the doctrine, confiscating sutras, and so on, these are unfortunate occurrences that cannot be avoided in the revolutionary stage: the central authorities are just now doing their utmost to rectify things." Anyway, it said, the reason for such occurrences might be partly a failure on the part of Buddhists to make the cadres understand. They should remember that it was their "duty to help local cadres by rectifying [their mistaken ideas]. If a major case cannot be easily resolved at the local level, then it is all right to report to the Ministry of Internal Affairs the concrete facts (note these two words) and to ask that things be investigated and rectified."[15]

Probably such cases became less frequent as policy took clearer shape and penetrated to the lower levels, but, unfortunately for the Buddhists, as it took shape it also became less protective than they had originally hoped. This too was reflected in the pages of *Modern Buddhism.* For example, in 1951 a reader wrote to complain about the cadres' "elimination" of small temples around Wusih, which had made Buddhists respond less enthusiastically to appeals that they undertake political study. "It is our duty," he concluded, "to issue correct instructions that will let them, on reasonable conditions, enjoy the right to religious freedom and make them realize that the weeding out now underway is not haphazard." He was answered by Chü-tsan, the editor-in-chief.

> Freedom of religious belief is stated as clear as day in the Common Program and it will not be compromised. However, one must realize that the Common Program is a charter for the era of the New Democracy; and the New Democracy takes as its premises the struggle against imperialism, feudalism, and bureaucratic capitalism, the overthrow of the reactionary power of the Kuomintang, and the purge of open and hidden counterrevolutionary forces. Buddhists who do not accept these premises are either reactionaries or backward elements.

> Reactionaries have no political rights; backward elements do not understand the times and, since in their thinking there is not much trust of the government, the government cannot treat them with the respect and concern that would otherwise be appropriate. Only if they become progressive and join the people of the era of the New Democracy can they fully enjoy all the freedoms in the Common Program . . . Some Buddhists think that, because the Common Program provides for freedom of belief, they can do anything they like and that anyone who corrects their thinking or actions is infringing on their freedom of belief. This is a very big mistake and really is the thinking of backward elements. If something like this can be found in Wusih Buddhist circles, it must be corrected as forcefully as possible. Anyone who does not listen must be denounced to the government. May the joy of the dharma be praised![16]

This statement by Chü-tsan is important because it underlines the fact that freedom of religious belief was not a universal and inalienable right, but a right only to be enjoyed by persons whom the government considered progressive. Chü-tsan himself was such a person.

CHÜ-TSAN

Chü-tsan had been progressive even before he became a monk in 1931. (The reasons why he became a monk are explained in the report translated in Appendix A, on which the following pages are based.) He had studied under the leading Buddhist reformer of the Republican era, T'ai-hsü, and edited a reformist journal in Kweilin during the war. In 1947 he tried unsuccessfully to get support for reform from the Nationalist authorities of Chekiang. The next year, while he was lecturing in Hong Kong, he had a chance to discuss his ideas with men who were soon to become important figures in Peking–Kuo Mo-jo, Shen Chun-ju Chang Po-chün, and Li Chi-shen. Li, whom he had gotten to know in Kweilin, was to be one of the six vice-chairmen of the People's Republic of China.

They agreed that the reform of Buddhism was a major problem, but said that unfortunately no plan for it was yet in sight. Chü-tsan then visited Taiwan to see if the Japanese influence on Buddhism there had been a good one: he concluded that Japan could not provide a model. In the first days of 1949 he was back in Hangchow, drafting a formal proposal for the reform of Chinese Buddhism under Communist rule—the first of several such proposals that he was to make. On January 10 came the great victory that brought the People's Liberation Army to the banks of the Yangtze. Alarm spread through south China and, curiously enough, Chü-tsan was not immune to it. Although he claimed to be sympathetic to the new regime and saw in it a possible patron of the reforms he was planning, he made a hasty exit to Hong Kong. There he polished his proposal and sent it through various intermediaries to the headquarters of the Chinese Communist Party. Perhaps reassured by its reception, he sailed to Peking on April 3 with the wife of Li Chi-shen.

During the next eighteen months he worked with skill and determination as a lobbyist for Buddhism. This was the critical period when policy began to take shape. Chü-tsan may have had a certain influence on the shape it took. His first step was to draft a comprehensive plan for reform, which was sent to Mao Tse-tung himself in May 1949. In an accompanying memorandum he tackled the basic question: why should Buddhism be preserved at all? His answer was that, although it had previously been corrupt, commercialized, full of superstition and feudalism, and infiltrated by heterodox sects, nonetheless its nature "is different from other religions. It is atheist, and advocates the 'realization of selflessness.' This completely corresponds to the spirit of the times. In addition, Tibet and Taiwan, which are awaiting liberation, both revere Buddhism. Neighboring countries such as Indochina, Thailand, Burma, Ceylon, India, Korea, and finally Japan are out-and-out Buddhist countries. If in the course of Chinese revolution the element of Buddhism is ignored, difficulties may arise in liberating Tibet and Taiwan and promoting world revolution. If, on the contrary, in the territory of the New China, Buddhism appears under a new aspect, then it may well facilitate the liberation of the whole country and the promotion of world revolution."[17]

The offer to place Buddhism at the service of world revolution may seem strange and even pitiful, but in actuality it followed a well-established Chinese tradition that religion should serve the goals of the state, and, whereas world revolution was a new goal, consolidation of ties with outlying areas like Tibet was not. Buddhism had been used for this purpose by both the Ch'ing and the Republican governments,[18] as Chü-tsan, of course, knew.

In his memorandum to Mao, Chü-tsan tried not only to show that Buddhism could be useful to the state but also that it could be cleansed of most of the defects that made it objectionable to Marxists. "Two slogans–'shift to production' and 'shift to scholarship'–should be advanced as the targets towards which the reform of all Buddhist institutions should aim. Shifting to production will smash the old feudal economic organization of the monasteries; shifting to scholarship will strengthen Buddhists' knowledge of Buddhism and their orthodox faith so as to eliminate superstition. Only when feudal organization and superstitious ignorance have been done away with can the revolutionary nature of Buddhism come to the fore. This will not be without effect in winning backward people to join the revolutionary forces."[19]

We do not know whether Mao Tse-tung ever read this memorandum, but it was probably read by officials of the United Front Work Department, who were now directly concerned with the formulation of religious policy. In June 1949 Chü-tsan handed them a proposal to set up a "National Committee for the Reorganization of Buddhism." They told him that it was premature, so in October he proposed to set up a local Buddhist association for Peking. They told him that this was premature too.

These disappointments did not mean that his efforts led to nothing. During the summer of 1949 he was chosen one of the two Buddhist delegates to the CPPCC. In the following spring he used the meetings of its Religious Affairs Section as a forum for his ideas. Because the meetings were attended by high ranking officials and because he kept discussing his successive proposals with the United Front Work Department, he became the monk they knew best and were most likely to employ as an activist. He was jockeying to get an advantage over lay Buddhist leaders like Chao P'u-ch'u–competing for leadership against the men with whom he was at the same time collaborating. Thus he repeatedly pointed out that "according to Buddhist scriptures, monks and nuns who have left lay life are in charge of the dharma, whereas Buddhist devotees who remain laymen merely protect the dharma . . . Therefore if we are talking about the reform of Buddhism, discussion must first focus on monasteries and temples headed by monks and nuns, and lay groups headed by devotees must come later."[20] That is, monks were the people who had authority in Buddhist circles and who should be put in charge of whatever the regime wanted to have done.

The denouement of his efforts to influence policy and win power came on June 18, 1950, when seventeen persons, Buddhists and CPPCC delegates, met for dinner at the Sen-lung Restaurant in Peking. Chü-tsan began by presenting his latest reform proposal—the fourth by my count—apparently hoping to win the endorsement of these important people and at last get some action. Chao P'u-ch'u, the Shanghai devotee, countered by saying, in effect, that it was all very well to keep formulating such proposals and presenting them to the government, but it would be better if Buddhists followed the example of Christians and took the initiative in reforming themselves without waiting for government approval and support. Other laymen present suggested that reform should be tried out first in a few localities; that local groups should be set up before a national association; and, in any case, that plans should be further discussed before anything was done. Shirob Jaltso, the most important lama then in Peking, added that it was fine to reform the organizational side of Buddhism but that Buddhist doctrine could not be reformed. Again one of Chü-tsan's proposals was shelved.

There was a good reason for the continuing resistance to his efforts at reform and re-organization. This was still 1950. The Party did not want to be rushed into formulating its policy towards Buddhism, how much protection and scope to give it and, in particular, whether to let it have a national association. In the end the only concrete result of the meeting on June 18, 1950, was the decision to publish a monthly, *Modern Buddhism,* with Chü-tsan as editor-in-chief. This was much more than just another Buddhist journal like the seventy-odd that had been come and gone during the Republican period. It was the nucleus of a Buddhist front and the precursor of the national Buddhist association that was to be established in 1953. It was chronologically the first of the several channels of government control whose history will be traced in this chapter.

MODERN BUDDHISM

Modern Buddhism transmitted government policy to Buddhists throughout the country; handled their complaints about their treatment by local cadres; promoted the reform of Buddhist doctrine and the monastic system; and cultivated contacts with foreign Buddhists who were friendly to Peking. All these activities were expressed or implied in the statement of goals that was published in the first issue.[21]

Its sponsorship was broadly representative. The names of its founders suggest that the United Front Work Department decided, probably in the summer of 1950, that both the magazine and the Buddhist front for which it served as a nucleus should capitalize on continuity with the past, not sweep it clean away; and not only should they enjoy the respect of Buddhists throughout the country, but they should have a certain political weight in the capital as well. Thus ten of its nineteen founders were men whose commitment to Buddhism was well known, including conservatives as well as progressives.[22] Fourteen of them were delegates to the CPPCC and six of them held high governmental posts.[23] The editorial committee, which actually put out the magazine, was also a serious group that included prominent Buddhist scholars and devotees.[24]

An article published at the end of 1954 traced three phases up to then in the development of *Modern Buddhism.* The first phase, from September 1950 through May 1953, was one of groping for the right focus, when "theoretical writings sometimes showed deviations and news reports were neither carefully checked nor prudently selected." In the second phase, which lasted for a year after the establishment of the Buddhist association, there was better focus and "much improvement in theoretical writings and news reports." The third phase began in June 1954, when the magazine was taken over by the association. "Serious mistakes are no longer being made, but some defects in our work still cannot be avoided."[25]

What had those "serious mistakes" been? Evidently they were indiscretions in printing readers' complaints and official reaction to them. Too much was revealed that could eventually be used in books like this one. We have already seen some examples,[26] but they were not the worst. In May 1951 an article contributed by a certain Wen Kuang-hsi stated openly that Buddhist scriptures were being sold for waste paper; that study of the "new thinking" had caused monks in some big monasteries to smash their Buddha images; and that intellectual development had to be accompanied by the development of reason (*li-hsing*) if life was to have a meaning—intellect without reason merely became a means to an end and served to increase human cruelty.[27] The phrase "human cruelty" was a not too delicate reproach to local cadres.

Until mid-1953 *Modern Buddhism* published many other articles, letters, and news reports that alluded to the difficulties monasteries were having.[28] The letters were printed in a question-and-answer column edited by a small group of monks, who usually took a hard line, telling their readers, in effect, that *Modern Buddhism* could do nothing to help them against the local authorities: they had to take care of themselves. Thus in September 1951, when the so-called "heterodox Taoist sects" were being ruthlessly extirpated, a reader in Chahar wrote that the monks and nuns in his area were "encountering a lot of suspicion from the lower level cadres who confuse Buddhism with the heterodox Taoist sects. For example, both keeping to a vegetarian diet and reciting buddha's name are restricted, and there are some doubts about the monthly [*Modern Buddhism*]. How can the situation be saved and things restored to their former stability?" He was given the following answer: "Cadres at the basic level have not studied Buddhism and confuse it with the I-kuan Tao [a heterodox sect] because the latter's members are also vegetarian and recite buddha's name. The only effective way to save the situation is for Buddhists themselves to show the points on which they differ from the I-kuan Tao . . . by helping the government ferret out counterrevolutionary elements and by responding to all the government's appeals. Also the I-kuan Tao uses superstition to cheat people of their money. Buddhists should eliminate superstition, serve the people, and seek the reasons for the situation in themselves rather than one-sidedly blaming others."[29] Several similar passages can be cited.[30]

If indiscretion was one kind of "serious mistake," another was a lingering conservatism that crept in when there was no need to defend government actions. One reader was told, for example, that although naturally monks ought not to make their living from rites for the dead, "still they have no other way to live, their cultural level is low, they are used to a life of freedom and wandering about, so it is difficult to expect them to change their occupation voluntarily and lead a life of productive labor."[31] To an inquiry whether bee-keeping was permitted from the standpoint of contemporary Buddhism, the editors replied that it was and then added: "What you call 'contemporary Buddhism' (*hsien-tsai fo-chiao*) cannot go beyond the scope of Buddhist norms, that is, it must honor the teachings that have been handed down from the Buddha. If you say that the modernization of Buddhism means that everything can be done in whatever way you please, then what would Buddhism become? So in modern Buddhism we are eliminating the bad things that have accumulated and restoring the original glory of the Buddha Sakyamuni in order to bring it into tune with modern life."[32]

Such passages cannot have pleased the officials in charge of religious affairs who monitored *Modern Buddhism*[33] and the question-and-answer column—the biggest source of trouble—was dropped in March 1952.[34] A column of local Buddhist news was retained, but in October 1953 readers were notified that they should not submit any more "exaggerated reports" on Buddhist activities, since, even though errors were few, they could affect the whole new Buddhist movement. "We hope that from now on all comrades submitting manuscripts will, in a strictly responsible spirit, make honest reports."[35] This call for self-censorship was effective:

next month the only contributions from readers were articles entitled "The Phases in My Ideological Transformation" and "Buddhists Begin to Purge the Reactionary Taoist Sects!"

Another step towards censorship was taken on August 31, 1955, when the Chinese Buddhist Association passed a resolution that "the contents of all publications . . . whether books, periodicals, or pamphlets, must consist of Buddhist doctrine and material that is patriotic. Nothing that contravenes Buddhist principles, distorts state policies, spreads rumors, sows discord, nor any other writing that damages the interests of the people can be permitted."[36] The immediate cause for this resolution may have been the "rumors" spread by a Buddhist journal that had just been suppressed in Shanghai, but the crackdown had its effect on *Modern Buddhism* too. Originally it had opened its pages to all Buddhists, asking them to send in materials of every kind.[37] Now it excluded anything implying criticism of the regime.*

In May 1956, nine months after the 1955 crackdown, began the period when "a hundred flowers bloomed and a hundred schools of thought contended." Many Chinese intellectuals accepted the invitation to put their grievances into print. The Buddhists were more cautious. They "bloomed" by making themselves useful to the regime and winning more of its patronage. The period of the Hundred Flowers coincided precisely with the celebration of the 2,500th anniversary of the Buddha's death (the Buddha Jayanti). Already a year earlier a Chinese Buddhist delegation had gone to Burma and made a good impression at the Sixth Buddhist Council (the sixth in 2,500 years). Now in May 1956 another delegation was sent. That month *Modern Buddhism* came out like Cinderella with twenty more pages than the month before, on heavy stock of good quality (which is still white, whereas the April issue has turned brown and brittle), and accompanied by an English translation of the table of contents. I have a copy that was sent to the Maha Bodhi Society in Calcutta with Chü-tsan's calling card; I believe that complimentary copies now began to be distributed

*The word "regime" is occasionally used in this book to refer to the Party and government together. It is not meant as an aspersion on the legitimacy of the government.

widely abroad. The English table of contents became a permanent feature and quality of paper was maintained until 1959.[38]

Suddenly in July 1960 publication was suspended. This was partly because of the paper shortage that followed the Great Leap Forward, but also, I think, because the enthusiastic reports of monks' labor and study during the Great Leap seemed in retrospect to have been indiscretions. The editors were instructed to re-orient the magazine towards making a better impression on Buddhists abroad. When it reappeared at the end of 1960 as a bi-monthly, it had become a kind of Buddhist counterpart to *China Reconstructs* with some articles translated into English. Instead of concrete details on how monks lived, it carried international Buddhist news and abstruse articles on Buddhist doctrine and history.[39] Yet even this was not enough of a change and at the end of 1964 it ceased publication entirely. Just why this happened will become clear in Chapter XI when we take up the Cultural Revolution.

Aside from its role as the initial nucleus of a Buddhist front, what was the importance of *Modern Buddhism*? How much influence did it have on its readers over the years and how many readers did it have? Its first issue was printed in two thousand copies. This figure had doubled to four thousand by 1953.[40] Thereafter it did not increase except on special occasions: six thousand for the issue on the establishment of the Chinese Buddhist Association and five thousand for the issue of May 1956 that celebrated the Buddha Jayanti year. Usually, however, after one allows for foreign distribution, only a little over three thousand copies were available to the Buddhists of China. If the number of monks and nuns was five hundred thousand (as was officially claimed) and if most of the nearly five million devotees before Liberation were still interested in Buddhism, then there was not one copy per thousand for the persons who might be considered potential readers. Even if we assume that the Buddhist community had been decimated (as will be suggested in Chapter II), the printings seem small. The reason was never officially explained, but it is likely that the government would not approve or make paper available for large printings of a religious magazine. No matter how carefully it was edited, it still served to keep an interest in religion alive. Hence placing a subscription was made more difficult than for major periodicals like *Study,* which could be obtained through any post office. Readers had to write to *Modern Buddhism* directly or, if they lived in Peking or Shanghai, they could buy their copies month by month at one of the several Buddhist bookshops there.[41] The government only wanted enough copies in circulation for the Buddhists who were to be kept abreast of the policy on Buddhism—enough for the larger monasteries, local Buddhist associations, and the political study classes that used it for reading assignments.[42] Yet that meant that the influence of *Modern Buddhism* was much greater than printing figures would suggest. It may even have had an influence on lower level cadres, to whom, in the first years after Liberation, the heads of monasteries could show their copies as evidence that the central government had extended a kind of recognition to Buddhism. Some Buddhists presented subscriptions to local government offices.[43]

Although the pages of *Modern Buddhism* were more revealing in its early years than after 1955, it was never so free as its competitors. The three most important of these were published in Shanghai, which, as the biggest city and largest industrial complex in China, provided the shelter for a certain independence. The pages of *Chüeh yu-ch'ing* carried far franker reports on the hardships monks were undergoing than any that appeared in *Modern Buddhism* or the national press.[44] Either for this reason or because of financial difficulties it ceased publication sometime between March 1953 and April 1954.[45] The same frankness could be found in *Chüeh-hsün,* a monthly published by the Shanghai Buddhist Youth Association. When officers of this group were arrested for counterrevolutionary activities in 1955, *Chüeh-hsün* ceased publication.[46] That left only *Hung-hua yüeh-k'an,* the organ of the Shanghai Buddhist Association, which in turn ceased publication between October 1957 and March 1963[47]—the last of the seventy-odd independent Buddhist periodicals that had been started in China since 1912.[48] Since *Chüeh-hsün* and *Hung-hua* were each printed in more copies than *Modern Buddhism,*[49] it may seem surprising that printings of the latter did not go up as competition from them was eliminated. This is one of the reasons for thinking that the government placed limits on the number of copies that could be printed.

THE CHINESE BUDDHIST ASSOCIATION

We shall now go back to the beginning and trace the development of the second channel of government control: the Chinese Buddhist Association. It was the Buddhists themselves who felt the need for it and tried to set it up as early as 1949.[50] Especially from the point of view of monks and nuns, it was not enough to have a journal in Peking like *Modern Buddhism.* They wanted a successor to the old Chinese Buddhist Association, which, whatever its defects, had concentrated on protecting monastic property during the two decades before Liberation.[51] Now its defects were often criticized, but this was probably because it had been established under the Kuomintang and its headquarters had moved to Taiwan. When a new association was finally set up, the presidency went to the monk who had founded and long served as president of the old one.

In 1950–52 inquiries about a new association were often printed in *Modern Buddhism,* which would explain to its readers that there were two reasons why the time for it had not yet come. Agreement had still to be reached on the exact manner in which Buddhism should be reorganized; and local associations had been formed in too few cities.[52] In other words, although the central authorities had decided that Buddhism should not simply be suppressed and that Buddhist cultural monuments should not be destroyed, they had yet to decide what to do in a positive way; and, before any national association was formed, they wanted "sound organizations at the basic level . . . 'Soundness' means that there are no questions about the people who belong and that they have shown their ability to do concrete work for the government and for Buddhism."[53] Ability to work for the government was the first criterion in judging potential leaders.

Another abortive attempt to set up a national association was made in May 1951, this time by Chao P'u-ch'u, who had been well known in Shanghai Buddhist circles since the 1930's[54] and was one of the lay devotees against whom Chü-tsan was competing for leadership. He proposed that eighteen eminent monks should sponsor a preparatory conference to be held that summer, August 1-7, 1951. This was approved first by the Religious Affairs Section of the CPPCC and then by the Ministry of Internal Affairs and the Religious Affairs Division. "There was complete agreement that a Buddhist association for the whole country should be organized." Yet when August came, there was no conference and nothing was done about a national body for another sixteen months.[55] News of this abortive attempt was not even printed in *Modern Buddhism,* a fact indicating that at a high official level—higher than the ministry—there continued to be uncertainty about how much scope Buddhists should be given.

By the autumn of 1952 the policy on religion had taken shape. Government organs had been set up with specific responsibility for religious affairs. It was also becoming clear that Buddhism could be profitably utilized, just as Chü-tsan had suggested. China was starting to play an active part in the international peace movement led by the Soviet Union. In September 1952 the Peace Conference of Asia and the Pacific Regions was held in Peking, attended by Buddhists from eight countries. Chinese monks entertained them and joined them in signing a joint appeal to Buddhists throughout the world for support of the resolutions of the conference.[56] This action offered an occasion to point out to the Party's Propaganda Department that China could be called the world's leading Buddhist country, since it had more Buddhists than any other, and that, if a national association were set up, it could speak for them with a single voice, calling for the defeat of the American aggressors in Korea and their withdrawal from Taiwan.[57]

In November 1952 twenty Buddhist leaders "happened" to be in Peking. Meeting November 4-5, they formed the preparatory committee for the Chinese Buddhist Association (CBA). They took this action "under the precious guidance" of Li Wei-han, the head of the Party's United Front Work Department, and with the help of Chao Fan of the Nationalities Affairs Commission and Ho Ch'eng-hsiang, the director of the Religious Affairs Division.[58] The reason for Chao Fan's participation becomes clear when we see that among the twenty sponsors were six lamas. This was the first evidence of another way in which the Party had decided to utilize Buddhism: as a counterweight to separatist tendencies in border areas. The following spring, when the CBA was officially inaugurated, a special eleven-man Tibetan delegation arrived in Peking from Lhasa, after a journey that had taken nearly eight weeks. They helped elect twenty-nine Tibetans to the CBA council, which had ninety-three members in all. Thus there were far more Tibetans than could be justified by their percentage of the population.[59] Two of the four honorary presidents were the Dalai and Panchen Lamas, and the third was a Mongol. The actual president was a Han Chinese, but when, within four months of the inaugural meeting, he died, he was replaced by another Tibetan, Shirob Jaltso.[60] Among the officers there were also a good number from the Thai region of Yünnan. The CBA rightly claimed to be the first Buddhist organization in Chinese history to include representatives of all the national minorities among whom Buddhists were to be found.[61]

The CBA's inaugural meeting, held May 29-June 3, 1953, adopted a constitution that set the course for the next four years. Its most noteworthy feature was that it did not provide for ordinary membership. The council of 93 *was* the CBA. Chao P'u-ch'u explained that having ordinary members would lead to inequalities between the sangha and the laity.[62] The explanation is obscure, but clearly the CBA was not set up to be a mass organization like the Youth League or the Women's Federation, with branches at the local level that the rank-and-file of Buddhists could join. There were no local branches. Chao explained that it would be "inappropriate" to set them up.[63] We may infer, therefore, that delegates to national conferences were selected, not elected from each locality. Who selected them was never revealed. In all likelihood, it was the Party's religious affairs apparatus, working in consultation with Buddhist leaders. Article 3 of the constitution states merely that council members were to be "elected at a conference of delegates from Buddhist circles within China."[64]

This did not mean that the council was unrepresentative. Analysis of the names on it shows that there was a fair proportion of elder monks and well-known devotees. The CBA could serve the government best if it *was* representative. A collection of Buddhist quislings would have had no influence over the Buddhist community; widely respected monks and devotees could be far more effective in persuading their followers to accept government policy. To the extent that they were a microcosm of the Buddhist community, the community could be changed as they were changed.

The goals of the CBA were set forth in its constitution: "to unite all the country's Buddhists so that they will participate, under the leadership of the People's Government, in movements for the welfare of the motherland and the defense of world peace; to help the People's Government fully carry out its policy of freedom of religious belief; to link up Buddhists from different parts of the country; and to exemplify the best traditions of Buddhism."[65] What this meant in terms of its day-to-day work was that the CBA served as an intermediary between Buddhists and the government. It passed government instructions down to Buddhists and reported upwards what Buddhists were doing and thinking. Sometimes when they were upset by "incidents violating religious policy," it would attempt to intercede with the government so that the violations could be rectified and prevented from recurring.[66] In 1957 Chao P'u-ch'u reported to the second national conference that not infrequently in the preceding three years "obstacles had been placed in the way of freedom of religious belief and national religious policy had been violated." In this connection, he said, the CBA staff had put a good deal of work into handling reports sent in by local Buddhists and had sometimes gotten "definite results." At other times their handling of situations had "not been sufficiently timely and complete—and this had affected the prompt and rational solution of certain problems."[67] These cryptic sentences presumably referred to incidents that it would have been embarrassing to describe more specifically, such as damage or confiscation of monasteries, which the CBA tried to prevent. From the point of view of Buddhists, this was the positive side of its work. There was also a negative side.

According to its constitution, one CBA goal was to get Buddhists to participate in "movements for the welfare of the motherland." Among these was included the movement for the suppression of counterrevolutionaries. We know that it was included because the inaugural conference agreed that "at present the most basic problem is making a clear distinction between the enemy and ourselves . . . Erroneous thinking and behavior has resulted from not making this distinction. For example, there have been people who felt sympathy for monastery officers who were struggled against by the peasants during land reform; and there have been people who chanted sutras for the salvation of souls of counterrevolutionaries after they had been suppressed . . . Buddhism has only one standpoint, the people's standpoint, which we must firmly take. There can be no middle ground in distinguishing the enemy from ourselves . . . We must sever all connections with counterrevolutionary elements and [help to] suppress counterrevolutionary elements. Not one of them may be given shelter or special consideration."[68]

There were also other goals of the CBA that sounded acceptable to Buddhists as formulated in the constitution, but were much less so in practice. The goal of "defending world peace" actually meant support for the Korean war, with monks and nuns contributing towards a Buddhist fighter plane. The goal of "carrying out the policy of freedom of religious belief" actually meant renouncing the freedom to preach Buddhism in public places.[69]

"Defense of world peace" was the goal on which the CBA was to spend more and more of its time. Whenever Peking took a strong stand on an international question—attacking, for example, the U.S. landings in Lebanon—the CBA would issue a statement of support. It arranged for frequent exchanges of delegations with other Buddhist countries. It appointed a committee to draft an article on China for an international Buddhist encyclopedia. It sponsored a pagoda to house the Buddha tooth relic that had toured Burma and Ceylon. Even such an apparently domestic activity as publishing a set of cave rubbings (from Fang-shan) was undertaken as part of the international celebration of the 2,500th anniversary of the Buddha's birth.[70]

1. The entrance to the Kuang-chi Ssu, headquarters of the Chinese Buddhist Association, whose sign can be seen to the right of the door. The photographer, who went there unannounced, found it "well kept but rather sad and deserted"—except for a few monks, who questioned him suspiciously about the reason for his visit. Peking 1962.

The CBA staff had grown to thirty or forty persons by 1957,[71] and they seemed to spend most of their time on such support for people's diplomacy. Except to the extent that they served as intermediaries in conveying policy down and complaints up, they do not appear to have had much to do with Buddhists at the local level. This was partly because there were no ordinary members. Even after 1957, when branches were permitted by the revised constitution, very few were set up, and whether they had ordinary members is unclear. Some *local* Buddhist associations did have, but for such associations the CBA bore no responsibility; they were supervised by the Party and government in their area.[72] From time to time the CBA would urge them to carry on political study; but it did little to help them with it.[73] It urged them to reform the monastic system, but I have read of no individual monastery where the CBA itself became involved in reform. It set up the Chinese Buddhist Seminary, but the latter then functioned as an independent entity, with its own staff and its own premises.

The premises of the CBA were in the Kuang-chi Ssu* in Peking, where the inaugural meeting had been held in 1953. The staff was headed by Chao P'u-ch'u, who was secretary-general during the whole life of the organization. He was assisted by two deputies, Chü-tsan and Kuo P'eng. One gets the impression that these three men actually ran the CBA and that the president, vice-presidents, standing committees, and council—on the principle of democratic centralism—merely assented to what they did.[74] If so, the preponderance of monks on the council did not assure (as in the case of the old CBA) that the association was dominated by the sangha. What dominated it was the Party, both directly and through the Religious Affairs Bureau. The Party held the purse strings. In theory, the operating expenses were "to be voluntarily contributed by Buddhists in different parts of the country."[75] In actuality, like its organ, *Modern Buddhism,* the CBA depended on a government subsidy.[76] At least one trusted Party member was in the inner circle of its leadership, where he was privy to all that went on. This was Kuo P'eng, the deputy secretary-general.[77]

The creation of the CBA had been a huge relief to Chinese Buddhists, especially to monks and nuns. They had assumed that they now were to have a place in the new China and that their problems with hostile cadres would come to an end. They were therefore all the more disappointed to find that this was not the case. As a member of the council said in 1955: "Two years ago when the CBA was founded, Buddhists all over the country greeted it with immense joy and enthusiastic support. But the great majority harbored the incorrect hope that with the founding of the CBA Buddhists would not have to undergo socialist reform, and that they could still return to their old way of life. They hoped that all their difficulties could be solved through the good offices of the CBA. The CBA, of course, could not satisfy the

**Ssu* means monastery; *shan* means monastery or mountain. For further details, see Welch, *Practice,* p. 467, n. 4.

hopes of these people. Then those who had been so 'enthusiastic' began to turn cold towards the CBA, becoming suspicious and dissatisfied."[78] This statement was made at the second plenum of the council, held August 16-31, 1955, the longest meeting in the history of the association. Here, much more than at the inaugural conference, the hard facts of the government's religious policy were driven home to the delegates, who were expected to transmit them to Buddhists in the provinces. Ordinations were to be restricted, wandering monks discouraged, local associations purged under the guidance of the local government.[79] Many of the sessions were spent discussing the Buddhist Youth Association in Shanghai, which had just been exposed as a hotbed of "sinister and vicious counterrevolutionary activities." Delegates were urged to assimilate the lessons to be drawn from this "serious case."[80]

We have seen how *Modern Buddhism* used to answer complaints about the cadres from some readers by suggesting that they might be themselves to blame. The same point was made at meetings of the CBA. For example, at the second national conference in March 1957 Chao P'u-ch'u, after speaking about the difficulties Buddhists had experienced, went on: "Some [of these cases] have occurred because the personal conduct of Buddhists has got out of line or they have made indiscriminate use of religious freedom or they have acted to the detriment of the interests of the masses. There have also been bad elements who have slipped into Buddhism and caused cases to occur. Therefore the first thing Buddhists should do is to ask whether they themselves have been patriotic and law-abiding and clearly distinguished between the enemy and themselves, between the heterodox and the orthodox. They should do nothing that will cause difficulties in getting the religious policy to be thoroughly implemented."[81] What this meant, I think, was that because Buddhists were an ideologically backward element of the population, the presumption of guilt always lay with them and they would only cause greater difficulties for themselves—and for the CBA—by appealing to the constitutional guarantee of freedom of religious belief.

The third national conference of the CBA was held February 1962. Its agenda was much the same as at earlier conferences: a report by Chao P'u-ch'u on the work of the headquarters; statements by delegates about the condition of Buddhism in their respective areas; and resolutions of gratitude and support for the government. Although the political climate was mild in 1962, it was still considered necessary, three years after the event, to condemn the rebellion in Tibet. The ratio of Tibetans elected to the council that year was sharply reduced.

Looked at in the perspective of history, the CBA played the same role of intermediary between Buddhists and the government as had been played by the sangha officials of the Ming and Ch'ing and by earlier Buddhist associations under the Republic. Like the sangha officials, but unlike earlier associations, it was supposed to keep Buddhist ranks free of counterrevolution and heterodoxy;[82] and again like the sangha officials, it was essentially a servant of the government, on which it depended for money and direction, not a servant of the Buddhist community like the Republican CBA. Therefore, far more than any earlier Buddhist associations, it served Chinese foreign policy.[83] Together with its official organ, *Modern Buddhism,* it had to depend increasingly on this to justify its existence as the number of monks and monasteries dwindled. From 1961 through 1964, as we shall see in Chapter VI, more Buddhist delegations than ever came to China and the leaders of the CBA found themselves cutting a wide swath in diplomatic entertainment. It must have been gratifying for them to read appreciations like the following, written by a Japanese Buddhist after a tour of the mainland: "Because of China's position in Asia, we can safely say that the Chinese Buddhist Association is the center of Asian Buddhist circles."[84] Yet concrete results were few, and people's diplomacy was "put on ice" during the Cultural Revolution. In the summer of 1966, a year and a half after *Modern Buddhism* had published its last issue, the CBA ceased activity too.

LOCAL ORGANIZATIONS

Inasmuch as the CBA had been created "to unite the country's Buddhists," one might have expected it to set up branches at the local level as rapidly as possible. The old CBA had had several hundred.[85] Yet, as we have seen, none were set up under the Communists for four years. Until 1957 the Buddhist groups established in many cities and some provinces were independent and purely local. Even after 1957, when the constitution was revised to permit branches, more of such purely local groups continued to be set up.

They came in a variety of forms and went under a variety of names (of which the most common was probably *fo-chiao hsieh-hui,* parallel to the name of the national association in Peking).[86] Some had ordinary members and were not (like the national association) a head without a body.[87] Their officiers were mostly local abbots and other high-ranking monks; laymen were in the minority and only in one case have I read of a layman as president.[88] All officers had to be approved, if not selected, by the local authorities, who also provided operating funds when the Buddhists could not provide them on their own.[89]

Despite the fact that these associations were not branches of the CBA, they operated in many ways as if they had been. Generally one or two of their officers sat on the CBA council and attended its meetings in Peking. After each meeting they would return to transmit the results to their own membership.[90] Therefore conferences of local associations usually took place within a few months after a CBA conference. Where there was a provincial association, its president might serve concurrently as president of the association for the provincial capital, so that he was active at three levels–national, provincial, municipal.[91] One report said that the first task of a local association was "to carry out the directives of the CBA."[92] Yet all this was apparently regarded by the authorities as significantly different from having a national association with local branches.

The activities of local associations were mainly secular.[93] Some of them started small factories and handicraft coöperatives so that monks and nuns, as pious donations dwindled, could become self-supporting.[94] Some became involved in the administration of monasteries, handling their land-reform papers,[95] registering their property,[96] collecting rents on it,[97] distributing livelihood subsidies to their needy monks and nuns,[98] helping to select new officers, and, in one case, helping to reorganize the personnel structure.[99] It was quite common for local associations to start "patriotic study classes" and to mobilize the Buddhists of the area to take part in political and economic campaigns.[100] They also entertained foreign Buddhist visitors and issued statements of support for Chinese foreign policy. It was activities such as these that prompted one refugee informant–a monk who left Wuhan in 1957–to remark that the association there was "just a name." That is, he said, all it did was to act as agent of the municipal religious affairs division.

When CBA branches began to be set up after 1957, they carried on many of the same activities.[101] They were headed by the same kind of prominent local monks, who also served on the CBA council and, after each of its meetings, returned to transmit the results.[102] Indeed there seems to have been no inherent difference between CBA branches and the purely local groups. Why then were they not all integrated into a single structure? This is a most interesting question, the answer to which testifies again to the cautiousness of the government's religious policy.

At the CBA's inaugural conference in 1953, Chao P'u-ch'u said: "Ours is a vast country of many nationalities and the situation of Buddhism varies according to regions and nationalities. On the basis of the CBA's present situation, it is deemed inappropriate (literally, not safe, *pu t'o-tang*) to set up branches. Local Buddhist organizations should be guided by the local people's government. They may establish relations and develop a certain liaison in their work with the CBA, but they are not branch organs of the CBA and may not enjoy the relationship of subordinate to superior."[103] Local Buddhists were actually eager to "enjoy the relationship of subordinate to superior" because it would place them to some extent under the umbrella of Peking's authority. That is why, even before the inaugural conference, a group in Hunan had begun to call itself the "Ping-chiang chapter of the CBA." It was soon ordered to stop doing so on the grounds that it violated the CBA constitution.[104] At about the same time other local groups sent delegations to Peking to talk their problems over with the CBA headquarters. Despite Chao's statement (just quoted) that they could get into liaison with the CBA, they were sharply reprimanded and told not to send delegations in the future without first getting written consent.[105]

Evidently the CBA had to be very careful about its relations with local Buddhists—but why? When branches were finally authorized in 1957, Chü-tsan commented that they had not been possible earlier because local Buddhists were "not sufficiently well informed and local branches would simply have caused a lot of confusion."[106] What he meant, I think, was that the Party considered it safer to leave Buddhists atomized in groups that were entirely under local government control, rather than to give them independent access to a national headquarters in Peking, through which they could by-pass the local government and "cause confusion." There was less to be gained in control than lost in security by sanctioning even the germ of a Buddhist *imperium in imperio.* This last phrase may sound farfetched, but in 1957, when Liu Ya-hsiu was attacked as a rightist, one of the crimes he confessed to was that he and Ch'en Ming-shu had talked about "establishing as many local Buddhist associations as possible and then linking them up. He [Ch'en] said: 'You seize control of them wherever you can, take over their leadership, then find a way to get more of them into the CBA. We must put our own people into leading positions in the CBA headquarters.' "[107]

Fear of such ambitions would explain why even after 1957 purely local groups were set up in more places than branches of the CBA; and why only a few of the existing local groups were converted into branches.[108] It would also explain why the establishment of all groups took such a long time. Readers who wrote to *Modern Buddhism* in the early 1950's asking when they could start a Buddhist association were told that it was better just to organize a political study group or a branch of the Resist America Aid Korea Committee, which could nevertheless function like a Buddhist association.[109] Only when "conditions were ripe" could regular associations be established. Even then their establishment was often a frustrating process. A preparatory committee would have to be set up first and operate for up to five years before its leaders were considered reliable enough for the group to be formally inaugurated.[110] Sometimes there were additional steps, and a step backward might have to be taken when a step forward proved premature.[111] Usually groups were first established at the municipal level and only when these were operating smoothly would a provincial association or a CBA branch be set up.[112] The whole process of getting organized was supervised by the Party,[113] and it must have made Buddhists feel occasional impatience; but they had no choice, for they could not start any group—even a reading room—without registering it.[114] Once it was registered, however, they enjoyed a certain security, which perhaps made the delays and trouble seem worthwhile.[115] Just as the Party had mixed feelings about Buddhist groups, Buddhist groups had mixed feelings about the Party and, in particular, its agency for controlling them—the Religious Affairs Bureau.

THE RELIGIOUS AFFAIRS BUREAU

It is not clear whether any cadres were assigned exclusively to the supervision of religious affairs during the first year or so after Liberation. Since no policy had taken shape, there was little to be done. At the national level it could be handled by high-ranking Party members for whom religion was merely a sideline. Thus it was Li Wei-han, the director of the United Front Work Department, who decided about the Buddhist delegates to the CPPCC in the summer of 1949; and it was Ch'en Ch'i-yüan, a vice-minister of Internal Affairs, who acted as head of the CPPCC's Religious Affairs Team in the spring of 1950.[116] This team had no real power, but at that time it came closest to a separate government organ with responsibility for religion.[117]

The need for a separate organ was already apparent. Although only a few local cadres may have been involved in "deviations" like the destruction of monasteries, the majority of them were still too hostile to be effective in dealing with religion. They openly scoffed at religious rites as superstitious; would not listen to monks who tried to explain the good points of their doctrine; and excluded them from volunteer labor projects and people's organizations.[118] This ran precisely counter to the ideas about the control and utilization of religion that were then winning acceptance in the capital. These ideas were, for example, that popular beliefs and customs had enormous power, which could only be countered by education; that religious groups had to be integrated rather than excluded from the united front of people's organizations; that the foreign ties of Christian churches made them a potential fifth column, which should be kept exposed rather than pushed underground; and that important foreign visitors to China, especially from Buddhist and Islamic countries, would be interested in what had happened to their religions there and so an effort should be made to give them a good impression. The control of religious affairs was therefore going to involve indoctrination, united-front work, public security, and foreign relations. Particularly able cadres would have to be trained to undertake it; and then given sole charge of it so that their less sophisticated colleagues could not interfere. A special bureaucratic hierarchy would have to be created, reaching from the capital down to the countryside.[119]

The first step was taken in January 1951, when the Religious Affairs Division (Tsung-chiao Shih-wu Ch'u) was set up in Peking, ostensibly under the Committee on Cultural and Educational Affairs of the Government Administration Council. Actually, however, it did not get its orders from this or any other part of the government, but from the CCP Central Committee. Because its work was so delicate and many-sided, the Party wished to control it directly. In 1954, after the new Constitution was adopted, it became a bureau (*chü*) of the State Council, but retained its confidential status as a Party organ. By then its staff had increased to several dozen persons, assigned to seven sections and supervising the activities of many provincial, municipal, and county branches.[120] Every year the heads of these branches, who were all Party members of long standing, came to Peking for a "national religious work conference." The sessions were highly confidential: lower ranking staff members were not allowed to enter the hall and the very fact that such conferences were held was kept out of the press. The decisions reached were transmitted orally by the heads of branches to their own staff and to local Party and government leaders. The first such conference was held in the winter of 1953-54.[121]

Provincial and municipal branches had begun to be established a few months after the central organ in Peking. The first that I have seen mentioned in the press was the Hunan Province Religious Affairs Division, which started operating June 1, 1951. Like the central organ, it ostensibly came under the Department of Culture and Education. It assumed full control of all religious groups in the province, which were instructed to "report to it directly." It had evidently been ordered to use its power with caution, for even on such an obvious thing as political study for monks (long since underway in Peking), it planned to postpone action until it had "better understood the Buddhist situation in the province."[122]

At the end of 1951 the CCP Central Committee ordered that religious affairs divisions be created in all provinces and municipalities where they did not already exist.[123] So in Canton, for example, the Provincial-Municipal Religious Affairs Division opened its doors in February 1952. This is the only one about which I have been able to collect a good deal of concrete information through interviews with a former member of its staff. The following pages are based mainly on what he saw take place in his own city or what he believed to have taken place throughout the country.[124] Wherever possible, I shall cite supporting evidence from the Mainland press, which has, however, been reticent about organs for the control of religious affairs.

My informant was the cadre who set up and served for half a year as acting head of the division in Canton. He had already been dealing with religion during two years in the Civil Affairs Bureau.[125] The other three members of his staff, however, came from the Propaganda Department and had had no such previous experience. This was typical, he said, of what happened everywhere: religious affairs organs had to be staffed mostly by tyros because there were so few cadres who had dealt with religious problems.[126]

All members of his staff—even the office boy—belonged either to the Party or the Youth League. Therefore none was an adherent of any religion. Their job was not to represent religious circles, but to control them. They could not do so effectively unless they learned something about them; so once a week they held a four-hour seminar to study the history of the major religions in China and the right methods for carrying out the government's religious policy. Each of them was expected to gain some familiarity with the sacred writings of the particular religion that came under his jurisdiction and to read the journal that its followers published in Peking. (Besides *Modern Buddhism,* journals were published by the Catholics, Protestants, and Muslims.) Senior cadres like my informant also received confidential circulars from Peking entitled "Reference Materials on Religious Work," which covered all its aspects, including the personal histories and habits of Buddhist leaders. In 1954, for example, he received a circular about the complications arising from the Dalai Lama's visit to Peking. The Dalai Lama, it said, defecated into a gold-plated receptacle. The feces were sent to Tibet for making medicine. When he bathed, he lay on the bed naked and was washed with hot water by eight senior eminent lamas—like a king of old. The washcloths were then taken back to Tibet to be kept for presentation to lamas who had made big contributions. Afterwards he was annointed with perfumed oil, wrapped up in gauze, and moved to a second bed, where he was dressed by another eminent lama. It seemed very strange to the Canton cadres that such things would be discussed in a Communist Party circular, but it served to show them how feudal and reactionary Tibetan Buddhism was, yet how carefully its leaders had to be handled.

The size of the Canton division gradually increased until by 1957 there were about twenty people working in four sections.[127] Two signs hung outside the door—"Kwangtung Province Religious Affairs Division" and "Canton Municipality Religious Affairs Division"—but the same four sections handled the work of both (until they split up in 1958). The chain of command was complex. Vertically the division was subordinate to the Religious Affairs Bureau in Peking, but horizontally it received instructions from local departments of the Party (United Front and Propaganda). The vertical links grew stronger as the bureau in Peking acquired experience and personnel and carved out a niche for itself in the central bureaucracy; so that more and more the Canton division acted as its agent and simply informed the local departments of what it was doing. However, since its staff salaries came from the Municipal Party Committee, it was never free from horizontal control. It does seem to have enjoyed freedom from control by local units of *government.* Because it came under the Party, consisted of Party or Youth League members, and dealt with such a variety of delicate matters—"as if it were a small government on its own"—its staff had a sense of superiority and treated ordinary government cadres as their subordinates.[128]

To most units of the local government, according to my informant, they had the authority to issue instructions on any question that came within their purview. For example, they could tell the Nationalities Affairs Commission what to do on a question that involved Islam;[129] or request the Bureau of Public Buildings Administration to vacate a "borrowed" temple; or order a residents' committee to recruit more monks and nuns for a sanitation campaign. Even the mayor had to be satisfied with information copies

2. Cadres of the Religious Affairs Bureau watch the National Day parade at the T'ien-an Men on October 1, 1957. These two accompanied the first Japanese Buddhist delegation on its long tour of China.

of their orders; the religious affairs cadres felt no obligation to consult him on anything.[130]

In the case of public security organs, the relationship varied. For example, the material in police files on Buddhist monks and nuns–which monk was returning late at night or known to be playing around with a woman–were open to inspection by the Religious Affairs Division, but not vice versa. Monks who wanted to hold a funeral service in somebody's home (which was contrary to government policy but permitted in Canton until 1958 as a long established custom) would first get permission from the division. Then if a crowd gathered to watch and the police became uneasy ("crowds were what the Party feared most"), the division would explain that it had authorized the service and the police would not interfere. Any important matter involving a religious group or individual–from the backward thinking of a Buddhist monk to the foreign contacts of a Catholic parish–would be referred by the police to the division. The referral would not be direct but through the first division of the Public Security Bureau. The latter was in charge of political security and worked closely with the religious affairs cadres, who regarded its staff as their equals. They had a similar close relationship with the Foreign Affairs Division of the municipal government, which was actually (like their own) an organ of the Party. They often coöperated in the handling of foreign visitors who had an interest in religion.

In 1954 religious affairs sections (*k'o*) began to be set up in those special districts and counties of Kwangtung where there were many religious believers. The sections were nominally subordinate to the head of the district or county but actually came under the division in Canton, to which they submitted regular plans and work reports and from which they received policy instructions and certain funds (like subsidies for elderly or incapacitated monks and nuns, which the division, in turn, received from Peking). Daily matters they decided on their own. I do not recall seeing any printed reference to religious affairs sections at the county level, but there is no reason to doubt that they were set up, as my informant believed, in many parts of China at about this time.[131]

At all levels the mission of religious affairs organs was the same: to act as agent of the Party in controlling religious activities and groups. No religious group could be formed without their approval; nor could any religious book or periodical be published.[132] They nominated all religious representatives to political bodies—people's congresses and councils and committees of the CPPCC. They intervened to prevent violation of the laws that were gradually passed to protect religious property; and maintained files on the status of such property. In Canton, for example, every monastery, temple, church, and mosque had been required to submit a report in 1950 that summarized its history, rules, and system of organization, and listed its land, buildings, books, sacred images, and other valuables. These dossiers went to the Religious Affairs Division when it was set up and facilitated action when a government organ tried to "borrow" a building or when a monk tried to raise money by selling a book or image. The division also maintained files on individuals who had some religious affiliation: each file included a biography, a résumé of political activities, a photograph, and a sample of handwriting. These dossiers were necessary because no government department could employ such persons without first obtaining the approval of the division, which, conversely, sometimes interceded to provide them with jobs. Similarly, they could not be arrested or detained by the police without the division being consulted; and it had overall responsibility for finding out whether any of them were counterrevolutionaries, spies, or "backward elements." Once a resident of Canton had been classified as "religious," there were few aspects of his daily life and his long term future that did not come under the purview of the religious affairs cadres.

These cadres devoted the largest part of their time to the control of internal activities of religious organizations. They oversaw the elections of abbots and other officials of Buddhist monasteries and tried to make sure (without employing overt coercion) that those elected would be ready to coöperate with the division. When a monastery reorganized its rules or personnel, the cadres might exercise "leadership." Sometimes they even came to live in a monastery.[133] Although Buddhist monks were not required (as were Christian pastors) to submit in advance the text of every sermon, a cadre would drop in from time to time when they lectured on a sacred text, in order to make sure that they were not giving undue emphasis to "negative, feudalistic ideas" that would undermine the political re-education of their disciples.[134] However, even a Buddhist monk had to submit in advance the text of an address that he was giving to a large audience on an important occasion, as, for instance, an abbot's address during an ordination. The cadres devoted a lot of time to getting monks of all kinds into political study and to successive movements and campaigns. As we shall see in Chapter III, this was often a difficult, frustrating task, since those whose commitment was otherworldly were not easily made into enthusiasts for Marxism and socialist construction. In connection with study and campaigns, as well as with the entertainment of foreign Buddhists, the Religious Affairs Division often enlisted the services of the local Buddhist association—whose personnel and other activities it also had to supervise.

What was particularly time-consuming for the cadres was the complicated "case," like the long drawn out troubles at the Liu-jung Ssu, which provide a good illustration of day-to-day problems. The Liu-jung Ssu was the principal monastery of Canton and the troubles there involved the three monks who headed it in the early 1950's. Since their names are confusingly similar, they will be referred to simply as abbots *X, Y,* and *Z.*

In September 1950 abbot *X,* after a quarrel with some of the older monks in the monastery, resigned, disrobed, and entered Nan-fang University. This was the largest training school for cadres in Kwangtung; he wanted to become a cadre himself, ostensibly in order to "get close to the people." All student cadres had to write out a "self-examination" (*chien-t'ao shu*) from the age of eight. When he wrote his, he was not at all critical of the influence of Buddhism on his life. Within a few months he was expelled from the university for being "difficult to reform" and "obstinate in his religious thinking." He then went back to live at the Liu-jung Ssu, but found that the monks there would not accept him because of what they considered his apostasy to Marxism. In a moment of despair he committed suicide.[135] Naturally this embarrassed the religious affairs cadres and made them worry about abbot *Y*, who, only a few months after succeeding *X*, had also gotten into a quarrel, disrobed, and entered Nan-fang University. Although he was not expelled for obstinacy, he did too poorly to qualify for anything better than a minor job in the anti-illiteracy program.[136] From 1952 to 1956, as a lower-level cadre, he went from county to county teaching peasants the rudiments of reading and writing. In 1956 the program was discontinued and the Provincial Department of Culture and Education, under which he had been working, refused to give him another job. It had come to consider him backward in his thinking and lacking in political enthusiasm—a "rice cadre." They said as much in a chit that they sent to the Religious Affairs Division.

The chit ended up on the desk of my informant, who was then in charge of the section that dealt with Buddhism, Taoism, and Islam. He decided that in the circumstances he could not recommend *Y* to any governmental employer; and urged him to go back to his monastery. *Y* was reluctant to try this. Especially after what had happened to *X*, he was afraid of the way he would be treated by the monks. Finally, however, after a promise of help from the cadre, he shaved his head, put on a monk's robe again, and walked into the Liu-jung Ssu asking to be re-admitted. Abbot *Z* (his successor) was indignant. He put his bag out in the street and hustled him down to the police station, where he told the station chief that here was a person who was not registered as a resident of the monastery and for whom there was no food ration there: would the police be good enough to bar him from attempting to move in? The station chief telephoned my informant, who pointed out that *Y* had been trained by and worked for the Party for many years and now had nowhere else to go. He was also an orphan without relatives. If the Party did not look out for its own people, it would lose face. Accordingly the station chief told *Z* that the return of *Y* was permissible so far as the public security organs were concerned and was the monastery's internal affair. That is, it was lawful for *Y* to live there since he had come from there in the first place. *Z* had no choice but to let his predecessor move back in.

3. Hsin-ch'eng (left), the monk referred to as *Y* in the text, shows a Japanese priest around the Liu-jung Ssu in 1965. The image of Maitreya can be seen inside the front entrance.

My informant, however, wanted no repetition of the suicide of *X*. So, over a period of six weeks, he called three meetings of all monks of the monastery, each lasting several hours. His purpose was to make them accept *Y* "voluntarily." He criticized *Z* for trying to exclude someone who had served as a cadre for many years and was therefore a glory to Buddhist circles. If they regarded him as an apostate from Buddhism, then that made themselves and Buddhism apostates from the government, since he had been serving the government. To force him out would show that they had taken a reactionary stand. Confronted by these arguments, the monks could only agree to *Y's* permanent residence. He was given the title, if not the duties, of guest prefect and lived in the temple supporting himself by doing odd jobs in a metal work factory. The case quieted down. Yet it was to have later reverberations. *Z* was sent to labor reform in 1958;[137] and the same thing happened to my informant, the cadre. One of the charges against him was that he had violated government policy in helping a rural resident, *Y*, return to live in the city.

This case illustrates how much time the religious affairs cadres could spend once they became involved in the problems of internal administration of monasteries, which had formerly been settled by the monks among themselves. It also illustrates the caution with which these cadres–in Canton, at least–tended to act. The need for caution had been dinned into them by the central authorities. My informant recalled how in 1953 a high Party official told the first religious work conference: "Outright prohibition of religion is useless; it will only hurt our Party . . . Religion is a form of social consciousness. If we prohibit it by administrative order, fanaticism will result, possibly bringing with it religious disorders. Therefore, if we are to destroy it, we must do so gradually by other methods."[138] The United Front Work Department often cited a sentence it attributed to Lenin: "The customs of hundreds of millions of people are a most terrible power."

In the spring of 1957, when Chao P'u-ch'u, the secretary-general of the CBA, was passing through Canton, he summoned my informant to his luxurious room at the Ai-ch'ün Hotel and cross-questioned him about his handling of Buddhist problems, in particular the problem of ordination. My informant said that his ultimate goal was to stop ordinations altogether, but the next best thing was to reduce their scale and influence, as he had been able to do. Chao commented: "It is very difficult. You must be cautious. Otherwise they [Buddhists] might report to the central authorities, who would find it a difficult matter to handle." He added that the methods to be adopted in dealing with religious problems should not be too obvious, but rather should be indirect. "Of course," noted my informant in recounting the conversation, "we already knew this. He was just reminding us." The reminder was impressive, however, because Chao said he was speaking not as an officer of the Buddhist association, but as the representative of the Religious Affairs Bureau in Peking, with which he had no overt connection. My informant had been summoned to see him by the head of the Canton United Front Department and found that he was extremely polite but behaved like a high-ranking member of the Party. If this was what Chao was, it illustrates another precaution taken by the Party to assure its control; it wanted to have more than one of its members holding key positions in each religious group.[139]

Caution was the thing most emphasized by this former cadre in all his testimony. He said that the Party genuinely feared the power of religion; felt bound by the constitutional guarantee of freedom of religious belief; and tried to protect legitimate religious groups from "deviations" committed by local cadres. If so, Buddhists do not seem to have been particularly grateful. They often felt that the religious affairs organs, instead of protecting them from local cadres, committed deviations themselves. Thus a progressive abbot from Shanghai told the second national conference: "With regard to the cadres who carry out the government's religious policy, in a country as large as ours it is hard to avoid having deviations in various localities and an inadequate understanding of the policy on religion. For this reason we hope that the CBA will suggest to the government that the cadres concerned with carrying out religious policy should step up their study of that policy."[140]

Most of the time monks kept silent about what they thought of the way they were treated. They were afraid of getting into more trouble. An outstanding example was Hsü-yün, the eminent Ch'an monk, who was nearly beaten to death by some local cadres in the spring of 1951. When a team of investigators was sent down from Peking, he refused to lodge a complaint, and the guilty cadres got off with a reprimand. In 1952 he was introduced to Mao Tse-tung, who inquired whether local cadres had made difficulties for him. Again Hsü-yün said: "No, everything has been fine."[141]

Chapter II

The Decimation of the Sangha

The goals of the official policy on Buddhism were not only to protect and control it (as we saw in the previous chapter), but also to reform and utilize it. The first step in reform was to turn monks into productive members of society who supported themselves by growing what they ate and weaving what they wore rather than by getting fees for serving people's religious needs. This had been the hope of the Confucian critics of Buddhism for many centuries: it was the Communists who finally realized it as part of the transition to socialism.

LAND REFORM

In the three decades before the Chinese Communists came to power, their agrarian policy had often changed, responding again and again to the circumstances of the moment. It began in 1922 as a modest program for reduced taxation; leaped forward in 1927 to a demand for the confiscation and nationalization of land; and pulled back in 1937, when Mao announced that "the confiscation of landlords' land shall be discontinued." In the next decade landlords were repeatedly guaranteed their rent and interest, although at reduced rates. The seesawing resumed in 1947 and it was not until June 30, 1950, that the final regulations for land reform throughout the country were promulgated.

Buddhist monasteries were among the largest landholders in China. Some received income from up to 12,000 mou of paddy (about 2,000 acres)—if not up to 200,000.[1] More than most landowners they had benefited from the oscillation of Communist agrarian policy during the preceding decades. In 1927, when confiscation of their land was specifically called for, only small areas were under Communist control. By the time of the Kiangsi Soviets of 1931-35, monasteries enjoyed a kind of exemption: their land was to be confiscated only after "obtaining the voluntary support of the peasants, so that the latter's religious feelings might not be offended." The first real blows do not seem to have been dealt until the Party saw victory within its reach. A new law was passed in September 1947 specifically abolishing the ownership rights of monasteries (along with other landlords) and, in the winter that followed, their holdings began to be redistributed to the peasants in "liberated areas." By June 1950, when the final Agrarian Reform Law was promulgated, redistribution had taken place throughout most of north China, in areas inhabited by a third of China's rural population.[2] But Buddhism had been weak in the north. Its stronghold lay in the east and central parts of the country. As late as December 1950 what monks in Chekiang were worried about was the reduction of rental income.[3]

The third article of the Agrarian Reform Law referred specifically to monasteries: "The rural land belonging to ancestral shrines, temples, monasteries, churches, schools and organizations, and other land owned by public bodies shall be requisitioned (*cheng-shou*)." The property of ordinary landlords was not to be requisitioned, but "confiscated" (*mo-shou*).[4] This distinction was significant. A landlord's fields were the private property of an individual. The fields of a monastery, on the other land, were institutional property or, as it is expressed in Chinese, "common property" (*kung-ch'an*).[5] They were registered in the monastery's name and were considered to belong either to the sangha as a whole (in the case of large public monasteries) or to a religious "family" (in the case of small temples).[6] In neither case did ownership lie with an individual: it lay collectively with a group of monks. One of the more interesting questions about land reform in China is whether the government permitted this kind of collective ownership to continue or whether it distributed all the land involved to the monks as individuals, so that a period of private ownership intervened before final collectivization. The evidence points both ways, and the central authorities seem never to have settled the question, or at any rate not to have enforced a consistent policy.

For example, when the eighteen monks at the Chü-lung Ssu in Ming-hsi, Fukien, got their plots, "a land certificate was issued to each of them, showing the fields [he had received]. They were no different from a mutual aid team of eighteen households."[7] In a mutual aid team, of course, each household retained ownership of its own land. Towards the end of 1951 a monk near Soochow wrote to the question-and-answer column of *Modern Buddhism*, asking in various ways whether the land that had been distributed to him and his brethren belonged to them as individuals—or was it common property like monastery land in the past? No, came the reply, it belonged to the monks as individuals, just the way what had been distributed to the peasants belonged to each of them. It was different from monastery property in the past. Individual ownership was in accordance with the provisions of the Agrarian Reform Law.[8]

Actually the law was ambiguous. Article 13 (e) stated: "Monks, nuns, Taoists, priests, and Akhungs should be given shares of land and other means of production equal to those of the peasants if they have no other means of making a living and are able and willing to engage in agricultural work."[9] While this clearly called for land being distributed in accordance with the *number* of monks, it did not specify that they should receive it as *individuals*. In practice, it would seem, they received it more often as a group. The same question-and-answer column informed its readers in June 1951: "The land that has been distributed to monks and nuns during land reform is . . . collective private property that does not belong to any one monk or nun. All those who work a piece of land are its owners." It was like the allotment to a lay family, which belonged to the family as a whole, not to any one member of it.[10] Buddhist monks themselves saw an advantage to this: it pointed up the communal element in the monastic tradition and made the latter seem more in tune with the new times.

The question of whether ownership was to be individual or collective seems to have been left up to the cadres of each locality. They also decided on the acreage that local monasteries were to receive. Thre was wide variation in this. Some received ten times more per capita than others. Presumably this reflected a favorable ratio of land to population in the area, but there may have been other factors, such as the attitude of the cadres towards Buddhism. I have been unable to find any area averages—not for a hsien, not for a province, and certainly not for the country as a whole. All I can offer is a table of individual cases (see pp. 46–47).

Throughout the country what mattered was less the amount of land than its fertility, availability of water, and convenience of location. Monks who went through reform have told me that the acreage requisitioned from their monasteries had been of good quality, while what was distributed to them was poor—usually gravelly, on hillsides, without abundant water, and too far away.[11] Furthermore, if the number of its residents declined, a monastery's allotment could be reduced. For example, Chiu-hua Shan had 200 resident monks and 64 mou in 1950; by 1953 the population had dropped to 178 and the number of mou to 45.[12] That meant they had about a third of a mou per capita, which was far too little to maintain life and necessitated a government subsidy.

If, on the other hand, the number of monks increased, this was not considered to justify a request for additional land. It was made clear in 1950 that once a monastery had gotten its share in accordance with the number of resident monks at the time, it could not ask for more in the future, no matter how many new residents had moved in.[13] A striking example of the inequities this could cause is provided by the Nan-hua Ssu, the population of which fluctuated wildly. It had been 200 before Liberation, dropped to 8 at the time of agrarian reform—so that the monastery only received 21 mou—and then rose to 90 by 1958.[14] Such fluctuations were not uncommon. The reason was that, as small temples were confiscated, many of their monks moved to those large public monasteries that remained in operation.[15]

Yet there were a few cases of generous treatment. Certain monasteries in Chengtu were allowed to exchange plots with neighbor-

Table 1. The redistribution of monastery lands

Area	Institution	Original holdings (in mou)[a]	Holding on completion of land reform[b]	Number of residents at time of land reform[c]	Number of mou per resident	Source
Rice area						
Anhwei						
Chiu-hua Shan[d]	All temples	–	64	200	0.3	*HTFH* 11/50, p. 32
Chekiang[e]						
T'ien-t'ai Shan	All temples	–	337	203	1.7	"Hōchū Nihon," p. 15
	Kuo-ch'ing Ssu		124	109	1.1	*HTFH* 10/58, p. 33.
Ningpo	Yü-wang Ssu	802	129	109	1.2	*HTFH* 4/53, p. 10
P'u-t'o Shan	All temples	–	c.180	c.200	0.9	*Chüeh yu-ch'ing* 13.2:20 (October 1952) and *HTFH* 6/62, p. 41
Fukien						
Foochow	Ku Shan	2,000+	180	148	1.2	H.K. *Ta-kung pao*, April 15, 1957
Ming-hsi	Chü-lung Ssu	–	30	18	1.7	*HTFH* 9/53, p. 21
Amoy	Nan P'u-t'o Ssu	80	15	45	0.3	*HTFH* 6/53, pp. 40-41
Hunan						
Changsha	Yen-shou An	–	c.5	3+	c.1.7	*HTFH* 3/51, p. 32
Changsha	T'ung-hsi Ssu	–	c.7	6	c.1	*HTFH* 3/51, p. 32
Ning-hsiang	Pai-yün Ssu		c.27	28	c.1	*HTFH* 8/51, p. 32
Kiangsi						
Yün-chü Shan	Chen-ju Ssu	–	9	4	2.2	*HTFH* 7/53, p. 18
Kiangsu[e]						
Nanking	Ta Mao-p'eng	400	9	6	1.5	former resident
Nanking	Pao-hua Shan	3,000	140+	130+	c.1	*Chüeh yu-ch'ing* 12.5:20 (May 1951) and 12.8-9:24 (September 1951)
Chenchiang	Chin Shan	4,800	60	100+	c.0.6	*Chüeh yu-ch'ing* 13.2:9 (October 1952)
Soochow	Ling-yen Ssu	3,000	100+	130+	c.0.8	*Chüeh yu-ch'ing* 13.2:20 (October 1952)

Kwangtung						
Ch'u-chiang	Nan-hua Ssu	60+	21	8	2.6	*Chüeh yu-ch'ing* 13.2:20 (October 1952)
Szechwan						
Chengtu	Chao-chüeh Ssu	1,000+	180	63	3	*HTFH* 6/53, p. 49
TOTAL			1590	1482		
AVERAGE					1.1[f]	
Wheat area						
Shansi						
Wu-t'ai Shan	All temples	–	622	374	1.7[g]	*HTFH* 6/53, p. 52
Taiyüan	Nan Shih-fang Yüan	80	120	28	4.3	*HTFH* 6/53, p. 28
Ninghsia						
Yung-ning	Cheng-chüeh Ssu		20	4	5	*HTFH* 6/53, p. 32
Chung-ning	Wan-fo Ko	–	30	4	8	*HTFH* 6/53, p. 32
TOTAL			790	410		
AVERAGE					1.9	

[a]Most of these figures on pre-Liberation landholdings were supplied by monks from the monasteries in question. Those for Pao-hua Shan, Chin Shan, and the Ling-yen Ssu are probably reliable. See Welch, *Practice,* pp. 461 and 498 note 44. The acreage for the Yü-wang Ssu is given by the source cited in the table. A dash means that no figure is available.

[b]I have lumped together grain and vegetable land, since the breakdown is often omitted. Therefore the grain land per capita is usually less than the figure given in this column.

[c]This is the total number of residents. The official figures for the average share they received might differ from those given in the table. That is because under the Agrarian Reform Law only able-bodied monks were entitled to receive land. But we know that the law was not always followed. For example, elderly monks and nuns in the Peking area, although they were incapable of labor, did receive shares in land distribution: see *HTFH,* 9/50, p. 29. In any case, the purpose of the table is to show how many mouths had to be fed from each mou. Thus Chin Shan had only 50 monks with labor capacity and they received 60 mou of land, or an average of 1.2 mou apiece. But what they produced had to support an additional 50 monks who were incapable of productive labor. See *Chüeh yu-ch'ing,* 13.2:19 (October 1952). This is similar to what happened at Omei Shan, where only 136 out of the 292 monks and nuns who were still there in 1953 had received land during agrarian reform: see *HTFH,* 6/53, p. 56.

[d]The low allotment per capita at Chiu-hua Shan may have been necessitated by a shortage of arable land within working distance of the monasteries; and the hope may have been that it would be offset, as in the past, by the large pilgrim traffic that used to be enjoyed there. But in the years following Liberation this traffic sharply declined. Hence in March 1951 the monks and nuns of Chiu-hua Shan appealed to the Buddhists of Shanghai to relieve their distress: see *Chüeh yu-ch'ing* 12.3:24 (March 1951).

[e]The most significant figures in this table are probably for Kiangsu and Chekiang, where the monasteries with the largest number of monks and most extensive landholdings in China had been located before Liberation. The drop in Chin Shan's holdings from 4,800 to 60 mou is particularly striking, since this was the leading meditation center in China. Meditation takes time and time takes unearned income.

[f]Since the rule of thumb was a catty per day of hulled rice, a man consumed about 500 catties a year of unhulled rice, which meant that he ate the produce of one to one and a half mou.

[g]In 1958 the peasants around Wu-t'ai Shan "handed over several hundred mou for the monks and nuns to cultivate": see *HTFH,* 10/59, p. 14. This must have been because what the latter had received in land reform was insufficient. Owing to the aridity around Wu-t'ai Shan, 6 mou was "the lowest amount of grain-producing land needed to maintain the life of one person": see *HTFH,* 6/53, p. 52. Therefore the 622 mou distributed to the 374 residents was only enough to feed about 100 of them.

ing peasants after the completion of land reform. Plots at a distance were exchanged for those nearby, scattered plots for clustered ones, and at one monastery there was actually a large increase in total holdings.[16] Somewhat similar was the case of the Wo-lung Ssu, a famous temple in Sian. In autumn of 1950 its monks lost all their suburban land—"just like any urban residents." For almost two years, living partly on a government subsidy, they carried on ideological studies so as to get a "labor viewpoint" and to realize that "the world is created by labor." In July 1952, when they were ready to plow and sow, the government returned to them 66 mou which, two years earlier, had been distributed to the peasants. They were also given the equivalent of US$6,350 to buy wagons, horses, donkeys, and a treadmill water pump.[17] Sian was important, of course, in the history of Sino-Indian relations,[18] but an additional reason for such generous treatment could have been friendliness to Buddhism on the part of local cadres or the influence of national Buddhist leaders.[19]

On the other hand, even when monasteries ended up with more land than they had had before, they were not necessarily better off. This was because the monks, having spent their lives in chanting and meditation, simply did not know how to farm, and even if they had known, too many of them were old and feeble. It was the younger monks who tended to disrobe as conditions worsened. The older ones were less able to face the adjustment to lay life and, as the small temples closed down, it was mainly they who collected in the large monasteries. Often they amounted to 70-80 percent of the residents.[20] Then the inferior land, the lack of skill, and the shortage of strong backs caused difficulties the seriousness of which we can sense from their desperate appeals for help.

Pao-hua Shan, for example, was the most famous ordination center and one of the model monasteries of central China. In the spring of 1951 its monks "were suffering virtual starvation—there was not even diluted congee to eat." Unable to get seed, cattle, and farm implements, they appealed for donations to Buddhists "in all circles."[21] The Kuo-ch'ing Ssu in neighboring Chekiang was an equally famous monastery, since it was considered the birthplace of the T'ien-t'ai sect. In October 1952 land reform had been completed there, but "productive labor had not been fully launched." Its hundred-odd monks were reported to be "about to run out of food" and they too appealed to Buddhist circles for help.[22] So did the eighty monks of Yün-men Shan who had been going with "only one meal a day of diluted congee." There was such a shortage of food that those who were strong enough used to collect firewood nearby and then carry it six miles to sell in Juyüan for sixteen cents a hundredweight, so that they could get money to buy rice. The able-bodied could just support themselves this way: the weak went hungry. When it rained or there was no market for wood, they all went hungry.[23] In their desperation they sent a letter to Li Chi-shen in Peking, a vice-chairman of the People's Government, and complained about the inferior quality of the plots they had received in land distribution. After investigating, he replied by telegram that nothing could be done about it.[24] At the end of 1952 his religious master, Hsü-*y*ün, the abbot who had restored Yün-men and was soon to be made honorary president of the Chinese Buddhist Association, told people in Shanghai that "things at the monastery are bad. The sixty monks still left there spend their days reclaiming wasteland."[25]

The problem of hunger became particularly acute when monasteries lost not only their land but their stores of grain—even the grain that they had grown themselves. During 1950, for example, the monks of the Chu-sheng Ssu on Mount Nan-yüeh collected no grain rents whatever. Instead they harvested 7,000 catties from the 200 mou of land they were cultivating. This was a tenth of the normal rate of yield and testifies to their lack of skill—or will—as farmers. Their hearts must have sunk when they compared it to the 200,000 catties they used to receive from tenants. But it was enough to feed twenty of them. (The number of monks is not stated in the account on which I am drawing, but the monastery used to have over a hundred residents.) Then, in the first days of 1951, former tenants from a neighboring township came to demand the return of their deposits. This was money they had left with the monastery from year to year as security for the payment of rent. They claimed 14,800 catties of unhulled rice—more than the total the monks had on hand. What was to be done? When they asked the local authorities, they were told: "According to what we know of the situation, this really does create difficulties. Please handle them as best as you can." All the monks could do was watch as their grain got lugged away. The cadres urged them not to be unhappy: if the time came when they really had nothing left to eat, the government would think of some way for them to manage and it would certainly not let them starve to death. But next day the same tenants were back again, this time to carry off the hulled rice and cooking oil and to seize some of the monks as hostages for the rest of the deposit fund.

In response to desperate pleas from the monks, the head of the local land reform office got the hostages released and obtained an order from the government of the township, which stated that "people in towns and villages inside or outside the Nan-yüeh special district, if they come to Nan-yüeh to arrest monks in connection with the return of deposits, must first get consent of the township government; indiscriminate arrests are absolutely not allowed." The monks of the Chu-sheng Ssu quickly delivered to the land reform office 140 canceled leases and then some of the seized rice was returned to them "so that they could continue to live." The monk who described all this in an article printed in *Modern Buddhism* was abject in his praise of the wonderful protection he and his brethren had received from the cadres. "Who," he concluded, "would now dare to say that Communism was a threat to Buddhist monasteries?"[26]

Some of the difficulties just described can be attributed to the fact that this was a transition period. Land reform was completed, except in minority areas, by February 1953. An average of 2.3 mou per capita had been distributed to 300 million peasants.

LABOR FOR URBAN MONKS

In urban areas a different kind of pressure had been exerted on monks to engage in productive labor. If they did not do so, not their land but their buildings might be confiscated. Ch'en Ch'i-yüan, a vice-minister of Internal Affairs, told a Buddhist audience on October 6, 1950: "On the average two persons are occupying one temple. When one compares this with the way government employees are crowded together into their offices, it seems rather unfair. But if in the future we borrow monasteries and temples as they are needed, we can still do so after consultation (*hsieh-shang*), whether we are borrowing or renting. We feel it is better that way. The people will not permit the alternative situation in which empty temple rooms stand idle and unoccupied."[27] Of course, the right to be consulted did not mean that the temples could be unreasonable. If they did in fact have empty rooms, they could not make up excuses for refusing to let government offices and army units move in. What they could do was to "get together and start using their empty space for production. Then the problem would take care of itself."[28] There was nothing new in the confiscation or occupation of monastery premises. All during the Republican period empty rooms had tempted government officials who needed space to house schools and bureaus. Unless there was opposition from other officials who were friendly to Buddhism, monasteries had often been taken over, in whole or in part.[29]

On May Day, 1951, one of the tasks undertaken by Buddhist monks was to organize light industrial enterprises and become self-sufficient.[30] The kind of light industry best suited to them was one that required little skill, a low investment, and offered the possibility of a good market. One such seemed to be the manufacture of gunnysacks (jute bags). China had been buying them from India at a cost of US$50,000,000 a year—her fourth largest import. Jute plantations were now to be expanded in the southern provinces.[31] So in September 1950 the Ta-hsiung Gunnysack Factory went into operation in Peking with hopes to "solve completely the problem of productive labor for the monks and nuns of the municipality."[32] Soon gunnysack factories were being started elsewhere, not only in urban, but in rural monasteries to offset the shortage of income from agriculture.[33] Other things that seemed relatively easy for monks to manufacture were cloth or toweling and finished clothing.[34] Sometimes the monks put up their own capital to get production started;[35] sometimes they rented part of the monastery premises to an outside enterprise, by which they were then employed;[36] sometimes they did not engage in manufacture at all, but simply continued to provide the hotel and restaurant services that were traditional in centers of recreation and pilgrimage.[37]

COLLECTIVIZATION

Collectivization was an essential part of the transition to socialism. In agriculture the first step towards it was to form mutual aid teams; the second was to combine them in coöperatives, Buddhist monasteries, were, in a sense, coöperatives already. They had the tradition not only of common ownership but of unpaid labor for the common good. The monks who worked in the kitchen and the vegetable garden were compensated only by the good karma they earned—and by their share in the food and shelter that the monastery provided to all. After Liberation it was natural for the same arrangement to continue. At least one monastic coöperative—industrial rather than rural—was set up even before Liberation. At the Tzu-tsai An in Changsha fourteen nuns established the First Sewing and Weaving Production Coöperative on March 31, 1949; yet Changsha was not taken by the Communists until the following August.[38] Actually, most of the light industrial monastery enterprises mentioned in notes 34-36 were coöperatives in fact if not in name. They came under the financial control of the municipal coöperatives federation, which audited their accounts and helped them to get equipment, raw materials, and technical instruction.

In rural areas, where mutual aid teams preceded coöperatives, they too engaged in handicrafts,[39] and they too were not necessarily called mutual aid teams. They simply functioned as such. Since an agricultural coöperative was larger—consisting usually of several teams—it could only be formed by a large monastery or in a place where several small monasteries lay close together. The first of which I have found mention was started at the Yü-wang Ssu (the Asoka Monastery) near Ningpo on September 1, 1952—three years before the big push for coöperativization began in the country as a whole. Indeed, it appears to have been one of the very first agricultural coöperatives set up in central China,[40] and its monks argued that the monastic tradition specially qualified them to provide a model for others: "Because we own our property in common and do productive labor in common, the labor-capital relationship does not exist in our monastery." They used this argument to secure approval first at the county level and then from the Federation of Coöperatives of Chekiang province. The Yü-wang Producers' Coöperative, as they called it, included teams for handicrafts as well as agriculture; and thirty-five of its members joined the local peasant association. The peasants of the area are reported to have been inspired by what the monks had accomplished and to have said: "Indeed collective production is very effective. We must run our mutual aid teams well in order to catch up with them."[41] (Actually, as we shall see below, some aspects of collective production at the Yü-wang Ssu were a failure.)

Most rural monasteries formed or joined coöperatives later on. Many must have done so after Mao delivered his famous speech of July 31, 1955, calling for rapid collectivization of the countryside. Yet I have found no overall figures—only individual cases. In 1956, for example, the Chang-hua Ssu, Shashih, Hupei, applied for membership in the local APC (agricultural producers' coöperative);[42] and in Sian by September 1957 the four largest monasteries had joined together to form the Sian Buddhists' Higher-Level APC.[43] One reason it was easier for monks to form their own coöperative rather than join an outside one was that hostile cadres would sometimes refuse them admission.[44]

Overall figures also appear to be unavailable on the final and highest stage of collectivization—the communes. Each commune was made up of many higher-level coöperatives, just as each of the latter had been made up of several lower-level coöperatives, and these in turn had brought together several mutual aid teams.[45] We know of individual monasteries that joined communes and of clusters of monasteries that joined, including some on a sacred mountain.[46] Yet we can read accounts of other monasteries, published at the same time, that make no mention of commune membership and, when listing future plans, do not include it among them.[47] Refugees and travelers reported that by 1959 monks all seemed to be working on commune production teams, no different from other citizens, but the official statements I have read tend to avoid quantification: for example, Shirob Jaltso said at the end of 1959 that the monks and nuns "who live in rural areas engage in production under the unified leadership of the people's communes there."[48] One of the very few descriptions of what this meant in practice was an article about the Ling-shan Ssu in Loshan, Honan. Entitled "The People's Commune Is Creating a Paradise on Earth," it dealt only with the benefits monks and nuns were receiving, not with the work they were expected to contribute. Special vegetarian mess halls had been set up for them, so that they could still observe their dietary rules. In addition to food, clothing, and bedding, they were given medical care if they fell ill. This was said to contrast with the difficulties they had faced in the past. Furthermore, with private ownership eliminated, the roots of the Buddhist "three poisons" (greed, hatred, and ignorance) had been pulled out; and the breaking down of village and country boundaries had fostered a communist spirit of broad coöperation so that, as scripture has it, "When a single buddha appears, a thousand buddhas emerge to help him."[49]

DIFFICULTIES AND FAILURES

The fact that monks started productive labor and set up coöperatives did not always assure success. A case in point is the Asoka Monastery near Ningpo, where the first Buddhist coöperative was established in 1952. Already in January of 1952 all the rice that the monks had produced the previous year (their first year of manual labor) had been eaten and the economic situation was "very serious." With money raised by selling the timbers from a bombed-out building and with some donations from Shanghai, they bought enough rice to survive until the next harvest. But something more had to be done. About half of the monks who were too old or feeble for regular farm work still had some labor capacity—enough at least, for light-industrial production.

> In order to avoid a waste of manpower and to solve the problem of too many people for too little land, we decided to

set up a gunnysack factory as a subsidiary occupation. To take advantage of the experience of the gunnysack factory of the Ningpo Municipal Buddhist Association we sent two of our men to Ningpo to learn the craft and at the same time bought ten looms. Since this was an industry that did not require heavy labor and where five or six men could work on one loom, it was easy to learn the needed skills, and the older monks could participate in the stranding of jute. Our preparations for the establishment of the factory began in spring. Inasmuch as the form of organization remained a problem, approval did not come from the county central coöperative until after the early rice crop was harvested in August [1952]. We started training on August 20, and the factory commenced operation in September.

For training purposes, we bought 700 catties of jute. . . . We began by making it into burlap and then sewed the burlap into gunnysacks. The first order we received was to process 1,100 catties of jute for the central coöperative. Because the batch was dark in color and fragile, and the elderly could not keep up in the stranding, our production was very low. In order to make a success of it, we enlisted a number of village women to help in the stranding . . . After we filled an order from the central coöperative for 600 salt bags, the jute crop that our coöperative had planted was ready for harvesting and we obtained a total of 1,098 catties, in addition to which we had the 700 catties that we had originally bought for trial production. A second sales agreement with the central coöperative was filled at the end of October, and it then gave us a new order for 5,000 salt bags. Delivery was to be made at the end of December, but we were not able to meet this deadline owing to the fact that a number of our workers had to take part in the harvesting of the rice crop and the drying of public grain; then there was a sudden onset of cold weather, a lack of farsightedness on the part of the leadership, an absence of any overall plan, insufficient attention paid to the execution of the contract, carelessness and bureaucratism in our work, and our failure to go deeply into problems and solve them.

> The achievements made in our work since the establishment of the gunnysack factory four months ago can be summarized as follows. First, we have utilized the surplus manpower of fifteen monks in their forties, thirteen in their fifties, and eleven over sixty years old. In the old society these monks were only consumers, whereas in the New China they have all become fighters on the production front. Second, wealth has been created for the nation. Third, the monks who have participated in production have all felt the greatness of the working class; and the attitude of indifference to production increase in the economy has been curbed and corrected.
>
> Yet owing to the rapid development of society there is no longer any market for our handmade burlap.[50]

The plan for the following year was to convert to the semi-mechanized production of heavy cotton yarn, to gear production to sales, and to institute cost accounting and inspection procedures.[51] We do not know how well this plan was carried out. At any rate one of the defects in past work had been the following:

> We planned for the sake of planning. We put into our plan [for 1952] a provision for the establishment of an inspection system merely in order to make the plan look better, and we did not carry it out, treating it merely as a decoration. This subjective formalism must be resolutely rectified. Another example of it was the provision in our plan to assist the growth of 150,000 young pine seedlings. This was based on an estimate of the number of trees that had already seeded themselves on the hills; and although the figure was accurate, our plan did not take into consideration in a concrete way *whether* they would grow and *how* they could be assisted.[52]

These disappointing results in gunnysack production and afforestation work have parallels elsewhere. Quite a few total failures are reported.[53] The impression is inescapable that the government, after ordering Buddhists to become self-supporting, often did not give them the means to do so. It is easy to see why. With their lack of skill, their "old mentality," and the limitations imposed by their rules (like not handling animal products), they presented a messy problem to which it was natural for the cadres to give a low priority.[54]

In agriculture too coöperatives were dissolved. One such had been set up at Nan-yüeh on February 17, 1957, two years after the "high tide" of coöperativization in the country as a whole. The reasons why it was set up so late were made clear in a revealing article that shows the kind of resistance encountered with the monks.

Nan-yüeh was the site of the Chu-sheng Ssu, whose monks had been helpless to prevent their grain reserves being lugged away by tenants after Liberation. The two hundred who stayed on in the many big monasteries of the mountain had depended mainly on subsidies from the government after 1953. It was apparently late in 1956 that "young, able-bodied monks and nuns led the way to the establishment of an APC." They received vigorous support from the local Party and government.

> However among the religious there were still many who could not see the point. Some considered that Buddhist monks and nuns were "outside the secular world," whereas running a coöperative was something distinctly secular. Monks and nuns had renounced even their own small "families": how could they enter the big "family" of a coöperative? There was a *bhiksuni* named Te-hsiu who thought up another reason: "nuns want solitude; if they don't have it, they're not nuns." Her idea was to invoke "solitude" in order to oppose collective activity. Some considered that, since for decades past they had done no manual labor, trying to do it now would be like an eighty-year-old man trying to learn to play a musical instrument—they couldn't do it well even as individuals, so how could they do it in this "coöperative"? Others talked in a more intelligent way about the shortage of labor power, the lack of experience, the difficulty of getting people together on it—but their conclusion was the same: not to have a coöperative. The people in charge of monasteries and temples where the income

> from donations was on the high side were even more sharply opposed to "running a coöperative for the general welfare." Then there were those who said: "Your coöperative simply means making everyone do manual labor, but when we help people by chanting sutras and striking the bronze bowl, and by kneeling until our backs ache, this is also manual labor. People pay to get rid of their troubles [literally, to avert disasters]. We work hard to help them get rid of their troubles; this isn't taking their money for nothing." Some considered that if a coöperative were started, then whenever there was a peak in production, religious practice would not be kept up. And there were even people who twisted the precious instructions of their ancestral master, Pai-chang, so that instead of his saying "On the day you do not work, you should not eat," they had him say "On the day you do not sit, you should not eat."[55] A small number of people also had thoughts about a change of regime and wondered if Chiang Kai-shek might not come back, so that it would be best to keep their individual status and be ready for whichever way the wind blew. One monk, Miao-yün, said: "I am only going to join the coöperative after the intercalary eighth month"—and when people asked why, he whispered: "In the intercalary seventh or eighth, the emperor Lao-tzu will slay them all."[56]

The persistence of such ideas illustrates the difficulty of thought reform in the case of the Buddhist and Taoist clergy. Of course, we are not told how many of the monks on Nan-yüeh felt this way, but that it may have been a majority is suggested by the fact that the APC there was joined by only 83 out of the 200 monks and nuns on the mountain. Presumably the article discusses their opposition at such length in order to point up the skill with which the activists overcame it, just as it goes into detail on the other problems faced by the coöperative in order to point up the activists' resourcefulness in solving them. The problems were certainly staggering, as the following passage shows.

> This APC had many special points of its own.
>
> 1. Its members were few and labor power was low. In all it

had only 83 members, of whom 22 men and women had full labor power, 15 had half labor power, 16 could do less than half labor or light labor, and 30 had no labor power.

2. Its arable land was small and scattered and there was not the skill to cultivate it. Some fields were so small that you could not get a plow into them; if a water buffalo went in there, it would be unable to turn around. It took 20 or 30 such bits to make one mou [about a sixth of an acre]. The arable land of the coöperative lay within an area that extended 30 Chinese li [about ten miles] in one direction, from the Chu-jung Peak down to the Great Temple in the town of Nan-yüeh; and ten li in the other direction, from the Nan-t'ai Ssu to Kan-lung. Natural disasters were, of course, much commoner on the mountain than they would have been on valley land. When mountain floods came, there was damage from water; when it did not rain for a long time, there was damage from drought—not to mention the ravages of wind, insects, and wild animals. There were only three monks [on the mountain] who knew how to handle a plow and harrow—and of these one absolutely refused to join the coöperative, saying that if he had to join, he would hang himself; the second went through the motions of joining, but did not join with his heart; and only the third and last monk, named Heng-shu, taught the art of ploughing to some disciples and really contributed something to the coöperative.

3. Members' hearts were not united and there were many ideological problems. Except for the handful of people who started the coöperative, whoever was elected a coöperative cadre would refuse to serve—on the grounds that "monks and nuns do not have enough time to secure their own release from birth and death, so how can they look after other people?" It was each monk to his own pot: when one person had finished half a day's work, another person had not yet cooked his breakfast. Sometimes the head of a production team could not assign work because the women would not go down into the fields, the men would not lug anything by shoulder-pole, and all that anyone wanted to do was to pull weeds and loosen the soil. A woman judged to have full labor power only did forty

> days work in a year. The number of "five guarantee" households was too large, which affected people's attitude toward production.[57]

One might have thought that the outlook for this coöperative was gloomy, but not all! In 1957, its first year, good harvests were reaped (360 catties of grain per mou) and members ended up after taxes with an income of 100-230 JMP apiece. They could buy new clothes, bedding, flashlights, thermos bottles, and even wristwatches. In 1958, under the stimulus of the Great Leap Forward, the accomplishments in production were twice as great and for 1959 the plan was to make them twice as great again. Three blast furnaces were started, a mess hall was set up, and the Buddhist-Taoist APC of Nan-yüeh was the first in its area to apply for membership in the people's commune. Before the end of 1958 it was accepted as a production team, and soon it was the model team of the commune. It is a surprise, therefore, to read that in 1962 it was dissolved by the local Buddhist association so that its members, who were too old, could return to the care of their temples, perform religious duties, and cultivate their own vegetable gardens.[58]

The reason I have chosen to treat at length the cases of coöperatives at Nan-yüeh and the Yü-wang Ssu is not because their "success stories" reveal a good deal of failure, but because these are the only two coöperatives on which I have found such detailed accounts in the mainland press. At each the same kind of difficulties are reported and the same claims of victorious achievement are presented to offset them. Regardless of the veracity of these claims, it is clear that monks felt a deep-seated resistance to coöperativization. During its "high tide" some of them pretended to be deaf and dumb and said: "This is something for worldly people that has nothing to do with us who are outside the secular world." Others, when visited by cadres who urged them to enter a coöperative, explained: "Our habits are different. Morning and evening devotions and the practice of the dharma do not go well with collective labor. It is still best for us to work in our own way."[59]

This attitude was totally unacceptable to the regime. Again and again the old way of life was called "parasitic." Monks were accused of having "eaten without plowing and dressed without weaving . . . There used to be a saying in big monasteries: 'if the oil bottle beside you tips over, don't lift a finger to pick it up.' "[60] Yet the Buddha himself, it was pointed out, had swept the floor, repaired the lintel of his front door, made clothes for one disciple, and taken care of another when he was ill.[61] The rebuke was really unfair. Chinese monks had always swept and cooked, grown their own vegetables, made minor repairs, and taken care of sick brethren; and they had done so in accordance with a coöperative tradition that went back 2,500 years.

THE PERSISTENCE OF "PARASITISM"

In view of the pressure from the regime, exemplified most concretely in land reform and in the threat of confiscation, we might suppose that monks throughout China had started productive labor (if they were physically capable of it) by early 1953, when land reform had been completed. Yet I have found no nation-wide statistics to confirm this. As usual, only a few scattered figures, all local, seem to be available. For instance, in September 1952 it was reported that 70 percent of the 2,000 monks and nuns in northern Anhwei were carrying on agricultural production.[62] In several cities 70 to 80 percent of the sangha were said to be engaged in light industry.[63] In the case of individual monasteries, sometimes all the monks were said to be involved,[64] but usually it was simply stated that production was being carried on; whether by some or all the monks is seldom clear.[65]

If monks did not take part in production, then from where did they get the money to buy their rice? According to *Modern Buddhism,* at least, their old sources of income had dried up. An authoritative article, published at the end of 1952, pointed out that in the past Chinese monks had depended for their income on four sources: (1) pious donations; (2) fees for performing rites for the dead; (3) rents from urban real estate; (4) farm rents. Since Liberation, it said, the sums donated by the pious had dropped to nearly nothing, not only because people's attitude towards religion had greatly changed (so that they no longer had any wish to donate money), but also because the financial circumstances of many of the people who used to make donations had also greatly changed (so that they could no longer afford to). As to fees for the performance of Buddhist services, these had also dropped to nearly nothing for the same reasons—that is, people were less interested in the afterlife and less willing to incur extravagance for the sake of the dead. As to urban rents, the amounts that could now be collected were negligible—and, of course, land reform had wholly eliminated rents from farm land.[66]

This gloomy picture is confirmed by reports from individual monasteries,[67] and the reasons it cites seem largely accurate. Landlords and rich peasants had indeed provided the bulk of donations and fees; and they certainly were, as a Communist newspaper put it, "classes on their way out."[68] In the old days it had not been uncommon for a prosperous Shanghai family to pay 2,000 silver dollars for the performance of a plenary mass at a large Kiangsu monastery or to contribute handsomely to the repair of one of its halls. As more and more money for national construction was squeezed out of the bourgeoisie and as its members fell victims to successive campaigns (like the Five-Anti) or were reduced to salaried employees of the businesses they had once owned, such lavish support of monasteries became increasingly rare and finally out of the question. Even small gifts from ordinary devotees were gradually discouraged.[69] Finally, while we may be skeptical whether people really were now less interested in the afterlife, there is no doubt that they had come to realize that it was a dangerous interest. Monks were warned against "doing business in superstition (*mi-hsin ying-yeh*)"[70] and laymen were warned that they "must discard rites that could easily be considered superstitious, like burning paper money and ingots, divination with bamboo slips, and so on."[71] In 1951 a young monk in Hunan enrolled in a school for construction workers, saying: "Why should I lead a superstitious life in this dreary temple and *put my future in danger*?" On this *Modern Buddhism* commented: "By 'superstitious life' he meant performing rites for the dead."[72]

These are the reasons why it would be reasonable to suppose

4. Devotions are recited at the Yung-ho Kung by lamas, old and young. Peking, 1956.

that by 1953 all Chinese monks were supporting themselves through productive labor. The fact, however, is that although most of them had entered production, some still managed to avoid it and a few continued to do so for a long time. Strange as it may seem, their rents, donations, or fees continued. In a few cities monasteries did not even have to bother collecting rent; it was collected for them by a management committee, which pooled their real estate and passed on to them part or all of the revenue. Especially lamaseries, like the Yung-ho Kung in Peking, enjoyed this privileged treatment, which enabled them to carry on religious exercises much as usual.[73] In other cities and sometimes in the countryside monks continued to receive pious donations, revenue from rites for the dead, and even fees for interpreting the divination tallies and other "superstitious practices."[74] At the Kao-min Ssu near Yangchow, as late as 1956, the income from pious donors in Shanghai was still large and regular enough so that many monks there did not have to engage in productive labor at all but could maintain the old schedule of religious activities, centered in the meditation hall, where those enrolled spent seven to fifteen hours a day in mental exercises. Some of them had not been outside the monastery walls for decades. The reason for the continuing lay support was that Kao-min was one of the four model monasteries of China, renowned as a center of Ch'an practice.[75]

Such "parasitism" was sometimes openly admitted in official Buddhist circles. "Of course, there are still quite a few monks and nuns who devote themselves exclusively to religious practice and to the study of the doctrine, their livelihood being maintained by donations (*pu-shih*) from believers and by other forms of religious income that their monasteries and temples receive. Because of the constant rise in people's living standards, these monks and nuns who depend on pious donations (*kung-yang*) are also enjoying a secure livelihood."[76]

Yet to call their livelihood secure was oversanguine. Policy oscillated, and each time it turned hard, some of the remaining "parasites" lost their unearned income and had to join the rest of their brethren in productive labor. In the very month that *Modern Buddhism* carried the statement just quoted, it also carried news of the suppression of the Shanghai Buddhist Youth Society, three of whose leaders had been arrested. One of their crimes had been to post appeals for donations to support the sangha.[77] Donations were sometimes discouraged by the monks themselves. In March 1954, for example, when large crowds came to the Kuan-yin Ssu, Liaoyang, to celebrate the birthday of Kuan-yin, they found the monastery covered with posters warning them against superstitious practices such as burning paper effigies, consulting the bamboo divination slips, and purchasing charms. "Do not think that through the buddhas and bodhisattvas you can obtain good fortune, cure disease, or avoid disaster. No matter how big a donation you make, they cannot grant you such requests. Keep your good money for buying Patriotic Bonds and you can create infinite happiness for society." The number of bonds purchased is not recorded, but the monks' donations and fees dropped to half of what they had been the year before.[78]

The biggest drop in donations, fees, and other traditional forms of monastic income came in 1958—the biggest drop, that is, since land reform. There were many reasons for it. Policy had turned very hard. Certain Buddhist leaders, including the former publisher of *Modern Buddhism,* were attacked in 1958 as rightists; and the anti-rightist movement made all Buddhists feel renewed fear that if they patronized monks and monasteries, they would be accused of "backward thinking." In at least one city where monasteries had been continuing to get rental income, their real estate was formally confiscated and such income came to an end.[79] Throughout 1958 pressure increased on monks to join communes and become self-supporting. Finally in the autumn a directive was sent by the Religious Affairs Bureau in Peking to its local offices throughout the country. This directive outlawed the donation boxes that had been a regular feature of the Buddhist shrine-halls; forbade the use of bamboo divination slips or their interpretation by the monks; and prohibited "improper religious activities." The latter was taken to refer to rites for the dead, especially those performed in people's homes.[80] Many of the small urban temples that had survived until 1958 by performing such rites were now forced to close down; others were simply confiscated. Large monasteries passed resolutions to the effect that rites for the dead "should not interfere with production."[81] Even the materials needed to perform them became suddenly scarcer and more expensive, including incense, candles, and paper ingots, on all of which taxes are reported to have been imposed by local authorities.

But after two steps forward in 1958-1959, there came—rather predictably and paralleling what happened in almost all phases of Chinese life—a big step back during the three years of 1960-62. People discovered that they would no longer be criticized for going to temples and they began to go in great numbers. Donation boxes re-appeared and rites for the dead were freely performed in the large cities. Those monks who had somehow managed to survive up to now without engaging in productive labor found that it was somewhat easier to go on doing so. There was a shift from the hard line to the soft line that shows up well in three official statements, printed within a ten month period. In October 1959

Shirob Jaltso, the president of the Chinese Buddhist Association, said: "There is freedom both to give and to accept legitimate donations and pious offerings. But when it comes to collecting money with the Buddha as a pretext and concocting tricks to cheat Buddhists of donations, that is called in Buddhism 'a heterodox livelihood (*hsieh-ming*)'; how can such people be so lucky as to win the pardon of the masses!"[82] This sounded very threatening to any monks who had been depending on rites for the dead.

Three months later *Modern Buddhism* published a New Year's editorial that included the following statement: "More and more monks and nuns with labor capacity have joined in productive labor and begun to walk the road of self-support . . . Those monks and nuns who have not yet joined, although they have the qualifications to, must quickly discard their parasitic life of eating without working and participate in some form of production under the leadership of the local government."[83] Here one is struck, first, by the admission that two years after the Great Leap Forward, despite their pledges, there were still monks leading a parasitic life; and second, by the rather perfunctory tone of the appeal for them to join productive labor.[84]

By April 1960 Shirob Jaltso was saying: "In Shanghai there are so many requests for Buddhist rites for the dead that monasteries, both large and small, are too busy to fill them all."[85] Foreign visitors saw them underway and overseas Chinese reported that wherever they went, the monks showed not the slightest reluctance to accept donations.[86] Although this relaxed mood was gradually dispelled by the developments that led up to the Cultural Revolution, there were still reports in 1965 and early 1966 of donations and fees being received at some of the remaining monasteries, especially in Shanghai.

"Parasitism" persisted, then, for many years after the regime had decided to eliminate it. As one Buddhist leader said in 1959: "It is indeed not a simple matter to raise monks' enthusiasm for labor."[87] The income that the sangha received aside from labor did not terminate abruptly and completely but declined gradually according to the circumstances and the locality in an uneven, oscillating pattern that can be seen in many other aspects of the treatment of Buddhism under Mao. This oscillating decline, however, should not make us lose sight of the fact that for most monks most traditional sources of income were eliminated in 1950-52. We may be more intrigued or surprised by the other side of the coin—that for some monks they continued in the years that followed—but it is historically less important. The same applies to the exodus from the sangha—a process directly caused by the decline in revenue. The great majority of monks returned to lay life in 1950-52, but defections on a smaller scale continued as others too found that there was not enough to eat at the monastery and they had to work so hard to grow it that they had too little time for religious practice.

THE RETURN TO LAY LIFE

The earliest reference that I have seen to the initial exodus comes from Shanghai, where the San-mei Ssu, like many other monasteries, was being used to quarter Nationalist troops at the time of Liberation. On May 27, 1949, the Nationalists marched out and the People's Liberation Army marched in. This might seem to have meant nothing more than the replacement of one group of uninvited guests by another. But the PLA was less open-minded about "superstitious activities," and so laymen stopped calling for Buddhist services, which here as elsewhere were the main source of income. Food soon became scarce and 90 percent of the resident monks left. Even then there was not enough for the remaining monks to live on. Among those who left was a certain Ts'ui-fang, who, after listening to speeches by Ch'en Ming-shu and Chao P'u-ch'u, "realized that his old life was wrong and resolved to engage in production. Since a monk's gown would get in his way, he took it off and started selling soy sauce, fruits, and cookies. He looked back with shame on his old life of making money by the salvation of souls."[88]

Some of those who disrobed went to the countryside to "serve agriculture."[89] Others preferred to join the army[90] and in Canton two were admitted to a university.[91] Nuns also disrobed in order to marry or enter production.[92] To disrobe did not necessarily mean that they had to move out. Some former monks and nuns went on living at their monasteries, although they let the hair grow on their shaven heads and wore lay dress. A few even married, raised livestock for slaughter, and spent monastery funds for their own pleasure. When that happened, the local Buddhist association was called in to set matters right.[93]

The return to lay life was never specifically ordered by the authorities. All they did was to make it easy for those who disrobed and hard for those who did not. Thus in 1951 *Modern Buddhism* explained to its readers how easy it was for a monk to renounce his vows. He did not have to make a long journey in order to do so in front of the masters who had originally ordained him; he could do it before any venerable old monk—or even on his own while making a reverence to the Buddha.[94]

In contrast to this, anyone who wished to remain in the sangha faced economic and psychological pressures. Some of the economic pressures have already been discussed: the shortages of food that were chronic when monks tried to raise it themselves; the failures in light industrial production; and the decline in traditional forms of monastic income. Psychological pressures were more subtle. The cadres did not threaten a monk with punishment if he stuck to his vows. They would just question his motives and deplore his feudal thinking. "Why don't you marry," they would say, "and lead a normal life? Otherwise you will be unable to fulfill your responsibilities to society."[95] In fact, of course, many monks were fulfilling them, since they worked as hard as laymen. What then was the point in their remaining monks? The monastery no longer offered a refuge from the dust of the world. And what sort of future lay ahead for those who stayed in it? A grim form answer to this question seemed to be given by the struggle against senior monks.

STRUGGLE AGAINST SENIOR MONKS

The Chinese sangha was organized not as a national hierarchy but as a loosely connected series of pseudo-families. In each of them the master was "father" or "grandfather" and the disciples were "sons" or "grandsons." The disciples felt many of the same filial obligations to masters as to parents. They obeyed them, took care of them in their old age, and made offerings to them after death, sweeping their graves at Ch'ing-ming.[96] At most monasteries the majority of younger monks were disciples of older ones who, like fathers in lay life, held all the power.

In the lay sector of society the policy of the Communist Party was to destroy the family system and bring about a transfer of loyalty to the State; it had a parallel program in the religious sector. Land reform provided a convenient opportunity. Abbots and officers of land-owning monasteries could be classified as landlords and thus become one of the targets of the vast persecution that was designed to break the power of the landlord class. That senior monks were to be classified as landlords was made clear in the very first issue of *Modern Buddhism.*[97] Refugees supply accounts of what this meant in practice.

For example, a monk who spent the year after Liberation at a landed monastery near Nanking told me: "Our abbot was sentenced to prison after being struggled against . . . I did not go to the struggle meeting, but in most cases they would strip the clothing from the upper half of a man's body and bind his hands behind his back and his feet too, and then he would kneel facing the masses and confess his crimes." I asked if the abbot in this case had been elderly. "Yes, he was elderly—but actually the treatment he got was quite polite. That was because the local people had a good impression of him. They did not punish him, they did not beat him. Ordinary landlords were beaten."

Another account gives more details on how struggle meetings were conducted and reveals a rather chaotic alternation of harshness and leniency in the treatment that monastery officers received. The monastery involved was the Ling-yin Ssu, the largest in Hangchow and one of the most famous in China. For six months after the Communists took Hangchow in May 1949, they did nothing to interfere with the operation of its temples: they simply "investigated." Then on December 11, 1949,[98] the cadres collected a crowd of about 4,000 people in a big open space outside the Chi-ch'eng Ssu. Tables were piled on tables to make a high platform and one by one five monks from the Ling-yin Ssu–including my informant–were led up to it. The abbot was not among them (he had once been a Communist Party member and was apparently considered still to be a progressive). The five were the prior, guest prefect, proctor, and two subpriors–in other words the officers most concerned with the day-to-day administration of the monastery.[99] As each one stood facing the crowd, a statement of his past misdeeds was read aloud by a representative elected by the people. "On such-and-such a day, month, year [perhaps twenty years ago] you gave such-and-such a monk a cruel beating."[100] Then this monk would spring to his feet in the crowd and shout: "Yes, it is true. He should be shot." At the end of the testimony a cadre would give the verdict in words like the following: "You see how fat and pretty he is. Why is he so fat? He has been eating the blood and sweat of the people. He is an exploiter, an evil person. Everyone says he should be killed. But the People's Government is magnanimous. It will send him to labor reform."

Then, according to my informant, the five of them were locked up in a Hangchow prison. Every day they went out to work on a road gang. After a week of this, for no apparent reason, the cadres sent them back to the Ling-yin Ssu, appointing some of the people who lived near the temple to act as their guarantors. Ling-yin had bought fourteen looms and its monks were now working at these as well as in its vegetable garden and tea plantations. But there was no market for what they produced: the cloth just piled up. The cadres then began to hold meetings three times a day, lasting two to three hours each. They accused the leading monks of being reactionary and against the government. They locked up the prior, Tung-lin, and beat him "until the blood flowed from his buttocks." Then they released him and locked up my informant. They asked him where the money was kept, beat him when he could not say, and kept him on rice water for forty-nine days. Then they sent him back to prison to do labor for reform. This time it consisted mainly of constructing more buildings to take care of the influx of prisoners–thirty or forty persons each day. Every night all of them would attend "examination meetings" (*chien-t'ao hui*), where the day's work figures would be compared.

"I carried 150 catties, but he carried 300. He is a glorious model worker," someone would say. A person had to be praised as a model for thirty consecutive days to be let out. My informant, however, did not want to kill himself (a few prisoners had, in fact, died from overwork and malnutrition). He did as little work as he could get away with. Finally, because the cadres still did not have accurate information about the Ling-yin Ssu, they decided to release him. He was brought before a judge who said: "You know your errors. You have failed to pay the taxes due the government. Do you admit this?" At first he protested that since the monastery could not sell its products, it could not pay any taxes. When he saw that this got him nowhere, he finally admitted that he was in the wrong. The judge returned him to the monastery, cautioning him to "do better in production and pay taxes to the government." Back at Ling-yin, he found that about one hundred soldiers were guarding valuable government property that had been stored in caves nearby for security against Nationalist air raids. Their commander was from his home town and advised him to flee while there was still time. He said that the cadres had discovered that there was still a six months supply of rice (200 *piculs*), flour (100 *piculs*), and cloth (300 bolts), and because these had not been surrendered, they planned to execute the leading monks. So my informant fled to Hong Kong, arriving in June, 1950.[101] The prior fled to Shanghai, was recaptured, brought back, struggled against, and executed. Two others escaped punishment without leaving the country, one by going to West T'ien-mu Shan, one to his home.

I have searched the Mainland press for something that might confirm this account, but have found nothing even remotely relevant, except, perhaps, the explanation given for the sharp drop in the number of monks in Hangchow: many head monks were said to "have fled for political reasons or because of tax obligations."[102] Struggle against monks is seldom even mentioned.[103] Perhaps because of the policy of freedom of religious belief, it was a more delicate matter than in the case of laymen. There is certainly no published information that indicates how many senior monks became its object.

But not many had to be struggled against to give the younger monks a sobering object lesson and make them wonder if they would be next. That is, how could they be sure that they, too, were not going to be classified as landlords? There were occasional hints in this direction[104] and in some areas harsh treatment seems to have been given to all monks, including the rank and file. The following account of what happened in one district in Anhwei should be read between the lines:

> The monks in charge of the temples were mostly in the landlord category. Last year when the reactionary Taoist sects were being suppressed, [Buddhist] monks and nuns were affected along with them. The masses did not distinguish white from black . . . and considered that all monks and nuns were superstitious, backward elements. Up to now this has still not been completely cleared up, and so difficulties have unavoidably occurred in individual cases with respect to the handling of monasteries and the problem of monks and nuns. At the same time we think that the cultural level of the monks in the villages is not high. They do not understand government measures. Also, ordinarily there has been no question of their diligently keeping the monastic rules, and many of them have lived the life of landlords. Therefore it is inevitable that they should incur the dissatisfaction of the masses.[105]

The safest thing for monks to do in the period of land reform was to disrobe, leave the monastery, and become workers. That way they might even be able to conceal their past and avoid being classified as "religious or superstitious practitioners." This classification excluded them from many desirable jobs, but it was required under regulations promulgated on August 4, 1950. Article 10 stated: "All those people who for three years immediately prior to Liberation, derived the main part of their income from such religious and superstitious professions as those of clergymen, priests, monks, Taoists, lay Taoists, geomancers, fortune tellers and diviners, are to be classified as religious or superstitious practitioners."[106] This was not as bad as being classified "landlord" or "rich peasant," but it was certainly less desirable than "poor peasant" or "worker." For landlords (and perhaps for superstitious practitioners) it took five years of "strenuous devotion to labor" to qualify for reclassification.[107]

OCCUPATION AND DESTRUCTION OF MONASTERIES

Perhaps the most conclusive reason for returning to lay life was the occupation or destruction of the monastery in which a monk had been living. He could, of course, try to gain admission to some other monastery, but the reduction of monastic income was so widespread that in most places he would be refused.

The forcible occupation of monasteries violated the policy of freedom of religious belief. It was forbidden, as we have seen, by the directive of January 1950, which required that cadres get permission from the head monk before they moved in, although his permission was not to be unreasonably withheld.[108] Yet forcible occupation unquestionably did occur: there are clear statements to this effect.[109] Even when it was not forcible—when the monks gave their permission—they may have done so because they had been told that to withold it would be "unreasonable." One way or another, many monasteries were occupied. Cases were reported in the Mainland press[110] and by visitors and refugees. A progressive Indian visitor in 1951 noted that "many of these [Buddhist] temples had been converted into schools or museums or government offices by the free and voluntary choice of the people concerned." When he went to a large Buddhist temple in Shanghai, he noted that "at the time the large adjoining halls at some distance from the main temple were being used as barracks for the military."[111] A monk who visited P'u-t'o Shan in 1956 found that most of the monasteries there were partly or wholly occupied by the PLA, since this was a front line area, facing Taiwan. Gun emplacements and chambers for ammunition storage had been blasted out of the hillsides. Another monk, who was in Ningpo in 1962, said that the Kuan-tsung Ssu had been turned into a factory: no monks were left there. The meditation hall and adjacent buildings of the T'ien-ning Ssu, Changchow, were said to have become a "People's Jail."

The Lung-hua Ssu in Shanghai, according to a reliable informant who visited it in 1962, had become a barracks and parade ground for the public security forces; and in 1950 the Kuang-hsiao Ssu, Canton, began to be used as a cadres' school for the South China Drama Troupe.[112] There seems to have been a particularly large number of such cases reported from Peking—perhaps because there were more visitors to do the reporting.[113]

All these were famous monasteries, but their conversion to secular uses may not have been so shocking to Chinese Buddhists as we might think. Under the Kuomintang the Lung-hua Ssu, for example, had already served as army barracks and the Kuang-hsiao Ssu had long been a judicial school.[114] In some cases, the Communists

5. The Hsiang-chieh Ssu, one of the loveliest temples in the Western Hills, now converted into a municipal teachers' sanatorium. Peking 1962.

6. The Wo-fo Ssu, a T'ang dynasty temple of the Sleeping Buddha in southwestern Peking 1962.

a. The main shrine-hall, which the photographer, peeking through a window, found stacked from floor to ceiling with buddha images, presumably from other temples that had also been closed down.

b. The back buildings, in which many families of ordinary citizens were living.

7. The great stupa at the Huang Ssu was built for the Panchen Lama who died there under Ch'ien-lung. In the early 1960's visitors were allowed to enter this part of the enormous temple compound, but the rest had been taken over by the People's Liberation Army to house troops and a radio transmitter. Apparently no lamas remained. Peking 1962.

8. In 1962 this part of the famous Lung-hua Ssu, the oldest monastery in Shanghai, looked empty but well kept. Other parts were being used as barracks by the Public Security forces, members of which could be seen (but not photographed) parading there in uniform. Shanghai 1962.

9. The gate of the Ts'ung-hsiao Ssu, which had been converted into a primary school as the sign indicates. Foreign visitors were not allowed to enter. Peking 1962.

10. The windows of this bell tower at the Wan-shou Ssu were sealed, since the bell was no longer struck to call monks to devotions. The monastery had become part of a commune and was used as a kindergarten and experimental school. In the 1920's it had still been an active monastery with several dozen monks. In 1934 it was taken over to house units of Northeastern University after the Japanese occupied Manchuria. Peking 1962.

followed the Nationalist precedent in permitting a few monks to remain, using a back part of the premises; in other cases all the monks were expelled.

The physical *destruction* of monasteries, although it was a far more serious violation of government policy, was also reported in the Mainland press.[115] In at least one case a large, famous monastery was involved: the Shang-feng Ssu on Mount Nan-yüeh was burned soon after Liberation.[116] Readers of *Modern Buddhism* were told that when the cadres did this kind of thing, it was an unfortunate occurrence, unavoidable in a revolution, and that the central authorities were doing their best to rectify matters.[117] After 1952, when the Preparatory Committee for the Chinese Buddhist Association was set up, such "distortions" do not seem to have recurred, but we have no way of knowing how many monasteries fell victim to the overenthusiasm of the cadres in the early years after Liberation and how many monks were therefore deprived of a place to live.

Whether they were destroyed in the early years or occupied later on, small private temples suffered the highest casualty rate. Wei-fang told the second CBA conference in 1957: "The rights of large public monasteries are being respected. The problem arises in the case of smaller temples. Some people consider that these temples are owned collectively by Buddhists; other people consider that they are the common property of society, so that not only may they be requisitioned by the State when it needs them, but also they may be taken over for use by others too . . . Actually, when this has happened in some localities, it has started wrangles within the ranks of the people. Buddhists consider that this shows imperfect implementation of the policy on religion."[118] The next year, when the wind was blowing from a different direction during the Great Leap Forward, this same Wei-fang co-authored an article noting with approval that "at present because of the big increase in the number of factories and the consequent urgent demand for factory premises, many temples have voluntarily surrendered their surplus premises for use in production". He called on others to follow their example.[119] According to oral informants, almost all the remaining small temples were occupied during 1958.

Since few small temples were of historical or architectural importance and since most of them had only a handful of monks, their loss might not seem important. In fact, however, they had played a crucial role in the Chinese Buddhist monastic system by serving as the schools that prepared monks for ordination. In the old days unordained monks had not even been allowed to stay at large public monasteries, where their ignorance of the rules would have disrupted the good order that was necessary when so many people lived together. Thus confiscation of small temples eliminated the traditional channel for entering the sangha.[120] Furthermore, while there were only a few hundred large public monasteries in the whole country, the small temples had numbered in the tens of thousands. They had provided living quarters for perhaps 90 percent of Chinese monks; and so closing them was an important factor in the decimation of the sangha.[121]

THE DECIMATION OF THE SANGHA

Nothing like the decimation of the sangha was referred to in the Mainland press, for reasons that will be made clear in Chapter VI. The official policy was to continue claiming more or less the same monastic population for China year after year—500,000 in 1950, still 500,000 in 1958.[122] Yet not only were there strong pressures for people to leave the sangha; there were also pressures, as Chapter IV will show, against holding ordinations so that people could enter it. As a result, its numbers could only decline.

The evidence of this decline is not to be found in statistics on cities or individual monasteries. For example, the fact that monks and nuns in Hangchow dropped from 2,000 to 1,090 in the ten months after Liberation[123] could mean simply that many had gone elsewhere, not necessarily that they had left the sangha. There was indeed considerable movement from place to place, as the monks and nuns in temples that had been confiscated or closed down collected in those that remained operating, so that the population at some monasteries actually increased at certain times. A good example is the K'ai-fu Ssu in Changsha. Because of its historical importance, the government allocated a large sum to have it repaired soon after Liberation. Then in 1952, when 13 of the smaller temples in the city were closed down, their 118 monks and nuns were moved into the K'ai-fu Ssu—so that it had more inmates than in the 1920's.[124] Similar cases can be found in Appendix C. The policy of concentrating the monastic population in a few large monasteries was not publicized, probably since it would have suggested that the sangha was declining.[125]

The hard evidence of its decline comes from Kiangsu and Chekiang. In these two provinces, which had the largest monastic population in China, the number of monks and nuns dropped about 90 percent in the first eight years after Liberation.[126] Not much of this drop can be attributed to their moving elsewhere. Fifty-five percent of all Chinese monasteries and temples also lay in these two provinces, and there would not have been space in the rest of the country to house such an exodus. Most of the drop has to be explained by secularization. It is probable that the figures for Kiangsu and Chekiang are representative for the country as a whole: that is, about 90 percent of the monks and nuns in China had died or returned to secular life by 1957.[127]

This had a different significance than it would have had in Southeast Asian countries (Thailand, for example) where almost all young men enter the sangha for a period of three months before they come of age, so that virtually the whole male population—except for monks—could be said to have returned to lay life. China did not have this custom. Before 1949 monks rarely disrobed: despite repeated inquiries I have only learned of a score of cases. When it happened, the reasons were not what they were after Liberation, but rather that a monk's parents needed caring for; or that the death of his only brother left no one else to maintain the family line; or that his poor health made a vegetarian diet inadvisable. Under these conditions he would be willing to disrobe; otherwise he saw it as a source of embarrassment. After all, he had accepted the support of lay devotees who counted on benefiting from the merit that his austerities would generate. Furthermore, to come back to the world after renouncing it might show that the austerities had been more than he could cope with. (The only two ex-monks that I have met myself stoutly denied that they had ever been in the sangha.) Anyway, most people became monks and nuns in China because they were genuinely disillusioned with life. The monastery was a refuge where they came to feel at home and its austerities were something to which they grew attached. Evidence of this crops up even after Liberation. The main reason that some nuns in Harbin were afraid of joining a coöperative in 1956 was that if they did so, people would want them to return to lay life and then they would have to endure the smell of garlic and onions (which were excluded from the monastic diet) and be dragged into dancing the *yang-ko* (forbidden by the monastic rules).[128]

The decimation of the sangha was the most important of the many consequences of land reform for Buddhism in China. Along with the Buddha and the dharma, the sangha was considered one of the Three Jewels; if it ceased to exist, it could be argued that Buddhism, as conceived by the Buddha, had ceased to exist. The laity would no longer have a religious elite to which it could look for refuge, for a model, for instruction, and for the accumulation of transferable merit. On the other hand, though it may be true that 90 percent of the monks and nuns in China returned to lay life, this fact must be viewed in historical perspective. Secularization was not a new phenomenon in China. During each of the great persecutions of Buddhism (in 444, 572, and 845 C.E.), hundreds of thousands were forced to disrobe. Almost every dynasty had made efforts to reduce the size of the sangha and get some of its members back onto the tax rolls and into production. It was not the Communists who first tried to turn monasteries into factories and monks into workers; it was the Nationalists. In 1931 the Ministry of the Interior held the first Internal Affairs Conference. The delegates noted that there were "large numbers of Buddhist and Taoist clergy in China's monasteries and temples, who all dress without weaving and eat without tilling, which seriously affects the nation's economy." The head of the Hupei Department of Civil Affairs called for an economic survey of monasteries in all provinces. Those that had the necessary resources, he proposed, should start schools where monks would be given vocational training and then they should be "forcibly directed" (*ch'iang-ling*) to follow their vocations. Factories should be set up in monasteries, so that "not a single monk would just sit and eat." The proposal, only a little softened, was passed by the delegates and sent to the ministry for implementation. At this point the Chinese Buddhist Association stepped in. It was far more independent than the one set up in Peking in 1953, and often fought hard for the interests of the sangha. In a telegram to the ministry it referred to the freedom of religion promised by the Kuomintang Program and protested that the industrialization of monasteries would violate it. Probably less because of this telegram than because of help from the association's powerful Buddhist friends in government, the proposal was watered down and it appears never to have been seriously implemented.[129]

Instead it was the monks themselves who took the initiative. When the Japanese attacked in 1937 and the income of many monasteries was reduced by disorders in the countryside, the need for greater self-sufficiency became apparent. A "work-study center" was started by the Kuang-hsiao Ssu, the largest monastery in northern Kiangsu, where monks and nuns operated ten looms, turning out cloth and towels. Unfortunately there was no one to teach them how to do it and the products were of such poor quality that they had to be given away—an omen of what was to happen on a much larger scale after Liberation.[130] Nonetheless the trend was clear and it seems likely that even without a Communist victory, fewer and fewer monks could have supported themselves on rites and donations, and more and more would have had to enter production and spend a large part of their time in the field or workshop.

Chapter III

Making Monks into Good Citizens

Productive labor as such did not conflict with the Buddhist tradition in China, where monks had long ignored the ancient monastic rule (still observed in southeast Asia) forbidding them to till the soil.[1] In the T'ang dynasty the famous Pai-chang, who gave the Chinese monastic system its form, said: "On the day you do not work you shall not eat." He particularly advocated farmwork, and Ch'an monks pioneered in settling some parts of southwest China, where they turned the wilderness into rice fields.[2] Examples of "farming Ch'an" (*nung-ch'an*) occurred as recently as the early Ch'ing dynasty, when a dormitory for "monk farmers" was built at Yün-chü Shan in Kiangsi.[3]

Yet for a century—or perhaps for several centuries—before the Communist victory, it had been exceptional for monks to work regularly in the fields cultivating staple crops. This was left to tenants or hired laborers. Otherwise there would not have been enough time for religious exercises and for the rites expected by the laity. The only manual labor regularly performed by monks—and then only by a dozen or so in each large monastery—was cleaning, cooking, waiting on table, and working in the vegetable garden. In case of an urgent job that required more hands, many or all the monks would help out. If the rice fields lay nearby and a storm threatened, they might even help the tenants bring in the harvest. Normally, however, they were busy with religious or administrative duties.

After 1949, as monasteries had to make themselves economically self-sufficient, labor by many or all the monks became regular rather than exceptional. The result was not an unprecedented reform in the monastic system but rather a return to the T'ang dynasty ideal of Pai-chang. At any rate, that was the official line and it contained enough truth so that some monks made a sincere and even enthusiastic effort to revive "farming Ch'an."[4] What was unprecedented was that monks had to come out of the monastery and take part in social and political activities like other citizens. Part of the *raison d'être* of monasteries had been to provide an environment insulated from the secular world, from its temptations and distractions and, most of all, from its values, so that monks could more easily detach themselves from the attitudes that bound them to the cycle of rebirth. This insulation was precisely what the Communists refused to countenance; and it was in this respect that the reform of monastic life after 1949 represented a sharp break with the Chinese Buddhist tradition.

It is true that already during the Republican period a small progressive wing of the sangha, led by T'ai-hsü, had called on monks to become socially involved—to start orphanages, schools, hospitals, homes for the aged, to visit prisons and do relief work. Yet T'ai-hsü had not advocated that monks become active politically; and even his social activism, though it won increasing support, was not accepted before 1949 by a majority of the sangha. Most monks feared that it would vitiate the purity of their detachment from the world, which in the past had not only been of advantage to their spiritual life, but also had been the basis for financial support by the laity and saved monasteries from encroachment or suppression by suspicious officials. T'ai-hsü argued that conditions had changed and that if the sangha was now to survive, it had to become relevant and useful to modern society; and that social service was in accord with the highest principles of Mahayana.

After 1949 these arguments were taken up by Chü-tsan, who had once been T'ai-hsü's pupil,[5] and by other Buddhist leaders. Chü-tsan told his fellow monks in 1950 that they had to cleanse their religion of "pessimism and escapism."[6] Salvation was to be sought not by withdrawing from the world but by contributing to it. The idea of withdrawal was a misunderstanding of what the Buddha taught. "When someone gets sick of the turmoil of secular life and afraid of worry and trouble and then withdraws far from living creatures to hide in the caves and cliffs of forest and mountain, hoping to win purity and peace—that is not in accord with the teaching of the Buddha."[7] What the Buddha had taught was to benefit living creatures. One sacred text stated: "If you bring happiness to living creatures, you bring it to all the buddhas."[8]

In the past the term "living creatures" had meant sentient beings in the several planes of rebirth—including gods and men, ghosts and animals, even the least of whom should be treated with compassion. Now it was reinterpreted. "What the term 'living creatures' means for us humans is the masses of the people. Buddhists must go deeply into the masses of the people and serve the masses."[9] Thus "productive labor exemplifies the bodhisattva vows and . . . coincides with the Buddhist principle that the highest conduct for a bodhisattva is to benefit living creatures."[10] So,

11. This sign, posted in the street at the entrance to the Ta-pei Yuan, Tientsin, tells passers-by that Buddhists help to protect world peace and carry out their duty of paying back the motherland for its kindness to them. Tientsin 1957.

for example, to volunteer for work on a water reservoir was "to carry out Samantabhadra's vow to beautify the land and benefit living creatures."[11] In 1953 a monk who had immured himself for eighteen years of meditation emerged to march in a May Day parade and said: "All Buddhists today must take part in the patriotic movement. In the past we could stay inside the monastery and recite buddha's name. Today we must study how to serve the people."[12]

Chinese monks had always served the people, though not in a way that would have redeemed them in the eyes of dialectical materialists. By their pure lives and religious practice they had accumulated merit that could be transferred to avert natural disasters and procure for the dead a more favorable rebirth. By preaching the dharma they had tried to make people realize that the world was illusory and that the only salvation lay in seeking release from it, just as the monks were doing themselves. This was precisely the kind of "pessimism" that they were now supposed to discard: they were supposed to believe instead that only the material world was real[13] and no salvation could be found outside it. Here progressive Buddhists were able to cite the Sixth Patriarch of the Ch'an sect: "The dharma is in the world and enlightenment is not something apart from the world; to seek for enlightenment apart from the world is like looking for the horns of a rabbit."[14] There was indeed an apparent similarity between what was advocated by Communists and by the early Ch'an masters. Both insisted on the importance of practical activities—"to draw water, to carry wood."[15] Both saw practical activities as leading to the goal of salvation through egolessness. However, the egolessness of Ch'an enlightenment was something ineffable that liberated a man from all attachments, all striving, all partisanship, whereas what the Communists meant by egolessness was to lose one's self by self-identification with the masses. Since the Party was the mystical body of the masses, embodying their will and their essence in a way impossible for living peasants and workers, who were often backward, misled, wavering, therefore identification with the masses really meant identification with the Party—including its intense partisanship in class struggle, its striving against imperialism, and its attachment to wealth and power for the New China. The result was the very opposite of transcendental egolessness towards which Ch'an masters had guided their disciples.

From the Communist point of view, on the other hand, this transcendental egolessness was a trick. "It was feudal rulers who created the slogan: 'Monks belong to the transcendental, they are a class of people pure and above the world, and they cannot take any interest in politics.' That was imposed on the monks, so that their main idea came to be that it was all right for them to while away their days and there was no need for them to do anything about the nation—no need to engage in production so long as they had rice to eat. This concept of the clergy was harmful both to the nation and to Buddhism, and we must vigorously carry on political education in order that, bit by bit, the misconception can be corrected."[16] Political education was, in fact, the first step in the reform of monastic life that began in 1949.

POLITICAL EDUCATION FOR MONKS

The standard method of political education was "study"—*hsüeh-hsi.* This included not only study (*hsüeh*) in our sense of the word, but also drill or practice (*hsi*) in what had been learned. Students first did reading assignments and listened to lectures, and then discussed the content with fellow students in relation to their own experience. Although the topic might be a particular program or campaign, the underlying purpose was always for people to "remold themselves" and to "raise their level of awareness."

Buddhist monks and nuns began to engage in study immediately after Liberation. As one of them put it a year later, "under the impact of the great changes in the new era, a great wave of study rose in every corner of the New China. Buddhists too became acutely aware of the necessity for study and remolding." So in Peking the progressive monk, Chü-tsan, got the consent of the Civil Affairs Bureau to organize a Buddhists' Study Society that held classes three times a week from September through November 1949. They were conducted by Chü-tsan himself and by Chou Shu-chia, a well-known scholar and the head of the Lay Devotees

Club, which provided the necessary classroom. The curriculum included dialectical materialism and Mao's "On the People's Democratic Dictatorship," published the summer before.[17] On the basis of this pilot program a more highly structured series of classes began in January 1950, and similar efforts soon followed in other major cities.

It is difficult to generalize about the conduct of study throughout the country in the ensuing years. I have been unable to get answers to the obvious questions: What percentage of the sangha took part? How many hours a week for how many weeks or years? What did they study? Who taught them? Under whose sponsorship? And finally—most important of all—how much were they actually "remolded"? There does not seem to have been a uniform or nation-wide plan with publicized targets. *Modern Buddhism* is full of references to the fact that here and there study was underway and it carries occasional reports of the details, but there is no way of knowing how typical those details were.[18]

For example, as to sponsorship, it came sometimes from the Civil Affairs Bureau or (later) from the Religious Affairs Bureau; sometimes from the United Front Department or the CPPCC or the local Buddhist association. Some classes were conducted by cadres (usually those in charge of religious affairs[19]); others by progressive Buddhists; and at least one by demobilized soldiers. In most big cities study began in the years 1949-51[20] and continued intermittently until 1958 when it became continuous and intensive during the Great Leap Forward. Before 1958 class schedules varied enormously: in about equal numbers, reports specify once a week, three times a week, and every day; in some cases for a few weeks, in others for a few months.

As to *what* was studied, it depended on the year. In 1949-51 there seems to have been more of an effort to teach the basic concepts of Marxism-Leninism as found in works like *The Communist Manifesto, A History of the CPSU(b), A Short History of Social Evolution,* and the works of Mao.[21] Later on, attention went increasingly to campaigns in which the sangha was expected to participate; land reform, the suppression of counterrevolutionaries, the anti-rightist movement, the Great Leap Forward; or to topics of the day, like the Marriage Law, the General Line, the Draft Constitution, or the latest congress of the NPC or CPPCC, the Tibetan rebellion, and so on. Materials on these would be culled from newspapers, particularly the *People's Daily,* more particularly its editorials; magazines like *Current Affairs* (*Shih-shih-shou-ts'e*), *Study,* and *Modern Buddhism.* Usually these materials would be read aloud by monks who were good at reading. The others just sat and listened until the discussion period when everyone was supposed to join in. Sometimes discussion led to concrete action; sometimes to passing a resolution. For example, monks would put up wall posters to show what they had learned; or they would draft "patriotic compacts" to codify what they had resolved to do—perhaps to increase production, to practice economy, to expose the reactionaries in their midst, and (in 1950-53) to oppose America in the Korean War.[22] Many a study program began and ended at the same time as the campaign on which it focused—and then there might be no more study until the next campaign.

This spasmodic pattern of effort shows up clearly in an account that was given me by a former cadre of the Religious Affairs Division in Canton, who used to conduct study meetings himself. I have relegated the details of his account to a note,[23] but it testifies to the difficulty of trying to teach monks the abstract points of Marxist theory. When they were given an editorial to read in the *People's Daily,* it simply proved over the heads of most of them. The questions they would ask during discussions were simple: "What was life like in the Soviet Union? How was religion treated there?" This was what really concerned them, what made them pay attention once study got underway. They wanted to know how they were going to be treated, how government policies would affect them, what was expected of them. They realized that the Communists were much more severe (*yen-su*) than the Kuomintang; so they were anxious to avoid violating State policy and expressing opinions that would get them into trouble, especially if they were called on to express their opinions in a small group meeting. Of course, there were some whose attention would still wander and who might even fall asleep during study. They would be reported to the cadres by their group leaders, and in flagrant cases they might be warned. Also reported were those who showed a high degree of awareness and activism. They could be groomed for greater responsibility.

In the second half of 1957, as the anti-rightist movement got underway, more cadres were assigned to study and its pace was stepped up throughout the country. In Canton plenary sessions were often held four days in a row. During the first half of 1958 in Peking, Shanghai, Wuhan, Sian, and Chengtu five regional colloquia were held to provide models for dozens of counterparts at the local level.[24] The goal was not merely to step up the pace and bring in stragglers who had stayed out so far, but to promote the Great Leap Forward and expose class enemies. The Wuhan colloquium, for example, "exposed a small bunch of rightist elements who had been taking advantage of study meetings among Buddhists in order to launch a vile attack on the Party's leadership and on socialism and who were plotting to use religion as a cover for dragging Buddhists down an anti-Party, anti-Socialist road."[25] This is an interesting admission that study could be double-edged: it could be used against as well as for the Party by those who had the skill and courage.

The best description of what the 1958 campaign meant at the local level comes from a monk who was then living in Hankow. Although classes had begun there in 1950,[26] he had never attended them. Now in March 1958 he and all the other monks and nuns in the city were required to start ten months of intensive meetings. Every day except Sunday they went on from eight in the morning until six at night. Up to two hundred persons came from all the city's big monasteries and nunneries to take part. Some of their time was devoted to reading and discussing the newspapers, but more to composing big-character posters and writing confessions. Each of them was expected to write an accurate account of his political and ideological past, going back to the age of eight, and including any bad things he had said about the Communist Party. Other students were expected to point out omissions, and the two cadres in charge (a man and a woman) were harsh towards those who were insufficiently enthusiastic or frank. Thus study meetings often became struggle meetings. Every few days they would go to the municipal auditorium to watch the much harsher struggle meetings that were being conducted there against "big rightists" and counterrevolutionaries.

In rural monasteries too there was the same intensification of study in 1958. At Yün-chü Shan, for example, even the evening meditation period, which was the most important in the schedule of Ch'an monasteries, was replaced by classes. Instead of listening to the Venerable Hsü-yün give one of his famous Explanations, the monks drafted big-character posters; and extra classes were held in the morning and afternoon.[27] After sixty days of intensive study the monks there signed a "patriotic compact."[28]

This was the year when patriotic compacts were signed at many, many places.[29] As in the early 1950's they promised greater efforts in productive labor, the practice of economy, the acceptance of Party leadership, and so on, but more emphasis was placed now on eliminating superstition and cleaning out reactionaries; and some compacts contained, for the first time, commitments not to accept disciples carelessly and not to offer indiscriminate hospitality to wandering monks, of which more will be said below.[30] It is hard to convey the pounding quality of the rhetoric that was generated in 1958, the year of the Great Leap Forward. "In this era of the Great Leap Forward everyone is making a flying leap forward. According to what Buddhist delegates to the [National Youth] Conference report about their work and thinking, Buddhist youth throughout the country, intently following the march of the Great Leap Forward, are stepping forward." Whenever they were speaking in public that year, Buddhists promised every kind of self-improvement with boundless enthusiasm and repetitiousness. The refrain was: "We surrender our hearts to the Party."[31]

The intensity of study dropped off in 1959, and it seems to have become a more or less perfunctory exercise in the period 1960-1963.[32] We do not know whether it re-intensified during the socialist education movement that led up to the Cultural Revolution. Possibly the remaining monks and nuns, most of them elderly, had already been written off as unfit for any serious effort at remolding. At any rate after 1963 I have found no mention of study by the sangha either in the national press or in *Modern Buddhism,* the sole surviving Buddhist journal.

This leads back to what I referred to earlier as "the most important question of all"–how much was the sangha actually remolded by study? Even the cadres could not be certain of the answer, since they had no way of reading people's thoughts. If they went by the accounts that were published in the press, they might conclude that a good deal of remolding had taken place. Here, for example, is a passage taken from the work report of the Hangchow Buddhist Association for 1950-51. "Monks and nuns, as they have gone through the stages of study, have realized how unreasonable and shameful their parasitic life used to be in the past. A good example is a monk called T'ien-chu, who said at a discussion meeting: 'If I had realized a little earlier the greatness of labor, I would certainly not have betrayed the laboring class and become a parasite.' A nun from the outskirts of the city said: 'I want to leave the life of depending on income from rents. I must exert myself to take a post in productive labor. Only then can I really stand erect . . . I will certainly not fold tinfoil into paper ingots again for the dead; I want to struggle to become self-sufficient on my income from growing vegetables.' "[33]

Of course cadres did not necessarily take reports like this at face value and sometimes their skepticism was justified. In 1953, for example, study at the Ling-shan Ssu in Kwangtung was reported to be underway two hours every afternoon, seven days a week. Acting in accordance with Chü-tsan's appeal, the abbot led his monks in reading newspapers and discussing political issues; and in the mornings they engaged in productive labor. Five years later it turned out that all along he had been the head of a reactionary Taoist sect.[34] In 1957 a study committee was set up in Kirin "to carry on a ruthless struggle against the bourgeois rightists." Soon its deputy head was attacked as a rightist himself–an ex-landlord and army officer who had previously had two wives.[35] There was nothing unusual about such turnabouts: they happened in all circles of society, not just among Buddhists.

Some reports of study are frankly negative. They are in a minority, but significant for the clues they give to certain underlying obstacles. For example, the first class in Peking "had few concrete results" because of irregular attendance and a lack of leadership; and the second class, which had been designed to train a small group as leaders, suffered from a lack of interest in the work and from the inability of cadres in charge to steer discussion.[36] At Wu-t'ai Shan, one of the earliest Buddhist centers to come under Communist control, study by 1953 had still not gone beyond group reading of the *Shansi Daily* and *Modern Buddhism.* Six group leaders had been elected who were real paragons–"enthusiastic, responsible, quick on their feet, quick with their hands, quick with their tongues, and of a relatively high cultural level". Yet the cultural level of those under them was not so high; there were language difficulties; the monasteries were widely scattered. Therefore newspaper reading was as far as study could go.[37] In other places it did not go that far. Since one of the pledges monks took in 1958 was to guarantee that every monastery and nunnery would get at least one newspaper, some must have not been getting any before then.[38] Monks in large cities were often able to avoid study altogether–like the monk in Hankow (see p. 91). Informants who lived in Peking and Shanghai until 1957 have told me that they never attended classes of any kind.

What is probably the fullest description of the obstacles to study involves the Asoka Monastery near Ningpo, the one that set up an agricultural production coöperative in September 1952 (see Chapter II at note 40). To prepare the way for the latter the leading monks organized a class to go over the draft regulations for APC's in East China. They met from seven to eight each morning. "At the beginning everyone was in high spirits; pacts and plans for study were decided on. But later on this study system was driven out of existence by the fact that everyone was too busy with other things and up to now [March 1953] it has not been reactivated." Newspaper reading at the Asoka Monastery started in 1951, but "because the persons who were in charge did not know the correct methods and because the masses [that is, the monks] did not very well understand the importance of newspaper reading, it produced very few results." Another study activity there was the writing of wall posters. A wall-poster editorial committee was appointed in

1952. Its progressive young members "went deep into the masses," and there was a weak-long campaign of composing and criticizing posters. "But there were certain defects in our work. First . . . most members [of the committee] did not fulfill the responsibilities entrusted to them and some of them felt the work to be a burden. Second, some of the masses did not attach enough importance to wall posters. When the time came to show their high sense of duty, they would draft a set of posters, but as soon as the storm died down, they left the work to take care of itself . . . Many wrote statements that they were determined to obey the organization, obey the leadership, go anywhere they were assigned, but they would forget all these pretty pledges when the day approached for carrying them out."

The basic trouble at the Asoka Monastery seems to have been that its monks did not *want* to engage in study. They were ready to do productive labor because the alternative was to go hungry, but no such pressure impelled them to read editorials in the *People's Daily* or compose wall posters. According to the monastery work report, the monks fell into five categories. The first two categories were progressive and studied hard. The third category "knew only that they should do what they were told . . . They found it troublesome to attend meetings and to study." The fourth category "discovered pretexts for avoiding newspaper-reading groups and meetings. They sometimes used a couple of modern terms, pretending that they were not backward elements." The fifth category was like "canned goods." They remained hermetically sealed. "There were only very few of them. They did not attend meetings or newspaper readings. Even when they were forced to attend, they neither heard nor spoke. New things held no attraction for them."[39]

In organizing political study by monks, the cadres were in a dilemma. Many monks had genuinely turned their backs on the secular world when they entered the monastery. It was almost impossible to interest them in the Five-Year Plan or dialectical materialism. Other monks, whose attitude was less otherworldly and who were more apt at political study, simply accepted the Marxist view of religion and returned to lay life. This left the cadres with the task of re-educating the ideological dregs–those who were too opportunistic to be sincere in political study, and those who were too old-fashioned to engage in it at all–so that the best that could be expected was conformity or dissimulation. That made it all the more necessary to find monks who were really competent as study leaders. Here again the cadres were in a dilemma. The monks who were best qualified (in Marxist terms) because they came from the lower strata of the sangha were usually the least literate and therefore the least able to read aloud or conduct discussion of an editorial in the *People's Daily*.[40]

Probably the only thing that would have made study more palatable was sweetening it by the inclusion of religious as well as political materials. At some monasteries this was done–perhaps not regularly, but at least when no objection was raised by the cadres.[41] It was even given temporary encouragement by the Chinese Buddhist Association. At its second national conference in 1957, Chao P'u-ch'u criticized overemphasis on the otherworldly but also criticized study programs that suffered from a contrary overemphasis and did not include Buddhist doctrine.[42] Speaker after speaker at the conference took this as a license to complain: "In the past we have only emphasized the study of politics and current events and slighted research in the doctrine: starting now, this must be corrected."[43]

Within a couple of months at the K'ai-yüan Ssu, Chaochow, "cultural classes" were being conducted which were, in fact, simply lectures on the *Heart Sutra*. The stated purpose was to improve monks' understanding of this particular text (which they recited daily during their devotions), to give them the technical vocabulary they would need to read other sacred texts, and to improve their religious practice. Nothing was said about political study.[44]

Study of doctrine had become increasingly important to the monks of China in the preceding forty years, as they had come to realize that their future depended less and less on self-cultivation and more and more on their ability to expound the scriptures. The delegates to the 1957 conference may even have felt that under the guise of study they would be able to reopen, in effect, some of the Buddhist seminaries that had been closed down at the time of Liberation. In this they were disappointed. Indeed the whole idea of increasing the doctrinal content of study evaporated the next summer in the heat of the anti-rightist movement.

When the third national conference was held five years later, not much progress seems to have been made in finding ways to interest monks in their own remolding. Chao P'u-ch'u's work report contained the same kind of complaint as before. In 1957 he had said that there were still "quite a large number" of monks who were opposed to study and considered that the things being studied belonged to the secular world and had no bearing on release from life and death.[45] In 1962 he said: "Some Buddhists still lack a clear understanding of the development of the situation . . . Some still have doubts about the official policy towards religion . . . These phenomena remind us that it is necessary to step up our study and remolding."[46] After 1963, as I have already mentioned, the whole subject of political study by the sangha seems to have been dropped from the Mainland press.

CIVIC PARTICIPATION

With Liberation monks and nuns found that they had the same rights and duties as other citizens: to vote and hold office, to serve in the army, and to take part in movements and campaigns, from afforestation to the suppression of counterrevolutionaries. Young and progressive monks were delighted with this evidence of their equality. Conservative elders, however, viewed with mistrust what seemed to them one breach after another in the wall of isolation that used to protect the monastery.

Public office for monks and nuns was indeed a new phenomenon. Under the Republic they had seldom even voted, and before that, under the Ch'ing dynasty, the only posts they had held were ecclesiastical.[47] But in 1949 they began to be elected to the Chinese People's Political Consultative Conference, to its local committees, and to the people's representative conferences of provinces, counties, and municipalities; then in 1954 to the people's congresses and councils that were provided for in the new constitution.[48] In these local bodies they represented not only the sangha, but all the citizens of their districts, to whom they reported back on measures that had been passed.[49]

Only at the national level do we know the total number of monks and nuns who held office—and it was negligible. There was one Chinese monk, Chü-tsan, in the first CPPCC; and one again, Neng-hai, in the first National People's Congress. There were, however, a good number of Tibetan and Mongolian lamas, outnumbering Chinese monks many times over.[50] If anyone, it was they who represented the sangha in national political bodies, but since they were primarily concerned with Buddhism in the borderlands, such protection as Chinese monasteries received at the national level came not from them, but from the lay Buddhist leaders mentioned in Chapter I.

At all levels the monks and nuns who stood for election were picked by the Party and government organs concerned. The United Front Work Department and the Religious Affairs Bureau would first set quotas for the representation of each religion in local bodies and then they would fill them with candidates who were either progressive or enjoyed enough popular support so that it was politic to incorporate them in the power structure. The progressives could be put to work, the conservatives used for decoration. Some conservatives, of course, were legally excluded from holding office. The Election Law of 1953 disenfranchised "elements of the landlord class whose status had not yet been changed." Since the change of status required five years of productive labor, it would have been difficult for senior monks, classified as landlords during land reform, to be rehabilitated in time for the elections of 1954.[51]

Ordinary monks and nuns could not only be elected to office but could also join a wide variety of people's organizations, depending on their work, age, and sex: labor unions, peasant associations, the Youth League, the Women's Federation, the People's Relief Association, and so on.[52] Whether they were able to join the Communist Party is a different question. Party membership was supposed to preclude religious belief or commitment of any kind.[53] This rule may have been relaxed in the case of a few

Tibetans, but probably not for Han Chinese. One is entitled to doubt the story given to Edgar Faure when he visited Peking in 1956—that there were practicing Buddhists who were at the same time militant members of the Communist Party.[54] He could not learn their identity, but if there really were such people, then the Party must have assumed—and perhaps we should too—that their Buddhist practice was only for show.[55]

If the Communist Party was the secular body that was least accessible to Buddhists, the most accessible was the army. In the years just after Liberation there was no better way for young monks to purge themselves of their feudal past than to take off their robes and join the People's Volunteers. Here is a typical case, involving a novice in Shansi, named Wu-jan.

> As soon as comrade Wu-jan realized that the government was now calling for volunteers to join the army and defend world peace, he immediately signed up. His old master and his brother disciple were very pleased and had encouraged him to enlist. This was because they knew that the purpose of entering the People's Volunteer Army was to exterminate the American imperialist demons, to realize the Pure Land here on earth, and, later on, to hasten the liberation of the peoples of the whole world. Buddhist youth *can* join the army and, in particular, it can win glory for Buddhism.[56]

Monks who enlisted were given a big send-off by their former brethren, dozens or hundreds of whom would light fire-crackers, beat drums and gongs, and wave red flags in honor of the occasion.[57] This drew attention to the sangha's contribution to the war effort—to the glory that was being won for Buddhism—and thereby relieved, perhaps, some of the pressures being exerted on monasteries. It also gave heart to the volunteer, who was not always as enthusiastic as comrade Wu-jan was said to have been.

An illustration of such a lack of enthusiasm is provided by an informant from Szechwan who was seventeen when China entered the Korean War. During the campaign to clean out KMT bandits and overturn petty tyrants (*ch'ing-fei fan-pa*), cadres came to his monastery and talked to its younger inmates, saying that many Buddhist monks were KMT spies dressed up in religious robes and that all monks had exploited the people with superstition. Exploitation was a serious crime, but if the youngsters would confess to it and then join in accusing their elders at a public meeting, they would be given immunity. If not, they would be shot. So when struggle began, the senior monks were attacked from two sides, first by tenants, who accused them of oppressive rent collection, and second by their own disciples, who testified to the harsh punishments they had administered. Struggle, however, was not the end. Afterwards the cadres said to the younger monks: "You have been the people's enemies and you must make up for the crimes you have committed against them. The way to do that is to join the People's Liberation Army and go to guard the Korean border." My informant had been frightened by the struggle meetings and welcomed the chance to prove his desire to reform. He enlisted along with several of his comrades for duty in Manchuria. When they got as far as Hopei, there was a new demand: since white Americans were attacking their yellow Asian brothers, they should volunteer to go to the front in Korea itself. If they refused, it would show they were still infected with bourgeois thinking and loyal to the Kuomintang. All of them volunteered. Nine months later my informant was captured as a prisoner of war and chose to go to Taiwan, where he became a monk again. He looked back with shame on his term as a soldier, not because he had fought on the Communist side, but because he had fought at all.[58] The first commandment of Buddhism is not to kill; and even to witness a battle violates the monastic vows.[59]

Under the Nationalists, although monks were legally subject to conscription, they had been allowed to remain monks and to avoid regular military service by volunteering for a Buddhist ambulance corps.[60] No such exemption was available after 1949.[61] To enlist was to disrobe; it meant becoming like any other soldier. The only consolation was getting the same honors in death. A young monk from Kansu who "went to the Korean front to kill the enemy and died honorably fighting in battle" was posthumously awarded Mao Tse-tung's Glorious Hero's Award.[62] We do not know how many monks in all entered the PLA and the militia. They presumably amounted to a small percentage of the sangha but a larger percentage of those whose youth qualified them for military service.[63]

No less offensive to Buddhist principles was participation in campaigns against the "enemies of the people"—rightists, counterrevolutionaries, and spies. Monks and nuns were called on to take an active part and to expose one another as well as outsiders. Despite their compunctions, they had no choice but to coöperate, not merely in order to show their loyalty to the new regime but also to cleanse their ranks of "bad elements" who might get them all in trouble. It is unnecessary to doubt the sincerity of appeals like the one made at a meeting of Buddhist circles in Hangchow on March 19, 1951, when the last speaker called on everyone to help the people's government prevent reactionaries from carrying on counterrevolutionary activities in the name of Buddhism.[64] More details will be given in Chapter VIII to explain how progressive Buddhists tried to justify action against reactionaries by arguing that the Buddha had not intended compassion to be indiscriminate but had advocated "killing bad people in order to help good people."

The other forms of civic participation required of monks by the regime may have been equally startling, but they presented less of a problem for the conscience. Buddhist publications, for example, sometimes printed photographs of monks and nuns taking part in a demonstration or parade—perhaps for National Day, perhaps for world peace, or perhaps to protest some action by the imperialists. Often they would carry emblems like paper doves or lotus fronds (see Fig. 12); and sometimes the photographer caught them with their mouths open as they shouted the slogans of the day.[65] Such photographs were intended to show how broad a base of popular support the regime enjoyed—even Buddhists were part of it. They also showed that even Buddhists could contribute something to demonstrations and parades, which may be the reason for the look of enthusiasm on their faces—a rather strained enthusiasm, I think, for this was a sharp break with Buddhist tradition. In the old society any monk who had been seen shouting a slogan in a demonstration would have been expelled from his monastery and

12. Buddhist monks march with their neighbors in the National Day Parade. Peking 1958.

cut off by horrified devotees from any financial support that they had been giving him. After Liberation, however, there were fewer monks who depended financially on devotees, and devotees themselves probably understood the necessity for monks to participate in a wide range of secular activities, even when it meant violating their vows. Under the seventh monastic vow, for example, monks were committed not to attend theatrical performances of any kind. Therefore, "it used to be hard for monks and nuns to see a play. In the new era they not only can often see progressive plays and films, but they themselves have organized classes in the literary arts that include the waist-drum dance, drama, Shaohsing opera, and song-recital teams." For the 30th anniversary of the Chinese Communist Party in 1951 monks in Ningpo put on a play entitled *Stop Hesitating* and sang songs as well. After the 700 people in the audience saw this, they said: "There are really lots of new things in the new society. One even has monks and nuns singing opera." On August 1, 1951, which was Army Day, all the city's masters of the waist-drum entertained servicemen's families "and our nuns' waist-drum troupe got a glorious reception."[66]

There were some activities, on the other hand, that could give offense to no one. An example is afforestation. Already for centuries the trees on sacred mountains and around important monasteries had enjoyed the protection of the sangha. At larger establishments there had been a special officer, the grounds prefect, who with his several assistants made sure that no wood was cut and removed by trespassers. The planting of new trees may not have been part of their duties, since China was silviculturally backward, but it was a logical extension of them.[67] As early as 1951 Buddhists made it one of their May Day tasks to organize tree-planting teams in the countryside under the guidance of the local government.[68] Although some teams planted their trees badly or not at all,[69] there are reports from three of the four sacred mountains that suggest solid achievement in actually getting seedlings to survive. The numbers were small compared to the areas involved and the monks available to do the work, but this may be because a hole was carefully dug for each tree. On Wu-t'ai

Shan 14,000 willows were set out, as well as many fruit trees;[70] on Omei Shan 50,000 cedar and gum trees.[71] This activity seems to have reached peaks in 1956 and in 1958-59. After that much less is said about afforestation by Buddhist monks.[72] In any case it was useful and appropriate work for them–indeed it is pleasant to write about an innovation in Buddhism under Mao that seems so wholly good. Even when elderly monks were pressed into service, as they were in 1958, they could handle the lighter tasks, like carrying seedlings.

Some monks did so well in afforestation that they were elected labor models, as, for example, the one who singlehandedly replanted five barren mountains in Jehol.[73] Others became models in flood prevention, irrigation, seed selection, grain payment, and there were some who distinguished themselves in several different lines at once. For example, in 1956 a certain monk in Kiangsu sold more than his share of public grain, bought more than his share of National Construction Bonds, and planted so many trees that he was put in charge of afforestation for the whole of his village.[74] The Great Leap Forward brought about an enormous increase in the sangha's participation in all kinds of work projects–or at least an increase in reports of it. In February 1958 a group of monks from Changchow went out to the countryside to do five days of farm work. It was the first time that such a thing had happened. "Everyone had thought that our study of the Agricultural Development Program had just been a theoretical exercise."[75] By the end of the year they were doing their part in the operation of backyard blast-furnaces, as were monks in many other places.[76]

The above illustrates how monks were encouraged to contribute to the public welfare in campaigns sponsored by the government. It was more difficult for them to contribute independently and privately. Before 1949 a small number of monasteries had started schools, clinics, and orphanages, but it was foreign to the Chinese Buddhist tradition and monasteries seldom had enough income for it.[77] After 1949 monastic income plummeted; and at the same time the government decided to assume control of all forms of education and social welfare, so that even when the monks managed to start something, it was closed down or taken over.[78] A monk who tried to set up a mutual assistance group for elderly

Buddhists in 1951 was accused of "bluffing and deceit, extorting money from the masses, and impairing social order . . . His activities were curbed."[79] Better luck was enjoyed by I-fang, the abbot of the Tung-yai Ssu on Chiu-hua Shan. In the spring of 1950 he started the Chiu-hua Primary School for the children of the peasants on the mountain, who had never been able to get an education before. He persuaded two laymen to serve as teachers, apparently without salary. The first year or so they worked under great difficulties: all they had to eat was congee flavored with a tenth of an ounce of oil a day. Then in fall of 1952 the operation of the school was taken over by the government and by 1953 it had 106 pupils. In the meantime I-fang had become the head of the whole school district, in charge of eleven primary schools. This showed that the government "had no prejudice against Buddhist monks."[80] It also showed that the government did not intend to have education left in private hands. I have seen no references to monastery schools later than 1954.[81]

The extent of civic participation by the sangha, regardless of the program or campaign in question, is difficult to estimate. All we have to go on are, as usual, individual cases, which may have been reported in the press because they were common or because they were uncommon; because they provided models to be followed, or because the purpose of the report was to make it *look* as if they were being followed. There is no reason to doubt that monks wanted to make a good impression on the government: their own future depended on it. Thus in 1951, when monks and nuns were excluded by unfriendly cadres from taking part in a project to enlarge a stadium and public garden in Wuhan, the local Buddhist Association interceded with the authorities and a hundred of them were finally permitted to carry hods of earth for seven days running—and twenty-eight became labor models. That made "them realize that the government did not discriminate against Buddhists at all."[82] Under the Kuomintang they might not have been so enthusiastic about earth moving; now they were eager to find ways in which they could prove their usefulness. One can sense this especially in local news printed by *Modern Buddhism* during the Great Leap Forward. An example is provided by the Ling-chiu Ssu, Kiangsi.

> Back in July [1958] when the sixteen monks [of the monastery] heard the news that an [iron-smelting] plant was to be established on Ling-chiu Shan, they were all extremely happy. But they were worried about one thing: "We are people who chant Amitabha's name. Will the government take us on to work in the plant?" Later on when Comrade Yang Hsi-jung, deputy secretary of the county [CCP] committee, came to Ling-chiu Shan to inspect the site, Ching-ju, the prior, went quietly up to Comrade Yang and anxiously asked him: "Please do me a favor–could I join in the work at the plant?" Comrade Yang encouraged him by answering: "You and all your brother monks will be welcome to join in the work. In this way we shall increase the plant's capacity." When the rest of the monks heard this good news, they bubbled with joy.
>
> At the beginning of September an army of over a thousand iron workers came to Ling-chiu Shan and built nearly fifty earthenware furnaces inside and outside the monastery. The monks were kept busy cleaning up and making fragrant tea for them; and they also moved out of their own rooms so as to make them available for their guests. In addition, they loaned firewood and tools to the plant. All the sixteen monks took part in iron smelting and one of them was even elected leader of a work team.

The next item of local news printed in this issue of *Modern Buddhism* came from Nanchang. "The monks of the Yu-min Ssu were the first to start a mushroom farm. After fighting hard for fifteen days, they harvested a second crop of mushrooms. One of these had seven big heads and weighed 7.2 ounces. It was a miracle of mushroom raising. With happy hearts and their good harvest of mushrooms, these monks went to the Municipal Religious Affairs Division and the CPPCC to announce the joyous tidings."[83]

The eagerness of Buddhists to prove their usefulness had begun long before 1958, of course. Consider the extraordinary range of activities carried on by members of the Kansu Buddhist Association between 1950 and 1953. Among other things they:

–collected winter clothing and relief money for disaster victims in four provinces during the winter of 1950;
–organized an anti-American demonstration of Buddhists and Taoists on March 13, 1951, in which 2,500 people took part, afterwards signing a patriotic pact;
–published a written protest against the draft peace treaty between the United States and Japan [presumably in April 1951];
–took part in the May Day parade [1951];
–organized anti-espionage teams and teams to combat KMT bandits;
–mobilized Buddhists, Taoists, and welfare workers, three thousand in all, to attend a meeting that welcomed home representatives of the Korean volunteers;
–started study sessions on the duty to study;
–celebrated the "liberation" of Tibet on June 2, 1951;
–started an urgent drive for members to donate money for weapons to be used in the Korean War;
–took part in the celebration of the thirtieth anniversary of the Chinese Communist Party [July 1, 1951];
–set up a Sino-Soviet Friendship Association within the Buddhist Association;
–volunteered to write letters to soldiers in Korea on Army Day [August 1, 1951] and to visit wounded soldiers in local hospitals;
–took part in National Day celebrations [October 1, 1951];
–accused the imperialist spy P'u-teng-po [otherwise unidentified];
–took part in the Three-Anti and the Five-Anti campaigns;
–attended the public trials of persons accused of corruption;
–attended a public trial of counterrevolutionaries and the subsequent execution of their sentences;
–attended the opening of the T'ien-shui-Lanchow Railway;
–participated in the patriotic hygiene drive and accepted the patriotic hygiene pact;
–took part in the anti-narcotics campaign;

–took part in land reform work and the recheck;
–carried out propaganda on the Marriage Law.[84]

In all, the members of the Kansu Buddhist Association participated in over 350 campaigns and activities from 1950 to 1953–probably more than the total number of monks and nuns in the province.[85]

Chapter IV

The Reform of Monastic Life

It was inevitable that as an increasing number of monks had to support themselves by productive labor, as political study was intensified, and as more and more participation was demanded in secular movements and activities, there would be less and less time left over for religious practice. Yet Buddhist leaders often claimed that religious practice was being carried on just as it always had been—or even more rigorously. At first the purpose of such claims seems to have been to reassure Buddhists who had not yet been drawn into production and study and were nervous about the demands on their time that these would make. In 1951, for example, when the first gunnysack factory advertised its product in the pages of *Modern Buddhism,* readers were told that its monks and nuns "every day, besides doing eight hours work, do not neglect their religious exercises (*pu-fei tien-t'ang*), and also carry on religious and political study."[1] Somewhat the same desire to reassure may be seen in a 1953 work report on Buddhism in Changsha: "Most monks and nuns, since beginning to take part in production and to lead a better life, have become more devout and punctilious *than they were before Liberation* with regard to devotions, reciting buddha's name, studying the dharma, and regular observance of the *uposatha.*"[2] To the question whether farm production had not affected religious life, the deputy head of a monastic coöperative replied: "Even while we are doing our productive labor, we can recite buddha's name or practice meditation. Wherever we may be working, we can go in the afternoon to a nearby temple and perform devotions. In this respect it is much more convenient than in the past."[3] Many similar reports can be cited from the Chinese press.[4]

Another purpose in emphasizing the continuance of religious practice was to facilitate contacts with Buddhists abroad. Friendly exchanges with people in countries like Burma and Ceylon could best be promoted by convincing them that Buddhism in China was flourishing as never before. Hence in 1954, when the English-language *China Reconstructs* printed its first article on Buddhism, it emphasized the protection that had been given to monasteries by the government: "In the temples there are lectures on the *Avatamsaka sutra* and incantations of the Buddhistic 'Seven.' Two week recitations of the Vinaya rules go on constantly. At the big monasteries ceremonies are held for the expiation of the sins of the dead." The author of the article, Chü-tsan, ended it by saying: "Since my own return in 1949 . . . my religious devotions have not been interrupted for a single day. It gives me joy to inform Buddhists from other countries of this fact."[5] The following year saw the first edition of what was to be the most important single piece of propaganda directed towards Buddhists abroad—a book of photographs of Chinese monks, monasteries, and Buddhist activities. Its foreword stated: "Chinese Buddhists of different nationalities and Buddhist schools in all their different regions are at present leading a free religious life, devoting themselves to the study of Buddhist scriptures in a happy and tranquil atmosphere." In 1956 when two new editions appeared, the foreword had been rewritten to make the same point, but more specifically: "Buddhists in China practice their religion in the traditional way—meditating in solitude, reciting sutras, studying the Buddhist scriptures, paying homage to the Buddha, holding religious ceremonies."[6] Foreigners who went to China and visited important monasteries were usually told at some length and with considerable emphasis how scrupulously religious practice was being maintained.[7] If productive labor and political study were mentioned, they were said not to interfere with traditional observances.

As skeptical books and articles began to be published abroad, particularly after the suppression of the Lhasa uprising in 1959, it brought a defensive, angry note into Chinese statements on this question. Three such appeared in the October 1959 issue of *Modern Buddhism.* The one by Shirob Jaltso expatiated on how well religious practice was being kept up throughout the sangha—"In all the monasteries, large and small, that I went to [on a recent tour] there was regular chanting of the sutras"—and then he noted how the government's patronage of Buddhism "had forcefully exposed the slanders spread by the professional rumor mongers of the capitalist world against the Communist Party."[8] More will be said about this in Chapter VI.

Whether or not the foreign "slanders" were true, progressive Chinese Buddhists had a good reason for protesting them: they reduced the usefulness of Buddhism to the government in winning friends abroad and therefore raised the chances that it would change its policy to outright suppression, as it finally did in 1966. This growing defensiveness made it even less likely that frank statements about the reduction of religious practice would be printed in any mainland periodical or made orally to any foreign visitor. It is to refugees that one must turn for the facts.

THE REDUCTION OF RELIGIOUS PRACTICE

According to several monks who lived on the Mainland during the first few years after Liberation, the reciting of sutras that used to be obligatory twice a day at large public monasteries soon became optional in the afternoon; or, both morning and afternoon, only a brief formula was chanted.[9] After the Great Leap Forward began in 1958, nothing at all was chanted except on the first and fifteenth of the lunar month.[10] As to Ch'an meditation, one informant had an opportunity to observe it at several monasteries in 1956. At the Kuang-chi Mao-p'eng he found that three periods were being held daily—one less than had been reported in the press three years earlier.[11] At the Kao-min Ssu elderly monks were still sitting for eight periods a day; the only change, even at this late date, was that no evening snack (*fang-ts'an*) was served to them because of the need to save food. At nearby Chin Shan, on the other hand, the meditation hall had simply been closed down.

Some refugees report that in south China, even though a couple of meditation halls stayed open until 1958, the quality of their work and number of participants declined.[12] Monks found that at the end of a day of hard physical labor they were so tired that they did not feel like sitting; or if they did, they were too sleepy for the concentration that was needed to make progress in Ch'an. Before Liberation in the best meditation halls the full schedule had varied with the season from seven to fifteen hours a day and any monk could enroll. Now, throughout China, this was a privilege enjoyed only by those who were too old or too weak to work—and their enjoying it meant that the young monks had to work so much the harder and had so much the less chance to come to the hall. So even where it remained open, it was no longer the training ground for the young elite of the sangha as it had been before 1949.

A particularly interesting informant was an émigré who had left before Liberation and settled in Pnom Penh, where he started a temple for overseas Chinese. In 1962 he felt free to return to China and visit Mainland monasteries, including some large ones that he had known before he emigrated (on his tour, see Appendix G). In most of them devotions were being performed twice a month. When he visited the Ling-yen Ssu, Soochow, which had been the most important center of Pure Land practice in the country, he found that almost all the young monks had returned to lay life and taken factory jobs. Those in middle age were kept busy cultivating the land that the monastery had received in land reform. The elderly ones operated a restaurant, where they sold carbonated drinks, tea, noodles, and sweets. During the Great Leap Forward daily devotions and the reciting of Amitabha's name had been halted so as to free the monks for more production and study. However, the autumn before he arrived—that is, in 1961—devotions had begun to be performed again every morning and afternoon; and early in 1962 the work schedule in the restaurant had been adjusted to allow groups of elderly monks, in

13. The meditation hall (*chien-hsing t'ang*) of the P'i-lu Ssu. The shape of the board hanging under the bell shows that the monastery belonged to the Lin-chi sect. The layout, however, is not what it should be in a proper Lin-chi hall, where a sleeping platform is found behind the benches for sitting. Probably this made no difference, since meditation was not being regularly carried on. The monk in the picture is Hung-liang, the senior prior of the monastery, who had spent two years at the Chinese Buddhist Seminary in Peking. Nanking 1962.

rotation, to hold four periods a day of reciting Amitabha's name. This did not represent as much practice as before Liberation, when there had been six periods a day, in which the young monks had joined too, but it is a good example of the fluctuating pattern characteristic of so many trends in Chinese Buddhism after 1949.

The same pattern can be seen when it comes to rites for the dead. Their frequency of performance fell and rose and fell again. Here, however, monks were discouraged not only by competing demands on their time, but also by legal and financial obstacles. When such rites were performed in people's homes, it violated the rule that religious activity should not be carried on outside religious establishments.[13] Wherever they were performed, it wasted time and materials. The paper ingots, cars, and houses that were burned for use by the dead, took hours to prepare and, especially in the case of tinfoil ingots, consumed valuable metal. To reduce this waste the government not only imposed taxes and

14. Paper tablets for the dead in the hall of rebirth of the P'i-lu Ssu. Note the photograph of Hsü-yün in front of the glass reliquary. Before Liberation there would have been offerings and incense burning in front of the altar. Nanking 1962.

raised prices on tinfoil and incense, but taxed the fees that monks charged for their services.[14] It also issued warnings from time to time against "rites that could easily be considered superstitious," that is, rites for the dead.[15] Some Buddhists tried to reform them in such a way as to overcome government objections. In 1954, for example, the Shanghai Buddhist Youth Society held a week of buddha recitation during which soul tablets were installed free of charge and the burning of paper money, houses, and cars was banned "in order to eliminate the superstitious activities that are incompatible with the dharma."[16] Yet this does not seem to have been widely copied. The people who could afford to hire monks and buy paper money and paper houses continued to have rites for the dead performed in the old-fashioned way,[17] except when a campaign against "feudal superstition" made it too dangerous. Such a campaign was held in 1958-59, only to be followed by a period of permissiveness in 1960-62.[18]

Despite such fluctuations the long-term trend was towards a reduction in religious practice of all kinds, if only for the reason noted at the outset: monks who spent more and more time on labor and political study had less and less time for chanting, meditation, rites, and the study of Buddhism. Occasionally this was openly referred to in the pages of *Modern Buddhism.* For example, before Liberation the monks and nuns of a county in Kwangtung, because their only income had come from rites for the dead, were said to have known less than nothing about the theoretical side of Buddhism. "After Liberation they had no choice but to go into production and then there was even less chance of their leading a religious life of Buddhist practice and study, so that they gradually lost the character of monks and nuns."[19]

One of the guarantees that monks gave in 1958 was not to let religious practice interfere with production.[20] Yet in statements designed to reassure Buddhist devotees at home and abroad, it was maintained that production had not interfered with religious practice.[21] Behind such contradictions, official policy was clear: "Religion hampers full implementation of the Party's general line for socialist construction and holds back the development of

Communist ideology among the workers . . . All religions insist on a great many troublesome religious exercises and rules."[22] Antipathy towards traditional exercises and rules can be sensed also in the sardonic tone of the following excerpts from Chü-tsan's article "A Brief Discussion of the Future of Buddhism."

> To treat labor as a religious practice—this is something that ordinary Buddhists cannot accept. But let us ask them: "What is the real goal of meditation, of reciting Buddha's name, and of other religious practices? If the goal is the purification of actions, words, and thoughts, then how long does one have to carry on these practices before he can attain purity, and when he has attained it, what comes next? Furthermore, if his goal is complete enlightenment, or release from birth and death, or rebirth in the Western Paradise, then what is this complete enlightenment? After he has been released from birth and death, what does he do then? After he has been reborn in the Western Paradise and looked with his own eyes upon Avalokitesvara, Mahasthamaprapta, and Amitabha, then what?" Unless these questions can be answered, religious practice can be carried on for a hundred thousand kalpas [eons] and they will be a waste of time. Let me tell you this: it is not in some far off place that the mind can get complete enlightenment. You have to be willing to die before can you be released from birth and death. The goal of rebirth in the Western Paradise is to reform this human world in the East. Purification of actions, words, and thoughts must be pursued in the midst of activity, trouble, and worry. It is to be sought here and now. There is no need to look elsewhere. In short, it is pernicious to talk about religious practices in isolation from everything on the concrete side of life, from carrying wood and drawing water, from all our acts and gestures. To talk about religious practices isolated from the multitude of living creatures is like a catching at the wind and clutching at shadows. For decades now Buddhist circles had been doing this and that practice and they have not yet practiced up anybody [with talent]. Otherwise Buddhism would not have

> fallen into its present shattered state. If we look at the Avadana section of the Tripitaka, we can see the moving way in which Sakyamuni resolutely faced all kinds of hardships in his previous lives when he was sowing the seeds of buddhahood. Thus we may know that absolutely no one becomes a buddha while enjoying leisure in an ivory tower. Trying to become a buddha in an ivory tower of leisure and contentment—this is just another pastime and opiate of landlords, bureaucrats, and petty bourgeoisie when they are surfeited with wine and food. It has nothing at all to do with Buddhism.[23]

RESTRICTING ORDINATION

Among the sangha's religious exercises the one that could, in a sense, be considered prerequisite to all others was the admission of new members, for without it there would not continue to be a sangha. The decimation of the sangha in the first eight years after Liberation took place not only because so many monks and nuns returned to lay life but also because their numbers were not replaced. Very few ordinations were held.

There were several reasons for this. The first was that the traditional ordination had been attended by such a large number of people. Dozens or hundreds of novices came to be ordained, and there were also many lay devotees, some of whom took a set of simple vows and some of whom had mortuary rites performed for their late kinsmen. They too would stay the whole time the ordination lasted—one or two months. Even in pre-1949 China the large number of people had created a problem of "public order." Thieves, for example, would prey on them as they traveled up to the monastery or mingle with them to slip into the monastery itself. After 1949 a prolonged gathering of such size involved additional problems. Although the Constitution guaranteed freedom of assembly, it also provided for the suppression of counterrevolutionaries. The public security office, from which a permit was required, could not be sure when an ordination would serve as cover for counterrevolutionary activity. It was therefore reluctant to issue such permits.

The second reason so few ordinations were held was the drop in monastic income. To feed the ordinands, to present them with books, robes, and bowls, and to provide hospitality for those lay visitors who could not make a sizable donation meant a heavy expenditure for the ordaining monastery.

A third reason was the decline in the number of applicants. This resulted not only from economic change, but from the confiscation of small temples, referred to in Chapter II. They had been the traditional channel for entering the sangha. A layman who wanted to become a monk would ask the head of a small temple to shave his head, give him a religious name, and thereby accept him as disciple. Then he would live at the small temple long enough to receive his basic training. Only when he had learned how to wear his robes, how to eat, sit, walk, chant, and so on, would he go to a public monastery to be ordained. After 1949 the small temples that were confiscated ceased to be available as places for tonsure and training. The monks who had headed them, rather than accepting new disciples from the laity, returned to lay life themselves—or moved to a public monastery where taking disciples was traditionally barred. In the few small temples that kept going, there were already too many mouths to feed and little incentive to recruit more. All this helps explain why I have noted very few cases of recruitment—the initial tonsuring of novices—after 1949, either in oral or documentary sources.[24] Without novices to ordain, there could be no ordinations.

Just after Liberation, of course, there was a carry-over of novices awaiting ordination from before 1949. The period of training in the small temple was supposed to last three years. Thus some of the candidates for the first ordination to which I have found reference under Communist rule may have been tonsured in 1947. This first ordination was due to be held at the Kuan-tsang Ssu, Ningpo, towards the end of 1950. In October *Modern Buddhism* published the news that it would start on the 18th of the tenth lunar month. The three sets of vows would be administered over thirty-seven days, "still in the old way." The editors added the following comment.

> This follows the former practice. Whether it helps in raising the standard of the sangha and in spreading the observance of the monastic rules is quite doubtful. The pains that the Kuan-tsung Ssu is taking on behalf of the future of Buddhism are, of course, praiseworthy. But the old mercenary method of ordaining indiscriminately (*lan ch'uan-chieh*) is to be blamed for the decline of Chinese Buddhism and the mixed caliber of monks. Whether it should be employed in this new era is a question that deserves the attention of Buddhist circles. Therefore it is hoped that the Kuan-tsung Ssu will make public some measures for the "strict screening" of ordination candidates as reference materials for Buddhist circles. For instance, the clause "I resolve to separate myself from lay life and to spend the rest of my days in the study and practice of the dharma" is something that really needs careful consideration. This is because anyone who makes such a resolve should have acquired adequate faith in and knowledge of Buddhism. By what means does the Kuan-tsung Ssu assess the faith and knowledge of the ordination candidates? If it should simply employ a written declaration of intent, how could it tell whether this was not merely another empty formality? It would still be difficult to avoid criticism for indiscriminate ordination.[25]

I have not found any report that Kuan-tsung Ssu went ahead with its plans, which may have been canceled because of the warning just quoted. At any rate within a few weeks the Culture and Education Section of the Preparatory Committee of the Ningpo Buddhist Association was conducting propaganda at this monastery.[26]

The first ordination that I know to have taken place after 1949 was held at Yün-men Shan in the summer of 1951. Originally it had been scheduled to start in spring, but the monastery was surrounded, its abbot nearly beaten to death, and some of its leading monks imprisoned or executed. Although this did not happen because of the plans to hold an ordination, the influx of ordinands undoubtedly helped attract the attention of the cadres; and the outcome cannot have given Buddhists the feeling that they were free to ordain as they pleased.[27] Their uneasiness may have been reinforced by further hints in *Modern Buddhism.*[28] In any case, the next ordination to which I have found reference did not take place for three years. When it did, it provoked sharp criticism.

> Last winter with great fanfare a certain monastery held the triple ordination. It did so in an ignorant and careless way, so as to destroy the future of Buddhism rather than to preserve it. First it did not examine the past life of the candidates and it did not make certain that they had sufficient faith. Thus (a) members of syncretistic sects, who could no longer survive in the new society, transformed themselves into bhiksus; (b) elderly and indigent people, who originally had no faith, acquired the status of bhiksu simply in order to have enough food to eat, so that a Buddhist monastery was made into a home for the aged (whether it had the *capacity* to provide for the aged remains a question); (c) the "great gate of expedient means" was opened wide for people with mental diseases, low competence, and extremely backward thinking, so that they could become "bhiksus who spread the dharma and benefit all living creatures." Second, the ordination was not given in successive stages from lower to higher on a gradual scale; rather, without making distinction between individuals, the full bhiksu ordination was given to everyone. Some of them did not even qualify as human beings–how could they be given the title "bhiksu," which is reserved for those who serve as teachers and models for heaven and earth? . . . It is hoped that everywhere those responsible for ordination will fully discharge their responsibility.[29]

In 1955 the council of the Chinese Buddhist Association passed a resolution that made official some, at least, of the reforms that had been called for. First, ordinations were now to be held strictly in accordance with Buddhist rules. Second, only persons from within the province of the ordaining monastery should come there to take their vows–unless they lived in a province where no ordinations were held; and, to reinforce this, widespread publicity in seeking candidates from far-off places was forbidden. Third, "indiscriminate ordination" was to come to an end.[30]

One reason for the geographical restriction may have been the fact that hundreds of candidates had just come "from different parts of the whole country" in order to be ordained at Pao-hua Shan, not far from Nanking. Not only did this show that Buddhism still had a following, but it meant that a lot of people were traveling about the country for their own private purposes, perhaps spreading rumors, perhaps worse. It is a little ironic that at the very time when their travel was being criticized, their ordination was being used to advantage in preparing propaganda directed at Buddhists abroad. A handsome photograph was printed in *Buddhists in New China.*[31]

Despite the CBA resolution, the next two years saw a spate of ordinations—more than in any comparable period since 1949. This happened because of the political detente (the blooming of the Hundred Flowers) and the celebration of the Buddha Jayanti—the 2,500th anniversary of the Buddha's death—when efforts to use Buddhism in people's diplomacy were at their height. The following monasteries were among those involved.

Monastery	*Date of Ordination*
Kiangsi, Yün-chü Shan Chen-ju Ssu	1955, end
Kwangtung, Canton Liu-jung Ssu	1956
Kwangtung, Shao-kuan Nan-hua Ssu	1956-57, winter
Shensi Hsing-chiao Ssu	1957, spring
Chekiang, P'u-t'o Shan P'u-chi Ssu	1957, spring
Fukien, Ku Shan Yung-ch'üan Ssu	1957, spring
Kiangsu Pao-hua Shan	1957, autumn

The authorities tried to keep those ordinations within reasonable limits, both as to how long they lasted and how many people were involved. It was important to prevent the waste of the time that might have been used for production and also to forestall any large gathering that would testify to the continuing strength of religion. Buddhists, of course, tried to resist such limitations. They wanted to replenish the sangha; and the length of ordination was a measure of the seriousness with which its members would begin their new careers (before 1949 the best monks had tended to be those whose ordination had lasted longest).[32] In this contest between Buddhists and cadres the outcome varied. For example, before it ordained in 1956, the Liu-jung Ssu in Canton applied to the Religious Affairs Division for a permit. According to a cadre who was privy to the negotiations, the division "was afraid that the ceremony would lead to a rapid increase in Buddhist influence, but at the same time it did not want to stop the ceremony openly. Therefore it resorted to the tactic of prolonging discussions . . . with the head monk and the other monks for many weeks hoping that this would lead them to abandoning it voluntarily. At first the Communists argued that since the lay believers were very busy working in various circles, it was not advisable to take them away from their work. When this approach failed to yield the desired result, they reminded the monks that their religious activities were not consistent with the 'current social situation' and even warned them by asking whether the temple could be sure that there would be no counterrevolutionaries among the new believers. The result was, as usual, that the temple made a series of concessions: (a) to cut down the number of participants, (b) to reduce the schedule to a shorter period, and (c) to omit some of the subsidiary ceremonies and programs. In return the Religious Affairs Division granted the permission . . . This was typical of what the Communists call the 'legal struggles between materialism and idealism.' "[33]

At Yün-chü Shan the cadres were equally successful in limiting the number of participants,[34] but at the Nan-hua Ssu, where three hundred had been expected, six hundred came—half of them to take their vows, half as spectators.[35] At the P'u-chi Ssu the monks had been prepared to ordain one hundred, but three hundred showed up. As a result there was not enough food and housing, and "It was a good thing that everyone was really set on taking their vows and ready to endure all kinds of hardships."[36] At Ku Shan, the cadres were in for a different kind of surprise. The hundred and fifty candidates came from all parts of Fukien, as well as from Kiangsi, Chekiang, and Southeast Asia. This, of course, violated the 1955 resolution against ordaining people from other provinces. What went even more against the official policy was that the ordination lasted the full fifty-three days (which was rare even under the Republic) and was conducted in the traditional manner by a full complement of ordination masters, who administered all three sets of vows.[37]

While the ceremonies at Ku Shan were still underway, the CBA held its second national conference. Four council members spoke up for stricter control of ordination and a committee was established to work out procedures that could be adopted by monasteries throughout the country—procedures for screening candidates and, after they were ordained, instructing them in the Vinaya. Even the progressives evidently hoped that ordinations would continue to be held, though modified in form.[38] Just after this conference, however, the period of the Hundred Flowers came suddenly to an end. At the same time the Religious Affairs Bureau began to digest the implications of the unexpectedly large numbers who had been coming to be ordained whenever the opportunity was offered. They showed that the bureau had not done enough to reduce the influence of religion on the masses. It decided, therefore, to halt ordination altogether. The evidence indicates that this decision was reached by mid-1957. Yet the largest ordination of all was held at the end of the year: vows were administered to 373 monks and 430 nuns who had gathered at Pao-hua Shan from eighteen provinces.[39] Though no word about it appeared in the press, the cadres must have known of it and given their permission for it. In view of the quickening anti-rightist movement, it seems an anomaly—an anachronism—that is hard to explain.

During the next year monks began to sign patriotic compacts

guaranteeing that they would not accept disciples "in a careless way" (*luan*) or ordain "too many of them" (*lang*), lest it lead to infiltration by bad elements and counterrevolutionaries.[40] It was pointed out that "in the past people only became monks because they were so oppressed by the reactionary despotism of the old society that there was nothing else they could do. In today's socialist society they can be peacefully and happily employed."[41] The implication seems clear: there was no longer any valid reason to be ordained. Nothing further was heard of the committee established at the CBA conference to formulate acceptable procedures. So far as I know, no ordination was held in China again.[42]

RESTRICTING HOSPITALITY TO WANDERING MONKS

The first step after being ordained had traditionally been to spend several years as a wandering monk, often called a "cloud-water monk," because he was supposed to drift about China as unattached as a cloud and to follow his inclinations as naturally as water follows the inclinations of the land. If he was inclined to meditate, he would stop at a center of Ch'an practice; when he wanted to study the doctrine, he would move on to attend the lectures of a famous canon-master; should he feel the need for self-mortification, he could go to a place like the Yü-wang Ssu, where he would get expert help in burning off one of his fingers as an offering to the Buddha. Once there had been dozens of such monks staying in the "cloud-water hall" of every large public monastery. The distances and the dangers of the road made their life a hard one, but they learned a lot from it and some kept it up for decades.[43]

After 1949 China again had a strong central government, acutely concerned about internal security. As with candidates for ordination, it did not like to have people wandering about the country on private missions. Not only could they spread rumors and stir up trouble, but some might be spies and counterrevolutionaries wearing monk's robes to elude detection. Hence the government attempted first to keep track of them and then to discourage monasteries from admitting them. Not that much discouragement was necessary: early on, large public monasteries which did not have enough food for their permanent residents had been forced to abandon the tradition that they would house and feed any wandering monk for as long as he chose to stay. After 1952, for example, Chin Shan could not offer hospitality for more than three or four days "because of livelihood problems," whereas before Liberation it had had fifty to a hundred monks staying for weeks or months in its cloud-water hall.[44] At other monasteries, particularly those where monks grew their own food, visitors could stay longer, but were expected to join in productive labor. Readiness for labor, however, gave no assurance that they would be allowed to stay. They had to show that they had received permission from the authorities to change their place of residence. This can be seen from what happened at the Ta-hsiung Gunnysack Factory. So many monks flocked to Peking illegally in hopes of getting work there that an announcement finally had to be published in *Modern Buddhism* forbidding anyone to come unless he had received formal permission.[45]

In the old days the only duties of wandering monks had been to attend meals, devotions, and perhaps three periods of daily meditation; and occasionally to help out with chores that the regular staff was unable to cope with—for example, lugging in sacks of grain after the harvest or helping out in the kitchen in case of a vegetarian feast. In general, they had enjoyed a lot of free time to rest their sore feet, to relax, and to study. The likelihood that instead of this they would have to work in the fields along with their hosts must have made the wandering life a lot less attractive.

It must also have been made less attractive—at least less cloud-like—by the requirement that wandering monks be registered by the monastery and reported to the local public security office. Before Liberation they had not been registered; they had not even been required to give their true names. So long as the guest prefect was satisfied that they were properly ordained and of good character, they could stay for as long as they liked without any record being kept of them. Only when and if they joined the permanent staff of the monastery were their names recorded. After 1949, according to the few informants who observed the admission procedures, each visitor had to produce his residence permit; its particulars were entered on a "temporary residence register" (*lin-shih hu-k'ou pu*), and then transmitted to the police; when he left, his name was checked off. If he wished to stay longer, he had to produce a police permit for a change of residence.[46]

A new deterrent was created in 1955 by the introduction of rationing. Visitors now had to bring their ration coupons with them, particularly at urban monasteries that purchased their grain rather than growing it. Since the standard coupon was valid only in the place where it was issued, a monk who wanted to wander from place to place had to go to the police, explain the reason for his trip and his projected itinerary, get their approval stamped in his residence permit, and take it to the grain-rationing office. Then, if all went well, he could get coupons of nationwide validity.[47] According to some informants, it was easier to do this if one were already living in an urban monastery. Country monks were supposed to stay "down on the farm."

None of the above resulted from a government measure that was specifically designed to discourage monks from wandering about the country. They simply represented the effect on Buddhists of changes that affected almost everyone.[48] In 1955, however, the CBA passed a resolution specifically calling on monks and nuns to cease wandering about the country and "permanently settle down" in one place. This would "insure their peaceful pursuit of religious practice and leave no opening through which bad elements could bore their way in." The resolution did not prohibit wandering monks absolutely, for it went on to say that, when they applied for admission at a monastery, their credentials and background should be carefully examined and thus bad elements would be kept out. The closest it came to a prohibition was to state that it was "not good to travel without an adequate reason."[49]

When the second national conference of the CBA was held in 1957, no further step was taken.[50] Only in 1958 was something approaching a ban incorporated in the patriotic compacts then being signed by many monks and nuns: for example, "We guarantee that our monasteries and nunneries will not let suspicious wandering monks set foot inside them."[51] According to my informants, this ban was in effect from 1958 to 1961 or 1962.

One of my informants did a remarkable amount of wandering himself. He was a young monk, who had been ordained in 1951. In 1956 he was living in Hankow from which he set out to visit all the "four famous mountains"–a traditional goal of Buddhist pilgrims in China. He was quite open about his plan when he applied to the police, which did not object to helping him get coupons of nationwide validity. As a result he was able to travel to P'u-t'o Shan and Chiu-hua Shan, stopping off at well-known monasteries along the way. Where there was none to stop at, he slept on the train. Everywhere he wore his monk's gown and it caused no difficulties. The next year in the same way he traveled to Wu-t'ai Shan in the north, and then down by Sian, Chung-nan Shan, and Chengtu to Omei Shan.[52] What struck him most on his wanderings was the fact that he never met another monk doing the same thing. He met many lay pilgrims: he went to Wu-t'ai with a group of ten from his own city; and there were hundreds at Omei, not only pilgrims, but tourists, students, and even cadres. Monks at the monasteries where he stayed often told him that he had a lot of courage to "go running around like this." They would have liked to, they said, but either they did not dare or they were committed to productive labor. In many respects the experiences of this informant contradict what I have heard from others. For example, at no monastery did he have to join in productive labor himself, even where most of the permanent residents were doing it, as at Chiu-hua and P'u-t'o. At Chiu-hua his hosts would not accept his ration coupons; and whereas at P'u-t'o the manager of the Hou Ssu asked to look at his residence permit, elsewhere this regulation was not followed. P'u-t'o, of course, was in a front-line area, facing Taiwan.

In 1958, 1959, and 1962 the same informant traveled again, but things had changed. He no longer found it possible to get hospitality at monasteries, presumably because of the ban that started to be enforced in 1958. He wore lay clothes because, he said, if the cadres had seen him in monk's dress, they would not have been very polite to him. In their eyes he was simply a lay worker, moving from job to job. Indeed the only members of the sangha I have met who, after 1958, traveled about staying at monasteries and wearing monastic dress were overseas Chinese. They could do so until 1966.[53]

REFORM OF THE SANGHA SYSTEM

In this century the Chinese monk best known outside China was T'ai-hsü (1890-1947). He traveled abroad, made a point of meeting foreigners in China who were interested in Buddhism, and cultivated contacts in the Nationalist government, particularly in the Foreign Ministry. At the time of his death he had just succeeded in winning control of the earlier Chinese Buddhist Association, which during the Republican period had come closest to representing Buddhists throughout the country. Tai-hsü's aim was to bring Buddhism up to date, to make it scientific, socially conscious, and respected by intellectuals and the youth. This could not be done, he believed, unless the monastic system was cleansed of commercialism and superstition. His ideas on how to do this were first formulated in 1915 when he wrote *The Reorganization of the Sangha System.* It aroused opposition from conservative monks, who felt that T'ai-hsü was not out to reorganize the sangha but to destroy it.

The controversy between the conservatives and reformers continued after Liberation and became particularly sharp in 1953, when the new Chinese Buddhist Association was about to be inaugurated and the future was therefore taking more definite shape. In the pages of *Modern Buddhism* a month before the inaugural meeting a Hunanese monk (the one who had revealed the difficulties on Nan-yüeh during land reform–see Chapter II at note 26) attacked the members of the sangha who "demand that they be able to marry and even have children while still in the monastery. Those who claim to be 'ideologically progressive' criticize the recitation of buddha's name and the chanting of sutras as feudal, backward, and superstitious. They make such wild attacks on the grounds of freedom for the individual."[54] In the same issue there was a report of young monks of this kind in Fukien who not only were eating meat, wearing lay dress, and letting their hair grow but who "talked constantly about Buddhism being superstitious, feudal, and despotic. One of them said about the people who were destroying copies of the Buddhist canon, 'these sutras are the poison left behind by society over several thousand years, printed with money gained by exploitation of the working class. Now that the new era has come, we no longer need such poison around to harm the people. What is wrong with our destroying it?' " Even the most radical followers of T'ai-hsü had treated the Buddhist canon with respect. Indeed one of his chief goals had been to have monks study it more thoroughly. The report from Fukien concludes: "These incidents, which violate the Vinaya rules and the monastic system, have caused deep anxiety among Buddhists. It is hoped that something can be done promptly to remedy the situation."[55]

Perhaps it was because of excesses like this that, when the CBA held its inaugural meeting in June 1953, T'ai-hsü's most eminent surviving follower came to the defense of the Vinaya. This was Fa-tsun, a specialist in Tibetan Buddhism who was later to become a vice-president of the CBA and deputy principal of the national Buddhist seminary. "The monastic system that we are going to build in the future," he said, "must be based on the Vinaya that the Buddha Sakyamuni prescribed with his golden tongue. When because of time, place, or circumstances there are [rules] we feel we cannot follow, then we must study the reasons for the dispensations mentioned in the Vinaya in order not to violate the Vinaya's [principle of] dispensation. We cannot ignore what the Buddha prescribed or make capricious changes on the excuse that the time and place are not the same. But to follow the Vinaya is no easy matter, and because most people today do not study the Vinaya, it is even harder . . . The three basic Vinaya practices to be regularly followed are the semi-monthly *uposatha,* the confession that begins the three-month summer retreat, and the confession that concludes it. If in the future we can reorganize the Buddhist monastic system in accordance with the Vinaya and really make it more important in our discussions than other considerations, so that we take the Buddha's words as our criterion, then we can avoid a lot of useless wrangling and we will be doing the right thing."[56]

To adopt the Vinaya as the criterion for the reform of Buddhism meant sharply limiting the scope of reform. Yet after some initial hesitation,[57] this seems to have been acceptable to the regime (except where it interfered with production) for reasons that can be imagined but are never spelled out. First, it would bring Chinese monks closer to their brethren in Theravada countries, with which the regime wanted to build friendly relations. Second, the idea of strict discipline may have had an inherent appeal to the Leninist mentality. Whatever the reason, the fact is that monks who married and ate meat were forced by local Buddhist associations to leave the monastery,[58] and sometimes the government itself saw to it that the Vinaya was followed. For example, in the winter of 1954-55 the local authorities at Omei Shan, working through the Omei Study Committee, made sure that "where a temple has more than five residents, it will conduct devotions. Smoking, wine, and meat are prohibited. The *uposatha* is performed twice a month; monks and nuns wear monastic dress."[59] This was done in the name of reform, but it was certainly not innovation. For example, it is true that the *uposatha,* which in China meant the semi-monthly recitation of the monastic rules,* had not been performed at most Chinese monasteries before 1949, but it had been a regular practice at certain monasteries of the Vinaya sect that specialized in ordination and at a few others that were already interested in an ecumenical rapprochement with the Buddhists of Southeast Asia. After 1949—precisely for this purpose—it became a regular practice at more and more monasteries.[60] The counter-tendency—to shorten or revise traditional liturgy—never seems to have won formal approval.[61] In practice, as we have noted, devotions were indeed shortened—or entirely admitted at some monasteries—but in theory the liturgical schedule remained unchanged.

*In Theravada Buddhism the term *uposatha* (Sanskrit *upavasatha*) is used to designate the *days* on which the Pratimoksa is recited. Chinese monks use it to refer to the recitation itself.

The issue of open innovation came up at the plenary meeting of the CBA council in 1955. According to a cadre of the Religious Affairs Division in Canton, a group of Shanghai monks appeared in lay dress and called for revising the Vinaya so as to give formal sanction for monks and nuns to marry. They argued that the children of such unions would assure the future of Buddhism, just as in the case of Christian pastors and the married clergy of Japan; that child-bearing was a social obligation; that many monks and nuns now wanted to get married and to prevent them from doing so was a violation of the new Marriage Law. These ideas were successfully opposed by the delegations from Peking and the interior provinces. Although the controversy does not appear to be mentioned in published reports of the meeting, the issue of *Modern Buddhism* that published them was prefaced by a page in large type, purportedly written by Hsü-yün, the honorary president of the association—and the staunchest of old conservatives. "I believe," he states, "that in the daily life of monks and nuns—in their clothing, meals, and living arrangements—there can be some modifications, but that in our approach to the three disciplines, that is, in the basic principles of following the rules, practicing meditation, and studying philosophy, there can be no change."[62]

With respect to the Vinaya rules, at least, this idea seems to have prevailed. Open changes were minor. One, for example, was in traditional monastic dress. Before Liberation only the followers of T'ai-hsü had worn anything but robes and gowns cut with a y collar. After Liberation, however, it became common for monks and nuns to wear "Lenin suits" or "Sun Yat-sen uniforms" with a Y collar, like ordinary laymen, partly to show that they were progressive and partly to avoid the "ridicule of the populace."[63] By April 1951 this had reportedly became the garb of 80 percent of the sangha in Changsha.[64] At the end of 1952 *Modern Buddhism* was telling its readers that the problem of appropriate clothing had not yet been solved, but it recommended wearing traditional garb *only* when performing ceremonies.[65] This recommendation was not necessarily followed. In fact, there seems to have been no general rule. Up until the Cultural Revolution visitors to Chinese monasteries saw their residents dressed in different ways,

15. This individual escorted a party of visitors about the Ta Hsing-shan Ssu. Although he was dressed as a layman, he said he was a monk. Sian 1965.

some in Lenin suits, some in T'ai-hsü suits (which were similar), some in traditional Chinese monastic robes and gowns, and some in the robes and gowns worn in Theravada countries or those worn in Tibet.[66]

When it came to meals, the vegetarian rule was still observed. In this respect Chinese monks continued to be more scrupulous than the Vinaya requires—and than their Theravada brethren. Now, however, at least one Chinese institution also began to observe the Theravada rule that no solid food should be eaten after twelve noon.[67] (One may surmise that the authorities approved not only because it served people's diplomacy, but because it saved food.) There were more widespread changes in the rules and arrangements for eating. Prayers were no longer recited before and after meals. Monks could talk while they ate, whereas in the old days they had had to eat silently, reflecting on the debt they owed to those who had provided food, and the proctor stood watchfully by the door, ready to punish anyone who even whispered. In general, except where rice was still offered to hungry ghosts before eating began, the ritual character of meals was abandoned.[68]

All these changes could easily be considered "some modifications of clothing, meals, and living arrangements." They were scarcely revolutionary. Revolutionary change in the rules seems to have been exceptional. Here and there monks and nuns were permitted to live together—not to cohabit sexually but to reside within the walls of a single institution on a permanent basis. Before 1949 this had been strictly prohibited at reputable monasteries except in Kwangtung, where it had been allowed by local custom. After Liberation it did not become universal or even common, but it did occur in several provinces with official approval.[69]

The strictness with which the monastic rule of continence was enforced after 1949 depended on the political stand of the person who had violated it. This, at any rate, is suggested by the following story from Canton, reported by a cadre of the Religious Affairs Division. One of the most famous monasteries in the city was the Hua-lin Ssu, known also as the "Temple of the Five Hundred Lohans." It had suffered from occupation and depredation under the Nationalists but, when the Communists took Canton, it still had seven or eight monks in residence. The abbot was young and handsome and had a wife. The fact that he lived with her openly did not trouble the cadres, since they found that he was an apt student of Marxism. They made him chairman of the Canton Buddhist Study Committee, set up in 1953.[70] One of his collaborators was a progressive and very pretty young nun from the Yao-shih An. She was about twenty years old. Before too many study sessions were over, she had fallen in love with the abbot and a year or so later became pregnant. This put the cadres in a quandary. Although the Marriage Law permitted divorce and remarriage, it would have reflected badly on the sangha. Some cadres wanted to have the abbot arrested, but because he was so obligingly progressive and did whatever the Party asked him to, he was allowed to

16. Monks at the Hsüan-chung Ssu eat informally at a small square table, not in silence at long tables as before 1949. Shansi 1957.

remain in his post and, two years later, was even made a vice-president of the Canton branch of the CBA. The nun was sent to a hospital, where she had her baby, and then stayed on to work as a nurse.

Such flagrant violations of the monastic rules had been severely punished under the Ch'ing dynasty, which expected monks by their pure lives to accumulate merit that could be transferred to increase the longevity of the emperor and protect the community against natural disasters. The Communists, of course, did not believe in the transfer of merit. The reason they were disappointed by the immorality of a monk like this Cantonese was that it reduced his usefulness as an agent for the remolding of Buddhism. The kind of remolding that especially concerned them was not disciplinary but organizational: they wanted to recast the power structure of monasteries.

17. At the Ling-yen Ssu, the long tables remain, but Mao instead of the proctor watches over the monks. This old monk sits silently waiting for the others to bring their bowls from the kitchen. Soochow 1965.

Before 1949 power had been concentrated in the hands of the abbot. Usually he had preferred to reach important decisions after consulting his senior officers, but he was entitled to decide things entirely on his own. Anyway, it was he who appointed the senior officers in the first place; and theoretically he could dismiss or expel them or anyone else in the monastery. Yet despite his power (he also controlled the finances) and his perquisites (he had his own private kitchen and comfortable, spacious quarters), his religious and administrative duties were so heavy that many who were qualified for the job would refuse to take it. Since if the wrong man took it, the monastery soon went down hill, picking the right man was the most critical problem in monastic administration. It used to be solved in different ways at different monasteries: each had its own tradition. The incumbent might choose his successor single-handedly; or he might do so after broad consultation and compromise; or his successor might be chosen from among a small group of self-perpetuating trustees; or an open election might be held in which all the monks of the monastery took part.[71]

After Liberation the first proposal for recasting the power structure was presented by Chü-tsan in October 1950. He called for a "new type of public monastery" (*hsin ts'ung-lin*) to be run by a "management committee" (*shih-wu wei-yüan-hui*) of seven to nine members, elected to serve for a term of three years. Three years had formerly been the term of the abbot, whom Chü-tsan's proposal did not even mention. The right to elect and be elected to the management committee would be enjoyed not only by all resident monks but also by devout laymen who had some historical connection with the monastery. Only the head of the committee and his deputy would have to be in the sangha.

Under the management committee there would be five teams. The "general business team" (*tsung-wu tsu*) would do the work formerly done by the business office and the guest department.* The study team (*hsüeh-hsi tsu*) and production team (*sheng-ch'an tsu*) would engage in the new kinds of work their names indicate. The religious practice team (*hsiu-ch'ih tsu*) would make arrangements for elderly monks and lay devotees to concentrate on religious exercises. Younger monks who wanted to participate in

*The traditional monastery was organized in four departments: the meditation hall, the sacristy (or abbot's private office), the business office (in charge of receipts, disbursements, and supplies), and the guest department (in charge of all other aspects of daily operation). See Welch, *Practice,* chap. I.

the latter would have to do so "in the time that could be spared from labor." Finally there would be a research team (*yen-chiu tsu*), in which monks of a high cultural level and research experience would be permitted to devote themselves entirely to Buddhist research—provided they produced an important dissertation every six months (a proviso that I am glad has yet to cross the Pacific).

Monks *and laymen* would be admitted to such a "new monastery" after they had been carefully investigated and won the approval of the management committee. They would be allowed to withdraw "only after persuasion had failed to change their minds." Food would not be provided free of charge: except for the elderly, all would have to earn their keep by eight hours of physical or mental labor each day, besides which they would have to attend daily devotions and study. A certain percentage of everyone's income would go into a welfare fund. Monastery receipts and expenditures would be published twice a month. If any members owned small temples, they would have to turn them over to the management committee.[72]

This proposal of Chü-tsan was new and striking in many ways. Before 1949 laymen had sometimes been consulted about a monastery's affairs, but they had never formally held office at any orthodox institution.[73] Younger monks, instead of being prohibited from taking part in religious exercises except in their spare time, had always been *required* to take part. Admission and departure had been free and easy. Any guest prefect could admit; and departure simply required notification. (What Chü-tsan proposed would not only have eliminated casual visits by wandering monks, but the right to depart "only after persuasion had failed" made membership sound like a kind of indentured service.) Before 1949 all the monks in a monastery received their meals free of charge. To pay for them would have been unthinkable since monastic property and income was considered to belong to the whole sangha. Even more unthinkable would have been the requirement that monks hand over the small temples that were, in effect, their "family homes."

I have found no evidence that Chü-tsan's proposal was officially approved or generally adopted—not, at any rate before 1957. Some monasteries remained in the hands of conservative abbots and senior officers who successfully resisted change. This is shown by complaints like the following, from some monks at "a certain monastery in a certain district of Chekiang" in 1953. "Now that people throughout the country, young and old, are leading a frugal life and doing their utmost to step up reconstruction of our beloved fatherland, we nonetheless still get most of our livelihood as before from performing Buddhist services and collecting donations. The monks responsible for our monastery do not permit anyone in it to have contacts with lay society, which are considered violations of the code of rules. All newspapers and magazines are banned. They say that those who practice religious cultivation are superior to others and tell us not to read things from the lay world, lest we be contaminated by them and lose our religious faith. Whoever says anything good about the Communist Party is discriminated against. The monastery finances are controlled by this small minority and never made public. The main body of monks are leading a life of hardship, while the few are singled out for material comforts. Truly they resemble owls who like to prey in the darkness on their own species."[74]

It is true that in 1950-52 committees and teams began to be set up in a few places (production teams, study teams, and so on), but this did not necessarily have much significance.[75] That is, they may have amounted to no more than renaming the traditional departments, so that the business office became the "general business team" and the meditation hall became the "religious practice team." Similarly, it is noteworthy that while there was frequent talk about "abolishing the abbot system," abbots continued to hold office.[76] It may be that for several years reorganizations were usually nominal—a facade behind which the old power structure remained intact. This would help to explain why in 1957 a delegate to the second CBA national conference urged that "the system of new public monasteries be introduced at an early date."[77] He would hardly have urged it if it had been done already. Also in 1957, after the whole of T'ien-t'ai Shan had been under committee-team management for five years, the abbot of the largest monastery there told a Japanese delegation that he was pressing for the reform of the monastic system on the mountain—thus revealing that really substantial changes had yet to take place.[78]

Substantial changes do not appear to have been widespread until the anti-rightist movement of 1957 and the Great Leap Forward of 1958.[79] A case in point is Yün-chü Shan, Kiangsi, an especially conservative monastery that had been restored by Hsü-yün, whose eminence enabled him to preserve the old administrative structure. Although productive labor was started in 1953, it did not bring about any change of offices or rules. Only in July 1957, after the anti-rightist movement started and lay cadres came to the monastery in force, was a "leadership team" set up with a cadre as its head, under whom other cadres began to supervise the work of the subsidiary teams for production, general business, and so on.[80]

One factor facilitating change in 1958 was the graduation of the first class of students to receive two years training in monastic administration at the Chinese Buddhist Seminary in Peking (see Chapter V at note 42). This meant that there were now monk cadres ready to be assigned by the Buddhist association to serve as priors of monasteries, large and small. Once they took over, it was they who showed visitors around and exercised real power in the monastery. Although they would consult the abbot on important decisions, he had no choice but to acquiesce.[81] This did not mean, however, that they were necessarily able to reorganize their institutions into the "new type of public monastery" that Chü-tsan had envisaged in 1950. The trend towards reorganization was offset by the trend for the number of resident monks to decrease. At many places there were simply too few people left to run anything but a museum. In any case, regardless of how monasteries were organized—whether they were headed by an abbot or a prior or a committee—real control had passed out of the sangha to the government, at first, to the civil affairs bureau, later to the religious affairs division.[82] Monasteries had lost their traditional autonomy.

We should try to see the Communists' reform of the monastic system in the perspective of history. Attacks on the sangha for parasitism were as old as the Mahayana in China. Control of the

18. One of the monasteries that became a museum was the Chieh-chuang Ssu or West Pavillion in Soochow, here shown in a series of photographs taken in March 1962.

a. Casual visitors enter the outer gate.

b. The great shrine-hall has been well restored, but visitors can be made out sitting on a bench inside the door where no bench would be found in a living monastery.

c. A flower pot stands on the seven-sided pillar where grains of rice used to be offered to the hungry ghosts.

d. Outside the refectory hang the *huo-tien* gong and *pang* wooden fish, just as they should be. The pang, however, looks freshly painted and shows no mark of being struck to summon the "pure multitude" to meals.

e. The monastery now houses the Museum of Buddhist Culture, whose sign hangs to the right of the moon-gate.

f. Inside the museum one of the six resident monks snoozes in a chair. Before 1949 this monastery had been an important center of Buddhist practice where ordinations were held every two or three years. When J. B. Pratt visited it in October 1923 there were 200 monks in residence, 110 enrolled in the meditation hall. "Discipline is very severe and breaches of it are punished by beating," Pratt wrote in his notes.

sangha, whether aimed at purifying it or preventing sedition, was also nothing new. Some of the measures taken by the Communists were no more than a restoration of controls that had existed under the Chinese empire, and those that were new would probably have come anyway, even without a Communist victory. More will be said about this in the last chapter.

In 1928 when Chü-tsan first met T'ai-hsü, he submitted a thousand-word statement on his four purposes in becoming a monk, one of which was "the reform of Buddhism." T'ai-hsü commented on it: "Here is a scholar who has set himself on the way, and, if well taught and guided by a teacher, he will go far." Later Chü-tsan studied under him at the South Fukien Seminary and was introduced by him to the master under whom he became a monk. (The full story of Chü-tsan's efforts as a reformer before

1949 is given in Appendix A.) Other leaders of the new CBA in Peking had also been T'ai-hsü's followers–men like Fa-tsun, Shih Ming-k'o, Li Jung-hsi. Yet he cannot be considered responsible for what happened to monastic life under Mao. A cadre formerly in charge of Buddhism in the Religious Affairs Division in Canton had never even heard of his seminal work on reform, *The Reorganization of the Sangha System.* Although much of what he advocated was realized after 1949 (productive labor, public service, political activism, the elimination of commercialized and superstitious rites), it was not realized in his name or because he had advocated it, but rather because it suited the needs of the regime.[83] Nor, I think, would T'ai-hsü have been pleased by the way it was realized. He had not approved of coercion and terror. He had not wanted to see the sangha turned into a servant of the government in power or to see monasteries turned into museums. He would probably have judged much of the reform of Buddhism after 1949 to be contrary to the Vinaya and to the ethic of compassion, as we shall see in Chapter VIII. This is not to say that, if he had still been alive, he would have been able to resist the pressure to follow the leadership of the Party. Perhaps, however, he would have looked back ruefully on his former enthusiasm for bringing the sangha into the world and would have felt inexpressibly uncomfortable reading, for example, what Shirob Jaltso wrote in 1960: "Monks have discarded their tolerant, transcendental, 'negative attitude of rejecting the world,' which has been handed down from the past, and they have been stirred into a 'positive attitude of entering the world,' so that they have a completely new mentality."[84]

Chapter V

Preserving Buddhist Culture

Whenever they had the opportunity, Buddhist leaders would point out what Buddhism had contributed to Chinese culture.[1] This was because they wanted to draw attention to a way in which they could be useful. They realized that Buddhism as a living religion had little or no future, but that its past had a future. Marxist historiography required that everything in the past be sifted and analyzed so as to show whether it had been a progressive or reactionary force at its stage of history. Because of their knowledge of Buddhist contributions to literature, phonology, printing, medicine, astronomy, art, and architecture Buddhist intellectuals could help Marxist historians do this for Buddhism—and even learn to do it themselves. Furthermore, national pride required that past cultural achievements be preserved. In the case of art and architecture—that is, monasteries, images, pagodas, and rock carvings—Buddhist monks could act as custodians. It was part of what they had been doing all along.

THE CONSERVATION OF ART AND ARCHITECTURE

Buddhist art and architecture were important to preserve not only on grounds of national pride but because they offered the masses esthetic enjoyment and lessons in cultural history, just like the network of new museums. Thus the Pi-yün Ssu was repaired because it was famous for its Ming sculpture, housed a memorial to Sun Yat-sen—and lay just outside the capital, where every

19. In 1962 repairs were still going on at the Pi-yün Ssu, the Buddhist showplace outside Peking.

visitor could be taken to see it. The Shao-lin Ssu in Honan was repaired because it was where the Shao-lin school of boxing started and where Bodhidharma, the patriarch of the Ch'an sect, lived and taught.[2] As to the Pai-ma Ssu near Loyang, it was the oldest monastic site in China,[3] while the Beamless Hall of the Fo-kuang Ssu on Wu-t'ai Shan was one of the oldest wooden buildings.[4] Whether or not monasteries had historical importance, it could be argued that they deserved preservation since they had been built with the toil and talent of the working people.[5] Once repaired, they could serve as headquarters for Buddhist associations and museums.[6]

They could also serve as showplaces for foreign visitors. This was the second reason for repairing them. Handsomely restored monasteries convinced Buddhists from Southeast Asia that the Chinese government felt concern for Buddhism and had a policy of freedom of religous belief. Many such visitors were deeply impressed to learn that on the restoration of the Ling-yin Ssu, Hangchow, the government had spent the equivalent of US$200,000.[7] By 1958 there was at least one monastic showplace in every major city on the tourist route; and monasteries elsewhere were repaired if they had special significance abroad. During the first millennium much of China's contact with the outside world had come through Buddhist monks. Restoring the monasteries that were connected with them provided a useful reminder of historical links with foreign countries. For example, the Hsüan-chung Ssu in Shansi, which had become dilapidated under the Republic (like so many monasteries in north China), was rebuilt in 1954-56 at an outlay equivalent to US$110,000 "specially because it is the mecca of the Japanese Pure Land sect, thus possessing international significance."[8] In 1957 it was visited by the first of several Japanese delegations.[9] The White Pagoda in Peking was supposed to have been designed by a Nepalese architect, Arniko; hence it was given state protection as "an impressive monument to the cultural intercourse and old-age friendship between our two countries."[10] The Ta-yen Pagoda in Sian had been built in the seventh century for China's most famous Buddhist pilgrim, Hsüan-tsang, to house the texts he brought back from India. After the equivalent of more than US$20,000 had been spent on its repair, it was shown to a series of Indian delegations.[11] At the Kuang-hsiao Ssu in Canton, where an Indian monk had planted a sapling of the Bodhi Tree in the sixth century, an historical shrine was set up "attesting to the cultural exchanges between India and China."[12] The influence of Indian and Central Asian art on Chinese sculpture could best be seen in the vast cave temples of North China, which were virtually dead as centers of religious practice but were among China's most impressive monuments. Between 1955 and 1961 nine hundred

20. In 1954-56 the Hsüan-chung Ssu, Shansi, was completely rebuilt. In 1957 it was visited by the first Japanese delegation.

a. The newly restored entrance-hall, the banner over which reads: "Welcome to the Japanese Buddhist Friendship delegation to China."

b. Inside, Chinese monks chant sutras to give thanks for the gifts brought from Japan.

c. These gifts include three portraits of Pure Land patriarchs: in the center, T'an-luan.

guests from forty countries visited the Yün-kang caves, to which a special highway was built.[13] In many of the caves the guides took the opportunity to point to their neglect under the old Kuomintang government and to the depredations of the "Western imperialists." Aspersions could even be cast on Western art historians, "who were preoccupied with biased opinions and unwilling to delve into the subject from the Buddhist approach."[14]

Another purpose of conservation work was to support the government's policy towards border areas like Tibet and Mongolia. Tibetans and Mongolians looked to several sacred mountains in China proper as places of pilgrimage. At Wu-t'ai Shan in Shansi, for example, lamas sometimes outnumbered Chinese monks. Between 1951 and 1959 the government spent the equivalent of over US$400,000 on restoring temples there.[15] Almost as much was spent on one temple alone in Peking—the capital's largest lamasery.[16] This was done partly to win the favor and loyalty of

21. Monks carry roof tiles to repair the Hsing-shan Ssu. Like the Ta-yen Pagoda nearby it was called a place of great importance in the history of cultural exchange between China and India. Sian 1957.

the lamas who had so much influence over the Tibetan and Mongolian populations.

In all over a hundred odd monasteries and pagodas in China were repaired, mostly between 1951 and 1958.[17] This is not a large number compared with the 230,000 monasteries and temples that had monks and nuns in residence before Liberation; and it becomes even smaller if one deducts the pagodas, which had no connection with religious practice and may have accounted for a third of the total. Of the sixty-odd monasteries that are identified by name, many seem to have been small or defunct; major repairs are reported at very few that were large and active.[18] This was only natural, since large and active monasteries had usually been well maintained before Liberation, but it meant that in terms of religious practice the big sums spent on restoration by the government had little significance. They were significant for people's diplomacy and the study of the history of Chinese art and architecture, but not for Buddhism as a living religion.

THE MACHINERY OF CONSERVATION

There were three aspects to the conservation program: legal protection from damage; maintenance; and restoration. Most of the protective laws were passed by 1954 and most of the restoration work was completed by 1958. Thereafter conservation seems to have consisted of the minimal repairs that were necessary to maintain buildings as they were.

At first the laws protecting monasteries were a patchwork of overlapping national and local decrees and directives. They began to be passed in the summer of 1949, when damage to monasteries was strictly prohibited in the municipality of Peking. This prohibition was made nationwide in July 1950,[19] but damage continued and further decrees were addressed to various localities and regions.[20] At the end of 1951, in order to make them more effective, monasteries were asked to submit lists of all their property.[21] There were few indications of damage after 1954.

On March 4, 1961, the Provisional Regulations Governing the Protection and Administration of Cultural Treasures were promulgated by the State Council.[22] Superseding previous measures, they laid down two important principles. First, large-scale alterations and repairs were to be avoided, both in order to save money and manpower and to prevent over-ambitious restoration that destroyed more than it conserved.[23] Second, all buildings under government protection were "normally to be used only as sites for museums, sites for institutions for the protection and care of cultural objects, or places of interest to tourists."[24] Although this clause was partly designed to deter government organs from requisitioning monasteries for office space, it could also be invoked to put an end to religious activities in them. Attached to the 1961 regulations was a list of 180 monuments that were the direct responsibility of the Ministry of Culture, including about 45 Buddhist monasteries and pagodas—mostly those that had no monks to care for them.

The responsibility for protecting monasteries—and for repairing and renovating them—often shifted. In the first few years after Liberation it had lain with local united front and civil affairs organs, perhaps because they were responsible for the monks who lived in them.[25] Gradually it had been taken over by the cultural divisions of municipal and provincial governments[26] or, in the case of certain sacred mountains, by commissions specially set up for the purpose. For example, the Wu-t'ai Shan Monastery Repairs Commission was formed in 1951 and took charge of all restoration work there. The same kind of special office was set up at Omei Shan, also an important place of pilgrimage—for Tibetans as well as Chinese.[27] The budgets of both came from their respective provincial governments.

All local organs could ask for help from the Institute for the Preservation of Ancient Architecture, set up by the Ministry of Culture in 1953. By 1961 its experts had advised cultural divisions in twenty-two cities and provinces as to which buildings were valuable and how they could best be repaired.[28] However, when the repairs needed were too large for the local budget or when a monument was simply too precious to leave in the hands of local authorities, the responsibility for it passed upward. For example, the restoration of the Beamless Hall of the Fo-kuang Ssu on Wu-t'ai Shan was to be so costly and its architectural importance was so great that the central government took direct charge of it, provided the money needed, and made sure that the job was well done.[29] The list of objects that had been placed under the central government's protection by 1961 included not only 45 Buddhist monasteries and pagodas, but nearly all the famous Buddhist caves—Yün-kang, Lung-men, Maichishan, Tunhuang and seven others.[30]

The 1961 regulations underlined the obligation to report upwards. Local organs, after selecting the monuments to be preserved in their own areas, had to report their decision to the provincial authorities, just as the latter were obliged to do with respect to the national authorities. In each case the higher level might choose to assume responsibility. If it did not, the local authorities had to continue to bear the cost of maintenance. It is surprising that they were willing to do this with 8,000 "cultural objects" and that only 180 had been transferred to the Ministry of Culture by 1961.[31]

Even when the central government did not assume responsibility, it might take an interest. This happened most notably with the renovation of the main shrine hall of the Ling-yin Ssu, the largest monastery in Hangchow. In July 1949 termites had caused the roof to collapse, irreparably damaging the three main images. It was decided to replace them with a single image, which was designed by Professor Teng Pai of the Chekiang Fine Arts Institute so as "to reflect the spirit of the new society." The monks of the Ling-yin Ssu did not like his design, and work came to a halt. Then Chou En-lai, on a visit to Hangchow, happened to look at the clay model and heard about the dispute. He sided with the monks, saying: "The feet should show more, the legs should be extended wider, the hair should be in whorls, and everything should be in accord with the Buddhist tradition." Naturally, Comrade Chou's advice was heeded and, when the image was installed in May 1958 (25 meters from its base to the top of the ornamental canopy and fully gilded–see Fig. 35c), it was said to testify to "the radiance of the religious policy of the Party."[32]

NEW CONSTRUCTION

A phenomenon that has had no parallel, so far as I know, in other Communist countries was the construction of buildings–not minor buildings incidental to a restoration project but entirely new structures created to house relics and commemorate eminent monks. The outstanding example was the Buddha's Tooth Pagoda outside Peking. Standing 50 meters high, its gleaming roofs tiled in green, its finial covered with gold leaf, it looked like such a perfect example of traditional Chinese architecture that it was hard to believe it dated from 1957.[33] Perhaps because it might someday be embarrassing for a Communist regime to explain why it had created "a new holy place," complete with altars, images, and guardian gods, the initiative for its construction was said to have come from the Chinese Buddhist Association, which supervised the work of a "pagoda-construction committee of architects, artists, and sculptors."[34] In fact, however, the entire cost–equivalent to US$560,000[35]–was paid by the government. The

22. The Tooth Relic Pagoda. Peking 1962.

reason is not far to seek. In 1955-56 the Buddha's Tooth Relic, about which more will be said in the next chapter, had been sent on a tour of Burma and had proved a boon to people's diplomacy between the two countries. By building a pagoda to house it the Chinese government was able to demonstrate its patronage of Buddhism in the most concrete way. Once the pagoda was completed in 1961—just before the tooth relic went off on a tour of Ceylon—it was shown to almost all Buddhist visitors. They no longer had to make a tour of the renovated monasteries in the provinces in order to be given "proof" of the policy of freedom of religious belief. An English-language booklet about the pagoda was published by the Buddhist Association and circulated abroad. In 1964, when the tooth relic was finally installed in it, the occasion was used to have Buddhists from eight countries issue a statement condemning U.S. bombings in Vietnam.[36]

It is impressive evidence of the value placed on propaganda by Communist leaders (who certainly did not have the pagoda built out of reverence for the Buddha) that they were prepared to spend such large sums for propaganda gains that seem so small. The same can be said in the case of the other new buildings erected or planned.

On October 25, 1963, the cornerstone was laid for a memorial hall to honor Chien-chen, the T'ang monk who had helped to

23. The service to commemorate Chien-chen on October 15, 1963. A Chinese monk, presumably the abbot of the Fa-ching Ssu, faces the altar. On his left is Kongo Shuichi, administrative head of the Soto sect; on his right is Onishi Ryokei, the 88-year old abbot of Kiyomizu in Kyoto. Yangchow 1963.

bring Buddhist culture to Japan. The 1,200th anniversary of his death, May 1963-May 1964, was declared "Chien-chen Year" and four Japanese Buddhist delegations came to China to plan and take part in commemorative ceremonies. His memorial hall was to have been a large and imposing set of buildings— like the memorial planned for Hsüan-tsang in Sian. With the onset of the Cultural Revolution, work on both was abandoned.[37]

In the 1950's government patronage went not only to Buddhist art and architecture, but to literature and scholarship. A subsidy was provided so that the wood-block printing of sutras could start again in Nanking; Buddhist bookshops, if not subsidized, were at least permitted to stay in business in a few cities; contributions were prepared for a Buddhist encyclopedia; and, most important of all, the Chinese Buddhist Seminary was set up in Peking.

CHINESE BUDDHIST SEMINARY

During the Republican period at least seventy seminaries had operated in twenty-two provinces. Their purpose was to raise the educational level of monks and, in particular, to teach them how to expound the sutras to the laity. Most survived only a few years because money and good teachers were hard to find, and the economic changes after Liberation closed down the last of them.[38]

The Chinese Buddhist Seminary,[39] which opened its doors in September 1956, was located in a large and beautiful Peking monastery, the Fa-yüan Ssu.[40] It was established by the Chinese Buddhist Association and headed by CBA leaders.[41] Initially its main purpose was not to train preachers, but administrators, and thereby to help the CBA serve the government. Thus most of its students during the first five years of its existence took a course that prepared them to go back and do administrative work in their own monasteries and local Buddhist associations.[42] The curriculum was weighted towards political indoctrination, partly in order to qualify them to make administrative decisions that conformed to government policy and partly so that they might better answer questions from foreign visitors.[43] Several informants who visited Chinese monasteries were, in fact, shown around by priors who

24. The Chinese Buddhist Seminary was housed in the Fa-yüan Ssu. Peking 1962.

a. The entrance gate with the seminary's sign.

b. The back part of the temple, which had been made into an old people's home, as the sign by the gate shows.

had taken this course. After 1961 it was no longer mentioned and had perhaps been discontinued because enough administrators had been trained.

In September 1961, with the establishment of a "research department," the emphasis shifted.[44] Students now began with a "basic course" in Buddhist doctrine, history, and art; the history of China's foreign contacts; and four foreign languages–Japanese and English, Pali and Tibetan.[45] Afterwards the best of them entered the research department where they apparently did not take courses, but worked on their own or collaborated on special projects such as the compilation of a Pali-Chinese dictionary.

The purpose of this shift of emphasis seems to have been to provide better support for Buddhist people's diplomacy–to turn out monks and nuns who knew foreign languages, understood Theravada Buddhism, and could contribute to international Buddhist exchanges, either by personal contact (talking to Southeast Asian visitors, for example) or by writing articles with English summaries that would interest the foreign readers of *Modern Buddhism.* This was only one facet of the increasing orientation towards people's diplomacy that now began to characterize all the activities of the CBA.[46] In September 1962 the seminary opened a department of Tibetan Buddhism in the Yung-ho Kung, the largest lamasery in Peking. Its students, including Han monks as well as lamas, set out to do a five-year course in Tibetan language and texts.[47] This too may have been connected with people's diplomacy–reflecting a desire to show that China, far from persecuting Tibetan Buddhism, was fostering its study.

The faculty of the Chinese Buddhist Seminary consisted of about a dozen persons, many of them laymen.[48] Its 50 to 120 students were given free room, board, books, and medical treatment, as well as an allowance of pocket money.[49] A half-hour of devotions was held each morning, but it is not clear whether attendance was compulsory. Those in the basic course then had seven hours of classes and three hours of homework. A European visitor who was shown the seminary one day at noon in 1962 heard a calisthenics program being broadcast over the public address system. There seems to have been no organized meditation.[50]

Presumably the Chinese Buddhist Seminary was closed down by the Cultural Revolution. In January 1966 it was stated that 361 students had graduated to date and that, except for 18 who had stayed to do advanced research, all had returned to the temples and local Buddhist associations that had originally sent them to study at the seminary.[51] It would appear that not more than a tenth as many monks graduated annually as in the many seminaries that existed before Liberation.[52] Suggestions that other seminaries be set up and more monks be enrolled were ignored.[53] The government evidently saw no need to train more than were needed for people's diplomacy and the administration of the few monasteries that remained operating. It certainly did not intend to subsidize the spread of Buddhism.

THE CHIN-LING SCRIPTURAL PRESS

Somewhat the same economical approach can be seen in the case of publishing. Prior to Liberation there had been several establishments that specialized in the traditional wood-block printing of Buddhist texts. The best known was the Chin-ling Scriptural Press in Nanking. After many years of inactivity, it was reopened in 1952, apparently in connection with the plan to permit a revival of representative Buddhist activities. At any rate its reopening coincided with the first steps to establish the Chinese Buddhist Association and its managing board was headed by Chao P'u-ch'u, who also headed the CBA Preparatory Committee. In 1957 it was formally taken over by the association—thus joining *Modern Buddhism* and the Chinese Buddhist Seminary as part of the officially sponsored network. By this time its buildings had been restored and enlarged for the equivalent of US$8,500, provided by the Nanking Municipal Government. It had acquired the printing blocks of most of the other scriptural presses—in Peking, Tientsin, Yangchow, Soochow, and Chungking—which were now closed down for good. The centralization of these 111,600 blocks, it was claimed, would greatly facilitate the future spread of Buddhism. At least it provided an impressive sight for Buddhist visitors. "Visitors, Chinese and foreign, who are interested in Buddhist cultural activities, usually come to see the Chin-ling Scriptural

25. A Japanese Tendai delegation visits the Chin-ling Scriptural Press. Nanking 1965.

a. Its manager, Hsü P'ing-hsüan (front center), stands with them for a group picture.

b. They are shown a workman writing out the characters to be incised. The rectangular frame helps to guide him and holds the paper in place.

c. Another workman incises the characters on a woodblock.

Press."[54] They were shown workmen cutting blocks and were given complimentary copies of some of the books they printed. These seem to have been limited to a small number of titles: the largest item appears to have been a set of the works of Hsüan-tsang.[55] In 1957 Hsü P'ing-hsüan, the manager, suggested that the press should print a "People's Tripitaka" to commemorate the 2,500th anniversary of Buddha's death. Nothing was done about this—or about any of the other proposals for reprinting the Buddhist canon after Liberation.[56]

The function of the Chin-ling Scriptural Press was primarily symbolic. It was meant to symbolize, as Hsü P'ing-hsüan expressed it, the fact that "the Chinese Communist Party is the most loving protector of China's cultural legacy and has the greatest respect for the religions in which the people believe. How grateful we must be—we Buddhists of China—to the Chinese Communist Party and the People's Government!"[57] To a visiting Japanese Buddhist the Chin-ling Press symbolized even more. Reflecting on how its buildings had been used by the Japanese army as barracks after the rape of Nanking in 1937, he concluded: "I could not quite imagine until I came here [to the press] that the Chinese people really had faith in the People's Liberation Army and the People's Government as their saviors."[58]

Buddhist bookshops in Shanghai and Peking were also shown to visitors as evidence of freedom of religion.[59] Guides did not mention the bookshops that had been forced to close down. A particularly striking example of the latter was the Central Scriptural Press in Peking, which announced in December 1950 that "because of the present situation we will have to go out of business in order to avoid incurring further losses." Its huge inventory of 30 million volumes (ts'e) of sutras was being disposed of at the equivalent of 40 cents a pound, postage paid. If the purchaser did not insist on specific titles, the price was 20 cents a pound. Buddhists throughout the country were asked to help out by taking advantage of this offer and thus to "support the future of Buddhism," since the alternative was for sutras to be destroyed—as some were anyway by unfriendly cadres.[60]

The five Buddhist bookshops that survived into early 1950's were amalgamated into two, one in Peking and one in Shanghai.[61] Formerly they had sold not only sutras, but sacred images, rosaries, liturgical instruments, and all kinds of other religious goods. The same articles were on sale in the amalgamated shops, but since these were under government supervision, lay devotees may have felt less secure about making purchases that might be condemned as superstitious. This could have been precisely one purpose of the amalgamations: to exercise tighter supervision over the public sale of religious books and articles. It was easier to supervise two bookshops than five, just as the use of printing blocks could be more easily controlled when concentrated in Nanking than when scattered in half a dozen places around the country.

From government's point of view the best place for Buddhist books was a library, where access was permitted only to those who would not be harmed by reading them (that is, who read them as an object of academic research); or where they were simply put on display as lessons in cultural pride. An example of the latter was the sole surviving copy of the Chin Dynasty Tripitaka that the PLA had snatched from the Japanese army during the war. "A fierce encounter took place in which eight Eighth Route Army fighters gave their lives, but the Buddhist classics were safely transferred." In 1949 they were brought to Peking and placed in the National Library, where, after nine years' work, 3,000 out of the 4,000 chüan were restored. The remaining sections had been irreparably damaged when the PLA stored them in a coal mine.[62] One cannot help reflecting that this loss would not have occurred if the Japanese had seized and sent them back to Japan; and microfilms would be available abroad today.

Some fifteen sets of the Tripitaka were stored at the headquarters of the CBA, which probably had the biggest collection of Buddhist books outside the National Library—over 50 thousand volumes (ts'e).[63] This kind of concentration made the books less, not more available to the Buddhists of China. In 1957 Chao P'u-ch'u suggested that sutras be translated into the modern vernacular so that they could be read by more people.[64] This had been done in Hong Kong and Taiwan, but it was never done under Mao.

THE DESTRUCTION OF ART AND ARCHITECTURE

The destruction of monasteries has been mentioned in earlier chapters.[65] Most of it took place in the first two or three years after Liberation, before the government's conservation policy had been effectively impressed on local cadres. Later on, some monasteries were razed with the approval of the government because their sites were needed for factories and housing.[66] From first to last, however, almost all the monasteries destroyed were small or decaying. I know of only one that was large and prosperous, with many resident monks—the Shang-feng Ssu on Nan-yüeh.

In the case of images, too, the most flagrant cases of destruction, in which the cadres invaded the monastery to smash them or cart them off, took place in the earlier years.[67] A different kind of threat developed in 1958 during the Great Leap Forward. Monks were put under pressure to make voluntary contributions to the scrap metal drive, and many images were undoubtedly melted down.[68] Again, however, from first to last, destruction does not seem to have befallen important images from large, active monasteries.[69]

This was probably of little comfort to the monks in the small monasteries that suffered the greatest losses. Yet what especially bothered them was to be blamed for the cadres' excesses. For example, a Hangchow monk wrote to *Modern Buddhism* in 1951 saying that "during land reform there have been villages where people have taken advantage of the slogan of 'opposing superstition' to destroy cultural objects. Is this a deviation?" The editor answered: "The fact is that rural cadres have seen too much 'praying to gods and worshipping buddhas' and it is very natural for them to consider it superstitious. Therefore, in handling questions connected with monasteries, they cannot have a firm grasp of government policy and it is hard to avoid deviations. Buddhists have the duty of protecting Buddhist cultural objects. When faced by their destruction, they should on the basis of the Common Program and the declarations of the central authorities, apply persuasion and, if persuasion does not work, refer the matter to the local government for investigation and correction. Do not be emotionally biased. You must look at both sides of the matter."[70]

26. The pagoda of the T'ien-ning Ssu was one of the most famous in Peking.
a. In 1962 it stands forlornly next to a coal yard, surrounded by barbed wire. Some of the temple buildings are being used for a factory and living quarters. The others (shown in b) have entirely disappeared.

b. The temple in 1906.

In 1953 the monks of the Pao-kuo Ssu in Le-chih, Szechwan, were accused of "not having protected national cultural treasures like the apple of their eye at the time when the masses were not yet aware of the government policy on religion and on protection of cultural relics. Hence [the masses] had parts of the precious stone sculpture destroyed, mistakenly thinking them to be superstitious. Better informed cadres told the county government about it and a policy of protection was instituted."[71] In this account, as so often, "masses" means "local cadres." It is hard to see how the monks, whom they looked down on, could have persuaded them to respect buddha images. Yet perhaps that was not really the point. The point, I think, may have been to make the monks see that, no matter what the cadres did, the blame lay with the sangha, because of its long record of otherworldliness. Chü-tsan expressed this well in his work report of 1950:

> In the past year, although I have received many letters from fellow Buddhists all over the country, I only recall one, from the Reverend Ming-chen, that took the following tone. "The Shang-feng Ssu met with a cruel fate when it was burned down. It was certainly most lamentable. Yet if we go to the

27. The temple of the Yung-an-shou Pagoda has also disappeared and grass sprouts from the roof. This and the T'ien-ning Pagoda evidently served as models for the new pagoda of the tooth relic, which they still outshine. Peking 1962.

root of it, it happened because we ourselves had forgotten the dharma and had not been able to apply compassion in ordinary life nor to attract and teach people. Why should we be resentful towards them? . . . We can now only blame ourselves for the fact that our work in the past was too far divorced from the people. Everything in the way of punishment for this must be born and accepted." The Reverend Ming-chen's attitude of looking for the fault in ourselves deeply moved everyone who read his letter and I believe that only by adopting an attitude like this can Buddhism extricate itself from its present problems and find a bright future.[72]

28. The Ch'i-hsia Ssu, Nanking in 1962. Visitors were told that the Nanking Municipal Government had spent 20,000 JMP to restore its buildings, which here look in mint condition. Actually they had all been built new in the 1920's and 1930's.

a. The entrance gate.

b. The Sui dynasty pagoda.

The information is not available to reach a balanced judgment of how much damage was done to Buddhist monuments after 1949 and how much was done in the way of conservation. Only in a few cases can we compare the state of repair in 1949 with, say, 1966. One does find evidence, however, that Mainland sources have exaggerated the amount of conservation after 1949 and the degree of neglect before it.[73] Buddhists working on their own before Liberation kept up far more buildings than the government did afterwards.[74]

Three general conclusions seemed warranted. First, after 1949 there was undoubtedly a net diversion of national income away from temple maintenance in favor of industrial construction. Second, since donations from the laity "dropped to nearly nothing"[75] and the monks were forced to contribute to the State the money they had put aside for repairs[76] and since they could make only minor repairs themselves without the purchase of building materials,[77] the future maintenance of monasteries depended entirely on the government, which thus acquired yet another lever for bringing the monks into line. Finally, it was disingenuous of the government to claim that its restoration of temples demonstrated its support for Buddhism, any more than the millions spent on Abu Simbel showed that the nations involved supported the religion of ancient Egypt. The art historian will be pleased that so much restoration was done, but the historian of religion may be less impressed. What interests him is not how many temples were restored but the degree to which they remained in religious use.

Chapter VI

Buddhism in Foreign Relations

From the point of view of the Chinese People's Government, Buddhists were of no use domestically. Its goal was simply to integrate them into its social and economic programs and to remold them ideologically, so that, as soon as possible, they would cease to be Buddhists. Foreign policy was something else again. For example, when diplomatic relations or a trade pact or a border settlement was being negotiated with the leader of a Buddhist country in Southeast Asia, he could be made more amenable if he were given the impression that China was not an alien country but shared a common religious tradition; and that Chinese leaders, though not religious themselves, respected Buddhism and gave Buddhists religious freedom. More generally, when there was a need to influence public opinion abroad, it helped to have developed friendly relations—through the exchange of visits—with politicians, students, businessmen, and other social circles, all of whom could be called on to coöperate in agitation and propaganda. Among these other social circles Buddhists were not the least important. In any Asian neighbor, whenever a segment of society like the sangha came to look to China as a model or fell under the domination of a pro-Chinese faction, it slightly increased the internal pressure on the government of that country to adopt a pro-Chinese foreign policy. At any rate, such reasoning appears to be the only explanation of Chinese efforts to use Buddhism in foreign relations from 1952 to 1966.[1]

The success of their efforts depended on persuading foreigners that Buddhism in China was flourishing as never before. Different foreigners were offered different kinds of evidence, but some methods of persuasion were used with almost everyone.

METHODS OF PERSUASION

Almost everyone who came to China with an interest in Buddhism was shown the spacious headquarters of the Chinese Buddhist Association and told about its work—how it represented and protected the interests of all the nation's Buddhists; how it had branches in different localities: and how its leading members had been elected to people's councils and the CPPCC. Then they were shown the Chinese Buddhist Seminary and told how its graduates would go out to spread the dharma among the people.

Another kind of evidence was the renovation of monasteries. In each of the twenty-odd cities that Buddhists visited,[2] at least one monastery was kept in fine repair, usually at government expense. This was especially impressive to visitors whose own temples at home were shabby and whose own government offered them no aid. From their point of view it did not make much difference whether the Communists were motivated by national pride rather than by concern for Buddhism as a religion. What mattered was that aid was given—and what was wrong with national pride?

At many monasteries visitors saw monks dressed up in clean robes, chanting the sutras.[3] Japanese visitors would sometimes be invited to join in the chanting, which reminded them of the links between the Chinese and Japanese Buddhist liturgical traditions.[4] If they asked about the livelihood of the monks, they were told that the sangha had become self-supporting, which would not strike them as strange, since so many members of the Japanese sangha held secular jobs. On the other hand visitors from Southeast Asia, where it was considered wrong for monks to do manual labor, were told that monks in China lived on donations and rents and could count on government subsidies if these became inadequate.[5] No picture of monks working in field or factory—or engaging in political study—was ever included in the books and exhibits

29. This was the kind of photograph released for publication abroad. The caption released with it reads: "Rhythm of worship. Maintaining their centuries-old rites of worship, these Buddhist monks somewhere in Communist China chant the dialogues of the Buddha." The photograph was probably taken in 1956, perhaps in Peking.

on Chinese Buddhist activities that were sent abroad.[6] In their pages and in what most visitors were told, the emphasis was on the continuation of traditional religious practice—meditation, rites, and study.[7]

An effort was made to show visitors as many monks and nuns as possible—ocular evidence that the sangha was not declining. Thus for the arrivals of Premier U Nu and Prince Sihanouk, monks and nuns were collected from all over Peking and trucked out to the airport.[8] Many of the monks whom visitors saw chanting at one monastery had sometimes been collected from others.[9] The regime avoided admitting the decline in the sangha. That is why deceptively similar figures on its size continued to be given out year

30. At the Soochow railway station in 1957 a cadre of the religious affairs division checks off the names of monks to make sure that all are present to greet a Japanese delegation.

after year.[10] It was the same with the laity. Officially there were as many practicing Buddhists as ever. Some visitors were taken to the houses of devotees in Shanghai, who put on lay robes and recited sutras in front of their home altars while the visitors looked on.[11] This happened as late as 1966 when most Shanghai devotees had dismantled their altars and no longer dared to worship either at home or anywhere else (see Chapter IX).

The prosperity of Buddhism in China was not the only theme used to win Buddhist friends abroad. With each visitor the Chinese emphasized the historical links with his country. In earlier centuries monks like Hsüan-tsang had gone to India, Fa-hsien to Ceylon; Buddhabhadra had come from Nepal, Mandala and Sanghapala from present-day Cambodia. So important was Hsüan-tsang considered as a symbol of Sino-Indian friendship that the temples connected with him in Sian were among the first in China to be repaired and at once began to be shown to Indian visitors.[12] Other examples of the interconnection between foreign policy and the conservation of antiquities have been given in Chapter V.[13]

The anniversaries of Buddhist pilgrims made good occasions for exchanging gifts. For instance, in 1960 on the 1,500th anniversary of Fa-hsien's pilgrimage, the Chinese ambassador presented a set of scriptures to a Buddhist university in Ceylon as a gift from the Buddhist seminary in Peking. He did not miss the opportunity to point out that the Chinese government had a policy of freedom of religious belief, that monasteries had been renovated, sutras re-

31. The White Pagoda. Peking 1962, attributed to a Nepalese architect.

printed, and relics protected.[14] Since we do not have a complete transcript of his remarks, we cannot tell if he also mentioned another historical link: the first Chinese nuns had been ordained in the fifth century by nuns from Ceylon. This was frequently brought up in connection with Sino-Sinhalese friendship. What was not brought up was the fact that Ceylon, like Nepal, Burma, and Indonesia, had traditionally been regarded by the Chinese as a tributary state, and that the Ming fleet had actually carried off the king of Ceylon to end his days in Peking.

The Chinese liked to talk about affinities of doctrine. When Shirob Jaltso addressed the Sasana Council in Burma in January 1961 he said: "Chinese Buddhism and Burmese Buddhism despite the differences between southern and northern tradition, both still make the Three Seals the foundation, take the Four Noble Truths as the standard for accepting or rejecting things, and cultivate in common the Eightfold Path."[15] This was the main point of an address he made later that year in Colombo, as well as of the speech he had given at the Sixth Buddhist Council in 1955.[16] In order to underline such affinities, Chinese monks often wore Theravada robes when traveling abroad; and their delegations were sometimes led by bhikkhus from the Thai region of Yünnan.[17] A course in Pali was given, as we have seen, at the Chinese Buddhist Seminary; and Pali texts were translated into Chinese.[18] Historical links and doctrinal affinities were both emphasized in the Chinese contribution to the International Buddhist Encyclopedia being compiled in Ceylon under the editorship of G. P. Malalasekera. By 1962 a special committee, with headquarters in Nanking, had sent in 1,500,000 words.[19]

The wooing of Southeast Asian Buddhists may have been carried furthest by Chou En-lai. In 1961 he intimated to a Sinhalese bhikkhu that the purpose of the new Buddhist seminary in Peking was actually to introduce Theravada into China and gradually do away with Mahayana. Chou averred that he himself had seen the wisdom of this after a discussion with U Nu. Of course it would be difficult to achieve, he circumspectly added, since Mahayana was so deeply ingrained in the customs of the Chinese people, but the effort should still be made. The bhikkhu was overwhelmed. He saw the prospect of wiping out a dangerous heresy (as many Sinhalese considered Mahayana to be) and spreading the true doctrine among seven hundred million people—what a windfall of merit there would be![20]

Another theme invoked by the Chinese was common suffering at the hands of the Western imperialists. Although China had never become a colony, she had been subjected to the same indignities and exploitation as Ceylon, Burma, and other Southeast Asian countries. It was the imperialists who had prevented ancient Buddhist contacts from being renewed between these countries and China. It was the imperialists who had shelled and destroyed the pagoda near Peking in which the Buddha's Tooth used to be kept. It was the imperialists who now insinuated their agents into international Buddhist meetings so that China was deprived of her rights. This theme often found a ready response.[21]

The most pervasive Chinese theme was friendship—friendship among Buddhists, friendship between China and other Asian nations, friendship that would be strengthened and consolidated by the visit or gift or conference of the moment. It provided the

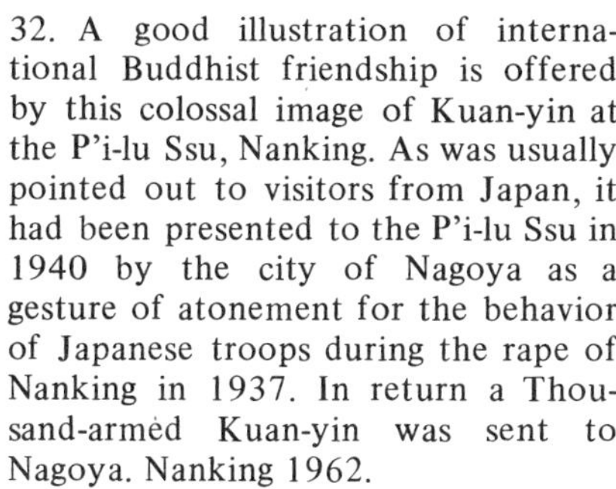

32. A good illustration of international Buddhist friendship is offered by this colossal image of Kuan-yin at the P'i-lu Ssu, Nanking. As was usually pointed out to visitors from Japan, it had been presented to the P'i-lu Ssu in 1940 by the city of Nagoya as a gesture of atonement for the behavior of Japanese troops during the rape of Nanking in 1937. In return a Thousand-armed Kuan-yin was sent to Nagoya. Nanking 1962.

33. A nun of the T'ung-chiao Ssu opens the gate so that the limousine of a foreign visitor may drive in. After being shown the immaculate main altar (right), the visitors were briefed by the abbess, who told them that this was the only nunnery in Peking and that it housed 61 nuns and two lay sisters.

refrain for many cordial speeches and touching scenes, as in Burma when Shirob Jaltso, after conveying the greetings of the Chinese people to a cheering crowd, held hands for a long time with a 90-year-old bhikkhu, saying he hoped that they would be comrades in the dharma from life to life and world to world until they reached enlightenment.[22]

It was possible for genuine friendship to arise between individual Buddhists who had been brought together by people's diplomacy.

Nuns were much better off since Liberation, she said, since they could earn money by productive labor, join the Women's Federation, and even be elected to the CPPCC.

It has to be recognized, however, that even if it did not arise, it was going to be reported; and that while friendship can exist between individuals, to speak of it between nations involves a misleading personification. Nations have no hearts. They act—or rather their governments act—on the basis of national self-interest. The purpose of people's diplomacy was to obscure this fact, to create the illusion that nations are capable of loyalty and deserve trust in the same way as individual friends. One thinks of the enormous pageants of friendship staged by India and China during the 1950's (in which Buddhism played a role too) and, by 1960, the mockery of the chant of "Hindi Chini bhai bhai"—"the Indians and the Chinese are brothers."

Even friendship between individuals was unlikely to arise in the course of the kind of Buddhist exchanges that China permitted. Too many obstacles stood in the way of personal contact. In the first place, almost no foreign Buddhists could speak Chinese, and so, when they met a Chinese monk or devotee, they could only converse with him through their interpreter. Even if they did speak Chinese, they were almost never allowed the chance to converse alone. Even if they had the chance, the Chinese Buddhist had no way of knowing whether they might not repeat what he said or publish it in the paper after they returned home, perhaps in such a way that he could then be identified. It was safer to stick to the exchange of civilities, not to open his heart, not to say anything that could possibly cause trouble.

Everything that foreign Buddhists saw and heard was, in fact, carefully arranged. Some of them knew that they were getting a "guided tour," but they may not have appreciated how much trouble their hosts had gone to. Whenever they were about to visit a monastery, the religious affairs cadres would prepare for them by drafting a list of the questions they might ask and formulating the appropriate answers. This catechism was committed to memory by everyone who might have contact with them, especially the monks who would receive them in the monastery. It was not always easy to formulate the appropriate answers. For example, if the visitor asked the abbot whether the number of Buddhists was increasing or decreasing, he had to reply that sometimes it increased and sometimes it decreased. The reason was that if the number was simply said to be increasing, it would look ridiculous for a Communist country; while if it was said to be decreasing, it would appear that there was no real religious freedom. If a visitor then asked why it fluctuated, the answer was that the mood and the needs of believers fluctuated.[23] After 1958 most foreign visitors were shown about monasteries by monks who had been trained at the Chinese Buddhist Seminary in how to answer every kind of question but they too would still be briefed by the religious affairs cadres. Some visitors were unaware that these cadres had played any role in their reception. They did not understand the political system in China and they assumed that the Buddhist Association, not the Communist Party, was taking care of them. Others—particularly the Japanese, who liked to exchange calling cards and could read the titles printed on those they received—realized that everywhere they went religious affairs cadres were on hand.[24]

To a visitor who did understand the political system in China, it was quite obvious that the red carpet being rolled out for them could not have been furnished by the Buddhists acting on their own. For example, the Sinhalese delegate to the 1952 Peace Conference was given three rooms at his hotel, with a telephone in each. It happened that a trade delegation from Ceylon was also in Peking at the same time and having difficulties in arranging for the barter of rubber for rice. They asked him to intercede. When he did so, the deal went through immediately. This made a very favorable impression on him: it showed that the Chinese government took Buddhist monks seriously.[25] In October 1955, when a Burmese delegation in Peking was short of cash, its leader found that Chao P'u-ch'u (who had not impressed him favorably in Burma) was a very influential person: he could pick up the phone and get thousands of JMP. Anything they asked for was given to them. In 1958 Rahula Sankrityayana, the Indian Buddhist scholar, had a heart attack during a visit to China; the Chinese brought his wife all the way from India to take care of him. It is important to realize that most Buddhist visitors were neither rich nor important in their own countries, and many resented the decline in deference to the sangha from both government and laity. They were simply overwhelmed by the wonderful hospitality they received in China and did not care to look further than friendship for the motive.

Friendship was also symbolized by gifts—images, scriptures, and relics—that were exchanged when foreign Buddhists came to China and when Chinese Buddhists went abroad. There was a special room in the Buddhist Association where all foreign gifts were kept in a kind of permanent exhibit of "the friendship of Buddhism."[26]

As might be expected, the Chinese were the more munificent donors, especially when it came to gifts of money. Foreign Buddhists, so far as I know, never gave any money at all,[27] whereas the Chinese donated large and small sums to their hosts and guests. In 1956, for example, they gave 600,000 rupees towards the construction of a memorial hall for Hsüan-tsang in India; 10,000 towards rebuilding the Buddha's birthplace in Nepal; 2,000 towards the construction of a peace pagoda at Hiroshima.[28] In 1960 they gave 500,000 rupees for a school run by the Nepalese bhikkhu Amritananda, who had published a very favorable report on the state of Buddhism in China the year before.[29]

Money was welcome, of course, but relics were probably the gifts most prized by devout Buddhists abroad, and, from the Chinese point of view, some of them had the advantage of being good reminders of historical ties. For example, in 1964 the ashes of Atisa, who had spent seventeen years in Tibet lecturing and writing commentaries on the Tibetan scriptures, were returned to Pakistan "as yet another move to cement the friendship between China and Pakistan."[30] China's most precious relic was the Buddha's Tooth, for which the new pagoda was built in Peking (p. 153). At least three other "Buddha's teeth" had been shown to visitors in different parts of China during the hundred years or so before Liberation. One had been kept in a crystal casket at Ku Shan, Fukien; it appeared to be made of whitish stone and was about six inches square.[31] Another—at the Wan-nien Ssu, Omei Shan—was of ivory and so large that it covered a man's chest.[32] One monastery in Peking had a large piece of rose quartz that it exhibited as "the Buddha's Tooth."[33] Perhaps because of the improbable nature of these articles, a Sinhalese bhikkhu who asked Chü-tsan in 1952 whether there were any relics of the Buddha in China was told that there were none at all.[34]

Early in 1955, however, a somewhat less improbable tooth—only two inches long—came to the notice of the Chinese Buddhist Association. It was identified as one brought from Udyana to Khotan and thence to China in the fifth century C.E.; kept in Ch'ang-an during the T'ang dynasty; and enshrined in the pagoda of a monastery outside Peking from the eleventh through the nineteenth centuries. In 1900 the pagoda was destroyed during the Boxer Rebellion. The monks found the tooth in the ruins and hid it. It remained hidden until 1955, when it was handed over to the CBA. The CBA put it on exhibit at the Kuang-chi Ssu in a simple display case, without any fanfare. It was noticed, however, by the Burmese ambassador. He reported its existence to U Nu, who mentioned it to Chou En-lai, saying that in the eleventh century the Burmese King Anuruddha had sent an expeditionary force to China in order to get it. Chou replied: "What you could not get through war you can now get through friendship. Take it—we have no use for it." So in September 1955 U Nu sent a delegation of fourteen persons to bring the tooth back to Burma where, they assumed, it would remain. When they arrived at the headquarters of the CBA, they found that it was no longer housed in a simple hexagonal case (glass sides on a wooden frame), as it had been when the Burmese ambassador saw it in the spring. Now a reliquary made from nearly 350 pounds of solid gold (*sic*) and encrusted with jewels had been brought from the Imperial Palace. Instead of being given to the Buddhists of Burma, the tooth was to be loaned. Apparently the Chinese had regarded it as a mere curiosity at first, but then realized its potentialities. The delegation was disappointed about the change of plan, but took it with good grace and carried the tooth back to Rangoon on a special plane.[35] Here is a description of what happened when it arrived.

> A sea of welcoming flags was waving in the bright sun and the roar and reverberations of drum-beating, horn-blowing, and the chanting of scriptures was like "thunder rending the sky." Among those who had come to welcome the tooth were President Ba U of the Union of Burma, Premier U Nu, members of the Supreme Court, congressmen, senators, secretaries of the Army, Navy, and Air Force, ministers of the various departments of the government, foreign diplomats, monks, nuns, and others. As soon as the jeweled pagoda containing the relic was carried to a specially made gold-plated carriage, a solemn ceremony of welcome was held at the airport. After Chao P'u-ch'u had presented the Buddha Tooth Relic to the

34. The reliquary of the Buddha's Tooth. Peking 1965.

> Burmese government, President Ba U and the whole crowd responded three times in unison with a voice like thunder: "Sato!" (It is good indeed!). President Ba U then said: "Many thanks to Chairman Mao, Premier Chou, the Chinese government, and the Chinese people. Through their profound friendship the historic wish of the Burmese people is now fulfilled . . . The people of modern Burma are fortunate indeed, for the tooth of the Buddha is now visiting our land . . . Long live the friendship between the peoples of China and Burma!"
>
> Then the jeweled pagoda containing the tooth relic was carried personally by President Ba U, Premier U Nu, and other high-ranking officials into a decorated car, which moved slowly through the streets of Rangoon in a parade with the government dignitaries walking alongside according to their ranks. A convoy of motorcycles, troops from the Army, Navy, and Air Force, policemen, scouts, and others marched in front, behind, and around the decorated car, safeguarding the tooth relic. The whole population of Rangoon was standing out in the street, beating drums, blowing horns, singing, chanting, bowing, and burning incense as the car went by. The Buddha Tooth Relic was then taken to the Peace Pagoda where it was enshrined for people to see and to worship.[36]

For the next eight months it toured Burma attracting large crowds and sharing in the international attention given to the Sixth Buddhist Council. With the pious offerings from those who worshiped it a pagoda was built in Myitkyina, where a replica of the tooth was installed in 1958.[37] For hundreds of thousands of devout and simple-hearted Burmese all this created a very favorable impression of China and its new government.

With the hope of another such success the tooth relic was sent to Ceylon in 1961. By now the CBA had published a handsome booklet giving its history, explaining that its size was about the same as the tooth relic kept in Kandy, and including photographs of the beautiful new pagoda that had been built near Peking to house it.[38] This booklet was distributed in Ceylon (and other countries) while the tooth was on tour there. During the tour the New China News Agency released a torrent of despatches about the enormous crowds that came to pay their respects to the relic, the high officials who made up the delegations escorting it, the receptions given by the Prime Minister, Mme. Bandaranaike, and the somewhat predictable speeches.[39] Chao P'u-ch'u, for instance, said that the reuniting of the two teeth in Ceylon "signifies that the peoples of Ceylon and China, after having freed themselves from the shackles of colonialism and imperialism, have not only revived a profound and historic friendship, but also developed it."[40]

On the whole, however, the tooth was less successful in Ceylon than in Burma. The suppression of the Tibetan rebellion two years earlier had left a residue of suspicion (which, of course, the tour was partly designed to allay). Furthermore the Chinese relic competed in a sense with Ceylon's own Buddha Tooth. Several leaders of the sangha in Kandy refused to allow their followers to escort it, and they let it be known that they did not consider it to be genuine. The pious donations collected on its tour were less than a tenth of those that had been collected when the relics of Sariputta and Moggallana had been brought to Ceylon in 1948.[41]

Perhaps some Party members in Peking were not altogether happy about the tour either. This would help explain why such an enthusiastic account of it was written for the *People's Daily* by Kuo P'eng, who was one of the people responsible to the Party for the activities of the Buddhist Association.[42] He was trying to counteract, I suspect, a feeling among the more uncompromising Marxists that it was shameful for such heavy expenditures to be made in order to have China represented abroad by an object that, from the materialist point of view, could only be a fraud. They may have felt like Han Yü in the T'ang dynasty, who said, when a Buddha relic was brought into the imperial palace, that it did not deserve to be worshipped but to be taken out and burned.[43] Men like Kuo P'eng, however, saw nothing wrong in taking advantage of the credulity of foreign Buddhists. The previous year the CBA had published a book by its Nepalese friend, Amritananda, in which he described how relics brought back by Chou En-lai from Nepal in 1958 had miraculously multiplied. "The Buddhists of the world will not be surprised to hear this news because it often happens that the relics sometimes increase or decrease according to the circumstances. The Buddhists believe the relics may be increased if they are kept at the right place in a right manner, and they may also disappear, if they are not kept at the right place and the right manner.[44] Presumably the CBA, where the relics had been kept, was a "right place" and their multiplication was another bit of evidence that Buddhism in China was flourishing.

THE PATTERN OF EXCHANGES

From 1952 through 1966 at least thirty-six foreign Buddhist delegations visited China; and eleven Chinese Buddhist delegations went abroad. During the same period twenty-five or more individuals were invited to China as Buddhists (other Buddhists came as officials and tourists); while from the Chinese side one individual—Chao P'u-ch'u—went abroad repeatedly.[45] The Chinese sent fewer individuals but more exhibits. For example, Chinese Buddhist art was exhibited in Japan in 1956 and photographs of Buddhist monuments and activities in China were exhibited in Colombo in 1960.[46]

To describe these exchanges one by one would be tedious. In any case most of them received good coverage in the English-language releases of the New China News Agency, to which the interested reader may refer for details.[47] As Table 2 shows, there were peaks in activity in 1956, 1961, and 1963-64. The year 1956 was not only the year following the Bandung conference, but it was also the 2,500th anniversary of the Buddha's death; 1961 saw China trying hardest to make friends abroad after the breakdown of relations with India and Soviet Union; and in 1963-64 the CBA was engaged in a final effort to justify its existence by mobilizing foreign Buddhists against the United States. The countries in Table 2 fall into three groups: those with which there were frequent Buddhist exchanges over a long period (Cambodia, Ceylon, Japan, and Nepal); those with which exchanges ended because of a shift in foreign policy (India after the border dispute began in 1960, Burma after the government decided on a policy of isolation in 1962); and those with which exchanges were sporadic, either be-

Table 2. Buddhist exchanges (*D*=delegation, *I*=individual)[a]

Place		1951	1952	1953	1954	1955	1956	1957	1958	1959	1960	1961	1962	1963	1964	1965	1966	1967	1968	1969	1970	Total
Burma	from	—	?I	—	—	D	D	—	I	—	—	D	—	—	—	—	—	—	—	—	—	3D, 2I
	to	—	—	—	—	D	D	—	—	—	I	D	—	—	—	—	—	—	—	—	—	3D, I
Cambodia	from	—	—	—	—	—	I	—	D	—	—	—	—	D	D	—	—	—	—	—	—	3D, I
	to	—	—	—	—	—	—	D	—	—	—	D	—	—	—	—	—	—	—	—	—	2D
Ceylon	from	—	I	—	—	—	I	I	—	2I	—	D	—	—	D	—	—	—	—	—	—	2D, 5I
	to	—	—	—	—	—	—	—	—	—	—	D	—	—	—	—	—	—	—	—	—	D
India	from	—	—	—	—	—	2I	—	I	—	—	—	—	—	—	—	—	—	—	—	—	3I
	to	—	—	—	—	—	2D	—	—	—	—	—	—	—	—	—	—	—	—	—	—	2D
Indonesia	from	—	—	—	—	—		—	—	—	—	—	—	D	D	—	—	—	—	—	—	2D
	to	—	—	—	—	—	—	—	—	—	—	—	—	—	—	D	—	—	—	—	—	D
Japan	from	—	—	I	I	I	—	D, 2I	—	—	—	D	—	3D,2I	3D	2D	2D	I	I	—	—	12D,9I
	to	—	—	—	—	I	—	—	—	—	I	2I	—	D	I	—	—	—	—	—	—	D, 5I
North Korea	from	—	—	—	—	—	—	—	—	—	—	—	—	D	—	—	—	—	—	—	—	D
	to	—	—	—	—	—	—	—	—	—	—	—	—	—	—	—	—	—	—	—	—	—
Laos	from	—	—	—	—	—	I	—	—	—	—	—	—	D	D	—	—	—	—	—	—	2D, I
	to	—	—	—	—	—	—	—	—	—	—	—	—	—	—	—	—	—	—	—	—	—

Place		1951	1952	1953	1954	1955	1956	1957	1958	1959	1960	1961	1962	1963	1964	1965	1966	1967	1968	1969	1970	Total
Mongolia	from	—	—	—	—	—	—	—	—	—	—	—	—	—	D	—	—	—	—	—	—	D
	to	—	—	—	—	—	—	—	—	—	—	—	—	—	—	—	—	—	—	—	—	—
Nepal	from	—	—	—	—	—	I	—	—	D	—	—	—	D	D	—	—	—	—	—	—	3D, I
	to	—	—	—	—	—	D	—	—	—	—	—	—	—	—	—	—	—	—	—	—	D
Pakistan	from	—	—	—	—	—	—	—	—	—	—	—	—	D	D	—	—	—	—	—	—	2D
	to	—	—	—	—	—	—	—	—	—	—	—	—	—	—	—	—	—	—	—	—	—
Thailand	from	—	—	—	—	—	I	—	—	—	—	—	—	D	—	—	—	—	—	—	—	D, I
	to	—	—	—	—	—	—	—	—	—	—	—	—	—	—	—	—	—	—	—	—	—
Vietnam	from	—	I	—	—	—	I	—	—	—	—	—	—	2D	2D	—	—	—	—	—	—	4D,2I
	to	—	—	—	—	—	—	—	—	—	—	—	—	—	—	—	—	—	—	—	—	—
Other	from	—	—	—	—	—	—	—	—	—	—	—	—	—	—	—	—	—	—	—	—	—
	to	—	I	—	—	—	—	—	I	—	—	—	—	—	—	—	—	—	—	—	—	2I
Total	from	—	3I	I	I	D,I	D,8I	D,3I	D,2I	D,2I	—	3D	—	12D,2I	12D	2D	2D	I	I	—	—	36D,25I
	to	—	I	—	—	D,I	4D	D	I	I	2I	3D,2I	—	D	I	D	—	—	—	—	—	11D, 9I

[a]The purpose of this table is to show the number of visits regardless of how many visitors were involved in each. Only Buddhist delegations are counted as delegations. One or more Buddhists coming in a non-Buddhist delegation are counted as one individual visit.

cause delegations could only come from areas under Communist control so that there was no need to woo them with Buddhist people's diplomacy (Laos, Mongolia, Thailand, Korea, and Vietnam); or because the countries were predominantly Muslim (Indonesia and Pakistan).

With each country there were different reasons and occasions for exchanges to take place. For example, Japanese delegations came most often to return the remains of Chinese prisoners who had died in Japan during the war; and to celebrate the anniversaries of Chinese patriarchs who were important in Japanese sects. The Japanese looked to China as the motherland of their kind of Buddhism—far more than to India; and the study of Chinese Buddhism was nowhere so highly developed as in Japan. Also, because many Japanese saw China as a potentially important trading partner or resented American influence at home, Buddhist groups in the two countries coöperated in calling for the re-establishment of diplomatic relations, opposing Japan's security treaty with the United States, and protesting the U.S. use of nuclear weapons. Some Japanese felt a special kind of war guilt towards China—not unlike what would be felt by a filial son after a patricidal outburst. For all these reasons, as can be seen from Table 2, Japan was the country with which China had the largest number of Buddhist exchanges going on the longest.[48] It was also the only country with which the Chinese set up joint bodies: three Japanese-Chinese Buddhist associations were operating in the years before the Cultural Revolution.[49]

In the case of Burma, the occasions for exchanges were the Sixth Council in 1955, the Jayanti celebrations and the tour of the tooth relic in 1955-56, and the Sino-Burmese Boundary Agreement in 1961. Behind the earlier exchanges lay U Nu's piety and his hope that Burma would become the center of world Buddhism. His successor, Ne Win, was simply glad to have Buddhism contribute to the friendly atmosphere in which the Boundary Agreement was signed.

Many Sinhalese considered that their country was already the center of world Buddhism. Ceylon had sent the largest number of Buddhist missionaries to India and the West; it published the most

35. A Japanese delegation in China.

The following pages are a pictorial record of what a typical group of Buddhist visitors saw on their tour of China. In 1963 the Chinese Buddhist Association had presented a copy of the *Lotus Sutra* to the Tendai sect of Japan in commemoration of the 1100th anniversary of its third patriarch. In 1965, to convey its thanks, the Tendai sect sent to China a six-member delegation led by Sokushin Shutan, the abbot of Enryakuji. Accompanied by Chou Shu-chia, they visited Canton, Hangchow, Shanghai, Nanking, and Peking. While in Hangchow they were driven out to T'ien-t'ai Shan—in Japanese Mt. Tendai and the place of origin of the sect. This was the first time that the sect's representatives had been there since 1936, before the outbreak of the Sino-Japanese War. Most of the following photographs were taken by the Reverend Mibu Shojun and the captions are based on his description of the trip, especially in "Chugoku Tendai-san Junreiki."

a. On the steps of the Ling-yin Ssu, Hangchow, crowds await the Japanese visitors.

b. People look more curious than devout. After all, it is May Day.

c. Inside the shrine-hall the visitors photograph the gigantic image of the Buddha, in the design of which Chou En-lai played a part (see Chapter V at note 32).

d. Afterwards, while a monk lights incense, the visitors inspect the other images in the shrine-hall, like these devas (here shown on another day).

e. Then they repair to the monastery's reception room for a cup of tea. Chou Shu-chia is third from left. At the end of the table is the number-one interpreter, who does not wear a cadre's suit.

f. Their visit to T'ien-t'ai Shan had first been discussed here four years earlier, when Mibu Shojun (standing) met Tan-yün, abbot of the Kuo-ch'ing Ssu (left), with Ta-pei, abbot of Ling-yin (center) and Yüeh-t'ao, abbot of Hsia-t'ien Chu (right).

g. On that occasion Tan-yün and Mibu Shojun exchanged gifts.

h. On May 2, 1965 at 8:00 A.M. four cars are waiting to transport the delegation straight from Hangchow to T'ien-t'ai Shan.
i. Before leaving, one of the delegates takes this photograph lest he forget that in China not everybody has a car.

j. Seven hours later they arrive at the Kuo-ch'ing Ssu, where dozens of monks are lined up to greet them at the outer gate.

k. As they pass through successive courtyards, they note how well everything has been repaired at the government's expense.

l. They enter the monastery proper through the Hall of Guardian Kings. The great drum and bell are sounded to receive them.

m. Soon they see the monks going to afternoon devotions, wearing their *kashaya* robes, all in good order.

n. They inspect the hall where lectures on sacred texts are said to be given once a month.

o. After chanting sutras in the great shrine-hall, which reminds them of Enryakuji, they go to a reception room where a speech of welcome is made by Chou Shu-chia. On the wall hangs a familiar face, flanked by two mottoes: "Obey Chairman Mao" and "Follow the Communist Party."

p. From the Kuo-ch'ing Ssu they drive to the Chen-chüeh Ssu and go on foot to pay homage to the mummified body of Chih-i, founder of the T'ien-t'ai school. Sokushin says: "This is where our T'ien-t'ai forbears have lived, and their tradition is still bright. When we compare it to Hieizan [site of Enryakuji and now partly a vulgar amusement park], we are grateful that this sacred place is still preserved just as it was. We are impressed by the fact that the road up the mountain was built with labor furnished by the people's commune."

q. From Hangchow the delegation goes to Shanghai, where it takes part in the celebration of the Buddha's birthday (see Figure 50) and then to Nanking (see Figure 25). Its last stop is Peking, where it is given a banquet by Kuo Mo-jo. Later Sokushin is photographed standing with Chü-tsan (left) and Chao P'u-ch'u (right) in front of the Tooth Relic Pagoda.

books and periodicals on Buddhism in English;[50] and it was the birthplace of the World Fellowship of Buddhists. The Bandaranaike governments sought to win popular support by giving patronage to Buddhism and at the same time, because of their Marxist leaning, wished to develop better relations with China. Both ends were served by the exchange of visits and the tour of the tooth relic.

Cambodia, in the eyes of Prince Sihanouk, needed the friendship of China in order to secure greater independence from the Western powers. He was himself a Buddhist monarch. He therefore welcomed a Buddhist delegation that was sent to attend Cambodia's Jayanti celebration in 1957; and in 1958 dispatched the Venerable Huot Tath as head of the first Cambodian delegation of any kind to go to China and the only Buddhist delegation ever to be received by Mao Tse-tung.[51] Within a month China and Cambodia established diplomatic relations. In 1961 Sihanouk played host to the Sixth Conference of the World Fellowship of Buddhists and saw to it that the Chinese were invited (they had not been to the Fifth Conference in Bangkok).

As to Nepal, although its population was predominantly Hindu, a small Buddhist revival enjoyed the patronage of King Mahendra, who played host to the Fourth Conference of the WFB in 1956—the first to be attended by the Chinese. The Nepalese saw China as an enormous neighbor facing them over a border that was long, unpatrolled, and—until 1961—undemarcated. Tibetan lamas and refugees had flooded across it after the Lhasa uprising in 1959. Almost immediately the first Buddhist delegation left Kathmandu for China—perhaps in order to reassure the Chinese of Nepal's friendship. It was led by the Venerable Amritananda, a Theravada bhikkhu trained in Ceylon, who became one of the leading advocates of the idea that Buddhism was flourishing in socialist countries.

PRAISE OR SILENCE

The CBA, which played host to most Buddhist visitors, was gratified when they went home with the impression that Chinese

Buddhism was flourishing; it was even more gratified when they said so in public statements that the New China News Agency could circulate in Asian Buddhist countries; and it was most gratified of all when its success with visitors could be shown to have resulted in a gain for Chinese foreign policy. U Nu testified to such a gain in 1961 when he said: "Buddhism is not only surviving in China but it is still in the course of development . . . It is *because of this* that I am all the more intimate with the Chinese government and I praise it more."[52] The CBA was seldom handed such concrete evidence that it had been useful to the regime and that Buddhism in people's diplomacy paid off. Yet as the domestic importance of Buddhism declined, it needed more and more to be able to cite such evidence in order to justify its existence to the authorities.

It was fortunate for the CBA that Buddhist exchanges tended to result in either praise or silence. One reason for this was that most delegations were selected by the governments of the countries from which they came. Since these governments wanted friendlier relations with China (otherwise they would not have coöperated), they expected the delegates they chose to make favorable statements when they returned home—or to say nothing.[53] Visitors who had not been chosen by their own governments had been chosen by the CBA, which was even more careful to avoid inviting people who might take a negative view of what they saw. Even among those who did take such a view, many were reluctant to publicize it, partly because it might decrease the chances for Chinese Buddhism to survive and partly because it might get them into trouble with leftist groups at home (this applied to especially to Japanese Buddhists, many of whom were in academic life). In any case, a visitor who wanted to publicize his unfavorable impression of the state of Chinese Buddhism was handicapped: he did not have the New China News Agency standing by to circulate it throughout Asia.

The kind of statement that the Chinese particularly liked to circulate was one that referred to the overcoming of earlier doubts, so that the reader, in case he had doubts himself, would feel that, if he too went to China, they would be overcome. For example, in 1958 the head of the first Cambodian delegation, the

Venerable Huot Tath, told reporters when he returned home that the Chinese people enjoyed freedom of religious belief and the government helped to restore ruined temples. "What I saw in China was entirely different from the rumors I had heard before."[54] The next year Amritananda, as head of a Nepalese delegation, made the same point. Before coming, he said, he had heard "rumors that there was no freedom of religious belief in China and that Buddhism had decayed in China . . . Now . . . it is evident to us who are here in China that these rumors are quite groundless."[55] Since he had only passed one day on Chinese soil at the time he said this, his conclusion might seem to have been reached hastily, if not eagerly, but it was confirmed by what he observed on his tour, in the course of which he made three more similar statements–in Liaoning, Kirin, and Shanghai–each of which was picked up and distributed in English by the New China News Agency.[56]

In 1961 a party of Buddhist women from Singapore made a tour of the Mainland in which they saw that "the life of monks and nuns was secure and peaceful." Afterwards they said in surprise: "Seeing is better than believing. We have seen with our own eyes that the Chinese government is really protecting freedom of religious belief . . . Chairman Mao in building happiness for the people is also building happiness for Buddhists. The merit of Chairman Mao is immeasurable–may he live forever! . . . You [monks] are really lucky to be carrying on religious practice in such a good place."[57]

The naive enthusiasm in the statement can be explained by the fact that this was a group of illiterate devotees–and perhaps also by the fact that, like the statements by Huot Tath and Amritananda, theirs has come to us through a Mainland source.[58] However, even when sophisticated visitors wrote in the Western press about their tours of China, their critical faculties were often given the day off. For example, after his tour in the spring of 1959, G. P. Malalasekera reported the following:

> As for China, before I went there, I was told that religious practices as a whole were frowned upon, that the activities of religious institutions were being greatly curtailed, if not en-

> tirely suppressed, and that monks were forbidden to carry on their work. In spite of this, my trip to China was the result of an invitation of a state-sponsored organization called the Buddhist Association of Peking, and as their guest I was given every facility to visit many parts of China, including Shanghai, Nanking, Soochow, Hangchow, and Peking. At an institution called the Buddhist Academy I found that Tibetan, Chinese, Japanese, Sanskrit, and Pali were all taught, and the study of Buddhist scriptures and the training of monks and nuns were going forward. The important Buddhist monasteries have been taken under state patronage and state funds are being spent for their restoration and preservation, monks are allowed to carry on their work unhampered, and several publications both in Chinese and in other languages are being issued regularly . . . Thus Buddhism remains of continuing importance in China since the revolution, and interest in it has not flagged.[59]

The assumptions implicit in this statement were (1) that if religious activities were being curtailed, there could be no such thing as a state-sponsored Buddhist association; (2) that the Chinese Buddhist Seminary performed the same functions as schools for monks in Ceylon; (3) that the state's restoration of monasteries showed monks could carry on religious practice unhampered; and (4) that the number of schools, publications, and monasteries was not much less in 1959 than it had been before Liberation, ergo, interest in Buddhism "had not flagged." As we have seen, all these assumptions were erroneous.

The same sort of assumptions underly the statement made by Amritananda in Shanghai: "The traditional Buddhist ceremonies are observed in the life of Chinese Buddhists. The temples are not only protected by the government, but in many cases are repaired with the help of the government. What astonished me the most are the many Buddhist pictures and books of Buddhist teachings in the Buddhist Publishing House here and the fact that many Buddhists are found reciting scriptures every day at the Buddhist Believers Society here. All this proves that there is freedom of religious belief."[60] Similarly, other members of Amritananda's delegation remarked that the existence of the Chinling Scriptural Press and the monasteries they had seen "proves that there is full freedom of religious belief in China."[61]

These and many other visitors were less than rigorous in their concept of proof. They do not seem to have considered the possibility that what they saw had been specially arranged to convey a false impression to them; or they deliberately rejected the possibility because of their gratitude for the kindness shown them by their hosts. Amritananda said: "We feel quite at home here among the Chinese brothers and sisters, who are as kind and friendly to us as our brothers and sisters in Nepal."[62] When he passed through Hong Kong on his way back, he had a heated argument with Chinese monks who suggested that he had been given a guided tour. This made him angry—perhaps because he knew that he had, but to admit it would cast an embarrassing light on his enthusiastic statements and on the gift he was soon to receive—500,000 rupees for his school outside Katmandu.[63]

Yet even when visitors to the Mainland had no reason to fear embarrassment, many of them resisted the notion that they had gotten a guided tour. It was more agreeable to suppose that their visit was exceptional or that their perspicacity had enabled them to learn about what they were not shown as well as what they were shown so that they had been able to arrive at a balanced judgment. For some visitors (and this includes not a few Buddhists), to adopt a skeptical attitude towards what they had been shown in China was to fall into a trap set by the American imperialists.

The most negative element that one can find in published accounts is an occasional reservation or expression of skepticism. André Migot, for example, after a five-month tour of China in 1957, concluded that Buddhism was "better off" after the first ten years of revolution. "Many people are becoming monks and nuns. Buddhist associations and journals have multiplied. Large crowds participate in religious ceremonies and pilgrimages." He noted that Buddhist monuments were carefully protected and repaired, although "the other side of the coin is that most temples have the atmosphere of a museum and this, I think, is what the government considers them." From Migot, however, this was not so much of a reservation as it may sound, since he considered that "if the theistic, ritualistic Buddhism that was established among the masses of the Chinese people is called upon to disappear—but is it not dead already?—the original Buddhism can perfectly well continue to prosper, pursuing the same goal: the complete realization of the liberated human being."[64] To anyone with this elitist view of religion, the conversion of temples into museums was actually a step forward.

Sometimes reservations were less complacent. For example the leader of a Japanese Buddhist delegation in 1957 reported that he got the "impression that Buddhism is certainly alive in China . . . Unlike the Soviet authorities, which have made it their policy to suppress religion, the Chinese Communist government has spent a lot of money, not only for reconstructing the Yung-ho Kung and Kuang-chi Ssu in Peking, but even for such temples as the Hsüan-chung Ssu in a remote part of Shansi province . . . We in Japan, on the contrary, cannot even hope for things like this. How I wish we could! . . . I was pleased to learn that Chinese Buddhism was so healthy. However there is the opinion that there may be something else behind what one sees. Of course, Communists do not recognize any necessity for the existence of religion. Their protection of Buddhism does not mean that they are encouraging Buddhist worship. What the authorities are trying to do is to preserve the nation's cultural treasures. Anyway, by their preserving these things rather than ignoring them, faith will still be kept alive."[65]

This may not sound particularly critical, but, so far as I know, it is the most negative statement published before 1966.[66] Buddhist visitors preferred to convey any negative impressions in private. For example, another member of the 1957 delegation wrote in a personal letter: "Chinese Buddhism is practically dead on the Mainland." The letter was published without his permission in an anti-Communist magazine.[67] This made him very angry, since it cut him off from future travel to the Mainland. Also, like many other foreign Buddhists, he believed that one way he could help keep Buddhism alive in China was to appear to be convinced by the guided tour and "pleased to learn that Chinese Buddhism was so healthy." That would provide evidence that Buddhist people's diplomacy was working; and the CBA would be able to use this evidence not only to justify its own existence, but to persuade the government that a few temples should be kept open for worship and a few monks should be available to dress up and greet visitors. That, after all, was better than no temples and no monks.

Yet how did negative impressions arise? How could some visitors get to feel that Buddhism was "practically dead" in China when their hosts took such pains to convince them of the opposite? It was not because they found out that the sangha had been decimated, monks arrested, temples closed, religious practice restricted, and so on. This kind of fact they had no way of learning. Instead they seemed to light on trifles. For example, when the tooth relic was handed over to the Burmese delegation in Peking, the ceremony was witnessed by a crowd of about a hundred Chinese spectators, mostly very old or very young. One of the Bur-

36. This former temple of the Japanese Pure Land sect in Tientsin had become a workers' sports club by 1957. Some of the Japanese Buddhist visitors who saw such buildings felt sorry that they had not been reserved for some religious use.

mese reflected that in Burma there would have been thousands of people present, led by the highest officials. It made a bad impression on him.[68] Later he asked Chou En-lai why he had seen no monks under thirty in the monasteries he had visited—since without a steady inflow of novices the sangha would disappear. Chou replied that young people were not interested in becoming monks and, since there was freedom of religion in China, the government could not force them to be ordained. This was a reasonable reply, but it struck the Burmese as evasive. An eminent Sinhalese bhikkhu, who lectured to a lay audience in Peking, was also distressed to see no young people in the audience—no children of farmers or factory workers. It was to them, he felt, that the dharma would have to be preached if Buddhism was to survive in China. In Shansi, when the rebuilding of the Hsüan-chung Ssu was celebrated in 1957, no ordinary believers attended: there were only monks and cadres. A Japanese guest asked why and was told that there would have been too big an influx of people, tens of thousands of whom came there every year for Ti-tsang's birthday. The Japanese knew that the monastery had been in ruins, could find no image of Ti-tsang, and wondered.

Some visitors were put off by the restriction of personal contact. For example, a member of the International Buddhist Monks Delegation in 1956, who knew Mandarin, found that he was not supposed to talk to Chinese monks except through his interpreter.[69] Others were put off by the solicitude of their guides, who never seemed to leave them alone.[70] Yet the presence of guides and interpreters did not always prevent disagreeable impressions. A visiting Indian scholar once met a Chinese devotee, who said through the interpreter: "Your coming to China has given us strength." The Indian sensed a hidden meaning and replied: "I hope I may come to your house and call on you." Immediately the Chinese answered: "Oh no—no. I shall not be at home."[71] Similarly, a Sinhalese bhikku who asked if he could stay at the Kuang-chi Ssu while he was in Peking (monks expect and prefer to stay in monasteries when they travel) was refused on the grounds that "we could not provide you with the proper comforts there. Our bhikkhus lead a primitive life. There are no good latrines."

The same request by a Nepalese bhikkhu was refused a few years later. Indeed no foreign monk, so far as I know, has spent the night in a Chinese monastery since Liberation—except in places of pilgrimage where no other accommodation was available. The Chinese Buddhist Seminary refused an offer to exchange students with the Pali Institute in Nalanda. Foreign students were common enough in Peking until 1966, but there were none who had come to study Buddhism.

Buddhist visitors usually did not know the names of any Chinese monasteries, so that they had to be satisfied with those that their hosts selected to show them, but when they could name one that they wanted to see, their request was often denied in a way that aroused suspicion. They were told that it no longer existed or was too far away or that a visit would be "inconvenient."[72] The more enterprising visitors then found their own way with the help of old

37. At least three different foreign delegations saw Pure Land practice being carried on at one monastery in China—the P'i-lu Ssu, Nanking. As here in 1957, it often seemed to be a kind of exhibition.

guidebooks. Sometimes the monastery had been converted to a nonreligious use. Sometimes it was in good repair, with incense burning on the altar and one or two monks in evidence—so that it was hard to see why it had not been included in the list of places open to visitors. On the other hand, sights that it would have been much better to keep from them lay within the twelve-mile radius of Peking, where foreigners were normally allowed. Some who went out to see the beautiful new Tooth Relic Pagoda, built "as a symbol of compassion and peace,"[73] found that the area around it was swarming with soldiers. The soldiers had even taken over the Ling-kuang Ssu, whose monks had preserved the tooth relic and originally offered it to the Buddhist Association. Now they had been evicted.

Once a visitor's suspicions had been aroused, he tended to find confirmation of them. For example, on another occasion the Indian scholar mentioned above invited a Chinese abbot to visit him in New Delhi. The abbot replied: "I would be happy to accept the invitation. My arrival in India would be the happiest day of my life." The Indian had no doubt of what he meant. About 1959 the Chinese ambassador to Ceylon was in conversation with an iconoclastic bhikkhu there, who said that the sangha should be eliminated because it was too primitive. "Well, you see," happily chimed in the ambassador, "we're *trying* to do away with it in China." This made a deep impression on the bhikkhu, who soon thereafter switched from being very pro to very anti-Peking.[74] Foreigners were so unpredictable!

THE WORLD FELLOWSHIP OF BUDDHISTS

Contact with Buddhists abroad was not limited to the exchange of delegations. The Chinese also took part in some of the conferences held every two or three years by the World Fellowship of Buddhists. The roots of this organization, founded in 1950, went back to the ecumenical ideals of Dharmapala and T'ai-hsü, both of whom wanted to create a worldwide movement that would strengthen and spread Buddhism.[75] The WFB, however, was not a center of hierarchical authority—nothing like a Vatican—but rather what its name implied: an organization whose meetings offered Buddhists the chance to become acquainted with one another and talk over common problems. (Its meetings, loosely referred to as "world Buddhist conferences," should not be confused with successive councils of the sangha that have been held in the 2,500 years since Buddha's death. The Sixth Council in 1955-56 coincided with the Fourth Conference of the WFB.)

At first the Chinese do not seem to have realized the opportunities offered by the WFB for people's diplomacy—for making many new friends quickly. After its inaugural conference *Modern Buddhism* printed a sharp attack saying that although not everyone who had attended was a running dog of the imperialists, the meeting had been manipulated by the imperialists. G. P. Malalasekera, who had convened it, did so after attending an East-West Philosophers' Conference in Hawaii, following which he visited the United States and Britain, where "he obviously asked for orders from the British and American imperialists and therefore, as soon as he returned to Ceylon, released the news of the convocation of the conference . . . His thinking is pro-British and pro-American." There was also reference to the "running dogs in charge of the conference."[76] This hostile tone was maintained by the Chinese at least until 1952.[77]

Early in 1954, however, when the Burmese were making plans to hold the Third WFB Conference in Rangoon, they asked the Chinese embassy if a delegation would not attend it from Peking. No answer was received, but when it opened on December 3, 1954, the CBA sent a congratulatory cable, expressing "hopes that the meeting will make great contributions towards spreading the dharma and safeguarding world peace, basing itself on the Buddha's doctrines of compassion, equality, relief for all the world, and salvation for all men."[78]

This was a turning point. Thereafter the Chinese attempted to win a leading role in the WFB. They sent a 15-member delegation to its Fourth Conference in Nepal in 1956, at which the CBA was recognized as a WFB regional center and Shirob Jaltso was elected a vice-president. There was a setback in 1958, when the Chinese were unable to attend the Fifth Conference, held in Bangkok,

38. Between sessions of the Sixth WFB Conference Chao P'u-ch'u chats diplomatically with an elderly devotee from Singapore who had visited many Mainland monasteries the year before. Pnom Penh 1961.

39. During a session of the conference Chü-tsan, Chao P'u-ch'u, and Li Jung-hsi listen to pleas that Taiwan be allowed to remain in the WFB. Soon afterwards they walked out of the conference. Pnom Penh 1961.

40. The author and a delegate from Hong Kong. Pnom Penh 1961.

because the Thai government would not give them visas; and at this conference Taiwan too became a regional center. However the Sixth Conference, scheduled for Pnom Penh at the end of 1961, promised favorable conditions for recovering lost ground. Treaties of friendship had recently been concluded with Burma, Cambodia, and Nepal. The tooth relic had made its tour of Ceylon. Within China Buddhism was enjoying the period of relaxation.

The Chinese delegation arrived in Pnom Penh with two assignments: to have Peking chosen as the site of the next conference and to have Taiwan expelled. The first might seem to have been the more important, since the host country controlled invitations and, by excluding unfriendly delegates, Peking could have gotten the WFB headquarters moved to Peking and won permanent control over the organization. Chao P'u-ch'u, however, gave priority to expelling Taiwan, presumably on instructions from the Foreign Ministry, and pushed for it so aggressively that he antagonized many of the delegates and was voted down. Then, in order to show China's indignation, he felt it necessary to lead his delegation dramatically out of the auditorium. Unfortunately, having walked out, he was not in the position to offer Peking as the site of the next conference. (A full account of this episode is given in Appendix E.)

Peking did not react for a month.[79] Then on December 19, 1961, the *People's Daily* denounced the conference in Pnom Penh for having been "obviously manipulated by US conspirators who had wormed their way into it."[80] Chinese Buddhist leaders tried to claim (perhaps for the benefit of their own Foreign Ministry) that U.S. schemes had been "firmly rebuffed,"[81] but failure became harder to conceal after the WFB headquarters were moved to anti-communist Bangkok in 1963. The Chinese protested the move and requested "all friends of different regional centers of the WFB to pay attention to this matter . . . lest the intriguing evil forces should utilize the world Buddhist organization to endanger Buddhism and to destroy the friendship among Buddhists of different countries."[82] When it became obvious that not only would the headquarters remain in Bangkok, but the Seventh Conference would be held in India, with which China was on equally poor terms, more protests were issued. Chao P'u-ch'u threatened to boycott the conference, and, when it was held as scheduled, protested again.[83] Because many of these protests called on other Asian Buddhists to take action and none did, the CBA was placed in an embarrassing position. If it was effective as a tool of people's diplomacy, then why did not foreign Buddhists rally to its side? This question was also raised by its indifferent success in holding two international Buddhist conferences in Peking, for which the occasion had been offered by the persecution of Buddhists in South Vietnam.

THE VIETNAM CAMPAIGN

On May 8, 1963, Buddhists in Hué, South Vietnam, attempted to celebrate the Buddha's birthday by holding a parade at which they displayed the international Buddhist flag. On the grounds that they had been denied a permit to do this, government troops fired on them and eleven persons were killed. The demonstrations that followed led to arrests and the closing of temples in many parts of the country.

The regime of Ngo Dinh Diem had been persecuting Buddhists for several years, but without attracting attention abroad. Chinese propaganda against Diem had made no mention of it.[84] Now, however, its possibilities become apparent. By encouraging Buddhist resistance to Diem, the Chinese could further divide his country and weaken his government. They could also portray the United States as a champion of Roman Catholicism against an indigenous Asian religion. They could turn the tables on all who had been decrying the persecution of Buddhism in China: every accusation made against the Chinese in Tibet could now be thrown back at the other side of South Vietnam. Finally there was the possibility that the WFB could be outmaneuvered by setting up an international body to help the Buddhists of Vietnam—a body that might eventually displace the WFB and bring the international Buddhist movement under Peking's influence or control.

Despite these interesting possibilities, the Chinese proceeded cautiously. Perhaps they feared that if they came out as the champion of freedom for the Buddhists of South Vietnam, it would provide leverage for Buddhists in China to demand more freedom.[85] At any rate their first reaction to the Hué massacre did not come for nearly a month. On June 3, 1963, the CBA sent a cable to the Vietnamese Unified Buddhist Association (in Hanoi) censuring "Diem's trampling upon the people's freedom of worship." It did not particularize beyond saying that troops had "suppressed a peaceful demonstration."[86] Then on June 21 the CBA issued a statement that widened the target to include the United States as a partner in Diem's crimes. The "U.S.-Ngo Dinh Diem gang," it said, had arrested eminent monks, besieged temples, and slaughtered Buddhists to the point where "the Reverend Thich Quang Duc had even burnt himself to death to protest against the persecution." (Eight years earlier, ironically enough, *Modern Bud-*

dhism had carried an article ridiculing self-immolation.[87]) Also on June 21, a religious service in memory of Diem's victims was held at the Yung-ho Kung.[88]

In August the Diem regime carried out a new wave of arrests. Peking responded on September 1 by issuing another statement and holding another service, this time at the Kuang-chi Ssu, where a shrine was set up for Vietnamese martyrs.[89] The September 1 statement contained no call for concrete action, only for moral support.[90] Yet plans may already have been underway to convoke a conference on Vietnam, the first international Buddhist conference to be held in Communist China. Curiously enough not a word was said about it in the press until the day it closed. The arrival of delegations one by one between September 29 and October 17 was announced without explanation; or it was explained that they had come "for a visit." Notably absent were any representatives of Burma, Ceylon, and India;[91] and notably present were the first Buddhist delegations ever to visit China from Pakistan, Indonesia, North Korea, Laos, Thailand, and North and South Vietnam. The more nations were represented at a conference, the more impressive it became, but in this case there was the additional advantage of getting delegations that could be counted on to vote as the Chinese wished.[92]

The delegation of whose vote the Chinese were most uncertain was the Japanese. It had arrived at the end of September supposedly in order to join in commemorating the T'ang dynasty monk, Chien-chen (see p. 155). Officially representing the Japan Buddhist Federation, it was led by a conservative priest, and, although the Chinese had managed to nominate four of its members, the remaining four were conservatives too. All were kept apart from the other Buddhist delegations that had arrived and none were told about the conference. It was probably for their benefit that any advance word of it was kept out of the press. In fact they did not learn of it until they were at the very door of the room where it was to be held. This tactic backfired, and when the time came to draft a manifesto, the Japanese dug in their heels. Their leader said that they had been invited to China for the sole purpose of commemorating Chien-chen—not to engage in politics.

Though it meant arguing the whole night, they refused to approve a text that condemned—or even mentioned—the United States. All that came out of the final session of the conference was a condemnation of Diem's atrocities and an appeal to the world's Buddhists for help—and, at that, the leader of the Japanese delegation would not sign it. He left this to an associate who felt friendlier towards the Chinese.[93] Naturally the New China News Agency did not report the difficulties behind the scenes. Instead it emphasized religious unity and solemnity—how the delegates had gathered at the Fa-yüan Ssu, where "clasping their hands, they chanted sutras for the salvation of the Buddhist victims in South Vietnam from the 'ocean of sufferings and for their early attainment of Nirvana' (eternal peace)."[94]

After the conference most of the delegations went on a tour of Nanking, Soochow, Shanghai, and Hangchow, where they took part in further religious services for South Vietnamese victims.

41. On October 17, 1963, after a solemn service at the Fa-yüan Ssu, Buddhist delegates from eleven nations attend a banquet given for them by the Chinese Buddhist Association. The places of honor on either side of Chao P'u-ch'u are occupied by Kongo Shuichi, leader of the Japanese Buddhist Delegation (left), and Ando Kosei, leader of the Japanese Cultural Delegation (right). Chao was trying hard to get Kongo in a good mood for the surprise conference to which he was about to escort him. At the extreme right is the head of the newly activated China-Japan Friendship Association. Peking 1963.

42. The final session of the Conference of Eleven Nations on Vietnam. Peking 1963.

43. During the same week there is an exhibit of photographs in Peking showing the sufferings of the Buddhists of South Vietnam at the hands of the authorities.

Since all expenses were borne by the CBA, this was the most elaborate and costly of its ventures in people's diplomacy, which must have increased the embarrassment of its leaders about the somewhat meager results. The following June they were given one more chance to show what they could do. This time there was no mystery about why Buddhist delegations were arriving in Peking. It was announced that they were coming to attend the opening ceremonies of the Tooth Relic Pagoda on June 25, 1964, and the commemoration of the 1,300th anniversary of the death of Hsüan-tsang on June 27. The pagoda had been completed in 1961, but there had been a long delay in finishing the interior and the relic itself had remained at the Kuang-chi Ssu.[95] Now its installation provided a reason to invite foreign Buddhists to Peking. Similarly, although a solemn memorial service had already been held for Hsüan-tsang on March 18 (the actual anniversary of his death), the only foreigners present had been Japanese.[96] Holding another memorial service provided a second reason to issue invitations. Of the ten delegations who accepted, six were led by the same persons who had come the previous October. Korea and Thailand were replaced by Ceylon and Mongolia; so that there were again eleven countries represented in all, including China.

This time there was no conference. Instead, the installation of the tooth and the commemoration of Hsüan-tsang provided a solemn backdrop for issuing political manifestoes.[97] On July 1, representatives from eight countries (excluding Mongolia, Pakistan, and Nepal) issued a statement that condemned the bombing of monasteries and Buddhists in Laos, South Vietnam, and Cambodia and specifically named the United States as the party responsible.[98] On July 6 there was another statement, this time by delegates from only five countries, which criticized the WFB for moving its headquarters to Bangkok and planning to hold its Seventh Conference in India.[99] These two statements seem to have been the only fruits of the second and last international gathering of Buddhists in Peking. During the ensuing half-year the CBA continued to issue occasional protests on behalf of Buddhists in South Vietnam, the final one on February 11, 1965.[100] By then the South Vietnamese Buddhists had split into factions and ceased

44. On June 25, 1964 a procession of Buddhists from eleven countries approaches the new Tooth Relic Pagoda outside Peking to install the Buddha Tooth Relic.

to threaten the stability of the government. Both factions had sent representatives to the Seventh WFB Conference in India. This eliminated their utility to the Chinese as a peg either for propaganda or for ecumenical activities. Public concern for Vietnamese Buddhist martyrs ceased in China as suddenly as it had begun.

OTHER FOREIGN POLICY FUNCTIONS

The functions of Buddhism in foreign policy can be divided into the general and the specific. One of its general functions was to provide the right atmosphere for entertaining Asian leaders and making them feel at home. For example, when U Nu went to Yünnan for a little vacation in 1961, he worshiped at Buddhist temples and took part in the local water festival with Chou En-lai. "Thousands of festival-makers danced and sang to greet them. Some people began to sprinkle water on Prime Minister U Nu and Premier Chou En-lai with cypress twigs from silver bowls, as an auspicious sign. The enthusiastic crowds soon tossed basin after basin of water on them. Prime Minister U Nu and Premier Chou En-lai mingled with the crowds, throwing water back at the joyous people, everyone got drenched. While splashing water, the people danced and cheered rhythmically, 'Long life Sino-Burmese friendship.' "[101]

During the visit of Madame Bandaranaike, the Prime Minister of Ceylon, in 1963, she worshiped at the Kuang-chi Ssu in Peking and in Shanghai she had a Buddhist memorial service performed for her late husband at the Jade Buddha Monastery. Some sixty-four Buddhist monks recited sutras for the salvation of his soul, while Chou En-lai, Mayor K'o Ch'ing-shih, and others "paid tribute . . . before his portrait." I can recall no other occasion when Communist Party members of this rank were present during a Buddhist rite, and Buddhist leaders must have felt that this was one of the high points in their prestige and usefulness to the regime.[102] They had helped to entertain Nehru, Sihanouk, Souvanna Phouma, and U Nu, but for no visiting chief of state had they been able to provide so personal a service.

The specific functions of Buddhism in foreign policy were

usually carried out by the Buddhist association. Besides acting as the official host to Buddhist groups, it played an ancillary role in the entertainment of all kinds of other visitors from Buddhist countries–not only chiefs of state, but trade, economic, cultural, and parliamentary delegations, and even a table tennis team. When receptions were given for them, CBA leaders were likely to be among those present, often in their role as officers of the friendship association that had been set up with the country involved.[103]

The CBA also provided the Foreign Ministry with statements of Buddhist support on specific issues–demanding, for example, the liberation of Taiwan, the withdrawal of the United States and Britain from Jordan, the suppression of the Tibetan rebellion, the rebuff of the "Indian reactionaries" and their border claims, and an end to the persecution of the U.S. Communist Party. It endorsed domestic acts of the regime that had been criticized abroad, like the imprisonment of Catholic Bishop Walsh. Sometimes it invoked Buddhist doctrine, as in 1958 when Chao P'u-ch'u told a Burmese peace delegation that withdrawal of U.S.-British forces from the Middle East "was in conformity with the teachings of the Buddha."[104]

The CBA not only issued statements but organized meetings and demonstrations to coincide with them. These were designed to mobilize public opinion at home as well as to provide evidence of it for use in propaganda beamed abroad. For three years–from 1950 through 1953–Buddhists throughout China held frequent meetings to protest the U.S. presence in Korea and promise continuing support for the People's Volunteers. In 1954 there was a massive campaign to collect Buddhist signatures for a worldwide declaration against the use of atomic weapons. On September 7, 1958, during the Taiwan Straits crisis, 130 Buddhist monks and nuns were among the three million persons who demonstrated against the United States in Peking, and the next day some of them attended a meeting at the Kuang-chi Ssu, where they expressed their indignation. One of them said: "If American imperialism does not withdraw at once, it will spell the end of its filthy life." The abbess of the principal Peking nunnery stated: "We nuns of the T'ung-chiao Ssu will do great things in our sewing work! Extraordinary things! Stake our lives on it! So as to give practical support to the liberation of Taiwan."[105]

Until the Sino-Soviet split opened up in 1960, Buddhists played their part in friendship with the Soviet elder brother. Not only did they join Sino-Soviet friendship associations, but they had chapters of their own. One such chapter during Sino-Soviet Friendship Month in 1952 carried on propaganda which "taught the masses [that is, the monks] that, in order to have a happy life, they must learn the advanced experience of the Soviet Union and understand the close connection between the success of China's revolution and altruistic help from the Soviet Union."[106] Anniversaries of the Great October Revolution were often celebrated in Buddhist circles, which also went into "deep mourning" at the death of Stalin. Chü-tsan wrote his obituary for *Modern Buddhism,* ending: "According to Buddhist scriptures, a real leader and guide of the people, whether the country he governs is large or small, is in every case the avatar of a bodhisattva. We Buddhists, heedful of this fact and reasoning, are in a deep mourning for the death of the great Marshal Stalin. With absolute sincerity we guarantee to increase our efforts to learn the spirit of the great Marshal Stalin and the Soviet people, in dedicating hearts and minds wholly to seeking happiness for all mankind, and, when necessary, to be on guard against the schemes of the American imperialists so as to contribute all our strength to building the nation and defending world peace." Buddhists in Peking wore mourning for Stalin, just as the Buddha's disciples did for him, "because Marshal Stalin's radiance shone on us Buddhists too."[107] Elsewhere Buddhist rites for the salvation of the marshal's soul were performed in some monasteries.[108]

The aspect of foreign policy in which it was most natural for Buddhists to become involved was the peace movement. After helping play host to Buddhist delegates at the Peace Conference of Asia and the Pacific Region held in Peking in 1952, Chinese Buddhists went to the Vienna Peace Conference in 1953 and the Stockholm Conference in 1958. Chao P'u-ch'u himself represented China at the 1961 meeting of the World Peace Council in New Delhi. He also attended three of the annual conferences held in

Japan to prohibit nuclear weapons—in 1955, 1960, and for the last time in 1961. Then the Chinese got nuclear weapons of their own.

The Chinese formula for peace was not pacifism. When Chao addressed the Second World Conference of Religious Believers for Peace, held in Tokyo in 1964, he said: "In the final analysis imperialism is the source of the present threat to peace. One's attitude towards imperialism is the touchstone of whether one is really for peace of not. We religious believers who bear the real responsibility for mankind should treat the wrecker of peace as the Buddha treated devils or as Jesus treated Satan. Therefore it is very important for the movement in defense of world peace to develop in a correct direction and for it to be unified."[109] The correct direction meant support for wars of national liberation, as in Vietnam. A declaration was issued by the conference, "the main content of which was opposition to U.S. imperialism and support for the liberation movements of oppressed peoples."[110]

Chinese Buddhists had already years before declared their support for these movements. One of the tasks they assumed on May Day 1951 was "to help Southeast Asia complete national liberation. The peoples of Southeast Asia, even to the southern archipelagos, have long received a Buddhist education. Some of the peoples in this region have already risen up and some are just now rising to carry on the struggle for national liberation. The Buddhists of China have been liberated relatively early. We ought all the more, on the basis of our advanced position, urge them on and support them, get them to cast off the fetters of the old society at an early date, create a renascence of the Buddhist religion, and take refuge in the Great Vehicle."[111] Sometimes the geographical scope of liberation was expanded, as during the protest in 1958 against the U.S. presence in the Straits of Taiwan, when a monk told his brethren: "We are going to liberate Taiwan, Asia, Africa, and Latin America."[112] It might seem far-fetched to suggest that Buddhists could help liberate Latin America, yet they did have a small contribution to offer: the old theory that the New World had been discovered by a fifth century Chinese monk, who made his way to Mexico by the Aleutian Islands and returned to China with an account of what he had seen. This meant that

China was linked to Latin America, just as it was to India and Southeast Asia, by the travels of ancient Buddhist pilgrims.[113]

The way in which Buddhists might seem to have been best able to contribute to the liberation of Southeast Asia was through the overseas Chinese. For many decades before the Communist victory Chinese monks had toured their communities, giving lectures, raising money, and building temples. Some of these temples were branches of large monasteries in China, which appointed their abbots and controlled their finances.[114] This might have offered a more concrete channel for political penetration than people's diplomacy. Unfortunately, however, after Liberation the lecture tours ceased.[115] Overseas branch temples, instead of accepting the authority of the CBA, severed relations with their parent institutions—as in Penang, where a monk sent out to take over a branch found himself isolated and ignored. No more success was enjoyed by another monk who came to Hong Kong with the assignment of building up a progressive faction in the local sangha.

The reason appears to have been the presence of refugee monks from China—about a thousand, according to one estimate. They took care of all the religious needs of the overseas Chinese: so lecturers from the mainland were no longer needed. Furthermore, whether they had fled with the PLA at their heels in 1949 or escaped in later years after land reform, struggle, and the restriction of religious practice, they were anti-Communist. Under their influence the religious and political conservatism of Chinese Buddhists in Southeast Asia grew stronger. This did not mean that overseas Chinese ceased to care about Buddhism in the motherland. Albeit in smaller numbers than before Liberation, they continued to come on pilgrimages, visiting sacred mountains and making donations to monasteries in their home towns. None of them came as guests of the CBA with all expenses paid, as foreign delegations did. Still, the cadres were very polite to them until 1958.[116] They were looked on as a source of foreign exchange rather than potential converts to the idea that Buddhism in China was flourishing as never before.[117] Tours of the mainland were even made by a few overseas Chinese monks. They were allowed to travel about in monastic dress and to go where they wished.[118]

In its early issues *Modern Buddhism* printed occasional news of Buddhist monks in overseas Chinese communities. After 1951 it ceased to do so, presumably because it decided that it was wiser to ignore them. For their part they ignored the CBA and avoided public attacks on the Communist regime until the Cultural Revolution.[119] Then, however, during the Hong Kong riots of 1967, the Hong Kong Buddhist Sangha Association was the second among six hundred social groups petitioning the governor to suppress the disorders that had been called for from across the border. This apparently angered the Communists, who began a serious effort to infiltrate and intimidate the sangha, not only in Hong Kong, but in Singapore and Malaya.[120]

The future of such efforts obviously depends on the overall policy towards Southeast Asia. Since 1951 Peking has treated overseas Chinese as more of a liability than a potential Fifth Column.[121] This could change, especially in Singapore and Malaya, when and if China grows stronger and begins to tidy things up in what it considers to be its sphere of influence.

THE USEFULNESS OF BUDDHISM

In 1950 one of the claims made by Buddhist leaders when they sought the patronage of the regime was that they could help it to develop relations with Asian Buddhist countries (Chapter I at note 17). As we have now seen, they made good this claim in two ways. First, they played one instrument in the orchestra of friendship that provided the background music for state visits and for the conclusion of trade, border, and other treaties with Burma, Cambodia, Ceylon, and Nepal. Second, they worked to persuade Buddhists in all Asian countries that the new form of Buddhism developed in China was superior, that it was only possible under a Communist government, and that wherever the Communist Party took power, Buddhists would be better off than they were now. Those who were persuaded of this joined forces with local leftists; or, if they were less activist or less than completely persuaded, they added their voices to those who were calling on their government to coöperate with China internationally.

How much real effect this had is hard to prove. Common sense tells us that Buddhist "background music" must have helped negotiations with certain countries, but cause and effect are very difficult to demonstrate here (U Nu's testimonial above at note 52 is the rare exception). It is equally difficult to show how much foreign policy was affected by public opinion; and how much public opinion–even in the most devoutly Buddhist countries–was affected by the Chinese use of Buddhism (as distinct from other Chinese efforts in propaganda). If the Chinese use of Buddhism was efficacious, the first place where it might be expected to show would be at international Buddhist meetings. Yet, as we have seen, the Chinese lost out in the WFB and succeeded in creating no rival to it.[122] At the international Buddhist meetings they themselves called in 1963-64 their efforts to have the United States publicly condemned were first turned down and then received only partial support. By the mid-1960's Buddhists from Southeast Asia were making trips to Taiwan.[123]

When Chinese Buddhist leaders sought for an explanation of the meager results achieved, they must have wondered whether the published statements of foreign praise for the People's Government's treatment of Buddhism were being outweighed by criticism circulated abroad by word of mouth. This would account for their sensitivity to foreign "slanders." The first manifestation of such a sensitivity came in 1954 when Chü-tsan referred indignantly to "slanders about how the Chinese Communist Party was 'destroying religion' . . . None of the Kuomintang tales about acts against our religion are true. No temple has been destroyed. No monks have been driven out. Neither have any of the monks and nuns been forced to marry, as has been asserted by ill-disposed rumor mongers."[124] (Unfortunately for Chü-tsan, his denials were belied in part by reports that had appeared in his own journal.[125])

After the Tibetan rebellion in 1959, Chinese sensitivity increased. They tried to convince people at home and abroad that Buddhism had not been persecuted in Tibet–it had not even been an issue.[126] Ceylon's Dr. Malalasekera was invited to Peking, where Chou En-lai spent two hours explaining that the issue had been social reform.[127] Amritananda was invited from Nepal to observe and testify to freedom of religious belief in China, contrary to the "rumors" he had heard.[128] Yet the Chinese continued to feel harrassed and frustrated by foreign criticism. In a single issue of *Modern Buddhism*—for October 1959—there were three articles complaining about the "slanders from our enemies abroad to the effect that our Party and government are persecuting Buddhism."[129] The effort to refute criticism—or forestall it—remained high through 1961.[130]

In 1963-64 the effort became more positive. In those two years the English language releases of the New China News Agency included far more items than ever before of three kinds: mentioning the performance of Buddhist religious services; describing the government conservation of Buddhist culture; and recalling how the imperialists had pillaged Buddhist art and how the Kuomintang had neglected Buddhist temples.[131] In the same two years the traffic in Buddhist delegations reached its all-time peak, as can be seen from Table 2.

In the second half of 1964 the New China News Agency stopped printing such articles;[132] the traffic in delegations sharply declined; and attacks on religion began to appear in the Mainland press. Thus Peking abandoned its drive, begun after the Tibetan rebellion, to convince Buddhists abroad that, contrary to what they might have heard, Buddhist practice was flourishing in China. Instead of reading how Chinese and foreign Buddhists joined in offering incense to the Buddha, one began to find articles describing how incense production was being stopped and prostration to the Buddha discouraged.[133] The main reason for this sudden change was the approach of the Cultural Revolution. Yet its approach coincided, I believe, with a feeling by Mao and others that the use of Buddhism in foreign policy had been more trouble than it was worth. In the long run Buddhists abroad could not be won over by Potemkin villages. The continuing "slanders" and the poor support received by the CBA showed that to win them over effectively, the government would have had to do more than repair monasteries and entertain delegations; it would have had to allow Buddhist monks actually to keep up more of their religious practice—but this would mean giving them special privileges, which, in the case of the returned overseas Chinese, had already proved troublesome. Furthermore, if the government continued its policy of systematic deception of foreigners about the state of Buddhism, it ran the risk of undermining its own credibility and it was a government more concerned than most about the claim to being truthful.[134] This was one reason, I think, why it decided to abandon (or at least suspend) the whole messy effort. It was easier to convince visitors that bridges had been built and tractor production had risen—since, in fact, they had—and it was simply too much bother to have a basic conflict between the internal policy on Buddhism (suppression) and the external policy (utilization).

Another reason for abandoning the effort may have been the realization that most Buddhists abroad fell into two categories. First, there were those who were—or might become—friendly to China. Their friendship, however, sprang not so much from admiration for the Chinese treatment of Buddhism as from their admiration of Mao and from their own resentments—resentment of colonialism, disaffection from their own government, and the frustrations of being a monk in an increasingly urban society. The second and much larger category were those Buddhists who were and probably always would be simply indifferent to Buddhism in China.[135] If they had heard of China and knew that Buddhism existed there, they probably also knew that it was Mahayana Buddhism, the fate of whose adherents was about as much concern to them as the fate of Russian Baptists to the Catholics of Spain. Even if they were tolerant of Mahayana, China was too far away; and there were too many questions about the future of Buddhism at home.

Mao was entitled to ask, therefore, how much harm would really be done if Chinese Buddhism was liquidated? In what foreign country would there be a serious reaction? At one extreme there was Burma, sunk in autistic isolationism, and at the other extreme there was Japan, where concern for Chinese Buddhism was the liveliest, but where the majority of those concerned were professors who did not want to antagonize their leftist students. Only in Thailand was there an environment that favored the public expression of concern for the fate of Chinese Buddhism; and yet such was the Thais' aversion to mixing Buddhism and politics that it was hardly expressed. The chances of a serious reaction abroad thus seemed minimal. This calculation proved to be correct. When Buddhism was suppressed during the Cultural Revolution, not a single voice was raised in protest abroad.

Chapter VII

Suppressing Buddhist Opposition to the Regime

During the great persecution of Buddhism in 445-446 C.E., monks were put to death simply because they were monks; and in the persecutions of 574 and 845 monastic property was confiscated simply because it belonged to monasteries. Nothing like this happened after Liberation. The policy of the regime was not to attack Buddhism as such. Monasteries lost their property in a program of land reform that was not directed against them in particular, but against all landlords. Monks were punished not for being monks, but for becoming implicated in one of the many forms of opposition to the regime. There was no repetition of the atrocities reported during the Republican period—as, for example, in 1928, when Communist troops were said to have locked up three hundred monks in a temple in Changsha, set it afire, and burned them alive.[1]

The regime suppressed its opponents in a series of campaigns, some brief, some continuing intermittently over many years. In certain cases Buddhists lay outside the target. None of them, for example, fell into the categories of cadres and businessmen, against whom the Three-Anti and Five-Anti campaigns were directed in 1951-52. In other cases the targets were broader and monks fell within them. This was true, for example, of the suppression of evil landlords (1950-53); the suppression of spies and counterrevolutionaries (1950-51 and intermittently thereafter); the suppression of heterodox Taoist sects (1951-55 and intermittently thereafter); the elimination of hidden counterrevolutionaries (in 1955); and the anti-rightist movement (1957-59). First I shall try to show how these campaigns affected Buddhists in general, and then give three case histories to make their concrete effects clearer.

CAMPAIGNS

Much has been written about the violence of land reform in China. Some have argued that it could have been carried out gradually and peacefully, as in other countries, without struggle meetings, arrests, and mass executions. Mao Tse-tung, however, believed that only violence could permanently break the power of the landlords. In the case of monasteries this was best exemplified in the armed attack on the T'an-che Ssu near Peking, which used to own 360 villages and was assaulted by 4,000 militiamen in July 1947. Its "evil monks" were denounced at mass meetings and then "taken care of" by the government.[2]

In most places the monks were powerless to resist. Some were arrested; some were executed. One informant, for example, gave the following account of the execution of his master, who was the head of a small but very rich temple that lay in the "Liberated area" of northern Kiangsu. Early in 1948 a struggle meeting was held to deal with him. The cadres accused him of being a reactionary who had exploited the people and then asked: "Shall he be killed or not? All in favor of killing raise your hands." A few hands were raised, mostly by cadres in the audience. The ordinary people, said my informant, did not raise theirs. The old monk was then publicly strangled by having a noose wound around his neck and pulled by two men, one standing on each side. The heads of many temples in northern Kiangsu were killed during this period, often in savage ways. He himself had seen a monk being stoned to death and he had heard of others who were forced to eat ground-up pottery so that their stomachs could be seen to churn and blood came from their ears and noses before they died.

Such things may have happened, but one cannot read about them in the Mainland press. During the campaign against counter-revolutionaries that began in 1950, the arrest of monks and nuns was occasionally mentioned but no details were given.[3] One counterrevolutionary monk was "executed"—the only execution of a monk that I have ever seen referred to in the Mainland press.[4] The press does describe the efforts to expose bad elements in the sangha. In 1953, for example, Shanghai monks were suddenly ordered to answer questionnaires about their past political affiliations. "To those who had belonged to a reactionary party and who did not have a clear political face, this provided an opportunity for giving a frank account of themselves"—and, of course, it provided the cadres with the leverage to force them to denounce those who had not been so frank.[5] Yet neither in Shanghai nor elsewhere were totals ever published for the number of people exposed.

Shortly afterwards began the campaign to suppress the "heterodox Taoist sects." These were syncretistic religions that were organized somewhat like secret societies and claimed to encompass Confucianism, Buddhism, and Taoism, and in some cases, Christianity and Islam.[6] Although orthodox Buddhists rejected them as heterodox, they for their part did not reject orthodox Buddhism. Their doctrines and terminology were partly or largely Buddhist and in some areas they had taken over Buddhist temples[7]—just as Buddhist monks had taken over Taoist temples. Especially after the campaign against them began, the sectarians openly called themselves Buddhist and adopted Buddhist-sounding names for their groups—like the Way of the Great Vehicle.[8] When the danger became too great, they would disband and, as individuals, enter Buddhist monasteries or clubs, seeking congenial shelter. This made it more difficult to identify and expose them, which the government was determined to do. It regarded their secrecy and millennial fanaticism as a potential threat and remembered that comparable religious groups had started many of the great rebellions in Chinese history.[9] When the campaign against them got under way,[10] the government put on exhibits of their alleged crimes. It showed films in which their rituals were acted out by former members, so as to reduce the glamor and mystery. All members, former as well as present, were ordered to register with the local authorities; and various measures were taken to prevent them from evading registration. Buddhist groups, for example, were prohibited from admitting them as members within a certain period of time, and Buddhist monks were prohibited from taking them as disciples—lest they acquire membership cards or certificates of initiation that might enable them to pass themselves off as Buddhists.[11]

The government's policy was thus to make a clear distinction in its treatment of orthodox Buddhists and members of the syncretistic sects. Yet because the latter occasionally did succeed in passing themselves off as Buddhists and because all religions looked alike to many local cadres, the distinction was not always honored. In some areas where the sects were being suppressed, monks and nuns were "affected" and "hardships occurred in individual cases."[12] When they complained, they were told that it was up to them to help the cadres avoid mistakes. They should inform on the sectarians, especially on those who had sought shelter in Buddhist groups.[13] A few Buddhists were so frightened that they did so. In Amoy there were even two devotees who, after attending the trial of some sectarians, protested the leniency of the verdict and called for a retrial and heavier sentences.[14] Most Buddhists, perhaps out of a reluctance to harm people, did no more than to issue noisy statements expressing their approval of the fact that the sects were being suppressed;[15] or, when the campaign against them was renewed in 1957-59, protested the attempt to use Buddhism as a cover and made public pledges that they would exclude sectarians, denounce them to the authorities, and "leave them no place to hide."[16] Next year, the abbots of two Buddhist monasteries were arrested as hidden sectarians.[17] Yet one cannot be sure whether these and other victims of the campaign were in fact sectarians who had been exposed by anxious Buddhists; or were conservative Buddhists whom the cadres chose to get rid of as sectarians; or were simply monks who had been denounced by their brethren to settle old scores.

The next campaign was against "hidden counterrevolutionaries," that is, against opponents of the regime who had heretofore been regarded as its supporters—cadres, intellectuals, and above all the writer Hu Feng, whose call for greater literary freedom had provided the spark that set the campaign going in the spring of

1955.[18] The target quickly widened, and Buddhists too were expected to show their activism by finding counterrevolutionaries concealed in their midst. Just as the campaign reached full swing, the Chinese Buddhist Association held its second enlarged council meeting (August 16-31, 1955). Delegates reported that counterrevolutionaries who had wormed their way into Buddhist circles in Kweichow, Szechwan, Ninghsia, and other provinces had now been arrested. "The government," they said, "deserves our thanks for this." No details, however, were given about the counterrevolutionary activities involved, except in the case of some Inner Mongolian lamas who had been stamping the New China's national emblem on the soles of their feet, so that they would stand on it when reciting sutras; and had been saying prayers for the early downfall of the Communists and for a Nationalist restoration.[19] The only other case on which the details were given involved the Shanghai Buddhist Youth Society, whose crimes will be described below.

The anti-rightist campaign of 1957-58 began as an effort to suppress the opposition that had come into the open when the Party invited the "hundred flowers to bloom and the hundred schools of thought to contend." Buddhists had been circumspect in accepting the invitation. At the CBA's second national conference, held in March 1957, not one delegate is reported to have lodged a serious complaint–although many Chinese intellectual and political leaders were then accusing the Party of monopolizing power for itself and denying freedom to others. Perhaps the Buddhists felt that their position was too weak; and their caution was rewarded, for when the anti-rightist campaign began in June, no monks and nuns came under attack. Although three lay leaders of the CBA found themselves in trouble for demanding a liberalization of the regime, they had not made the demand as Buddhists, but as members of democratic parties.[20]

In 1958 the anti-rightist movement grew in intensity and broadened to include all opposition to the Party, open or covert, past or present. The monks too began to have difficulties. In Fukien, for example, two of them had to "bow their heads" when they were exposed as "anti-Party, anti-people, anti-socialist, and pro-capitalist." What this meant was that one of them had frowned on the execution of landlords during land reform and recited sutras for the salvation of their souls; and the other had tried to start a welfare project for the elderly and harbored a grudge against the Party when it was suppressed.[21] Four monks in Kirin were struggled against for having criticized agricultural coöperatives, grain distribution, and the suppression of counterrevolutionaries. They had also, it was alleged, collaborated with the Japanese during the war and more recently attempted to "overthrow the leadership of the People's Government and the Chinese Buddhist Association."

Descriptions of struggle meetings make it sound as if they were used to settle old scores, as can be seen in a passage from the report on the Kirin case that has just been cited. "Ever since Liberation Jui-t'ao, who consistently harbored hatred against the Communist Party and the People's Government, tried every means to sabotage the various political movements launched in the country, and also nursed strong resentment against government cadres. He repeatedly said of them: 'When the Kuomintang comes in the future, they will be the first to be executed.' He looked upon activists leaning to the side of the Party and the government as a thorn in his side. A rascal by nature, he often strutted down the street before Liberation carrying an axe at his waist and wearing dark glasses. After Liberation he did not change a bit, but proclaimed himself the 'living buddha' of the Po-jo Ssu. Three of the monks there were given a sound beating by him. One, Pao-hsiu, held up a blood-stained bedspread to denounce him. Cheng-kung had also been assaulted by Jui-t'ao, but had been intimidated into keeping quiet. Furthermore Jui-t'ao had tied up Hsi-fan, forced him to drink pepper water, and pierced his nose with a long needle."[22] In the cases discussed so far there was no mention of arrests.

Indeed only one case involving the arrest of monks seemed to have been reported in the press in 1958: it was a very important case (Pen-huan's) and will be described below in detail. However oral informants tell not only of arrests, but of suicides and executions.[23] Some of those arrested have not been heard from since. Others were sent to labor reform, came through it well, and returned to their old monasteries.[24]

It seems characteristic of the campaigns from 1949 to 1958 that the official target was only a point of departure. Once struggle had begun and a "tense atmosphere" had been created, the cadres could attack any monk who had caused them trouble and the monks themselves could denounce any of their brethren against whom they bore a grudge.[25] Struggle, arrests, and executions also served to intimidate the rank and file of Buddhists and to increase their enthusiasm for carrying out government policies that might otherwise been distasteful to them—on the principle of "killing the cock to warn the monkey."

The best way to see how Buddhists were affected by successive campaigns is to examine the "big cases," about which many details are available. Each had its distinctive features, but all of them point, I think, to the inevitability of conflict between progressive cadres and those Buddhists who were determined to go on doing things in their old way.

THE SHANGHAI BUDDHIST YOUTH SOCIETY

The Shanghai Buddhist Youth Society was one of the most active Buddhist groups in the country's largest city.[26] For sangha and laity alike it served as a center of study and practice: its monthly, *Chüeh-hsün,* enjoyed a good circulation. Although eleven of its members—or at any rate eleven persons it was "sheltering"—were arrested in 1954 as counterrevolutionaries,[27] this was not publicized at the time, and the society seems to have continued operating as before.

Then in May 1955 came the campaign against the writer Hu Feng, which turned into a movement for exposing counterrevolutionaries hidden in the Party, government, and people's organizations, including the CBA. When the latter held its second enlarged council meeting in August, the main target was the Youth Society. We know that the attack on it was part of the Hu Feng campaign because it was said to be "exactly like the Hu Feng clique,"[28] and one delegate attributed its unmasking to the "important lessons we learned from the affair of Hu Feng."[29]

The charges against the Youth Society were first presented to the CBA's East China Subcommittee.[30] Most of them sound vague and melodramatic. It was castigated as "an opium den that has poisoned the youth and a rendezvous for counterrevolutionaries in religious dress who have carried on activities against the Party and the people." Its publications, particularly *Chüeh-hsün,* had been "hostile to the new society, opposed the government, slandered the Party, attacked progressive persons, distorted facts, spread rumors, and sowed hatred and dissension."[31] No particulars were given. There were, however, more concrete charges. The society had "put up notices appealing for donations to support the sangha at important monasteries in order to hoodwink monks and nuns whose political awareness was low."[32] (It was quite true that in 1951 the monks at some monasteries had appealed for donations to be sent to them through the Shanghai Buddhist Youth Society. Presumably their claim to be suffering from "virtual starvation" made this appeal an attempt to hoodwink people.[33]) Also, according to the accusation, the society had obstructed land reform; sheltered counterrevolutionary elements (like the eleven arrested in 1954); instigated students to neglect their studies and resist the job assignments given them by the government; and "conducted sabotage under the cloak of spreading and defending Buddhism."[34] This last charge was illuminated by Lü Ch'eng, the elderly scholar and devotee who was then supervising the Buddhist Encyclopedia in Nanking. He said that the society "had fooled people into taking the road of negativity, pessimism, and escape from reality—thinking that these were Buddhism." Its publications, he went on, had harped on "suffering, emptiness, impermanence, illusion, everything being like a play, the real world being ephemeral, without value—as if worldly things and Buddhism were separated by an unbridgeable gap. This," he concluded, "is all nonsense. When have the doctrines of Buddhism been like this?"[35] (The answer, as he well knew, was that Buddhist doctrines had always been like this.[36]) In the same vein a young monk, not yet twenty, testified how the publications of the society had undermined his morale by painting the new China as a place full of sorrow, its glorious programs a pack of illusions; and by spreading hopes for the return of Chiang Kai-shek. This had caused him a mental struggle that kept him awake at night—until he read some issues of *Modern*

Buddhism, which had enabled him to "conquer the demons of negativity and pessimism."[37]

Such were "the sinister and vicious activities of the Shanghai Buddhist Youth Society's counterrevolutionary clique." One of the council members remarked at the meeting, perhaps with irony: "We residents of Shanghai often met them [the society's leaders], shook hands and chatted with them, and yet we were unable to discern their true political identity."[38] To make up for their lack of discernment, he and everyone else present "angrily called for a resolute and thorough purge of the hidden counter-revolutionary elements."[39] The government obliged by arresting Cheng Sung-ying, the editor of *Chüeh-hsün;* Ch'en Hai-liang, the manager of the Ta-hsiung Buddhist Bookshop; Li Hsing-hsiao (unidentified); and Ch'ing-ting of the Vajra Shrine.[40] Chao P'u-ch'u, when summing up the case in his work report for 1955, said that it had given Buddhists "a profound education" and clarified for them "the dividing line between the enemy and ourselves."[41] *Chüeh-hsün* appears to have been closed down for good. Nothing more is known of the fate of its editor or any of the others arrested. The society itself, however, seems to have changed its name to the Religious Believers Society (Hsin-tsung Hui) and slowly recovered. At any rate, a group by this name was visited by an overseas Chinese monk in 1962, who was told that it had once been known as the Buddhist Youth Society. It had over two thousand members, all lay devotees, who pursued religious study and practice in its premises "under the guidance of the Chinese Buddhist Association."[42]

THE PEN-HUAN CASE

The most famous monastery in Kwangtung province was the Nan-hua Ssu, where the Sixth Patriarch had lived in the T'ang dynasty and where his mummified body was still preserved. In the 1930's Hsü-yün had restored it and, when he retired, left it in the hands of a series of able abbots.[43] In 1948 he decided that the succession should go to Pen-huan, a monk from Hupeh who was both well trained in meditation practice and experienced in monastic administration.[44] Pen-huan remained abbot for the next ten years. He appeared to be able to adjust well to the many changes after Liberation. Early in 1955 he was named to the Kwangtung CPPCC as one of the three representatives of religious circles in the province.[45] Later in the year he became a CBA council member.[46] During the period of the Hundred Flowers he does not seem to have been especially outspoken—not, at least, in statements published at the time. At the CBA's second national conference in March 1957 he expressed warm gratitude for the help given by the government during the recent ordination at the Nan-hua Ssu.[47] He reiterated this sentiment at a meeting of the Kwangtung CPPCC held a month later; and in addition he praised the government for its aid in repairing his monastery and for its overall policy of respect for freedom of religious belief. It is true that in the same speech he deplored the "technical errors" made in certain localities, such as the failure to preserve buddha images and to provide well enough for the livelihood of monks and nuns, on whom excessive pressure was exerted to engage in political study—and yet when they did so, he said, they were not given adequate guidance. All these errors, however, were simply shortcomings in the *implementation* of policy: the policy itself was correct.[48] After the CPPCC meeting he was appointed to an inspection team of the provincial people's congress and communicated its findings to the religious affairs section in Shao-kuan. Interviewed by a reporter, he expressed satisfaction over the way the government was encouraging free criticism. "The Communist Party is truly determined to accept the advice of the masses of the people in overcoming shortcomings and blunders."[49]

Almost exactly a year later Pen-huan was arrested and charged with so many crimes going back so many years that, if the charges were true, the public security cadres had been shockingly negligent. The dispatch reporting his arrest deserves to be read in full.

> Acting on information from the masses and after verification of charges, the public security organ of the Shaokuan Special Administrative District has recently arrested abbot Pen-huan of the Nan-hua Ssu, who was found to have been a counter-revolutionary hiding under the cloak of religion.

The facts uncovered prove that Pen-huan was originally a traitor and rascal who sneaked into Buddhist circles. During the Japanese occupation he did counterrevolutionary work for a Japanese puppet organization. He collected information on Chinese guerrilla forces for the enemy and made a lot of treasonable propaganda. He did not change his reactionary stand after he came to the Nan-hua Ssu, but persistently spread rumors, engaged in sabotage, and acted as an enemy of the people. Taking advantage of his religious position, he even engaged in smuggling, grain profiteering, and the illegal sale of gold.

According to charges brought against him by Buddhists* and confirmed by the public security department, Pen-huan was a habitual rumor monger at the Nan-hua Ssu, who attacked the policies of the Party, particularly the religious policy, and tried to drive a wedge between the Buddhists on the one hand and the Party and people's government on the other. For years now the government has implemented the policy of freedom of religious belief and the Nan-hua Ssu has freely carried on many kinds of religious activities. Yet Pen-huan covertly slandered the motherland in front of his own monks and devotees from overseas,** saying that there was no religious freedom. To preserve the religious monuments of the Nan-hua Ssu, the government has spent several thousand yuan each year on repairs. Yet Pen-huan started the story that the government was making no repairs. In the past few years the monastery has repeatedly conducted "ordinations" and Pen-huan himself has accepted forty to fifty disciples. Yet he slandered the government by saying that it would not allow him to conduct "ordinations" or to accept disciples.*** He also tried to incite Buddhist dissatisfaction with the government by conducting "secret ordinations" and by refusing to issue "ordination certificates" to ordinees. There were thousands of "ordination certi-

*It is significant that throughout this report, the Buddhists themselves are represented as outraged by Pen-huan and as taking the initiative in his prosecution.

**Complaining to people from abroad was regarded as particularly treacherous because it undercut the government effort to make them believe that Buddhism was more flourishing than ever.

***In fact, of course, the government did restrict ordinations and taking disciples (see Chapter IV).

ficates" in his room, but in order to attack the policy of freedom of religious belief, he declared that they had to be issued by the government.*

To help the monks of the Nan-hua Ssu with their livelihood difficulties, the government distributed farmland to them, provided medical care at state expense, and gave Pen-huan himself a monthly living allowance.** However, in order to incite the monks to dissatisfaction with the People's Government, Pen-hua put out the lie that they had a hard life—while squandering the monastery's property as if it were his own.

For the birthday of the Sixth Patriarch in June, 1954, many people came to the Nan-hua Ssu to worship. The public security organ, concerned about maintaining public order, had a talk with Pen-huan and the others, asking them to help make a good job of public security work and to register all persons in accordance with the law. On his return to the monastery, he venomously declared to the monks that this was a trap set by the People's Government and that its religious freedom was a fraud.

Pen-huan also constantly spread rumors and nonsense in order to attack political movements. He harbored the deepest resentment of land reform, often saying that "it left a resentment that would be with him as long as he lived." He visited Nan-hsiung to investigate the "hardships" of a woman landowner (who later became a nun), and afterwards went about vociferously championing her cause. During the high tide of agricultural coöperativization, he again spread a lie—that there would be no future to joining the higher-level coöperatives—and he used his religious position to prevent Buddhist

*These accusations of Pen-huan's "covert slander" contrast sharply with his public praise for the policy of freedom of religious belief, the government's aid in repairing Nan-hua, and for its help during ordinations (see this chapter at note 47). The use of quotation marks around the word "ordinations" suggests that the government regarded them as in some way a bogus practice.

**On the totally inadequate allocation of farmland to the Nan-hua Ssu, see Chapter II at note 14. Allowances like that received by Pen-huan were given to monks who were making themselves useful to the government. "Rumor mongering" was the last thing expected of them. See Chapter X at note 25.

monks from joining. As monks and nuns began to realize the necessity to support themselves and actively joined in productive labor, he criticized them, in his capacity as abbot, for caring only about production and not about religious practice. He made reactionary statements such as the following: "During the Kuomintang times there was no need for manual labor";* and "It is not as good now as it used to be." Last year, at the time when the bourgeois rightists were frantically attacking the Party and the People's Government, Pen-huan blatantly made frenzied efforts to inflame Buddhists by saying: "The Communists have been too dictatorial." He also indicated that he would concentrate his attack on the weak spots of the Communist Party.

According to what Buddhists reported and to what has been uncovered, Pen-huan used his position in the monastery to take in a large number of reactionaries and other bad elements. Among the disciples he accepted, there were three counterrevolutionaries and nearly ten reactionary bureaucrats, despotic landlords, and thieves. He used these men as his trusted lieutenants in preventing Buddhists from getting close to the People's Government, in keeping watch on and attacking the activities of progressive Buddhists, and in building up his own power in order to resist the government. Moreover he gave them a free rein and protected them when they violated nuns, stole valuables, and committed murder.

Pen-huan once took in a man just released from labor reform whose name was Li Tsung-wen and who had a counterrevolutionary background. Although the monks were all opposed to his even being accepted as a disciple, Pen-huan deliberately promoted him to be one of his personal attendants [acolytes], allowing him to put on airs and bully the monks. Another of his close disciples was Yeh Chung-t'ing, who was a counterrevolutionary with four "blood debts" against him. Yet Pen-huan administered the Refuges to him and made him his disciple. When he spread rumors and carried

*This statement may have been reactionary, but it was perfectly true.

on sabotage at the monastery, showing his hostility to the people's regime, many monks demanded that he be expelled, but Pen-huan openly and boldly shielded him. When the government helpfully advised him not to make his monastery into an asylum for bad people, Pen-huan took a completely hostile attitude.

In addition, Pen-huan imposed on the monastery a feudalistic and barbarous rule and resorted to many illegal practices. He forbade the monks to read new books or newspapers and threatened them by saying that anyone who read the *Selected Works of Mao Tse-tung* was unworthy of being considered a monk. He regularly beat and railed at monks and nuns, infringed on their human rights, and even made vulgar advances to nuns.* All the monks and nuns therefore felt gagged and suffocated, unable to speak or breathe. After Pen-huan was arrested, they shouted with joy: "Today at last Liberation has come to us!"

Recent investigation has revealed that during the Japanese occupation of China, Pen-huan was a shameless traitor in the service of the enemy. As early as 1942 he was in charge of reception and arrangements for the "Sixth Month Festival of Wu-t'ai Shan," run by Japanese intelligence agents.** His special assignments were to find out if there were any Communists or members of the Eighth Route Army among the worshipers who came on pilgrimage to Wu-t'ai Shan; and to report to Japanese agents the condition of our guerrilla forces. Later, he acted as head of the construction department of the traitor organization called the "Wu-t'ai Shan Restoration Committee," in which capacity he circulated among Buddhists a series of treasonable and reactionary propaganda themes, such

*Beating, as has been mentioned earlier, was a normal punishment in Chinese monasteries. Sexual advances to nuns was an accusation often made against Chinese monks by those who did not like them (which does not prove, of course, that it was unjustified in this case).

**It may have been run by Japanese agents this year, but it was a traditional festival for which pilgrims used to come from many parts of China and even from overseas. See, for example, John Blofeld, The *Wheel of Life* (London, Rider and Company, 1959), pp. 122-155. Pen-huan may well have collaborated with the Japanese: many Chinese holding responsible posts in occupied areas had no choice but to do so.

> as: "Let us celebrate victory in the greater East Asian War," "Unprecedented triumph of the Japanese army on the anniversary of the sacred war in greater East Asia," "The sacred war in greater East Asia is a blessing for the whole people of East Asia," "Strive to exterminate the Communist bandits," "Purge Communist thinking," and so on. Pen-huan and Company also ruled that every monastery had to write out material on these themes and post it up; and that speeches had to be made along the same line. Failure to do so would incur penalties up to expulsion from the mountain. In October 1942, after a traitor monk named Ching-hsi had been executed by our guerrillas for passing information to the Japanese, Pen-huan held a big funeral service for him.* After the Japanese surrender Pen-huan used his priestly robe to shelter another notorious traitor [by taking him as a disciple]. When Wu-t'ai Shan was liberated, Pen-huan fled south, fearing retribution for his crimes. He intended to sneak into Hong Kong, but his plan did not work out and he became the abbot of the Nan-hua Ssu.** Since then, under the cloak of religion, he has carried on the criminal activities recounted above, always concealing his counterrevolutionary past. Even now he has not confessed to the government.[50]

What seems to have been at the root of the charges against Pen-huan was his refusal to coöperate with the public security organ. It wanted to know who the pilgrims were that came to the Nan-hua Ssu. Pen-huan, realizing that this might some day cause them difficulties, refused to turn in their names. He regarded the monastery as a place of asylum, outside the secular world, as it had traditionally been in China, where not only pilgrims could safely come, but also where people who had lost out in politics, business, and love—and even criminals—could put the past behind

*Performing funeral services for a fellow monks was a duty from which the prior of a monastery was not relieved by the fact that the deceased was considered a traitor by the Communist Party.

**In fact, of course, he could easily have gone to Hong Kong like so many other monks at this time, but he appears to have deliberately chosen to assume the heavy and risky responsibility of the Nan-hua abbotship.

them and seek solace in the dharma. The public security cadres could tolerate no place of asylum, nc right to cut oneself off from the secular world, and they were particularly suspicious of monasteries, since Communist leaders themselves had been given shelter there under the Kuomintang.

The government realized that the arrest of Pen-huan could lend substance to the very rumors that he had been spreading, since it could be interpreted as an infringement of freedom of religious belief. He was an influential monk in a prominent post, appointed by Hsü-yün. Therefore he had to be completely discredited. That is why the charges against him were so comprehensive and why Buddhists met to endorse them. The meetings not only provided a chance to show that the government had acted justly, but also a chance to smoke out other hidden opposition. Realizing this, monks showed lively enthusiasm in denigrating their former master and colleague.[51] "All the monks at Nan-hua Ssu supported the government's arrest of Pen-huan, a counterrevolutionary element dressed up in Buddhist robes . . . and unanimously asked the government to punish him according to the law." This was echoed in wall posters and in statements by individuals, only one of whom sounded a little wistful: "I used to think Pen-huan was a good man and became his disciple. All along he was a counterrevolutionary element, a traitor! I must take a firm stand and draw a clear line of demarcation between myself and him."[52]

In Canton, Buddhists were joined by Taoists in condemning the culprit and declaring that "there is no contradiction between freedom of religious belief and the lawful arrest of a counterrevolutionary element in religious circles. Only by arresting such counterrevolutionaries . . . can freedom of religious belief be safeguarded."[53] Almost the same thought was voiced at a meeting held thousands of miles away in Sinkiang, showing how well Buddhism had been unified under Communist rule.[54]

The outcome of the case was that Pen-huan was sent to a labor camp and that many monks left the Nan-hua Ssu. They may have "shouted for joy" at the news of his arrest, but their number dropped from ninety to sixty in the next four months.[55] According to word that reached Hong Kong in 1962, Pen-huan's thinking had by then been successfully reformed and he had been allowed to resume his activities as the abbot of Nan-hua Ssu.[56] I have seen and heard nothing of the fate of those who were arrested with him.

THE HSÜ-YÜN CASE

Hsü-yün was the most revered monk in China. No other had so many lay disciples. No other had such renown for the practice and teaching of meditation. No other had rebuilt so many ancient monasteries.[57] No other was believed to be so old. This last was particularly important not only because age has always been powerful evidence of sanctity in China[58] but also because, if Hsü-yün was born in 1840, his life had spanned the entire period of China's painful entry into the modern world. He was the living embodiment of the pre-modern Buddhist tradition. As one looks at photographs of his gaunt, ascetic face and reads the story of his career, full of suffering, miracles, and transcendental experiences, one feels that he *lived* hagiography. To some extent, of course, his biographers have added highlights and embroidery in order to express their admiration and to make his career conform to the *Lives of Eminent Monks,* but far more, I think, he himself made his life conform. He did so with a stubborn vigor that stayed with him when he was a hundred years old. It was his stubbornness that got him into trouble with the cadres of northern Kwangtung.

At the time of Liberation he was living at the Yün-men Ssu, a monastery in the north of Kwangtung. He had recently returned from Hong Kong against the wishes of his disciples, who had warned him that the monastic life would be much disrupted by Communist rule. That was precisely why he decided to return: in order to do what he could to protect the sangha. The next year passed uneventfully. As yet little affected by the change of regime, he held an ordination at the Nan-hua Ssu and then spent a lot of time putting his papers in order for publication. Land reform had been proceeding slowly in Kwangtung. In any case, the monks of the Yün-men Ssu had already started to work in the fields them-

45. Hsü-yün and four of his disciples at the Nan-hua Ssu in 1949. Left to right: Chu K'uan-ching, Pen-huai, Hsü-yün, Hui-chang, and Miao-yün. The latter, his most promising disciple, was executed as a counterrevolutionary in 1951.

selves, since Hsü-yün realized that they would have to become self-supporting.[59]

In the spring of 1951 the Central-South Land Reform Committee decided to speed up land reform in Kwangtung and take a harsher line towards landlords there. This was necessary because the prestige of the United States, now China's enemy in the Korean War, was making many people wonder whether there might not be a Nationalist restoration. Peasants were timid, landlords stubborn, and local cadres dilatory. At the end of March the first of six thousand northern cadres began to be sent into Kwangtung to get things moving.[60] This could help explain what happened at the Yün-men Ssu starting on March 31. An ordination was then being held there. A large number of lay devotees and about forty novices had joined the eighty monks normally resident in the monastery. The following account is translated from Hsü-yün's biography.

On March 31, 1951, the monastery was suddenly surrounded by over one hundred people, who forbade anyone to leave or enter. They confined the Venerable Hsü-yün to the abbot's quarters and set a number of people to guard him. The sangha was separately imprisoned in the meditation hall and the dharma hall. Then followed a great search of the monastery from roof tiles to flagstones. The images of the patriarchs, the liturgical instruments, and the sacred books were all minutely searched. After two days of painstaking work by over one hundred persons, nothing was found. Thereupon they arrested the prior, Ming-k'ung, and the following officers of the monastery: Wei-hsin, Wu-hui, Chen-k'ung, and Wei-chang. They took them all away. They also took documents, correspondence, and Hsü-yün's commentaries, lectures, and sayings, going back a hundred years, tied them up in burlap bags and went off with them. They made all sorts of accusations because of the fact that they had heard false rumors abroad that arms and radio transmitters had been hidden in the monastery, as well as gold and silver, and these were their objective. In the course of several days they arrested twenty-six members of the sangha and used different kinds of torture on them to force them to hand over arms and hidden gold. When the monks protested their ignorance, Miao-yün was beaten to death; Wu-yün and T'i-chih were also repeatedly pummeled until some of their ribs were broken; and several monks disappeared. This turmoil went on for ten days until finally, when they found nothing, their resentment turned to the master.

On April 6, 1951, they moved the master to confinement in a single room. They sealed up the windows and doors and cut off his food and water, nor did they allow him to leave the room to go to the toilet. Day and night there was a single dim light burning. It was like somewhere in hell. On the 8th ten burly fellows came in to force the master to hand over the gold, silver, and guns. The master said that there were none. Finally they gave him a cruel beating, first with wooden sticks, then with iron rods. They beat him until his head and face were covered with blood and some of his ribs were broken.

While beating him, they interrogated him. The master sat in lotus position [so that he might enter] trance. While blows with wood and iron thudded down, he closed his eyes unseeing and closed his mouth unspeaking: he assumed the aspect of someone in *samadhi.* On that day he was beaten four times in a row. [Finally] they threw him on the floor and, seeing the terrible state he was in, thought he was dead and went off boisterously. The guards left too. His acolytes waited till night came, then helped him up into a sitting position on his bed.

On April 10 those people heard that the master was not dead. Again they came into the room. When they saw the old man sitting upright in trance as before, they got even angrier and beat him with wooden truncheons, pulled him down on the floor, and then more than ten of them kicked and trampled on him with their leather boots. Blood was running out of his body everywhere as he lay overturned on the floor. They thought that there was no doubt that he was dead and again went off boisterously. Once more the acolytes came at night and picked the master up in their arms and set him on the bed upright as before. On the morning of the 15th he gradually assumed an auspicious position (like images of the Buddha in nirvana [that is, reclining on his right side]). At the end of another day and night he was motionless and still. When the acolytes held a filament of lampwick to his nostrils, it did not waver. They would have believed that he had passed away except that his body was still warm and his color was good. Two acolytes guarded him. On the morning of April 16 he groaned slightly and was helped to sit up. The acolytes told him how long he had been in trance and lying on the bed. The master slowly told the acolytes, Fa-yün and the others, that his spirit had made a journey to the Tusita Heaven and heard the dharma [expounded by Maitreya who told him that the time had not yet come for him to die: he had to return to his monastery][61] . . .

The thugs now gradually began to get frightened when they saw with their own eyes the master's miraculous survival. They began to talk about it, and one man, apparently their leader, asked the monks: "Why is it that the old boy can't be beaten to death?" The monk replied: "The venerable master has accepted suffering in order to help all sentient beings. For you people he has averted natural disasters. He cannot be beaten to death. Some day you will understand these things yourself." The man became frightened and did not have the master tortured again.

Things had gone to this point without their getting what they were after. That made them all the more afraid that the news would leak out. Hence they kept the monastery surrounded as before and continued their investigation and search. Not one of the monks was allowed to talk or to leave the premises. Even their food and drink was inspected and checked. It went on like this for over a month. Then the master began to feel the effect of the injuries he had received during torture. His illness grew worse from day to day. His sight and hearing failed. His disciples feared the worst and urged the master to give them an oral account of the main events of his life, with result that they wrote down the draft of the present autobiography.[62]

During May news of what had happened at Yün-men gradually trickled out to Shao-kuan. The monks of the Ta-chien Ssu in Ch'ü-chiang informed the master's disciples in Peking and other disciples overseas, who made a concerted effort to save the situation. The local government received a telegram from Peking ordering an investigation and only then was the blocade gradually relaxed—but a large part of the monastery's supplies of food and clothing had already been seized and made off with.

Since he received his injuries, the master had taken neither congee nor rice. Every day he drank plain water. When he learned that the food supplies were gone, he said to the monks: "My heavy karma has dragged all of you down too. Now that things have turned out like this, you probably should go your separate ways and try to live out your lives." But none of the monks were willing to leave the master. So they went together into the hills behind the monastery and

> collected faggots, which they carried five miles or so to the city and sold. The money they used to buy rice, which the monks ate as congee. They kept on with morning and afternoon devotions and continued to sit in the meditation hall.
>
> In mid-June the government in Peking sent a special commission to Kwangtung, where it met with officials of the provincial government. On the 27th they arrived at the Ju-yüan county office. On the 28th they reached the Yün-men Ssu. In order to conduct an investigation on the spot, they brought with them technicians, tape-recorders, cameras, and so on. First they solicitously inquired about the master's venerable health. The master was still sick in bed. Since his hearing and vision were impaired, he did not realize that these were high officials dispatched from Peking and Canton. As soon as he saw the local police [who were with them], he was unwilling to say anything. They asked him whether or not he had been maltreated and whether anything had been taken [from the monastery]. To both questions he answered: "No." Later, when they had made their identities clear to him, he simply requested them to conduct a thorough investigation and report back to Peking. The officials continued to be most solicitous towards him and ordered the local authorities to be sure that they released all the monks who had been arrested. Thus the difficulties of the Yün-men Ssu, which began on March 31 did not end until June 28, 1951."[63]

There were many reasons why the central government intervened so powerfully on Hsü-yün's behalf. In May Chao P'u-ch'u had proposed that eighteen eminent monks be convened to discuss the establishment of a national Buddhist association. The proposal had been approved by the Ministry of Internal Affairs and the Religious Affairs Division (see Chapter I at note 55). The first name on the list of eighteen was Hsü-yün's and it was more than a little embarrassing to find out that he had just been nearly killed by local cadres. Furthermore, some of the most influential Buddhists in the capital were Hsü-yün's disciples and had taken the Refuges with him—including Li Chi-shen, one of the six vice-chairmen of the Chinese People's Government. It even appears that Chu Teh, second in rank only to Mao Tse-tung, owed his life to Hsü-yün. Many years earlier, as a defeated army officer in Yünnan, he had been given asylum in the Hua-t'ing Ssu, of which Hsü-yün was then abbot. Chu had thought of becoming a monk (like so many other officers whose factions had lost out), but Hsü-yün refused to accept him as a disciple, saying that he was not suited for the monastic life. Chu was safely hidden for a few days and then left for the west.[64] Nor is this the only story about Hsü-yün protecting Communists in danger.[65] He followed the Chinese monastic tradition of providing compassionate shelter for anyone—which, as has already been pointed out, made the Communists particularly suspicious of monasteries once they became the hunters and not the hunted.

I have interviewed two of the monks who were living at the Yün-men Ssu when Hsü-yün was beaten. Their statements fit with the excerpt from the biography translated above, which mentions one of them by name. The second was among the ordinary monks locked up in the meditation hall. They too were subjected to daily interrogation. They would sit in their places as if for meditation while a cadre encouraged them to speak out by saying such things as "You are big landlords. You are an espionage organization and have a lot of guns. Be honest and hand them over, along with the gold." There was no way to reply.

This second informant stayed on at the Yün-men Ssu for another two years. In his view, the greatest loss in the spring of 1951 had been Miao-yün, whom the police must have killed precisely because he was Hsü-yün's favorite and most promising disciple (see Fig. 45). He was a university graduate, which was rare in the sangha, and the even rarer combination of being both an intellectual and a religious devotee.[66] His death, however, was only part of a much larger tragedy: 28,332 persons were executed in Kwangtung between October 10, 1950, and August 10, 1951.[67]

In the year after Hsü-yün's beating, once Peking had intervened, he was treated with the highest favor and consideration. In the spring of 1952, when he had recovered somewhat from his injuries, he received an invitation to come to Peking and help form the Chinese Buddhist Association. Officials were sent to accompany him and make sure he was well cared for on the journey.[68] He decided to go because he believed that the sangha "was disintegrating and unless it could unite into a strong organization, what had happened at Yün-men would not be the worst." He reached Peking on September 16, 1952, and two weeks later, on behalf of the Buddhists of China, he presented a silver stupa to the Sinhalese bhikkhu, Dhammaratna.[69] A photograph of the presentation was later published in *Buddhists in New China* (p. 162). Dhammaratna told me years afterwards that he had had no idea of the identity of the silver-haired Chinese monk who gave him the stupa and, of course, had been told nothing about the reasons he appeared to move with difficulty.

Hsü-yün remained in Peking until December, staying at the Kuang-chi Ssu and lending his prestige to the meeting that set up the CBA preparatory committee.[70] Immediately thereafter he submitted a petition to the government urging that it prohibit the destruction of monasteries, images, and sutras, and the forcible laicization of monks and nuns; and that it give them either subsidies or enough land so that they could support themselves. According to his biography, "the petition was approved by the authorities and so monks and nuns enjoyed a little more security."[71] There may be some exaggeration in this claim, which resembles an earlier passage describing how Hsü-yün, during the first days of the Chinese Republic, had interceded with the government to protect Buddhism.[72] Still, he probably did exert some influence through disciples like Li Chi-shen,[73] and he is said to have had an interview with Mao himself. This is not impossible, since Mao may have felt a certain curiosity about this fellow-Hunanese of whom he must have sometimes heard. According to the story, he asked whether the local cadres had made difficulties for Hsü-yün, who answered: "No, everything has been fine."[74]

There seems to be no doubt that many Chinese Buddhists looked on Hsü-yün as their protector. When he went south in December 1952, it became the occasion for the biggest Buddhist ceremonies that had been held since Liberation. In Shanghai, Hangchow, and Soochow, thousands of people took the lay initia-

46. Hsü-yün as he sat at the Kuang-chi Ssu in 1952, a year and a half after he was nearly beaten to death by local cadres and shortly before he was made honorary president of the new Chinese Buddhist Association. Peking 1952.

tion with him, and some of the country's most famous monasteries invited him to serve as abbot.[75] When the CBA was formally inaugurated in May 1953, Hsü-yün became one of its four honorary presidents, along with the Dalai and Panchen Lamas and the Mongolian Chagangegen. Thus he became the highest ranking Han Buddhist in Communist China just two years after Communist cadres had nearly beaten him to death.

He refused the invitations to serve as abbot (on the grounds of ill health), but accepted the task of restoring the Chen-ju Ssu at Yün-chü Shan in Kiangsi. This famous T'ang monastery had been burned by the Japanese: almost nothing was left except a giant bronze image of Vairocana, standing alone in the grass. Hsü-yün settled in a nearby cowshed and there he remained as monks and money poured in—much of the money coming from Chinese devotees abroad—until a complete set of monastery buildings had been erected. This was, in fact, much larger than any of the Buddhist construction projects undertaken by the government described in Chapter V. Hsü-yün devoted himself to it wholeheartedly and exclusively. He kept aloof from the activities of the Buddhist association,[76] and, partly because of his special position and partly because Yün-chü Shan lay in such a remote spot, he managed to keep politics out of the monastery. His monks worked hard in the fields and on their new buildings, yet kept up religious exercises and practiced meditation under Hsü-yün's personal guidance. Theirs was probably the last meditation hall left operating in China.

In 1957, when the anti-rightist movement got underway, the local authorities took over the land that the monks had worked so hard to reclaim. This violated the original understanding that whatever they reclaimed they could keep for their own use. Hsü-yün protested to Peking, and the land was restored. However, this so angered the local cadres that they resolved to discredit him for good. By this time the anti-rightist movement had become a widespread purge in which, as we have seen, monks connected with Hsü-yün were arrested and detained. One of them was persuaded to denounce Hsü-yün for corruption, reactionary and erroneous thinking, indiscriminate ordination, and homosexual relations with young monks.[77] Wall posters were pasted up at the monasteries that he had restored, his quarters were ransacked again, and more of his followers were arrested.[78] His case was due to be brought up at the National People's Congress in April 1959. It happened, however, that the charges against him were shown to Mao Tse-tung, who (so the story goes) asked Li Chi-shen about them: "You used to respect Hsü-yün a great deal. What do you think of the old man?" Li did not dare to say anything, although he knew the charges were false. "I don't know," he replied, "I am guilty of making a mistake." Mao sensed that something was wrong. "Oh, what a mess!" he said. "We are having an NPC meeting. Why bring up this stuff? Take it away, take it away." The dossier of accusations was then stored at the Kuang-chi Ssu for possible future use.[79] In October 1959, however, Hsü-yün died. His death was reported by the New China News Agency, which still described him as the honorary president of the CBA. A memorial service was held at its headquarters in Peking.[80]

About a year later it turned out that the cadres had been partly right back in 1951. Hsü-yün did indeed have gold hidden at the Yün-men Ssu—some $28,000 worth that he had collected in the 1930's for the restoration of the Kuang-hsiao Ssu in Canton. It was buried under a tree. Shortly before he died, he gave his acolytes a map of the location, told them to dig it up and give it to the government, explaining the purpose for which it had been put aside. After his death they did so—but the Kuang-hsiao Ssu had long since become a museum.[81]

BUDDHIST UTILIZATION OF GOVERNMENT PROGRAMS

The case of Hsü-yün illustrates the two sides to the policy on Buddhism. When he was regarded as hostile to the regime, he was vigorously suppressed; when it appeared that he could be used to rally Buddhists behind domestic programs and to win friends abroad, he was accorded favor and patronage. Similarly, monasteries were first impoverished in land reform and then repaired at government expense. The associations, seminaries, journals and bookshops that Buddhists had created for their own purposes with their own money before Liberation were forced to close down; and successors were set up that could be relied on to serve the government's purposes, operating on official subsidies.

To some extent, however, they served the purposes of Buddhists too. There was the rub. No matter how carefully the government dispensed its patronage to religious groups, it kept them in being. A monastery that had been repaired as an architectural monument and had monks living in it to impress visitors from Southeast Asia was—in terms of religious practice—more alive than one that had been converted into a police station. *Modern Buddhism* did useful work in transmitting directives and study materials to Buddhists, but in order to qualify as their journal it also had to publish articles that presented, however abstractly or distortedly, Buddhist doctrines. The CBA was the agent of the government in dealing with Buddhists at home and abroad, but its very existence gave a certain legitimacy to Buddhism. Thus the short-term program to utilize Buddhism conflicted with the long-term program to let it die of its own accord.

What made matters worse was the ingenuity of Buddhists in using a wide variety of official policies and campaigns as screens behind which they could carry on traditional religious activities.[82] For example in October 1950, only a year after Liberation, a group of thirty-one prominent Buddhists got together in Peking and decided to hold a series of religious services. The stated purpose was to protect world peace against the American aggressors. As they put it, "we Buddhists of Peking together with peace-loving persons who include representatives of the Mongolian and Tibetan minority nationalities, consider that the imperialists are demons who threaten world peace and must be subdued by the power of exorcism. Only then can one speak of permanent world peace." So for seven days some of them chanted liturgy and others lectured on the sutras—including the *Diamond Sutra,* perhaps the most popular subject of traditional Buddhist lectures. We are told that "those who attended were all overjoyed at this, the first large-scale Buddhist religious event since Liberation."[83]

How should this be interpreted? Had the People's Government succeeded in using Buddhists for its own purposes—in whipping up an anti-American campaign? Or was it the other way around–had Buddhists used the peace movement as the screen behind which they could chant and lecture on the sutras to large gatherings of the faithful just as they always had done in the past? Had they even, perhaps, been "trying something on"–seeing whether the new regime would accept the idea of using exorcism as a weapon with which to fight the American imperialists?[84] In that case, they had a vast store of ceremonies on which they could draw to exorcise China's enemies and justify their existence. This part of it did not succeed. At any rate we hear no more about exorcism; but on the whole, the services went off well, and it was suggested that similar ones be held in other places. They soon were. In Tientsin, for example, the *Heart Sutra*–another popular text–was lectured on for eight days in November, and many manifestoes were issued calling on the people of the city to realize that it was true compassion to aid the Korean War effort and repel the American imperialists.[85]

One purpose of the ceremonies in Tientsin was to "dispel disasters" (*hsiao-tsai*). This was a catch-all term that could refer to floods, droughts, or anything else that people were afraid of. But which were Buddhists more afraid of at this time–American imperialists or overenthusiastic local cadres, who were then holding struggle meetings against Buddhist abbots, smashing Buddhist images, and taking over Buddhist monasteries? It is conceivable, at least, that in the minds of some who participated the real purpose of the ceremonies was not to dispel the Americans but the Communists.

For the next decade monks and devotees continued to contribute to the peace movement. Not only did they hold religious services, they attended conferences. In 1952, as we have seen, Yüan-ying, the future president of the CBA, headed a delegation to the Peace Conference of Asia and the Pacific Regions, held in Peking that October. It was an important occasion–the first contact between Chinese and foreign Buddhists since Liberation. The foreign Buddhists who came to attend saw Chinese monks and nuns marching in a parade before the T'ien-an Men and carrying cardboard doves and big placards with the slogan "Protect world peace." Afterwards Yüan-ying said: "Because we are Buddhists, we must do Buddhist things. What are Buddhist things? Safeguarding world peace is the biggest Buddhist thing."[86] The catch is that "to do Buddhist things" was the standard phrase for performing rites for the dead–the principal source of income for most Chinese monks and an activity that many cadres were now suppressing as superstitious. Here was a chance to try and put it into a more respectable category–or rather to put peace propaganda and Buddhist funeral rites into the same category so that both would be permitted. The point is not that the effort was successful–since funeral rites were only permitted to continue in a few of the largest cities–but rather how quick Buddhists were in seizing every opportunity to turn Communist slogans to their own advantage.

Another example of this is their use of the slogan "miss none of the three" (*san pu-wu*), the three being production, study, and religious exercises. By tying these into a package, the authorities had thought that they were elbowing the sangha towards reform–making religious exercises a *privilege* that depended on satisfactory performance in the field or the classroom. The sangha, however, reversed the stratagem; it claimed that the package made religious exercises a *right* to which production and study entitled them. Thus we read of monks in Shanghai who "insisted on upholding the principle of 'missing none of the three',"[87] and elsewhere too monks saw the advantage of treating religious and secular activities as interdependent.[88] Even the call to reform monastic life could, as we have seen, be utilized by conservatives to preserve activities that might otherwise have disappeared, like the *uposatha* and summer retreat (see Chapter IV at notes 56, 59).

The best way, however, to carry on traditional activities was to protect them with a screen like the peace movement. Buddhists participated in half a dozen peace conferences–including those in Vienna, Hiroshima, and Stockholm. Foreign peace delegations visiting China were usually received by the CBA, and Chinese Buddhists throughout the country pitched into the huge campaign of 1955 to collect signatures opposing the use of atomic weapons. All this was useful to the government; and it was therefore useful to Chinese Buddhists. For example, in November 1952 a "peace service" was held by two hundred monks and devotees at a monastery in northern Kwangtung. A neighboring abbot, Pen-huan, came to lecture. (This was the same Pen-huan whose arrest in 1958 has been described above.) What he lectured on was *partly* world peace, but his main topic was methods of self-cultivation. The audience then proceeded to practice these methods: they chanted the sutras and recited Amitabha's name.[89] A much bigger service—the longest and most elaborate to be held since Liberation—started in Shanghai on December 12. While eminent monks expounded the sutras, rites for the dead were held at seven altars for forty-nine days. Among these was the "release of burning mouths" in which hungry ghosts in hell were fed sweet dew and released from their torment. This rite was performed five times, twice with five monks presiding—an unusually elaborate arrangement. All the activities during these seven weeks were believed to generate enormous merit, on which devotees could draw for the benefit of themselves or their families by paying to have soul tablets installed at one of the altars. The charges varied from the equivalent of US$85 (a month's salary for ordinary workers in Shanghai) down to less than a dollar. Collecting such charges had been clearly labeled "cheating the masses with superstition," and yet two future leaders of the CBA took part; and eight were to be found among the lecturers. Hsü-yün, still frail from his beating, presided over the whole affair and administered the bodhisattva vows to the living and the dead. (Chinese Buddhists believe that the dead too can thus be helped towards a better rebirth.) So confident was the mood of the monks in Shanghai (because of the honors accorded Hsü-yün and the plan to set up the CBA) that they did not feel it necessary to erect a particularly elaborate screen for this particularly elaborate ceremony. They announced that it was being performed to deter aggression and to promote world peace. No aggressors were named, but they did endorse the recent Peace Congress in Vienna and point out that among the dead who would benefit from the services were soldiers who had died in the Korean War and whose rebirth in the Western Paradise would now be facilitated.[90]

The living too wanted to facilitate their rebirth in the Western

Paradise. Hence devotees recited Amitabha's name during this and other peace services.[91] According to the official line, the Western Paradise was being built here on earth by the Communist Party and the means to reach it was to participate in socialist construction, not to recite Amitabha's name. This did not deter Buddhists from reciting his name in the old way. Sometimes they even practiced the intensive form of recitation that went on day and night for seven days—in four cases as a contribution to the peace movement[92] and in two cases as a measure to bring about the liberation of Taiwan.[93]

The "liberation" of Taiwan also provided a basis for celebrating the Buddha's birthday on the 8th of the fourth lunar month—one of the major religious festivals of traditional China. A tiny statue of infant Sakyamuni would be placed in a basin and then everyone present would pour some holy water over it. After Liberation this was sometimes done as an act of self-dedication to world peace,[94] sometimes to bring about the "liberation" of Taiwan and in one case to celebrate the achievements of the First Afro-Asian Conference.[95] Some of the Chinese delegates to this conference were said to have been killed en route to it by U.S.-Chiang agents and, when a memorial service was held for them, it too was a celebration of the Buddha's birthday.[96] Amitabha also had a birthday (on the 17th of the eleventh lunar month) which was celebrated in 1951 at a peace service held by the Buddhist branch of the Resist America Aid Korea Committee.[97]

Many different kinds of screens could be used to protect traditional activities.[98] If an activity seemed to be particularly risky, Buddhists sought protection several screens deep. For example, in October 1954 some monks and devotees in Hupeh had had the main images of their temples re-covered with gold leaf. Although they wanted to hold an inaugural ceremony, they knew that they might be criticized for having spent money on images that had not declared important by the cultural administration. Therefore they announced that the purposes of the ceremony would be: first, thanksgiving to the Buddha and to the State; second, commemoration of patriots who had died for the country; and third, self-dedication to world peace and to the hope that the people of

China could always live an independent, free, democratic, and happy life in a Western Paradise here on earth.[99]

Buddhists could use the rhetoric of the regime not only to camouflage religious activities, but also to exert counterpressure on cadres who were making trouble for them. In 1957, for example, a delegate to the CBA's second national conference compared the lot of monks in the New China with their lot under the Kuomintang. Such comparisons were a standard exercise in political study, designed to make people count their blessings. "What is especially true," he concluded, "is that the monasteries we live in today are peaceful and solemn whereas in the past they were invaded and despoiled by Kuomintang troops. In this respect there is even less of a comparison with the past."[100] Now everyone present, including the cadres, knew that *both* the Communists and the Nationalists, despite laws to the contrary, had taken over monasteries for barracks and offices. By talking about the superiority of life under the Communists, this delegate seems to have been reminding the cadres that, if they really wanted to be considered superior to the Kuomintang and to abide by the law, they should be more considerate of monasteries in the future. The speech was not servility but a curious kind of intimidation—almost like jiu-jitsu, in which the weaker tries to use the strength of his opponent to defeat him.

Praise of the regime was often loaded this way. The very next month at the Kwangtung Provincial CPPCC, Pen-huan praised it for helping with the ordination held at his monastery the previous winter, to which six hundred Buddhists had come to be ordained, including some from Southeast Asia. He ended by saying: "This should help convince the overseas Chinese of the government's good faith with regard to religion."[101] Yet in reality the ordination had been held without government permission and afterwards he had been prohibited from holding another one. So what he actually seems to have been getting at was: "Look out, cadres, unless you lift your prohibition and let us ordain when we like, it will jeopardize your relations with the overseas Chinese."

The cadres could deal with a tricky individual like Pen-huan by arresting him, but what must have caused them to scratch their heads were the efforts by many Buddhists to do exactly what the cadres expected of them—efforts that could represent submission as easily as camouflage. For example, soon after Liberation monks began to refer to themselves as "the masses"—*ch'ün-chung.* This was only a slight phonetic change from the traditional term for the monks who held no monastic office—*ch'ing-chung,* the "pure multitude." Did this change of terms mean that monks had really begun to identify themselves with the broad toiling masses? Or did it just mean that they wanted the cadres to think they had? Yet how could the cadres forbid the monks to adopt a proletarian stand, since that was the whole purpose of socialist study? All the cadres could do was to go along, maintaining their vigilance. In the end their vigilance was often rewarded, but in a way that only showed greater need for it.

An example is provided by the Ling-shan Ssu in eastern Kwangtung. About 1951 its monks started a farm. They called it an "experimental farm," which sounded very progressive, and they announced that they were leading a communal life of political study and productive labor.[102] From the cadres' point of view here was a group of model Buddhists. Yet in 1956 the abbot was expelled for having given asylum to counterrevolutionaries, and in 1958 he was arrested as the head of a reactionary Taoist sect.[103] His "experimental farm" and his fine slogans had apparently been just a screen, which the cadres finally penetrated.

In 1954, a year before the Buddhist Youth Society came under attack in Shanghai, its magazine, *Chüeh-hsün,* was being read in socialist study classes as far away as Shensi, where its articles on politics and current events were said to have "raised the patriotic fervor" of local monks and nuns.[104] The group that published it was congratulated for consolidating the unity among Buddhists.[105] Yet, as we have seen, among the charges against it in 1954 was that it "sowed dissension to undermine patriotic movements, destroyed the unity between Buddhists and the government and the unity among the Buddhists themselves."[106]

Perhaps the Chinese are more adept than other people at using screens and protective camouflage because they have had such long experience at it—two thousand years of survival of those who were fittest at espousing the philosophical orthodoxy of a strong central government. Among Chinese the Buddhists have had to develop especially high survival skill, since they were, after all, heterodox. Just as in earlier centuries they used to justify their existence on Confucian grounds, now in the 1950's they could point out that their monasteries had been collectives for a thousand years. Monks had lived in buildings communally owned, worked together, eaten together in their mess halls, and decided things together. By a little judicious selection, Buddhist doctrines could be presented as denying the existence of God, of the soul, and advocating the overthrow of privileged classes. It is no wonder that, as we shall see in the next chapter, the cadres became suspicious of the effort to reconcile Buddhism and Marxism. They also became suspicious of the Buddhist use of government programs and slogans in connection with traditional religious rites. This reached peaks in 1952-53 and during the peace movement in early 1955.[107] It dropped off when the Hu Feng movement got into full swing and, so far as I know, ceased entirely after the anti-rightist movement began in mid-1957.[108] Yet the memories of it probably lingered on in the minds of the cadres; and when Buddhism came to be suppressed during the Cultural Revolution, the reason was not only because it was no longer of much use in foreign policy and its domestic strength had been sharply reduced, but also because of long frustration in trying to control and utilize the few Buddhists who remained. To some cadres they must have seemed like really slippery characters who held traditional rites on the most cynical pretexts, and who, when they took part in political study, in productive labor, and in people's diplomacy, managed to use the programs of the regime for their own purposes, which was just the reverse of what the cadres wanted.[109]

Let me try to anticipate a misunderstanding. It may seem that I have painted a one-sided picture of the monks manipulating the cadres—as if the cadres were almost helpless in their hands. Needless to say, that is absurd. It was the monks who were almost helpless when their monasteries were occupied, their lands confiscated, their ordinations forbidden, and the greater part of religious practice displaced by productive labor and political movements.

They were almost, but not quite helpless. This "not quite" is the point. I think that people who have written about the fate of Buddhism in Communist China (including myself) have tended to overlook the resourcefulness of Buddhists in trying to survive. They were certainly very weak; they did not have strong popular support—certainly not strong enough so that it was strengthened by persecution—but they did have ways of temporizing, compromising, and dissembling that enabled them to postpone the end for seventeen years—and the Cultural Revolution may not have been the end, as we shall see. Nor do I wish to assert that Buddhist use of government programs and slogans was always mere dissembling. For fifteen hundred years the sangha had had to justify its existence by transferring the merit it created to serve the government—to procure the defeat of external enemies, long life for the emperor, avert floods and droughts, and so on.[110] To recite buddha's name for the liberation of Taiwan followed an ancient tradition. Sometimes the continuity was striking. In the first lunar month of 1955, for example, the Ch'ing-liang Ssu in Chin-yang, Shensi, held a religious service of self-dedication to peace and opposition to the use of atomic weapons.[111] During the week it lasted, besides performing the Thousand Buddhas Penance (a general preventive against accidents and disasters), the participants chanted the *Jen-wang hu-kuo ching.* This had been used for centuries to protect the nation from external threats—and had continued to be so used under the Republic.[112] Again in 1957, abbot Ching-kuan was probably being sincere when he told the CBA national conference that "rites of prayer for the peace and happiness of the people and for a year of good harvests should be considered by Buddhists to be among the religious activities that repay the kindness of the motherland and of all living creatures."[113] Yet his sincerity may have been questioned by the cadres. In August 1966 his monastery was wrecked and, after being struggled against by a crowd of a hundred thousand people, he was arrested.[114] The Cultural Revolution was launched partly to deal with such slippery practitioners of superstition.

Chapter VIII

Interpreting Buddhist Doctrine

During the time that the Communist Party was waiting for Buddhism to disappear of its own accord (as socialism eliminated the reasons for its existence), Buddhist monasteries could be utilized in people's diplomacy—and gradually converted into museums. Buddhist monks could be utilized in socialist construction—and gradually be converted into good citizens. But how could Buddhist doctrine be utilized? There seemed to be a similar answer. By selecting and emphasizing its positive elements (positive from the Marxist point of view), by making the less positive more positive, and by discarding the negative, cadres could utilize Buddhist doctrine to increase the enthusiasm of monks and devotees for participation in the programs of the regime; and, perhaps, to provide a model for those Buddhists abroad who were trying to adapt the dharma to serve nationalism and modernization.

Progressive Buddhists in China were eager to see their doctrine utilized in this way, because they were on the defensive and wanted to show that their doctrine was not superstitious, but scientific, not feudal and reactionary, but eminently compatible with Marxism. From the Party's point of view, however, this was dangerous in the long run. It was true that pointing out what Buddhism and Marxism had in common might help turn a few Buddhists into Marxists; but it would confirm far more in their adherence to Buddhism, to the truth of which Marxism merely offered a new testimonial. There was even the danger that Marxism itself might become contaminated. Mao had foreseen this danger when he warned in 1940: "Communists may form an anti-imperialist and anti-feudal united front for political action with certain idealists and even with religious followers, but we can never approve of their idealism or religious doctrines."[1]

The full import of this warning was scarcely felt during the first decade after Liberation. Cadres and progressive Buddhists alike cited religious justifications for monks and devotees to participate in the programs of the regime, and they were rarely censured for doing so. One of the exceptions came in 1951 when *Modern Buddhism* printed a couple of items suggesting that Buddhist landowners should practice charity by "taking all their land and tools and enthusiastically giving them to the People's Government for distribution to the peasants."[2] At the end of the year the editors, evidently on orders from above, retracted this on the grounds that it "blurred class consciousness in the class struggle. The essence of land reform is for the peasant class to wage a revolutionary struggle against the feudal landowning class. It is not a question of the landowners offering charity to the peasants."[3] If land had been distributed on the basis of the Buddhist ideals of charity and compassion, some peasants might have credited their gains to Buddhism rather than to the Communist Party. Yet such purism was exceptional. Usually during the first decade under Mao religious justifications and scriptural authority for the programs of the regime were invoked quite freely and even with official encouragement.

SCRIPTURAL AUTHORITY FOR SOCIALIST CONSTRUCTION

After the Religious Work Conference in the winter of 1953-54, a directive was issued by the CCP Central Committee ordering local cadres to go through canonical literature and find passages that could be used to mobilize the faithful.[4] It did not matter if a passage had to be taken out of context and given a meaning that was inconsistent with the main body of doctrine. In fact, the cadres were warned *not* to try to construct a new doctrinal schema that would be self-consistent and compatible with Marxism, for that would, in effect, salvage the religion.[5] Rather they were to utilize individual passages to introduce Marxist principles to the faithful in the most acceptable way—and step by step eventually convert them from wavering Buddhists into committed Marxists.

For example the following passage was frequently quoted from the *Avatamsaka Sutra:* "That which has really caused all the buddhas and bodhisattvas to become what they are is their mind of great compassion. It was because of all living creatures that their great compassion arose; it was because of their great compassion that their bodhi mind was born; it was because of their bodhi mind that they reached true enlightenment. This may be illustrated by a great tree in the desert. If its roots get water, its branches, leaves, and fruit are all abundant. It is the same with the desert of life and death and the great tree of bodhi. All living creatures are the roots of the tree; all the buddhas and bodhisattvas are its branches. If all living creatures are nourished with the water of great compassion, then it results in the flowers and fruit of the wisdom of buddhas and bodhisattvas."[6] When Chao P'u-ch'u quoted this in 1955, he said it was summed up in a second passage: "Without all living creatures a bodhisattva could never obtain supreme enlightenment."[7] What relevance does this have to socialist construction? This becomes clear as soon as we recall that the term "all living creatures" (*chung-sheng*) is now taken to refer to "the masses" (*ch'ün-chung*).[8] Chao went on to quote Chou En-lai's speech to the first NPC, in which Chou said that the goal of the Communist regime was to serve the people and to improve their material life. "This makes us realize," Chao P'u-ch'u continued, "that our dependence on living creatures means that we must do our best in every kind of work under the leadership of the People's Government we have today."[9]

This may sound vague and jejune, but the meaning was sometimes made more explicit, as when the readers of *Modern Buddhism* were told in 1959 that "productive labor accords with the Buddhist principle that the highest conduct for a bodhisattva is 'to benefit all living creatures.' "[10] Buying national construction bonds was "to carry out the *paramita* of charity and Samantabhadra's vow to 'beautify the land and do good to sentient beings.' "[11] The kind of patriotism that was expected of Buddhists as of other Chinese citizens was "surprisingly similar" to the Buddhist idea of protecting the state, based on the concept of *dharmadhatu* (dharma realm).[12] The Communist Party exemplified the Buddhist ideal of compassion.[13] Thought reform was the same as the Buddhist practice of "purifying one's own mind." This last was explained most clearly in a riposte sent to a magazine in Ceylon that had printed an article critical of "brain-washing."

> The Buddha taught us with special emphasis to "purify one's own mind"[14] and to progress with unslacked energy. We do not understand why one who professes to be a follower of the Buddha should be so terrified by the term "remolding" and joins in the clamor against it as "brain-washing." In fact, if dirt is found in one's thought (just as it is on one's body), what harm would it do to advise him to have a wash . . . After all the question is with regard to what things are to be washed off . . . The things that we advise people to wash off are: concern for individual interests at the expense of the collective interests; concern for immediate interests at the expense of long-term interests—in other words, lack of patriotism, disdainfulness towards the masses and the like thoughts, which are concrete manifestations of greed, hatred, and ignorance.[15]

Thus after a nine-day socialist study symposium in 1958 a Kiangsi monk described the benefits he had gotten: "It was as if the lock of my mind had been opened; I felt completely relaxed and full of joy." In this condition he and the other participants in study resolved to "surrender their minds to the Party."[16]

Most of these references to scriptural authority came from progressive Buddhists—or Buddhists who were trying to appear progressive—but the same thing could be heard from religious affairs cadres when they exhorted monks and devotees to participate more enthusiastically in the programs of the regime. At any rate this is what oral informants have asserted. Unfortunately few such exhortations have appeared in print.[17]

Scriptural authority was also cited by progressive Buddhists when they wished to brighten the reputation of Buddhism in the eyes of cadres and win a more honored place for it in the New China. They argued, for example, that the Buddha and his followers had been among history's leading dialecticians and materialists;[18] that he had anticipated Marx by rejecting belief in a soul that survived after death and in a God who created and ruled the world.[19] Since there was no such thing as a soul, the individual only existed insofar as he belonged to the masses (hence to have individual feelings was un-Buddhist–like, for example, the sympathy that some Buddhists had felt for the thousands of landlords who were killed during land reform).[20] Since there was no God, prayer was useless; to cope with sickness Buddhists should consult a physician, and to cope with natural disasters, they should promote relief work.[21]

In a word, Buddhism was a scientific religion. Whatever was unscientific in it belonged to the superstitious accretions of 2,500 years, which should now be washed or explained away.[22] The miraculous events described in the canon were merely metaphors and propaganda devices designed to spread the doctrine.[23]

Socially too Buddhism was modern and progressive. It embodied strong democratic and collective traditions. The early sangha had been the world's first participatory democracy, in which decisions were reached by majority vote at meetings that all could attend.[24] Monks not only led a collective life, but their concept of selflessness qualified them to lead it better than anyone else.[25] Gautama–the historical Buddha–was in fact a social revolutionary, and the reason his teachings had spread so rapidly in ancient India was that the new classes of landlords and merchants wanted to throw off Brahmin domination. "The power arrogated by the nobility, which was supported by the sacramental privileges of the Brahmins and by the caste system, seriously impeded the growth of the agricultural irrigation system and the development of external and internal trade. Therefore Buddhism, which opposed these sacramental privileges and the caste system and advocated the equality of all living creatures, received the support of the people of that time and was especially welcomed by the newly arising landlord and merchant classes."[26]

Many articles on this theme were published in 1959-1960. Another explained that Gautama was probably of non-Aryan stock and hence naturally hostile to the caste system that the Aryans had created. He preached in the colloquial, not in the elegant literary language of the Brahmins. When he begged, he accepted food from the lower castes and even took a common laborer as his disciple.[27] In other words, his life and teaching, in Marxist terms, constituted a progressive force that moved history forward.

From portraying the Buddha as an opponent of the caste system, it was only a step to depicting him as an advocate of class struggle.[28] This made his teachings more relevant to good citizenship in the New China, but it posed a serious problem for traditional Buddhists, since it brought them face to face with the first precept—not to take the life of any sentient being.

KILLING COUNTERREVOLUTIONARIES AND IMPERIALISTS

In 1958 *Modern Buddhism* printed a long article by Ming-chen in which he discussed Gautama's opposition to the caste system and then went on to refute "those among us who twist the Buddha's egalitarian teaching so as to assert in a forced way that we Buddhists must 'eliminate the concepts of the nation and nationality,' 'eliminate the concept of social classes'—on the grounds that these concepts are the root causes of war and human cruelty and are utterly bad." Traditional Buddhists might argue that it was Ming-chen who was guilty of twisting, since one of the Buddha's fundamental teachings was the danger of all attachment (including attachment to a nation or class), since it led to dualism and partisanship. Yet dualism and partisanship were precisely what Ming-chen believed the Buddha had favored. He had loved the working class, sympathized with oppressed nations, and, in effect, taken their side—just as Chinese Buddhists should today. "To advocate eliminating the concepts of nation, nationality, and class is really to advocate that we eliminate the concepts of good and evil, right and wrong, so that Buddhists will inevitably fall into ideological paralysis and into an attitude where the difference between the orthodox and the heterodox are obscured. This will render them unable to distinguish the enemy from ourselves. Then the 'infinite mercy and compassion' that these people talk about can only become empty words on paper. After all, is it not true that the existence of exploiting classes is the root cause of all the evil and wrongdoing in the world?"[29]

The effort to make monks more class conscious and readier to participate in class struggle had been going on since Liberation. It was one of the main themes of political study. Yet political study and articles like Ming-chen's probably had less effect on monks than certain object lessons. Movements like land reform made many of them see that unless they were *against* landlords and other enemies of the people, they might be suspected of being *for* them or even *among* them, with all the frightening consequences that this entailed. That, I think, is why one Buddhist leader wrote in 1953 that "after going through [land reform] my hatred for the feudal landlords' exploitation of the peasants was deepened and my awareness and understanding of class struggle was raised."[30] Here is an episode reported by some monks in Kiangsi.

> In the spring of 1950 a former battalion commander of the bandit army [that is, the defeated Nationalist army] escaped from a labor reform team and came up the mountain. He thought that monks would easily be taken in, but we saw through his devilish tricks and, pretending to be hospitable, secretly went down and reported to the village government, which in due time had the bandit commander arrested. In the autumn of the same year a reactionary who had sabotaged land reform came up the mountain to hide. Although he was well acquainted with an old abbot here, we paid no attention to this and had him arrested in the same manner as the bandit battalion commander. Since the bandits had not yet been mopped up and our mountain monastery was far removed from any human habitation, the government was worried about our safety. Luckily, however, the Liberation Army vigorously finished off the remaining bandits within a few months.
>
> At that time most people viewed these actions of ours in the light of old-fashioned ideas. On the grounds that monks should

> avoid anything that leads to the death of living creatures, this person and that person charged us with doing wrong. But we had faith in the policies, decrees, and measures of the Communist Party and the People's Government, which everywhere serve a great cause, the general good rather than private gain, and have as their aim the salvation of the nation and mankind. Only those who have lost heart and sanity will not have faith in them and support them. What is more, our actions had their basis in scripture. The *Jnanottara-bodhisattva-pariprccha Sutra* says: "Our master, Sakya Tathagata, when practicing the way of the bodhisattva, killed one bad man in order to save five hundred men." This is the best example to follow. Our vow not to destroy life cannot be viewed dogmatically. Killing for personal fame and profit is a breach of the vow. Killing in order to save people is in the greatest conformity with the vow. Armed as we were with these correct beliefs, the common run of accusation did not shake our resolve in the least and we were more determined than ever to remain on this mountain wilderness and help the government catch bandits and spies. Government functionaries, when they held meetings, often paid tribute to our conduct, saying that our awareness was high and that we abided by the laws and decrees of the government. People no longer looked down on us *and never again talked about our being superstitious.*[31]

I shall have more to say below on the scriptural authority for killing that is cited here.[32] A somewhat similar episode occurred the following year when another "bandit" sought asylum at a nunnery in Kwangsi. The nuns urged him to surrender himself and, at the same time, discreetly sent word to the militia. When the militia arrived and surrounded the building, he made a dash to the river in hopes of getting across it and escaping, but he was shot dead. "This shows that not only had the nuns firmly taken the people's side and sworn to destroy the enemies of the people, but also that they had understood the spirit of Buddhist compassion, namely that 'to kill a bad person and save many good persons gives rise to great merit,' which is the highest compassionate principle."[33]

Not all Buddhists were so ready to violate the first precept. For example, the Ningpo Buddhist Association reported in 1952 that "in the movement for the suppression of counterrevolutionaries all the monks and nuns in our association had first clung to the concept of 'compassion' (*tz'u-pei*). They considered that it [the movement] would bring down upon them Heaven's displeasure. They were not clearly informed on the evil deeds done by counter-revolutionary elements to harm the country and the people. It was only after taking part in political study *and attending several public trials* that they began to take the movement seriously." Then, allegedly inspired by patriotism (but more probably by the fear that unless they accused others they themselves might become victims), they lodged accusations against seven persons, including two of the leading monks of Ningpo, who were consequently arrested.[34] At about the same time in nearby Hangchow monks and nuns were "taking the first step towards a clear understanding of how to draw a line between the enemy and ourselves and adopt the standpoint of the masses. For example, in the campaign for the suppression of counterrevolutionaries the abbess of the Ch'ing-lien An exposed the wicked conduct of a counterrevolutionary and of her own disciples in sheltering counterrevolutionary elements. A nun of the Lien-ju An gave evidence of the evil deeds of a traitor under the Japanese occupation. The government therefore arrested these enemies of the people . . . [The above] is enough to show that the Buddhists of today are no longer blindly compassionate."[35]

Again and again in 1950-52 we see progressive Buddhist leaders trying to persuade the monks and nuns that neither the ideal of compassion nor the prohibition against taking life should deter them from enthusiastic participation in political movements. Even the youth, who might have been expected to be more open towards new ideas, had reservations. Wei-fang (see Fig. 51) addressed the following words to a crowded meeting of young monks in Shanghai on May 18, 1951.

> "We Buddhists are not well enough informed about the suppression of counterrevolutionaries. Our thinking is still be-

numbed and we cling to the concept of compassion. Actually there is no conflict between the suppression of counterrevolutionaries and Buddhist doctrine, since the suppression of counterrevolutionaries promotes orthodoxy and crushes heterodoxy. As the sutras put it, 'unless you crush heterodoxy, you cannot make the orthodox shine forth.' The founder of our religion, Sakyamuni, once had no qualms about killing a bad element in order to save five hundred merchants. Not only was there nothing wrong in so doing, but it produced considerable merit. Why did this act of killing produce considerable merit? Because it was done to protect the lives and welfare of many people and the one person killed was a bad element. This completely corresponds with the present campaign to suppress counterrevolutionaries. The purpose of suppressing counterrevolutionaries is to protect our peaceful, happy life. Therefore we must raise our vigilance and be on the lookout for any possibility that the American imperialists and the Chiang bandit clique are utilizing religion to carry out plots and sabotage. Everyone must unite so as not to let one counterrevolutionary—not one member of a syncretistic sect—infiltrate our Buddhist circles . . . "

When his speech was over, all the Buddhists waved their arms and shouted: "Strengthen the people's democratic dictatorship," "Support the People's Government in severely suppressing counterrevolutionaries," and "Right on!"[36]

The idea of "crushing heterodoxy"—which could also be rendered as "crushing heretics"—was closely linked with another concept invoked by progressive Buddhists to justify killing counterrevolutionaries. This was the concept that "the Buddha and demons cannot co-exist."[37] In the original Buddhist tradition demons were personifications of the *klesa,* the obstacles to enlightenment, particularly hatred, greed, and ignorance. Just before Gautama's enlightenment, he was tempted by whole armies of demons, led by Mara, whose power he subdued. This was counted as one of the eight great events of his career. After 1949 the phrase "subduing demons" (*hsiang-mo*) was used in a different sense. It no longer referred to the struggle against enemies in one's own mind, but against external enemies, not only Chinese counterrevolutionaries but American imperialists. The implication was that by killing them one could become a buddha.[38] Soon after China entered the Korean War, the country was swept by a wave of meetings and demonstrations to resist America and support Korea. On January 21, 1951, Ch'en Ming-shu addressed a meeting of 2,500 Buddhist monks, nuns, and devotees in Wuhan and explained how the activities of the United States revealed its ambition to "rule the whole world. Its goals are gradually to expand its armed aggression, sabotage world peace, slaughter the peoples of the world, and destroy their cultures. Thus the American imperialists are demons, without a trace of humanity, a hundred thousand times more murderous and evil than the Fascists. Since the Buddha and demons cannot co-exist . . . resisting the Americans is the clear obligation for Buddhists." That is, in order to follow the bodhisattva path, they should sacrifice their lives for peace.[39]

We have already seen how monks went off to fight in Korea (Chapter III at note 56). Now we can begin to see the religious justification for doing so. On March 11, 1951, Hsin-tao addressed a meeting of 187 Nanchang Buddhists as follows. "We know that the People's Government absolutely guarantees the freedom of religious belief. We Buddhists must unite as quickly as possible and, with the followers of other religions, completely support the Chinese Volunteer Army and the Korean People's Army. The best thing is to be able to join the army directly and to learn the spirit in which Sakyamuni, as the embodiment of compassion and our guide to buddhahood, killed robbers to save the people and suffered hardship on behalf of all living creatures. To wipe out the American imperialist demons who are breaking world peace is, according to Buddhist doctrine, not only blameless but actually gives rise to merit."[40]

However, just as with the campaign against counterrevolutionaries, there were some monks who still had doubts about killing. These were dispelled by arguments like the following. "Buddhist compassion is not without guiding principles. One has to be compassionate to good people, but if one is also compassionate to bad people, it will indirectly help evil people to do bad things. Therefore Buddhism has the ancient precept: 'To kill evil people is a good resolve.' "[41] The same "ancient precept" was used to justify a rather extraordinary performance put on by the monks of Ningpo during an anti-American demonstration in March 1951. Some of them formed a "war-drum squad" that marched in the parade beating their temple drums—the ones normally used to accompany the recitation of sutras. Others formed an "axe squad," carrying twenty-four raised axes to show the demon-subduing power of Buddhism. As they marched, all of them shouted "Kill kill kill kill kill the American wolves!"[42]

In 1951-52 Buddhists throughout China raised money for a fighter plane to be used against the Americans in Korea. Individual pieces of equipment, like its cannons, were paid for by individual temples. It may seem hard to believe, but the plane was named the *Chinese Buddhist.*[43] The money for it, however, had not been raised without an effort at education, as Chü-tsan admitted in 1952.

> Our Buddhist circles do not have a wholly positive attitude when it comes to certain aspects of the government's appeals. For example, in the matter of contributing towards airplane cannons, we understand that the response has mostly been quite enthusiastic, but that some individual groups consider that Buddhism prohibits killing and their contributions towards airplane cannons violates this prohibition. Therefore some people advocate that the objects to be purchased with the contributions should be changed from airplane cannons to medical supplies; and others advocate contributing towards ambulances rather than fighter planes and bombers. These ideas naturally have their points, but the government is asking us to contribute towards airplane cannons for the purpose of resisting and annihilating the American imperialists who are striking at our country's security and the people's welfare, that is, for the purpose of "subduing demons." Subduing demons requires a strong Vajra eye (*chin-kang nu-mu*). Killing is permitted under the Yoga bodhisattva vows; and the *Nirvana*

> *sutra* advocates wielding the spear and starting battle. Therefore there is nothing contrary to Buddhist doctrine in a Buddhist responding to the appeal to contribute towards fighter planes, bombers, cannons, and tanks . . . I ask my fellow Buddhists throughout the country to give this some thought and hereafter not to harm a great cause for the sake of some petty scruples.[44]

The end of the Korean War did not mean an end to Buddhist militance. During the Middle East crisis in 1958 Chü-tsan told a protest meeting in Peking that "Buddhist scriptures preach compassion and pity, but advocate resistance to aggression and regard it as a just cause. That is why we Buddhists stand firmly by the side of the people in the Middle Eastern countries and strongly condemn the aggressive actions of the United States and Britain."[45]

I have quoted so many of these passages that justify killing counterrevolutionaries and imperialists because I would not want the reader to suppose that they were isolated "deviations" (like the destruction of monasteries and the burning of sutras). In order to turn Buddhists into Marxists—or at least into patriotic good citizens—it was necessary to interpret their ideal of compassion in a rather special way. This was possible thanks to the help of the Communist Party. "Only under the leadership of the Party, unwaveringly following the Party's leadership and taking the road to socialism, can we exemplify the best traditions of Buddhism and Taoism and realize the spirit of doing good to sentient beings."[46] Since compassion towards good people now meant ruthlessness towards bad people,[47] it was possible to give a positive content to the first precept. As explained by a former religious affairs cadre, the commandment not to kill could be utilized in the peace movement—since the imperialists were killing thousands in their wars of aggression—without inhibiting the People's Government in its tasks of national defense and internal security. The people that *it* killed were all bad. At study meetings, when Buddhists objected to this interpretation, the cadre in question used to silence them by asking: "In laying down this precept, what was the Buddha's purpose? His purpose was peace."[48]

THE SCRIPTURAL JUSTIFICATION OF KILLING

Readers who have always thought of Buddhism as a religion of peace and nonviolence may be surprised at the way progressive Buddhists in China interpreted the ideal of compassion.[49] They may suppose it to be a Communist-inspired distortion of what the Buddha originally taught. In actuality, however, although it may be a distortion, it is not a new one. For two millennia the philosophers of Mahayana Buddhism have been providing increasingly ingenious justifications for breaking the first precept. The history of this lamentable process—parallel to the process by which the teachings of Christ have been interpreted to sanction the violence of war and revolution—has been traced in a masterly article by Paul Demiéville, which I shall now summarize, noting the parallels in China under Mao.[50]

Demiéville begins by pointing out that in the early canonical tradition "killing is the gravest of all offenses," not only for monks but for laymen.[51] Simply to be a soldier—whether or not one kills with one's own hands—is to be an accessory to killing; and unless one has been forcibly conscripted, one is as guilty as those who wield the sword.[52] This idea is implicit in the vows of the *Sutra of Brahma's Net*—vows that were taken by every Chinese monk. These forbade him to participate in a war or rebellion, to possess weapons, and even to watch a battle being fought.[53]

Yet under both the Hinayana and Mahayana traditions war has sometimes been tolerated or even encouraged. The great Sinhalese King Duttha-Gamani led his troops into battle with a relic of the Buddha on his spear. Monks were encouraged to disrobe and join his army: one became a general. When he grew troubled at having slain so many of the Indian invaders, eight arahats told him that actually only one and a half human beings had been killed in the battles. The rest had been wrong believers and men of evil life, who could be considered animals.[54]

In China there were monks who did not even disrobe before they went into battle. Demiéville cites the case of Fa-ch'ing who led fifty thousand troops in a rebellion against the Northern Wei in 515 C.E. He proclaimed that each of his soldiers would become a bodhisattva as soon as he had killed one of the enemy.[55] Fa-ch'ing, like most rebel monks in Chinese history, cannot be considered an orthodox Buddhist, but there were orthodox monks who bore arms. At the start of the T'ang dynasty those of the Shao-lin Ssu helped T'ai-tsung win power; and military honors were conferred on them.[56] At the end of the Sung, some monks in Kiangsi fought against the Mongols under a banner inscribed "Subdue demons!" (*hsiang-mo*)[57]—anticipating by several centuries one of the justifications we have seen advanced by progressive Buddhists under Mao. In the Ming dynasty the monks of the Shao-lin Ssu (another monastery by this name in Fukien, I believe, rather than the one in Honan) battled savagely against Japanese pirates who infested the coast of China's southeastern provinces. With their hair dyed red and their faces painted blue, they advanced on the pirates twirling their single-sticks (one of the arts of Shao-lin boxing) and, when they caught them, cut them in two with their swords.[58]

In China fighting monks were rare; in Japan they became a national institution.[59] Probably this was not because Chinese Buddhists took their vows more seriously than their brethren in Japan, but rather because the Chinese government was too strong and too centralized for any rival military power to exist. However, if monks in China had been allowed to fight—and if they had wanted to—they could have cited many passages from scripture to justify it. These passages are the last and, for our purpose, the most important topic discussed by Demiéville.

The *Mahaparinirvana Sutra* (not the Hinayana, but the Mahayana text by that name) describes how the Buddha in one of his former lives killed some heretical Brahmins, first in order to protect Buddhism from their slanders and second in order to save them from the punishment they would have incurred if they had continued to slander it.[60] The same sutra explained that, when the dharma was in danger, then the person who held back because of the five precepts (including the one against killing) was no follower of the Mahayana: the true Mahayanist (as Chü-tsan pointed out in 1952) ignored the precepts.[61] That explains how the Buddha could say that devotees must be ready to take arms in order to defend the sangha.[62]

The second scriptural justification for killing was the one that we have seen used so often by progressive Buddhists. It was good to kill one man in order to save the lives of two. This was illustrated by the story of the Buddhist traveler whose caravan was about to be waylaid by brigands. A brigand scout, apparently an old friend, recognized him and warned him of the danger ahead. The Buddhist then reasoned as follows: if he told the five hundred people in his caravan what the situation was, they would kill the scout and suffer in hell for doing so. If he did not tell them, they would be killed themselves by the five hundred brigands, whose sufferings would be even greater. Therefore, perpetrating what is surely one of the dirtiest tricks in fable or fiction, the Buddhist killed the scout who had been kind enough to warn him. When the scout failed to return, the brigands did not attack the caravan and so 999 persons benefited from the death of one—and from the tortures that the Buddist himself later had to suffer in hell for the murder he had committed.[63]

The great Mahayana philosopher Asanga added a certain refinement to this kind of "preventive killing" when he said that the bodhisattva should wait until his victim's mind was empty of evil thoughts and then kill him with a feeling of horror and compassion—horror for the sin he was committing and compassion for the sinner whose further sins he would prevent. By killing in this fashion the bodhisattva actually gained merit[64]—a thought that we have seen echoed in Nanchang fifteen centuries later (at note 40).

These justifications for killing were essentially utilitarian and hence well-suited to the needs of progressive Buddhists in the 1950's. Because the third justification was metaphysical, it did not suit their needs. Its essential point was that since there was no soul—no permanent self—there was nothing to be killed. One particularly striking passage tells how Manjusri pretended to run his sword through the Buddha. The latter then congratulated him for realizing that he, the Buddha, was "merely a name, without substance, without reality, a trick of the senses, as empty as an illusion. There was no sin and no sinner. Who could be punished for having killed someone? Between the Buddha and the sword there was non-duality."[65] Even the father of the Pure Land school, the Venerable Hui-yüan, known for his devotion to the compassionate

Buddha Amitabha, accepted this reasoning and commented that if Manjusri had run his sword through the Buddha, he would have *seemed* to do wrong, but actually he would have been following the Way.[66] During the T'ang dynasty there was a famous Zen master who cut a cat in two so that his disciples might see the danger of dualistic thinking.[67] Demiéville notes the paradox that "the Lesser Vehicle, which tends to condemn life, has remained strict in its prohibition of killing; and it is the Greater Vehicle, which extols life, that has ended up by finding excuses for killing and even for its glorification."[68]

When I began to collect material for the present book, I was ignorant of this aspect of the Mahayana tradition and I expected that my Chinese refugee informants, who were all religious conservatives and only too ready to find fault with whatever was happening in the Mainland, would express indignation at the passages quoted in the preceding section. I can report no indignation at all. Only one monk, the Venerable T'an-hsü, said to me: "Although the alternative is your own death, you are not permitted to kill—no, not a poisonous snake either—and if you can save a life, then you must save it even at the cost of your own. Otherwise you violate the dharma." Doctrinaire as this seems and difficult to follow, it is a view that deters human aggressiveness more than what I heard from a disciple of T'ai-hsü, who said: "According to the Mahayana it is guiltless to kill from compassion. If I kill you, the objective is not to kill you, but to save you, because if I do not kill you, you will kill a great many other people, thus causing great suffering and incurring great guilt. By killing you, I prevent you from doing this, so that I can save both you and them. To kill people from compassion in such a way is not wrongdoing." I heard this—or something like it—from most of the refugee monks I talked to about the question.[69]

Thus we see that progressive Buddhists in China, faced with the need to justify killing imperialists and counterrevolutionaries, did not have to step entirely outside their own tradition or to look far for scriptural authority. As historians they were less resourceful in finding precedents than Demiéville,[70] but as students of scripture they located many of the same passages he did[71] and even a few that he did not. They referred to the story of how the Buddha, when incarnated as a lion, killed a poisonous dragon who was insatiably devouring the people of a certain country.[72] They cited King Anala as one of the "model people whose example we should follow." King Anala was "said to have made killing into a divine service . . . The various kinds of severe punishments that he employed to chasten [the wicked] made them realize the majesty of the law and kept them from uncircumspect behavior, so that they reformed and became new people."[73] King Anala was indeed a model who deserved to be cited in the New China. When one entered his palace, one found his subjects having their hands and feet cut off, their eyes gouged out, getting boiled in oil or roasted, so as to "make them follow the example of the bodhisattvas without sliding back into sin."[74] A Sung dynasty monk wrote a picture book about the Buddhist text in which King Anala is described. The poem under his picture contained the lines:

> Swords, halberds, knives and mountains performed
> their miraculous function,
> Boiling water in cauldrons and glowing charcoal
> in braziers displayed their divine merits.
> False speech and evil tongues were here cut off,
> Murder, theft, depravity, and licentiousness were
> here put to a stop.[75]

The scriptural authority to which progressive Buddhists referred most often was the passage describing how the Buddha killed a heretical brigand in order to save five hundred merchants. This is not the story cited from the *Ta fang-pien fo-pao-en ching* by Demiéville, but one that seems even more apt, since the denouement is that *everyone* goes to Heaven—the killer, the victim, and those for whose sake he was killed. Let me offer a tentative translation:

> Again [the Buddha] said to the Bodhisattva Jnanottara: "In the world of long ago people did not know the good and bad fruits of karma and therefore I showed people the evil fate [that bad karma led to].

"A tathagata [a buddha] once said: 'If I, as a dharma king, have not been free from the bad karma arising out of past lives, then how can people like you be free from it?' [Yet] it is said: 'A tathagata is eternally without evil karmic residue.' [This sounds contradictory but] it is like a teacher who is proficient in reading, writing, and arithmetic and who teaches children, wanting them to master these things. There is nothing he does not know or that is an obstacle for him. The children, watching him and listening to him, acquire some learning and gradually get to the root of things. In the same way a tathagata masters all the dharmas so that he knows everything. He [merely] makes a display of evil karmic residue, wanting thereby to have all living creatures realize the pure dharma. Or take a doctor who has studied medicine and understands drugs and herbals. He uses the cure that answers the disease. Because he is able to heal himself [as the Buddha enlightened himself], he is able to heal people at large."

He [the Buddha] then turned to something that he found most admirable. "In the time of the Buddha Dipankara there were once five hundred merchants who went to sea in search of treasure. [Among them] was a miscreant whose evil mind had led him to evil deeds and who had mastered sinister arts of murder and robbery. When he had seen the merchants, he had boarded the boat . . . thinking 'presently I will kill all the merchants and get the treasure for myself alone.' The captain, who came from Jambudvipa in the south, was named Mahakaruna [?]. He now had a dream in which a sea god spoke to him, saying: 'Among the merchants there is a robber who has conceived a most wicked thought. He wants to do away with all the five hundred merchants and get the treasure for himself alone. If he makes this come to pass, his sin will be immeasurable. Why is this? These five hundred merchants have formed an irrevocable resolve to achieve the supreme perfect enlightenment (*anuttara samyak sambodhi*). If they meet harm, their resolve will not be turned aside. Such harm will simply mean that, one by one, following the bodhisattva path, they will attain the supreme perfect enlightenment. However, the robber will fall into hell, and it will be many ages before his sin is

> expiated. Now you, good captain, should resort to the magic of means in order not to let this man go through suffering in hell and so that the merchants may be saved from harm.'
>
> "He reflected for seven days and could think of but one way to deal with the situation. 'The only thing to do is to take his life. If I tell the merchants, they will get angry and certainly kill him, but the result will be that they drop down to an evil plane of existence.' Then he thought to himself: 'If it is I who kill him, I will have to take the consequences of my wrongdoing, but I would prefer this because, even though I suffer in hell for ten thousand kalpas, I shall prevent the merchants from meeting harm and the robber from going to hell.' The captain was so pleased at this righteous solution that he jumped out of his bed with joy."
>
> The Buddha said [to Jnanottara]: "Oh you son of a noble family, in that captain there sprang up great compassion (*mahakaruna*) for the merchants and, applying expedient means, he took the robber's life. When he came to the end of his days, he was reborn in the Twelfth Heaven of *abhasvara.* That Mahakaruna was myself. For more than a thousand kalpas, whenever I have died, I have been reborn in heaven because I applied expedient means in this way. The five hundred merchants who were then on the boat with me were the five hundred buddhas of our present kalpa."[76]

Quaint and obscure as this story may sound, it was utilized by progressive Chinese Buddhists as an important scriptural sanction. Its moral was echoed by Shirob Jaltso, the president of the Chinese Buddhist Association, when he told a reporter in 1957: "I do not advocate killing and do not persuade others to kill. But Buddhism must not be interpreted in a doctrinaire way and under certain circumstances killing is permissible. Should flies be killed? They should when they act as a carrier of contagious diseases . . . Especially destructive are locusts and rats: they come in swarms over our plains. The killing of locusts and rats is compatible with our religion. We kill not only locusts but also any other harmful elements, such as imperialists and counterrevolutionaries. The killing of those that must be killed is not incompatible with the spirit of our religion. If killing the wolf is the taking away of a life, we should think of this when we put him to death. Pity the wolf: his guilt is certainly heavy because he has eaten so many sheep. Let us kill him to alleviate it."[77]

Yet one gets the impression that it was harder to persuade monks and devotees to help kill rats and wolves than counterrevolutionaries. At any rate, there are almost no reports of monks taking part in the campaigns to rid the country of animal pests.[78] Perhaps this was because animals did not represent a threat to the leadership of the Party.

If we accept the reports printed in *Modern Buddhism,* educating Buddhists to help kill was sometimes quite successful. For example in 1951 Chü-tsan chaired a forum in Peking on the movement to suppress counterrevolutionaries. He began by saying to the sixty monks and nuns present: "The government is suppressing counterrevolutionaries so as to preserve revolutionary order. It is a necessary measure. But Buddhism advocates the prohibition of killing. Is there a clash here? Please express your views as fully as possible." One after another the participants in the forum responded. One monk said: "Buddhist sutras say that unless the bad is eliminated, the good cannot come into its own . . . We should help the government by exposing secret agents." Another monk said: "Not only is there no shaking in my heart, but it dances with joy." Another pointed out that Sakyamuni had done his utmost to control heterodoxy. A nun remarked that the nation's resolve to shoot counterrevolutionaries was like coping with spinal meningitis or tuberculosis: unless one killed it quickly, one's own life was in the greatest danger." When the forum was over, Chü-tsan summed up by saying that everyone present had come to the opinion that there was no conflict between the government's actions and "our Buddhist doctrine."[79]

Thus at last Chinese Buddhists led the way for Christians after a century of copying them. In Christianity another decade was to pass before progressive priests, at the end of a century of increasing lip service to the principle of nonviolence (inspired in part by the impact of Buddhism on the West), began talking about a "revolutionary theology" to justify their participation in national liberation movements in Latin America and elsewhere, and about the necessity—in a good cause—to kill.

THIS WORLD ONLY

As we have seen, the justification for killing that Buddhist leaders in the New China did not and could not utilize was the metaphysical one—to look upon the killer and the killed as illusions that disappeared into nonduality. In the new Buddhist thinking the phenomenal world was very real indeed and the dualism of good and evil, progressives and reactionaries, was of the first importance. Idealism, nonduality, and otherworldliness of any kind reduced the enthusiasm of monks and nuns not only for class struggle, but also for socialist construction.

Before 1949 the goals of most Chinese Buddhists could only be called otherworldly. A few sought release from this world through nirvana, but the great majority, since nirvana was too difficult to achieve in our degenerate age, sought it through devotion to the Buddha Amitabha. That is, they hoped that after death they would not have to be reborn in this world of suffering but would be accepted into the Pure Land over which Amitabha presided. From the point of view of the Communist Party, that hope was no less otherworldly than the metaphysics of idealism.[80] The Party wanted Buddhists, like other citizens, to see the phenomenal world as the sole object of valid knowledge, not as illusory; as full of challenge, not inevitable suffering; and as the only paradise that man can expect. Progressive monks explained that "the sole aim of Buddhists is to reach the truth . . . The truth is reached only through [phenomenal] reality . . . Knowledge from perceptions automatically becomes rational knowledge and this leads the masses to reform the world . . . Buddhism certainly does not take the world and human life as objects of cloistered metaphysical study. Rather what it aims at is patriotism."[81] This was because patriotism meant "beautifying the land as an offering to the Buddha."[82] Only by beautifying the land and "promoting the welfare of sentient beings can we win the grace and wisdom we need in order to become buddhas ourselves . . . Looking for it [buddhahood] in any other way is as fruitless as looking for horns on a rabbit. Therefore . . . now that the socialist construction of the motherland is in full swing, every Buddhist must live up to the spirit of the Buddha's teaching . . . and, united with the people of the whole country, actively contribute to the great task of the nation's socialist construction so as to . . . make our motherland into a fair and happy 'Pure Land on earth.' "[83]

It would appear that the ideal of the Western Paradise—also known as the Pure Land or the Land of Bliss—was so powerful that the cadres decided to adapt it rather than discard it. This was all the easier for them to do because sophisticated Buddhist thinkers had long argued that the Western Paradise was not another universe, but here and now, created by our own minds when we began to see the everyday objects around us shining like the jewels described in the *Sukhavativyuha.* As interpreted by progressive Buddhists, however, this ideal was exteriorized and concretized. Old objects did not shine with new radiance: instead, through socialist construction, new objects were created. Their radiance came not because the mind had been freed of all delusions, but because it had surrendered itself to the Party. The result was a curious kind of materialist millennarianism in which Marxist and Pure Land phraseologies were mixed. Here is an example:

> From now on all the people of China, under the leadership of the People's Government, will be unfolding criticism and self-criticism, positive remolding, and vigorous self-renewal. Since all the people will be producing directly through physical labor or indirectly through mental labor, there will be no question about food, clothing, housing, and transport from now on. Everyone will cherish peace and treasure freedom. From now on there will be no wars, no disasters; all the sufferings of human life will be eliminated forever. Is this not to transform the world into a peaceful, happy, free, and beautiful Pure Land? In their writings Buddhists have long liked to speak of wishing to transform the Saha world into the Pure Land. Their wish is the first step towards a Pure Land on

> earth. The [actual] transformation will come by [self] remolding and [socialist] construction . . . The *Vimalakirti-nirdesa Sutra* says: "If you wish to reach the Pure Land, you must make your mind pure. Once the mind is pure, the land becomes pure by itself."[84] This tells us that if we want to transform the world into the Pure Land, then we must start with the "masses of the people" purifying their own minds. The way to purify their minds is by the "remolding," "self-renewal," and "straightening out one's thinking" that have already been mentioned.
>
> But is it not enough to say that we seek for rebirth in the Western Paradise [after death]? Why must we speak of wanting to construct a "Western Paradise on earth"? We have to realize that constructing a "Western Paradise on earth" is a duty that Buddhists cannot escape . . . [because] if they only seek rebirth in the Western Paradise for themselves, feel no concern for the masses, do not vow to transform the world into the Western Paradise, then they are self-seeking, they are spoiling the seed and scorching the sprout—what's the use of it? So Buddhists must feel concern for the masses; they must vow to transform the world into the Western Paradise. That alone is the path of the Mahayana bodhisattva. Fellow Buddhists! Arise with your hearts set on rebirth in the Western Paradise and help the government build a Pure Land here on earth.[85]

The high point in this kind of invocation of the Pure Land ideal came in 1955 when the first Five-Year Plan was being launched. In July 1955 the leaders of the CBA proclaimed that the successful fulfillment of the plan "would mean realization here on earth of the Western Paradise that is spoken of in the sutras."[86] This was frequently reiterated in the year that followed,[87] and as late as 1959, Ho Ch'eng-hsiang, the Director of the Religious Affairs Bureau of the State Council, told students at the Chinese Buddhist Seminary: "All Buddhists have a splendid ideal—to go to the 'Land of Bliss,' where suffering in its many forms does not exist but instead there is every kind of happiness. Today this 'Land of Bliss' is being gradually realized in our great motherland. I hope that during the coming term students will make a really positive effort to advance fearlessly and tirelessly towards the creation of a 'Land of Bliss' here on earth."[88]

If the Communist Party was building the Western Paradise in China, then Mao Tse-tung was presumably taking the role of Amitabha. There were, indeed, occasional attempts to identify Mao with a Buddhist divinity, but they were made mostly by Tibetans.[89] Even after the so-called "cult of Mao" developed during the Cultural Revolution, he was revered less as a buddha than as a Confucian sage.[90] One reason for the hesitation to elevate him to the Buddhist pantheon was that it would have carried Buddho-Marxist syncreticism much too far.

THE DEMISE OF BUDDHO-MARXIST SYNCRETICISM

At the beginning of this chapter we noted Mao's stricture: "Communists may form an anti-imperialist and anti-feudal united front for political action with certain idealists and even with religious followers, but we can never approve of their idealism or religious doctrines."[91] This was an early warning that Buddho-Marxist syncreticism of the kind discussed in this chapter would not, in the long run, be tolerated.[92] Another warning was given in 1958 by Chang Chih-i, then deputy director of the Central Committee's United Front Work Department and a leading theoretician, especially in minority and religious affairs. In one of the first authoritative articles on religious policy to appear in several years, he cited the statement by Mao and wrote: "Any propaganda attempt to twist Marxism to suit religious tenets or serve as a decorative front for religion should also be strongly opposed. Any views tending to stimulate the religious feelings of believers or propaganda purporting to dress up religion in new finery is apt to strengthen their blind adherence to religion and to encourage their erroneous religious views. Such a procedure, practically speaking, means helping religion to conduct deceptive propaganda. Communists should not take such an attitude."[93]

In 1959 Chu Ch'ing, a specialist in border areas, rebuked Party members there who "either think that religious belief and Communism are not contradictory or that religion does not play a bad role at all in a socialist society. These ideas are, of course, completely mistaken . . . The religious view of the world is reactionary, unscientific, anti-socialist, and anti-Communist . . . In a socialist society it is, now as before, completely contrary to the welfare of all the workers, completely contrary to Communist thinking . . . A Communist must be a thoroughgoing atheist."[94] This seems to have been addressed to Tibetan nationality cadres in Tsinghai and Szechwan who were getting restive because of the increasing persecution of lamas, but it presaged a gradual hardening of the government's religious policy in China proper. Buddhists tried to save themselves by offering to modify their doctrines even further,[95] but what was now starting to build up was intolerance of Buddhism even in its most modified form. At the beginning of 1961 a leading theoretical journal published an attack on the Avatamsaka school, saying that its doctrines had been designed to "anesthetize the people" and "lay the theoretical foundation for the corrupt, reactionary, and cruel exploiting system of the T'ang."[96] This attack came less than four years after the *Avatamsaka Sutra* had been liberally cited as an authority for Buddhists to participate in socialist construction.[97]

In 1963 the guns were turned on Confucius but the target was actually larger. "Confucius was, after all, a thinker of the exploiting class, living more than 2,400 years ago. There is no doubt that he did not and could not advance scientific principles of epistemology. These could only evolve from Marxism . . . Neither can we hang the label of Marxist principles under the name of Confucius or any other ancient figure . . . It is likely to lead people down the road of worshiping the ancients blindly . . . To modernize the ideologies of the ancients and to say that there is almost no difference between them and Marxism and that their ideas transcend classes and time will result not in inheriting the valuable things of ancient times, but inevitably in affixing a proletarian label on the thought of the exploiting classes . . . and will inexorably lead people to worship the ancients blindly."[98]

This echoed a piece that had come out in an anti-religious journal in the Soviet Union. (Particularly now, the Chinese were determined to keep up with the Russians in Marxist orthodoxy.) The author of the article, A. N. Kochetov, revealed that "the attempt to demonstrate affinities between Communism and Buddhism, officially encouraged among the Buryats of Soviet Asia between 1926 and 1928, is not now regarded as serviceable." He then "criticized efforts among the surviving lamas to make the best of it by 'polishing up' Buddhism as something which is 'not in contradiction with Communism.' Anything of this nature was doomed to failure."[99] At the end of 1963 Hu Nien-i, in an article entitled "Do Not Modernize the Ideas of the Ancients," made the same point with regard to literature—and yet the implications for religion are not hard to see. Hu criticized people for interpreting "certain ideas of the ancients as being in complete agreement with modern Marxist literary theories, as if the literary viewpoint of Marxism had already been stated by people one or two thousand years ago . . . Divorced from class analysis, there can be no correct explanation of the historical phenomena of literature . . . We must not just take one or two sentences from this or that chapter, pick out the incomplete meanings therein, and develop them at random."[100]

The gradual rise of pressure against Buddho-Marxist syncreticism—and against religious tolerance in any form—will be further discussed when we come to the Cultural Revolution. Neale Hunter recounts how, shortly before the latter, he was being shown around a Buddhist monastery by a woman cadre. When he asked what she thought of it, she replied: "Buddha belongs to the past. He has nothing to do with our society today." Hunter then suggested that the Buddha simply meant someone who understood all things with perfect clarity. "Why, Chairman Mao, if you like, is a kind of buddha," he went on. "Thereupon, she swung around on me, with a look of utter horror on her face, and snapped: 'Chairman Mao and the Buddha have nothing whatever in common!' "[101]

THE ECUMENICAL CONSEQUENCES

The reason why progressive Buddhists in China tried to make their doctrines more relevant to national goals was not simply that they were under pressure to do so from the regime. They had been doing so for thirty years before the Communists took power. Furthermore, in countries where Communism was not a factor and where the state did not interfere in religious affairs, Buddhists had long been making similar efforts. All over Asia there were those who felt that their religion was old-fashioned and ineffective and who wanted to reform it in such a way that it would better serve nationalism and modernization. In the eyes of such Buddhists the most modern political theory—and the one least tainted by the colonial past—was Marxism. Therefore, as far back as 1930, Buddho-Marxist syncreticism had been developing in several Asian countries.

A good example is Burma. Many of the technical terms of Marxism did not exist in Burmese, and Burmese Marxists found that Buddhist terms were both convenient and acceptable for use in translating them. Thus *bhava*—liberation in the sense of nirvana—was applied to social liberation through revolutionary struggle. Lokka Nibban—nirvana on earth—was used to describe the paradise that would be created by socialism in Burma—just as in the case of the Western Paradise being created in China under Mao.

Once terms were borrowed, concepts began to be equated. The Buddhist concept of causally governed cyclical history was equated with dialectical materialism. Capitalism was identified as the root of the three *klesa* (the impediments to spiritual progress—greed, hatred, and ignorance). If capitalism were eliminated, everyone would be able to advance more easily towards nirvana.[102] This was not only because there would be less *klesa,* but also because nirvana required the realization that the self did not exist, and the notion of the self was fostered by private property. The socialist ideal of communal ownership, which gave no fuel to the self, was best exemplified by the sangha, whose monasteries had been owned in common for 2,500 years. Productive labor was a form of meditation. The Burmese Association of Marxist Monks welcomed the advent of socialism as the dawn of the age of Maitreya, the next Buddha, when nirvana would again be easy to attain—just as progressive Buddhists in China considered agricultural collectivization an aid to nirvana and selfless service of the state an exemplification of the bodhisattva path.[103]

There were also parallels to the Chinese reinterpretation of Buddhist history. Gautama was portrayed as a social reformer who lifted the yoke of the Brahmins and their gods from the back of the masses. He was a great rationalist whose view of the world was consistent with science and Marxism.[104] Indeed science and Marxism were only lower, partial truths, whereas Buddhism was higher and all-inclusive: it alone could save the world.[105]

To claim primacy for Buddhism was something that progressive Buddhists in China did not dare to do (although they had done so before 1949),[106] nor could they promise marvels like the return of the Wishing Tree, from whose branches had dropped whatever was needed by primeval man, so that all he had to do was pick it up. (It is hard to tell whether U Nu's prediction that socialism would bring back the Wishing Tree was intended figuratively or literally.)[107] A more important difference was that the Burmese rejected violence. They seem to have made no attempt to find a canonical justification for "killing bad people to help good people." U Nu himself tried to kill as few people as possible, and in the end he turned away from Marxism in the harsh form it had assumed in China and the Soviet Union.[108] Yet he continued to endorse its economic theories and to believe that they were the most appropriate modern economic expression of Buddhist ideals. Furthermore, if Buddhism was as flourishing in China as he had found it to be, then it must be compatible even with the harsher forms of Marxism, and this provided important evidence of its adaptability and of the great future that lay before it. Therefore not only U Nu, but progressive Buddhists in other Asian countries (Japan, Ceylon) were disinclined to accept the rumors that Buddhism was *not* flourishing under Mao.[109] Although most of them deplored violence, they felt that excesses were unavoidable during a great revolution.[110] Although some of them disapproved of the way Chinese monks flouted the Vinaya by putting on plays and marching in parades, others recalled that the Buddha himself had changed the Vinaya rules to suit the circumstances; and they did not see political activities as violating the spirit of his teaching so long as the monks involved did not take sides. For example, to demonstrate against nuclear weapons was permissible since it was nonpartisan and for the benefit of all mankind.[111]

One reason why the Chinese People's Government permitted a decade of Buddho-Marxist syncreticism was, as we have seen, to make Buddhists easier to mobilize. Another reason, I suspect—although I can offer no evidence—was the hope of influencing Buddhists abroad by providing them with a model for the modernization of Buddhist doctrine. How could progressive Buddhists in Southeast Asia fail to be favorably impressed by scriptural slogans like "beautifying the land," "purifying the mind," "subduing demons," and "benefiting all creatures"—so long as they were kept from seeing what these slogans meant in practice. (English language publications distributed to foreign Buddhists were as silent about hating and killing as about productive labor and political study).[112] This was, perhaps, a more pernicious feature of the systematic deception of foreign Buddhists than the guided tours of well restored monasteries with monks chanting the sutras. It was also a more pernicious distortion of what the Buddha taught, comparable to the medieval distortion of Christ's teachings to sanction the burning of heretics and crusades against the pagans. "Subduing demons," which had originally included subduing the demon of hatred was turned into a justification for the hatred of counterrevolutionaries and imperialists—those heretics and pagans of the New China. Compassion, which had originally meant compassion for all without distinction of good and bad, was turned into a justification for killing the bad to save the good—a fallacy that even Confucius had seen through.[113] The criterion for telling the bad from the good was what side they were on, although the Buddha had repeatedly warned against the attachment of partisanship; while the surest way to be on the right side was to surrender one's mind to the Party—the mind that the Buddha had taught should submit to no external authority, mortgage its future to no external goals, but devote itself to seeking out salvation with diligence.

Mao Tse-tung was not the first Chinese ruler under whom Buddhist doctrine was interpreted so as to serve the state. In 581 C.E.

soon after Wen-ti established the Sui dynasty, he issued an edict in which he proclaimed himself a Cakravartin King. "With the armed might of the Cakravartin King We spread the ideals of the ultimately benevolent one [that is, the Buddha]. With a hundred victories and a hundred battles, We promote the practice of the ten Buddhist virtues. Therefore We regard weapons of war as having become like incense and flowers [presented as offerings to the Buddha] and the fields of this visible world as becoming forever identical with the Buddha land."[114] Of course there are many differences between the Sui dynasty's use of Buddhism and its use by the Chinese Communist Party. Wen-ti, unlike Mao, was a genuine devotee who lavishly patronized temples, built pagodas, ordered Buddhist services for the dead, himself took the bodhisattva vows, and accepted the title "Bodhisattva Son of Heaven." Mao did none of this. He simply permitted his underlings to use Buddhism for strictly limited political purposes until he grew impatient with the charade and let it be swept away with the rest of the Four Olds.

Chapter IX

The Laity

Much less is said in this book about the laity than about the sangha. This is not because I consider the sangha to be more important, but because there is more information available about it; and it is easier to treat a precisely defined body of persons with an organizational structure than an entity as hard to define as the Buddhist laity in China. It is so hard to define, in fact, that estimates of its size since 1949 have varied from ten to a hundred million.[1]

Most of the laity was wholly unorganized, belonged to no Buddhist groups, and had made no formal commitment to Buddhism. People simply worshiped in temples or at home; many also carried on various forms of self-cultivation and religious practice, mostly at home, but sometimes in temples. The amount of these different kinds of religious activity fluctuated sharply in the first seventeen years after Liberation. We have already seen how the domestic political atmosphere and the needs of foreign policy affected the sangha. They affected the laity in the same way at the same time.

PATTERNS OF LAY ACTIVITY

From 1949 until September 1952 lay activity sharply contracted. The policy of freedom of religious belief was not yet clear. In the city local cadres criticized people for superstitious feudal thinking if they went to worship at temples.[2] In the countryside they were simply forbidden to worship. This was not because the cadres were being overzealous. It had been ordered "from the higher level."[3]

In the first three quarters of 1952 religious policy crystallized and religious affairs organs began to enforce it locally. At the end of September that year Chinese Buddhists played a useful role at the Peace Conference of Asia and the Pacific Regions. It was probably not a coincidence that on October 12, when Tz'u-chou was installed as abbot of the Nan P'u-t'o Ssu in Amoy, over five thousand Buddhists attended the ceremony—the first large turnout that I know of after Liberation.[4] A month later the decision was announced to set up a national Buddhist association, which Buddhists took as a sign that their rights and institutions were to receive the protection of the government. Overt religious practice was resumed on a scale that had not been seen for three years, and large crowds of the devout gathered to watch the ceremonies presided over by Hsü-yün during his triumphal tour of the east-central provinces. Because he had just represented China at an international conference, helped start the Buddhist association, and had spoken with Chairman Mao himself, the local cadres were reluctant to interfere. A resident of Soochow recalls the day when the venerable old abbot—then believed to be in his one hundred and thirteenth year—was driven from the railroad station to rededicate the tomb of an abbot at Hu-ch'iu that had been destroyed by some over-enthusiastic cadres and rebuilt at government expense. Tens of thousands of people, my informant said, lined the streets along Hsü-yün's route, most of them holding yellow flags. "I saw this with my own eyes"—and indeed twenty thousand onlookers are mentioned in *Modern Buddhism.*[5]

In 1955 with the onset of the campaign against Hu Feng, the trend was reversed. An Indian Buddhist scholar who toured China from April through August saw no lay worshipers at the many temples he visited except in Canton.[6] The next year, with the blooming of the Hundred Flowers and the celebration of Buddha Jayanti, there was another reversal. A hundred thousand persons attended the plenary mass that went on in Shanghai for two weeks (versus the usual seven days for such ceremonies) and included both the Chinese and the Theravada anniversaries of the Buddha.[7]

It must have been the biggest public manifestation of Buddhism since 1949, and nothing on that scale was to take place again.

When the anti-rightist movement was launched in June 1957, overt Buddhist activity became more dangerous than it had been at any time since 1951. Oral informants recall that very few people offered incense at temples in the period 1958-60, partly because they were afraid of being called superstitious and partly because they were simply too busy. During the Great Leap Forward, campaigns and movements followed hectically one upon the other, each with its meetings and activities, until finally there was a campaign to have fewer meetings. Also, because so many temples were now taken over for secular uses, there were fewer places left to worship in; and the incense and paper used in worship became scarcer and more expensive.[8]

The period of relaxation that began in 1960 and faded in 1963 was the last during which people in many places worshiped freely. An informant from Shanghai said that the crowds at temples grew rapidly in the second half of 1961, especially at the Yü-fo Ssu, Ching-an Ssu, and Hung Miao, where there was an enormous turnout on the Buddha's birthday in 1962. "It was as if everybody were pinning his hopes on Kuan-yin," he said. This was also a time when pilgrims were streaming to sacred mountains, and, according to confidential Party documents from Fukien, many new temples were being constructed on the southeast coast. The enthusiasm of the masses for superstitious activities was so great that some of the cadres were themselves taking part in them.[9] Such "spontaneous religiosity" (like "spontaneous capitalism") was one of the reasons for the socialist education campaign that began in 1963 and gradually restored the masses' fear of public worship, which ceased altogether in 1966.

The pattern described above seems to be one of inverse correlation between political movements and religious activity. That is, whenever people grew frightened that public worship would lead to accusations of feudal thinking or worse, they stayed away from Buddhist temples. Yet according to a former cadre of the Canton Religious Affairs Division, the pattern was not so simple. In the latter part of every political movement, he said, overt religious activity actually increased. More people began going to temples in order to consult the bamboo divination slips so as to find out whether they—or any members of their families—would be among the movement's victims and in order to pray that they might not be. Although the persons involved were mostly housewives (perhaps worried about their husbands), there were also university students, which greatly surprised the cadres.[10]

There was not only a temporal but a geographical pattern in lay Buddhist activity. It was immediately noticed by foreign residents of Peking when they visited Shanghai. Most temples in Peking seemed to them like museums; in Shanghai they often found crowds of people offering incense, consulting divination slips, and having Buddhist rites performed for the family dead. Such rites were seen under way at the Yü-fo Ssu and Ching-an Ssu as late as August 1966, just before the Cultural Revolution closed these temples down.[11] One reason for this contrast was that Peking, as the capital, felt the force of government decrees most strongly, whereas Shanghai enjoyed such importance industrially, commercially, and intellectually, that the central government was reluctant to impose conformity that might needlessly "upset things" there.[12] However, a more important reason was to be found in tradition. The whole of east-central China, as far west as Wuhan and as far south as Fukien, was the region where Buddhism had flourished in the century before the Communists took over. There was nothing new in the contrast between Shanghai and Peking.[13]

The third pattern involves age. A young refugee who was the son of a poor urban worker and had been employed by a ministry in Peking until 1962 told me once: "None of the young people in China today have any interest in religion." A man who left Soochow in 1961 said: "Young people find it amusing to see someone kneeling before a statue of the Buddha." A middle-class engineer from Shanghai agreed, but added that in the periods of economic hardship (1960-61) or political struggle (1966-68) many of the young people he knew wondered why their problems were so difficult to solve and tended to think that the reason was bad luck, which made them interested in divination, if not prayer.[14] Even in early 1957, when the atmosphere was relaxed, the prior of

47. Traditional religious activities were freely carried on in the liberal atmosphere of 1956, as can be seen at this Shanghai temple, properly called the Pao-an Ssu-t'u Miao, but usually referred to as the Hung Miao.

a. Two old women (left) burn paper ingots as offerings to the souls of their departed
b. Inside, women offer candles

c. and incense,
d. as do men too.

the Ling-yin Ssu, Hangchow, said that "under the bright radiance of the policy of freedom of religious belief, the number of worshipers coming to the Ling-yin Ssu to do reverence to the Buddha has grown larger every year for several years now; in the past older people were in the majority among them; now younger people are also coming in large numbers. We are terribly happy about this."[15] The evidence here is contradictory, but we should at least be cautious about accepting the idea that all young Chinese simply scoffed at religion after 1949. Public scoffing and private piety have been a Chinese religious syndrome since the Sung dynasty.[16]

TEMPLE WORSHIP

In the old days the laity had gone to temples for many different reasons, but most often to attend funeral rites; to pray for help from the gods; and to celebrate Buddhist festivals. After Liberation they went for exactly the same reasons, except when fear deterred them. In February 1962, for example, a foreigner who dropped in unannounced at the Yü-fo Ssu, Shanghai, found about

48. A service for the dead being performed at the Jade Buddha Monastery (Yü-fo Ssu), Shanghai in 1963.

twenty monks chanting a funeral service. The family of the deceased was present and had brought the children dressed in white gowns. Other visitors saw separate services being performed there in five or six separate alcoves, each with five or six monks. The mourners sat on benches around the sides of the alcove and afterwards had a vegetarian meal.

On March 18, 1962 a foreigner visited the Ling-yin Ssu, Hangchow, and took the photograph reproduced in Fig. 49. It was the 13th of the second lunar month, which was a Sunday but not a Buddhist festival. In and around the temple there were about five thousand people, many of whom had obviously come to pray. They carried yellow pilgrim's bags and went from altar to altar, lighting incense, burning paper money, and prostrating themselves before the Buddha image. At each altar one or two monks stood by to help them. "Both the main halls were scenes of tremendous activity—people bowing three times and then kneeling, and then doing the same thing three times and then going away. There were young men too. But the worshipers were very much country bumpkins. The city people stood around watching." This could be a description of the temple before 1949.[17] A Japanese visitor to Ling-yin—also on a crowded Sunday—noted "many young men and women," some of whom burned incense and worshiped.[18] A European visitor saw groups of pilgrims with yellow bags and students in a holiday mood. "Incense was burning everywhere."[19]

These accounts come from 1960-62, but in other periods too temple worship was impressive when the regime was not discouraging it. In the winter of 1956-57, for example, a European accompanied by his Chinese wife dropped in at the temple of the city god in Shanghai. They found it "humming with activity—people even had to queue up and await their turns to kowtow before the dusty idols. Even the large dark hall on the first floor, where people seldom came in the old days [he had been married in Shanghai in 1937] was crowded. Incense and smoke from the many little fires of paper money made the eyes smart . . . During the first few years after the Liberation [according to an attendant] the temple operated at a loss . . . About a year ago it somehow became known that it was all right to go to the temple again. People came

49. The Ling-yin Ssu, Hangchow, on March 18, 1962.

streaming—on certain festivals the crowds were bigger than they had been before the Liberation."[20]

The biggest Buddhist festival was the Buddha's birthday, celebrated on the 8th of the fourth lunar month.[21] In some places, just as in the old days, lay devotees would join monks and nuns in the major temples to chant sutras and perform the rite known as "bathing the Buddha." A large basin of shallow water was placed on the altar. In the middle of it stood a statuette of the infant Sakyamuni. One by one the devotees would go up and pour a dipperful over his head. Probably only a few did this in Peking,[22] but in Shanghai and Hangchow tens or hundreds of thousands came to watch or take part year after year, and the monks often performed elaborate rites for seven days or more.[23] Outside there were temple fairs, which had been common in many parts of China before 1949.[24]

Besides the Buddha's birthday, devotees continued to celebrate the anniversary of his enlightenment[25] and the birthdays of Kuan-yin and other divinities.[26] The people at large tried to keep up observances on the 15th of the seventh lunar month, the Feast of Hungry Ghosts. A Shanghai resident recalled that during this festival in 1959 flaring candles and sticks of incense could be seen "in every Shanghai street." A book on Canton published the same year mentioned that there it was the occasion for special ceremonies performed by monks and nuns in the larger temples.[27]

The very next year, however, a Canton newspaper printed the following letter just before the festival began.

> Don't Waste Any Rice on the Ullambana Festival
> —Reader's Suggestion—
>
> The Ullambana festival (popularly known as the "Feast of Hungry Ghosts") is approaching. Some superstitious people, after making "offerings" to the gods and ghosts that night, will, in accordance with established custom, dump rice and other offerings on the streets, thereby causing great waste.
>
> It is my opinion that, although the government does not forbid people to worship gods and make offerings to ghosts, yet a wasteful custom can be gradually abolished by means of

50. The Buddha's birthday, on May 8, 1965, is celebrated at the Jade Buddha Monastery (Yü-fo Ssu), Shanghai.
a. A woman devotee pours water over an image of the infant Sakyamuni.

b. Monks and devotees chant together.
c. Outside a crowd mills about. The sign "1965 Buddha's Birthday Celebration" may have been put up on the great shrine-hall for the benefit of the Japanese delegation that was brought to attend.

> propaganda and education. I therefore suggest that, in conjunction with the present movement to increase production and practice economy, propaganda be conducted with fanfare against superstition and, above all, against the waste of food during the Ullambana festival.[28]

Although the government had long been making sporadic attempts to discourage the celebration of Buddhist festivals,[29] the really serious effort was not to begin until 1963, as will be made clear in Chapter XI.

PILGRIMAGES

Because monks found it harder to travel about after Liberation (see Chapter IV), very few of them went on pilgrimage to "famous mountains" as they used to in the old days. Pilgrimages by laymen, however, continued. In 1956 over 37,000 visited Omei Shan and, on the average, stayed three or four days—barely long enough to climb to the summit and back.[30] An informant who was there for a week in August 1957 saw "several thousand people a day."[31] In 1960-62 there were reports of devotees traveling from Shanghai to far-off Wu-t'ai Shan,[32] thronging the island of P'u-t'o Shan,[33] and trudging up Nan-yüeh at the rate of seven to ten thousand a day.[34] Usually such crowds would be seen only during the pilgrimage season, which varied from mountain to mountain and centered on the birthday of the presiding bodhisattva, whom pilgrims came to worship.[35]

Travel to a sacred mountain was tiring and expensive. There was not only the expense of train and bus tickets but of hotels along the way and of room and board in the monasteries of the sacred mountain.[36] Furthermore, pious Buddhists wanted to make a donation at every shrine. One purpose of their long journey was to gain the merit that arose from supporting the sangha in a holy place. Since they had less money than before 1949, they gave less, though probably as much as they could afford.

Not all who visited sacred mountains were pious Buddhists. Some claimed to be traveling for their health or recreation—or as surrogates for elderly relatives who did not feel up to making the trip themselves but to whom the merit from it could be transferred. At Nan-yüeh, for example, Rewi Alley saw one 14-year-old boy carrying, at his grandfather's request, a large iron roof tile, "rather a rare thing today, as the practice is dying out." Such tiles had once been brought in great numbers, with the name of the donor engraved on each. Alley makes no estimate of the ratio of tourists to devotees. He says only that as the crowds walked up the path, "some" chanted sacred texts; and people "often" carried sticks of incense. "Every temple and grotto was paid respects to."[37]

One of the most vivid descriptions of a pilgrimage comes from a European who visited the Baths of Yang Kuei-fei near Sian during the Lantern Festival in 1966. There were big crowds in one of the many temples there, so big that she could not get in. Inside she could hear the music of a percussion orchestra of drums, gongs, and wooden fish, and many of the people outside were mumbling prayers rhythmically and in a low voice. They were mostly extremely poor, wearing only a tattered jacket over the bare skin, with no outer garment, and having dirty towels wrapped around their heads. "Their faces were hard and *abruti.* They stared about, more like animals than human beings—quite different from the townspeople."[38] On other occasions she saw worship going on at several of the famous Buddha caves—something that had seldom been reported even before 1949.[39]

RELIGIOUS PRACTICE

Some lay devotees went to temples not for worship but to take part in some form of religious practice or self-cultivation. We have already seen instances of this in Chapter VII: many of the activities for which government programs provided a screen in 1950-57 were carried on by laymen as well as monks.

The commonest form of practice was to repeat the name of the Buddha Amitabha in a rhythmical chant, for hours on end, so as to dedicate oneself to rebirth in the Western Paradise. Many instances can be cited.[40] The least common practice was Ch'an meditation. Two weeks of it were held at the Yü-fo Ssu, Shanghai, in February 1953. Hsü-yün himself presided and gave an explanation of Ch'an methods every evening.[41] Laymen sat in the meditation hall together with the monks—the only time, so far as I know, that this happened after 1949. Even before 1949 it had been a rare though promising phenomenon.[42]

In 1950 Chü-tsan had proposed that laymen should be admitted to monasteries for permanent residence and allowed to hold all but the highest positions.[43] There is some evidence that this was done: at any rate, men and women devotees were occasionally reported to be living at monasteries and nunneries and to be helping the monks with productive labor.[44] Yet it is hard to tell whether they were permanent residents co-equal with the monks (as Chü-tsan proposed) or whether they were more like the lay guests who had always been permitted to live at monasteries with which they had some connection.

From an orthodox Buddhist point of view one of the most appropriate forms of religious practice in which laymen could participate was the study of the dharma. Already in the Republican period there had been a marked increase in public lecturing on the sutras. Formerly confined to monasteries and attended largely by monks, such lectures had begun to be held in lay Buddhist clubs and, even when they were held in monasteries, to have lay audiences. In either case, the religious character of the occasion was preserved. Dressed in a red robe and seated in lotus position on a high and spacious chair, the dharma master would expound the meaning of a text word by word.[45]

I have seen almost no mention of this kind of lecturing before the first resurgence of Buddhist activities at the end of 1952.[46] In December of that year, in connection with the elaborate plenary mass that was held at the Yü-fo Ssu, Shanghai, seven eminent monks began to expound seven different texts in a lecture series that lasted for nearly seven weeks.[47] Thereafter, in this place and that, lectures were given intermittently,[48] but not on a large scale again until May 1956. Then, again at the Yü-fo Ssu in Shanghai, five eminent monks successively expounded the sutras from 2:00 to 4:00 P.M. every day for two weeks.[49] Among them, as in 1952, were Ying-tz'u, who had been expounding the *Avatamsaka Sutra* for forty years,[50] and Ching-ch'üan, who was already attracting good audiences in 1919.[51]

Reports of sutra lecturing can still be found in 1960 and the practice may have continued until 1965.[52] Yet the authorities had long been uneasy about it. In 1956 the Canton Religious Affairs Division, according to one of its former cadres, became alarmed because Chüeh-ch'eng was attracting such large audiences and told him that his goal had better be to strengthen the belief of the disciples he already had rather than to increase their numbers. If he continued to be "undiscriminating" about who came, he might "give an opportunity to counterrevolutionaries" (to pose as Buddhists). From then on he gave fewer lectures to more select audiences.[53] In 1958 Fukien Buddhists signed a patriotic compact that included the clause: "We guarantee that the occasions when we hold lectures on the sutras and carry on religious activities will not be utilized to spread any reactionary words or deeds that are disadvantageous to the Party and the nation."[54]

The authorities were uneasy about sutra lecturing because it showed that there was still some popular support for Buddhism and also because it could be used to spread anti-materialist ideas. They preferred to see it replaced by inspirational talks in a Buddho-Marxist vein. Some Buddhist leaders were ready to oblige. Thus on the afternoon of August 14, 1958, when the Great Leap Forward was beginning to soar, the Venerable Neng-hai went out to inspect the afforestation work being carried on by some of his monks. During one of their rest breaks he made the following speech:

> "The Venerable Pai-chang Huai-hai spoke of 'the old monk preaching the dharma beside the mattock,' and today we are going to have a taste of this farming Ch'an. Is everyone a bit tired? After this rest break, your fatigue will be gone. The merits of the trees we plant and Bodhi forest we are creating will last forever. Thanks to the leadership of the Party, we are able to contribute a portion of our energy to the socialist construction of our motherland and to adorn the holy place of

the Bodhisattva Manjusri. We are really accomplishing two things at the same time. Even as we show a fearless adventurous spirit by following our compatriots in three years of bitter struggle to transform our mountain area, we are transforming ourselves as individuals into people who love labor. This means we are creating the Pure Land on earth, in which the builders of the socialist paradise will at last realize the dream of 'the beautification of the land and the betterment of sentient beings.' Bodhisattvas! These are not words that we can sit pat on. They can only be realized by going through the phases of faith (*hsin*), release (*chieh*), action (*hsing*) and attainment (*cheng*)—that is, by throwing ourselves into the high tide of the Great Leap Forward in a fearless spirit of daring to think and to act."

After he had finished his explanation, the Venerable Neng-hai ordered his acolytes to give each monk six pieces of fruit candy. All who had heard the Explanation had long since ceased feeling tired. Their spirits were revived and, after eating the fruit candy, they redoubled their efforts. They were all so happy.[55]

LAY SOCIETIES

In Chapter I we saw how local Buddhist associations were set up in many cities and provinces. These were associations of the sangha and laity together. Although the sangha usually predominated, they served all elements in the Buddhist community as intermediaries with the government, transmitting instructions downwards and reports upwards, and mobilizing Buddhists to participate in government programs. Thus their activities were largely secular.

Quite different were the devotional societies whose primary goal was to enable their members—all lay people—to carry on religious practice. They were of two kinds. Small informal groups—like religious "sewing circles"—had existed for centuries. Starting about 1920, much larger and well-organized groups had sprung up in the major cities to carry on not only religious practice, but also social welfare work that exemplified the bodhisattva ideal.[56]

After Liberation the informal groups survived especially in Kiangsu, Chekiang, and Fukien, where the number of lay devotees had been largest.[57] About most of them we know only their names, which indicate that their purpose was usually Pure Land practice.[58] About one we know somewhat more. This was the Mu-kuang Lotus Society in Nantung, Kiangsu. Its seventy-six members got together to recite buddha's name once a month; and on other occasions to celebrate Pure Land festivals. Although the members were all laymen, a monk came to lead them when they wanted to perform complicated rites. They seem to have been winning converts, for on the birthday of Amitabha in 1952, twenty-two persons took the lay initiation. Perhaps the cadres were mollified by the fact that on this occasion prayers were said for world peace, just as on National Day, when the members celebrated the birthday of Yin-kuang (of whom fourteen had been Refuges disciples), they also "studied the significance of Sino-Soviet friendship"—and during their rites for Kuan-yin subscribed to National Construction Bonds.[59]

The members of the Mu-kuang Lotus Society were luckier than their neighbors in She-yang, where the New Fourth Army had won control even before the Japanese withdrawal. In 1951 *Modern Buddhism* published a letter from a devotee there who said that several flourishing devotional groups set up by disciples of Yin-kuang "had all of them been inactive since 1944 because of the progress of the revolution." He asked whether a regular Buddhist group should not be set up now "so that Buddhists might be more clearly distinguished from members of the syncretistic sects." This rather naively mealy-mouthed question drew a harsh reply: "If Buddhists want to draw a clear line of demarcation with syncretistic sects, then the best thing for them to do is to denounce the members of the latter to the government; or persuade them to withdraw and confess . . . Buddhist groups should be organized in connection with the patriotic movement . . . As to [devotional] activity or inactivity, that is their own affair and of no concern to outsiders."[60] It seems clear that even seven years after the Communist occupation of this strongly Buddhist area, small devotional groups did not yet feel free to resume activity.

Things were very different in Peking and Shanghai, where the larger, more formal lay societies were to be found. In these two cities they continued to operate more or less as they had under the Nationalists. It is true that in Peking the emphasis shifted from religious practice to scholarship. For example, the members of the Peking Lay Buddhist Club, who at first had continued to perform Buddhist rites and recite buddha's name six days a month, launched a research program in August 1954. Thereafter as many as a dozen members were hustling back and forth to the National Library in order to get epigraphic and historical documents which they were editing to publish as a collection of Buddhist cultural materials–monastery histories, biographies, the sayings of eminent monks, and so on. To give this work added luster, it was described as something that Chou Shu-chia (the head of the club) had tried unsuccessfully to pursue under the reactionary rule of Kuomintang and which had only become possible in the New China, "thanks to the Communist Party and Chairman Mao!" While promoting scholarly activity, the club decided to discontinue the observance of Buddhist festivals that had no basis in history or doctrine–presumably such festivals as Kuan-yin's birthday. The birthday of the Buddha (a more historical figure) was acceptable, and members celebrated it in May 1956.[61]

The San-shih Study Society, the second major group in Peking, had always emphasized research. Its only nonacademic activity after 1949 appears to have been the provision of Chinese medical treatment for needy patients–a thousand a year in 1953.[62]

In Shanghai things were different. Religious practice and social welfare work were both kept up. The best illustration is the Pure Karma Society, whose headquarters housed a "beautiful shrine hall with an image of Amitabha. There were monks in residence–several dozen perhaps–who practiced the recitation of buddha's name and the chanting of Pure Land sutras." Arrangements for lay members who took part were made by the "religious activities committee," which had subcommittees for recitation, chanting, and the performance of penance services. There was also a study committee that organized seminars for the study of doctrine (by members) and lectures designed to spread the doctrine (presumably among nonmembers who came to listen). Finally there was a clinic that daily treated 100-200 outpatients, who were given a choice of Chinese or Western medicine. So active was the society that it employed a full-time staff of ten, each of whom received 40 JMP a month plus food. Operating expenses were met from the dues paid by the two thousand members, from fees for Buddhist services, and from donations.[63] This description of the Pure Karma Society, provided by a Japanese priest who visited it in 1956, might have been written twenty years earlier. The biggest change was that the membership and the number of resident monks had doubled.[64]

Just as twenty years earlier, there was an overlap with the membership and activities of the other main Buddhist group in the city, the Shanghai Lay Buddhist Club. The same men, Yu Yu-wei and Li Ching-wei, were president and vice-president of both; and the club, like the society, had sections for religious practice, research, propaganda, and social welfare work.[65] By 1962 the two groups may have amalgamated.[66] Other lay Buddhist groups simply dropped out of sight. Many of them are mentioned in the press during the early 1950's but not later on. Presumably they ceased to exist. If this happened in Shanghai, where there was the maximum freedom and support for Buddhism, it happened elsewhere too.

Not only organizations but practices disappeared—for example, the release of living creatures. It had long been a Buddhist tradition for laymen to purchase animals destined for the cage or abattoir and release them as an expression of compassion for all sentient beings. This was done on Buddhist festivals, especially the Hungry Ghosts festival, when the merit created could be transferred to the benefit of the dead. It was a very common practice during the Republican period.[67] After Liberation, however, it was considered to violate the principle that no religious activities should be carried on outside the premises of religious institutions, and I have heard of only one case of it. After the ordination held at the Liu-jung Ssu in 1956, buckets of live fish, shrimp, and turtles were poured into wooden tubs at the monastery (to symbolize the fact that the release took place there) and then the tubs were taken to be dumped into the Pearl River. Because the Hundred Flowers were blooming, the Religious Affairs Division issued a special permit for this and told the police about it so they would not interfere.

Chapter X

The Individual Buddhist

The preceding chapters have dealt with broad institutional changes after 1949 and shown their effect on different categories of Buddhists. We have yet to consider their effect on the individual—the ordinary monk or devotee. What, for example, was a monk's daily schedule? How did he go about coping with practical problems like food and clothing? How had his life goals been altered since 1949? Only unsatisfactory scraps of information are available to answer such questions, and the answers depend in any case on the time and place and on the position of the monk.

Consider, for instance, the abbot of a large monastery. His daily routine was so full that he had few chances to think about life goals. He was expected, whenever possible, to lead the other inmates in production, setting the same kind of example in manual labor that he used to set in religious practice. Depending on what the monastery produced, he had to deal with the cadres in charge of agriculture and forestry or industry and commerce. On the maintenance of buildings, he had to deal with the cadres of the cultural administration; on rations, with the food cadres; on admissions, with the public security cadres; and on all problems, with the cadres of the religious affairs division, who often acted as intermediary when he dealt with other cadres too. In the old days, when life in China had been less bureaucratized and monasteries had been autonomous, their affairs had been simpler to manage.

The abbot was expected to attend all kinds of meetings—meetings of teams and committees (if his monastery had been reorganized as described at the end of Chapter IV); meetings of the political study class, if one were underway; of the local Buddhist association; of the provincial and national associations, if he was a member; and, if he had been elected to a people's council or congress, he had to attend its meetings too. Most of these activities were new and made the burdens of office that much heavier than they had been before 1949, when monks had avoided involvement in secular life. At the same time, many of the abbot's old responsibilities remained, like receiving visitors and leading the monks in whatever religious practice continued.

Even in the old days the internal politics of monasteries had been a "headache": factionalism and rivalry had existed there as elsewhere. Now the factionalism became more threatening to the abbot personally, since a hostile faction could enlist the help of the cadres and invoke sanctions that had been unknown in monastic life before 1949. This is illustrated by what happened at the P'i-lu Ssu, Nanking, in the spring of 1951. The incumbent abbot was impeached by two monks whom he had antagonized when he canceled their right to succeed him. They submitted a written complaint of his "criminal conduct" to the Nanking Buddhist Reform Committee. The accusations sound tendentious, but they were enough to bring about his confession and resignation: "After Liberation he [Ju-ying] succeeded to the abbotship through the use of flattery. At first he seemed to be doing a good job and showed himself able to endure hardship and work hard, but this was a false front . . . and soon his true character began to appear. He was simply a sharp hand at corruption. He would do nothing for most of the monks, kept putting his own cronies and brothers in monastery offices, gave beatings to the workmen and old monks who did the menial work around the monastery, and for no good reason arbitrarily canceled the position of his younger dharma brothers, Yin-t'an and Yung-p'ei, in the dharma lineage." It was on these grounds that Yin-t'an and Yung-p'ei had him denounced as a "devil who had been strangling Buddhism." Soon afterwards he disrobed and returned to lay life.[1]

In the Republican period it had been difficult enough to find men who were willing as well as competent to assume the burdens and worries of the abbotship.[2] Now it became much more so.[3] That is probably one reason why this office changed hands so seldom after 1949. Replacements could not be found.

A MONK'S DAILY LIFE

The life of the ordinary monk was less difficult. If he was lucky enough to be living in a small temple in one of the main cities of central China where there were still lay people who could afford rites for the dead and where the cadres did not put early pressure on the sangha to enter production, then he perhaps lived very much as he used to before Liberation—until 1958. Two or three days a week he would perform a penance service in the afternoon and a "release of burning mouths" in the evening. He would have to do his part in housekeeping (cooking and cleaning), since monks could no longer afford servants, but he had a good deal of free time to spend on study and on gossip—although not on meditation, since this had never been carried on in the ordinary small temple.

If he was enrolled in the meditation hall of one of the few large monasteries where Ch'an was still practiced, then his day might be spent as follows.

A.M.	3:00	Up
	4:00	Morning devotions
	5:00	Breakfast
	6:00	Meditation
	7:30	Farmwork or other productive labor
	11:00	Lunch
	11:30	Meditation
	12:00	More labor
P.M.	4:00	Afternoon devotions
	6:00	Meditation
	9:00	Retire

This was the daily schedule followed at Yün-chü Shan in the seventh lunar month of 1957, according to an informant who then lived there. He explained that attendance varied in the different meditation periods. Only about twenty monks came in the morning, whereas the evening period was attended by almost all of the hundred-odd monks in the monastery. Hsü-yün himself gave an Explanation at 8:00. It was the sole contact that most of them had with him. He was too weak to go to the shrine hall for devotions or to the refectory for meals.[4]

Afternoon devotions were omitted at Yün-chü when the monks had too much work. Work–aside from housekeeping–consisted of growing the monastery's food, and making the bricks, tiles, and tar (*t'an-yu*) that were needed for new buildings. At night they were free to stay up after the retiring hour. This was when some twenty of them who were studying the *Surangama Sutra* every morning under Hsü-yün's guidance used to copy out the notes they had taken.

Schedules similar to the above are reported at a few other monasteries. Perhaps there were half a dozen in the whole of China where meditation was carried on, as here, four or five hours a day (about half as long as before 1949).[5] Elsewhere too the study of sutras was reported. For example, in 1954 at the Po-jo Ssu in Shenyang every day from 7 to 9 A.M. the monks worked on a text entitled "An Explanation of the Main Points about Amitabha" (*Mi-t'o yao-chieh*).[6] In 1957 the monks of the K'ai-yüan Ssu, Chaochow, were holding a weekly class on the *Heart Sutra.*[7] In other places there were occasional series of formal sutra lectures, attended by devotees as well as monks, as described in the last chapter (at notes 46-51).

The daily life of the monk who lived alone, either in a hermitage or a furnished room, was not necessarily so different from that in temples. For example, soon after Liberation the abbot of an urban temple in Hupeh decided to retire to an abandoned nunnery in the mountains. Every morning he chanted the *Diamond Sutra* and every evening he recited buddha's name, but what he spent most of his time on was productive labor–first reclaiming land, then planting it to rice, sesame, and cotton, buying tools, gathering medicinal herbs for supplementary income, and, after selling all his surplus grain to the government, being chosen a leading model for the township. Thus he seems to have been a good citizen first and a hermit second—very different from the eccentrics and iconoclasts who used to play an important role in Chinese life by providing a counterweight to Confucian conformity.[8]

A somewhat sadder case involved the head of a small temple in Kiangsi, which had formerly received sixty bushels of grain a year in farm rents—enough to assure a comfortable life for himself, his eleven disciples, and their two servants. After land reform everyone left but one of his disciples. In 1952 the two of them were ordered to vacate their temple (which obviously had more space than they could use), so that it might be converted into a farm building. Pigs moved in as they moved out. At first they were allowed to take over a smaller temple nearby, left vacant by the death of its owner. There they lived on the equivalent of US$4 a month that the master received as a government subsidy because of his age and frailty. Soon, however, the cadres decided that they wanted this smaller temple too (for a nursing home) and allocated the two monks a single room in a dilapidated house about ten kilometers away—too far for easy contact with friends and former donors. For some reason the subsidy was terminated, and they had to feed themselves by growing vegetables on a plot of land they had been assigned and cutting firewood to sell in the nearest town. Working hard and lacking a shrine hall, they were too demoralized to keep up any religious practice. Neither in dress, housing, nor daily routine did they retain any vestige of the monastic life. Yet they still considered themselves monks and remained vegetarian and celibate.[9]

Before Liberation Buddhist hermits had not only been vegetarian and celibate, but had often practiced austerities like striking a bell day and night, sealing themselves up in a room for three years, keeping silent or facing a wall, copying sutras with their own blood, branding sacred patterns on their skin, and burning off fingers as offerings to the Buddha. I have heard little of such practices since 1949,[10] presumably because they reflected an otherworldly orientation that was being discouraged—and it is certainly true they would not have contributed much to socialist construction.

A MONK'S LIVELIHOOD

Chapter II indicated how, as old sources of income were gradually eliminated, more and more monasteries had to become self-supporting. What this meant for the individual monk differed from city to countryside. In the country monastery he simply ate the food he had helped to grow.[11] In the urban monastery he had to pay for it from his own pocket—and provide ration coupons as well.[12] (Rationing was introduced in 1953, and by the end of 1955 all basic necessities required coupons as well as cash.) In addition, whether he was in city or country, he needed at least a little pocket money to buy clothes, toilet articles, writing materials, and to pay for travel. Before Liberation he had been able to earn this by performing funeral services, for which he received 20-40 percent of what the monastery charged the bereaved; and he often enjoyed other sources of personal income.[13] All these were now eliminated (except for a few lucky monks until 1958), so that it became necessary to find new ways of getting cash. Some got it by working in a monastery coöperative, making towels or gunnysacks. Those in the textile coöperative of the K'ai-fu Ssu, Changsha, averaged 30, 40, and 50 JMP a month in 1959 (1 JMP = US 45¢). They were thus not so well off as the average urban worker (who averaged about 55 JMP), though presumably their needs were simpler. Yet they were not necessarily free to spend everything they earned. "They responded to the nation's call by depositing any money they did not need in the savings bank."[14]

Those who took jobs on their own, like the monks at a monastery in Shenyang (see above at note 6), were probably better off.[15] Others were worse off because they had neither a monastery coöperative nor the opportunity for more than occasional outside work. This was true at Wu-t'ai Shan, for example, where the soil was poor and there was no market for handicrafts. Sometimes the government paid the monks there for doing afforestation work. At one monastery, for example, thirty to forty monks together earned 6,000 JMP planting trees in March through June 1959. Since it was piece work, the stronger and more efficient monks made as much as 4 JMP per day.[16]

When the absence of regular employment led to serious hardship, the government often stepped in to give temporary relief. At Wu-t'ai Shan, for example, in 1952-53 the equivalent of 18,500 JMP was allocated to provide for three hundred hungry monks and lamas (mostly in the spring of 1953 when their supplies were running low).[17] Similarly in Lanchow, when the forty-four nuns of the city were unable to earn enough from rope making to feed themselves in 1952, the government twice gave them the equivalent of 20 JMP apiece.[18] Such temporary relief was reported in several other localities.[19] Sometimes relief was not in the form of cash or grain but abatement of obligations. Some nuns in Shantung, for example, harvested a poor crop in 1953, and the government—like a benevolent landlord of old—reduced their public grain quota by 40 percent.[20]

A different problem was presented by the many monks and nuns in all parts of the country who were unable to support themselves even when jobs were available, because they were disabled or too old and feeble to work. They needed a living allowance throughout the year and every year. On certain conditions (which will be discussed below), such persons received the equivalent of 5-10 JMP per month starting in 1952 or 1953.[21] Out of this they were expected to cover their expenses, including food. It may sound difficult to live on $2 a month, but food was cheap. If, for example, the monthly grain ration was 24 catties and grain cost 0.14 JMP a catty, then an old monk would give the prior of his monastery 3.36 JMP (plus the coupons) and have 1.50-6.50 JMP left over—or even more.[22] Sometimes, of course, he might be under pressure to invest most of what was left over in National Construction Bonds.[23]

The real problem for the elderly was whether they could qualify for a living allowance. In theory they qualified by age and infirmity. Shirob said in 1959: "Monks and nuns in people's communes who have lost their labor capacity are treated in the same way as 'five-guarantee households' [who were guaranteed food, clothing, fuel, care of children, and a decent burial.] Those who have not joined the commune and whose income from productive labor is insufficient to meet their expenses are completely cared for by the People's Government . . . Monks and nuns who are unable to support themselves and who have been subsidized in the past will continue to be subsidized in the future and the subsidy will be steadily increased in accordance with the development of production and the rise in living standards."[24]

In practice, however, according to a former cadre of the Religious Affairs Division in Canton, living allowances were only given to monks and nuns who were patriotic. This was because the money came from a central government appropriation for the support of patriotic groups and activities.[25] If a monk's political thinking was "backward" or he gave no evidence of political thinking at all, he simply did not get an allowance: it did not matter how hungry he was.[26] On the other hand, he was almost sure to get one (even though his need was slight) if he was playing a constructive and patriotic role, as, for example, serving in a representative body or in a people's organization like the local Buddhist association.

An illustration is the case of Chüeh-ch'eng in Canton. He received no allowance until 1956, partly because he was getting adequate donations from the laity, who greatly revered him, but also because he did not have a coöperative attitude towards the Religious Affairs Division—which, on the other hand, did give an allowance to Abbot Ch'i-shan, despite his two wives, since he always did whatever it asked (see Chapter IV at note 70). In 1956 it decided to utilize Chüeh-ch'eng's popularity by having him elected to the CPPCC. He then began to get an allowance of 20 JMP per month (slightly more than Ch'i-shan) and seemed (to the cadres at least) more dependable. Soon afterwards he was made abbot of the Liu-jung Ssu, a council member of the CBA, and president of the preparatory committee of the Canton Municipal Buddhist Association. Besides him, there were 20-25 other monks and nuns in the city who received allowances—5-10 percent of the sangha.[27] Outside Canton, so far as this informant knew, no one was getting an allowance except for a few monks at the Nan-hua Ssu.[28]

Allowances varied according to the time and place and did not always come from the religious affairs office.[29] In a few areas homes for the aged were set up.[30] There was a certain irony in this, since before Liberation every small temple had been a home for the aged–and a real home, because it belonged to the tonsure family. Elderly members of the family could live there in comfort, without responsibilities of any kind, surrounded by their "sons and grandsons," and devote themselves to the religious exercises that were considered the proper preparation for death.[31]

Only occasionally after Liberation do we hear of an elderly monk who could devote himself to religious exercises. In 1955, for example, there was a retired abbot in Szechwan, seventy-nine years old, who was chanting homage to Kuan-yin five thousand times a day and to Amitabha ten thousand times; reciting the Mantra of Great Compassion seven times and the Mantra of Rebirth two hundred times; and making a hundred prostrations to the Buddha.[32] We hear more about elderly monks who spent their day in a very different manner. An example is I-hui, a resident of the Asoka Monastery. When the late autumn harvest was being collected in 1952, he "carried bags of rice as if he were flying. When asked to rest, he said, 'I am not old at all.' The masses wrote the following song to praise him: 'The old monk will not give way. Lugging or drying the rice, he struggles to be up ahead. He is sixty-eight, but he works harder than the rest of us. He may be old in years, but his heart is young. He wants to vie with everyone to carry off the honors. It is good to have the leadership of the Communist Party; the kindness of Chairman Mao is unforgettable. Even the old have become young.' "[33] Especially in the Great Leap Forward, when miracles of labor by elderly monks became commonplace,[34] Shirob's picture of the elderly being "completely cared for" seems misleading.[35]

Regarding the final chapter of the monk's career–illness and death–I have seen information on only one locality. In Changsha any member of the sangha who needed medical treatment could apply to the local Buddhist association for a grant to cover the cost. After his death the association guaranteed that at one of the monasteries in the city there would be a recitation of buddha's name by all the monks and a "release of burning mouths," the merit to be transferred to his benefit. If he left no savings, the association would cover the cost of his burial.[36]

THE INDIVIDUAL DEVOTEE

The ordinary lay devotee, who played no role in a Buddhist association and took part in no other activity that would get his name into print, is someone about whom we know even less than about the ordinary monk. For information I have had to depend even more on the recollections of refugees—like a Shanghai woman who came to Hong Kong late in 1962 and whom I got to know well because she kept house for me. She recalled how she had stopped in at the Jade Buddha Monastery one day in 1961. She had never felt any special interest in Buddhism, but she went upstairs over the great shrine hall to view the image of the Sleeping Buddha. "When I saw how happy his face looked," she said, "I just wanted to stay there all the time." She began to go on the 1st and 15th of the lunar month to offer incense and pray for success in moving her family to Hong Kong—her main concern at that time. Although her husband had a good job, she often could not find enough food in the shops, and she hated to listen to her children crying from hunger after being put to bed. (They were not starving, just hungry.) She said that Shanghai temples were then crowded with other people praying for help with livelihood problems, just as earlier they had come to pray because they had gotten into some political difficulty.[37]

How many people felt drawn to Buddhism for such reasons we cannot tell. There is no doubt, however, that converts had been made, especially in the early years. We read of formal initiations where people "took refuge in the Three Jewels" (the Buddha, dharma, and sangha). This betokened their commitment to Buddhism as opposed other religions—and, perhaps, as opposed to Marxism. When two hundred persons were initiated in Sian during the summer of 1950, Shirob Jaltso told them: "Now that you have taken the Three Refuges, you must make a *special* effort to support the nation and serve the people."[38] During the first two years after it was announced that a national Buddhist association would be established, when its establishment was still interpreted as a sign of toleration for Buddhism, large numbers of people took the Refuges. Thousands did so during Hsü-yün's triumphal tour of central China in 1953. (This at any rate, is what we learn from unofficial sources.[39] Considerably smaller numbers are mentioned in the Mainland press.[40]) No breakdown as to the sex of converts is given in any of these reports, but already during the Republican period there had been far more women than men.[41] Under the Communists it must have taken a lot of courage for a man to commit himself to Buddhism in this public way. After mid-1957 it became risky for everybody.[42]

There were not only deterrents against public commitment to Buddhism but also against private religious practice. We have already seen the ways in which during certain periods people were discouraged from going to temples and taking part in the activities of lay Buddhist clubs. Yet even what they did in their own homes could cause them difficulties. In 1951 a lay reader wrote to *Modern Buddhism* asking how, since he worked in a government office, he could practice self-cultivation, such as reciting buddha's name and chanting the Mantra of Great Compassion. The reply began by saying that *Modern Buddhism* was constantly being asked by people what they ought to do if their interest in Buddhism was not tolerated in the government offices where they worked. The answer was that if they did as well as cadres and Party members in serving the people, then their interest in Buddhism would be accepted. However, if by self-cultivation they meant personal purity and aloofness, then they were merely *talking* about compassion while in their hearts they looked down on everyone and did not care about the happiness of anyone. "If this is the kind of self-cultivation it advocates, then Buddhism must be completely eliminated because its so-called self-cultivation comes down to the approach of the I-kuan Tao." Buddhists had to realize that "their first duty is to identify their interests with those of all living creatures [that is, the masses]. To recite buddha's name and chant mantras is a secondary duty for the individual."[43]

In 1958 the regime stepped up the pressure against religious practice at home. This is illustrated by the case of a peasant in Hupeh who for many years had worshiped and made offerings to a bodhisattva image and was still burning incense and prostrating himself before it. People called him "the champion of superstition." In August 1958 his village took part in a tool renovation campaign where the masses were called on to contribute metal for the manufacture of ball-bearings. The old man who had previously maintained that "without the help of the gods no one could walk a step," began to experience a violent ideological struggle. After considering how life had improved since Liberation and how he ought to obey the Party and smash superstition, he decided to contribute his image so that its thirty catties of bronze could be used to improve farm tools. As he was taking it off its dais, he sang a song:

> God, O God, be not angry,
> Step down as quickly as you can.
> I revered you for a long time,
> And yet you changed nothing and our farms were
> still plowed by the ox.
> Mechanization is now being carried out,
> I request you to transform yourself.[44]

Instances like this were seldom reported in the press, but oral informants confirm the trend. My housekeeper had a friend who was a devout Buddhist in her fifties. Her husband objected to her having many sacred images at home and wearing a devotee's black gown when she chanted before them. In or about 1961 she took one of them to the Jade Buddha Monastery, where it was placed in a room with other statues, some also owned by laymen. She paid the attendant of this room the equivalent of US$1.75 a month to burn three sticks of incense in front of it each morning. To purchase the incense she provided him with additional money. "She was rich and could afford it," said my housekeeper. On her altar at home she still kept one small Burmese buddha. Every morning she would get up before breakfast, take a bath (they had an electric hot-water heater), offer incense, and recite a sutra. On the 1st and 15th of the lunar month she would go to the monastery, put on her devotee's gown, and offer flowers and incense to her image there.

This was possible in 1960-62, the period of relaxation, but it might have gotten her into difficulties in 1958-59. Another informant told me that his aunt in Shanghai had felt free to go to a Buddhist temple in order to burn incense and candles only through 1957. After the anti-rightist movement intensified, she became afraid to worship in public and did it in her kitchen instead. In 1958 she would draw the curtains of the kitchen windows and light incense before the images there (which had been moved from the front part of the house soon after Liberation, in order to avoid arousing comment). After incense began to get scarce in 1963, she would simply sit at the kitchen table in silent prayer. She would appear to be looking out the window or at a wall, and no one except her own family would know that she was concentrating on the Buddha.[45]

THE BUDDHIST CAREER

So far this chapter has consisted of little more than random scenes from the lives of a few individuals. What about their lives as a whole—what sort of a pattern can we discern? Some Buddhists were important enough to be frequently mentioned by name in the Mainland press. They seem to fall easily into three types: conservatives, opportunists, and progressives. This, however, does not always enable us to say how they fared in the New China. Some conservative monks like Hsü-yün got into trouble because of their refusal to compromise, whereas others were discreet or lucky enough so that they did not need to compromise (like Tan-yün). Opportunists (from Wei-fang to Ch'i-shan) seldom had real difficulties but did not do much better than hold their own. It was the progressives who got ahead. Some had already been prominent before Liberation and it was quite natural for them to take a leading role in Buddhist circles now: examples are Chü-tsan and Shih Ming-k'o. Other progressives had been unknown and first made their name after 1949 (like K'uan-neng). A few people (Chüeh-ch'eng, for instance) resist classification and seem to partake of the character of several different types.

The careers of the individuals whose names have just been mentioned can be traced by means of the index. Let us turn now to some about whom less has been said so far. Among conservatives the most eminent monk in China next to Hsü-yün—and the one who, on his death, succeeded him as honorary president of the CBA—was the Venerable Ying-tz'u. After 1949 he stayed in Shanghai, where he was not exposed to the tumult of land reform and the militance of rural cadres. He was never struggled against or beaten like Hsü-yün. Yet he seems to have made no compromise with the new times and simply to have continued his lifework of teaching Avatamsaka doctrine.

Ying-tz'u was born in 1873 and brought up in Kiangsu, where his family was in the salt business. In 1898, apparently because they went bankrupt, he entered the sangha in Nanking and in 1902 he was ordained at the T'ien-t'ung Ssu under the illustrious Eight Fingers.[46] He enrolled in the meditation hall there for a year or so. Then he moved to another of the four model meditation centers of China, the T'ien-ning Ssu in Changchow, where he received the dharma in 1906. This entitled him to become its abbot—a high honor, since it was the largest monastery in the country. However, he refused to accept the post, which he considered an impediment to spiritual progress, and instead devoted his life to teaching.[47] The text in which he specialized was the *Avatamsaka Sutra.* He used to lecture on it all over China, not only in Kiangsu and Chekiang, but as far off as Wu-t'ai Shan—wherever he was invited to go. For six years in the 1930's he spent two periods each year back at the T'ien-t'ung Ssu. In the winter he would attend the seven weeks of intensive meditation (he believed that study and practice should go hand in hand) and in the summer he would lecture on the *Avatamsaka Sutra* during the three months of the summer retreat.

When Chao P'u-chu first attempted to start a new Buddhist association in 1951, Ying-tz'u was among the eighteen eminent monks proposed as its sponsors. Naturally he became a council member of the CBA when it was founded in 1953, and the next year, when a municipal Buddhist association was set up in Shanghai, he was elected its honorary chairman. In 1955 he was elevated to the CBA's standing committee, in 1957 to be a vice-president, and in 1962 to be one of the three honorary presidents—despite the attack on the Avatamsaka school that had begun the year before (p. 359).

Throughout this period he had been living in a small temple in Shanghai along with twenty to thirty monks and nuns, presumably his pupils. On at least one occasion he delivered a public lecture; a two-page spread in *Buddhists in China* shows him expounding the *Avatamsaka Sutra* on October 14, 1955, at the Jade Buddha Monastery. The English-language caption calls him "a master of the Hua-yen [Avatamsaka] school."[48] He wears the red robe of the dharma master, sits in lotus position on a high seat, and in every other respect seems to have given the lecture in the most traditional manner (rather than in the modern, less formal manner that had been introduced by T'ai-hsü during the Republican period).

In 1962 Ying-tz'u was listed as one of the 824 delegates to the Shanghai Municipal People's Congress. Apparently he was picked because of his eminence as a Buddhist.[49] At any rate it cannot have been because he had shown a high degree of political activism or awareness. There is no report of his speaking at any of the CBA meetings he attended. The closest he seems to have come to activism was to permit his name to be used as coauthor of an article on Buddhism in Shanghai during the Great Leap Forward.[50] All in all, his performance and treatment since 1949 showed that if a monk were eminent and circumspect enough, he could continue to play a prominent role without compromising his religious ideals.

The same seems to have been possible for a few laymen. An example is Chou Shu-chia who was already a prominent Buddhist scholar and devotee in the 1930's and continued to be until his death in 1970 at the age of 71. A lecturer at Peking University, he had published a history of Buddhism (1933), a study of Dharmalaksana philosophy (1934), and of Buddhist logic (1934). He knew fluent German if not English and collaborated on a translation of the *Yao-shih ching* that is still in print.[51] Apparently in the late 1930's he founded and headed the Chinese Buddhist Academy, where in 1941, for example, two hundred young monks were enrolled for religious studies. He was also an officer of several lay Buddhist societies and a patron of two or three monasteries.[52] He used his large private means (derived from his family's shipping line) for the support of all these organizations.

Within a year after the founding of the People's Government

51. Chou Shu-chia (far left) photographed with a Japanese Tendai delegation in front of the stupa of Yang Jen-shan. Nanking 1965.

Chou Shu-chia joined in the task of making a place for Buddhism in the New China. He helped start *Modern Buddhism* and served on its standing and editorial committees. A sponsor of the CBA, he was elected deputy secretary-general at its inaugural meeting. Similarly, when the Chinese Buddhist Seminary was set up, he became a deputy principal. Very few Buddhist visitors came to Peking between 1950 and 1966 without meeting him.[53] Tall and serious, courtly and with presence of mind, he made a good impression on foreigners. In 1955 he was among those who escorted the Buddha's Tooth to Burma. In 1959, in his dual capacity as vice-president of both the CBA and the China-Nepal Friendship Association, he accompanied the Nepalese delegation on its tour of China.[54] He also served in a wide variety of political fronts: the Sino-Soviet Friendship Association, the Asian Solidarity Committee, the Chinese People's Committee to Support Egypt's Resistance to Aggression, and the Chinese People's Association for Cultural Relations with Foreign Countries. Yet I have been unable to find attributed to him a single political pronouncement, either at public meetings or in the pages of *Modern Buddhism.*[55] I have questioned some of the foreign visitors whom he guided on tours of China and they too cannot remember his discussing anything political. He appears to have avoided politics as conscientiously as Chao P'u-ch'u embraced them. Perhaps the regime considered it useful to have at least a few Buddhist devotees who confined their activities to Buddhism. Another one was Hsü Sen-yü.[56]

Let us go now to the opposite end of the scale and look at a progressive who made his name under Mao: the Reverend Ming-chen. Born in Hupeh about 1900, he had been in the first graduating class of T'ai-hsü's Wuchang Seminary in 1925. In the 1930's he was teaching at a seminary at Nan-yüeh, the sacred mountain in Hunan. He first came to public notice just after Liberation, when he wrote Chü-tsan about the burning of the Shang-feng Ssu, one of the principal monasteries there. Ming-chen placed the blame not on the cadres who had apparently set fire to it, but on "Buddhism's feudal past" (Chapter V at note 72). The next year *Modern Buddhism* published his report on land reform at Nan-yüeh, replete with telling details on the difficulties then being faced by

52. In 1957 Hsü Sen-yü, a prominent Shanghai devotee helps Wei-fang, abbot of the Jade Buddha Monastery, entertain a Japanese Buddhist delegation.

the monks, but ending with warm praise for the protection given to Buddhism by the cadres (Chapter II at note 26). This show of political awareness apparently qualified him for membership on the first CBA council, to which he was elected in 1953. He was elevated to the standing committee in 1955 and became deputy secretary-general in 1962. By 1964 he had taken charge of administration at the Chinese Buddhist Seminary. Throughout his steady rise he had kept giving evidence of his progressive stand. In 1954, for example, when he was presiding at a meeting to promote the sale of National Construction Bonds, he compared their purchase to following the bodhisattva path (Chapter VIII at note 11). In 1958 he wrote an article warning against indifference to class distinctions and insisting on the importance of class struggle (Chapter VIII at note 29). In 1959 as chairman of the Changsha Buddhist

Association, he spoke in support of the government's measures to suppress the Tibetan rebellion.[57] In 1964 he addressed a meeting of religious circles in Peking and vowed support of the Vietnamese people's struggle against aggression.[58] By this time he was living in Peking and belonged to the inner circle of progressive Buddhist leaders.

The career of another progressive, Ch'en Ming-shu, followed the reverse pattern. He began as one of the most influential Buddhist laymen in China and ended up with less than no influence at all. The details of his life as a general, administrator, and politician can be found in any good biographical dictionary.[59] He was a nineteen-year-old member of the T'ung-meng Hui when the revolution broke out in 1911. He led detachments of the Northern Expedition in 1927, served as governor of Kwangtung 1928-31, fought the Communists in Kiangsi in 1931 and the Japanese in Shanghai in 1932, broke with Chiang Kai-shek by launching the Fukien revolt in 1933, and, after it failed, retired from active political life. Throughout the shifting alliances of the twenties and thirties he remained loyal to Li Chi-shen and helped him to set up what was to become the Kuomintang Revolutionary Committee. After Li was chosen a vice-chairman of the Chinese People's Republic in 1949, Ch'en held a series of important posts, especially in the central-south region, which included his native Kwangtung.

Ch'en had been a Buddhist devotee for many years, as had Li and several of the other men with whom he was associated.[60] It was only natural that he should want to make a place for Buddhism in the New China. We have seen how he helped found *Modern Buddhism* and served for three years as its publisher. Although he obviously hoped to have the sangha cleansed and improved (better monks and better trained), it is not clear that he regarded the socialization of monasteries as anything but a disagreeable necessity. He made a not too veiled protest against the way monks were being treated by the cadres[61] and is said to have been among those who intervened when Hsü-yün was beaten. In a pamphlet published in 1950, he ostensibly called for making Buddhism into something that would exemplify dialectical materialism, but this may only have been part of his effort to help it survive. His real feelings are hard to guess. Perhaps he was not so progressive after all. A man of his age and formation would find it hard to discard the transcendental elements in Buddhism and would probably not want to see the monastery turned into just another production team.

After 1953 he was excluded from Buddhist activities. The official explanation was that he had tried to use Buddhism as a base for building his own political power.[62] The real reason may have been that he had voiced his disappointment at the treatment Buddhism was getting from the regime, to which he had originally looked with such hope—like many other bourgeois idealists.

After being harshly struggled against as a rightist in 1957, he was nominally rehabilitated in 1963 and died in 1965. There is no mention of any of his Buddhist friends attending his funeral, nor of monks performing Buddhist rites for his soul. If there are such things as restless ghosts, Ch'en Ming-shu may be one.

Some Buddhist progressives had been followers of T'ai-hsü, whose impatience with the old order may have prepared them to accept the new.[63] Others had started out hoping to compromise with the new in order to conserve what was best of the old. Chao P'u-ch'u himself, I think, belonged to this latter category. He ended up a tragic figure, who had made himself into an instrument for uses that would probably not have been acceptable to him before Liberation. At any rate this was the way he appeared to some who had known him in the 1930's, when he was a benevolent young man who did much to help the poor and homeless in Shanghai. When I met him myself at a conference in 1961, I noticed that sometimes he would forget to keep his face arranged in the rixus of official friendliness and then his expression would change to one of anger (because the conference was going badly for him) or desolation. I have seen this desolate look again in photographs snapped later in the sixties. My guess is that his hospitalization with heart trouble in 1966 at the age of fifty-eight was caused by worry and internal conflict.[64] He was worried by his failure to achieve any conspicuous success in people's diplomacy but more deeply troubled, I suspect, by the thought that in his hope to save Buddhism he had betrayed it.

Throughout the Buddhist world today—and in Christianity too—there are people who do not wish to give up their religious identity yet who feel that their religions are largely outdated and irrelevant. They want to go on thinking of themselves as Buddhists or Christians but at the same time to be part of the future, which seems to them to belong to the Left. Hence they discount the plans of their leftist allies to extirpate religion and they even find ways to think of the latter as better Buddhists or Christians than they are themselves. In the hope of finding religious renewal in a political movement, they compromise more and more of their essential religious principles. How they may end up if the movement succeeds is illustrated, perhaps, by the fate of men like Ch'en Ming-shu and Chao P'u-ch'u.

Chapter XI

The Cultural Revolution and After

Events in China since 1949 have often had a dreamlike disconnectedness. When the first group of Americans visited Peking in the spring of 1971, they found an orderly city of pleasant people. It was hard to connect it with the wild events of the Cultural Revolution five years earlier when gangs of angry youths were looting houses and dragging their elderly residents out into the street to be publicly humiliated. It was a little like visiting the scene of a great earthquake and finding no trace. Similarly, foreigners in 1953 who saw smiling peasants in a peaceful countryside found it hard to imagine them screaming for the landlords' blood at public executions two years before; and visitors in 1960 saw little to suggest the millennial enthusiasm of the Great Leap Forward except for an occasional backyard furnace forgotten among the weeds.

The converse has also been true. When the Cultural Revolution broke out, many China specialists abroad found it hard to connect with what they had been reading in the Mainland press. Only when they went back over their reading again did they discern a pattern that had not been apparent to them at the time and that made the Cultural Revolution understandable, if not inevitable. This was true in my own case. When Buddhism disappeared from sight in August 1966, I was surprised at the sudden write-off of such a large investment in the restoration of temples and friendship with Buddhists abroad. Yet, when I re-examined the record, I could see that its disappearance had not really been so sudden. It culminated a process that had begun in 1962. Rather than being dreamlike, the disconnectedness was theatrical: it was as if I had been looking at a series of tableaux without noting the small signs that the author and the producer were arguing backstage.

What do I mean by "the disappearance of Buddhism"? The plan of this chapter is first to answer that question–to say what happened in the Cultural Revolution–and then to examine the process that led up to it over the preceding four years.[1]

THE DISAPPEARANCE OF BUDDHISM

On August 3, 1966, a brief dispatch was included in the English service of the New China News Agency. That day, it said, the CBA had given a banquet in honor of a group of visiting Japanese Buddhists, members of the Shingon sect, led by Onozuka Juncho. The day before they had joined in performing a religious ceremony at the Kuang-chi Ssu; and the day after, August 4, they were received by Kuo Mo-jo.[2]

So far as I have been able to discover, these were the last items of news on Buddhism to be printed on the Mainland press. Not only was there was no further mention of foreign Buddhist delegations (including this one, which was headed for Sian when it dropped out of sight), but nothing more was heard of the CBA or of the activities of monks and lay devotees.[3] What makes this remarkable is that the Cultural Revolution began two weeks later with the campaign against the Four Olds–old ideas, old culture, old customs, and old habits–and Buddhism was an obvious target. Yet we only learn about the attacks on it from foreign observers and a few radio broadcasts. Nothing appeared in the press. For example, in "A Hundred Examples of Smashing the Old and Establishing the New," posted at a Peking middle school on September 1, 1966, all sorts of things to be smashed are listed–even finger-guessing and Chinese boxing–but nothing is said about temples, monks, and festivals.[4] Perhaps the closest thing to a specific allusion to Buddhism was printed in Canton, where the Four Olds were said to include "altars for worshiping the gods," rites for the dead, and "feudal festivals," and where a shop that sold religious goods was forced to shut down.[5]

The consensus of foreign observers was that by the end of September 1966 every Buddhist monastery—and every temple, church, and mosque—in China's metropolitan areas had closed.[6] Of course monasteries here and there had been closing for centuries as they fell into disuse; and for fifty years more and more of them had been subject to government seizure and confiscation. However, this was the first time since 845 C.E. that nearly all the monasteries in China ceased to function. Some were simply closed; some also had their walls covered with revolutionary slogans;[7] some were stripped of images and religious paraphernalia;[8] some were converted into offices, factories, apartments, or barracks for Red Guards.[9]

Foreign observers saw some of this going on. For example, at the Ling-yin Ssu, Hangchow, a Canadian journalist watched a Red Guard, with a bucket of paste and brush in hand, slapping revolutionary posters over a Buddhist image (Fig. 53). His companions had already put up a slogan on the temple facade (Fig. 54). The

53. On August 27, 1966 at the Ling-yin Ssu, Hangchow, paper slogans were pasted over an image of Maitreya, the buddha of the future. The right-hand slogan reads: "Long live the dictatorship of the proletariat." On the face of the image is "Smash the old world."

54. A few days later the monastery was locked and its doors sealed. Over the plaque of the great shrine-hall (the "Ta-hsiung Pao-tien") was posted: "Long live the people." Compare Fig. 48.

journalist asked the abbot what he thought and he managed to say: "This is probably a very good thing." Because the Ling-yin Ssu was a cultural monument, the Red Guards did little serious damage there. They "made only the symbolic gesture of breaking one bench and throwing a small Buddha to the ground."[10]

The following year a survey of the state of Buddhist monasteries was attempted by Tokuda Myohon, one of the leading monks of the Vinaya sect in Japan, who went to China in August 1967 as member of an educational delegation. Originally he had planned to be in Sian for the 1,300th anniversary of a Vinaya patriarch, but on the night he reached Peking he was told that his itinerary had been changed to Tsinan and Shanghai. Nonetheless, whenever he got the chance, he slipped away from his guides to look for traces of Buddhism. In Shanghai he visited the Fa-tsang Ssu at 5 A.M. on August 19. He found that this important temple, which had been still a center of considerable religious activity in the early 1960's, was converted into an apartment house. Its lecture hall, where eminent monks used to expound sutras to large audiences, was partitioned into living quarters and the images had been removed. Next he went to the Yü-fo Ssu, which had been headquarters of the Shanghai Buddhist Association. He was not allowed to enter. He asked to worship its famous Jade Buddha and was told that it was no longer there.[11] People said that only one monk, the abbot, remained in residence (in contrast to the fifty who had lived there before the Cultural Revolution and the three hundred before 1949), but Tokuda could not meet him because he had been "summoned to a government office." Later, when he asked a taxi driver to take him to the Ching-an Ssu (the famous Bubbling Well Monastery), the driver said: "It is not there any longer."[12]

In Peking he went alone to the Kuang-chi Ssu, the headquarters of the national Buddhist association. He found it closed to visitors, its monks apparently expelled, posters and cartoons covering its walls. A lamasery near the palace had been converted into a museum on the evils of rent collection. He saw wall posters accusing Liu Shao-ch'i and his followers of "treating religion sympathetically" as part of their revisionist program, which had included the plan for a memorial hall to honor Chien-chen (Chapter V at note

55. The Jade Buddha of the Yü-fo Ssu, Shanghai in 1962. It had been brought from Burma in 1882.

37). Kuo Mo-jo told the delegation that "religion is the dog of capitalism and an opiate . . . Those who believe in a god carry on aggressive wars." Tokuda left China very much disheartened about the future of Buddhism.[13]

One of the things he could not find out was what had happened to the monks and nuns who used to live in the temples that had been shut down. A clue is provided by a poster that a foreign resident saw at the gate of the Kuang-chi Ssu on August 26, 1966. It announced that the personnel of all four "foreign religions"—the Catholic and Protestant churches, Buddhism, and Islam—must hand over all their records to the public security authorities and return to their native villages. Beginning with a rough "All you rotten eggs . . . " it was signed simply "Red Guards." It is significant that it was seen posted at the gate of this monastery, the CBA headquarters. A year later when Tokuda Myohon peered through the gates, he could see many youngsters hanging about the monks' living quarters. Presumably they housed Red Guards. Considering the fact that thirteen million young Chinese came to Peking in the autumn of 1966 and millions more moved about between other cities (in order to experience the hardships of the Long March), it would be not surprising if all urban monasteries had been converted into Red Guard dormitories. Yet informants found most of them closed rather than occupied.

According to an informant who left in 1968, Buddhist monks and nuns were ordered to "abandon superstition," shed their robes, let their hair grow, eat meat, marry, and enter production. Not all complied at once. For example, the fifty-year-old abbot of a monastery in Fukien, after resisting until 1968, finally married a woman devotee and resigned his post to move to Shanghai.[14] On the other hand, a Shanghai nun who changed into lay dress and went to work in a factory in 1967, still had not married or started to eat meat as of early the next year. All I have learned about forced secularization comes from refugees and visitors, but it is to some extent confirmed by a statement attributed to Chiang Ch'ing: "There are large numbers of monks and nuns in Chekiang streets. Let the nuns get married."[15]

Western journals have printed rather lurid reports of the physical destruction of Buddhist art and architecture during the Cultural Revolution. I am inclined to think it was rare. The contents of a large Taoist temple in Soochow were burned,[16] but I have heard of nothing comparable happening at a Buddhist monastery. On August 24, 1966, Buddhist images not in a monastery but at the Central School of Fine Arts were smashed by students who considered them to be "freaks and monsters."[17] Outdoor rock-carvings were defaced in Hangchow: many bodhisattvas lost their heads or noses. In Shanghai the stone lions of the Ching-an Ssu were reported to have been smashed, but before many objects *inside* the monastery were damaged, the PLA arrived to expel the Red Guards and lock it up. One reason for the locking up of monasteries and the posting of "no entry" signs may have been

56. Buddhist images in Hangchow that had had their heads knocked off during the Cultural Revolution.

precisely to avert damage. At the end of 1966 there were reports of a deliberate effort to preserve religious images by moving them to warehouses; and trucks loaded with them were seen in the streets of Peking.[18]

The policy of protection did not, however, extend to articles of little artistic value. It cannot be doubted that during the campaign against the Four Olds, many popular images were destroyed. On August 25, 1966, a European tourist saw an exhibit of "superstitious objects" in a village near Peking. Buddha images, each splashed with a black cross, were laid out on trestles beside broken frescoes and torn books, waiting to be publicly destroyed.[19] In Hunan, Kwangsi, and elsewhere, after buddha images had been destroyed, they were replaced by statues of Chairman Mao.[20] Shanghai had a famous temple of the city god, in one hall of which were sixty wooden statues representing the cyclical years of the old Chinese calendar. It had been customary to burn incense

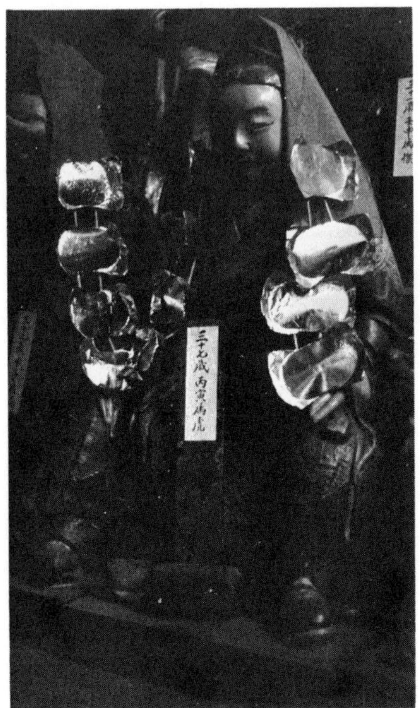

57. In the Temple of the City God, Shanghai, stood this image of the third year in the sixty-year cycle. In 1962, when the picture was taken, it would have been worshipped by persons thirty-seven years old by Chinese reckoning.

to the year in which one was born. According to a Shanghai resident, Red Guards forced devout old women to break up the statues with hammers and sticks. Afterwards an anti-religious exhibit was held there, containing (according to one visitor) the most vicious propaganda against Buddhism he had ever seen. A more bizarre story appeared in a Taiwan newspaper. During the Cultural Revolution in northern Kiangsu (where Buddhism had particularly deep roots) big-character posters were posted over images in local temples: a city god would be labeled "tyrannical landlord": Kuan-yin "a ruined woman"; Tathagatha the Buddha "a robber"; and so on. Then the Red Guards would bind the images with ropes and put them up on a platform where they would be struggled against like any other counterrevolutionaries. People were encouraged to curse them and vent their indignation and anger. After this the images had paper dunce-caps put on their heads, placards hung around their necks, and were pulled through the streets to the beating of gongs and drums—sometimes for several days on end. Finally a meeting would be held to announce the verdicts: this or that bodhisattva would be sentenced to be "shot to death." In the words of the ex-Red Guard who told this story, "How queer it was!"[21] Yet it was not really so queer in a country where district magistrates used to have statues of city gods publicly whipped for failing to bring rain during a drought. Furthermore, it is easy to forget the atmosphere of those hectic days in August and September 1966, when women were dragged off for having a permanent wave and graves were dug up because foreigners were buried in them. Chinese graves were also desecrated. The relation of a famous overseas Chinese, buried in Fukien, stopped the Red Guards at the very side of his tomb, with shovels in hand. "You cannot dig him up until you telegraph Chairman Mao," she said. They did so and, somewhat to their disappointment, found that he did not approve of the exhumation. The same woman saw Buddhist monks being forced by Red Guards to parade through the streets wearing the dress of Christian ministers (and vice versa).

There were also reports of much harsher treatment. On August 29, 1966, the abbot of a Buddhist monastery in Harbin, who was also a council member of the CBA, became the target of struggle by the "Eighty-eight Red Flag Combat Group." After collecting a crowd of a hundred thousand people in a public park, they read an indictment accusing him of frantic attacks on the Party and socialism and "carrying on counterrevolutionary activities under the cloak of religion." His punishment was swift. "Heeding the demand of the people at the rally, the public security authorities announced the arrest of the accused counterrevolutionary on the spot." This was not enough to satisfy the Red Guards, however. "The young fighters also wrecked his lair and threw away all the paraphernalia used for disseminating superstition and other feudal and counterrevolutionary ideas. This is indeed an event that inspires the people, a happy event that is exhilarating and thrilling." The above report was carried on the radio, but not in the press.[22] Similar reports come from refugees.[23]

The campaign against the Four Olds had an inevitable effect on lay devotees. Aside from the fact that they were afraid of becoming a target of Red Guard attack, they could no longer offer incense in temples that were locked up nor have rites performed by monks who had gone away. Worship at home became less satisfactory because religious images had been hidden or destroyed, either before the Cultural Revolution or during the campaign of August 1966 to search people's houses for feudal, bourgeois, or superstitious objects. Incense was even harder to buy than it had been in the past. Those who felt these changes the most were, of course, the "simple-minded old women" whom we tend to dismiss in discussions of religious practice as if their simple minds made their practice worthless. A broadcast from Kunming reported that "a woman of sixty-nine, who had for thirty years pinned her hopes on worshiping idols and being a vegetarian, has now hung up a portrait of Chairman Mao and sings revolutionary songs"—a touching story indeed.[24]

Since the temples and the various religious associations, journals, and bookstores had been shut down and since no religious delegations were coming to China, there was little to justify the continued existence of the Religious Affairs Bureau in Peking, and, in fact, like some other government organs, it apparently ceased to function. Neither its director, Hsiao Hsien-fa, nor his deputy, Kao Shan, was mentioned in the Mainland press after August 1966.[25] Since it had close connections with the United Front Work Department, it was natural that it should suffer along with the latter in the Cultural Revolution.[26] Early in 1967 and again in 1968 groups of Australian students touring China tried to get in touch with the Religious Affairs Bureau while they were in Peking. They did not succeed; and were given the impression by some of their hosts that it no longer existed.[27] It is interesting that a German visitor who was there about the same time found that there were two units concerned with Islam, one in the Ministry of Culture and one in the Ministry of Internal Affairs. This may represent a transfer of responsibility and personnel from an organ that had become defunct; and it would fit in with the fact that the first religious institutions to be reopened in China were mosques.[28]

All efforts by foreign Buddhists to re-establish contact with their brethren in China met with failure. For example, a Japanese priest who visited the Mainland four times between 1953 and 1965, was in the habit of sending an annual New Year's greeting to Chü-tsan. After 1966 he got no reply. Other Japanese had similar experiences. On visits to the Mainland they were unable to get in touch with Buddhist friends. Chinese monks in Hong Kong, who had previously got news from across the border in a variety of ways, claimed to be getting none at all; and to know of no Buddhist refugee who had emerged from the Mainland. Temple furnishings, including Buddha images, began to appear in Chinese Communist shops in Hong Kong. From the point of view of the outside observer, Buddhism had disappeared as completely as it had been swallowed up in a black hole of anti-matter.

THE BUILD-UP, 1963-1966

Let us now go back a few years and examine the events that gave warning of what was to happen to Buddhism. In August 1963 the *People's Daily* published an article entitled "On the Question of Religious Superstition" by Ya Han-chang (whose name suggests that he may have been a cadre of the Nationalities Affairs Commission). The article equated religious and superstitious activities but drew a distinction between those activities carried on "spontaneously" by the masses and those carried on by professionals "who swindle money and goods from the people through superstition." The latter had to be "strictly prohibited" and "forcefully hit" by the "methods of dictatorship"; whereas to cope with the beliefs and activities of the masses the only methods to be used were, as always, education and persuasion.[29] Two days later these points were repeated in another Peking newspaper, which called for a ruthless struggle against geomancers, fortune tellers, exorcists, faith healers, and the like. Then, however, it hinted at a broader target by saying: "We should also take the lead in doing away with superstition, educating the masses, and discouraging all kinds of superstitious beliefs. *We should not let superstitious activities take their own course.*"[30]

In retrospect these articles emerge as the beginning of a debate on religious policy and of a campaign against religion that reached its climax during the Cultural Revolution. This campaign was directed against a broad variety of "old customs and practices": not only divination, exorcism, healing, and their practitioners, but also against plays about ghosts, visits to clan tombs, elaborate weddings and funerals, and wasteful religious festivals that took time from production and money that could have been better used by the State.[31] In November 1963 cadres were criticized for taking no positive measures to discourage such customs,[32] and by the following February they had begun to act. For example, in Shanghai during the Spring Festival in 1964 a neighborhood cultural center organized propaganda teams that went about lanes, restaurants, and market places trying to persuade the residents to observe the Spring Festival—that is, the old Lunar New Year—in a revolutionary way. Particularly significant was the effort to get people to surrender the buddha images from their home altars. The last time such an effort had been made (in 1958), it had been an incidental feature of scrap metal collection.[33] Now the point was to get rid of images as such. The propaganda team marched through the streets beating gongs and drums and pushing two pedicabs loaded with "superstitious articles" contributed by members of the newspaper-reading teams of nine residents' committees. Among the articles were statues of Kuan-yin and the Buddha, incense burners, candlesticks, and so on. The team put on plays, one of which was called "Mother Huang Eliminates Superstition." It was about Mrs. Huang Chiao-yün of East Chien-kuo Road, whose husband had died a year earlier. Originally she wanted to have Buddhist rites performed for him, but after reading the newspapers with her team, she decided to send away the old woman she had engaged to perform them, not to buy any paper money, and to use for other purposes the money she saved. This play proved so effective that two old women and one old man handed over the buddha images before which they had been worshiping for years.[34]

In Shansi propaganda teams were sent out to reform temple fairs, which the *People's Daily* now attacked as a tool of the landlord class. It said that they had to be more closely supervised so that the people who came to them would stop praying to the gods and watching reactionary plays, but would instead receive an education in class struggle and absorb socialist culture. Even at this late date it appears that some thirty temple fairs a year were being held in a single county of Shansi. Farmers had been thronging to them to shop and to worship and also to enjoy the traditional music and the performances of Chinese opera that were put on across from the temple (so that the gods could enjoy them too). In order to bring a breath of fresh air into this feudal atmosphere, the propaganda teams replaced Chinese opera with plays against superstition and traditional music with revolutionary songs. They encouraged people with sick children not to pray but to see a doctor.[35] Thus new customs were supposed to take the place of old.

Starting in August 1964 there was a campaign to change "feudal" place names. This resulted in the disappearance of "Great Buddha Street," "the Street of Kuan-yin's Pavilion," and the "Lane of the Accumulation of Good Deeds." Residents of Hangchow who stopped at a tea house by the West Lake could no longer sigh over scrolls that praised the beauty of the four seasons there. These scrolls were now considered to "benumb the revolutionary fighting will of workers, peasants, and soldiers."[36]

At the end of 1964 parents began to be warned against bringing their children to worship in Buddhist temples. The *South China Daily* printed a letter from a reader who had seen an elderly woman getting a five-year-old to kneel and kowtow to the buddha image in the K'ai-yüan Ssu, Chaochow. This became the peg for an editorial saying that, although making three kowtows morning and evening and offering a full incense burner at sunrise and sunset were comparatively rare, yet "feudal and superstitious ideas of various types lurk more or less in the back of some people's minds. Certain persons . . . are inclined towards the idea of gods and spirits." This was bad enough, but it was even worse when they infected little children.[37]

Pa.tly to discourage religious practice, incense was now made harder to buy. In Chekiang the wood powder that had been produced in Yüyao county and used to manufacture incense sticks was allocated instead to plastic factories. One commune of Feng-

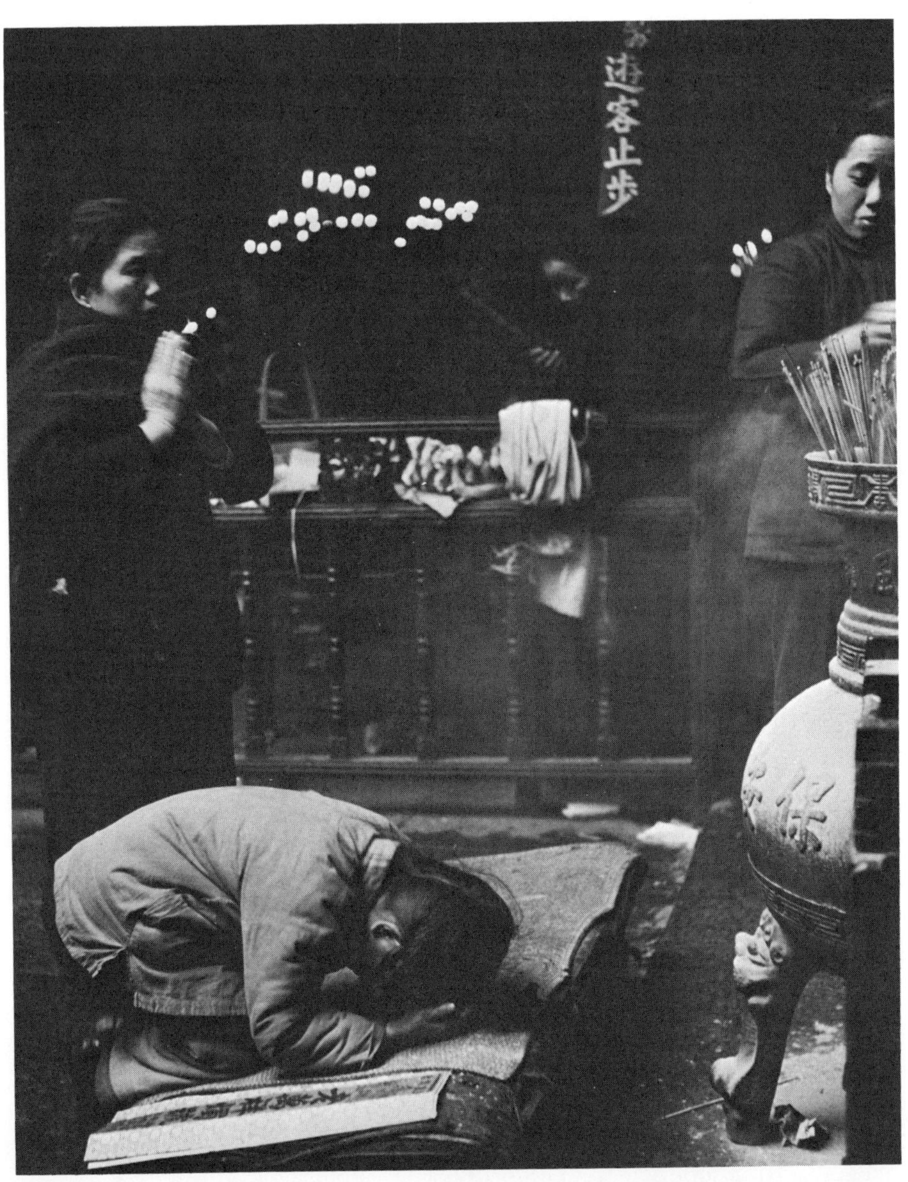

58. In 1956 a little girl prostrates herself before a smoking incense burner at the Hung Miao, Shanghai, while her mother prays and another woman looks pleased to see the young being well brought up.

hsin county, Kiangsi, which had formerly derived 40 percent of its income from the production of the paper used in religious offerings (mock money, clothing, and so on) switched to making toilet paper. Commenting on the news, an editorial in the Peking *Ta-kung pao* said that paper money and the like should no longer be sold in supply and marketing coöperatives or in other retail outlets—except where specially called for by the higher leadership (referring, perhaps, to outlets that served overseas Chinese or Buddhist groups performing ceremonies for foreign visitors).[38]

It is noteworthy how, in all these efforts to discourage "religious superstition," the target expanded from the professional practitioners to the practices themselves, including the "spontaneous" practices of the masses, with which Ya Han-chang had said the government should not interfere. We shall see in a moment how this paralleled the course of the debate on religious policy.

Some omens of change that appeared between 1963 and 1966 have already been noted in the preceding chapters. At the end of 1964 *Modern Buddhism*—the last surviving Buddhist journal in China—ceased publication. No reason was given: subscribers simply got their money back the following April. October 1965 saw the publication of a new *People's Handbook* which, unlike the previous editions, listed the CBA without the names of any of its officers.[39] This did not mean that their offices had been abolished, because some were mentioned in news items right up to August 1966. Yet it did suggest there had been some change in the status of the association. It was followed on November 30 by the dismissal of Shirob Jaltso as vice-governor of Tsinghai. We do not know whether he was also dismissed as president of the CBA, but he was not mentioned as such thereafter. He was the second Tibetan Buddhist leader to fall from grace in a year. The Panchen Lama had been attacked and demoted in December 1964.

Other events were not merely omens but causes of a change in the government's policy towards Buddhism. There was, for example, the series of disappointments in the use of Buddhism as a tool of foreign policy. Between 1954 and 1963, as we have seen, the Chinese had attempted without success to win an influential role in the World Fellowship of Buddhists. In 1963-64 they had tried to outflank the WFB and perhaps to set up a rival organization of their own. This too failed. One early reason for their patronage of Buddhism had been its usefulness in controlling Tibet. The rebellion of 1959 left them no option but military control. Another early reason had been the interest in Buddhism displayed by Prime Minister Nehru. The Sino-Indian border dispute had made this irrelevant by 1960. Still another reason had been the Buddhist piety of Prime Minister U Nu. He had been under house arrest in Burma since 1962. Similarly, relations with Ceylon had grown cooler with the election of the Senanayake government in 1965. The militant Buddhist movement in South Vietnam had once seemed to offer an apt tool to use against U.S. intervention there, but by 1965 it had disintegrated. China's role in the peace movement, which had been well served by the Buddhist delegates it sent to conferences against war and nuclear weapons, became more difficult to sustain after she developed nuclear weapons of her own.

Yet the more important reason for a change in the policy toward Buddhism was domestic. It was part of a change in the policy towards religion in general which, in turn, was part of the socialist education campaign. This campaign resulted mainly from Mao Tse-tung's increasing discontent with the embourgeoisement of the bureaucracy and the lack of revolutionary fervor among the youth, but he must also have been discontented with the persistence of superstitious beliefs and activities. That would explain the efforts that began in 1963 to suppress "religious superstition."

It can only have been deeply discouraging to Mao that despite more than a dozen years of educating the masses and suppressing superstitious practitioners, superstition still spontaneously reappeared whenever controls were removed. He may have read confidential Party documents like the following report of a Fukien Party committee in 1962:

> Superstition has been very active in areas along the coast. According to investigations made by the Huang-chi commune there are thirty-one new temples; eleven temples that have been repaired; and seventy-seven clay images [re-

> paired];–at a total outlay of 8,185 JMP.[40] Also, in the most recent period Taoist priests, propagators of religion, and religious bullies have been fiercely active. If this cannot be set right, then it will certainly be utilized by counterrevolutionary elements. Many cadres do not dare to do anything about superstitious conduct; there are also cadres and their family members who willingly take part in superstitious activities on the grounds of "freedom of religious belief" and "superstitious activities are demanded by the masses." We Communists are atheists. For Communists to carry on superstitious activities is not a question of freedom of religious belief, but of Marxist attitude. As for superstitious activities, most take place when a minority of people utilizes the masses' backward mentality.[41]

The distressing spontaneity of religious activity is made even clearer in the following passage.

> Although they have received ten years of education in socialist ideology since Liberation, the peasants fall back on the old customs when the opportunity occurs, thereby producing class struggle on the battle fronts of politics and ideology . . . Last year when we encountered difficulties, marriage by sale began to reappear and the masses once again began to engage in activities inspired by superstition, such as worshiping bodhisattvas, divination, and fortune-telling . . .
>
> The force of old customs not only asserts itself among the masses but also within the Party as well . . . Now as the nation is passing through a state of temporary difficulty, the great majority of Party members is good; nevertheless there is a minority among whom old ideas predominate. Take the problem of superstition, for instance. Communist Party members are fundamentally atheists. Yet a minority of members is inclined towards superstition.[42]

Mao would not have considered it necessary to launch the 1963 campaign against superstitious activities if the only people taking part in them had been a few simple-minded old women. He was, I

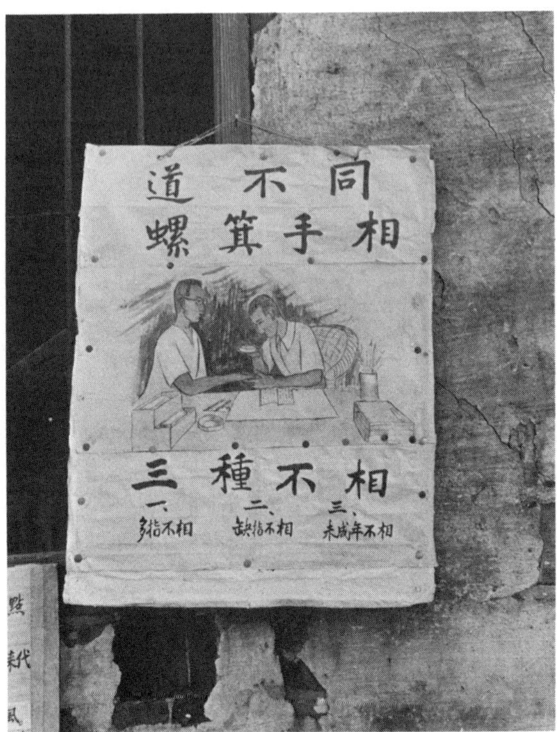

59. A fortune-teller's sign photographed in Soochow 1957. It says: "Tao Pu-t'ung [his trade name]. Palms read. Three kinds of palms will not be read: those with extra fingers, those with fingers missing, and those of minors."

think, impatient with waiting for the masses of the peasants to "throw out [the idols] with their own hands," as he had predicted nearly thirty years earlier.[43] He had lost confidence in the Marxist-Leninist "law" that religion must fade as socialism develops—the law on the basis of which the guarantee of freedom of religious belief had been included in the Constitution.[44] Therefore, I believe, he gave a nod to the "hawks" in the debate on religious policy that started in 1963. At any rate, without his approval it is unlikely that the debate would have gone as it did, ending in a revision of his own thesis that the Party should wait for religion to die of its own accord.

The debate was long and tortuous. The main spokesman for one side was Ya Han-chang, whose arguments were rebutted and finally defeated by Yu Hsiang and Liu Chün-wang. Dozens of articles were published, totaling a hundred thousand words—or many more if one includes the articles that led up to the debate. Back in October 1960, after several years of silence on religious policy, the *People's Daily* had printed a critique of the theory that religion had furnished the ideology and organization of peasant rebellions throughout Chinese history. On the contrary, wrote the authors, religion had never played more than an ancillary role in making peasants rebel and, because it was superstitious and backward, it had often weakened rebellions in their later phases. Furthermore religious beliefs about equality and happiness in the next world had been utilized by the exploiters to anesthetize the masses.[45] This latter idea was taken up in a harsh attack on the Avatamsaka school published in February 1961.[46]

These articles were counteracted by others sympathetic to Buddhism, if not to religion,[47] but only in 1963 did thrust and counterthrust become rapid and connected enough to be called a debate. Since an extensive summary of it has already been published, there seems no point in attempting another one here.[48] In any case, it is difficult to summarize because what divided the debaters was exasperatingly elusive: each side seemed to hold to the same theory and to be arguing only about slight differences of dialectical emphasis. Crudely put, these differences come down to the following. Ya Han-chang said that so long as religious believers did not engage in political activities detrimental to the regime, they should be persuaded rather than coerced to abandon their beliefs; and to this end anti-religious propaganda should be improved. He conceded that primitive superstition could and should be summarily destroyed but argued that higher religions like Buddhism should be tolerated until they died of inanition and irrelevance. Yu Hsiang and Liu Chün-wang rejected the notion of higher religion.[49] For them all religious belief was equally superstitious and had to be combated with equal force. They stopped short, however, of saying that it should be *destroyed* by force. This was left to someone of more rank: Fan Wen-lan, an alternate member of the Eighth CCP Central Committee and a full member of the Ninth. As the New China's leading historian-bureaucrat, Fan was preparing a revision of his *Simplified History of China,* for which he now wrote two chapters on T'ang Buddhism. Presumably because of their relevance to the current scene, they were published as a separate book at the end of 1965. The foreword appeared in the October issue of *New Construction.* It was the harshest condemnation of Buddhism that had appeared so far. Buddhism, said Fan, was a tool of the ruling class. It contained no elements that favored rebellion and the attempt to connect it with peasant uprisings was useless. On the contrary, the doctrine of karma made the peasants accept their sufferings as the inevitable fruit of former lives; and Buddhist monasteries were among the largest and cruelest landlords, oppressing not only the peasants but the lower ranks of monks. The working people of China had suffered from the evils of Buddhism for nearly two thousand years and had still not been able to throw off its yoke. Why was this? Fan answered with a flurry of mixed metaphor. "Religion . . . will not disappear of its own accord . . . [It] will rely on the force of custom to prolong its feeble existence and even plot to make a comeback. When a dying cobra bites a man, it can still wound or kill him. Therefore no matter how little of religion's vestigial poison remains, it is necessary to carry on a rigorous struggle against it on all fronts and to pull up and destroy all of its poisonous roots."[50]

This was the last word. No more of the voices sympathetic to Buddhism, which had been raised as late as the spring of 1965, were heard again.[51] The publication of Fan's article coincided with the new edition of *People's Handbook* in which the CBA was listed without the names of any of its officers. The debate on religious policy had been a debate about theory; but in this case there was unity of theory and practice.

THE AFTERMATH

China is a vast country. Foreigners seldom visit points outside a few major cities. A Japanese delegation in 1963 was astonished to learn that they were the first foreigners who had been in Yangchow since Liberation.[52] The fact that from 1966 to 1971 the only temples seen by foreigners were closed is not conclusive evidence that all temples everywhere were closed. In the winter of 1968-69, for example, a report was received overseas that the K'ai-yüan Ssu in Chaochow was still open. Fourteen monks were left (compared to nineteen before the Cultural Revolution). They wore lay clothes and worked on a nearby commune but continued to eat vegetarian food. Although the main shrine-hall was locked and no one could burn incense, the other buildings could still be entered. The monastery as a community of monks had survived. An even more remarkable report came from an elderly overseas Chinese who went back that same winter to her native place in east-central China—the heartland of living Buddhism. She found that some of the most illustrious monasteries—all in the countryside, none near a city—were still in operation, each with dozens of monks. The latter were elderly but able to perform Buddhist rites. She herself had a seven-day memorial service said for her late husband at one monastery and stayed there as a guest throughout that week. Everywhere she was able to offer incense. Of course, it was not like the old days; the monks lived a hard life, growing their own food, and some abbots had been replaced by CBA appointees before the Cultural Revolution began. Yet, again, these were living communities of monks. If they survived until the winter of 1968-69 after the massive *hsia-fang* movement of the previous autumn, when the urban youth went out to carry the Cultural Revolution to the countryside, possibly they were able to survive a few years longer.

There was nothing in the Mainland press that cast light on this possibility. On January 15, 1970, news of the death of Chou Shu-chia was carried by the New China News Agency. He was described as a vice-president of the CBA. It was the first mention of the association since August 3, 1966, and could conceivably have had some significance.[53] In the spring of 1971 the Sinhalese hosts of the Tenth Conference of the World Fellowship of Buddhists (which was eventually postponed to 1972 because of disorders in Ceylon) tried to make contact with the CBA in order to invite a delegation to attend. They had no success.[54] Japanese who went to China that spring were unable to learn anything of the fate of temples. In the summer, however, Kuo Mo-jo told an Australian visitor that religious institutions in China had not been "canceled" but were "in a state of suspension" and that their fate would be determined by the process of struggle, criticism, and transformation. Since museums and public libraries were still closed, it was hardly surprising that temples had yet to reopen. Of their eventually reopening there could be no doubt. Such large buildings would not be allowed to stand unused in People's China. But *how* would they be used? How many would be converted to production and how many preserved as cultural monuments cleansed of religious activity? Instances of each were reported.[55]

When one is writing a book, it is exasperating to have to depend on tomorrow's newspaper; and it is wiser to avoid any speculation about what one will find in it. Yet, as I wait for tomorrow's newspaper, I cannot help wondering why the foreigners who were in China during the wildest days of the Cultural Revolution saw no Buddhist monks or nuns being humiliated. There were dozens of them in Peking and Shanghai at the time and they were certainly easier to find (living in well-known temples and conspicuous by their robes and shaven heads) than the hundreds of people whom the Red Guards did find—and drove through the streets in trucks, their arms tied behind their back, wearing dunce caps and placards with inscriptions like "I am a cow-headed monster." If anyone was considered a cow-headed monster, it should have been the elderly Buddhist monk whose mind was full of idealism, superstition, and habits of exploitation two thousand years old.

I wonder therefore who saw to it that most monks and nuns were returned to lay life without being conspicuously molested. Was it the same person or coterie who saw to it that no important temples or images were seriously damaged? And behind this was there a reluctance to exclude the possibility that Buddhism could be used again in people's diplomacy? In Japan and Southeast Asia, there are Buddhists who still admire Mao and would welcome the chance to renew the visits exchanged in 1953-66. The Soviet Union and Mongolia, with whom the Chinese are competing for influence in the "third world," are still planning to make further use of Buddhism.[56] In other words I see evidence of conflicting views in the leadership. One view, perhaps supported by Mao, is that the use of Buddhism in people's diplomacy has proved itself more trouble than it is worth. The other view, perhaps supported by Chou En-lai, is that it should be kept ready for use again if the circumstances make it advisable. It is as if we were back where we started in 1949: the leadership has not made up its mind what to do about religion. Until it does, we cannot be sure whether the removal of the Buddhist tableaux from the repertoire is permanent. Some of the actors and props have been safely stored away. The management may yet decide to use them again.

Chapter XII

The Future of Buddhism in China

Before we can go more deeply into the question that the preceding chapters led up to—what is the future of Buddhism in China? —we have to ask what is meant by "Buddhism," and this is part of the larger problem of what is meant by "religion." Only when we have decided can we set up the criteria by which to judge the past and future prosperity of Buddhism in China, or of any religion in any country.

The difficulty is that not only the specialist in religious studies but every other thinking person defines "religion" in his own way and has different criteria for its prosperity. Some refuse to define it at all, regarding it as a misnomer that should be replaced by terms like "tradition" or "religiousness."[1] Others think of Buddhism not as a religion but as science or philosophy.[2] Realizing these differences of viewpoint, I have no hope of coming to a conclusion that most readers will find acceptable. What I have decided to do, therefore, is to offer several alternative conclusions, ending with my own, and let the reader pick the one that best fits his premises. First, however, we must be clear about the overall pattern of the state's religious policy.

THE PATTERN OF POLICY

Chapter I showed how religious policy took shape. The succeeding chapters have indicated how it fluctuated from year to year, in response to theoretical and practical factors. The theoretical factor—and the one that had the greatest importance in the long run—was the Marxist theory of religion. For more than a century this theory had seen little change, either with regard to the causes of religion, its evil effects, or the right way to eliminate it. Echoing Marx, Mao saw its causes in man's inability to explain and cope with nature;[3] and in the existence of social classes.[4] Echoing Engels, he early rejected its outright suppression as counterproductive and recommended instead that the people should be persuaded and educated to abandon their religious ideas. His most often quoted statement on religion was the following: "Any attempt to deal with ideological matters or questions involving right and wrong by administrative orders or coercive measures will not only be ineffective but harmful. We cannot abolish religion by administrative orders; nor can we force people not to believe in it. We cannot compel people to give up idealism, any more than we can force them to believe in Marxism. In settling matters of an ideological nature or controversial issues among the people, we can only use democratic methods, methods of discussion, of criticism, of persuasion and education, not coercive, high-handed methods."[5] This view, which he had first hinted at in 1927,[6] was exemplified in the guarantee of freedom of religious belief, enunciated in the Common Program of 1949 and then in Article 88 of the Constitution of 1954. At first Buddhists took it to imply freedom of religious *activity*[7] and so, when the Constitution was passed, they were enormously elated.[8] However, as we have seen in the preceding chapters, it soon became clear to them that religious activities were tolerated only to the extent that they did not interfere with socialist construction and public order and that religious belief was only free insofar as it had no political implications. No one was free to believe, for example, that Buddhists would be better off under a different regime. The most striking limitation of religious freedom was the rule that beliefs could not be propagated nor activities carried on *outside* the premises of religious institutions, just as anti-religious propaganda could not be carried on *inside* the premises—a division of space that gave the advantage to the latter.[9]

Little is known about the volume of anti-religious propaganda before 1958. It was not printed in national newspapers, but in pamphlets, which were presumably distributed to political study classes. Early in 1957 a Christian leader complained about twenty such pamphlets, which, he said, attacked religion as a weapon of the exploiters and as "the epitome of decadent reactionary thought." One of the pamphlets, interestingly enough, said that "progressive monks" were merely cleverer than their brethren and "consequently more skillful in concealing their hatred of science and of the development of mankind."[10]

In 1958-59 anti-religious propaganda began to appear in the national press. Perhaps in order to get ideas on how to improve it, a delegation from the Religious Affairs Bureau visited the Soviet Union.[11] Soon cadres were going into the villages to show people how much money their religious devotions were costing them each year (in one village 8 JMP per family for incense and candles alone!) and to convince them that gods and buddhas did not exist.[12] As we have seen, this was also the period when study and labor pre-empted the time that Buddhists had formerly devoted to religious practice.

Suddenly in 1960 the trend was reversed. Anti-religious propaganda seemed to disappear from the press, and religious practice began to be tolerated or even given a certain priority. Thus in April 1962, when a Buddhist association was set up for P'u-t'o Shan and a representative of the Chekiang Religious Affairs Division enumerated what the tasks of the monks should be there, he mentioned "to live a good religious life" before "contributing to socialist construction."[13] In other reports of local Buddhist meetings, references to socialist construction were vague or it was not mentioned at all.[14] Taken in conjunction with the increase in public worship and the official interest in Buddhist culture, this represented a considerable zag after the zig of 1958-59.[15] But then came the socialist education campaign, discussed in the last chapter. By April 1965 exhibits on superstition were being held in Shanghai and other cities, and anti-religious books were to be found in many bookstores.[16] The Cultural Revolution was on its way.

The zigzag course of the government's policy towards Buddhism resulted from the zigzagging of larger policies, internal and external: the policy on traditional culture (what portion should be thrown away and with how much force it should be thrown); the policy on enemies of the regime (which of the Buddhists were enemies and which were "people"); the policy on socialization (how fast and how forcefully monks and nuns should be converted into useful citizens and laymen discouraged from wasteful rites and festivals); and foreign policy (how much at any given time the regime cared about friendlier relations with Asian neighbors and how much it felt that Buddhism could help in this). The final shutdown of the Buddhist establishment in 1966 took place because of a zig to the left in all these larger policies at the same time.

Throughout the first seventeen years under Mao, Buddhists remained largely passive. Having no tradition of martyrdom, they never resisted anything that was done to them. The regime's fear that outright suppression would only strengthen Buddhism was based on a European precedent that did not apply. Just as the widespread removal of ancestral graves in 1958 caused not the slightest stir among the populace, we hear of no protest against the closing of temples in 1966. The monks had never gotten over the traumatic lessons of land reform and the suppression of counter-revolutionaries, which had taught them that China again had a strong central government with an apparatus of control that was more efficient than any in the past. It was simply pointless for them to resist, and I have seen no evidence that they were ever involved in sabotage or subversion, which would not only have been pointless but lay as far outside their tradition as martyrdom. The best they could do was to accomodate, coöperate, make themselves useful, and try to take advantage of government programs for their own purposes. This, as we saw in Chapter VII, they did with some skill during the first eight years.

In the first two or three years a few Buddhists like Chü-tsan were not entirely passive. They tried to exert an influence on government policy and perhaps some of their suggestions (as to how Buddhism could serve the regime, for example) were utilized. However, all important matters were finally decided by the leaders of the Chinese Communist Party. It was *their* attitude towards Buddhism that really determined its future.

The Attitude of CCP Leaders. The reason that nothing has been said about this so far is that so little is known. There are indications of a passing interest in Buddhism in the case of several early Party leaders and sympathizers, including Li Ta-chao, Ch'ü Ch'iu-pai, and Lu Hsün.[17] Chou En-lai's mother was a Buddhist, but then so were many other people's—including Mao's.[18] In 1915-16 Kuo Mo-jo attended lectures in Tokyo on *The Awakening of Faith in the Mahayana,* and at one point considered becoming a monk.[19] Whether this interest in Buddhism left any permanent trace is impossible to say. Kuo helped to entertain many of the Buddhist delegations that came to China, but it was his official obligation to do so. He does not seem to have gone out of his way to show a friendly attitude towards Buddhism. The only leader who did so, to my knowledge, was Chu Teh.[20]

What we would most of all like to know about, of course, is the attitude of Mao himself. Edgar Snow quotes him in the following reminiscence:

> My mother devoutly worshiped Buddha. She gave her children religious instruction and we were all saddened that our father was an unbeliever. When I was nine years old, I seriously discussed the problem of my father's lack of piety with my mother. We made many attempts then and later on to convert him, but without success. He only cursed us and, overwhelmed by his attacks, we withdrew to devise new plans. But he would have nothing to do with gods.
>
> My reading gradually began to influence me, however; I became more and more skeptical. My mother became concerned about me, and scolded me for my indifference to the requirements of the faith, but my father made no comment. Then one day he went out on the road to collect some money, and on his way he met a tiger. The tiger was surprised at the encounter and fled at once, but my father was even more astonished and afterwards reflected a good deal on his miraculous escape. He began to wonder if he had not offended the gods. From then on he showed more respect to Buddhism and burned incense now and then. Yet when my own backsliding

> grew worse, the old man did not interfere. He only prayed to the gods when he was in difficulties.[21]

Robert Payne may have been simply embroidering on this when he wrote that Mao's mother was "deeply religious, a Buddhist, and therefore averse to any form of killing. For a long period of his childhood and his early youth Mao Tse-tung attended Buddhist ceremonies with his mother, sang Buddhist hymns, and believed that nothing was more criminal than the killing of living things and nothing more necessary for salvation than the giving of rice offerings to the poor." When he was ten, his mother "still hoped that he might enter the Buddhist priesthood or perhaps, by becoming a merchant, support a monastery."[22] At thirteen, according to Payne, Mao was "growing skeptical of Buddhism," but he still "delighted in the incantations and prayers in the evening." Reading Han Yü's essay on the Buddha finger-bone finally turned him away from Buddhism.[23] This is different from what Mao told Edgar Snow: "Another influence on me at this time was the presence in a local primary school of a 'radical' teacher. He was 'radical' because he was opposed to Buddhism, and wanted to get rid of the gods. He urged people to convert their temples into schools. He was a widely discussed personality. I admired him and agreed with his views."[24]

Yet in 1917 Mao still felt a certain respect for the Buddha. In his essay on physical education he wrote: "Lao-tzu said that immobility [*wu-wei*?] was the ultimate goal; the Buddha sought quiet and methods of contemplation . . . The Buddha traveled continually, preaching his doctrine, and he died in old age. Jesus had the misfortune to die unjustly . . . All these men were called sages and are among the greatest thinkers."[25]

In 1927, as we have seen, Mao praised the expropriation of temples, the prohibition of religious rites, and bringing the peasants to the point where they would "pull down the bodhisattvas with their own hands."[26] Perhaps he still felt respect for the "higher aspects" of Buddhism, but by 1938 this too had vanished. In his essay "On Dialectical Materialism" he wrote: "Buddhism and all China's various fetishist religions attribute the movement and development of the myriad phenomena (*wan-wu*) of the universe to spiritual forces. All of these doctrines which think about movement apart from matter are fundamentally incompatible with dialectical materialism."[27] The attitude that Mao showed towards Buddhism hereafter was alternately cynical, sentimental, and dogmatic. He made sardonic use of Buddhist metaphors in his speeches.[28] To Buddhist visitors whom he had to entertain, he dropped appropriate phrases—but then sometimes could not resist pricking their balloon. For example, he remarked to the Dalai Lama in 1954 that "Buddhism was quite a good religion and Lord Buddha, although he was a prince, had given a good deal of thought to the question of improving the conditions of the people. He [Mao] also observed that the Goddess Tara was a kind-hearted woman." The Dalai Lama, who reported in his autobiography that he was "quite bewildered by these remarks," recalled another occasion when Mao "advised me how to become a leader of the people and how to take heed of their suggestions. And then he edged closer to me on his chair and whispered: 'I understand you very well. But of course, religion is poison. It has two great defects. It undermines the race and secondly retards the progress of the country. Tibet and Mongolia have both been poisoned by it.' I was thoroughly startled. What did he mean to imply? "[29]

In 1952 and again in 1959 Mao is reported to have shown a sentimental interest in the Venerable Hsü-yün, the most eminent monk in China, who also happened to be a fellow Hunanese.[30] Even during the Cultural Revolution the Buddhist elements of Mao's background were not concealed. The first thing that visitors saw when they entered his birthplace was the family altar with its high table and ancestor tablets. The guide would say that it was just as it had been when Mao was a child and added that his mother had been a devout Buddhist.

After 1957 Mao's published works contain no reference, so far as I know, to Buddhism in particular or to religion in general.[31] The course of the debate on religious policy in 1963-65 suggests, however, that whatever respect he may once have felt for Buddhist philosophy and whatever sentiment he may have kept for his childhood faith, his overriding concern was to see China's youth transformed into genuine revolutionaries. That was why he permitted the policy of freedom of religious belief to be abandoned in August 1966. The official line, of course, was that nothing had changed. In September 1966 the Party secretary of the Peking Foreign Languages Institute came to talk to the teachers there about the Cultural Revolution. Asked about religion, he emphasized that the Constitution guaranteed freedom of religious belief. "The Constitution stands," he said. "Nothing has changed. There is still freedom of religion in China." Then he paused, and added: "However, there is also freedom to oppose religion. This is a prerogative that cannot be denied to the people."[32]

In Historical Perspective. It is tempting to compare events since 1949 with the three great persecutions of Buddhism in Chinese history (446, 574, and 845 C.E.). Yet such a comparison is only superficially satisfying. It is true that during them ordination was halted and monks were laicized (in 574 and 845 so that they might return to production, just as in 1950-52); temple land and buildings were confiscated, scriptures burned, and images melted down (in 845 to make farm tools, again as under the Communists); and in 845 the elderly monks permitted to remain in the sangha were moved from small temples to the few large, culturally important monasteries that were left open, one in each prefecture (which is even closer to the pattern after 1949). Many other parallels could be cited. Yet the reasons for these earlier persecutions were less deep-seated and their effects less long-lasting than was the case under Mao. Each of them was brought about by plotting at court by Taoists and Confucians who caught the ear of the emperor and turned him against Buddhism for their own factional advantage. It was never the emperor himself who decided that religion as such was bad for the people and set about re-educating them. The ruling house, unlike the Communist Party, was not ideologically opposed to basic Buddhist doctrines like karma and rebirth. Therefore in all three cases, the anti-Buddhist decrees were reversed within a decade and (in two out of three cases) the anti-Buddhist plotters were executed. No such reversal was in the cards after 1949.

Until the Cultural Revolution the treatment of Buddhism by the Communists can be more aptly compared to its treatment by the Ch'ing dynasty, under which it was controlled but not persecuted. Like the Communists, the Ch'ing limited ordination, prescribed dire penalties for membership in syncretistic sects, forbade the erection of temples without permission from the capital, and banned performances of opera at temple fairs. With regard to wandering monks, the Ch'ing code demanded of sangha officials that they "should not allow strangers of doubtful character to stay in monasteries and should always be on watch for any that might be concealed there." It required every monastery to submit periodic lists of its residents and prohibited public solicitation of funds, preaching, or, in effect, any religious activity carried on outside the monastery.[33] All this was just as in the New China. Again like the Communists, the Ch'ing dynasty supported and utilized while it controlled and limited Buddhism. The K'ang-hsi, Yung-cheng, and Ch'ien-lung emperors were generous patrons of leading monks and monasteries. They too used Buddhism to strengthen links with Tibet. The function of the hierarchy of sangha officials that worked under the Board of Rites was close to that of Buddhist associations working under the religious affairs cadres.[34] Even some of the terminology is identical: the Ch'ing code, for example, prohibited monks from "taking disciples indiscriminately" (*lan shou-t'u*), the same phrase used after 1949.[35] The main difference lay in enforcement. Whereas towards the end of the Ch'ing many of the laws governing the sangha were allowed to lapse,[36] Communist enforcement was vigorous, especially in certain periods (like 1958-59) and with respect to certain innovations (like land reform).

During the Republican era (1912-1949) enforcement was weaker than before or after. Laws were passed to govern the sangha, but the central authorities simply could not determine what happened at the local level. There was no counterpart to the Religious Affairs Bureau that controlled but also supported and protected Buddhist monasteries. During the whole Republican period Buddhist monasteries were on their own, and what support or protection they received came mainly from individual Buddhists in influential posts.[37] Yet the Republican era was not devoid of precedents for what happened to Buddhism under Mao: there was widespread confiscation and destruction of monastic property; an effort to modernize Buddhist doctrine and make it scientific and progressive; a shift away from self-cultivation to social service; and a growing necessity for monks to support themselves by productive labor. Freedom of religious belief was guaranteed in the Nationalist as in the Communist constitution[38]—and was no more effective in protecting the sangha. Things got worse in Taiwan, where monastery land was permanently confiscated, monks were conscripted into the army, and religious activities were prohibited outside temple premises.[39] Buddhists in Taiwan were much freer than on the Mainland—let there be no mistake about that—but the trend, since 1912, had been towards limiting their freedom.

All in all I can think of nothing that happened to Buddhism after 1949 that was without precedent and wholly new. This applies to the cadres' contempt for "superstitious" beliefs and practices. It might seem to have been inspired solely by Marxism. Yet it was close to the attitude of bright young Nationalist officials in the 1930's, who were influenced by Christian missions and foreign education. In both cases, I think, the deeper reason for their attitude lay in China's century of humiliation, which they attributed to her technological backwardness and old-fashioned ways of thinking, best exemplified in "superstition." Still deeper lay the legacy of the literati's tradition of rationalist skepticism that went back to Wang Ch'ung in the Han dynasty and the literati's fear that Buddhism and Taoism would weaken their ideological grip on the people. Hostility to Buddhism is a bureaucratic syndrome that runs through a millennium of Chinese history. It was not invented by Mao Tse-tung. Until 1966 there was little in Mao's treatment of Buddhism that would not have won the applause of Confucians from Han Yü to K'ang Yu-wei. Only with the Cultural Revolution would they have drawn the line because of their reluctance to oppose the customs of the people directly—a reluctance that Mao had previously shared himself.

THE OPTIMISTIC VIEW

It testifies to the strength of Buddhism that it could have survived a thousand years of official hostility. Yet this is not the reason why some people today see a bright future for it. I have heard their viewpoint best expressed by an eminent Zen master in Japan. It all went back to his visit to China in 1957. Chao P'u-ch'u had told him then that the goal of Buddhism was to "benefit living creatures and beautify the land" and that, since the Communist Party had the same goal, Buddhists were coöperating with it. The Zen master thought to himself: "If both have the same goal, one of them is superfluous and will be eliminated, but that will be all right, because, so long as the other remains, the goal will be served." The one that he foresaw being eliminated was Buddhism—at least in its outward form. When this actually happened during the Cultural Revolution, he was not dismayed. "The policy of Mao Tse-tung *is* Buddhism," he said. Therefore to the extent that Maoism prospered, Buddhism prospered—and this made it very prosperous indeed.

In his view the prosperity of Buddhism should not be judged by the number of monks, by the condition of monasteries, or by the publication of Buddhist books, but rather by the presence of the Buddha mind—*buddhacitta.* When in China, he had often seen the slogan "Put the public welfare before one's own" (*hsien-kung hou-ssu*). This exemplified the Buddha mind. In his own country there were "so many scholars writing books on Buddhism, but how many of them are willing to die for the people? " In China, on the other hand, the model of every schoolboy was Wang Chieh, who had thrown his body on top of a land mine and thus saved the lives of the platoon of commune militia that he was training. This too exemplified the Buddha mind. Then in 1966, when he visited China for a second time and the leader of his delegation expressed concern that Chairman Mao might be suffering from old age and the approach of death, Chü-tsan replied: "Chairman Mao is thinking only of the people and nothing else. He cannot experience suffering." This most of all exemplified the Buddha mind.

Those who were capable of such unselfishness were bodhisattvas.

He considered that there were 700 million bodhisattvas in China. This did not mean that every thing was perfect there, especially during the Cultural Revolution. His visit in 1966 had taken place just before it broke out, but its effects were already beginning to be felt. For example, when he had asked to meet a famous abbot who was a calligrapher and poet like himself, his request was refused—in a way that made him think there was something wrong. Similarly, he had had no letters from Chao P'u-ch'u since he called on him in the hospital that year, and he had deemed it best not to write him. During the Cultural Revolution the Buddhists of China had been unable to voice their own thoughts, only Chairman Mao's, and this was bad. The Red Guards had undoubtedly committed excesses. Yet all such undesirable phenomena were due to the fact that certain people merely paid lip service to Chairman Mao. Yes, these people could not be called bodhisattvas. However, there were only a few of them, a small handful compared to the masses, the lower strata, who loved and followed Mao.

Mao was leading China in the right direction. Because the bad things that occasionally happened were due to the failure to follow him, they should be looked upon as minor, temporary deviations. To reject the main direction because of minor deviations would be short-sighted. The goal itself—a whole nation infused with the Buddha mind—was so good and Mao was so obviously pursuing it that he deserved the support of Buddhists everywhere regardless of what might actually happen in China from week to week.

Buddho-Marxist syncretism was discussed in Chapter VIII. Its tenets have been adopted and elaborated by the optimists of today, often quite imaginatively. The Zen master just mentioned reminded me that the Buddha had preached equality, and that the People's Liberation Army used no insignia of rank; "So," he said, "when I think of the ranks and privileges in my own monastery, I wonder which better exemplifies Buddhism, the Chinese army or the Japanese sangha?" A much younger Buddhist in Japan pointed out to me that behind the ideal of equality was the concept that every man had the Buddha nature. Was this not very close to Mao's idea that every man can be re-educated? Awakening to the Buddha nature was a process of continuing rebirth. Was this not like the continuing revolution called for by Mao? As a means to facilitate our awakening, the Buddha had taught us to moderate and eliminate our selfish desires. Was this not exactly what Mao taught—to have no desires for ourselves as individuals—to transcend the self? Then going back a little, when China had been liberated in 1949, it was as if the whole country had become a monastery, and as if the whole people had become the sangha—so that Buddhism was one with daily life.[40] Seventeen years later came the Cultural Revolution. This was as if the monastery were holding a *sesshin* (a period of intensive meditation). There were the same harshness and intensity, which were needed to help people break through to egolessness. Just as at a monastery, outside visitors had to be discouraged. The Cultural Revolution was a good omen for the future, for it was the first in a series. Perhaps the next would be launched to re-introduce Buddhism. Buddhist insights and methods of mental training transcended time, space, and history. They would enable Mao (whose mother, after all, was a devout Buddhist) to teach ordinary people how to cope better with certain problems—death, for example. Heroes like Wang Chieh could find meaning in death because of their self-sacrifice, but ordinary people did not die heroically . . .

It may seem capricious to cite so lengthily the opinions of just two Buddhists in Japan but I have heard similar opinions expressed in other countries at other times. Examples will be found in Appendix F. Opinions like these provoke immediate questions (from some of us, at least), but it is not always easy to get satisfactory answers; and there is a point beyond which it is useless to press for them. To illustrate this I have distilled a number of actual interviews with different people into an imaginary dialogue.

W. You put great store by Chinese Communist slogans. How can you tell whether they are actually put into practice?

X. I have been there and *seen* them being put into practice. The Communist Party exists in order to serve the people; it would not be serving the people unless it practiced what it preached; and the people would not support it.

W. But China is a big country where things vary from region to region and from year to year. How do you know that what you saw was representative?

X. I know many who have visited it in different years and received the same impression that I did.

W. But might not they have been shown things carefully chosen to give them that impression?

X. Yes, that happens to tourists in every country. When I went to China I was of course shown the good things and not the bad ones. Still, wherever I went people told me how much better off they were than before 1949. On the basis of my experience I believe that 90 percent of the people are grateful to Chairman Mao and the Communist Party.

W. What about violence? Mao has said himself that a revolution is not like a dinner party or painting a picture, but an act of violence that necessitates a brief reign of terror.[41]

X. The alternative was a continuation of a reign of terror that had lasted for centuries.

W. But do you believe that Buddhism permits killing, even killing bad people?

X. No—not even bad people. [Some answer: No unnecessary killing.] But you forget how much the good people had been suffering.

W. What is your criterion for whether the end justifies the means?

X. The feelings of the people—and I have seen how they feel. They are not only grateful to Mao, they are ready to die for the common good. That is the ultimate Buddhist principle.

W. But men and women in many countries and eras have been willing to die for others—Marie Curie, for example, died from her efforts to improve medical science. Was she a Buddhist?

X. Yes, she was a Buddhist.

W. Does Buddhism have no special feature that distinguishes it from ordinary altruism?

X. Yes, its special feature is *sunyata* [voidness].

W. Does Mao, being a materialist, accept *sunyata* as the basis for the self-sacrifice he advocates?

X. Mao's system goes under the name of materialism, but its real spirit is different.

W. But the Communists have condemned religion as idealism and a tool of the exploiting classes.

X. They are not talking about Buddhism but about superstition.

W. What do you think about events in Tibet?

X. Tibet is a good example of superstition. Buddhism there had become encrusted with it, as well as with formalism and aristocratic privileges. Things could not continue as they were.

W. In the final analysis do you think that Buddhism will survive in China?

X. Why does it matter whether what you call Buddhism survives? Buddhism is the Truth and the Truth cannot be destroyed.[42]

This dialogue could be continued for many pages, but the above is enough to show how it would go. The optimists who hold such views are intelligent men of good will whose influence is larger than their number. It is they who offer the Chinese government the best reason to start using Buddhism again in people's diplomacy and hence to allow a slight resumption of traditional Buddhist activities. I have noticed that the optimists are happy to recollect seeing traditional activities (worship and so on) and point to them as evidence that Buddhism is—or was—flourishing. This is a little inconsistent, perhaps, because they do not count the disappearance of such activities as evidence that Buddhism is on the decline, but it shows how, if they are invited to China again, their hosts can please them.

THE PRAGMATIC VIEW

In ordinary language the word "Buddhism" is not a synonym for the Truth, but refers to a complex of things that most people are accustomed to calling "Buddhist"—doctrines, literature, art, and architecture, as well as sangha, laity, worship, meditation, and so on. Given the trends of the past century and the factors that can now be discerned, it is not difficult to make a common-sense estimate of the future of these things. For example, there is obviously not going to be a restoration of the sangha as there was after its three earlier persecutions. The 200,000-odd monasteries and temples that once dotted the land and were converted to other uses after 1949 are not going to become available again as places for monks to live or laymen to worship. A small number of culturally important monasteries will probably be open as museums and parks. There is the possibility that a few old monks will still reside in a few of them, but they will be there as custodians, not to perform rites for the laity or to lead them in religious practice. It is also possible that the government will resume its effort to use Buddhism in people's diplomacy, but if so, the effort will be on a much smaller scale than before. The Buddhist association may reopen in Peking and a trickle of novices may be trained and ordained there, but a sangha large enough to play a role in the lives of the people will remain a thing of the past.

Except in periods of extreme liberalization, the government will continue to discourage popular worship; and modern education will continue to reduce the number of worshipers. Religious festivals, if they are permitted, will lose their religious significance much as Christmas has in the West.[43] Devotional clubs like the Pure Karma Society, Buddhist journals, and Buddhist bookstores will not revive—except for one or two that might be needed to show visitors. Since religious activities will no longer be carried on in temples with the assistance of monks and nuns or in devotional clubs with the encouragement of fellow members, they will have to be carried on privately and at home. Without the support of tradition that comes from clergy, community, and books, home practice is likely to be simplified, syncretized, and transformed. After a few years it may be difficult to decide whether it should be called "Buddhist."[44]

Buddhist art and literature will be preserved in museums and libraries. Museum visitors will look at a Sung dynasty image of Kuan-yin with more cultural pride than in London or New York, but for most of them her compassion will be merely a fact of art history. In philological studies of Buddhist texts, a few Chinese scholars will vie with scholars abroad, but it is unlikely that their studies will make them any readier to "die for the people." Buddhist metaphors will continue to be part of the language and Buddhist ideas like karma and rebirth will not be expunged from the popular mind for some years to come, but Buddhism as a living religion that is identifiably Buddhist will have disappeared.

A PERSONAL VIEW

I have sometimes asked Buddhist leaders whether it is logical for them to be so attached to Buddhism, which advocates nonattachment. I admire the consistency of the Zen master cited above who was not disturbed by the disappearance of monasteries, sangha, and practice. After all, these too must be subject to *anitya,* the law of impermanence. And how could a Buddhist retain his impartiality if he were opposed to the Communist Party because of its plan to expunge religion and idealism? That would only mean taking sides.

Where I find fault with the optimistic view of the future of Buddhism in China is in its appraisal of the facts, which seems to me unrealistic. I do not think that China has more implicit Buddhism—or more bodhisattvas—than any other country. I see no convincing evidence that Mao has created a New Man. I believe that monks labor in China in order to eat, not in order to benefit all sentient beings; and that while a person who is far advanced in religious practice can unite it with everyday life, to talk of ordinary people doing this is a cover for no practice at all. Similarly I believe that while true bodhisattvas may be able to kill with compassion, Mao's followers have killed his enemies with hatred. That, at any rate, is the emotion that the theory of class struggle has required them to feel.

Yet I would agree that the preceding chapters have failed to come to grips with a most important question: so what? What does it matter if the Chinese government has eliminated most of the things ordinarily called Buddhist? How do we know the Chinese people are not better off without them? It can be argued that religion is dying out all over the world. Why should we expect it to continue in China? Would it make us feel comfortably superior for China to remain backward and priest-ridden?

First, I personally do not think that religion is a sign of backwardness or that it is dying out all over the world. In the most advanced industrial countries, as some forms of religion die, others revive and new ones are born. New mythologies—from Superman to Tolkien—replace the old; people are using divination more, not less; interest in trance experience has never been higher than in the past decade; communities set apart from the secular world have never held more attraction for them; cults like witchcraft and peyote and complete religions like Soka Gakkai are spreading in the middle of the world's largest cities. The notion that man is on his way to become a dialectical materialist seems to me harder and harder to maintain. Wherever he is free to choose his own way, that is not the way he usually chooses.

Second, I would object to calling the Chinese people "priest-ridden." The religious situation is very different in China from that in Europe, where anti-clericalism has been closely connected with liberalism. In China it has been connected with Confucian orthodoxy. It is not the Chinese sangha that has tried to impose a set of dogmas on the populace, but its enemies, the anti-clerical literati. Monks have occasionally been involved in factional plotting at court, but the sangha has never even begun to hold secular power comparable to the clergy's in Europe. In this respect, therefore, it is inappropriate to see something liberal in Mao's treatment of Buddhism. On the contrary, if freedom of religion is considered a civil right, then that right has been violated.

For many centuries Chinese Buddhism has been more of a popular than an established religion. This is why it revived in 1960-62 with a spontaneity that was so vexing to the Party. Even today the Party cannot be sure what would happen if people were no longer afraid to be caught lighting incense and consulting fortune tellers. It is not yet clear that the Cultural Revolution has eliminated religious needs—like the need for purification, for rebirth, for a savior. The Party has tried to fill these needs by providing socialist substitutes like public confessions, the emulation of heroes, and the cult of Chairman Mao, but it is not yet certain that these substitutes are satisfactory. If they were, perhaps there would have been less "spontaneous religiosity" in 1960-62. It may be that the Party is barred from creating a satisfactory substitute for religion because of its insistence on materialism. The magical, the mysterious, and the transcendent have to be excluded from whatever it creates; and, of course, everything has to serve socialism.

I am not sure what religion is, but essential to it is an element of the otherworldly. That is why it is difficult to unite it completely with everyday life. It seems to me that Mao has begged the question: "What do people live for? " His answer—"They live to serve the people"—is circular.

The Communist Party may hope to dispose of religion by eliminating its objective causes, but there are some causes that it cannot eliminate—death, for example, as well as old age, disease, airplane accidents, and many of the other dangers and uncertainties of life. It has, however, eliminated the traditional ways of coping with them—ways that were irrational, unscientific, and materially wasteful, but which were effective enough to be very popular in China. It is all very well to educate people to see a doctor when they are sick, but it is foolish to exclude the therapeutical assistance of "superstitious" activities that predispose the mind to accept the cure in a way the doctor cannot. It is all very well to teach people how to make rational plans for the future, but it is foolish to eliminate fortune tellers, since doing so deprives the Chinese of a way to affirm their ancient feeling that they are part of a universe in which everything is interconnected and makes sense.

Then there is the effect of eliminating religious festivals. Perhaps no one starves in China today, but everyone works as hard or harder than under the Kuomintang. In the old days, however, work used to be interrupted by religious festivals that offered a complete change from everyday life. Socialist festivals do not offer such a change. On the contrary, their goal is to intensify people's commitment to the tasks of everyday life. This may not seem terribly important but I think it illustrates a broad misestimation of human psychology that the Party may some day regret.

To explain what I mean, let me compare the celebration of

National Day and the Festival of Hungry Ghosts. It is true that National Day is a day off and that there are parades and fireworks—and even something a little magical when the thousands massed in the stadium manipulate colored placards so that there appears, as if from nowhere, a huge portrait of Mao Tse-tung or one of his slogans. His slogans, however, merely urge higher production, renewed struggle, and greater sacrifice. Like the songs sung, the operas performed, the stories recited, the special issues published, the programs on radio and television, they simply drive home a little more forcefully than usual the messages that people have been hearing, day in and day out, for months or years. The celebration offers no release from the pressures of daily life, no outlet for the imagination, no hope for the individual.

In contrast to National Day, which is organized for weeks ahead of time by Party secretaries and street committees, the Festival of Hungry Ghosts just happened. People celebrated it as they wished and of their own accord. Dressed in their best clothes, they put the farm and workshop completely out of their minds as they thronged to the temples to pray to the gods and to offer them thanks for prayers answered. (Today their thanks go to the Party and Chairman Mao.) Many would consult fortune tellers about the present and the future. (Today they are supposed to learn about the future from the Five-Year Plan.) Across from the temple was a mat-shed tent with performances of Chinese opera that were continuous during the festival. The simplest peasant could name the heroes and villains who postured about the stage in fantastic costumes of rainbow colors, looking and acting like men from a different world. (Today the heroes are workers and peasants.) Everywhere there was bustle and excitement—hawkers with ices and water chestnuts, venders shouting up their wares from their stalls. (Today people are expected to save their money to increase production.) The festival took place in the seventh month, when the ghosts of the uncared-for dead were free to leave hell and roam about the earth. To feed them, offerings of food were left at the edge of streets, and paper money and clothing were burned for their future use. (Today anyone who wasted food that way would be considered a "backward element".)

It is an ancient feature of the Chinese religious tradition to treat the dead as living. Unrealistic as this would be considered today, it had an important psychological effect. This can best be seen in a Buddhist rite known as the "release of burning mouths" that was always performed on the Hungry Ghosts Festival. Using magical instruments the monks purported to unlock the gates of hell and enter to feed the souls being tortured there, who, after their pangs of hunger and thirst were allayed, could listen to the dharma being preached. As a result many of them were released and reborn on earth or in the Western Paradise. I imagine that the filial son who took part in this rite was helped in a variety of ways. To think of his father as a tortured soul expressed his unconscious resentment. To pay for the monks to feed him expressed his gratitude. To treat his father as still existing mitigated the sense of loss. To see his own son standing beside him reminded him that he himself would some day be dead and his son would be doing what he was doing now. Even if he only half believed in the ceremony, it offered functional equivalents for actions that there was no way to perform in the everday world–actions that coped with inexpiable guilt and ineluctable fear.

While this beautiful and mysterious rite, with its five hours of chanting, was taking place in the monastery, a much simpler one was being performed on the banks of rivers and streams. Thousands went there with little rafts of paper and wood, in which they placed lighted candles and then launched them on the current. As the rafts drifted slowly off, the stream became a moving sheet of tiny lights. Each person would follow his own with his eyes until he lost it among the others. They thinned out in the distance, as the candles burned down or the rafts sank, but one could not be sure of the moment when his own light disappeared in the darkness.

In theory the purpose of the ceremony was to guide the souls of the dead back to hell. As in the case of the "release of burning mouths" we cannot know what was going on in the minds of those who took part, but I imagine that besides enjoying the beauty of the summer night, they had a sense of free community–everyone doing something together, but doing it on his own–each making or picking his raft, deciding about its shape and seaworthiness, lighting it and launching it. More important was a sense of time. Another year had passed. How many had it been since one launched one's first raft as a child? How many would it be before one's own life went out in the darkness? For some people, at least, the immensity of that darkness and the flickering of the tiny flames that moved into it must have put daily preoccupations into perspective and released them from the insistence of everyday life.

It is this kind of perspective and release that is denied to the people of China by the requirement that their every word and action should serve the socialist cause. I am not referring simply to festivals. They are merely an illustration. In no phase of contemporary life are the Chinese given a chance to look for transcendental meaning, to see things *sub specie aeternitatis,* to exercise their power of fantasy and imagination. I wonder if the result is not an increasing and deep-seated uneasiness, comparable to that which results from the deprivation of dreams. What is really at stake here is the existence of the individual. Mao's goal is for the individual to lose himself in serving the people, in following the leadership of the Party, in having no ideas or wishes of his own. The religious goal is for the individual to find himself. Losing himself means to escape from the problem of who he is and what his life means: finding himself is to solve that problem. After it is solved, he feels it wondrous to carry wood and haul water—not because he is serving the people thereby, but because he rejoices in whatever he does for its own sake. Daily life is holy and samsara is nirvana. This is something he can only have reached on his own, as an individual, not in a mass movement. The masses cannot reach nirvana. The masses are an abstraction used to depersonalize a large number of individuals, deprive them of identity, and reduce them to manipulable elements in a political formula.

In general, I think that when people are suddenly cut off from the customs through which their lives have been kept in balance over many centuries, when the behavioral ecology, so to speak, is upset, the results cannot be foreseen. I believe that people have certain psychological needs—religious needs—which the Communist Party cannot fill. It seems to me that subtle pressures will build up to burst the Party's holistic grip on human life and goals.

I am interested by Jung's hypothesis that when "superstitions" (by which he means archetypal symbols) are repressed by the conscious mind, their energy, which appears to disappear, actually "serves to revive and intensify whatever is uppermost in the unconscious." This includes potentially destructive tendencies "that might in some circumstances be able to exert a beneficial influence but are transformed into demons when they are repressed."[45]

Some of these demons were loose, I suspect, during the Cultural Revolution and eventually they may burst out again in an explosion that could not only break the Party's holistic grip, but bring with it a recrudescence of "spontaneous religiosity," which will be all the stronger for the years it has been kept down. This will not necessarily mean a revival of Buddhism in its traditional form, yet elements of Buddhist belief and practice will surface, I think, as part of something which Marxists will call "superstitious" as well as "escapist," "negativistic," and "reactionary," but the need for which they cannot eliminate.

Appendices
Notes
Bibliography
Glossary
Index

Appendix A

Chü-tsan's Report

The following article[1] is a revealing statement of why and how a monk became "progressive." It is also important because the monk in question, Chü-tsan, was the one given the most authority by the Communist Party in 1950-66. Finally, it is useful to an understanding of the first critical years 1949-50—of the difficulties Buddhists were having and of the way the government's policy towards Buddhism took shape.

AN ACCOUNT OF MY WORK OVER THE PAST YEAR

Chü-tsan

"To offer my body and mind to innumerable realms
This is called repaying the Buddha for his kindness."

MY PAST

Perhaps it was because I was born into a decayed petit-bourgeois family that from the time I was young I was emotional and easily depressed.[2] Often in the gloom of a windy and rainy day I would run alone to the mountain two or three miles from my home, gaze up at the sky, and cry my heart out; or on a moonlit evening, when there was a fresh breeze, I would sit by myself bolt-upright on a dike between the fields and play my flute; or sometimes I sat under a tung-oil tree and sipped alone, facing the moon, until I was completely drunk. Sometimes I would give all the few pennies I had saved to some little beggar and still feel sorry for him for a good while afterwards. I recall that one day in winter vacation when I was fourteen or fifteen years old, I was reading in the study and, as I watched all the people coming and going in the street below my window, I asked myself: "What is the purpose of their coming and going?" Just by chance a friend of mine dropped in and I asked him: "After all, what is the purpose of those people in the street coming and going? " He answered by asking: "And what's your purpose in here? " It gave me a start: I felt as if I was carrying a heavy load on my shoulders that I could not put down, and from then on I thought of becoming a monk.

During the summer holiday when I was nineteen, I stole away from home and went to the Ch'ing-liang Ssu in Changchow to see the Reverend Ying-tz'u, in hopes of becoming a monk as his disciple.[3] Things were against it and my hopes were not realized. Then I tried to become a monk at the Ling-yin Ssu in Hangchow. It just happened that the Reverend T'ai-hsü[4] was there then. After he saw me, he asked me to write a statement of my purposes in becoming a monk. I wrote one of more than a thousand characters in verse, setting forth four purposes. (When leaving home, aside from some changes of clothing and an umbrella, I had only brought along three books—the *Lao-tzu, Chuang-tzu,* and the *Chao-ming wen-hsüan.*[5] One of my four purposes was the "reform of Buddhism" (*kai-ko fo-chiao*). Actually, what I knew then about Buddhism was only what I had learned from reading the several volumes of the *An-shih ch'üan-shu* when I was at the Ling-yin Ssu. Before then I had never studied it.[6] I really did not know the first thing about the "reform of Buddhism." (The original manuscript was destroyed during the fighting that broke out January 28, 1932 [in Shanghai].) However, T'ai-hsü thought a great deal of it, and in his comment he said: "Here too is a scholar who has set his heart on the Way; if he gets good guidance from a teacher, he will go far." A few days later I accompanied T'ai-hsü to Amoy, where I entered the South Fukien Seminary.[7] I still had no master and had not even taken the Refuges. Without knowing exactly what I was doing, I studied Buddhism there for a few months. As there was a series of big disorders at the South Fukien Seminary and as my father entreated me to return, I went back to Shanghai without having become a monk and I continued my schooling for a time, while secretly taking part in revolutionary work.

Actually, although I did revolutionary work, my thinking was not clear-cut and my behavior was not really progressive. All I had then was an honest sense of righteous indignation. We controlled the workers of two newspapers in Kiang-yin county, some of the workers in the textile mill, and the teachers at primary and middle schools, but we were too loosely organized. All our secrets were known to the village bullies and evil gentry, who joined in informing on us to the Kiangsu Kuomintang Provincial Party Headquarters. A warrant for our arrest was issued. While one comrade was lost, I took to my heels and did not get caught, but a lot of damage had been done. At this time my father had recently died. I was still suffering from grief, added to which was this new shock. The old question of the meaning of life again welled up in my heart, so I decided to go to Hangchow again and become a monk. Originally some friends had wanted to give me an introduction to study with Hsiung Shih-li or go to Shantung to work under Liang Sou-ming, but I politely refused. As luck would have it, T'ai-hsü again came to Hangchow, and through his introduction I formally became a monk as a disciple of Ch'üeh-fei, abbot of the Ling-yin Ssu, and received the full ordination at Pao-hua Shan. That was in 1931, when I was twenty-three.

Having become a monk, I began studying Dharmalaksana philosophy, which maintains that only consciousness exists. In a year and a half I read carefully the books of the Yogacarin school and their commentaries, and I also made many notes. I asked myself whether Buddhism would ultimately be of any use to me and at that point my answer was "no." Then I went on to ask myself why, if Buddhism would be of no use to me, I should be a monk? Would it not be better to retrace my steps? But I looked at it more closely: there were many in the past thousand years or more who had benefited by studying Buddhism, and could they all have been fools? This was something important and I could not afford to be hasty. My mental anguish continued to grow, and sometimes I even awoke from dreams weeping. Once I went to see Ma I-fou and asked him, "What is a man? " He said that no one had asked anything like this—"What is a man? " One had to find the answer to it oneself. At that point, since I had failed to get satisfaction on a question that meant so much to me, I could not keep myself from bursting into tears. From then on I stopped reading sutras and treatises and started careful reflection on the questions that I found in my own mind. How was I to know that one question would lead to another and that there would be so many of them? Mr. Chou Shao-yu introduced me to Mr. Ou-yang Ching-wu of the Metaphysical Institute, who helped me solve some everyday problems, but my mind was not yet at rest.[8] Having stayed at the Institute a few months, I was invited to teach at the Sino-Tibetan Buddhist Institute in Szechwan.[9] Since I only had a light teaching load, and no administrative duties, every day I applied myself seriously to reflection. Almost a year went by like this, and I gradually came to feel that many of the answers I had found to my questions were, without my intending them to be, consistent with the sutras and treatises. But the questions became more acute and profound. Then I returned to the Metaphysical Institute and began to read texts of the San-lun, Prajna, T'ien-t'ai, Avatamsaka, Ch'an, and Pure Land schools, Mahayana and Hinayana sutras and treatises. The questions lurking in my mind gradually became fewer, and I went out to look high and low for new questions. The sutras and treatises I had read up to then contained more than seven thousand chüan, and the questions I had solved were over five hundred. (While reading each sutra or treatise, I took notes, then recorded how I formulated each question and how I answered it. All this came to a boxful.) In the meantime I had also been to see three venerable monks, Chao-an, Yü-kuei, and Yin-kuang[10] and then I had felt peaceful about being a Buddhist. Yet with the condition of Buddhism I grew even more discontented. This was before 1937.

After the Japanese attack on July 7, 1937, I devoted myself to secular studies. Besides reading the pre-Ch'in philosophers and the neo-Confucianists of the Sung and Ming, I also began to relearn English and Japanese, which I had long since put aside; and I started German in hopes of reading Kant, Hegel, Marx, and Engels in the original. However, as the fierce flames of the Japanese invasion spread further with each passing day, I fled from Fukien to Hong Kong to Kwangtung (where, at the Nan-hua Ssu, I got to know the Venerable Hsü-yün and served as a secretary for a few months) to Hunan. Traveling by boat and train I was attacked alternately by poverty and illness and certainly had no way of doing any scholarly work. In 1939 I was at Nan-yüeh running the Buddhist Research Center. When Nanchang was threatened, I could no longer keep my mind patiently set on books and organized over twenty student [monks]into a Buddhist youth-service corps to join the war of resistance. In the course of my work I had many reverses and once I almost lost my life, but it only strengthened my faith in the dharma. In autumn of 1940 I found it impossible to continue living in Hunan.[11] I then left for Kweilin in Kwangsi, where I published the monthly named *Shih-tzu hou* (The lion's roar), which vigorously supported resistance against the Japanese and the movement for the reform (*ko-hsin*) of Buddhism. (The two slogans "shift to production" and "shift to scholarship" were put forward at this time.) My contacts in the world became even broader, and many people at that time thought that I liked being so active. Actually I was just trying to get to the bottom of every social stratum. The more I learned that proved the correctness of Buddhist doctrine, the more determined I became to attempt a thorough reform of the Buddhist establishment (*fo-chiao chiao-wu*).[12] In 1946 I returned to Hangchow, lived at the Ling-yin Ssu, and worked for the Chekiang Provincial Buddhist Association and the Hangchow Municipal Buddhist Association.[13] The inside goings-on of Buddhist circles thus became even clearer to me, and I realized that under the reactionary Nationalist government it was impossible to do anything about the reform of the Buddhist establishment. Shen Hung-lieh, who was then governor of Chekiang, encouraged me to draft a plan for the reform of the Buddhist establishment in that province. I felt that empty words would serve no purpose and did not pay any attention to him. Later Shen Hung-lieh was succeeded by Ch'en I, and Tu Wei, a Buddhist devotee, became head of the Civil Affairs Department. He twice told me that he would like to help me reform the Buddhist establishment in the city of Hangchow. I then wrote to him and raised a few questions, but as I got no reply, I dropped the matter. The fact is that since the economic foundation of society remained unchanged, since all the old forces were securely combined, it was just a subjective fantasy–a piece of pure idealism–to expect that the head of a civil affairs department could bring about reform. He could never have succeeded even if he had devoted his whole strength to it. As I write this, I cannot help thinking of the Reverend T'ai-hsü, who hurried about for decades making appeals without getting any results, because what he could do was limited by the time he lived in. Thus a great teacher of that generation died without having realized his objectives.

One cannot but look back in sorrow and one may even think of two lines of the elegy that Tu Kung-pu composed for Chu-ko Wu-hou.

> He died before the victory of his forces,
> To think of it fills a warrior's eyes with tears.[14]

In the spring of 1948 I lectured on the sutras in Hong Kong. I met Mrs. Li Chi-shen, Shen Chun-ju, Chang Po-chün and Kuo Mo-jo. When we talked about the problem of Buddhism, everyone agreed that it was a big problem. The People's Liberation Army would soon liberate the whole of China and the status quo of Buddhism would be shattered. How should things be done in the future? No new plan was yet in sight: it was really most disappointing. I was very worried about it then, and, having completed my lectures, I went to Taiwan to see what Buddhism was like when it had been made partly Japanese. I spent a month in Taiwan, traveled all over the island, visited a great many temples, and felt that it was questionable whether we could take Japan as a model. (For the details, see "My Travels in Taiwan" in *Chüeh yu-ch'ing.*) The reform of the Buddhist establishment in China had to be in tune with the times. In working out the right approach, the Japanese model could only serve as a point of reference. From Taiwan I returned to Hangchow and began to consider how to draft a plan for the reform of the Buddhist establishment throughout the country. Mr. Chao P'u-ch'u, the Buddhist devotee, came to Hangchow once to talk to me about it, and we thought of calling a secret conference of progressive Buddhists scattered in Shanghai, Hangchow, and Ningpo to decide on concrete measures. However I fell ill and because of other considerations too we kept putting it off. Then came the end of the battle of Hsü-huai. Alarm was spreading through the area south of the Yangtze River. Everyone was terribly nervous and had no time for a conference, so I left Hangchow and went to Hong Kong.[15]

At that time Mr. Li Chi-shen and the others had all left for the north. Mr. Hsia Yen and Mr. P'an Han-nien were in charge of the South China Bureau of the Chinese Communist Party. Mr. Hsia Yen was an old acquaintance of mine, whereas Mr. P'an Han-nien I have never met before. Once Mr. Ch'en Shao-hsien and Mr. Lü Chi-i mentioned me to him. They said that he was much interested in the Buddhist problem, had asked me to draft a plan, and would see what he thought after reading it. I then wrote a draft on the reform of Buddhism in the new China, which I asked Mr. Lü Chi-i to deliver to Mr. P'an Han-nien. After getting no news for a long time, I went to see Mr. Hsia Yen and found out that Mr. P'an Han-nien had studied the draft with people but had not expressed any opinion on it and, as someone happened to be leaving for Shih-chia-chuang, he had asked him to take it to the north. The truth was that my draft was just a hasty improvisation, for I knew nothing about the actual conditions in liberated areas. A lot of things were probably wrong with it, but there really had been no one then to discuss it with. The only thing to do was to forget it. It was lucky that I alone had signed it and that it did not represent the consensus of Buddhist circles.

The above is an account of my twenty years' work (*ts'an-hsüeh*), which may be summed up in four points. First, I have loved the study of Buddhism (*fo-hsüeh*) from the time I was young; and to reform the Buddhist establishment has been my long-standing wish. Second, although reform of the Buddhist establishment is needed, its basic spirit must draw on the fine old qualities to be found in Buddhist circles, such as the "sincere devotion" advocated by the Venerable Yin-kuang, the "serenity" advocated by the Venerable Hung-i, "conquering hardship" as advocated by the Venerable Hsü-yün and Chi-yün, what the Reverend T'ai-hsü called "never forgetting Buddhism for a moment," and Ou-yang Ching-wu's "shining enthusiasm and awesome will power."[16] These are all worthy of being adopted and developed. Third, to polish ourselves by practical use is the way to improve and can never hurt us: one can even call it true self-cultivation. On the contrary, if we divorce ourselves from practical affairs in order to seek for the truth (*li*), it is like creeping into a horn: the further we creep, the narrower the horn will get, and finally our spiritual future will be cut short. Fourth, the reform of the Buddhist establishment is not only an urgent task for Buddhist circles, but is also something that society in general considers to be full of big problems and extremely necessary.

BEFORE AND AFTER THE CPPCC

On April 3, 1949, with Mrs. Li Chi-shen and Mr. Lü Chi-i, I left Hong Kong for the north by ship. Prior to my departure Mr. Hsia Yen and Mr. Liao Mo-sha sent a cable on my behalf. Upon my arrival at Tientsin I was given a reception that greatly exceeded my expectations. I thought it might be because of my fellow travelers.[17] On April 13 I reached Peking and was put up at the Peace Hotel. At first I did not realize that this had been turned into a government guest house and wanted myself to pay for room and meals. This was refused, I was given perfect hospitality, and then I suddenly woke up to the fact that the Chinese Communist Party would not put anyone aside who had supported revolution and favored democracy, regardless of how much ability he had and what class he belonged to—just so long as he was willing to throw himself into the glorious enterprise. This was called the "united front." I felt such deep admiration and gratitude, but I was a little embarrassed. So, after staying in the hotel for two weeks, I moved to a place in the Pei-hai Park. Thereafter I would only take seventy-five catties of flour a month from the guest house and did not want any cash for minor expenses. Finally in February 1950, when we started our political study class, we were given our meals, and I did not want any more hospitality. Furthermore, I never asked Buddhists in Peking for one cent of money or one catty of flour. All the money that I spent, either in the public interest or for myself, with the exception of a small amount that had been sent me the October before by Buddhists in Shanghai, came from honoraria that I gotten for my lectures in Hong Kong. That way my mind was easier, for I felt my ability to be very limited and I was afraid that I was not contributing much either to the nation or to Buddhism.

When Buddhist circles in Peking found a stranger like me suddenly in their midst, they thought it very surprising and queer. Some suspected me of being a veteran cadre who had dressed up as a monk and come to do some work. There were also others who thought that I had come with an old set of tricks to make my way in the new society. Some who did not understand the meaning of the word "reform" were terrified that I had come to destroy Buddhism. There were even some who thought that I had come from the south to the north to get my hands on big temples. But there were also many who understood, like the devotee Chou Shu-chia and others. Once we had talked things over, we found that our ideas were extremely congenial. After a month of investigation and discussion, acting in the name of our fellow Buddhists in Peking, we sent a letter to Chairman Mao and the democratic parties calling for a nationwide reform of Buddhism. It had four main points.

1. The people's democratic revolution had wiped out the last fortresses of feudalism and superstition and had made the Chinese people struggle free from all their fetters and stand up firmly to build a new society and a new nation of freedom and equality. This was the most magnificent page in their five-thousand-year history. It had been achieved because of the correct leadership and heroic struggle of the Chinese Communist Party, and because of the enlightened and enthusiastic support of the democratic parties. We Buddhists all expressed our admiring and loving joy over the dawn of this new era.

2. Since Buddhism came to China over 1,800 years ago, it had gone through a close interaction and mutual harmonization with every aspect of Chinese culture. However, enjoying the support of feudal society for so long, Buddhism naturally could not have simply gone its own way, unaffected by the reality of its environment. Inevitably it had changed character, bit by bit, and ended up by betraying Sakyamuni. Especially in the last forty or fifty years, monasteries all over the country, large and small, had been transformed from feudal landlords into commercial establishments, into family enterprises. This had sharply aggravated the tendency towards superstition and decadence and made Buddhism an object of ridicule and scorn by society. The latter really caused us a lot of pain, and in the past we had sometimes acted to improve things. But the Buddhist sector was an integral part of society and so long as the whole of society was not changed by revolution, there was no way to move ahead with the internal reform of Buddhism. Therefore, although the reform of Buddhism had been going on for thirty years, one could say that nothing had been achieved prior to our present era. Now the government had cut for us the bonds of feudalism and superstition that used to hold back Buddhism and it had also eliminated all kinds of

heterodox sects, such as the I-kuan Tao, Chiu-kung Tao, P'u-chi Buddhist Society, and P'u-ming Buddhist Society, which in the past had borrowed the name of Buddhism to spread superstition and brought disgrace that Buddhism was helpless to prevent. From all this, Buddhism would emerge to build a vigorous new life for itself. So we gave ten thousand thanks for the present era and for the Chinese Communist Party.

3. The nature of Buddhism was different from that of other religions. It was "atheist" (*wu-shen*) and advocated "the realization of selflessness" (*shih-chien wu-wo*). This completely corresponded to the spirit of the times. In addition, Tibet and Taiwan which were awaiting liberation, both revered Buddhism. Neighboring countries such as Indochina, Thailand, Burma, Ceylon, India, Korea, and finally Japan were out-and-out Buddhist countries. If in the course of the Chinese revolution the element of Buddhism was ignored, difficulties might arise in liberating Tibet and Taiwan and promoting world revolution. If, on the contrary, in the territory of the new China, "a new form of Buddhism" appeared, then it might well facilitate the liberation of the whole country and the promotion of world revolution.

4. Two slogans—"shift to production" and "shift to scholarship"—should be advanced as the targets towards which the reform of all Buddhist institutions should aim. Shifting to production would smash the old feudal economic organization of the monasteries. Shifting to scholarship would strengthen Buddhists' knowledge of Buddhism and their orthodox faith so as to eliminate superstition. Only when feudal organization and superstitious ignorance had been done away with could the revolutionary nature of Buddhism come to the fore. This would not be without effect in winning backward people to join the revolutionary ranks.

The above statement of views was drafted by me and signed by twenty-one persons. Clearly the occasion was ripe for a nationwide reform of the Buddhist establishment. Although we had not yet reached the stage where we could settle the exact methods of reform, it had already won the approval of part of the Buddhist community, which would have been unimaginable prior to Liberation. The democratic parties considered that the ideas and measures we proposed were extremely reasonable. With regard to the organization [the Communist Party] it was not easy for them to comment openly, but when we talked with them, they expressed their sympathy. This was the first stage of my work over the past year.

Before the meeting of the Preparatory Committee of the CPPCC, I came across Mr. Lin Po-ch'ü [of the CCP Central Committee] at the home of Mr. T'ien Han [the dramatist]. He said that it had already been decided to have religions represented in the CPPCC and I was delighted to hear it. Mr. Lin also asked very solicitously what was the state of Buddhist circles in Peking. I said, "Not too tranquil." He said that if there were some concrete facts, I could report them to him and he would pass them on to a higher level. Not long after that the People's Municipal Government of Peking issued a proclamation strictly prohibiting damage to temples and ancient cultural monuments. Buddhist circles gradually calmed down. However, I considered that such negative protection had to be followed by positive reorganization before it could be effective. With this idea in view I had a long talk with deputy mayor Chang Yu-yü, who was very enlightened and also had quite a good understanding of the state of Buddhist circles. He said that positive reorganization would be beneficial both to Buddhism and to the government, but there had to be a Buddhist group to assume leadership from within. When forming the group it would be best to restrict its goal to the solution of the problems of Buddhism; there was no need to get involved with other matters. This was very good advice. Therefore, on the basis of his suggestion, I drafted a proposal for setting up a national committee for the reorganization of Buddhism and a charter for a preparatory committee and sent them to the United Front Department for approval. The comrades at the United Front Department said that to organize a nationwide group would necessitate bringing in many able people and to do this at that time might be difficult. It would be better to wait until after the CPPCC. For one thing there would then be the Common Program to go by and, for another, the CPPCC delegates themselves would bear a responsibility for dealing with this problem. This view was very correct, and therefore the question of forming a group was temporarily shelved.

On June 21, 1949, a plenary session of the CPPCC Preparatory Committee passed a resolution on the composition and numbers of delegates to attend. Seven seats were allotted to democratic personages from religious circles. When Buddhists in Peking heard about this, they all congratulated one another. At that juncture I wrote a letter to Mr. Li Wei-han. Its main points were that Buddhism was one of the three great religions of the world with a history of 2,500-2,600 years; that it had believers throughout Asia; that recently it had been taken up by Europeans and Americans and that even in the Soviet Union there were several noted Buddhist scholars; that it had a tradition of 1,800 years in our own country and today there were great numbers of believers; and so Buddhism qualified for representation in the CPPCC. It was true that we Buddhists felt ashamed that since the founding of the Chinese Republic we had been unable to break completely the bonds of feudalism, vigorously reform ourselves, and develop the inherent revolutionary spirit of Buddhism so as to serve the people. But now there had to be a fierce and thoroughgoing reformation. We believed that, unless all our hopes were in vain, Buddhists could still perhaps play an active role vis-à-vis the masses after they underwent reform and on the basis of their faith in its original form. At the same time we Buddhists would strive to take part in the CPPCC, both for the sake of our faith and to repay the Buddha's kindness. Later on I wrote to Mr. Li Wei-han another letter. Part of it read:

> I have learned recently from Mr. Li Chi-shen and Mr. T'ien Han that there would be Buddhists among the seven delegates to attend the CPPCC. Let me briefly convey why I am so overjoyed at this news. To have

religious delegates in the CPPCC is a boon of democracy. The religious delegates should be able to apply the theory of New Democracy to solve all problems with respect to religion in such a way that afterwards they have a clean conscience with respect to the people. Otherwise—if they just take things easy and look pretty in their seats—they will be a handicap to religion and a blot on the CPPCC. Take Buddhism for instance. Because its long history and large number of believers have resulted in an accumulation of abuses, it has more problems to solve than Christianity or Islam. The responsibility Buddhists delegates bear will be correspondingly heavy and difficult. Therefore it is obvious why the selection of Buddhist delegates must be very strict. According to Buddhist scriptures, monks and nuns who have left lay life are in charge of the dharma, whereas Buddhist devotees who remain laymen merely protect the dharma. Therefore a monk may become the head of a monastery, whereas devotees are only its patrons. Although for many decades past eminent monks and nuns certainly have not been lacking, the character of the general run has been deteriorating. In faith and knowledge some are even far below lay devotees. Their status, however, as those who have charge of the dharma remains unchanged. Therefore if we are talking about the reform of Buddhism, the discussion must first focus on monasteries and temples headed by monks and nuns, and lay groups organized by devotees must come later. This point has already been elaborated in the "draft proposal for the reform of Buddhism in the New China," which was attached to the statement submitted to Chairman Mao. So it is very clear why the Buddhist delegates to the CPPCC should consist principally of monks and nuns.

At this time Mr. Ch'en Ming-shu, the devotee, came to Peking. Regarding CPPCC representation, he thought that among the seven religious delegates three should be Buddhists, considering the long history of Buddhism and the number of its believers. He and Mr. Li Chi-shen also jointly propounded this view to Mr. Li Wei-han. It was not until August 31 that the final decision was taken: three of the religious delegates would be from Buddhist circles, one of whom would be in the category of "specially invited." Later, when devotee Lü Ch'iu-i [Lü Ch'eng] was prevented by business from coming to the capital, his name was not posted and so only two of us, devotee Chao P'u-ch'u and myself, attended the conference. I was well aware of the heavy responsibility I bore and of the difficulties beyond my powers of coping, but for the sake of Buddhism with its history of over 2,500 years, I could not but make an effort to cope with these difficulties. This was the second stage of my work over the past year.

On National Day, October 1 [1949], I met Mr. Ch'iao Mu[18] at the T'ien-an-men. He said that Buddhism was terribly important in the relation to Southeast Asian countries and that an association ought to be organized to carry on work. What a coincidence it was, I said, for we were just then thinking about starting the reform of the Buddhist establishment by first organizing a local Buddhist association. The draft constitution was already in proof and we were waiting for it to be printed so that we could submit it and get the reaction of those in authority.

We had embarked on this plan because we had been urged to by the Civil Affairs Bureau of the Peking Municipal People's Government, but it was necessary to get the prior approval of the United Front Department. From Mr. Wang Po-ping I learned that the United Front Department considered that the Buddhist establishment definitely needed reform but that no decision had yet been reached about what reforms should be carried out. There were two main reasons for this. First, the Central Government was still considering whether an organ should be created to handle religious affairs. Second, the religious affairs team of the CPPCC National Committee had not yet begun to function. Therefore we had better wait a little before organizing a Buddhist group. At that time the Buddhist lay devotee, Chao P'u-ch'u, had returned to Shanghai on business. Since there were many things that needed to be talked over between religous circles and the government, I had to remain in Peking.

Since the beginning of my stay in Peking, I had been having constant discussions with Peking Buddhists on the question of carrying out a reform of the Buddhist establishment. My efforts to this end can be divided into three phases. The first was setting up a temporary Buddhist Problems Study Society (Fo-chaio Wen-t'i Yen-chiu Hui) to help me collect materials and do research on the questions that arose during the session of the CPPCC. The second was organizing a symposium to get monks throughout the city started on collective discussion. It too was temporary in nature and thus was not registered with the government. At the symposium I addressed the audience as follows:

> I came to Peking to win a reasonable attitude towards Buddhism and proper role for it in the new nation and new society. Thus far on both counts the government has reacted satisfactorily in a concrete way. Chao P'u-ch'u and I have participated in the CPPCC as Buddhist delegates. This was not simply because we were Buddhists, but also because of certain contributions we had made in the past to the democratic movement. One might say that we were invited to be delegates because we were democratic personages, and, because we were Buddhists, we were invited to be the delegates who represented the democratic personages of Buddhist circles. How must we do things, then, in the future? We know that Buddhist circles have never had anything to do with imperialism and also have had very little connection with bureaucratic capitalism. On the other hand, society generally regards us Buddhists as closely connected with the feudal tradition. We do not object to self-examination. In the past, what

> did we depend on for our livelihood? There is not denying that the major part came from land rents. This proves beyond doubt that we Buddhists have been good friends of feudal imperialism. Henceforward if we continue in our old ways and do not make plans to improve, the times will not put up with us. We must be well aware that the founding of the new nation is not like a change of dynasties in the past, and that in the new society it is absolutely impermissible for man to exploit man and man to oppress man. We must really wake up to this. We must utilize the reasonable attitude and proper role we have won in order to exert ourselves in good time, truly to display Sakyamuni's revolutionary spirit, and truly to undertake production so as to serve society and the people. Only in this way do we have a future. The alternative is for us to be weeded out as unfit to survive. Looked at in the light of present objective conditions, Buddhism is by no means without a future, but it must be we ourselves who win that future. Buddhism is by no means without light, but again it must be we ourselves who try to find its light. Buddhism has many problems, but they are problems that we alone must try to overcome. Whether the future is to bring disaster or prosperity, fortune or misfortune, depends upon how we do things.

Following my address 238 major monasteries and temples individually put forward their suggestions for reform, which came down to four points: (a) thorough elimination of feudalism and superstition; (b) purging Buddhist circles of the heterodox sects concealed therein, as well as of the organizations that have borrowed the name of Buddhism to cheat the masses; (c) concentrating monks into groups to serve production; (d) [recognizing that] the property of every monastery and temple is the property of the Buddhist community (*chiao-hui*) and should be used in accordance with the wishes of the community.

Although this is the way we were talking, there was still the problem of how to put it into practice. Therefore the third phase began when I formally established the Peking Buddhists' Study Society and started to get people's thinking straightened out. The history of the study society and of the training class for monks and nuns is covered in a separate report and will not be discussed here. But there is one point I ought to mention. Although the training class for monks and nuns did not accomplish as much as we expected, it was not without results. Those who had been through training were more progressive in their thinking than those who had not. They understood the times and the true spirit of Buddhism, and they accepted the theory and method of reforming the Buddhist establishment. They also understood that the future of Buddhism had to be won with our own blood and sweat. Therefore we opened a gunnysack factory and got them into this sector of production. This fitted into the plan for a new type of public monastery and was the first step towards a new constructiveness on the part of Chinese Buddhism. That was the third phase of my work over the past year. There follows a draft outline of how a "new type of public monastery" should be organized.

1. If any monastery wants to become a new type of public monastery *(hsin ts'ung-lin)*, a management committee having specific responsibilities and consisting of seven to nine members shall be elected by all the monks of the monastery together with devout Buddhist laymen who have some historical connection with the monastery.

2. The head and deputy head of a committee shall be monks, but other positions may go to Buddhist devotees if there are no monks to fill them or if they are unable to fill them.

3. The term of committee members shall be three years and they may be re-elected for consecutive terms.

4. Under the committee there shall be teams for general business, study, production, religious practice, and research. The function of each team shall be as follows:

a. General business team. This team shall handle all manner of business, bookkeeping, disbursements, and visitors, so that it will be equivalent to the business office and guest department of traditional monasteries.

b. Study team. This team shall take charge of study of the new democracy and of the basics of Buddhism.

c. Production team. This team shall handle industrial and agricultural production.

d. Religious practice team. This team shall make arrangements for elderly monks and Buddhist lay devotees who wish to concentrate on keeping up religious practice. Young persons who want to participate must do so in time they can be spared from labor.

e. Research team. This team shall make arrangements for concentration solely on research by monks whose cultural level is high and who have a background in research on Buddhism. However, once every six months they must produce an important dissertation.

5. Once the committee is set up, anyone who wants to join this new type of public monastery shall only be admitted after he has been carefully investigated and passed by the committee. If anyone wants to withdraw after joining, he shall have the liberty to do so only after persuasion has failed to change his mind.

6. Those who have joined the new type of public monastery, with the exception of the elderly, shall earn their keep through physical or mental labor and [free] board shall not be provided in the monastery.

7. Income from the monastery's real estate, except for what is used to support the elderly and the research personnel, shall all be used to pay contributions and taxes (*chüan-shui*).

8. From each person's compensation for labor a certain percentage according to the circumstances shall be deducted and pooled for use as a welfare fund and for emergencies.

9. Finances shall be public; receipts and expenditures shall be published once a month.

10. An eight-hour day shall be the standard for all manual and mental laborers. In addition they shall attend devotions once a day; and once a day there shall be study of the new culture and of the basics of Buddhism. The form of devotions shall be separately prescribed.[19]

11. All small temples belonging to all members of the new public monastery must be entirely turned over to the committee for handling.

12. The reform of dress and of the "pure rules" (including stipulations about becoming a monk and receiving ordination) shall be separately prescribed.

After the CPPCC came to a close, conversations were continuously underway with the government on the problem of reforming the various religions, until on May 5, 1950, a second symposium convened by the Religious Affairs Team of the [CPPCC] National Committee formally began discussion. First Mr. Ch'en Ch'i-yüan, acting chief of the section, transmitted Premier Chou En-lai's instructions on the problem of religion. The main idea was: The government in its coöperation with religion was after political, not ideological (*ssu-hsiang*) conformity. Every religion should confine itself to religion (*tsai-chiao yen-chiao*). Christianity should resolutely oppose imperialism, in particular American imperialism. Occurrences in various places that impaired freedom of religious belief had to be censured and corrected with the utmost vigor. Mr. Pu Hua-jen,[20] the next to speak, said: "Of the cadres in various places, some have handled religious problems well, some have not. This has not only been true for religious problems, but for other problems. Religious circles should not be pessimistic. They should trust the government. Difficulties can be overcome and things may perhaps take the turn for the better after rectification." Finally Mr. Ch'en Ch'i-yüan answered the questions I raised by making three points.

1. The preservation of monuments was not a problem for Buddhism alone. The Government Administrative Council would soon be promulgating a directive.

2. Regulations on the registration of social groups had gone through repeated discussion and would soon be promulgated. They would cover religious groups too.

3. When government organs and army units borrowed religious buildings (including monasteries and temples), they should get the consent of the persons in charge; a directive [about this] had been issued in January this year by the Ministry of Internal Affairs. But monasteries and temples that had vacant rooms should take into consideration the widespread shortage of space and

should help the government in their area to resolve the difficulties arising therefrom.

In the case of Christianity, the reform of which was directed towards administration, financial support, and preaching by the Chinese themselves [rather than foreigners], the draft program had been revised eight times and not formally made public until September 23, [1949]. From this one could see how very cautiously matters of this kind were handled.[21]

On May 29, [1950], the Religious Affairs Team convened a third symposium to discuss three documents that I had presented, namely: (1) "The Present Situation of Buddhism"; (2) "Suggestions for Handling Common Religious Problems"; (3) "Suggestions for the Reform of Buddhism." The main goals in reforming Buddhism, said Mr. Lan Kung-wu, were productive labor, sweeping away the handicap of superstitious thinking, and eliminating the role of monasteries as landlords. Nor, he said, could we permit the survival of the system of hereditary temples, in which little children became monks. He expressed support for the suggestions I had made on reform. Mr. Hsieh Pang-ting[22] made four additional suggestions: to conduct propaganda; to get more voluntary effort; to provide a model at important centers that could be followed elsewhere; and to stress equally the teaching of the doctrine and support for those who teach it (? *–chiao-yang ping-chung*). I considered all this to be most correct and, after thorough revision, it became a paper entitled "Suggestions for the Reform of Buddhism," of which the preamble and basic points were as follows:

> Buddhists throughout the country loyally express their support and love for the commencement of a new era and the founding of a new nation. We feel neither complacent nor proud of ourselves because Buddhism has had a long history in our country, a multitude of believers, a large number of monasteries and temples, and has affected many aspects of society. On the contrary, we hold that the Buddhism of the past was inextricably bound up with feudalism and that the thinking and behavior of Buddhists were largely superstitious and backward. Therefore we sincerely support the Common Program, and under the leadership of the government we oppose imperialism, feudalism, and bureaucratic capitalism. Our purpose is to cleanse Buddhist circles of the parasitism, laziness, pessimism, and escapism which still survive there and which can hinder social development; to recover the revolutionary spirit of primeval Buddhism, which was realistic and practical; and to make Buddhism a force in the construction of the new nation. The following basic principles are proposed for the reform of Buddhism:
>
> 1. As Buddhism has been very deeply impregnated with feudalsim and superstition, hence in the early stage of reform, the main task will be to combat feudalism and superstition. At the same time, in order to safe-

guard a lasting world peace and to complete the victory of national construction, we must combat imperialism and bureaucratic capitalism.

2. The present Buddhist system must be thoroughly reformed in the direction of productive labor, so that elderly monks and nuns will receive support and young monks and nuns will have work. This will eliminate the role of monasteries as landlords, the system of hereditary private ownership [of temples] and doing business in superstition.

3. In theoretical work we should, according to Article 40 of the Common Program of the CPPCC, study Mahayana doctrines with a scientific-historical approach and discard what is false while exalting what is true, in order to purify our thinking. In our conduct, we should promote the positive spirit of the bodhisattva path and selflessly put theory into practice. With regard to our literature, while everything should be preserved, there must be weeding out and cleaning up so as to put the scriptures in order.

These suggestions were brought up for discussion again on June 10 at the fourth symposium held by the Religious Affairs Team, which considered them to be quite correct and consistent with the policy of [creating] a new society. But [the feeling was that] in carrying them out haste should be avoided, and they should be worded tactfully in order to avoid misunderstanding. When he had conveyed Premier Chou En-lai's instructions to us, Mr. Ch'en Ch'i-yüan had also called on us to solicit more suggestions from different quarters before deciding anything. Therefore seven persons—Li Chi-shen, Ch'en Ming-shu, T'ang Sheng-chih, Chao P'u-ch'u, Fang Tzu-fan, Chou Shu-chia, and I—jointly extended an invitation to those of the delegates to the second conference of the CPPCC National Committee who had some connection with Buddhism, asking them to a symposium at the Sen-lung Restaurant on June 18, [1950]. Besides the hosts, there were ten persons present: Yeh Kung-cho, Li I-p'ing, Chou T'ai-hsüan, Li Ming-yang, Lin Chih-chün, Tung Lu-an, Liang Sou-ming, Li Ken-yüan, Shirob Jaltso, Cheng Chen-to, and Sha Yung-ts'ang.[23] A summary of our discussion is given below.

Chü-tsan reported on his work to date in drafting the paper "Suggestions for the Reform of Buddhism" and on his two discussions with the Religious Affairs Team of the National Committee.

Chao P'u-ch'u said that the suggestions for the reform of Buddhism that had now been put forward might be called the draft of a draft, and only after a lot more discussion in various quarters could they become the consensus of Buddhist circles. The procedure should be like that followed in revising suggestions for the reform of the Protestant Church, where stress was laid at first on asking the government to solve problems, but at the end, after it had been revised for the eighth time, the stress was entirely on the work of the churches themselves. In reforming Buddhism this could be referred to as a model. But the reform of Buddhism was something that the force of circumstances did require and, instead of being made to act, it was better to take the initiative in action.

Yeh Kung-cho: A characteristic of Buddhism in the past had been its dispersion and being scattered over a vast area. There would perhaps be many difficulties if the work of reform were begun at once on a national scale. Simply in economic terms it would create problems. It seemed better to start with local work. It would be easier to settle on measures that would be applicable to a given district than to attempt a reorganization that would be uniform throughout the country.

Ch'en Ming-shu: Suggestions for the reform of Buddhism should now be discussed with fellow Buddhists in Peking. Later suggestions should be solicited from Buddhists throughout the country. After a decision had been reached, then plans could be made to organize a Buddhist association.

Liang Sou-ming: In the past Buddhists had been like a tray of loose sand. It was most necessary to link them up and create a center. Today's gathering might provide the foundation. He himself was exceedingly eager to contribute his utmost.

Shirob Jaltso: The word "reform" could never be lightly used in regard to Buddhism. According to what was contained in the suggestions paper, it was only a question of [reforming] the Buddhist establishment. Buddhists should seek to keep their behavior in tune with the time and place, but doctrine and religious cultivation (*hsiu-yang*), that is, the Buddhist religion as such, were absolutely not open to change and this point should be firmly maintained. To settle now on the term "the reform of Buddhism" would perhaps cause no problem in Chinese, but if it were translated into Tibetan, it could give rise to grave misunderstanding. As to how the [secular] activities of Buddhists could be made to fit in with the policies of the government, in his view this was, properly speaking, up to the Buddhists.

Chü-tsan: It was the custom in Buddhist circles in China proper that when one talked about "Buddhism" (*fo-chiao*), it generally meant the externals of Buddhism and its system of operation. If one were talking about doctrines and religious cultivation, one usually employed the terms "Buddhist studies" (*fo-hsüeh*) or the "dharma" (*fo-fa*). Therefore, the kind of reform we were talking about was consistent with the views of the Venerable Shirob.

Chou T'ai-hsüan: To reform the Buddhist system was a matter for the sangha. Monks and nuns from different localities ought to be called together to talk it over.

Chao P'u-ch'u: At present Buddhist monasteries in different localities were in danger of extinction. They had no organization and no way of maintaining themselves. One thing that could be done first would be to organize groups along the lines of fellowship societies for Buddhists—organs by which Buddhists in the different localities could get into touch with one another.

Li Chi-shen: If we were talking about the situation today, the reform of

Buddhism was more urgent than the propagation of Buddhist doctrines. Copies of the suggestions paper could be sent out to monasteries in the different localities, soliciting their views, and later representatives in the different localities could be convoked to talk things over together.

Chü-tsan: To organize Buddhist groups was, of course, very urgent. To solicit suggestions widely was also a must. But there always had to be some basic principles to go on before any of these could play a useful role; otherwise it would certainly lead to nothing. The suggestions for reform that had been under discussion there that day should be regarded as the basic principles to go on.

The outcome of this discussion was as follows. In order to avoid misunderstanding, the "Suggestions Paper for the Reform of Buddhism" was retitled "The Suggestion Paper on the Reform of the Chinese Buddhist Establishment." Chü-tsan would first solicit the suggestions of monks and nuns in Peking and devotee Fang Tzu-fan would solicit the suggestions of monks and nuns in Shanghai. Then a date would be fixed to hold a meeting in Shanghai at which the Buddhist delegates to people's representative conferences in the different provinces and cities and persons in Buddhist circles who were enthusiastic about reform would be invited to hold discussions together. At the same time we would sponsor the organization of the Modern Buddhism Publishing House, which would publish a monthly, *Modern Buddhism.* Ch'en Ming-shu was elected the publisher and Chü-tsan the editor-in-chief. Other details are given in the report on its origin and its articles of association and there is no need to repeat them there. Just one point should be made. The Modern Buddhism Publishing House was started June 18 and before three months had gone by, the first issue was out. Everything went very smoothly, perhaps thanks to the blessing of the "Three Jewels of the Ten Directions (*shih-fang san-pao*). This means that we have our own magazine in the capital with which we can transmit the government's religious policy, correct mistaken thinking in Buddhist circles, hold aloft the true spirit of Sakyamuni, and report conditions in Buddhist circles throughout the country. Thus our efforts were consummated successfully. This was the fourth phase of my work over the past year.

The above is the story of my year's work. Although it cannot be said that I accomplished much, I have really exerted my best efforts for Buddhism and it has not proved to be entirely fruitless. I cannot but feel grateful for the times we live in and for the all-embracing solicitude and wise direction of the government authorities. At the same time there was the support and encouragement of devotees Li Chi-shen, Ch'en Ming-shu, Chao P'u-ch'u, Li Ming-yang, Chou T'ai-hsüan, Yeh Kung-cho, Li Shu-ch'üan, Chou Shu-chia, and Sha Yung-ts'ang, and of abbots Sheng-ch'üan of the Hsien-liang Ssu and Ta-ju of the Chi-le An. Only because they gave every kind of attention and support was it possible to get such results. This is something that must be made especially clear in reporting to Buddhists throughout the country.

[The last page and half of Chü-tsan's report is not translated here, since the contents, which deal mostly with damage to Buddhist monasteries and the expulsion of monks, are covered in Chapters III and V. According to the colophon, the report was completed September 26, 1950, at the Chi-le Ssu, where Chü-tsan was presumably living.]

Appendix B

The Council of the Chinese Buddhist Association

The table below shows how the Han-nationality membership of the council of the CBA changed over the years. The names of all members of the standing committee are preceded by an asterisk. The names of lay persons are italicized. The names of persons whom I often saw mentioned as Buddhists before Liberation are printed in capital letters. The names of nuns and female devotees are followed by (f), heads of temples by "abbot" or "abbess." The locality that each member is from is not his place of origin but his domicile at the time of his election. A few members who were first elected at the enlarged council meeting in August 1955 are so tagged. The sources of the information in the table are *HTFH,* 6/53, pp. 14, 17; 5/57, p. 28; and 2/62, pp. 9-10 (May 1962). Few of the names are included in the glossary.

The table is significant in several ways. It shows that monks and nuns outnumbered the laity three or four times over in the CBA council, presumably as a token of the sangha's leadership of Buddhism. Yet in the secretariat (where real power lay) laymen outnumbered monks two or three times over until 1962. By then enough trustworthy monks and nuns had been trained so that they could be allowed a majority in the secretariat too.

Women were not given equality of representation. In the 1930's nearly half the sangha had consisted of nuns, and more women than men had worshiped at most Buddhist temples. Yet female members of the CBA amounted to 7-8 per cent. More important, perhaps, Peking (as the capital) and Shanghai (as the center of Buddhist activism) were represented by far more delegates (about 17 per cent each) than could be justified by their Buddhist population. In the 1930's Peking had had less than one-half of one per cent of the nation's Buddhists. Other places with disproportionately high representation were Shansi, Shensi, Honan, and Hopei, probably because they had historically important temples that were often shown to foreign visitors. Shantung was the only province with no representation at all.

The biggest inequity does not show up in this table, since it lists Hans only.

Some 40-50 per cent of the council members came from minority nationalities, though these amounted to but 6 per cent of China's population. (cf. Chapter I, note 59). The purpose was, of course, to counteract separatism in outlying areas.

Despite such inequities the namelists show that the CBA was intended by the regime to hold the confidence and perhaps to reflect the opinions of the conservative majority of the nation's Buddhists. Few members can be identified as clerical reformers or radicals and their number did not increase. More than half the members added to the standing committee in 1957 and 1962 were abbots. Throughout the history of the CBA a good proportion of the council consisted of persons who had been well known as traditional Buddhists before 1949. It is true, on the other hand, that membership in the council and promotion to the standing committee were usually granted in recognition of coöperativeness with the regime.

The table points up changes in the lives of those it lists. Chi-kuang, for example, began as an ordinary council member in Kiangsi. In 1957 he was promoted to the standing committee and that same year moved to Peking in order to become first the prior and later the abbot of the Kuang-chi Ssu. Lung-lien, who had headed a nunnery in Chengtu, also moved to Peking, where by 1955 she was one of the leading nuns of the T'ung-chiao Ssu. In 1962 she was back in Szechwan. Chou Yüeh-ch'ing lived in Peking during the years when her husband, Li Chi-shen, was a vice-chairman of the People's Government, but returned to Canton after his death.

HAN MEMBERSHIP OF THE CBA COUNCIL

1953-1957		1957-1962		1962-	
Member	from	Member	from	Member	from
A-t'an (abbot)	Shanghai	*A-t'an (abbot)	Shanghai	*A-t'an (abbot)	Shanghai
		An-hui	Liaoning		
				Chang Mu-hsiang	Shansi
		Chang Pen-ya	Yünnan	*Chang Pen-ya*	Yünnan
		Chang Po-lin	Shanghai	*Chang Po-lin*	Shanghai
				Ch'ang-ming	Shensi
**CHAO P'U-CH'U*	Shanghai	**CHAO P'U-CH'U*	Shanghai	**CHAO P'U-CH'U*	Peking
Ch'ao-ch'üan (abbess)	Hupeh	Ch'ao-ch'üan (abbess)	Hupeh	Ch'ao-ch'üan (abbess)	Hupeh
		Ch'ao-ming	Hupeh	Ch'ao-ming	Hupeh
		Che-po (abbess)	Liaoning	*Che-po (abbess)	Liaoning
		Ch'en-k'ung (abbot)	Chekiang	Ch'en-k'ung (abbot)	Chekiang
		Chen-fa	Hopei	Chen-fa	Hopei
		Cheng-kuo	Shanghai	*Cheng-huo (abbot)	Peking
				Cheng-shan	Anhwei
Chi-kuang	Kiangsi	*Chi-kuang	Kiangsi	*Chi-kuang (abbot)	Peking
Chieh-ch'eng	Kansu	Chieh-ch'eng	Kansu	Chieh-ch'eng	Kansu
				Chieh-yüan (f?)	Hunan
				Chih-ch'an	Kwangsi
				Chih-pei	Liaoning
CH'IH-SUNG (abbot)	Shanghai	*CH'IH-SUNG (abbot)	Shanghai	*CH'IH-SUNG (abbot)	Shanghai
CHING-CH'UAN (abbot)	Chekiang	*CHING-CH'UAN (abbot)	Chekiang	deceased	

		Ching-ju (abbot)	Shansi	Ching-ju (abbot)	Shansi
		*Ching-kuan	Heilungkiang	*Ching-kuan	Heilungkiang
Ching-yen	Honan	Ching-yen	Honan	Ching-yen	Honan
**CHOU SHU-CHIA*	Peking	**CHOU SHU-CHIA*	Peking	**CHOU SHU-CHIA*	Peking
Chou Yüeh-ch'ing (f)	Peking	**Chou Yüeh-ch'ing* (f)	Peking	**Chou Yüeh-ch'ing* (f)	Kwangtung
Ch'un-hsin (abbot)	Kwangtung	Ch'un-hsin (abbot)	Kwangtung	Ch'un-hsin (abbot)	Kwangtung
		Chuan-p'ien	Yünnan	Chuan-p'ien	Yünnan
		Chung-ch'üan	Kirin	Chung-ch'üan	Kirin
Chung Hui-ch'eng	Shanghai	*Chung Hui-ch'eng*	Shanghai	*Chung Hui-ch'eng*	Shanghai
Chung-ting (1955)	Shanghai	Chung-ting	Shanghai	Chung-ting	Shanghai
				Chung-yü	Shensi
*Chü-tsan	Kiangsu	*Chü-tsan	Peking	*Chü-tsan	Peking
		Chüeh-ch'eng (abbot)	Kwangtung	Chüeh-ch'eng (abbot)	Kwangtung
FA-TSUN	Peking	*FA-TSUN	Peking	*FA-TSUN	Peking
Fan-ch'eng	Kiangsu	Fan-ch'eng	Kiangsu		
Fang Tzu-fan	Shanghai	*Fang Tzu-fan*	Shanghai	*Fang Tzu-fan*	Shanghai
				Fu-hui	Fukien
				Fu-t'ien	Szechwan
Han Ta-tsai	Hupeh	*Han Ta-tsai*	Hupeh	*Han Ta-tsai*	Hupeh
		Hsiang-li (abbot)	Shansi		
		Hsien-tsung	Peking		
		Hsin-chuan	Hunan	Hsin-chuan	Hunan
		Hsin-tao	Kiangsi	Hsin-tao	Kiangsi
Hsing-fu (1955)	Kiangsi	Hsing-fu	Kiangsi	*Hsing-fu	Kiangsi
				Hsing-k'ung	Chekiang

Continued

1953-1957		1957-1962		1962-	
Member	from	Member	from	Member	from
Hsiu-yüan (1955)	Yünnan	Hsiu-yüan	Yünnan		
		Hsin-tsung (abbot)	Szechwan		
		Hsü P'ing-hsüan	Kiangsu	*Hsü P'ing-hsüan*	Kiangsu
Hsü Sen-yü	Shanghai	*Hsü Sen-yü*	Shanghai	*Hsü Sen-yü*	Shanghai
Hsü-tao (1955)	Hopei	Hsü-tao	Hopei	Hsü-tao	Hopei
				Hsüan-chih	Shansi
Huai-i	Kweichow	Huai-i	Kweichow	Huai-i	Kweichow
		Huang Ch'an-hua	Shanghai	*Huang Ch'an-hua*	Chekiang
				Hui-chüeh	Fukien
		Hui-kuan	Heilungkiang	Hui-kuan	Heilungkiang
		Hui-tsung	Shanghai	Hui-tsung	Shanghai
Hui-wen (1955-abbot)	Hopei	Hui-wen (abbot)	Hopei		
				Hung-liang	Kiangsu
Hung-san	Yünnan	Hung-san	Yünnan		
I-fang	Anhwei	*I-fang	Anhwei	deceased	
I-huan	Shanghai	I-huan	Shanghai	I-huan	Shanghai
Jen-hsin (1955)	Kirin	Jen-hsin	Kirin	*Jen-hsin	Kirin
Ju-san (1955)	Shanghai	Ju-san	Shanghai	Ju-san	Shanghai
		K'ai-i	Szechwan	K'ai-i	Szechwan
Kao Ho-nien	Kiangsu	*Kao Ho-nien*	Kiangsu	deceased	
		Kao Kuan-ju	Peking	*Kao Kuan-ju*	Peking
Ken-ch'üan	Kiangsi	Ken-ch'üan	Kiangsi		
		Ken-ju	Anhwei		

				K'uan-jung (abbot)	Chekiang
				KUAN-K'UNG	Peking
		K'uan-neng (nun)	Kwangsi	*K'uan-neng (nun)	Kwangsi
				Kuang-hsin (abbot)	Fukien
**Kuo P'eng*	Peking	**Kuo P'eng*	Peking	**Kuo P'eng*	Peking
				Lan-wu	Anhwei
Lang-chao (abbot)	Shensi	*Lang-chao (abbot)	Shensi	*Lang-chao (abbot)	Shensi
Li I-p'ing	Kiangsi	**Li I-p'ing*	Peking	**Li I-p'ing*	Peking
		Li Jung-hsi	Peking	*Li Jung-hsi*	Peking
		Li-k'ung	Shensi	Li-k'ung	Shansi
				Liang Wen-t'ung	Kwangsi
Lin Tsai-p'ing	Peking	*Lin Tsai-p'ing*	Peking	deceased	
Lin Yang-tseng					
Liu Ya-hsiu	Szechwan	*Liu Ya-hsiu*	Szechwan	dropped	
Lu Ho-fu (or Tibetan)	Shensi				
Lung-hai	Hopei	Lung-hai	Hopei	*Lung-hai	Hopei
Lung-kuang (1955)	Hopei	Lung-kuang	Hopei	Lung-kuang	Hopei
Lung-lien (1955, nun)	Peking	*Lung-lien (nun)	Peking	*Lung-lien (nun)	Szechwan
Lung-yü	Shansi	Lung-yü	Shansi	Lung-yü	Shansi
**LÜ CH'ENG*	Kiangsu	**LÜ CH'ENG*	Kiangsu	**LÜ CH'ENG*	Kiangsu
Man-tz'u (1955)	Hunan	Man-tz'u	Hunan	Man-tz'u	Hunan
		Mao-lin	Peking	Mao-lin	Peking
Mi-pao (1955-abbot)	Hupeh	Mi-pao (abbot)	Hupeh	*Mi-pao (abbot)	Hupeh

Continued

1953-1957		1957-1962		1962-	
Member	from	Member	from	Member	from
		MIAO-CHEN (abbot)	Kiangsu	MIAO-CHEN (abbot)	Kiangsu
		Miao-ch'üan	Hupeh		
				Miao-hsing	Anhwei
		MIAO-HUA (abbot)	Kiangsu	MIAO-HUA (abbot)	Kiangsu
Miao-k'uo (1955-abbot)	Shensi	Miao-k'uo (abbot)	Shensi		
		Miao-lien (abbot)	Fukien	*Miao-lien (abbot)	Fukien
				Miao-lien	Hupeh
Ming-chen	Hunan	*Ming-chen	Hunan	*Ming-chen	Hunan
				Ming-k'ai	Kiangsu
				Ming-ta	Shansi
		Ming-te	Honan		
Ming-yang (1955)	Shanghai	Ming-yang	Shanghai	Ming-yang	Shanghai
				Mo Yün-kang	Kweichow
*NENG-HAI	Szechwan	*NENG-HAI	Shansi	*NENG-HAI	Shansi
		Neng-pen (abbess)	Peking	Neng-pen (abbess)	Peking
		Nuan-jui	Shanghai	Nuan-jui	Shanghai
Pen-huan (1955-abbot)	Kwangtung	Pen-huan (abbot)	Kwangtung	dropped	
		Ping-ch'u	Anhwei	Ping-ch'u	Anhwei
Po-ming (1955)	Hunan	Po-ming	Hunan	dropped?	
		P'u-chao	Szechwan	P'u-chao	Szechwan
				P'u-yü	Fukien

		San-i	Shansi	San-i	Shansi
				Shan-chu	Hupeh
				Shen-jih	Chekiang
		Shen-te	Shansi	Shen-te	Shansi
Sheng-ch'üan	Peking	Sheng-ch'üan	Peking	dropped?	
Sheng-hui (abbot)	Fukien	Sheng-hui (abbot)	Fukien	deceased?	
Sheng-lien (1955-nun)	Shensi	Sheng-lien (nun)	Shensi	Sheng-lien (nun)	Shensi
		**Shih Ming-k'o*	Peking	**Shih Ming-k'o*	Peking
Shou-p'ei (1955)					
Sun Le-chai	Yünnan	*Sun Le-chai*	Yünnan	*Sun Le-chai*	Yünnan
				Sung-t'ao	Kiangsu
				Ta-ch'ang (abbot)	Shensi
Ta-hsin (abbot)	Hupeh	*Ta-hsin (abbot)	Hupeh	deceased	
TA-PEI (abbot)	Chekiang	*TA-PEI (abbot)	Peking (?)	*TA-PEI (abbot)	Chekiang
Ta-yüan	Shanghai				
T'ai-kung	Szechwan	T'ai-kung	Szechwan	T'ai-kung	Szechwan
		TAN-YÜN (abbot)	Chekiang	TAN-YÜN (abbot)	Chekiang
Tao-ch'en (abbot)	Liaoning	*Tao-ch'en (abbot)	Liaoning	*Tao-ch'en (abbot)	Liaoning
		Tao-hang (abbot)	Kiangsu	Tao-hang (abbot)	Kiangsu
Te-ch'in (1955-nun)	Fukien	Te-ch'in (nun)	Fukien	Te-ch'in (nun)	Fukien
		Ting-an	Kweichow	Ting-an	Kweichow
				Ts'eng-t'ai (abbot)	Hupeh
Ts'ung-shan (1955)	Chekiang	Ts'ung-shan	Chekiang	Ts'ung-shan	Chekiang

Continued

1953-1957		1957-1962		1962-	
Member	from	Member	from	Member	from
**Tung Lu-an*	Hopei	deceased			
				T'ung-mei	Chekiang
		Tzu-an	Shanghai	Tzu-an	Shanghai
Tzu-hsin (1955)	Yünnan	Tzu-hsin	Yünnan		
				Tsu-hsing	Yûnnan
		Tzu-ju	Honan	Tzu-ju	Honan
Tz'u-ch'ing (abbot)	Szechwan	Tz'u-ch'ing (abbot)	Szechwan	*Tz'u-ch'ing (abbot)	Szechwan
TZ'U-CHOU	Fukien	*TZ'U-CHOU	Fukien	deceased	
				Tz'u-fa (abbot)	Heilungkiang
Tz'u-tsang (1955)	Kiangsi	Tz'u-tsang	Kiangsi	dropped?	
Tz'u-yün	Shensi	Tz'u-yün	Shensi	Tz'u-yün	Shensi
		Wang En-yang	Szechwan	*Wang En-yang*	Szechwan
		Wang Tsan	Peking	*Wang Tsan*	Peking
		Wei-ching	Kiangsu		
WEI-FANG (abbot)	Shanghai	*WEI-FANG (abbot)	Shanghai	*WEI-FANG (abbot)	Shanghai
				Wu Chin-ting	Peking
		Yang Hai-lien	Kansu	*Yang Hai-lien*	Kansu
YEH KUNG-CHO	Peking	*YEH KUNG-CHO*	Peking	*YEH KUNG-CHO*	Peking
				Yeh-chün	Peking
				Yen-i	Szechwan
		Yin-ku	Hopei (?)		
		*Ying-ch'e (abbot)	Kiangsu	*Ying-ch'e (abbot)	Kiangsu

YING-TZ'U	Shanghai	*YING-TZ'U	Shanghai		
		Yung-kuang	Szechwan	Yung-kuang	Szechwan
				Yü Po-hsien	Shanghai
Yu Yu-wei	Shanghai	*Yu Yu-wei*	Shanghai	*Yu Yu-wei*	Shanghai
		Yü Yü	Peking	*Yü Yü*	Peking
Yüan-chüeh (nun)	Peking	*Yüan-chüeh (nun)	Peking	*Yüeh-chüeh (nun)	Peking
*YÜAN-YING	Fukien	deceased			
Yüeh-an	Kansu	Yüeh-an	Kansu		
Yüeh-hai	Anhwei	Yüeh-hai	Anhwei	*Yüeh-hai	Anhwei
		Yüeh-hsi	Chekiang	*Yüeh-hsi	Chekiang
		Yüeh-t'ao (abbot)	Chekiang	Yüeh-t'ao (abbot)	Chekiang
				Yüeh-ts'ang	Yünnan
				Yün-feng	Kwangtung

Appendix C

Monastic Population

The figures given below are intended to show how the number of residents in certain monasteries and areas changed after Liberation. Those without notes came from Mainland visitors and refugees.

A plus sign (unless otherwise indicated in the notes) means that information from the Chinese source was phrased in such a way that final zeros may be replaced by any digits from 1 to 9 so that, for example, 10+ can mean anything from 11 to 19, 100+ anything from 101 to 199. All round numbers should be considered approximate.

The successive figures for a monastery or area are not always comparable. Before Liberation 20-30 percent of the total number of residents often consisted of wandering monks and lay workmen. After Liberation both these categories were largely eliminated by the drop in monastic revenues. Another reason that successive figures may not be comparable is a desire on the part of the source to maximize or minimize; or differing degrees of carelessness.

This table is still, I think, of some value. It provides evidence of three different patterns of change in monastic population. First there is overall decline, seen in Chekiang and Kiangsu and at individual monasteries like Chin Shan and the Hua-t'ing Ssu, Kunming. Second there is the oscillation that took place as monks from monasteries that had been closed down were collected at those that remained open. This can be seen at the Kuo-ch'ing Ssu, T'ien-t'ai Shan; the K'ai-fu Ssu, Changsha; the Chen-ju Ssu in Kiangsi; and the Nan-hua Ssu, Shao-kuan. Third there are the monasteries that were at a low ebb before Liberation but were restored and enlarged by the People's Government for reasons of foreign or domestic policy and whose population therefore shot up. Examples are the Hsing-shan Ssu, Sian, and the Hsüan-chung Ssu, Shansi. Another thing of possible significance is the lack of oscillation at some monasteries from 1960 to 1966. These were the monasteries most often visited by foreign Buddhists. The unchanging figures given out to the latter could reflect a policy of maintaining the monastic population at these important spots; or at least of maintaining consistency in answering visitors' questions. Examples are the Ling-yin Ssu, Pai-ma Ssu, Ling-yen Shan, Hsing-shan Ssu, Yung-ho Kung, and Yü-fo Ssu.

Place	Year	Number of residents
Anhwei, Chiu-hua Shan	1930's	1,000
	1950	200[1]
	1953	178[2]
	1960	230
Chekiang province	1930	107,000[3]
	1955	11,100[3]
Chekiang, Hangchow municipality	1949	2,000+[4]
	1950	1,090[5]
	1953	1,177[6]
	1957	600[7]
	1961	800[8]
	1965	560[9]
Chekiang, Hangchow		
Ling-yin Ssu	1940's	400
	1951	40
	1955	30
	1957	53[10]
	1962	50
	1965	50[11]
Chekiang, Ningpo		
Ch'i-t'a Ssu	1937	300[12]
	1962	30
Kuan-tsung Ssu	1937	300
	1962	0
T'ien-t'ung Ssu	1929	400[13]
	1957	151[14]
Yü-wang Ssu	1940's	500-600[15]
	1953	109[15]
	1957	110[16]
	1962	100+
Chekiang, P'u-t'o Shan	1920's	2,000[17]
	1962	200+[18]
Chekiang, T'ien-t'ai Shan		
Kuo-ch'ing Ssu	1940's	100+
	1952	100+[19]
	1954	80+[20]

Continued

Place	Year	Number of residents
	1957	102[21]
	1958	109[22]
	1961	90+[23]
	1965	50-60
Fukien, Amoy		
Nan-p'u-t'o Ssu	1940's	200
	1953	45[24]
	1960	35
Fukien, Chüanchow		
K'ai-yüan Ssu	1957	15
	1965	19
	1969	14
Fukien, Foochow		
Ku Shan, Yung-ch'üan Ssu	1929	400[25]
	1946	12
	1954	148[26]
	1957	130[27]
	1965	50+
Honan, Loyang		
Pai-ma Ssu	1940's	25
	1949	4
	1955	9[28]
	1959	33[29]
	1960	15-17[30]
	1965	14[31]
Hunan, Changsha		
K'ai-fu Ssu	1924	45 monks[32]
	1954	122 monks and nuns[33]
	1959	114 monks and nuns[34]
Hunan, Nanyüeh	pre-1949	800
	post-1949	200
	1962	158[35]

Place	Year	Number of residents
Kiangsi		
Yün-chü Shan, Chen-ju Ssu	1949	10[36]
	1953	4[36]
	1957	100+[37]
	1958	60[38]
	1962	170
Kiangsu province	1930	171,176[3]
	1957	20,000[3]
Kiangsu, Chen-chiang		
Chin Shan, Chiang-t'ien Ssu	1940's	350[39]
	1952	100[40]
	1963	47
Kiangsu, Nanking		
Ch'i-hsia Ssu	1940's	110
	1955	22
	1959	30
	1962	40
Kiangsu, Nanking		
Pao-hua Shan, Lung-ch'ang Ssu	1932	200[41]
	1951	100+[42]
P'i-lu Ssu	1951	9[43]
	1962	25
Kiangsu, Soochow		
Ling-yen Shan	1942	150[44]
	1949	200
	1952	130+[45]
	1959	100[46]
	1962	125
	1965	100+[47]
Kiangsu, Yangchow		
Kao-min Ssu	1940's	200
	1952	190[48]
	1956	c.60
	1963	c.30

Continued

Place	Year	Number of residents
Kwangtung, Canton		
Hai-ch'uang Ssu	1879	200[49]
	1940	30
	1955	4
Kwangtung, Canton		
Liu-jung Ssu	1940's	80[50]
	Sept 1950	30[51]
	Nov 1950	18[50]
	Sept 1951	14[52]
	1957	10
Kwangtung, Ting-hu Shan		
Ch'ing-yün Ssu	1935	400
	1945	20
	1960	10
	1963	10
Kwangtung, Shaokuan		
Nan-hua Ssu	1945	200
	1950	60[53]
	Oct 1952	8[54]
	Dec 1952	6[55]
	June 1958	80[56]
	Oct 1958	60[57]
	1963	40
Ta-chüeh Ssu	1950-51	80[58]
	1952	60[59]
	1963	13
Shansi, Taiyüan municipality	1953	122[60]
	1957	96[61]
Shansi, Wu-t'ai Shan	1950	200-300[62]
	1953	374[63]
	1957	480[64]
	1962	350[65]
Shensi, Chung-nan Shan		
Ching-yeh Ssu	1953	40+[66]
	1954	55[67]
	1958	70[68]

Place	Year	Number of residents
Shensi, Sian		
Hsing-shan Ssu	1949	2[69]
	1957	33[70]
	1961	30[69]
	1963	20[71]
	1965	25[72]
Szechwan, Chengtu		
Chao-chüeh Ssu	1940's	150
	1951	90[73]
	1953	63[74]
Chin-tz'u Ssu	1940's	250[75]
	1951	151[75]
	1953	80[76]
Szechwan, Chungking municipality	1951	302[77]
	1952	256[77]
	1953	200[77]
Szechwan, Hsintu		
Pao-kuang Ssu	1932	200[78]
	1953	40[79]
Szechwan, Omei Shan	1951	1,000+[80]
	1953	292[81]
	1955	203[82]
	1957	216[83]
Yünnan, Kunming		
Hua-t'ing Ssu	1949	200[84]
	1950	63[84]
	1953	30+[85]
Peking municipality	1930	1,490[86]
	1954	470[87]
	1961	300+[88]
Peking		
Kuang-chi Ssu	1940's	200
	1959	50+[89]
	1961	40[90]
	1964	30[91]

Continued

Place	Year	Number of residents
T'an-che Ssu	1930's	300[92]
	1965	1[92]
Yung-ho Kung	1879	1,300[93]
	1940's	300[94]
	1956	83[94]
	1959	60[95]
	1964	50+[96]
Shanghai municipality	1930	6,200[97]
	1949 (May)	2,000[98]
	1950 (Feb)	1,500[99]
	1955	3,200[100]
	1957	2,800[101]
Shanghai		
Ching-an Ssu	1940's	100
	1955	30
Yü-fo Ssu	1940's	300
	1956	60[102]
	1964	60[103]

Appendix D

Monasteries Repaired

The following monasteries were reported to have been repaired after 1949. Where the information is available, the name of each is followed by the date when repairs began (e.g., 1955-) or were completed (e.g., -1956); and by the cost (in new JMP) or nature of repairs. (Where there is no indication of the cost or nature of repairs, they may have been minor.) Monasteries with an asterisk were placed on the 1961 list of important cultural properties to be protected by the central government. Not included below are monasteries where repairs were only made to a pagoda, stele, or other object that had no necessary connection with religious practice.

Anhwei

Anking: Ying-chiang Ssu
Fouyang: Tzu-fu Ssu
Hofei: Ming-chiao Ssu; Kuang-chi Ssu
Lang-la Shan: K'ai-hua Ssu

Chekiang

Hangchow: Ling-yin Ssu (1953-1958, 500,000 JMP)
P'u-t'o Shan: Ch'ien Ssu; Fo-ting Ssu; Hou Ssu; Tzu-chu Lin

Fukien

Amoy: Nan P'u-t'o Ssu (-1952, 1,000 JMP); Jih–kuang-yen Ssu
Chüanchow: K'ai-yüan Ssu (1952, 30,000 JMP)
Foochow, Ku Shan: Yung-ch'üan Ssu

Heilungkian

Harbin: Ti-tsang An

Honan

Loyang: Pai-ma Ssu (1952, 1954, 1957)
Sung Shan: Shao-lin Ssu
Teng-feng: Hui-sheng Ssu; Chung-yüeh Ssu

Hopei

Cheng-ting: Lung-hsing Ssu*
Tientsin: Ta-pei Yüan

Hunan

Changsha: Kai-fu Ssu (1950-1952, 13,000 JMP)

Hupeh

Wuhan: Kuei-yüan Ssu, Pao-t'ung Ssu

Kiangsi

Lu Shan: Ta-lin Ssu

Kiangsu

Nanking: Ch'i-hsia Ssu (1952-1954, 8,000 JMP); P'i-lu Ssu
Wusih: Hui-shan Ssu

Kwangtung

Canton: Kuang-hsiao Ssu*; Liu-jung Ssu

Liaoning

An-shan: Lung-ch'üan Ssu; Hsiang-yen Ssu; Tsu-yüeh Ssu; Tsung-hui Ssu; Ta-an Ssu

Shansi

Chiao-ch'eng: Hsüan-chung Ssu (1954-1956, 155,000 JMP)
Wu-t'ai Shan: Fo-kuang Ssu*; Hsien-t'ung Ssu; Lo-han Ssu; P'u-sa Ting; Shih-fang T'ang; Ta-yüan Ssu. (All Wu-t'ai monasteries, through 1952, 163,600 JMP; through 1958, 477,740 JMP; in 1959, 100,000 JMP; in addition to this 400-500,000 JMP were provided for the restoration of Fo-kuang Ssu and its Beamless Hall)

Shensi

Sian: Ta Tz'u-en Ssu and its Ta-yen Pagoda* (50,000 JMP); Kuang-jen Ssu

Szechwan

Chengtu: Chao-chüeh Ssu; Pao-kuang Ssu; Ta-tz'u Ssu; Ts'ao-t'ang Ssu; Wen-shu Yüan
Chungking: Hua-yen Ssu; Lohan Ssu; T'u-shen Ssu; Wen-ch'üan Ssu
Omei Shan: Ch'ing-yin Ko; Fu-hu Ssu; Pao-kuo Ssu; Wan-nien Ssu

Yünnan

Kunming: Hua-t'ing Ssu

Peking

Kuang-chi Ssu (1,550,000 JMP); Fa-yüan Ssu; Wo-fo Ssu (1955); Yung-ho Kung* (840,000 JMP)

Shanghai

Yü-fo Ssu

The repair of fourteen of these monasteries is mentioned in Chao, *Buddhism in China* (1960), pp. 31-32. Information about the rest is scattered through many sources, principally *Modern Buddhism.*

Appendix E

The Sixth WFB Conference

The following article is reprinted by the kind permission of the Far Eastern Economic Review *in which it originally appeared (Vol. 35, No. 9, March 8, 1962). Here and in Appendix F the text has not been altered to conform to the orthography—or approach—of the present volume.*

People still ask me about the Sixth World Buddhist Conference that I attended last November in Phnom Penh. They ask, presumably, because it has yet to be reported in the Western press. This is a rather puzzling oversight. The conference had interesting political implications, especially for China's future behaviour in international bodies. Since these implications are important, I shall suppress a certain reluctance to "tell tales out of school" (I participated in the work of the conference) and try to offer a fairly complete account of what went on there.

The WFB is the only world body that ignores the iron curtain: both Peking and Taiwan belong to it. So do North and South Vietnam. Though the Cambodian hosts had not sent an invitation to Taiwan, they had invited the two sides of other divided countries: North and South Korea; East and West Germany. Still, most delegates came expecting just another peaceful interchange of ideas on how to spread—and better exemplify—Buddhism.

I came with the Hongkong delegation, first as an observer, and later acting for the chief delegate who had been called out of town and left me in charge since I was the only remaining member of the delegation speaking the necessary languages. Although it was the first such meeting I had attended, I knew in general the history of the World Fellowship of Buddhists. It was founded in 1950 by Dr. G. P. Malalasekera of Ceylon who served as its president until he was appointed Ambassador to Moscow in 1958. His successor was U Chan Htoon, a justice of the Burmese Supreme Court. Meetings have been held every two years: 1950 in Colombo, 1952 in Tokyo, 1954 in Rangoon, 1956 in Kathmandu, and 1958 in Bangkok. The meeting in Phnom Penh was originally scheduled for 1960, but had to be postponed a year because of the death of the Cambodian king.

Under its constitution, the WFB has 44 "regional centres" throughout the world, of which some 36 have sent delegations to its world conferences. A few countries have more than one centre: India has six, for example. In other cases, a centre represents dependent areas (like the one for Hongkong and Macau) or whole continents (like the centre for South America, which is inoperative).

The purposes of the World Fellowship of Buddhists are given in its constitution:

1. to propagate Buddha's teachings among non-Buddhists;
2. to work for their strict observance by Buddhists themselves;
3. to organise welfare activities;
4. to work for peace.

In practice, although many excellent resolutions have been passed at World Conferences, few have been carried out. This is partly because the WFB has no permanent paid staff. Whatever there is to do has to be done by volunteers in their spare time. Furthermore, the very eminence of President U Chan Htoon means he has heavy responsibilities elsewhere. What, in effect, the WFB provides is a forum where Buddhists from all over the world can get to know each other and exchange information about the progress of Buddhism in their respective countries. Gradually, they have come to feel a sense of common identity as members of a new international movement—a movement in which the East is teacher and the West is pupil. That is not to say that the ideal of fellowship has been perfectly realised. One hears of rivalry between Ceylon and Burma. Ceylon is the country where it flourished in later centuries and where it has recently become the state religion. The WFB began in Ceylon; its seat and administration are now Burmese.

There are more fundamental differences, however, between the Mahayana Buddhists in Northern Asia and the Theravadins in the South. Generally speaking, the latter are purists in following the monastic rule. They beg for their food, abstain from sex and alcohol, and refuse to take life. In Japan, on the other hand, monasteries have (or had) vast endowments. Priests can marry (priesthood is, in fact, often hereditary). Some sects (like Nichiren) advocate not only killing, but war. Although in 1956 at Kathmandu the WFB passed a resolution to abolish once and for all the terms "Mahayana" and "Theravadin," these terms and the reality they represent continue to figure in its proceedings. I have heard adherents of each school say privately that they could not stomach representatives of the other. Yet, as in the case of Catholics and Protestants, common ground is emerging.

One might also have thought that the participation of countries with such different political systems would have resulted in dissension. But during the first ten years of the WFB, this did not prove to be the case. Delegates to its conferences generally tried to avoid political issues: their objective was to find what Buddhists could share, not what divided them. Sometimes dissension was avoided because of the place in which a conference was held. In 1958, for example, it was held in Bangkok. No communist delegation could get entry visas. (It was at Bangkok that the Taiwan Regional Centre was formally admitted.) This year the tables were turned. The delegation from Bangkok (since diplomatic relations with Cambodia had just been broken) could not attend, and Taiwan was not even invited. The only Chinese delegation came from Peking. In the circumstances, it was naive, perhaps, to expect a peaceful session.

The first day and a half seemed peaceful enough. But the Chinese delegation had let it be known almost as soon as they arrived that they would bid for Peking as the site of the next conference. Such a bid would appeal to those who had experienced or heard about Peking's hospitality to its guests. Delegates familiar with communist methods began to worry. Once in control of the conference organising machinery, the Chinese would be in a position to get their own candidates elected to office, and eventually to win control of the WFB. They would be able to give it massive infusions of the money, personnel, and purposefulness that it had lacked so far. Provided they acted with the same subtlety that they had shown over the past eight years, during which they had exchanged at least twenty-eight Buddhist friendship missions with other Asian countries, the WFB could serve them as a potent tool for political penetration. Unfortunately, however, the Chinese delegation had come not with one assignment but two. The second assignment was to get Taiwan expelled as a regional centre and they had evidently been ordered to carry it out at all costs.

After a day and a half of plenary sessions, devoted to ceremonials, speeches, greetings from chiefs of state, and reports on the condition of Buddhism in various countries, we began to meet in sub-committees. There were four: on education, propaganda, humanitarian activities, and unity. I chose to attend the fourth, which passed the following resolutions:

1. to fix the date for the universal celebration of Buddha's birthday as the first full moon in May (up to now the date has varied from country to country);
2. to organise a Buddhist boy scouts movement; and
3. to encourage parents not to take their children to motion pictures that feature killing, fighting, and other harmful acts.

Quite a few other worthy resolutions were submitted to our committee but we found that they had all been passed at previous world conferences and then forgotten so completely that they were being presented as new. (One, I remember, was: "To persuade parents all over the world not to buy war-weapon toys for their children.") To avoid a repetition of such embarrassment we suggested that the Secretary-General publish a cumulative list of all resolutions passed by the Fellowship since it was founded and indicate what, if anything, had been done about them. We could not, alas! suggest how the

Secretary-General was going to perform this task without a permanent staff to help him.

On Friday, November 17, at three o'clock in the afternoon the delegates re-assembled for the final plenary session. I do not think that even then they realised what was coming. The auditorium was full. I could see Manuel Sherman down to the left of me, holding his seven-foot staff upright beside him. Before us on the dais sat President U Chan Htoon in his Burmese tunic and white headband. He was flanked by the elders and patriarchs of the World Fellowship, venerable old monks with gentle smiles. On their left sat Shirob Jaltso, the head of the Chinese delegation and a Vice-President of the WFB. He was holding himself so erect and looked so much taller than his neighbours that I wondered if he were sitting on a pillow. He paid no attention to the speakers as they came up one by one to address us. He ignored the earphones that would have enabled him to tune in on one of the four conference languages–Cambodian, French, English, and Chinese. Instead, with his head tilted back and his eyes closed, he rapidly and constantly moved his lips, reciting (so far as I could make it out through binoculars) *Om Mani Padme Hum.* One might have thought that he had no connection with the world around him but for the fact that under the table one could see his two large feet, encased in brown leather shoes, planted firmly on the ground.

Down on the floor sat the rest of the Chinese delegation. There was only one monk, Chü-tsan, who had proved his political reliability years ago in the campaign for the suppression of counterrevolutionaries. By his side sat Chao P'u-ch'u, the lay Secretary-General of the Chinese Buddhist Association. He was a short, heavy, bloodless individual, a little like the film star Peter Lorre. He had taken a leading role both in the "remoulding" of Buddhism in China and in friendly contacts with foreign Buddhists. Then there was the extraordinarily tall, cadaverous young man named Cheng Mu-tien, across whose thin lips there never passed a smile. He had the forehead and pallor of an intellectual, but his role was unexplained.

All these gentlemen were looking grimly businesslike as the final session, in which they were to play a leading role, began. First we heard the reports of the sub-committes on education and propaganda. The report of the third sub-committee (on humanitarian activities) was read by its chairman, Rev. Riri Nakayama of Japan. In reading it he included the text of a resolution that warned against radioactive fall-out and called for a protest through the UN to all nuclear powers. He explained that, although it had not been passed by the Steering Committee, he wished to place it before the Conference. The delegate from North Vietnam rose to object. President U Chan Htoon acknowledged the validity of his objection and ruled that the resolution, since the Steering Committee had been unable to agree on it, could not be voted on by the Assembly. The World Fellowship, he explained, had always worked on the Buddhist principle of unanimous agreement.

At this point, it seemed that everyone in the hall wanted to speak. Various delegates protested that, whatever the Steering Committee may have done, the resolution had been passed unanimously by the Committee on Humanitarian Activities. The *bloc* delegates stuck to their point, namely that a warning of the dangers of radioactive fall-out implied criticism of the Soviet Union. Instead the conference ought to call for general and complete disarmament.

After ten minutes of increasing vehemence, Rev. Nakayama started towards the *podium* again. The President told him that continued protest could serve no useful purpose: he had had his chance that morning in the Steering Committee to say everything there was to say. Undeterred, the small, elderly Japanese priest, who usually looks a little absent-minded, shuffled up to the *lectern* and insisted on repeating that people down in this corner of the world might not realise the danger of nuclear fall-out. In Japan one was aware of it every day. Japan was the nation that had suffered most from atomic weapons and the Japanese delegates refused to be silenced. Unless this resolution was passed, how could they go home and face their fellow Buddhists? "If the conference will not accept this resolution," he ended, "then we shall have to withdraw." With that he folded up his notes and began walking off the *podium.* It was a dramatic moment. Before the rest of the Japanese delegates could rise from their benches and follow him out of the hall, the President announced: "We shall now recess to have our photographs taken." The hall emptied.

During the half hour of photography, the Japanese were caucusing and in conversation with other delegates. When we repaired to the auditorium again, we found they were still in our midst.

President U Chan Htoon resumed the proceedings by saying that, much as he disliked the thought, it might now be necessary to abandon the principle of unanimity on which the WFB had operated for so many years. We might instead have to begin following our constitution, which provides that all questions be determined by majority vote. It was for us, the assembled delegates, to decide. The *bloc* representatives, argued long and persuasively for unanimity, but when the ballot came they were defeated 24 to 3. This made it possible to vote on the fall-out resolution and here they were defeated 23 to 4. We had resolved that radioactivity was a bad thing.

Japan was therefore safely back in the organisation. Who would walk out next? We had already been given a premonition on the previous day. During the report on Buddhist activities in Mongolia, the Peking delegation had left as one man—rather an odd time to leave, since the Grand Lama was just attacking "certain countries" for maintaining relations with the "traitors on Taiwan."

We were all on the edge of our seats therefore when President U Chan Htoon turned at last to resolution No. 29: to cancel the membership of the

Taiwan Regional Centre. Though it had not passed the Steering Committee, it could now under the new procedure be voted on by the plenary conference just as the fall-out resolution had been. U Chan Htoon read it slowly and in full, giving his kindly Buddhist listeners a chance to mull over the flavour of sentences like this one: "As everyone knows American imperialism is trying to create two Chinas in order to occupy permanently China's territory Taiwan. They use ignominious means to cheat people at all places and try to carry out their shameful intrigues on all occasions."

Having read it, he said that he would like to avoid endless repetition of the arguments that had already been heard in the Steering Committee and would therefore attempt to sum them up, so that discussion now might be limited to procedure. He went on with the greatest earnestness: "I am by training a lawyer and also a judge. Thus I am used to summing up. But I am only human. If I use words or any nuance that is likely to suggest that I am giving an edge to one side or the other, may I be forgiven—because I feel completely unequal to the task and I know the feelings on this question are charged with emotion." He then proceeded to give a masterly resumé of the pros and cons along the following lines:

Pros	*Cons*
Recognition of the Taiwan Centre lends support to the claim that Taiwan is not a part of China.	Recognition of regional centres has no political or territorial significance: India has six, the United States has two.
The former WFB president had assured the Chinese in 1956 and 1957 that there was no regional centre in Taiwan.	At that time there was none. The former president made no commitment as to the future.
Peking was not invited to the Bangkok meeting at which the Taiwan centre was recognised; hence the action should be cancelled.	Absence of one delegation cannot invalidate a decision. If so, Thailand could some day ask that any decision taken now be cancelled.

And, in general, concluded the President, the purpose of the WFB is purely religious, that is, to provide affiliation and mutual contact for Buddhists wherever they are regardless of the political situation. As many groups as possible, he said, should be represented in our Fellowship, and no group should be shut out "so long as it exists as the organisation of the Buddhists of its area."

If the President hoped that his summing up would limit discussion, he was disappointed. After his *resumé* of the *pros,* he had asked the Chinese delegation whether it was an adequate statement of their case: had he left anything out? No, replied Chao P'u-ch'u, he had stated their case adequately. But now Chao felt called on to state it all over again. When he finished, the President explained that he sympathised deeply with the speaker, who was a very dear friend of his. Next the Venerable Huot Tath, the chief Cambodian delegate, gave a rambling, kindly address, in which he said that what should be considered was humanity and perhaps the admission of the Taiwan Regional Centre had not been so useful.

Ceylon suggested that voting should be deferred until the problem could be studied, perhaps suspending Taiwan's membership in the meantime. Hawaii pointed out that under the Constitution, no regional centre could be expelled until it had been given an opportunity for explanation. The President answered both the latter speakers by saying that the General Conference was the supreme authority and could expel anyone it wished whenever it wished, with or without study, and regardless of the Constitution. Singapore, Korea, and Malaya called for a decision now, probably because they felt (and quite rightly) that the tide was running against Peking. Teh Thean Choo of Malaya ended his address by saying: "I pray that all of you would try to remember that you are Buddhists. Please do not permit this organisation of ours to be turned into another international forum where we start quarrelling about political matters. I go down on my knees and beg all of you not to permit this" And indeed he did go down on his knees. There was an ovation.

Then up rose Chü-tsan, the brown-robed monk from Peking, to have the last word. He had apparently missed the significance of the ovation, and he certainly ignored the instruction he got from the President as he ascended the dais: "Please do not discuss the merits of the case, only the procedure."

"As you all know," began Chü-tsan, "Taiwan is a part of China's territory, but it is now surrounded by the armed forces of the American imperialists and it has been made into an independent state. It is the intention of the American imperialists to support the policy of two Chinas . . . ."

At this point the President struck his gong and said: "Please, please no accusations or mention of any place or individuals."

"It is the situation, and we have to talk about it," went on Chü-tsan inexorably. ". . . This organisation of ours should be a holy organisation devoted to the establishment of Buddha's holy teachings, but now it has become involved in political problems. The Chinese Buddhist delegation is of the opinion that this is against the teaching of Buddhism . . . Please let us withdraw from this political involvement. Let us restore the purity and holiness of this organisation." With that, he returned to his seat. U Chan Htoon said shortly: "We have said enough and heard enough," and called for a roll-call vote.

The Chinese resolution was defeated by 13 to 6 with 5 abstentions. Only Nepal and India joined the communist *bloc.* The abstentions, as I afterwards learned, were on differing grounds. Burma felt that the vote was in violation of the Constitution (as I did myself) since it had been taken without giving the Taiwanese a chance to defend themselves. Ceylon still favoured postponement for further study. France, in the person of René de Berval, the elderly editor of *France-Asie* in Tokyo, said that "he did not want to win the cold war." Cambodia, it was rumoured, later wished to shift its vote to the majority. Pakistan was non-communicative.

After the vote was announced, President U Chan Htoon, who, since the beginning of the Conference, had been urging the Chinese to drop their resolution, told the assembled delegates that the entire proceedings had pained him deeply. "I can assure you," he said with a sincerity that moved most of us, as we recalled the Nationalist irregulars in Burma, "that I have no reason to speak for Taiwan as a Burman. I have no reason to like Taiwan as a Burman. But as the head of the Buddhist movement, I have had to express my views directly and publicly, and if I have appeared to favour one side or the other it has been solely in discharge of the duties you have imposed on me."

At about that point, the Chinese delegation rose stonily from their seats and left the auditorium. It was the second walkout of the day, but this time there was no return, not, at least, a general return. Perhaps twenty minutes after the walkout, the young Tibetan cadre slipped back in through the door. That seemed odd. Then we realised what we, as well as the Chinese, had forgotten: old Shirob Jaltso was still up on the *podium* reciting *Om Mani Padme Hum.* Slowly the cadre led him down the steps and out of the hall. For all his dignity, he had rather a vacant look.

After passing a number of additional resolutions and electing a new slate of officers, we left the auditorium, a little bleary, at a quarter past ten. We had been in session for over seven hours.

The next morning the Chinese delegation, still not realising why they had been defeated, held a press conference. They handed out a mimeographed statement that said: "Due to the fact that this [present]conference was controlled by some elements who engaged themselves in conducting activities of political intrigues, they continued to follow their aggressive policy of American imperialism for creating 'two Chinas' and vetoed our proposal. For this we wish to express our regret and protest. These people claim to be Buddhists, but their act is contrary to the objects of the WFB for solidarity and peace and is also contrary to the teachings of the Buddha. This should arouse the vigilance and attention of all Buddhists. We hope that under the concern and supervision of all upright Buddhists of different countries, the WFB will come to the right path of light and purity as indicated by the Buddha.

"The Chinese Buddhists will continue to co-operate hand in hand and strive together with all the Buddhists of different countries for the protection of the purity of Buddhism, for international solidarity and world peace, and for the propagation of Buddha's teachings and the exchange of Buddhist culture.

"Finally, we wish to express our thanks to those friends who sympathised with and supported us in this conference."

For the Chinese to say that those in control of the conference had followed the aggressive policy of American imperialism would win few friends in Burma—or in Cambodia either, for that matter. Why gratuitously insult these people when, as the statement also makes clear, China intended to continue co-operating with them, presumably within the WFB?

The evening of the next day the Chinese turned up all smiles at a reception given by the Cambodian Buddhist Association. Their walkout was evidently not to be a total one. Many of us went up to chat with them and tried to make them feel at home. On Sunday, they flew up to Angkor with the other delegations to spend a day touring those magnificent ruins. They found it hard to keep smiling, however. I noticed that when the Malayan delegate, who had used his stentorian voice to keep politics out of the conference, used it now at the Elephant Terrace to give the Governor of the Province a vote of thanks for the sumptuous buffet provided for us there, Chao P'u-ch'u turned his back and looked straight in the other direction, white with anger. Was he angry because he had not thought of the graceful gesture himself? Or because his English was not good enough to make it? Or because the general amiability of the proceedings brought to his mind the frigid reception he would get from his superiors when he returned to Peking empty-handed? [1]

Evidently he continued to brood, for on the third day, after the delegation had returned to Phnom Penh, he addressed a letter to the chief Burmese delegate in which he called the President of the WFB a liar: "What U Chan Htoon has said in the meeting is not only contrary to the facts, but also annulled the facts of friendship between our two countries." This personal attack on the President of the World Fellowship was even harder to understand, for in making it he was leaving the field open for the Soviet delegates to be friendlier than ever. I remember that after the Chinese walkout when U Chan Htoon announced that he would be continuing in office for two more years, the Soviet delegates, who were in the best of spirits, clapped enthusiastically.

Mr. Chao and the rest of the Chinese delegation left for home a day early. They therefore missed the buffet dinner given at the Royal Palace by Prince Sihanouk, who impressed us all as a most considerate host. In fact, seeing the way he cared for his guests that night—getting a plate for this person or a chair for that one, giving us a second less formal performance of the Royal Ballet in the floodlit palace garden—I suspected that his hand had been very much behind other kindnesses showered on us during the course of the conference: the car, driver, and equerry at the disposal of every delegate 24 hours a day; the two Red Cross ambulances that followed the delegations wherever they went at Angkor; the banquets, planes, accommodation, all at the Cambodian Government's expense. Of course, there were occasional failures of organisation, but never did I see one of the Cambodian conference officers, though sorely tried, lose his temper.

I left for home with two overall impressions of the World Buddhist Conference. First, I was surprised by the ineptness of the delegates from Communist countries. It would not really have hurt the Soviet Union, for example, if it had been criticised by implication for its recent series of nuclear tests—at least, it would have been hurt less than it was by trying to stifle the criticism. As to the Chinese delegation, they could probably have scored a triumph if they had played the underdog. Many of the delegates from neutralist countries *wanted* to be friendly towards the Chinese: after all, this was a fellowship conference. That is why a resolution condemning the persecution of Buddhism in Tibet was bottled up in the Steering Committee. The word Tibet was never heard on the floor of the plenary conference.

Furthermore, although many Buddhists realise that Buddhism has been suppressed by the People's Government, they feel that its suppression would be even more total if the Chinese did not belong to the WFB. They know that the handsomely restored temples they see when they visit China are merely showplaces to impress visitors,but is it not better to have showplaces than no temples at all? They are therefore most reluctant to do anything that would cause Peking to withdraw.

If the Chinese had taken advantage of this widespread deference to their feelings, had argued mildly for their Taiwan resolution, had taken defeat sadly, had treated the fall-out resolution in the same way, and then had said in effect: 'Look, chaps, we have not made out very well here, but we do have one last plea. We would like the honour of having the next conference in Peking" . . . in that case, I think, it would have been a pushover for them. As it was, delegates who came friendly to China went away perplexed and even frightened by the snarl behind the smile. How could the spirit of fellowship be maintained at future conferences if the Chinese were going to behave as they had at this one? What would happen to the World Fellowship of Buddhists if the Chinese continued to insist that it was only purely religious when it was politically pure? What would happen at the next meeting if both Peking and Taiwan attended? Could the WFB survive?

At the end of the marathon closing session, a new slate of vice-presidents was presented for election. The first nominee, a distinguished Burman, withdrew on the grounds that the President was already from Burma. This created a vacancy. After electing eleven other vice-presidents (including two Americans, Gard and Miyabara), nominations were called for to fill the vacancy. Up sprang Miss Pitt Chin Hui of Singapore and said: "I nominate Dr. Paul Fung." The delegates were so stunned that before they knew what had happened, they had their third American vice-president—this in the sole organ of the world's Buddhists, less than one-tenth of one per cent of whom are to be found in the United States. One delegate quickly went across to Paul Fung and suggested that he withdraw in favour of a candidate from Japan, which was conspicuously unrepresented among the new vice-presidents. Paul Fung loftily ignored him.[2]

After the conference was over, others approached Dr. Fung with similar requests, including Miss Pitt Chin Hui, who had not realised when she nominated him that he would be the third American on the list. In the end, he offered a gracious compromise. He would withdraw, he said, on January 1, 1962 if Buddha's Universal Church was made a WFB Regional Centre (thus under the WFB constitution representing all the Buddhists in the United States)–but, he added, he would only do so "if his parishioners would permit him to." Like some others I left Phnom Penh wondering whether the World Fellowship of Buddhists would be turned into a tool of Peking or a branch of the Fung Brothers' Universal Church.

The same question appears to have occurred to Peking. After a whole month during which the mainland press said not a word about the World Buddhist Conference, except that it had taken place, the *People's Daily* printed a long angry article on December 19, 1961. First it recounted Chinese efforts to build friendship with Buddhists abroad, partly through the WFB. "However," the article went on, "dark clouds from the West appeared over the Sixth Conference of the World Fellowship of Buddhists . . . Strange figures who had never been seen in dignified Buddhist conference in the past made their appearance in the conference and were very active . . . All these people, without exception, came from the United States . . . The fact that these Americans in religious cassocks show such an 'enthusiasm' for Buddhism should arouse the serious vigilance of the Buddhists of Asian countries . . . It is regrettable that a small number of Southeast Asian personages were taken in by the Americans and failed to expose their intrigues in time. Consequently certain resolutions with ulterior motives were adopted haphazardly. Under the Americans' manipulations, three of the twelve newly elected vice-presidents of the World Fellowship of Buddhists are such Americans. Someone pointed out the ugly fact that, while the representative from Hong Kong and Macau was absent, an observer with U.S. citizenship posed as the representative and actually voted in that capacity.[3] What happened at the conference should arouse the vigilance and attention of all Buddhists." I think the *People's Daily* has a point.

The Chinese continued to brood. On January 16, 1962, when Shirob Jaltso spoke at a meeting held to condemn the "U.S. Government's persecution of the Communist Party of the U.S.A.," he recalled that "last November Kennedy despatched a horde of his unholy pawns . . . to turn the World Buddhist Association into a tool of the policy of aggression. However, they were firmly rebuffed by all just-minded Buddhists."

On December 19 Peking's line had been that "many Asian delegations" had expressed condolences for the Chinese defeat. Now it seems to have become that, on the contrary, there was a Chinese victory, made possible by the support of "all just-minded Buddhists." Is it possible that this revision of history has really been accepted by the leadership in Peking, just as a century ago defeats became victories for the eyes of the Emperor?

Appendix F

Asian Buddhists and China

The following article is reprinted in its entirety by the kind permission of the Far Eastern Economic Review *in which it first appeared (Vol. 40, No. 1, April 4, 1963).*

Buddhism is inherently disposed to co-operate in its own destruction. This is the conclusion that I came to after a tour of Asian countries at the end of 1962, in the course of which I talked with Buddhist leaders from Kathmandu to Kyoto.

Before this tour I had heard a good deal about "communist penetration" of Buddhism and I had assumed that it was exaggerated. I would still say that it was exaggerated. Penetration, in the sense of acquiring trusted agents in the Buddhist movement, scarcely exists. Instead there is an attitude among Buddhists that outsiders find it hard to understand. They call it "softness towards communism" or "fuzzy-mindedness" or "neutralist naiveté." I too found it hard to understand. As I had one long conversation after another with Buddhist leaders, I became more and more confused. What did they mean by their self-contradictions? Why did they seem so ready to rationalise?

I found the answer only when I considered my interviews in retrospect from a Buddhist point of view. The answer is that it is I who am "fuzzy-minded"—and so, perhaps, are my readers. Let me begin with a typical interview, to give the flavour, and then go on to some of the stranger conversations which, though they do not necessarily represent the thinking of the majority of Buddhists on all subjects, do represent the thinking of important minorities on some subjects. For reasons that will become apparent, I shall preserve the anonymity of the people I talked to.

In Ceylon there is a handful of elder monks of great eminence who know English as well as they know Theravadin Buddhism (Theravada is the Buddhism of Southeast Asia, in contrast to the Mahayana sects of China, Japan, and Tibet). The monk to whom I addressed myself one day late in 1962 belonged to this handful. A few years ago he had visited Peking and the immediate purpose of my interview was to ask him what he had learned about Chinese Buddhism under the new regime. I am writing a book on Buddhism in China since 1912.

As he began to answer my questions, I started taking notes. He immediately asked me to stop. He was worried about what use I might make of them. Perhaps I would quote only what was critical of conditions in China and not what was favourable. It was essential to be fair. Americans, he said, seemed to want to talk only about the bad things that the Communists had done, and I was an American.

For example, he too believed that Buddhism would die out in China, but this would happen not so much because the government was destroying it, as because Buddhists themselves were not keeping to their religion. He was very much concerned about the state of Buddhism in China—and in every country. It was his duty, he said—it was the duty of every Buddhist—to speak out when he saw that Buddhism was being harmed. I asked whether to speak out would not mean getting involved in politics. No, he replied, not if he confined his statements to the treatment of Buddhism. I suggested that in the case of China this could be taken as interference in her internal affairs. That did not matter, he said; it was still his duty to speak out. He asked me if I had read the report on Tibet by the International Commission of Jurists. I said that I had. He said he had read it too, and shook his head sadly.

I showed him some articles on Buddhism from the Chinese Communist press. They were rather frank articles, intended only for domestic consumption. He was surprised. This was not the kind of thing they had told him when he was in China. I suggested that one explanation might be that the People's Government was destroying Buddhism at home while using it to win friends abroad. He hesitated, and then told me in a confidential tone that actually he agreed with me. That was about what it amounted to. But, of course, he could not speak out about it publicly. I asked why. Because, he explained, that would mean getting involved in politics.

This is only a mild foretaste of baffling self-contradictions. One of the questions that I asked everywhere had to do with the Chinese Communist revision of the Buddhist doctrine of compassion. Enlightenment and compassion are the two threads that run through all of Buddhism, Mahayana as well as Theravadin. The first Buddhist rule is not to take the life of any sentient being. In China, however, from 1950 onwards, a new doctrine has been enunciated: it is compassionate to kill bad people if doing so helps good people.

TRUE COMPASSION

Thus, during the Korean War, Buddhist monks read in the Peking monthly *Modern Buddhism* that "the best thing [for monks] is to be able to join the army directly and to learn the spirit in which Shakyamuni as the embodiment of compassion and our guide to buddhahood, killed robbers to save the people and suffered hardships on behalf of all living beings. To wipe out the American imperialist demons that are breaking world peace is, according to Buddhist doctrine, not only blameless, but actually gives rise to merit" (*Modern Buddhism* 1951/4:35). During the Jordan-Lebanon crisis in 1958, the same Buddhist journal reported that Buddhists and Taoists had issued a joint statement in Peking, in which they said: "We good Buddhists and Taoists always love peace and abhor war; but we are never afraid of war. We must kill the war-provoking devils in defence of world peace. Only then will we be following the Buddhist and Taoist doctrine of true compassion" (*Modern Buddhism* 1958/8:28).

Over and over again in the last twelve years official Buddhist sources in China have referred to an obscure story about the Buddha in one of his earlier rebirths and used it as a justification for government policy. For example: "According to the scripture, 'our original master Shakya Tathagata, when practicing the way of the bodhisattva, killed one bad man in order to save five hundred men.' This is the best example to follow. The vow not to destroy life cannot be viewed dogmatically. Killing for personal fame and profit is a breach of the vow. Killing in order to save people is to observe the vow" (*Modern Buddhism* 1953/7:17). Here the story was being quoted to justify killing reactionaries and counter-revolutionaries, which is no less compassionate than killing warmongers.

I had assumed when I embarked on my tour of Asia that Buddhists there would be distressed, if not appalled by such doctrinal revision, particularly the Theravadin Buddhists, who take pride in the purity of their doctrine. I am afraid that I can hardly report any distress at all.

One monk in Ceylon, whose eminence is recognised in India and throughout the Buddhist world, began by expressing surprise when I showed him these and similar quotations. He could recall no episode in which the Buddha had killed anyone. The doctrine of killing for compassion could not, so far as he was aware, be justified by any of the Pali texts on which Theravadin Buddhism is based. But then he began to have afterthoughts. Did not the Bhagavad Gita advocate much the same idea? Had not Dr. Ambedkar (who revived Buddhism in India) written that the doctrine of non-violence meant that one did not kill *unnecessarily*? Monks in Japan married: why could not monks in China become soldiers (*sic*)? Had not Buddhist monks helped defend Ceylon against the British invaders? Had not Ceylon's most famous king, Duttha-Gamani, killed his enemies and earned the praise of the monks? (He had indeed. According to Rahula's *History of Buddhism in Ceylon* the king led his troops into battle with a relic of the Buddha in his spear. Monks were encouraged to disrobe and join his army: one became a general. When the king grew troubled at having killed so many thousands of the Indian invaders, eight *arahats* [Buddhist saints] told him that actually only one and a half human beings had been slain in the battles: the rest were wrong believers and men of evil life, who could be considered animals.)

Another of my informants, a left-wing monk in Japan, dismissed the quotations on compassionate killing as "taken from the early 1950's, when change in China was urgent." In other words, they were symptoms of a temporary excess of enthusiasm. Actually, half the quotations I showed him belonged to the period 1958-1961, but I was somehow unable to draw his attention to this fact. Besides, he and other Japanese asked me the following question: "What would you do if you were standing with a revolver in your hand behind the pilot of a plane that was about to drop a hydrogen bomb on a city of ten million? Would you shoot him? " This was a problem, they said, that was causing great perplexity to Japanese Buddhists. Perhaps there were circumstances in which saving life justified taking it.

THE ROAD TO BELIEF

When I was in India, a philosopher, sympathetic to Buddhism, though not a Buddhist (he was an old associate of Gandhi) told me that the doctrine of compassionate killing was absolutely wrong, but he was no less absolutely sure that the Chinese Communists would evolve away from it. "The road to belief lies through unbelief," he said. "Of course Marxism is the antithesis of Buddhism and spirituality, but it is necessary as a corrective for the excessive spirituality that preceded it: the branch must be bent in the other direction before it can be straightened." He was convinced (most recently from his conversations with Khrushchev) that Communists everywhere were moving towards spirituality. "They are evolving in the right direction," he said. "It is only a question of time."

I asked him if it was possible they might be evolving in the wrong direction. He said no, it was not. I was much struck by his "bent branch" simile. It allows him to assume that the worse things get under a communist regime, the more evidence he has that things are sure to get better. Strictly speaking, of course, this is true.

Other people that I talked to dismissed the doctrine of compassionate killing as just one more error of Mahayana Buddhism. They were Theravadins who looked on Mahayana as a heresy that had done great harm to the world and they were not in the least surprised, when they considered its past errors, to hear that Mahayana had now come to this. I found it hard to persuade them that most Buddhists in China—certainly up to 1950—would have opposed the sophistry of compassionate killing just as strongly as their fellow believers in Southeast Asia. One monk even told me that he heartily supported the efforts of the Chinese Government to wipe out Mahayana. Thus he was applauding the Communists' destruction of Chinese Buddhism because of a doctrine that the Communists themselves have imposed on it. What could be more ironic?

BUDDHISM AND MARXISM

One Burmese monk, considered a leftist, refused to discuss the question at all. It was irrelevant, he said. Buddhism was not concerned with killing. Neither was Marxism. Marxism was concerned with justice. In the administration of justice, methods of punishment differed with the time and place, and it was unimportant which method–killing or otherwise–was employed.

"Do you really mean," I asked, "that from a Buddhist point of view, killing is unimportant? "

"Yes," he said, "it is a minor point. What is important is the progress of science and whether Buddhism and science are compatible." He believed that they were. Buddhism, in fact, *was* science, though using a different terminology. For example, he said, Buddhists spoke of five elements instead of a hundred. This monk's attitude was not unusual. Many Buddhists consider that because the Buddha alluded to other universes and microscopic creatures, he anticipated and indeed surpassed recent scientific discoveries. There were no professional scientists among the people that I interviewed. I am not sure how many Buddhists appreciate the importance of the scientific method as opposed to its ever-changing results.

In my interviews with recent visitors to China, I discussed not only questions of doctrine, but also the actual practice of Buddhism. Almost none of them seemed to be aware that the few remaining monks on the mainland are forced to labour the same long hours as the rest of the population, take part in the same political campaigns, and learn "to put the service of their country above the service of their religion." All this and more has been spelled out in hundreds of newspaper and magazine articles published in China (in Chinese only) from 1950 to 1960. But some of the people I talked to were unwilling to believe that it could be so; others made the comment that when a great country industrialises, sacrifices must be expected from everyone. In Ceylon, a monk who always received me lying on his bed, where he lolled during the several hours of our interviews, said that the monks he had seen in China were too old to do manual labour, but if they were doing it, it would be good for them. "I wish we could labour here. It would be better for me than lying around my bed all day."

"Even if you had to labour eight or ten hours a day? " I asked.

"Yes," he said, with conviction, and then continued: "As I said when I came back from China, if our young men and women had the same opportunities for employment as in China, the number of monks and prostitutes would go down here too."

One might have thought that this eminent monk looked contemptuously on his own vocation, but in a previous talk he told me that ideally everyone should become a monk. The Sangha, that is, the congregation of monks, was "all important." Yet in another breath he expressed complete indifference as to whether the Sangha died out in China or not. "If it does, it can be revived there, as it was in Ceylon." He said this when I pointed out that virtually no ordinations had been held in China since 1957. "When I was in China," he said, "I was not interested in ordinations. I went to China to learn about schools, factories, and farms, not to learn about religion. I had seen enough of religion in other countries. I assumed that since ordinations were allowed in other countries, they were allowed the same way in China."

Thus I was also baffled in my interviews by an apparent indifference to facts that would be unfavourable to the Chinese Government, and a resistance to drawing conclusions from them. A Nepalese monk, for example, said it was probably true that fewer ordinations were being held and the Chinese Sangha was getting smaller, but this was a good thing: now only those who had really mastered Buddhist doctrine could become monks. It was no longer enough to be able to chant the scriptures, sweep the floors, and light incense. A conservative Sinhalese monk expressed a similar thought when he said that only those monks and monasteries that strictly followed monastic rules were allowed to exist as before. Hence he felt that the decline in the number of monks and temples in China was a good omen for Chinese Buddhism.

I remember another Sinhalese monk, whose opinion I asked about a Chinese Communist statement that "the religious viewpoint is reactionary, anti-socialist, and anti-communist." He was not in the least perturbed: "Oh," he said, "they are not talking about Buddhism. Buddhism is not a religion, but a science." (I wish that the Communists agreed.)

DALAI LAMA

The saddest rationalisation of all, perhaps, concerned the Dalai Lama. To many I put the question: who is telling the truth about recent events in Tibet—the Chinese or the Dalai Lama? The Dalai had few champions. In Japan, Nepal, India, and Ceylon, people told me that Tibet was not a part of their respective countries, but belonged to China. They should therefore express no opinion on the subject. In the words of a prominent Nepalese Buddhist layman: "We just do not think about the Dalai Lama." He went on to add that the Chinese action in Tibet was like President Kennedy's action in calling out troops to defend the rights of James Meredith at the University of Mississippi. In any case, he added, the whole business of incarnations and living buddhas was superstition.

The Chinese Communists themselves have suggested a somewhat more ingenious approach to the problem. A monk from Ceylon was told by Shirob Jaltso, the President of the Chinese Buddhist Association, that the Dalai Lama was his disciple's disciple and he, Shirob, was therefore the Dalai Lama's teacher's teacher. For this reason (*sic*) the Chinese Government was correct in doing what it could to develop Tibet. In the second place, when it came to any conflict in veracity, it was obviously the teacher and not the disciple whose words must be accepted. Shirob, of course, has fully supported Chinese actions in Tibet. I heard something similar from a Burmese monk: "Only if you ask the Panchen Lama," he said, "will you get the whole answer on Tibet. He is the Dalai's teacher." (He is also a Chinese puppet.)

A prominent monk in Nepal averred that he "pitied" the Dalai Lama, but as to who was telling the truth about Tibet he told me that he had "nothing to say." The Indian philosopher, whose faith in the growing spirituality of Marxism I have mentioned earlier, snapped that he had no respect for the Dalai, who was not worth talking about. An Indian Buddhist monk would comment only that the Dalai was suffering from the influence of a very unfavourable star called "Shami." On the whole, the reaction of most Buddhists in Asia towards the most dramatic persecution of Buddhism in a thousand years was a desire to change the subject.

Towards the end of each of my interviews I asked about the probable future of Buddhism in China. The clearest answer came from the leftist monk in Japan, who represents a sizeable body of opinion, particularly in the Nichiren Sect. Chinese Buddhism, he said, was not going to disappear, but would survive and develop. It would differ from Buddhism in other countries and from Buddhism in its original form. That is, it would incorporate elements of Marxism. But he would still call it Buddhism, though others might not. An equally clear statement came from a monk in Ceylon. He was the one who welcomed the Chinese Government's decision to wipe out Mahayana Buddhism. Since he also believed that they planned to introduce Theravadin Buddhism in its place, the future of Buddhism in China seemed to him very bright.

From most people the answers I got were much more equivocal. A Nepalese Buddhist layman, active in politics, told me that religion was a sign of weakness. Someday, when every need was satisfied it would no longer be necessary. (This, of course, is an orthodox Marxist view.) But, he added, religion would not completely die out. This was because, on the one hand, people would never lose their fear of illness and misfortune, while, on the other, there would always be a small minority who understood the true Buddhism, which is scientific. In fact, as a devout Buddhist, he felt that the survival of Buddhism was terribly important, both in China and elsewhere, since it was a force for peace. (He was not necessarily contradicting himself. It is logical to maintain that Buddhism, as a religion, is a sign of weakness, but as a science, it is a force for peace.)

I would say that the most common attitude towards the future of Buddhism in China, as towards the question of Tibet, was indifference. As the Nepalese monk put it: "Buddhism in China is not going forward, but neither is it going backwards very quickly . . . Religions are always decaying and being created." He said that he was concerned about the new generation of

Buddhists in China, but he was concerned about it everywhere. There must be changes in a country that is industrialising. And so on.

THE REASONS WHY

As an admirer and student of Chinese Buddhism, I found these interviews more and more exasperating. It was hard for me to understand how Buddhists, who advocate compassion for all creatures in suffering, should feel none for the sufferings of their fellow Buddhists.

One reason was, of course, that most of them did not know what their fellow Buddhists were suffering. Of all the many visitors to China that I interviewed, not one spoke Chinese. Not one brought his own interpreter. Not one ever stayed in a Chinese monastery or talked alone with a Chinese monk, and even if he had, he could not have made himself understood, since virtually no Chinese monks speak English. It is true that the Japanese visitors were able to *read* Chinese, but this did not mean that they took full advantage of their ability. The Nichiren monk whom I have quoted shrugged his shoulders when I asked about the Peking monthly, *Modern Buddhism,* and said that he never looked at it.

Many of the Southeast Asian Buddhists, on the other hand, cannot even read English. They have no access to translations from the Chinese mainland press or to international discussion of events in China. They have no way of knowing that their Chinese hosts publish one thing in Chinese for consumption at home and quite another thing in foreign languages for consumption abroad. When such visitors are invited to China and shown monastery after monastery, beautifully restored, with monks in immaculate robes reciting the scriptures, there is no possible corrective to the false impression they receive. The remarkable thing is how many of them suspect that it is false.

Actually, however, few people in Asia seem to feel much interest in what is going on outside their own national borders, and because of sectarian differences, this applies especially to the fate of Chinese Buddhism. In Southeast Asia, as I have already suggested, most people look upon Mahayana as a heresy, while in India most people look on Buddhism of both varieties, Theravadin as well as Mahayana, as mere deviations from Hinduism. Even in Japan, the leftist monk that I talked to said that he was not interested in the survival of Zen meditation in China, since he belonged to the Nichiren Sect.

Some readers may dismiss all these attitudes as "naiveté." Naiveté—or what seemed like it—I cannot deny. A Nepalese monk who was a most honoured guest in Peking several years ago told me that he had asked to stay in the principal Peking monastery. The request was refused on the grounds that he "would not be comfortable there." He assured his hosts that he was accustomed to hardship and would gladly put up with any discomfort in order to stay where, as a monk, he ought to stay. The request was still refused. They insisted that he would not be comfortable. So far as I could tell, he accepted this explanation, and the more obvious one (a fear that he might see or hear something that he was not supposed to) never occurred to him. He was the same person who assured me that his visit to Peking's showplace nunnery, with interpreter and driver, was "unannounced." Even if it was (which is unlikely) what he did not appreciate, perhaps, was the fact that one function of this nunnery is to be kept in perpetual readiness for visitors.

Several of the people I interviewed told me that if I wanted information on Buddhism in China, I should write to the Chinese Buddhist Association in Peking. "They don't tell lies, because they are dealing with the world," as a Burmese put it, and by this I think he meant that, if a lie were detected, they would be discredited before the whole world. I did not ask him how the whole world would hear about it. Similarly, when a prominent monk in Ceylon came across a quotation that was allegedly from a Soviet book, but seemed in conflict with what he had read about the Soviet Union, he decided to check whether or not there was such a book. To whom did he write? To the Soviet Embassy, of course, which assured him that the book did not exist.

I do not think, however, that ignorance, indifference, and naiveté really explain the attitudes that I found. The explanation, I believe, lies first in certain hopes and fears, and second, in the very nature of Buddhism. By "fears" I mean, for example, the fear of displeasing one's own government. In some countries, like Ceylon and Nepal, the government looks with distaste on anything that disturbs its policy of building better relations with Communist China. Buddhists who wish to be on good terms with their government must adjust to the political atmosphere. By "hopes" I mean, for example, the Japanese hope to re-establish trade with China, which causes many Japanese to cooperate in the Buddhist "friendship act" staged by Peking. Other Japanese cooperate in the hope that by making Chinese Buddhism useful to Peking, their cooperation will help keep it alive. In many countries Buddhists hope to build a world Buddhist movement that is truly international, and so they hesitate to say or do anything that would cause the withdrawal of the *bloc* representatives.

CHINESE CONTRIBUTION

Another hope is more material. The Chinese Buddhist Association has made frequent gifts to Buddhist organisations abroad. In one case they gave half a million *rupees* to a monk in Nepal who, by an odd coincidence, produced a book soon afterwards, praising Communist treatment of Buddhism. Part of the money he received was used to construct some much-needed school buildings.

Then there is the prospect of travel. Many Southeast Asians told me that they enjoy nothing better than travel. Since they are unable to get foreign exchange, their only hope is to go abroad as the guests of a government or institution. Some look towards the West, some towards the *bloc,* and some manage both. On the whole, the *bloc* seems better equipped to make a good impression on them. A left-wing Burmese Buddhist told me that in the U.S.S.R. there are thousands of laymen who crawl on their knees to kiss the foot of a Buddhist monk, while in the United States only one Buddhist monk is allowed into the country every two or three years, and when he gets there, he is "treated like a monkey."

An early Sinhalese visitor to China said that he was given three rooms in his hotel in Peking, with a telephone in each. He cut a grand swathe, even interceding on behalf of a Ceylon trade delegation that had been trying for weeks to get an agreement out of the Chinese. Within twenty-four hours of his intercession, the delegation got what it had been asking for. Many Buddhist travellers attend meetings and conferences and may enjoy the excitement of representing their own country with more privileges than the accredited ambassador.

The next hope is, on its reverse face, a fear. Communism has spread over half of the world in the last fifty years. Though it seems to be temporarily arrested, the Western powers are far away and, in any case, looking to them for one's own defence might mean the return of colonialism. Therefore Buddhists wonder what is going to happen to Buddhism—what is going to happen to them—if and when Communism reaches their countries? Is it not better to reach an accommodation now?

Furthermore, as I was so often told, Buddhism and Communism have many points in common: both deny the existence of God, the existence of the soul, and think dialectically. The Sangha practices some things that the Communists have so far merely talked about: no personal property, living a communal life, taking all decisions unanimously, and devoting oneself to the service of the people and world peace. It may be true that the Buddha differs from Marx on a few points, like the use of violence, but such differences can be rationalised.

CHOU EN-LAI'S VIEWS

With these thoughts in mind, therefore, some Buddhists feel as if they were already riding the wave of the future. They turn from fear to hope. Religion will always be necessary. Even the Marxists say that it cannot be eliminated in the near future, and the Marxists are sure to find, once material needs are satisfied, that something spiritual is required above and beyond. Is not Buddhism best suited to supply this spiritual something? No religion is so compatible with Marxism. In fact, like Marxism, Buddhism is not a religion at all, but a science. So perhaps Marxism, instead of destroying Buddhism, will spread it.

This idea is so intoxicating that sober heads are turned. Provided one is certain that Marxism is evolving—*must* evolve—in the "right direction", one can dismiss all Marxist pronouncements on religion as having only historical interest. I have already mentioned the monk in Ceylon who believes that the Chinese Government plans to replace Mahayana with Theravadin Buddhism. This is what he was told by Chou En-lai, he said, and Chou had come to favour such a plan after a talk he had with U Nu on the relative merits of the two kinds of Buddhism. Theravada was pure and scientific, while Mahayana was corrupt and superstitious.

According to Chou En-lai the reason that the Chinese Buddhist Institute was founded in Peking seven years ago was to introduce Theravada and gradually to do away with Mahayana. But Chou admitted that it would be difficult to convert the Chinese people to Theravada because their Mahayana habits were so deeply engrained (thus, in his usual farsighted way, he provided himself with an alibi should the conversion of China fail to materialise).

To spread the *dharma* among seven hundred million people—what a glorious prospect for any Buddhist monk! what enormous merit would be generated! and how resolutely any attempt at sabotage must be resisted! Only in these terms can I explain the extraordinary conversation that we then had. I asked this monk if it would not be a good idea for him to know more about the present situation of Buddhism in China. Would he like to see translations from Peking newspapers? He began by saying that he would. Then, after a few moments' reflection, he changed his mind. The Chinese Communists, he said, had been striving to put their country on its feet. Certain steps had necessarily been taken that were detrimental to Buddhism, but these steps were correct. Similarly, in the history of Ceylon, some kings had conducted wars of liberation. Though many were killed, the people were grateful and the monks chanted psalms of praise (*pitis*) to show that they sanctioned it. Some day in China, a stop would come to all these things: "one has to deal with the people, and so there will be liberalisation."

OUTSIDERS

Still, I asked, would it not be best for him as a visitor (he is going to China again this year) to have as much information as possible, particularly if he hopes to undertake such a vast programme of conversion? No, he said, if outsiders knew what was going on, the Communists would not be able to carry on their plans of reconstruction (*sic*). In the United States, too, outsiders were kept from knowing certain things. But, I persisted, was it not safer to know what the Chinese had been saying to one another in their own language? Was it wise to run even the remotest risk of being used?

That was not the way to look at it, he said. If he knew beforehand the real conditions in China, he might feel an aversion to going there. Also, it was like trying to find out too much about a man's weaknesses: it could spoil your relationship with him. Even in Ceylon, social and economic conditions made it impossible to practice Buddhism perfectly. Once conditions in China improved, the practice of Buddhism would improve too. And what was the alternative to the present regime? Twenty-five years ago he had seen Chinese dying in the streets, crying for water, and not one of the landlords came to give them any. Today the roads were straight and clean: even the most ordinary person had enough to eat. How could we entertain the suspicion the the Communists, who had done so much for their country, would not be sincere and honest in their dealings with outsiders?

And so it went for nearly two hours. Yet we parted on the best terms, and I think that he held no ill will for my persistent questions. I for my part did not consider that he was "naive," but simply that his good judgment had been overwhelmed by the hope of changing the world for the better.

I do not want the reader to be misled by the conversations recounted above, many of which I have selected more because they are striking than because they are typical. I do not consider that the *majority* of Asian Buddhists have sacrificed their good judgment or intellectual honesty for the sake of currying favour with their own government, or for the sake of foreign trade, Chinese donations, guided tours, or the prospect of converting Communists to Buddhism. Let me make this point very clear: the *majority* of the people that I talked to were more or less aware of the nature of the Chinese Communist regime and had doubts about the survival of Buddhism in China. They were not stupid, nor were they Communist dupes.

If they often seemed evasive and self-contradictory, it was because they were trying to observe a cardinal principle of Buddhism: avoid partisanship. Monks may not engage in partisan politics. If Buddhism is persecuted, they must, as always, obey Government decrees and wait for a suitable time to speak. At the right time they can and should speak out on all questions of right and wrong, even political questions, *provided they do so in a non-partisan way.* This proviso is the crux of the matter. Because it can be interpreted so differently, the outsider gets a bewildering variety of answers when he asks the Buddhist about the role of the Sangha in the modern world.

For example, Buddhist monks in Ceylon could take no action to help Buddhists in Tibet. They could merely express *sanvega,* "impersonal regret," and meetings were actually held for this purpose in Ceylon after the suppression of the Lhasa uprising. They were meant to be non-partisan, but some Buddhists would not have considered them so and certainly the Chinese Embassy did not.

If one follows the principle of non-partisanship a little further, one can finally see, I think, the underlying reason for so much of the apparent indifference and rationalisation that I encountered from Buddhists in many countries. I was an American, representing (in their eyes) partisanship personified. I was necessarily *against* the Soviet Union and *against* Communist China. I was a supporter of the world contest that now exemplifies the three primary Buddhist evils: greed, anger, and stupidity. How were these monks and laymen to deal with me? If they accepted what I had to say or, rather, if their thinking was moved in the direction indicated by my questions (for I tried to avoid the expression of my own opinions), they too would run the risk of being snared by partisanship and slipping back into the greed, anger, and stupidity which they had spent their lives overcoming.

Thus the monk who shrugged his shoulders when I mentioned the possible demise of the Chinese Sangha and said: "Well, if the Sangha is destroyed, it can be revived"—his concern at that moment was not for the Chinese Sangha, but for himself and for me. Would he allow my question to turn him against the Chinese Communists? Was there any way in which he could turn me, perhaps, away from my partisanship? It was not he who was "fuzzy-minded," but I. In his view, my efforts were directed towards criticising the People's Government, whereas they should have been directed towards criticising myself.

One difference between Theravadin and Mahayana Buddhism has been and still is that in the Theravada the first problem is oneself. For how can one help others until one has clarified one's own mind? Many (though not all) of the quirky statements that I have quoted above make perfectly good sense when seen as an effort on the part of the people I was interviewing to avoid falling into partisanship at the hands of a dangerous American diversionist. The more compelling the evidence such people are offered about the true status of Buddhism in Communist countries, the more rigorously they must discipline their minds to discount it. The greater the indignation that outsiders may feel over the treatment of Buddhism in China, the harder Buddhists must try to teach them the non-attachment which alone leads to true compassion.

I wish that I could leave it at that. But I must tell my friends in Southeast Asia—if any of them ever read these lines—that their approach seldom has the effect they hope for. To most non-Buddhists the Theravadin attitude to the problem of Communism is simply incomprehensible. Non-Buddhists are not stirred to self-examination, but to scorn. I feel not scorn, but sadness. One young monk in Ceylon told me that he and eighty *per cent* of his contemporaries hoped that their country would soon have a Communist government. If it did, he said, the Sangha would be much better off than it is now. It would have financial support and public respect, and it would become stricter in following the Buddhist rules. Other Sinhalese to whom I repeated his estimate felt that it was not very much too high.

I have made a special study of Buddhism in China. I know what has happened to it in the last twelve years, both the good and the bad. I think that I know what would happen to the Sangha in Ceylon if their government were Communist. Buddhism would die a painful death. This may, in fact, happen. There is nothing an outsider can do to warn the victims. Any warning will be regarded as partisan propaganda. Nor can he urge those Buddhists who know the facts to proclaim them publicly, for that would be engaging in partisan politics. Nor, for the same reason, can he expect them to take joint action in their own defence. The outsider can only sit by and watch.

It is my impression that the devout Buddhists of Southeast Asia, if confronted by a choice between self-defence and destruction, would choose destruction. They may remember the famous Jataka tale in which the Buddha, in one of his previous lives, felt compassion for a hungry tigress and provided his own body as a meal. Non-Buddhists may wonder what practical purpose was served by the sacrifice: they miss the point. The point was the change that it represented in Buddha's mind. Unfortunately this is not the kind of mental change that a Communist regime will permit.

Appendix G

A Visit Home

Although isolated bits of information provided by oral informants have often been cited in this book, I have given few extended accounts of their experiences. The following concerns the visit home in 1962 of a monk whom I interviewed several times immediately after he came out of the Mainland. As was occasionally possible, I tape-recorded these interviews and the summary offered below is largely in his own words.

This individual was born in Kiangsi about 1928 and became a monk at the age of fourteen about 1941. (His reasons are given in Welch, *Practice,* pp. 262-263.) After being ordained at the Nan-hua Ssu, he stayed on in its meditation hall for five years, first as an acolyte, then a recorder, then a succentor. In 1946 he acted as an ordination instructor and his name is given in the ordination yearbook. By that time he had become a guest prefect. In 1948, possibly because of uneasiness about the political future of China, he moved to Hong Kong and in 1956 to Phnom Penh. During the food shortage that followed the Great Leap Forward he began sending food parcels to his parents. However, it took two months for the parcels to reach them and the duty was prohibitive–24 reals on a can of oil that cost only 19, for instance. If he sent things by air, the shipping charges were also prohibitive–70 reals to send 12 ounces of vitamins. In the spring of 1962 he heard that his father was ill from malnutrition. Since he was in his sixties, he might not live much longer. Therefore my informant, who had not seen him since he became a monk twenty-one years earlier, felt that he ought to go back, taking as much food as he could, not only to give his parents but also to his masters' master (*shih-kung*), who was in his seventies. After several days of weighing the possible risks and gains, he decided to apply for a passport at Peking's embassy in Phnom Penh. (He still considered himself a Chinese citizen.)

Whereas most overseas Chinese could get their passports in a week, his took over a month. His entire past was thoroughly investigated and a check was made in his home town. He was interviewed by a representative of the Overseas Chinese Affairs Commission attached to the embassy. He explained to him that his purpose was first to visit his parents and second to see the progress of the motherland. The representative explained to him that he was being investigated so carefully because he was a monk and they had to be on the lookout for Kuomintang spies among people with this kind of background.

When he got to Hong Kong, someone in a local travel bureau advised him not to wear traditional monk's dress, but to get some "T'ai-hsü uniforms," now worn by Mainland monks. He also advised him not to take in the maximum amount of Mainland currency, but to purchase instead two wristwatches and two fountain pens. A wristwatch costing the equivalent of 100 JMP in Hong Kong could be sold for 480 in Canton or 600-1,000 in Peking. A pen costing 60 could be sold for 200-300. There would be no difficulty selling them, for once he reached his hotel in Canton, buyers would come to his room. Since the objects were small, they could take them away in their pockets with no one the wiser. The reason prices were so high, according to this travel agent, was that Soviet specialists were still living in places like Shanghai and getting high salaries with nothing to spend them on.

The same man arranged for fourteen packages of food and clothing, purchased in Hong Kong, to be handed to the Hong Kong branch of the China Travel Service, which, in turn, arranged to have them transported to Canton and placed in the warehouse there under his name. Later the packages were shipped to Nan-ch'ang, from where he picked them up to take to his home town in the southwestern part of the province. They weighed 600 pounds in all.

The reason that the Communists let overseas Chinese bring in such large quantities was, he thought, because the advantages outweighed disadvantages. They lost face when food and clothing were mailed, but not when they were brought by visitors who were returning anyway. Hence the weight limit on parcels did not apply to travelers' baggage. Similarly, the risk of having overseas Chinese get a bad impression was outweighed by the chance to acquire foreign exchange and alleviate the food shortage and by the effort that was made to see to it that every visitor got a *good* impression.

Thus, wherever he went, he was escorted by representatives of the Overseas Chinese Affairs Commission. They would meet him at the station, carry his bags, and be terribly polite. After he had registered at the local Overseas Chinese Hotel which, in Peking, for example, cost 7.50 JMP a night plus 2.50 for food, representatives would ask him what he wanted to see. He would explain that he was a Buddhist and wished to learn something of the state of Buddhism in the motherland since Liberation. They would then suggest the names of the local showplace monasteries (*chao-p'ai ssu-yüan*). In every large city, he said, one Buddhist monastery and one Buddhist nunnery had been preserved, along with a Catholic church and a Taoist temple. Once his itinerary had been fixed, they would call up the monastery and let its people know that an overseas Chinese monk wanted to pay them a visit and that they should "get ready." When he drove up—usually about 8:30 A.M.—the lamps would already have been lit in the great shrine hall, the monks would be lined up by the main gate, and as soon as the horn was sounded, it would open. He would be welcomed effusively, shown around the buildings, and then be taken to a beautifully appointed reception room that was always to be found in showplace monasteries. While cakes and tea would be served, he could chat with the abbot or prior.

In all monasteries he visited he was accompanied by people from the Overseas Chinese Affairs Commission. He was never allowed to talk alone to any of the monks. The only place he spent the night was the the Ling-yen Ssu in Soochow, but even there the only monks he talked to (well-chaperoned) were the abbot, the prior, and two retired abbots. There was a good side, he felt, to all this. He could not get into trouble, nor could the monks he talked to. Even so, he dared not ask many questions. If he had done so, they might have thought he was a spy and not let him out of the country. All in all, because of the tightness of controls, he had no way of finding out how many Buddhist monks had been successfully "remolded" and supported the new regime.

He reached his home town in May. Conditions there were grim—but not as grim as they had been in 1960, when one thousand of the total population of five thousand had starved to death. It was the able-bodied adults who starved, not the children or the aged, who required less food. In 1961 private plots had been introduced. Some land already under cultivation was given to the aged (2-3 fen apiece); waste land that had been reclaimed was given to the rest of the population, usually in far off mountainsides. Its soil was so poor that they could only grow pig fodder (*chu-p'o-ts'ai*) and sweet potatoes, but these literally saved their lives. Rations fluctuated and the full amount of the ration was not always available. His own family, for instance, had six members: his mother and father, brother and sister-in-law, and the latters' two children. Their total ration was 160 catties for a three-month period, but sometimes what they actually received was as low as 100 catties. In 1962 the oil ration had been reduced from four ounces a month to two ounces, but no oil had been actually purchasable since the end of 1961. His family lived by boiling up the pig fodder and sweet potatoes with a little rice and salt. Almost as soon as they finished eating they would feel hungry again. Pig fodder is not meant for human consumption and although they could eat as much as they grew, they told him that the food he brought with him enabled them to stop feeling hungry for the first time in years. He brought rice, flour, peanut oil, dried mushrooms, beancurd (which they had not seen since Liberation), and spices.

Besides visiting his home province, he went to Canton, Swatow, Chaochow, Ningpo, Hangchow, Shanghai, Soochow, Nanking, Wuhan, and Peking, which he reached on the day of the summer solstice. After three months in the Mainland, he arrived back in Hong Kong on July 1, 1962. Our first interview was on July 3. About a month later he returned to Cambodia, where he died in 1967. Although his report of the number of deaths from famine may give rise to skepticism, I found him an intelligent and honest informant. What a native can find out about conditions in the deep countryside must necessarily be very different from what foreigners can learn in the major cities.

Appendix H

The Debate on Religious Policy

The following articles, which appeared in 1963-65, seem most closely related to the debate on religious policy discussed in Chapter XI at notes 28-37, 43-45, 48. All Chinese titles are given below in English.

January 20, 1963 *Hsin chien-she,* "On the origin of the concept of the existence of gods," by Ya-han-chang

January 23, 1963 *KMJP,* "The problem of inheriting the ideological legacy in the light of discussions on Confucius," by the editorial department of *Hsin chien-she,* tr. in *SCMP* 2924:1-6

April 4, 1963 *JMJP,* "I no longer believe in the gods," by Yü Jung, tr. in *SCMP,* 2973:11-12

July 20, 1963 *Hsin chien-she,* pp. 38-46, "On the problem of the disappearance of the concept of gods," by Ya-han-chang

August 8, 1963 *JMJP,* "On the question of religious superstitions," by Ya-han-chang, tr. in *SCMP,* 3048:1-13

August 10, 1963 *Kung-jen jih-pao,* "Superstitions continue—we must suppress them," tr. in JPRS 22244:51-56 and *SCMP,* 3061:9-15

August 15, 1963 *JMJP,* "Draw the bow to the full without letting the arrows go, and be on the alert" by Yü Chün, tr. in *SCMP,* 3048:11-13

August 20, 1963 *Chung-kuo ch'ing-nien pao,* "Oppose superstition" by Chi Yü-chang, tr. in *SCMP,* 3062:11

September 20, 1963 *Hsin chien-she,* "Some questions concerning the Marxist-Lenist view of religion," by Yu Hsiang and Liu Chün-wang, summarized in *SCMP,* 3099:1-2

February 20, 1964 *Hsin chien-she* "On the distinction between the existence of the concepts of gods, religion, and feudal superstition, a reply to Yu Hsiang and Liu Chün-wang," by Ya-han-chang, tr. in *SCMM,* 413:1-7

February 25, 1964 Shanghai *Wen-hui pao,* "An understanding of several religious problems," by Ya-han-chang

February 26, 1964 *Hung-ch'i,* "The correct understanding and handling of the problem of religion," by Yu Hsiang and Liu Chün-wang, tr. in *SCMM,* 410:41-49

March 21, 1964 *KMJP,* "Religious and class struggle in the transition period," by Liu Chün-wang and Yu Hsiang, tr. in *SCMP,* 3202:1-7

March 23, 1964 *JMJP,* "Religion and idealist philosophy" by Tseng Wen-ching, tr. in *SCMP,* 3217:1-7

April 2, 1964 *KMJP,* "The problem of eliminating religious superstition," by Chou Chien-jen, tr. in *SCMP,* 3226:15-17

April 21, 1964 Shanghai *Wen-hui pao,* "The relationship between the concepts of god and superstition which exist together in religion," by Yu Hsiang and Liu Chün-wang

May 5, 1964 Shanghai *Wen-hui pao,* "The origins and the end of religion: another riposte to Comrade Ya-han-chang," by Yu Hsiang and Liu Chün-wang

June 15, 1964 Shanghai *Wen-hui pao* "Query about the origins of religion: response to Comrade Yu Hsiang and Liu Chün-wang," by Ch'en Yang-tung

June 17, 1964 *Tientsin jih-pao,* "Religion is superstition, but not all superstitions are religion," by Ya-han-chang

June 23, 1964 Shanghai *Wen-hui pao,* "The correct understanding of 'Religion is the opiate of the people': reply to Comrade Ya-han-chang," by Ping Ch'üan

July 5, 1964 Shanghai *Wen-hui pao* "Some ideas on the problems of religion and the concept of gods: reply to Comrades Ya-han-chang, Yu Hsiang and Liu Chün-wang," by Fang Tzu-p'ing

August 31, 1964 *Hung-ch'i,* review by K'ung Fan of Jen Chi-yü's "Collected essays on Buddhist thought from Han through T'ang," tr. in *SCMM,* 438:28

September 11, 1964 Shanghai *Wen-hui pao* "Religion and feudal superstition are not the same thing: another response to Yu Hsiang and Liu Chün-wang," by Ya-han-chang

December 10, 1964 Shanghai *Wen-hui pao,* "Superstition is a generic term including the concepts of gods, religion, and feudal superstition: third response to Yu Hsiang and Liu Chün-wang," by Ya-han-chang

January 20-30, 1965 Hong Kong *Ta-kung pao,* "Evil monks of an ancient monastery" by T'ang Hu-lu

February 8, 1965 Canton Nan-fang jip-pao, "Do not compromise with superstitious ideas," tr. in *SCMP,* 3423:18

February 11, 1965 Canton *Yang-ch'eng wan-pao,* "How man created the gods: a philosopher said, 'If big yellow oxen believed in gods, gods would be oxen,' " by Wan Hui-ts'ao

March 7-8, 1965 *KMJP* "On the problem of understanding religion—for consultation with Ya-han-chang," by Yu Hsiang and Liu Chün-wang, tr. in *SCMP,* 4326:1-11

March 8, 1965 *Yang-ch'eng wan-pao,* "What is the use of Buddhism," by Wan Hui-ts'ao

June 15, 1965 *Li-shih yen-chiu,* pp. 75-83, "Problems concerning the historical origins of primeval Buddhism," by Ch'i Hsien-lin, reprinted in *JMJP,* August 20, 1965

June 30, 1965 *KMJP,* "Draw a clear line of demarcation with the 'religious studies' of the bourgeois class," by Ya-han-chang, tr. in *SCMP,* 3501:1-9

October 20, 1965 *Hsin chien-she,* pp. 29-34, "Introduction to Buddhism in the T'ang dynasty," by Fan Wen-lan

December 7, 1965 *JMJP* "Fan Wen-lan on the evils of Buddhism in the T'ang dynasty," by Chang Chih-yen tr. in *SCMP,* 3599:15-17

December 20, 1965 *Hsin chien-she,* pp. 80-84, "Religion has always been the opiate of the people: a response to Ya-han-chang," by Liang Hao and Yang Chen, tr. in JPRS 34726:8-18.

Notes

METHOD OF CITATION

In this book English translations of Chinese names and terms are frequently used in the main body of the text—for the convenience of readers who do not know Chinese—whereas in the notes and appendices the same names and terms are given in romanized form—for the convenience of readers who want to know the Chinese original. For example, the text often refers to *Modern Buddhism*, the journal published in Peking from 1950 to 1964; it is cited in the notes as *HTFH* (*Hsien-tai fo-hsüeh*). *People's Daily* is cited as *JMJP* (*Jen-min jih-pao*).

As to the numerals used in citation, I have imposed consistency in certain cases where the system changed. For example, in January 1953 *Modern Buddhism* ceased to identify its issues by volume and number, so that the issue of that month—vol. 3, no. 5— became simply 1953, no. 1. I have cited all issues this way from the beginning, so that what is, properly speaking, vol. 1, no. 1 (September 1950) is cited as *HTFH*, 9/50. The same has been done with all Mainland periodicals that ceased to use volume and number. This leads to confusion when a monthly changed to a bi-monthly as *Modern Buddhism* did in 1960. I have continued to cite it by the number on its cover, but have added the month of publication: for example, *HTFH*, 5/62, p. 1 (October 1962).

Where I refer the reader to Chapter *X* at note *Y*, I mean to refer him to the passage in Chapter *X* for which note *Y* provides the source or comment.

Where material has appeared in a government translation, the reader should not assume that I have checked it against the original source unless I so indicate. I have, however, checked all items appearing in *Modern Buddhism*.

ABBREVIATIONS

CB	*Current Background*
CNA	*China News Analysis*
ECMM	*Extracts from China Mainland Magazines*
FBIS	*Federal Broadcast Information Service*
HTFH	*Hsien-tai fo-hsüeh* (Modern Buddhism)
JMJP	*Jen-min jih-pao* (People's daily)
JPRS	Joint Publications Research Service
KMJP	*Kuang-ming jih-pao*
NCNA	New China News Agency
SCMM	*Selections from China Mainland Magazines*
SCMP	*Survey of the China Mainland Press*
T	Taishō Tripitaka (*Taishō shinshu daizokyō*)
URS	Union Research Service

CURRENCY

In the text I have preferred to translate most monetary sums into the U.S. dollar equivalent for the benefit of readers who may not be familiar with Chinese currency reforms. The value of the yuan was reduced 10,000:1 on March 1, 1955, and was thereafter officially equivalent to about 45 cents U.S. Untranslated sums are followed by JMP (*jen-min-pi,* people's currency) rather than by "yuan" in order to avoid confusion with other Chinese currencies.

I. A POLICY EMERGES

1. The phrase "a state of terror" comes from a reader's letter to *Modern Buddhism.* He said that in his region "during the new era the number of lay people who follow Buddhism has quietly declined, while monks and nuns are in an even greater state of terror (*tan-chan hsin-ching*)." See *HTFH,* 8/51, p. 24. A guarded description of their difficulties was given by Ch'en Ming-shu in 1950. "Monks and nuns (*fo-chiao t'u*) are a class of people despised by the world [i.e., the cadres]; temples and monasteries are, for the world, a symbol of deadly poison; and the temple property that monks and nuns use to fill their stomachs, as well as their income from performing Buddhist rites, are looked upon as public property acquired by exploitation. For all three reasons, monks and nuns throughout China have become like prisoners of war [to be captured], monasteries are bandit strongholds [to be taken], and monastic property is booty . . . [monks and nuns] from ancient times have been unable to put up resistance; they have simply been pitiful weaklings, backward and ignorant. They have been despised as weak parasites, so everywhere they have been subject to merciless pursuit and encroachment, even to

the point of being punished like tyrants . . . Not only has 'religious freedom' become a dead letter; they do not even have the right to feel secure about their survival!" See *HTFH,* 10/57, p. 28. More detailed information on the difficulties encountered by Buddhists in the first years after Liberation will be found below at notes 15, 16, 27-29 and in Chapters II-IV and VII.

2. In 1951 a reader wrote to *Modern Buddhism* asking whether "some people" were correct in saying that Buddhist monasteries and sacred images were "symbols of feudal superstition": see *HTFH,* 9/51, p. 22. Here and elsewhere in materials I have read, anti-Buddhist cadres are often referred to by a euphemism like "some people" or "the world." See *HTFH,* 5/51, pp. 26-27, where a question about "people" destroying Buddhist property near Hangchow is answered by explaining why rural cadres would do such a thing.

3. Mao Tse-tung, *Selected Works* (Peking, 1961-65), I, 45.

4. *Ibid.,* p. 51.

5. *Ibid.,* p. 46 (slightly altered).

6. Conrad Brandt, Benjamin I. Schwartz, John K. Fairbank, *A Documentary History of Chinese Communism* (Cambridge, Mass., 1952), p. 22. The confiscation of monastery land was provided for in the Land Law: *ibid.,* pp. 225-226.

7. On the inclusion of religious believers in the united front, see "On the New Democracy" in Mao's *Selected Works*, III, 155. Landlords' holdings were exempted from confiscation in February 1937: see Mao, *Selected Works,* I, 269, and Chao Kuo-chün, *Agrarian Policy of the Chinese Communist Party, 1921-1959* (New Delhi, 1960), p. 38. Chao, p. 47, cites a resolution of the Central Committee of January 28, 1942, on special types of land problem: "Land that belongs to a religious group (Christian, Buddhist, Muslim, Taoist, or other sects) shall undergo no changes."

8. Mao, *Selected Works,* III, 313.

9. See *CB,* 9:2. Article 5 reads: "The people of the People's Republic of China shall have freedom of thought, speech, publication, assembly, association, correspondence, person, domicile, moving from one place to another, religious belief, and freedom of holding processions and demonstrations."

10. *HTFH,* 10/50, p. 21 (italics added), and see Appendix A. This is Chü-tsan's summary of what Ch'en Ch'i-yüan transmitted as Chou's instructions, so it is doubly removed from the force of the statement in Chou's own words.

11. *JMJP,* Sept. 23, 1950.

12. See Wang Tzu-yeh's article "The Basic Attitude of Marxist-Leninists Towards the Problem of Religion" in *Hsüeh-hsi,* 3.2:9-10 (March 16, 1951). According to a cadre then handling religious affairs in Canton, the *People's Daily* editorial of September 23, 1950, was the first statement and this was the second statement about religious policy to be printed in the national press after Liberation.

13. *The Agrarian Reform Law of the People's Republic of China and other relevant documents,* 4th ed., (Peking, 1953), pp. 9-10 (article 21).

14. On the GAC order, see *HTFH,* 11/50, p. 6. I have not found its original text. It may be identical with the order to the same effect that Chü-tsan later said had been issued in June 1950: see *China Reconstructs,* 1-2/54, p. 42. *HTFH,* 9/53, p. 19, referred to "Measures for the Protection of Ancient Relics, Cultural Treasures, Books, and Rare Plants and Animals," issued by the GAC on May 24, 1950. The very first move to protect the monasteries seems to have been taken, as might be expected, in the area around the capital. Probably in June or July 1949 the People's Municipal Government of Peking issued a proclamation strictly prohibiting damage to monasteries and ancient cultural monuments: see *HTFH,* 9/50, p. 25. More will be said in Chapter V about these and later measures for the protection of monasteries.

15. *HTFH,* 10/50, p. 30. The Soviet Constitution's guarantee of freedom to perform religious rites was invoked again in 9/51, p. 22. Article 124 of the 1936 Constitution reads: "In order to ensure to citizens freedom of conscience, the church in the U.S.S.R. is separated from the state, and the school from the church. Freedom of religious worship and freedom of anti-religious propaganda are recognized for all citizens." It was fallacious, of course, for Chinese Buddhists to argue that Soviet citizens enjoyed so much freedom because their rights were not delimited in their Constitution. Their rights were very strictly delimited—more so than by any published legislation under Mao—by the laws of 1918 and 1929 (amended 1932). See Richard C. Marshall, Jr., ed. *Aspects of Religion in the Soviet Union 1917-1967* (Chicago, University of Chicago Press, 1971), pp. 62-102, 437-462.

16. *HTFH,* 9/51, p. 24.

17. *HTFH,* 9/50, pp. 24-25, and Appendix A. Although this memorandum was signed by twenty-one persons who purportedly represented the Buddhists of Peking, it had been drafted by Chü-tsan.

18. See Holmes Welch, *The Buddhist Revival in China* (Cambridge, Mass., 1968), pp. 173-179.

19. *HTFH,* 9/50, p. 25, and Appendix A.

20. *Ibid.* The same point was repeated in *HTFH,* 11/51, p. 22.

21. This statement was: "We should use this periodical to work for the fulfillment of the six duties and goals listed below: 1. To transmit to Buddhists the government's policy on religion and the direction it is going in dealing with Buddhist problems. 2. To re-evaluate Buddhist doctrine (*fo-hsüeh*) from a scientific-historical viewpoint. 3. To investigate Buddhist property of cultural value, to put in order Buddhist historical records, and to clarify the close relationship between Buddhism and various aspects of China's national culture over the past two thousand years, for reference and utilization by academic circles. 4. To correct erroneous ideas in Buddhist circles . . . so as to advance the reform of the Buddhist system as it operates

today. 5. To discuss problems in Buddhist studies (*fo-hsüeh*) with progressive scholars at home and abroad. 6. To establish links with Buddhists at home and abroad in the struggle for lasting peace and people's democracy" (*HTFH,* 10/50, p. 32). These are an elaboration of the aims projected for the magazine when it was first conceived (see *HTFH,* 10/50, p. 23) and are quite similar to the aims with which the Chinese Buddhist Association was to be established in 1953. I take clause 3 above to mean that *Modern Buddhism* would try to keep track of monastic property and show why it should be protected.

22. Chü-tsan*, Li Chi-shen*, Ch'en Ming-shu*, Chao P'u-ch'u*, Shirob Jaltso*, Yeh Kung-cho*, Li I-p'ing*, Fang Tzu-fan*, Chou Shu-chia, and T'ang Sheng-chih*. As to the other nine, three (Li Ming-yang*, Li Shu-ch'eng*, and Chang Tung-sun*) were non-Communist intellectuals and political leaders who seem to have been well-disposed towards the preservation of Chinese culture, including Buddhism. Six I cannot adequately identify. Ch'en Lien-sheng has a name (literally "Lotus Born") that sounds like a devotee's. Lin Chih-chün wrote an article on the Tibetan canon in *HTFH* 2-3/53. Ch'a An-sun, Chou T'ai-hsüan*, and Yang Shu-chi do not turn up again in connection with Chinese Buddhist activities. Chou was a Paris-trained zoology professor at Chengtu University. Yang represented the Ministry of Health at a TB Research Conference in Leipzig in 1951. Sha Yung-ts'ang is elsewhere described as a "devotee": see *HTFH,* 10/50, p. 23.

23. The names marked with an asterisk in the preceding note were all CPPCC delegates (or, in the case of Yeh and T'ang, were soon to become CPPCC delegates). As to the six who held high governmental posts, Li Chi-shen was a vice-chairman of the Chinese People's Government; Ch'en Ming-shu was on the People's Government Council, the Central-South Military and Administrative Council, and held many other important posts; Li Shu-ch'eng was Minister of Agriculture. Shirob Jaltso was vice-governor of the sensitive border region of Tsinghai; T'ang Sheng-chih was a vice-governor of Hunan; and Li Ming-yang was on the East China Military and Administrative Council. It was perhaps with reference to such men that *Modern Buddhism* told its readers in 1951 that, whereas cadres studying for admission to the Party naturally could not hold any religious belief, "in Peking a really able cadre who was at the same time a resolute and orthodox Buddhist is subject to no limitation at all on his beliefs": see *HTFH,* 5/51, p. 27. He could not, however, join the Party.

24. The editorial committee consisted of Chü-tsan, Yeh Kung-cho, Li Shu-ch'eng, Chou Shu-chia, Chou T'ai-hsüan, Chang Chung-hsing, Yü Yü, Yu Hsia, Hsü Tan, and Lin Tzu-ch'eng. I cannot identify Chang. Chou Shu-chia was perhaps the most eminent lay Buddhist devotee in Peking. Hsü Tan had already been a devotee in the 1930's. Yu Hsia was a contributor to the International Buddhist Encyclopedia and wrote articles for *Modern Buddhism* on Yang Jen-shan and Ou-yang Ching-wu, to whose school in Nanking he

probably belonged. Yü Yü and Lin Tzu-ch'eng were members of the San-shih Hsüeh-hui, a lay Buddhist society specializing in the study of the Yogacarin school. Lin was a writer who had headed a Buddhist youth group in occupied Shanghai during the war.

The standing committee, to which the editorial committee was responsible, consisted of Li Chi-shen, Chü-tsan, Yeh Kung-cho, Chou Shu-chia, and Sha Yung-ts'ang. Two names are conspicuously absent: Chao P'u-ch'u, perhaps because he still spent most of his time in Shanghai; and Ch'en Ming-shu, the publisher of *Modern Buddhism.* In 1957, when Ch'en Ming-shu was criticized as a rightist, Chü-tsan said that "in the publishing house of *Modern Buddhism* everything was decided by the board of directors [presumably meaning the standing committee] and Ch'en Ming-shu's own opinions never affected what we did": see *HTFH,* 12/57, p. 28. By this time Chü-tsan was no longer editor-in-chief of *Modern Buddhism,* having been succeeded in 1956 by Shih Ming-k'o, an ex-monk who had also been a disciple of T'ai-hsü.

25. *HTFH,* 12/54, p. 30. On the take over of *Modern Buddhism* by the Study Committee of the Chinese Buddhist Association, see *HTFH,* 7/54, p. 30. Ch'en's name last appeared as publisher in the issue of December 1953, after which the publisher was given as Hsien-tai Fo-hsüeh She until the issue of July 1954, when it became the Chung-kuo Fo-chiao Hsieh-hui Hsüeh-hsi Wei-yüan-hui.

26. See above at notes 1, 2, 15, 16.

27. *HTFH,* 5/51, p. 25.

28. See for example *HTFH,* 3/51, pp. 32-33.

29. *HTFH,* 9/51, p. 21.

30. In 9/51, p. 21, the column editor, Yü-chih, replied to an inquiry about reorganizing Buddhism by saying that this had to be done by the Buddhists themselves, not by the government, and that its success would depend on their degree of awareness. The month before he had answered a complaint (see note 1 above) by saying: "The new era has not limited religious activities at all, since the Common Program clearly provides for freedom of religious belief. Why should monks and nuns be in a state of terror? Why should the number of lay people studying Buddhism have quietly declined? We think that the problem here is the Buddhists themselves and not the government in the new era." Cf. above at note 15 and Chapter V at note 72.

31. *HTFH,* 9/51, p. 20. This was also written by Yü-chih, the same editor who told the readers the month before not to "cheat the people with superstition," a phrase that usually referred to making money from performing rites for the dead.

32. *HTFH,* 10/51, p. 29.

33. One indication that they were monitoring it was the occasional correction to a political error in a previous issue. Two such were printed in *HTFH,* 12/51, p. 36.

34. It cautiously reappeared in April, June, and July 1954 and then was dropped for good.

35. *HTFH,* 10/53, p. 32.
36. *HTFH,* 11/55, p. 4.
37. In its first issue (*HTFH,* 9/50, p. 31) *Modern Buddhism* had appealed for correspondents to send in monthly reports on Buddhist activities from all provinces, municipalities, and sacred mountains. Anyone, whether he was a monk or a lay person, could become a correspondent, with good remuneration, after his articles had appeared in two issues (although the magazine would "not be responsible for his personal conduct"). In the summer of 1954, after it had been taken over by the Chinese Buddhist Association, *Modern Buddhism* seems to have made an effort to win back the favor of readers and to counteract the impression that articles were no longer welcomed from the public at large: in two consecutive months it printed appeals for news reports and feature articles "reflecting different opinions, so long as they are reasonable and provide evidence for what they say": see *HTFH,* 8/54, p. 30, and 9/54, p. 30. The last such appeal ever to appear was printed in *HTFH,* 3/56, p. 30, during the Hundred Flowers.
38. The quality of paper, which had risen in June 1953 when the CBA was inaugurated and dropped in 1955, strikingly improved with the issue of May 1956, and remained very good through 1957 and fair until 1959. One can see here a recurring pattern of the authorities deciding that *Modern Buddhism* was important and then allocating enough good stock for a year or two. The third time this happened was at the beginning of 1964; and those who decided to allocate good stock for that year may not have been the same people who decided to close it down in 1965. Drawing conclusions from the quality of paper is complicated by the fact that starting as early as 1959, issues were printed in two runs, one on good paper, one on poor. Generally speaking the copies on good paper were sent to foreign Buddhists and overseas Chinese.
39. The last monthly issue (118) was dated June 13, 1960, and it contained three and a quarter pages of local Buddhist news. The next issues were dated November 13, 1960 (119), December 13, 1960 (120), and April 13, 1961 (121). The only item of local news they contained was a brief obituary. It was during the second period of non-publication (January-March 1961) that the partial conversion to English took place. For example, issue 121 had both the Chinese and the English texts of an article by Lü Ch'eng, "The Origin and History of the Abhidharma Texts" and English summaries of two articles in Chinese "An Account of the Different Sects of Buddhism" and "The Establishment and Brief Content of the Four Dhyānas and Eight Samādhis of Śrāvakayāna Buddhism." Thereafter domestic Buddhist news was entirely absent from some issues: in others it consisted of obituaries or the most summary reports of the activities of the national or local Buddhist associations.
40. Of the first issue 1,700 of the 2,000 copies printed had been sold by the end of the year: see *HTFH,* 12/50, p. 35. The issue for June 1953 was printed in 6,000 copies on better paper (to report the inauguration of the

Chinese Buddhist Association). The figure dropped to 4,000 for the rest of the year. Press-runs in 1956 totaled 43,500 copies: 3,500 per month before May; 5,000 for the May issue to honor the Buddha Jayanti year; and 4,000 thereafter: see *HTFH,* 5/57, p. 6.

41. See *HTFH,* 4/54, p. 21.

42. It was the main source for the newspaper-reading team at a nunnery in Harbin: see *HTFH,* 7/53, p. 27.

43. See *HTFH,* 2/53, pp. 28, 29.

44. Compare, for example, the report on Yün-men Shan printed in the Hong Kong *Ta-kung pao* of May 3, 1950, with the reports that appeared in *Chüeh yu-ch'ing* for 12.10-12:32 (December 1951) and 13.2:20 (October 1952).

45. I have seen a copy of the issue of March 1953, but the magazine was not mentioned in a list of religious periodicals published in *HTFH,* 4/54, p. 21. Its financial difficulties are alluded to in *Chüeh yu-ch'ing* 13.2:16 (October 1953).

46. On the suppression of the Youth Association, see Chapter VII. On *Chüeh-hsün's* involvement, see *HTFH,* 10/55, p. 21.

47. Yu Yu-wei, the publisher of *Hung-hua* helped receive a Japanese delegation in October 1957. He was then deputy secretary-general of the Shanghai Buddhist Association: see "Hōchū Nihon Bukkyō shinzen shi-dan hokokusho," *Nitchu Bukkyo* 1.3:34. On February 1, 1956, it had been taken over by the Shanghai Buddhist Association (just as *Modern Buddhism* had been taken over by the national association two years earlier): see *HTFH,* 4/56, p. 32. In March 1963 a Chinese resident went to the Shanghai Buddhist Bookshop and asked if he could subscribe to *Hung-hua.* He was told that it was no longer published and that its place had been taken by *Modern Buddhism.* There is no way of knowing how many other Buddhist journals may have been published in the first years after Liberation. In 1951, for example, a monthly called "Buddhist World" (*Fo-chiao jen-chien*) was being published in Shanghai: see *HTFH,* 4/51, p. 36. A *Pure Land Monthly* resumed publication in southern Szechwan on January 1, 1951, with the permission of the local authorities, who had temporarily suspended it: see *Chüeh yu-ch'ing* 12.1:24 (January 1951).

48. On the periodicals published before Liberation, see Welch, *Revival,* pp. 279-284.

49. The issues of *Hung-hua* for March and April 1957 were printed in 4,600 copies; three issues of *Chüeh-hsün* in 1951-52 were printed in 6,200 copies.

50. The first attempt seems to have been made in May or June 1949 by Chü-tsan. See *HTFH,* 9/50, p. 25, and Appendix A. A second attempt was made at the dinner party on June 18, 1950, when it was decided to start *Modern Buddhism.* Although this is not mentioned in Chü-tsan's account (*HTFH,* 10/50, pp. 22-23), *Chüeh yu-ch'ing,* 14.1:6 (January 1953) clearly

states that the participants resolved to organize a national Buddhist association but were unable to do so "because the time was not ripe."

51. See Welch, *Revival,* pp. 40-49.

52. See *HTFH,* 3/51, p. 28; 9/51, p. 21. At the end of 1950 *Modern Buddhism* published an elaborate proposal for the reform of Buddhism by Chang Yu-ju (otherwise unidentified). One of his ideas was that municipal and county associations should be established first and assume firm control over local monasteries; then when the hierarchy was extended to the provincial and national level, it would not be a head without a body, like the old CBA. See *HTFH,* 12/50, pp. 27-28.

53. *HTFH,* 9/51, p. 21. At the end of 1951 it was stated that not even the name of the future national organization could yet be determined: see *HTFH,* 12/51, p. 21.

54. Chao P'u-ch'u was born in Huai-ning, Anhwei, in 1908; attended Soochow University; and in the 1930's was general manager of the Hua-t'ung Transportation Company in Shanghai. At the same time he was assistant head of the Pure Karma Society, one of the most important lay Buddhist groups. After the Japanese attack he worked in Chinese refugee camps and with the International Red Cross, still living in Shanghai. He continued to do relief work under the Communists and thereby was drawn into public administration. In 1950 he became deputy director of the East China M.A.C. Civil Affairs Department. After being in the CPPCC National Committee, he was elected an NPC deputy from Anhwei in 1954.

55. *Chüeh yu-ch'ing,* 14.1:6 (January 1953).

56. *HTFH,* 10/52, pp. 2ff, 5/56, p. 8.

57. I am only conjecturing that Buddhists made these points to the Propaganda Department. Chü-tsan had made similar points in 1950 (see Appendix A and cf. *HTFH,* 1/55, p. 28).

58. This meeting of the sponsors of the Chinese Buddhist Association was reported by the NCNA in English: see *SCMP,* 453:25. The roles of Li, Chao, and Ho were explained in *HTFH,* 6/53, pp. 4-5. The most detailed account of the meeting, however, seems to be in *Chüeh yu-ch'ing* 14.1:5-6 (January 1953), which reprinted the sponsors' appeal for support. Cf. *HTFH,* 11/52, pp. 26-27. The sponsors were Hsü-yün, Shirob Jaltso, Gelatsang (Ke-la-ts'ang), Yüan-ying, Leosha Thubtentarpa (Liu-hsia T'u-teng t'a-pa), Tan-pa Jih-ts'ang, Lo-sang Pa-sang, To-chieh Chan-tung, Neng-hai, Fa-tsun, Chü-tsan, Ch'en Ming-shu, Lü Ch'eng, Chao P'u-ch'u, Tung Lu-an, Yeh Kung-cho, Lin Tsai-p'ing, Hsiang Ta, Chou Shu-chia, and Kuo P'eng. The names common to this list and the list of eighteen eminent monks proposed by Chao in 1951 were Hsü-yün, Yüan-ying, Neng-hai, Fa-tsun, and Chü-tsan.

The personnel of the preparatory office of the CBA consisted of Chao P'u-ch'u (its head), Leosha Thubtentarpa (who was stationed in Peking as head of the Tibetan mission there), Tan-pa Jih-ts'ang, Chü-tsan, Chou Shu-chia, Kuo P'eng, and Li I-p'ing.

With regard to Tibetan and Mongolian names such as those appearing above, two methods of romanization are used in this book. If NCNA has romanized a name, its spelling is followed even if it is incorrect according to the method of transcribing Tibetan and Mongolian that is accepted in Western academic circles. If NCNA has not romanized a name, it is spelled according to the Wade-Giles transcription of its Chinese equivalent. For example, what many Western Tibetologists would romanize as Sherab Gyaltsho is spelled Shirob Jaltso by NCNA and in this book. In Wade-Giles it would be Hsi-jao Chia-ts'o.

59. The figure most often given for the number of Buddhists in China was 100 million: see Chapter IX, note 1. There were 4.5 million Tibetans and Mongolians: see *Handbook on People's China* (Peking, 1957), p. 15. Assuming that all Tibetans and Mongolians were Buddhists, then 5 percent of the nation's Buddhists held more than 30 percent of the seats in the CBA council.

60. The first president was Yüan-ying, who had founded the old CBA in Shanghai in 1929 and served as its president until the Japanese invasion. He died September 20, 1953, at the T'ien-t'ung Ssu, the famous Ch'an monastery of which he had once been abbot. His replacement as president, Shirob Jaltso, had lived in China for sixteen years and had been given high government posts by the Kuomintang: see Welch, *Revival,* pp. 177, 336. Under the Communists he became a member of the CPPCC National Committee, vice-president of the Nationalities Affairs Committee (almost the same position he held under the Kuomintang), and a vice-governor of Tsinghai.

61. See *HTFH,* 6/53, p. 7. Delegates were of the Tibetan, Mongol, Thai, Manchu, Miao, Sani, and Uighur nationalities.

The names of Han-nationality council-members of the CBA are given in Appendix B. Almost all the 93 members of the first council were among the 141 persons listed as delegates to the inaugural conference, of whom 21 could not attend because of illness or business. This was the pattern at later conferences: a few delegates would not be elected to the council, so that the composition of the council was a little more select than that of the conference.

62. What he said was that the CBA "should make no distinction between clergy and laity, either in name, rights, or responsibilities, and therefore there is no provision in the draft constitution for members": see *HTFH,* 6/53, p. 5.

63. *HTFH,*6/53, pp. 5, 27.

64. *HTFH,* 6/53, p. 16.

65. *Ibid.* An almost identical statement of purposes had been included in an appeal for support from the country's Buddhists that was put out by the sponsors of the CBA on November 5, 1952.

66. The words quoted come from a good definition of this aspect of the CBA's role made by Chao P'u-ch'u in 1957: "As a bridge between Buddhist followers and the government, the association makes regular reports and suggestions to the government, and conveys the policy, enactments, and plans of

the government to Buddhists, so that the interests and requirements of religion may be protected and satisfied, and that incidents violating religious policy may not happen, or, should they occur, may be rectified in time." See *HTFH,* 5/57, p. 7. This passage was incorporated in Chao P'u-ch'u, *Buddhism in China* (Peking, 1957), p. 41.

67. *HTFH,* 5/57, p. 7.

68. *HTFH,* 6/53, p. 8. The meaning of the term "struggle" as used in this passage will be made clear in the section of Chapter II entitled "Struggle against Senior Monks."

69. Details on the Buddist fighter plane will be given in Chapter VIII at note 43. With regard to preaching in public places, the policy was that just as atheists should not conduct anti-religious propaganda inside churches and temples, so believers should not conduct religious propaganda outside churches and temples. This was first hinted at in a summary of the CBA inaugural conference: "As to the problem of the scope of Buddhists' activities, in order to avoid anything affecting public order or undermining the policy of freedom of religious belief, Buddhist activities (religious rites and so on) should generally be carried out in monasteries, Buddhist groups, or the homes of devotees": *HTFH,* 6/53, p. 8. This was spelled out more clearly by Chang Chih-i in 1958: "Atheists should refrain from conducting anti-religious propaganda in churches or temples, while theists should also refrain from conducting religious propaganda outside churches and temples." See *Che-hsüeh yen-chiu* 1/58, p. 46, tr. in *CB,* 510:18. A clearer translation appears in *CNA,* 221:1. Compare also, *HTFH,* 12/58, p. 33, where Buddhists and Taoists in Heilungkiang "guaranteed to limit their religious activities to Buddhist and Taoist monasteries and temples, religious groups, and the homes of lay devotees."

70. Details on the foreign activities of the CBA will be given in Chapter VI. Regarding the Fang-shan rubbings, see NCNA, February 22, 1956, in *SCMP,* 1235:15, and Chao, *Buddhism in China* (1957), p. 43. There was also international benefit to be derived from the postage stamp of I-hsing, a monk-astronomer. To promote itself domestically the CBA drew the attention of Chinese musicologists to the fact that elements of T'ang dynasty music were preserved in Buddhist liturgy. See Chao, *Buddhism in China* (1957), pp. 30-31.

71. *Kuang-hui-ti pa-nien* (Hong Kong, 1958), p. 176. This figure did not include the staff of the Chinese Buddhist Seminary.

72. For example, when the Canton Buddhist Association was set up, the CBA in Peking was neither consulted nor officially informed of the fact, according to a former cadre of the Canton Religious Affairs Division. One of the few known instances in which the CBA became involved in matters at the local level occurred when it approved the promotion to higher ranks of Thai Buddhist monks in the Sibsong-Baana Autonomous District, where the CBA had a branch: see *HTFH,* 10/59, p. 18.

73. In 1957 Chao P'u-ch'u told the second national conference that the CBA had given little concrete help in the conduct of local study classes: see *HTFH,* 5/57, p. 4. In 1962 he told the third national conference that it had provided them with study materials: see *HTFH,* 2/62, p. 23 (May 15, 1962).

74. The structure of the CBA was the same before and after the constitution was revised in 1957. The president, vice-presidents, secretary-general, deputy secretaries-general, and standing committee members were all elected by and from the council. The council was elected at a national conference, to be held every three years, and was supposed to meet in plenary session every year. Nowhere in the 1953 constitution was it specified what powers the different officers had. A revised constitution accords to the national conference "the right to discuss and decide the course and tasks of the association": see *HTFH,* 5/57, p. 26.

75. This was according to Article 9 of the 1953 constitution. In the revised constitution—perhaps as a gesture to credibility—there was added the sentence: "When necessary, it may apply for help to the government." (*HTFH,* 5/57, p. 26). The scale of government help can be seen from the fact that in 1960 the CBA donated half a million rupees to a friendly Nepalese Buddhist for an addition to his school near Kathmandu (see Chapter VI at note 63).

76. Chao P'u-ch'u stated this to a Japanese visitor in 1957. Minor political parties in China also operated on a subsidy. At the beginning *Modern Buddhism* may have been privately financed. Li Ming-yang apparently made the first contribution to it, equivalent to US $40: see *HTFH,* 12/57, p. 28. There were occasional allusions to budget shortages in its first two years, as in *HTFH,* 8/51, pp. 24, 32, but as soon as the CBA was founded, the quality of paper improved. Therefore, although *Modern Buddhism* did not become the official organ of the CBA for another year, it seems likely that it began to benefit at once from whatever subsidy the association received.

77. Before Kuo P'eng joined the CBA staff, he had been a cadre of the Civil Affairs Bureau in Peking: see *HTFH,* 11/50, p. 21. In 1959 he was described (perhaps inadvertently) as "of the Bureau of Religious Affairs of the State Council": see NCNA English, May 21, 1959, in *SCMP,* 2021:46. In 1961 he was still listed as a deputy secretary-general of the CBA, but the next year he became secretary-general of the China-Ceylon Friendship Association. I have not seen his name in connection with the CBA thereafter. While serving as its deputy secretary-general, he was also vice-principal of the Chinese Buddhist Seminary, so that all its activities too were known to him. Chao P'u-ch'u may also have been a Party member (see below note 139), but Kuo P'eng, who had no known connection with Buddhism before Liberation, seems a purer *apparatchik.*

78. *HTFH,* 9/55, p. 22. The "immense joy" with which Buddhists had originally greeted the establishment of the CBA can be seen in the upsurge of religious activities that followed it. For example, a 49-day plenary mass was

held in Shanghai: see *Chüeh yu-ch'ing,* 14.1:7-9 (January 1953). Four hundred Buddhists recited Amitabha's name for two days in Fukien: see *HTFH,* 8/53, p. 25.

79. These changes were provided for in resolutions passed at the meeting: the details will be given in Chapters IV and VII.

80. See *HTFH,* 9/55, pp. 9, 14, *et passim.* Also in cities other than Shanghai there were "counterrevolutionaries who had wormed their way into Buddhist ranks and had been arrested by the local authorities" (*ibid,* p. 15). Details will be given in Chapter VII.

81. *HTFH,* 5/57, p. 7.

82. The occasional gestures in this direction by the old Chinese Buddhist Association had little force because they were not made under the pressure of an official proscription of heterodox sects. For example, in January 1937 the old CBA issued a circular to all its branches urging the sangha to change the names of temples when they were not properly Buddhist and to remove images that did not belong in the Buddhist pantheon. Temples where this was not done or that were occupied by non-Buddhist clergy would not get any help from the association. The purpose was to "prevent and correct improper beliefs and practices." See *The Chinese Year Book, 1937* (Shanghai, 1937), p. 74.

83. The sangha officials had had nothing to do with foreigners. The old Chinese Buddhist Association, so far as I know, did not get involved in exchanges of people with foreign countries. The Chinese Buddhists who went abroad during the Republican period were sponsored by devotees or devotees' societies. For example, Huang Mao-lin (Wong Mou-lam) was sent to Ceylon by the Pure Karma Society in Shanghai. Yüan-ying, when president of the old CBA, made a tour of Southeast Asia in 1939 to raise money for China Relief.

84. Mibu Shojun, "Jinmin Chūgoku no Bukkyō-o miru," *Shinri,* 27.9:8 (September 1961).

85. Apparently these all dissolved when the Communists won control of the Mainland and the headquarters of the old CBA moved to Taiwan. It is possible, of course, that some were quietly reorganized into the independent local associations that continued operating. At the end of 1952 there were still a Swatow chapter and a Kweichow branch of the Chinese Buddhist Association: see *HTFH,* 1/53, p. 22. During the early Republican period, when there was often no national association, what would have been branches were autonomous entities, but after a stable national association emerged in 1929, it was glad to accept them as its subordinate organs and they were glad to be subordinated to it. Here and below I used the word "association" not only for the national group (as in the preceding volume), but also for the local groups that were supposed to represent the Buddhist monks of their areas; and I use the word "society" for local lay groups that were mainly interested in religious study, devotions, and good works. These will be discussed in Chapter IX.

86. In 1951 there was a Buddhist "federation" (*lien-ho hui*) in Wuhan, a Buddhist "fellowship" (*lien-i hui*) in Kunming, a Buddhist work committee in Szechwan, a Buddhist "reform committee" (*ko-hsin wei-yüan-hui*) in Nanking, and in 1952 a "people's Buddhist association" (*jen-min fo-chiao hui*) was reported in Hai-k'ang, Kwangtung. See *HTFH,* 9/51, p. 24, and 9/52, p. 30. Many other examples can be found in *HTFH,* 1/53, p. 22. *Fo-chiao hsieh-hui* was nearly the universal name by 1957.

87. In 1950 the Hangchow Buddhist Association's preparatory committee had 1,800 members; in 1953 the counterpart in Changchow, Fukien, had 1,500 and in Amoy 215.

88. This was in Kweiyang: see *HTFH,* 6/62, p. 41. The sangha in Kweichow had been almost the smallest in the country. On the other hand in one county of Fukien the committee that organized the local Buddhist association consisted entirely of monks: see *HTFH,* 8/53, p. 25.

89. Aside from general statements to the effect that "local Buddhist associations should be guided by the local authorities": (see Chapter I at note 103), there is the testimony of a former cadre of the Canton Religious Affairs Division that it selected all the officers and furnished the entire budget of the Canton Buddhist Association. According to *HTFH,* 2/54, pp. 24-25, the Buddhist association of An-k'ang, Shensi, was receiving a subsidy from the United Front Department. Elsewhere, however, there is evidence that some associations were able to finance themselves by keeping a percentage of the rents they collected on monastery real estate or taxes they collected from the rites for the dead. See Chapter II, note 73 and Chapter IV, note 14.

90. A good example of this downward transmission is given in *HTFH,* 6/62, p. 39 (December 1962), tr. in JPRS 18158:13-15.

91. This was true for Liaoning and Shenyang in 1959; and for Hupeh and Wuhan in 1962. In 1962 the president of the Amoy Municipal Buddhist Association (not a CBA branch) was elected vice-president of the Fukien branch of the CBA.

92. This was stated to be part of the first task of the Buddhist association of the Sung-chiang special district: see *HTFH,* 3/54, p. 28.

93. Religious activities were seldom carried on by the local associations, perhaps because they would have exposed the officers to the charge of encouraging superstition. Almost the only cases I have seen came in early 1953 after the Peace Conference of Asia and the Pacific Region, when some local associations held rites to pray for world peace. Dharma meetings (*fa-hui*) to pray for world peace were organized by associations in Changchow, Changshu, and Min-ch'in (Kansu) in January 1953. Similar services were held in many more places, although not specifically under the sponsorship of the Buddhist association, as will be detailed in Chapter VII. In November 1957 the Amoy Municipal Buddhist Association permitted seventy converts to take the Three Refuges and Five Vows at the temple that served as its own headquarters: ten thousand people attended. See *HTFH,* 1/58, p. 27.

94. The Ningpo association organized textile factories (*HTFH,* 12/50, p. 32; 4/53, p. 11). The Tientsin association organized a productive labor coöperative (*HTFH,* 9/55, p. 33). In Kunming the association received the equivalent of nearly US$1,000 to get monks and nuns into productive labor (*HTFH,* 6/53, p. 51). In Chungking the association founded a restaurant in the Lo-han Ssu to give employment to twenty monks (*HTFH,* 6/53, p. 50).

95. In 1951 all Wuhan monasteries were required to fill out a form reporting their holdings of suburban land and send it to the Buddhist association for forwarding to the Suburban Land Reform Committee: see *HTFH,* 3/52, p. 7.

96. During April 18-27, 1950, the Ningpo Buddhist Association preparatory committee investigated the real estate, religious property, and number of residents of all the monasteries and nunneries in the municipality: see *HTFH,* 12/50, p. 33. In 1953 the Sung-chiang Buddhist Association was to make a survey of monastery property in order to protect national cultural relics (*HTFH,* 3/53, p. 28). Such surveys served the Buddhists' own ends, but they also fulfilled government directives.

97. See Chapter II, note 73.

98. In 1952 the preparatory committee of the Buddhist association of An-k'ang, Shensi, received the equivalent of US$325 from the county government and distributed it to monks and nuns who were in difficulties: see *HTFH,* 7/53, p. 27. Presumably no religious affairs section had yet been set up within the government, since this was usually the office that made such distributions. Cf. Chapter X, note 29.

99. In 1951 the Ningpo Buddhist Association sent one of its members to help the Yü-wang Ssu reorganize itself into a "new *ts'ung-lin*" as recommended by Chü-tsan in Peking: see *HTFH,* 4/53, p. 11.

100. More information on this will be given in Chapter III. In a somewhat exceptional instance, study as conducted by the Omei Buddhist Association was reported to have been mainly of Buddhist doctrine, history, the Vinaya rules, and the history and geography of that famous Buddhist center. "In addition political study was also carried on in a planned way." See *HTFH,* 5/57, p. 16.

101. A Japanese Buddhist delegation that toured China in the autumn of 1957 was not even aware of the distinction between the two kinds of local group: see "Hōchū Nihon," p. 35.

102. For example the Fukien branch's chairman was deputy abbot of Ku Shan, the largest monastery in the province; the first two vice-presidents were abbots of the K'ai-yüan Ssu in Chüanchow and Nan-ch'an Ssu in Changting. The other three vice-presidents were also monks and the name of only one layman appears in the whole standing committee. See *Chung-kuo hsin-wen,* October 16, 1962 (Foochow).

103. *HTFH,* 6/53, p. 5.

104. *HTFH,* 7/53, p. 27. Already in 1951 a Buddhist group in Amoy had registered as the "Amoy Municipal Branch of the Chinese Buddhist Associa-

tion (Chung-kuo Fo-chiao Hsüeh-hui)"–of which I have found no other trace: see *HTFH,* 3/51, p. 35.

105. It was stated that the unauthorized local delegations had caused "considerable difficulties" to the CBA preparatory committee and that "from now on when local Buddhist organizations have to consult the [CBA] preparatory committee on their problems, they must get in touch by letter first. Without the written consent of the preparatory committee, they must never recklessly send delegations to Peking." See *HTFH,* 4/53, p. 31. Two years earlier local groups had been told that after they were set up, they were "required to establish relations with the capital": see *HTFH,* 12/51, p. 21.

106. *HTFH,* 5/57, p. 21. Article 11 of the revised constitution read: "This association may, in accordance with the actual situation, establish branch associations (*fen-hui*) in the various provinces, municipalities, and autonomous areas": see *HTFH,* 5/57, p. 26. At the second national conference, which adopted the revised constitution, one monk had proposed that chapters (*chih-hui*) also be authorized for counties and small cities, since a three-level system would unify the country's Buddhists even better and improve their esprit de corps: see *HTFH,* 5/57, p. 17. This suggestion was rejected on the grounds that the necessary funds and personnel were not available (*ibid.,* p. 21). County level associations seem never to have been set up.

107. *HTFH,* 12/57, p. 29. At meetings called to criticize Ch'en Ming-shu, Chü-tsan said he had often spoken of trying to turn Buddhism into a political asset: *ibid.,* p. 28. Ch'en's main problem was not his plan for Buddhism but his criticism of Mao and of the Party's monopoly on education during the Hundred Flowers.

108. The new local associations set up in or after 1957 were for Hupeh, Kiangsu, Szechwan, Soochow, Canton, Tsamkong, Swatow, Sian, Chiu-hua Shan, and P'u-t'o Shan. Already before 1957 local associations had been set up in at least 34 cities and two provinces. In or after 1957 branches were set up for Fukien, Liaoning, and Yünnan, and local associations were converted into or replaced by branches in Kiangsu, Changsha, Yangchow, and Tientsin. The Tibet branch was set up in October 1956, before the constitution was revised.

109. In 1951, for example, a reader in Wusih wrote in asking how to set up a local Buddhist group. Chü-tsan answered that it was best to do what had been done in Peking, that is, set up a Resist America Aid Korea committee. The one in Peking, he said, had "a secretariat and a propaganda department which issue orders to the representatives of the various districts on how to carry on their work. Each district representative is chosen by agreement among responsible persons of the monasteries and temples in their district. Because of inequalities in the number of people, every such person is responsible for getting into liaison with several monasteries and temples to form a group. If something happens to come up, the committee informs the representatives and the representatives pass on the information to the monasteries and temples in their liaison group. It is extremely quick and convenient.

Every Saturday afternoon the district representatives hold a meeting, discuss their work, and carry on study. Besides this there are six study teams that are led in study by comrades from the Civil Affairs Bureau. The expenses of the committee are borne by the individual monasteries and temples and collected from them by the district representative. This is the way Buddhist circles are currently organized in Peking. Most people consider that it is better than the Buddhist association that used to exist before. Buddhist circles in different places can copy our method without difficulty." Later, Chü-tsan said, when the Resist America Aid Korea movement was concluded, the committee could be reorganized into a regular Buddhist association. In the meantime it would be able to work to overcome the otherworldliness of Buddhist circles through patriotic activities, to popularize productive labor, to bring out leaders, and to win the respect of the people. See *HTFH,* 9/51, pp. 23-24. Oddly enough, what seems to be the same Peking group was referred to the month before as the "Peking Committee of Buddhist Circles to Defend World Peace and Oppose American Aggression": see *HTFH,* 8/51, p. 23.

110. In Ningpo the preparatory committee was set up before September 1950 and the association was not inaugurated until September 28, 1955. In Hunan the dates were February 3, 1950, and August 5, 1955. There was a similar five-year interval in Soochow and a three-year interval in Chungking.

111. Such a step backward was taken in Kiangsu when the preparatory committee for the Kiangsu Provincial Buddhist Association was established on December 3, 1956: see *HTFH,* 5/57, p. 24. A Kiangsu Buddhist association had already existed in 1953: see *HTFH,* 6/53, pp. 30-31. In Changsha the initial group was the Buddhist Monastery Property Reorganization Work Team; after two years this was succeeded by the Changsha Buddhist Study Committee, which soon became the preparatory committee for the Changsha Municipal Work Committee, "with unified responsibility for all Buddhist work in the municipality." See *HTFH,* 6/53, p. 46. Not until several years later was the Changsha Municipal Buddhist Association formally inaugurated. A similarly complex series of reorganizations and changes of name took place in Amoy and in Canton. In one area of Chekiang where conditions were not ripe for the formation of a Buddhist association, a branch of the Sino-Soviet Friendship Association was formed instead. Its 376 members were all monks and nuns, and lay people were excluded "in order to distinguish friend from foe and make the organization strong and pure." See *HTFH,* 7/53, p. 27.

112. This was the sequence in Hupeh, Fukien, Kansu, Kiangsu, Liaoning, Shansi, and Szechwan.

113. *HTFH,* 8/51, p. 24, states the establishment of an association should be coordinated with the Civil Affairs Bureau, but from other cases it is clear that the actual decision was made by the United Front Department and later by the Religious Affairs Division.

114. In August 1951 a Shensi layman wrote to *Modern Buddhism* asking if government permission was required for some devotees to open a very small reading room and library or a study group—in view of the guarantees of

freedom of assembly, association, and religious belief in the Common Program. The answer he received was that no matter what kind of group was to be organized, registration had to be applied for with the local government. See *HTFH,* 8/51, p. 24.

115. In November 1951 *Modern Buddhism* published a letter from a nun in Lien-ch'eng, Fukien, saying that Buddhist groups in a number of villages had been dissolved by the local government and asking if anything could be done to help. The reply was that Buddhist groups not guilty of anti-governmental activities should apply for registration according to the law and that then the local government would be unable to dissolve them arbitrarily. See *HTFH,* 11/51, p. 23.

116. It appears that the Religious Affairs Team (Tsung-chiao Shih-wu Tsu) of the National Committee of the CPPCC was created in September 1949, when the CPPCC first met, but did not become active until the following spring. It then held four symposia on the future of religion in China, the last three on May 5, May 29, and June 10, 1950. Ch'en Ch'i-yüan presided as acting head of the team. See *HTFH,* 10/50, p. 21. Ch'en was a former Nationalist finance specialist who split with the Kuomintang in 1927 and lived for seventeen years in the United States. I have found nothing to indicate that he had a special interest in religion. His assignment to the team was apparently in his capacity as director of the Social Affairs Bureau within the Ministry of Internal Affairs. This ministry's local branches, the civil affairs departments of provinces and municipalities, were then involved in handling religious problems at the local level. It is worth noting that under the Nationalists there had never been a separate agency to deal with religious affairs, which had been the responsibility of the Ministry of the Interior and the Ministry of Social Affairs. A separate agency had last existed under the Ch'ing dynasty, i.e., the Board of Rites, under which came the hierarchy of sangha officials. In this, as in many other respects, the Communists restored Ch'ing institutions in the control of religion.

117. When the People's Republic of China was inaugurated on October 1, 1949, "the Central Government was still considering whether to set up an office to handle religious affairs": see *HTFH,* 10/50, p. 20.

118. For allusions to cadres' laughter and scorn, see *HTFH,* 10/51, p. 21; 11/51, pp. 23, 14; 12/51, p. 21. On cadres' refusal to listen, see *HTFH,* 4/51, p. 31. On the exclusion of Buddhists from women's organizations, see *HTFH,* 5/51, p. 26. On the exclusion of monks and nuns from a public works project, see *HTFH,* 3/52, pp. 8-9. This last citation is from a work report that *inter alia* expresses the hope that "the government will take the opportunity to get ordinary middle and lower level cadres better posted on religious policy." Cf. the discrimination referred to in *HTFH,* 5/57, p. 13.

119. Such inner workings of policy formation were not the kind of thing to be explained in the *People's Daily.* My source is a former cadre about whom more will be said below.

120. It should be noted that from 1951 to 1954 both the national and local organs of religious affairs were termed "divisions" (*ch'u*). According to the former cadre the seven sections of the national organ were the policy research office (*cheng-ts'e yen-chiu-shih*), the documents office (*tzu-liao shih*), the personnel office (*jen-shih shih*), the secretarial section (*mi-shu k'o*), the Catholic section, the Protestant section, and the Buddhist-Taoist-Islamic section. The last three were referred to by number. The Catholic was the "first section"; the Protestant the "second section." These were the two biggest, because foreign churches were considered to present the most important problems of control. Buddhism and Taoism did not have such loyal followers, such strong hierarchical organizations, or such close ties abroad.

The director of the Religious Affairs Division from the time of its creation was Ho Ch'eng-hsiang and the deputy director was Hsü Ning: see NCNA, January 14, 1951, translated in *SCMP,* 48:13. Ho Ch'eng-hsiang, who remained director until 1961, was an old Party member from Manchuria, who had served for the preceding year as head of the staff office of the Committee on Cultural and Educational Affairs and before that as deputy director of the first office of the United Front Work Department. There is nothing to indicate that he had any special knowledge of or interest in religious affairs. This may have been one reason why he was picked for the job. During the next decade, except for occasional activities in foreign relations, religious affairs were his main work. His photo appears in *HTFH,* 11/56, p. 5. His successor, Hsiao Hsien-fa, had already been working in the bureau at the time of his appointment and, like Ho, was active in the Chinese People's Association for Cultural Relations and Friendship with Foreign Countries (although he does not appear to have taken part in delegations to Communist bloc countries the way Ho did).

Hsü Ning, a former *Ta-kung pao* correspondent in Manchuria, served as deputy director at least until 1955. In 1957 he was expelled from the Party as a rightist and succeeded by Yang Ch'eng-sen. Yang was replaced in 1961 by Kao Shan, who had been in charge of the Catholic section.

121. The former cadre went to Peking for this first National Religious Work Conference (Ch'üan-kuo Tsung-chiao Kung-tso Hui-i) but was not allowed to attend the sessions, which were open only to division chiefs. His own chief told him that the decisions taken were: (1) to control efforts by religious groups to propagate their religion; (2) to emphasize the patriotic orientation of religious activities (so that "study classes" were soon renamed "patriotic study classes"); (3) to give more livelihood subsidies to elderly and disabled monks and nuns; and (4) to expose the members of reactionary Taoist sects who were using Buddhism as a cover. Presumably the conference also discussed the establishment of national associations of Christians, Buddhists, and Muslims, which was then underway. This informant recollected that already in early 1951 a conference on religious affairs had been called by the United Front Work Department (principally to decide how to handle the

property of foreign missions); that the 1953 conference had been called by the Propaganda Department; and that later annual conferences were called by the Religious Affairs Bureau itself.

122. *HTFH,* 8/51, p. 32.

123. An anomaly that seems hard to explain is the fact that in late August 1951, half a year after the Religious Affairs Division had been set up in Peking, all ordinary monasteries in the capital that had monks in residence were still under the control of the Civil Affairs Bureau: see *HTFH,* 10/51, p. 3. Similarly in 1953 long after religious affairs organs were exercising unified control in most of China, the sacred mountain of Wu-t'ai Shan was in charge of the Shansi Bureau of Culture and Education; monks there were guided in political study by the Nationalities Affairs Commission (presumably because so many were Mongol or Tibetan); relief of those incapable of labor came from the Provincial United Front Department; and the repair of monastery buildings was handled directly by the Central Government. See *HTFH,* 6/53, p. 52. By 1958 there was an Wu-t'ai office (*pan-shih ch'u*) of the Shansi Province Nationalities and Religious Affairs Bureau (*ch'u*)—the only case of such terminology that I have seen. See *HTFH,* 12/58, p. 27.

124. This informant wrote an account of his experiences as a cadre soon after he reached Hong Kong during the big exodus in the spring of 1962. A summary was printed in *China Notes* 2.1:3-8 (September 1963). My interviews with him took place in 1964 and in 1967-69. In successive interviews he remembered things differently and I have had to use my judgment in deciding when his memory served him best.

125. In 1950 he had worked on the registration of social groups, including Buddhist monasteries. In 1951 he had become chief of the subsection on social groups and handled a broader range of religious problems according to instructions that he received from the United Front Department. It was the head of this department who recommended him for the job of setting up the Religious Affairs Division in 1952.

126. The few cadres who had had experience in dealing with religion were to be found in the united front organs of local Party committees, in civil affairs bureaus, and in the police. There were exceptions, however. In September 1950 a Kunming monastery reported its re-organization directly to the Military Administrative Commission: see *Chüeh yu-ch'ing* 12.1:24 (January 1951). In 1951 the monks and monasteries of Omei Shan were considered to belong to a separate village and were supervised by something called the "specially assigned village office of the third district of Omei hsien" (*O-mei-hsien ti-san t'e-pien-ts'un kung-so*): see *HTFH,* 8/51, p. 23.

127. In 1951 the initial staff of four cadres plus one office boy was broken down into three sections, publicly referred to only by their numbers (cf. above note 120). The first section handled the Catholics, the second the Protestants, and the third handled Buddhists, Taoists, and Muslims. The third also included the secretariat. In 1957 the latter became the fourth section (or,

according to statements made by my informant at other times, the third remained the secretariat and it was the fourth that handled Buddhists, Taoists, and Muslims). As in Peking, the Catholic and Protestant sections were the largest. Although the staff had trebled by 1957, the Religious Affairs Division was still the smallest of the municipal or provincial organs. Technically speaking it had no chief but only a first and later a second deputy chief. The purpose of this curious arrangement was to emphasize that the work of the division was regarded as extremely delicate and that higher authorities should be consulted on all important matters. Sometime after 1957 the position of chief was nominally filled by the director of the first division of the Public Security Bureau (which handled political security).

128. I have found no clear evidence in the press that religious affairs organs came under the Party rather than the government, as my informant kept emphasizing. It is true, however, that where references to control over religious activities have specified an organ of control (other than religious affairs organs), it has most often been a united front department of the Party. See, for example, *HTFH,* 9/51, p. 23 (Wusih); 3/53, pp. 27-28 (Changchow); 6/53, p. 4 (CBA), p. 29 (Shansi); 7/53, p. 26 (Lin-hsien, Hunan); 11/53, pp. 31-32 (Nan-yüeh, Liu-chou, and Kwangsi); 2/54, pp. 24-25 (An-k'ang, Shensi); 10/57, p. 23 (Shansi); *NCNA,* March 11, 1958 (*SCMP* 1733:1); *KMJP,* August 8, 1958 (*SCMP* 1837:39); *HTFH,* 7/59, p. 34; 6/61, pp. 39-41 (December 1962–Szechwan, Liaoning, Hupeh, Shansi, Canton, Amoy). In 1953 the head of the united front department in a special district of Fukien was concurrently head of the local religious affairs division: see *HTFH,* 8/53, p. 25. Usually public statements about control were very general, e.g., Buddhists in Amoy were "under the unified leadership of the United Front Department, the Religious Affairs Division, and the Buddhist Association" (*HTFH,* 6/53, p. 42). Cf. Shirob's statement that in 1959 Buddhists everywhere were engaging in political study "under the leadership of local Party and government organs and of the Chinese Buddhist Association" (*HTFH,* 10/59, p. 11). A Harbin nunnery was said to have solved all important problems by "asking the Party and doing what the Party says" (*HTFH,* 6/60, p. 34).

129. The Nationalities Commission and the Nationalities Work Section of the Civil Affairs Bureau dealt with all problems that were considered to arise from the nationality of Muslims rather than from their religion. (The Chinese Communists have followed the curious theory that the Muslims who reside in the home provinces of China all belong to a single non-Han race.) Thus the Friday services in Canton's three mosques came under the purview of the Religious Affairs Division, but the nationalities organs handled the supply of beef and lamb (rather than pork), mixed marriages, and the difficulties caused by non-Muslims moving into Muslim districts.

130. In general I felt that my informant may have exaggerated the independence and authority of the Canton division, in which he took an obvious

pride. I do not doubt, however, that by 1954, wherever decisions about handling religious problems may have originated, it was the religious affairs organs that carried them out.

131. My informant only mentioned sections at the special-district, not the county level in Kwangtung: Shao-kuan, Kao-yao, and Swatow. Yet county branches must have existed if, as Ho Ch'eng-hsiang told a Japanese visitor in 1957, the Religious Affairs Bureau had 200-300 branches in all: see *Chūgai nippō,* November 29, 1957.

132. Approval to form a religious organization came from the Civil Affairs Bureau, and a permit to publish was issued by the Press and Publications Division of the municipal government; but in both cases it was the Religious Affairs Division that decided what should be done. Registration was expected of even the smallest group: see above note 114.

133. *HTFH,* 1/55, p. 29, states that the rules for daily operation of monasteries at Omei Shan were drawn up by a study committee "under the leadership of the local government authorities concerned." On the cadres who came to live at Yün-chü Shan, see Chapter IV at note 80.

134. I have seen no confirmation of this in published materials. In 1958 Fukien Buddhists guaranteed that they would "not utilize lectures on the sutras or religious activities to spread any reactionary words or deeds that are disadvantageous to the Party and the nation": see *HTFH,* 9/58, p. 28. Note that the Party came before the nation.

135. More details are provided in published accounts. The admission of *X* to Nan-fang University, after passing the entrance examination, was reported in the Hong Kong *Wen-hui pao* on September 26, 1950, where his name was given as Hsüan-ch'ung. Articles in the Hong Kong *Hsing-tao jih-pao* for September 6 and November 6, 1950, explained that his name had originally been K'uan-ch'iang and that he had been a disciple of Hsü-yün, the most influential monk in Kwangtung. Hsü-yün was said to have selected Hsüan-ch'ung to be abbot of the Liu-jung Ssu after Liberation because he was young (26), well educated (a graduate of Hua-nan University), and would know how to get on with the Communist authorities. This was what he did. He kept the monastery in good order. To feed its thirty monks he utilized the admission fees from the famous pagoda on the monastery grounds, which amounted to the equivalent to US$6-8 a day. Then, however, some of the older monks from outside Kwangtung, apparently resentful of his youth and ability, took him to court on the charge of pocketing the admission fees himself. He quashed this by appealing to the provincial governor, Yeh Chien-ying, who believed his version of what had happened and ordered military police to be stationed at the monastery to prevent the older monks from causing any further trouble. Hsüan-ch'ung then decided to enroll in Nan-fang University. The newspaper accounts explained this as a delayed reaction to his quarrel with the older monks—which is odd, since he had bested them. My informant had another explanation. Early in 1950, he said, Hsüan-ch'ung had proposed to the Civil

Affairs Bureau that a Canton Buddhist association should be organized, led by progressive Buddhists, with himself as president. The authorities approved of the idea but told him that, since he had only been to middle school (*sic*), he would have to be educated and indoctrinated. It was they who sponsored his admission to the university.

At the time he was expelled from the university, abbot Z–Chien-hsing by name–held the post of acting abbot. Chien-hsing attacked Hsüan-ch'ung as an apostate (*p'an-t'u*) who had become a cadre and was no longer a monk. The two of them even came to blows. The Civil Affairs Bureau did not dare to interfere because the government's policy on religion was not yet clear (this was probably mid-1951). It simply urged Hsüan-ch'ung to settle the dispute through discussion. Soon afterward Chien-hsing telephoned to say that Hsüan-ch'ung had hanged himself. My informant (who had been handling the case) immediately accompanied the head of the United Front Department and a representative of the police to the Liu-jung Ssu. They found that he had dressed himself in a new *kashaya* robe–the formal dress of Buddhist monks–and had tucked into it his ordination certificate. There he hung, with protruding eyes and a swollen tongue. They could not decide whether it was suicide or murder. It seemed to them likeliest that Chien-hsing had murdered him, but in absence of proof they could take no action.

I wonder if they did not overlook an alternative explanation of Hsüan-ch'ung's behavior–one that would have provided a deeper reason for suicide. Perhaps Hsü-yün had sent Hsüan-ch'ung to Canton specifically in order to work his way into the Communist apparatus and thereby provide greater protection to Buddhism than he could from the outside. That would account for his proposal for a Buddhist association and his enrollment in the cadres' school. He soon found that he was incapable of playing the anti-Buddhist role that was necesssary for success. Yet when he returned to the monastery, it was not safe to tell his brethren what he had been trying to do (for one thing it might make trouble for Hsü-yün). So when they too rejected him, he saw that he could go neither forward nor back and hanged himself, with his robe and ordination certificate as signs of where his true commitment had lain all along.

136. The name of *Y* was Hsin-ch'eng. He too was said to have been a disciple of Hsü-yün, but it does not seem likely that he enrolled in the cadres' school with the same motive as Hsüan-ch'ung. His lack of success there does suggest, however, how hard it was for a monk to acquire the mentality of a cadre.

137. What is more interesting than the fact that Chien-hsing was sent to labor reform is how long he had continued to hold office before then. After all, he had been suspected of the murder of Hsüan-ch'ung; and of an anti-Communist attitude that made him refuse readmission to Hsin-ch'eng. Yet it was not until October 1957 that we know him to have been replaced as abbot.

138. Hsi Chung-hsin, who made the statement, was vice-director of the Party's Propaganda Department, which according to the former cadre had called the conference; but he was concurrently vice-director of the government's Committee on Cultural and Educational Affairs, to which the Religious Affairs Division was nominally subordinate. For an example of the kinds of religious disorder feared by the Party, see *CNA,* 221:3.

139. I am assuming that Kuo P'eng was also a Party member (see above note 77). Although Chao's Party membership was never publicly acknowledged, arguing for it is the fact that from May 1951 to December 1952 he was deputy director of personnel of the Civil Affairs Department of the East China MAC. Personnel work was seldom left in non-Party hands. My informant believed that unless Chao had been a Party member, he would not have summoned him to his hotel room, but would have gone to see him at the Religious Affairs Division. My informant was also impressed by his nylon summer suit, with the trousers of a slightly different color from the jacket, and by his pointed shoes–things that were unobtainable and even dangerous to wear in Communist China. He had already heard that Chao was a secret Party member, which he found more impressive than regular membership.

140. *HTFH,* 5/57, pp. 13-14. Cf. Pen-huan's criticism of cadres' "technical errors" in carrying out government policy in *Nan-fang jih-pao,* May 13, 1957. Whether or not Buddhists really believed that the government's religious policy was intended to be cautious and protective, it was a good tactic to pretend that they did and they had long used it in self-defense (for an earlier example, see above note 118). Refugee monks have scoffed at the idea that the government's goal was to protect Buddhism. In terms of its long term goal, of course, they were right.

141. See Chapter VII, note 74.

II. THE DECIMATION OF THE SANGHA

1. See Holmes Welch, *The Practice of Chinese Buddhism, 1900-1950* (Cambridge, Mass., 1967), pp. 234, 460, and 495-496. According to a source dating from about 1700, nearly 14 percent of the cultivated land in China was owned by religious bodies other than clan temples: see *Agrarian China,* comp. and tr. the research staff of the Secretariat, Institute of Pacific Relations (London, G. Allen and Unwin, 1939), pp. 1-2.

2. For some of the high points on the early history of land reform under the Communists, see Brandt, Schwartz, and Fairbank, *A Documentary History,* pp. 63, 96, 122, 224-226, 276-278; Chao Kuo-chün, *Agrarian Policy,* pp. 14-93. Chao, p. 78, quotes the clause in the Land Law of September 13, 1947, that abolished monastery ownership of land.

3. *HTFH,* 12/50, p. 26, published a letter from a monk on P'u-t'o Shan, the Buddhist sacred island off the Chekiang coast, asking whether there was again to be such a reduction. According to a statement of the Ministry of

Finance previous reductions had been "fake measures of the Kuomintang's reactionary rule." The reduction then being enforced elsewhere varied with the locality, but was in the vicinity of 25 to 30 percent. Chao Kuo-chün, pp. 74 ff., divides the postwar period into four stages. From August 1945 to December 1946 the Party continued its wartime policy of suspending the confiscation of land and working merely for the reduction of rent and interest payments. From December 1946 to October 1947 it also carried on compulsory purchase of landlords' "excess land." From October 1947 to the spring of 1948 there was a brief period of harsh class struggle in areas under Communist control: land was rapidly confiscated and redistributed. Then in the spring of 1948 the emphasis shifted back to rent and interest reduction.

4. *The Agrarian Reform Law,* p. 15. In 1951 when a reader wondered why it had been announced that "the land of all the temples in his city would be confiscated," *Modern Buddhism* replied that the word "confiscated" must be a mistake for "requisitioned."

5. This term is sometimes mistranslated as "public property," which in Chinese is *kuan-ch'an,* "official [i.e., government] property."

6. On the distinction between small private temples and large public monasteries, see Welch, *Practice,* pp. 129-130, 137.

7. *HTFH,* 9/53, p. 21.

8. *HTFH,* 12/51, p. 21. Compare *HTFH,* 3/51, p. 34, which states that the Fukien People's Representative Conference passed a resolution that local authorities should "distribute land to monks and nuns in individual shares (*an ko-jen ch'eng-fen, fen-p'ei t'u-ti*)"; and *HTFH,* 3/51, p. 32, which states that at Nan-yüeh "all the monks and nuns with the capacity and readiness to do farm work may [each] receive alike one share of land." In some cases individual ownership was disapproved of, but nonetheless allowed. After Liberation the monks at the Hua-yen Ssu, Chungking, "insisted on engaging individually and separately in production." Only in August 1952 did they "hand over their land for coöperative [cultivation]": see *HTFH,* 12/53, p. 31. Even in 1953 each of the monks at two monasteries in Fukien was tilling his own separate share of land, distributed to him in land reform, reaping his own individual harvest, and even cooking on his own stove—with foodstuffs from the general stores! See *HTFH,* 5/53, p. 3.

9. *Agrarian Reform Law,* p. 6.

10. *HTFH,* 6/51, p. 29. A similar answer (though a little more tentative) had been given to readers half a year earlier: "monks and nuns are single persons who are highly mobile. Common ownership (*kung-yu*) should be promoted over the land that has been distributed to them. This will also be in line with socialism." See *HTFH,* 12/50, p. 27. Even when land certificates were issued, it did not mean that ownership was individual. They were issued at Chiu-hua Shan, for example, and monks were called on to submit individual production plans, but it is clearly stated that the land remained the property of the monasteries (*ssu-an so-yu*): see *HTFH,* 6/53, p. 54, and cf.

Chüeh yu-ch'ing, 13.2:20 (October 1952). Land distributed also remained monastic property in a case I have discussed with a monk who himself participated in land reform. This was at Yün-men Shan, Kwangtung, where neither he nor any of the other resident monks received a plot or certificate. Yün-men got its land as an institution, to be owned and cultivated collectively.

11. In the case of many of the rich monasteries in central and east China, it would have been impractical to give them back any of their best land in redistribution, since it was widely dispersed and lay up to thirty miles away. That was one of the reasons why before Liberation their monks, even if they had wanted to, could not have "eaten their own rice": it would have taken them too long to get back and forth to work. During agrarian reform such distant holdings were distributed to tenants and other farmers in the area where they lay. A refugee report of 1952 stated that in one area of Szechwan there was much resentment among the peasants because the richest land, which had formerly belonged to the temples, was now being used to set up state farms. Most state farms reclaimed and cultivated land in border areas. The few that were set up in the home provinces of China provided models for the introduction of modern farming techniques.

12. *HTFH,* 11/50, p. 32, and 6/53, p. 54. Chiu-hua Shan was one of the four sacred Buddhist mountains of China and had many monasteries on its slopes. What happened there is not perfectly clear. The second passage cited states that "the monks remained in possession of all the land that they had tilled themselves before land reform" and gave figures for this that included 11 mou of paddy and 34 mou of vegetable garden. But, according to the first citation, as of autumn 1950 the monks were tilling 26 mou of paddy and 38 mou of vegetable garden—which, it said, was "hardly enough." This is not the only report of a reduction of allotment. The paddy land of the Yü-wang Ssu was reduced from 129.33 to 121.08 mou after "readjustment" (*tiao-cheng*), apparently because the number of monks had gone down: see *HTFH,* 4/53, p. 13. An informant who had been through land reform confirmed that a reduction of allotment often did follow a reduction in the number of monks.

13. See *HTFH,* 12/50, p. 26.

14. See *Chüeh yu-ch'ing,* 13.2:20 (October 1952) and *HTFH,* 8/58, p. 31.

15. See this chapter at notes 124-125.

16. The monasteries involved were the Chao-chüeh Ssu, which increased its holdings from 70 odd to 180 odd mou, and the Chin-tz'u Ssu, where there was also an exchange of distant for nearer plots but where no net increase in acreage was reported. See *HTFH,* 6/53, p. 49.

17. *HTFH,* 6/53, p. 36.

18. The first Indian friendship mission had visited China in October 1951 but had not gone to Sian. That city was visited in 1954, however, by an Indian good-will delegation; in 1955 by an Indian cultural delegation and Raghu Vira; in 1956 by P. V. Bapat and Jagdish Kasyap; in 1957 by two Japanese delegations—and so on.

19. Neng-hai, for example, who had been abbot of the Chin-tz'u Ssu in Chengtu (see note 16), was one of eighteen eminent monks proposed by Chao P'u-ch'u on May 24, 1951, to organize a Chinese Buddhist association: see *Chüeh yu-ch'ing,* 14.1:6 (January 1953).

20. At the Yü-wang Ssu in 1952 75 percent of the monks were over 40, and half of those from 18 to 30 were disabled or too weak to work: see *HTFH,* 4/53, p. 12. Elderly monks were in the majority at P'u-t'o Shan and the Nan-hua Ssu: see *Chüeh yu-ch'ing,* 12.2:20 (October 1952). It was reported that at a monastery in Mukden in 1953 "most of the 11 resident monks are elderly, between 60 and 80. Only the guest prefect, aged 36, is in the prime of life. The capacity to engage in productive labor is on the whole rather limited": see *HTFH,* 12/53, p. 27. *HTFH,* 6/53, p. 52, notes that there was a large number of elderly and disabled monks at Wu-t'ai Shan, but even if there had not been so many, the land allotted would only produce enough grain to feed a hundred of the 374 lamas. In the ensuing years over 90 percent of them had to be given livelihood subsidies. See *HTFH,* 10/59, p. 12. In P'u-t'ien county, Fukien, only 20 percent of the 1,580 monks and nuns were classified as young or middle-aged in 1957: therefore 80 percent must have been elderly, presumably over 60. See *HTFH,* 5/57, p. 24. On the failure of the Nan-yüeh Coöperative because of the old age of its members, see this chapter at note 58.

21. *Chüeh yu-ch'ing,* 12.5:20 (May 1951). Cf. *ibid* 12.8-9:24 (August-September 1951).

22. *Chüeh yu-ch'ing,* 13.2:20 (October 1952). They finally got help from the government, which supplied them with 46,000 catties of rice until they began raising two crops a year and became self-sufficient, apparently in 1957: see *HTFH,* 10/58, p. 33. Similarly, two years after land reform Ku Shan, the largest monastery in Fukien, was producing only 20,000 catties of rice to feed its 120 resident monks (*HTFH,* 6/54, p. 30)–less than half their annual need.

23. *Chüeh yu-ch'ing,* 12.10-12:32 (December 1951). Some details are as of ten months later, when the situation was unchanged: see *ibid.,* 13.2:20 (October 1952).

24. This information comes from a monk who was at Yün-men Shan at the time. Despite his high position, Li Chi-shen was unable to save his own son from a twelve-year sentence in 1952 for exploiting the peasantry. See Howard L. Boorman, ed., *Biographical Dictionary of Republican China* (New York, 1967-71), II, 295.

25. *Chüeh yu-ch'ing,* 14.1:25 (January 1953). Cf. Hong Kong *Ta-kung pao,* May 23, 1950. Hsü-yün added that things were "even worse" at the Nan-hua Ssu, on the restoration of which see Welch, *Revival,* pp. 92-93.

26. *HTFH,* 3/51, pp. 32-33. I have figured one hundred catties of paddy to a *tan.* A *tan* by volume was heavier in many areas. The monk who wrote this article, Ming-chen, had already suggested that it was the fault of the

Buddhists themselves that the Shang-feng Ssu had been burned down (see Chapter V, note 72) and urged young monks who had to negotiate with peasants to feel remorse about the past and joy about the present and to realize that they were paying back debts. On his rapid rise thereafter, see Chapter X at notes 57-58.

27. *HTFH,* 11/50, p. 6.

28. *HTFH,* 5/51, p. 27. This recommendation to use empty space for production came in response to a reader's letter that asked: "People are now forcibly occupying monasteries and nunneries, whose rights are not clearly defined. The losses they have incurred are quite large. Please explain." The answer began: "According to the directive of the central authorities, organs and army units must get the consent of monasteries and nunneries in order to use their premises. But if the monasteries and nunneries have empty rooms, they may not make up reasons for refusing." The directive referred to here was issued in January 1950 by the Ministry of Internal Affairs: see *HTFH,* 10/50, p. 21.

29. See Welch, *Revival,* pp. 10-11, 23, 143-150. Friendliness to Buddhism was much less common in the new regime: nonetheless it was part of the religious policy to avoid the appearance of arbitrary action.

30. *HTFH,* 6/51, p. 30.

31. *HTFH,* 10/50, p. 31.

32. *HTFH,* 3/51, back page advertisement. "Ta-hsiung" is an epithet of the Buddha. The goal was to increase production from 200 bags a day to 10,000 a month. According to *HTFH,* 3/51, p. 27, the Peking gunnysack factory was intended to serve as a model for monks everywhere.

33. Such a shortage was the reason for starting a gunnysack factory at the Yü-wang Ssu in September 1952: see this chapter at note 50. At Chiu-hua Shan too monks tried to raise the jute: see *Tsu-kuo,* 26.7:18 (May 25, 1959).

34. In 1951 the Omei Shan Buddhist Spinning and Weaving Production Coöperative was said to be operating 36 pieces of textile machinery in four buildings. Daily production was over 50 catties of yarn and 140 of cloth. See *HTFH,* 4/51, p. 35. Dozens of Changsha monks and nuns wove cloth in the factory of the K'ai-fu Ssu, first started in 1949: see *HTFH,* 9/52, p. 18; 6/53, p. 47; 11/59, pp. 28-30. (This last item gives one of the fullest accounts of a light industrial enterprise operated by the sangha; it has been translated in JPRS, 6289.) In March 1950 some monks from the Nan-hua Ssu and the Yün-men Ssu started a factory in the Lay Devotees Club of the nearby town of Shao-kuan, which was soon turning out twenty dozen towels a day: see Hong Kong *Ta-kung pao,* May 23, 1950, and cf. *ibid.,* April 1, 1961. Many examples of enterprises started by Shanghai monks and nuns just after Liberation are given by Alfred Kiang in "A New Life Begins in the Temples," *China Weekly Review,* 116.11:173-174 (Feb. 11, 1950).

As to finished clothing, one of the earliest reports I have found involved the Ching-an Ssu, Shanghai (the famous Bubbling Well Monastery). There in

1949, soon after Liberation, the monks experienced an 80 percent drop in income. Many of them left, but those who remained began to spend six hours a day making stockings on hand-driven machines. See *New York Times,* August 23, 1949, p. 15. Perhaps an even earlier instance involved the twenty nuns of the Mi-t'o Ssu in Harbin, who started to work at a factory in 1949, making clothes and bedrolls for the army: see *HTFH,* 7/53, p. 27. Something similar was done by the nuns of the Pai-i An in Tsinan (*HTFH,* 2/53, p. 58) and by the nuns of Wuhan who first undertook production in the summer of 1950 (clothes, towels, and socks): see *HTFH,* 9/50, p. 20. In February 1951 the Preparatory Committee of the Wuhan Buddhist Association declared that it would make a survey, select temples where factories could be set up, and train monks and nuns to work there: see *HTFH,* 4/51, p. 34.

35. From mid-1950 to April 1951 the sangha in Hangchow collected the equivalent of US$3,000 as capital to start productive enterprises: see *HTFH,* 3/52, p. 16. During the Great Leap Forward one monastery in Fukien invested the equivalent of US$300, over five ounces of gold, a hundred silver dollars, and 8,000 catties of scrap iron and steel to establish a monastery cotton mill and chemical fertilizer factory: see *HTFH,* 11/58, p. 33.

36. In 1951 eight of the fourteen monks of the Liu-jung Ssu in Canton went to work in a clothing factory that had been set up on the premises rented from the monastery. (The other six monks were too old to work.) See *Chüeh yu-ch'ing,* 12.8-9:24 (September 1951). According to a cadre of the Canton Religious Affairs Division, somewhat larger enterprises were set up in Canton monasteries in 1956: a bindery, an umbrella factory, and in 1959 a crematorium. According to *HTFH,* 5/57, p. 16, a crematorium was also established at Tz'u-yün Ssu, Chungking, since more and more people preferred cremation to burial. (Actually crematoria had long been a standard feature of Chinese Buddhist monasteries.) In other cases the monks went out to work in a factory that lay at a distance from the monastery: for example, see *HTFH,* 3/51, p. 35 (Mi-t'o Ssu, Antung).

37. At Omei Shan, for example, there was very little arable paddy land. At first some of the monks there tried to set up textile factories (see note 34) but when these failed for want of a market (*HTFH,* 6/53, p. 57), they went back to helping their brethren care, as usual, for the tens of thousands of pilgrims who still came each year to spend a few days on the mountain (*HTFH,* 5/57, p. 16). Other sacred mountains—like P'u-t'o and Chiu-hua—were different in having fewer pilgrims and a little more land available. An informant who visited all four sacred mountains in 1957 said that labor at Chiu-hua was particularly arduous; whereas at P'u-t'o, so far as he could see, the monks did not farm the land they had received, but lived off subsidies and pilgrims. Some urban monasteries expanded their guest dining rooms into regular restaurants. Eighteen public mess halls were reported to have been set up by Shanghai monasteries in 1949: see Alfred Kiang, p. 173. The Hua-lin Ssu in Chungking opened a restaurant in February 1953 that employed

twenty of its monks (*HTFH,* 6/53, p. 50). Faure saw it still in operation in 1956: see Edgar Faure, *The Serpent and the Tortoise,* tr. Lovett F. Edwards, (New York, St. Martin's Press, 1958), pp. 153-154. He was told that the Hua-lin Ssu had three hundred monks, some of whom worked in its restaurant, others of whom made clothing and practiced Chinese medicine.

38. *HTFH,* 7/52, pp. 18-20. Cf. Chapter VII, note 106. This coöperative had been renamed the Changsha Nuns' Production Coöperative in 1950, when it was expanded to include four other nunneries. In 1952 it was combined with a monks' coöperative to form the Changsha First Dyeing and Weaving Production Coöperative and moved into Changsha's biggest monastery, the K'ai-fu Ssu, where by then monks and nuns both had living quarters. See *HTFH,* 6/53, pp. 45-47.

39. *HTFH,* 8/53, p. 27; 1/54, p. 29. The four mutual aid teams at Chiu-hua Shan produced tea and flowers to sell as well as sweet potatoes to eat: see *HTFH,* 6/53, p. 54.

40. Most of the coöperatives started before this were in Manchuria and in the north, where land reform had taken place earlier. Already in 1947 the Communists had set up a model farm east of Chia-mu-ssu in Sungkiang. It operated by voluntary mutual aid and coöperation until February 1951, when it became the first collective farm (*chi-t'i nung-ch'ang*) in that area. In the spring of 1951 an agricultural producers' coöperative was established in Kirin, and by April 1952 there were 1,200 in Manchuria; but there had still been no coöperativization of agriculture in densely populated farming areas like east China. See *CB,* 176:4-9; *SCMP,* 297:25-31, 322:10.

41. *HTFH,* 4/53, pp. 10, 15.

42. *HTFH,* 2/56, p. 30. In 1953 the thirty-odd monks there were reported to be supporting themselves by productive labor (*HTFH,* 6/53, p. 45), but it was only in 1956 that we read of their having formed a productive labor team, which was just then applying for membership in the APC.

43. Tsukamoto Zenryū and Makita Tairyō, "Chūgoku hōmonki," in *Tōhō gakuhō* 28:301 (March 1958). A coöperative operated by the Hua-t'ing Ssu, Kunming, is mentioned in *HTFH,* 6/53, p. 51. For other individual examples, see *HTFH,* 2/56, pp. 17-18; 2/56, p. 30; 3/56, p. 30.

44. On such a refusal see *HTFH,* 2/56, p. 17.

45. I use the term "collectivization" to cover all stages, from mutual aid teams to communes. Members of teams and lower-level coöperatives—which were not collectives—got more income if they had more land. In higher-level coöperatives they did not—although they theoretically retained ownership of their land. This latter was the chief difference between a Chinese higher APC and a Soviet Kolkhoz, where even in theory the ownership of individual plots was not retained by members. In the commune even this theoretical difference was eliminated, and no one owned farmland as an individual.

46. The Nan-hua Ssu became a production team of the Ma-pa People's Commune on October 1, 1958; see *HTFH,* 11/58, p. 31. About the same time the

Ching-yeh Ssu on Chung-nan Shan did the same: see *Tsu-kuo,* 8/65, p. 29. Communalization in Inner Mongolia is discussed in *HTFH,* 10/59, pp. 16-17. The joint coöperative set up by the many monasteries on the sacred mountain of Nan-yüeh early in 1957 became a production team of the local commune before the end of 1958. See this chapter at note 58. A Japanese delegation that visited the Kuo-ch'ing Ssu, T'ien-t'ai Shan, in May 1965 was told that the monastery belonged to the people's commune of T'ien-t'ai county and that all its monks except the elderly participated in the work of the commune as a production team. See Mibu Shojun, "Chūgoku Tendai-san junreiki," *Shūkyō kōron* 9/65, p. 32.

47. There is no mention of commune membership in articles on activities at Yün-chü Shan (*HTFH,* 11/58, pp. 33-34), Chiu-hua Shan (*HTFH,* 12/58, p. 32), and Wu-t'ai Shan (*HTFH,* 12/58, pp. 27-29), nor in the development plans of the sangha in two counties of Kiangsi and Fukien in August and September 1958, whereas elsewhere–Harbin, for example, on September 18–plans did include a pledge to join the people's commune (*HTFH,* 11/58, pp. 32-33 and 12/58, p. 33).

48. *HTFH,* 10/59, p. 11. *HTFH,* 1/60, p. 3 stated that "most (*i-pan*) rural monks and nuns have positively taken part in the movement to convert to people's communes."

49. *HTFH,* 4/59, p. 16 tr. in *ECMM,* 170:39. I have been unable to locate this quotation in the canon.

50. *HTFH,* 4/53, pp. 13-14.

51. *HTFH,* 5/53, p. 15.

52. *HTFH,* 4/53, p. 15.

53. For example, in November 1951 a chopstick factory was started in Hangchow. Three hundred monks and nuns applied to work there, but because of shortage of capital only half–the 150 who were facing the greatest hardship–were accepted. "There was little congee but many monks to eat it–and everyone was afraid." Within a few months they had to close down the factory altogether because they did not have the money to purchase the bamboo from which to make the chopsticks. Some of the monks went home to become farmers; others started to make socks and towels and pulp for paper; seven monks got together, bought a hammer, and crushed rock beside the road in the suburbs. Better luck was enjoyed by the 130 nuns who were given jobs at a nearby tea factory after the Hangchow Buddhist Association had invested the equivalent of US$2,500 in it. They were allowed to join the Tea-workers Union and were paid 20 cents a day. See *HTFH,* 3/52, p. 6, and *Chüeh yu-ch'ing* 13.2:19 (October 1952). In 1950 the monks and nuns of Ningpo who were learning to weave cloth and towels had great difficulties finding a market for their product: see *HTFH,* 12/50, p. 32. In 1951-52 one of the two sewing workshops for monks and nuns in Chungking was closed down, and 49 out of the 74 monks, nuns, and devotees who were working there lost their jobs: see *HTFH,* 6/53, p. 50. By 1953 three out of the four

spinning and weaving workshops that had been started on Omei Shan failed for want of a market; and the monks and the nuns who had been employed there became "surplus labor": see *HTFH,* 6/53, p. 57. Also by 1953 a weaving coöperative run by the local Buddhist association in Kunming had failed not only because there was no market for what it produced, but also because its members did not have the necessary production skills. The association's farm too was reporting heavy losses. See *HTFH,* 6/53, p. 51. Even the pioneer model effort in urban labor by monks—the Ta-hsiung Gunnysack Factory—may have failed. I have seen no mention of it after 1952. In the first five months after it was set up, its operating losses amounted to the equivalent of over US$1,000. Therefore no more jute could be bought and the shareholders had to put in more capital. The difficulties it experienced were described at length in *HTFH,* 8/51, p. 33, where, nonetheless, its value as a model for other factories was still insisted on. Two months later readers were told that starting similar factories in other cities "would not be so very easy." The one in Peking was "running constantly into problems." Since all its machines were hand-driven, the plan was to replace them with electrically powered machines. Yet the factory already suffered from a surfeit of hands, and monks from other cities who wanted to come and work in it were told to stay where they were. See *HTFH,* 10/51, pp. 11, 29. Many if not most of these unsuccessful enterprises were organized and financed by the Buddhist associations of their localities.

54. Already in 1950 Ch'en Ming-shu had complained: "For the past half year I have been getting a movement started in Shanghai for monks and nuns to save themselves through productive labor; and gradually it has begun to spread . . . but we know how inactive the government has been in carrying out this reform and how little effect has been given to the policy directive on entering productive labor." See *HTFH,* 10/57, p. 28.

55. "To sit (in meditation)" and "to work" are homophonous phrases. Actually, even without altering the character from *tso* "work" to *tso* "sit" there is the question of what kind of work Pai-chang had in mind. See Chapter III at notes 1-4.

56. *HTFH,* 11/58, p. 27.

57. *HTFH,* 11/58, pp. 28-29. Cf. 6/58, pp. 25-29.

58. See Rewi Alley, *Amongst Hills and Streams of Hunan in the Fall of 1962* (Peking, 1963), p. 18. The dissolution of the production team makes me even more skeptical about the harvests claimed at Nan-yüeh. The practical and psychological obstacles described seem too great to have been overcome so easily. The same is true of the Yü-wang Ssu, where the figures themselves are sometimes contradictory. For example, if production there in 1951 had really been the 501 catties per mou that was claimed on 121 mou, then why did the 120 residents of the monastery run out of food the following January?

59. *HTFH,* 2/56, p. 17.

60. *HTFH,* 4/53, p. 15.

61. *HTFH,* 5/55, p. 27.

62. *HTFH,* 9/52, p. 30. Another 10 percent were engaged in industrial production. According to *HTFH,* 7/53, p. 27, 80 percent of the monks and nuns in Haining *hsien,* Chekiang, were engaged in agriculture, and the rest lived in urban temples.

63. In May 1951, 70 percent of the monks and nuns at Nanking were supporting themselves by productive labor (making matches, for example) in factories outside their monasteries, since inside them factories had not yet been set up: see *HTFH,* 5/51, p. 27. In early 1952, 90 percent of the nuns (no mention of monks) in Changsha were said to be engaged in productive labor: see *HTFH,* 7/52, p. 19. In early 1954, 70 percent of the sangha in Shenyang were said to be so engaged: see *HTFH,* 1/54, p. 23. In 1959 productive labor such as bookbinding was being carried on by over 80 percent of the monks and nuns of Wuhan: see *HTFH,* 10/59, p. 11. Eight years earlier, only nuns had gone to work in the five factories that were set up in Wuhan before the end of 1951 (most of them making supplies for the army in Korea): see *HTFH,* 3/52, p. 8. Here as in Changsha it seems to have been easier to get the nuns into production than the monks, perhaps because they were naturally more tractable or because they felt more defenseless.

64. For example, at Ling-yen Shan: see *Chüeh yu-ch'ing,* 13.2:20 (October 1952). Cf. *HTFH,* 6/53, p. 40.

65. For example, *HTFH,* 4/53, p. 11; 6/53, p. 26. One of the few statements as to what portion of monks in a specific case were spending how much of their time on production was given to an Indian good-will mission, which was told in October 1951 that 13 out of 40 monks at a monastery in Hangchow spent the greater part of their day in agricultural labor: see Pandit Sunderlal, *China Today* (Allahabad, n.d.), p. 389. In 1958 one of the targets undertaken when the commune was set up at Nan-yüeh was to increase the number of persons working from 45 to over 60 percent: see *HTFH,* 11/58, p. 31. At the end of 1958 monks at Wu-t'ai Shan were said to be "taking part in organized labor for the first time": see *HTFH,* 12/58, p. 27.

66. *HTFH,* 12/52, pp. 7-8.

67. For example, a monk of the Yü-wang Ssu stated: "Since Liberation our monastery's income from performing Buddhist rites has been completely cut off. The threat to livelihood has increased the masses' enthusiasm for productive labor": see *HTFH,* 5/53, p. 14. The same experience was reported at the San-mei Ssu in Shanghai: see Hong Kong *Ta-kung pao,* July 12, 1950.

68. Hong Kong *Ta-kung pao,* April 1, 1950. Here it is stated that "the men and women who came in the past to worship were almost all landlords and rich peasants." This is a gross misstatement, but it is true, I think, that landlords and rich peasants provided much of the income that came in the form of donations and fees. See Welch, *Practice,* pp. 226-240.

69. In 1951 the readers of *Modern Buddhism* were told that it was not illegal for laymen to donate money to monks who had administered the Three Refuges to them or had lectured to them on the sutras or who were

having sutras printed or images made. Nor was it exploitation for monks to accept such money; but they should "conscientiously ask themselves whether they should really accept so much support from people and, if they did not feel they should, they should accept less. If they did feel that they should accept so much, then it was best to get incontestable proof [that it was a voluntary contribution] so as to avoid attacks from skeptical people." See *HTFH,* 10/51, p. 28. The "skeptical people" were presumably the cadres who had been "interfering illegally with donations" on the grounds that the monks were "parasites" (*ibid.*). The fact that this was discussed in the pages of *Modern Buddhism* suggests that these difficulties were not uncommon. Donations to monks remained legal, but they felt less and less free to accept them as the years passed. This is why, for example, the monasteries of Chung-nan Shan, which had received donations equivalent to US$128 during the Kuan-yin festival in 1952, presented the entire sum to the Resist America Aid Korea committee of their county "in order to show the fervor of Buddhists' patriotism": see *Chüeh yu-ch'ing* 13.2:20 (October 1952). Cf. notes 78, 79, 85.

70. *HTFH,* 10/50, p. 22.

71. *HTFH,* 12/51, p. 21.

72. *HTFH,* 8/51, p. 32 (italics added). Cf. the condemnation of mortuary rites in *HTFH,* 5/57, p. 21 and Chapter IV, note 18. Already in June 1950 one of the topics for discussion by a study group in Wuhan was "how monks and nuns could stop supporting themselves by performing rites for the dead": see *HTFH,* 9/50, p. 20.

73. One of the rare statements about this in the Mainland press concerned the real estate owned and rented out by the fifty-six Buddhist temples in Changsha. It was taken over by a municipally established committee that collected the rents for them—averaging 15,520 catties of rice per month in 1950-52 and apparently, reaching 18,900 catties per month in 1953, enough to feed 630 persons. See *HTFH,* 6/53, pp. 45, 47. This seems to have been the same as the arrangement referred to in Article 2.3 of the Provisional Measures for the Management of Monasteries and Temples in Peking, passed August 23, 1951, which stated that "the real estate belonging to monasteries and temples shall be separately managed." See *HTFH,* 10/51, p. 3. On the tax paid by Peking temples on their income from real estate, see *HTFH,* 9/51, p. 21.

In 1961 I met a monk from the Kuang-chi Ssu in Peking, who was then a vice-president of the Chinese Buddhist Association. When I asked him if he did productive labor, he laughed and said that his labor was mental and that his monastery (the seat of the association) still received rents from urban real estate. Along with that of some other temples in Peking, he said, its real estate was managed by the Temples Management Committee (Ssu-miao Kuan-li Wei-yüan-hui), which collected the rents and distributed them to the owners. He assumed that this was the case with temples in all Chinese cities.

From a refugee informant, I have heard that in Soochow ownership of all temple real estate was transferred to the local Buddhist association immediately after Liberation. It collected the rents, kept the lion's share, and gave the monks an allowance equivalent to about US$5.00 a month. All this fits in with what Chao P'u-ch'u told a Japanese visitor in 1957: –that real estate continued to be the largest source of income for urban monasteries. See *Chūgai nippō* (Kyoto), October 19, 1958. An earlier Japanese visitor was informed in 1954 by the abbot of the Ching-an Ssu, Shanghai, that monks in the cities did not engage in labor, whereas those in the countryside did farming and afforestation. See Ōtani Eijun, *Shin Chūgoku kenmonki* (Tokyo, 1955), p. 120. The logical result of such differences would have been a shift of monastic population to the city, but the only place where I have found evidence of it is Shanghai (see Appendix C).

Reports of continuing unearned income are particularly credible in the case of lamaseries because of the policy of special favor towards Tibetan and Mongolian Buddhism. The lamas of the famous Yung-ho Kung in Peking were said to live partly on donations and partly on renting out some of their temple premises as living quarters: see P. V. Bapat, "A Glimpse of China Today," *Maha Bodhi,* 64.8:388 (August 1956). A Western visitor was told the Yung-ho Kung received the equivalent of about US$1,200 a month in rents, plus subsidies to individual lamas: see Peter Schmid, *The New Face of China,* (London, 1958), p. 56. (The same information was given to Fernand Gigon.) Another Western visitor reports being told by the lamas at the Yung-ho Kung in 1966 that their income came from real estate rented out *to the government.* A foreign visitor was told in 1955 that the Kuang-jen Ssu, a lama temple in Sian, had received 404 mou in land reform, which it still rented out to tenant farmers for 25 percent of the crop. This is confirmed in *HTFH,* 6/53, p. 36.

74. In 1951 the temples of Yü-lin (a town in the desert borderland of northern Shensi) were all hereditary and depended on Buddhist services, which were in demand by the masses, "whose awareness had not yet been universally raised": see *HTFH,* 9/51, p. 20. In 1952-53 two monasteries at Mount Nan-yüeh netted the equivalent of US$640 a year from donations (*hsiang-yu*): see *HTFH,* 11/53, p. 32. In 1953 the Hua-yen Ssu, Chungking, received the equivalent of more than US$170 from pious laymen (*chai-hsin*)–probably meaning laymen who had asked the monastery to serve them a vegetarian meal in connection with Buddhist services; see *HTFH,* 12/53, p. 31. Professor Bapat (see preceding note) mentions that the monks at the Yü-fo Ssu, Shanghai, and Liu-ho T'a, Hangchow, were being "supported by their followers." In 1953 a "certain monastery" in Chekiang was said to be deriving the majority of its income from rites for the dead and donations: see *HTFH,* 5/53, p. 3. In 1957 the T'ien-t'ung Ssu, a famous meditation center in the Ningpo countryside, was still receiving fees for performing Buddhist services: see *HTFH,* 5/57, p. 19. At the second national CBA conference in

1957 one delegate complained that divination by bamboo slips was still being carried on as a profitable business by the monks of southern Kiangsi—as well as the even more heterodox practice of breaking open the blood-bath hell in order to release the women who had been imprisoned there for contaminating the earth with their blood during childbirth. See *HTFH,* 5/57, p. 21, and Henri Doré, *Researches into Chinese Superstitions,* tr. M. Kennelly (Shanghai, 1914), I, 84-87. Visitors and refugees report that in Canton, Shanghai, Soochow, Yangchow, and Wuhan donations and fees were common until 1958. One informant, who lived in a small temple in Hankow from 1954 to 1958, said that he and his five or six fellow monks performed three or four Buddhist services each month, which brought in more than enough to support them. In 1957 a lay informant then in Soochow paid 2 JMP apiece to the five monks and nuns who performed a Buddhist service in his home.

75. Much of this information abut the Kao-min Ssu comes from a monk who stayed there in 1956. It is supplemented and partly confirmed by the following item published in *Chüeh yu-ch'ing,* 13.2:20 (October 1952). "The Kao-min Ssu was founded in the Sui dynasty and restored by Yü-lin [in the early Ch'ing]—a restoration that has lasted until today. Along with the Chiang-t'ien Ssu at Chin Shan it is considered a great model and a place where achievements [in meditation] are attested to (*kung-hsing yin-cheng*). The reverend elder of the present generation is Lai-kuo, who has headed the monastery for more than forty years. Over 190 persons are still living here. Those who have labor capacity take part in labor. There are twenty or thirty persons who are adepts in meditation and have not gone outside the monastery walls for decades. Meditation is carried on just as it always has been. Last winter there were ten meditation weeks: the work was not interrupted. Three meals of congee are served each day. This consumes 1.4-1.5 piculs of polished rice. Fuel must be bought outside." Note that monks are not said to take part in *productive* labor. Labor in the form of chores and menial tasks had been a regular feature of Chinese monastic life for centuries. The quantity of rice consumed averaged over a catty per head per day—a more than ample diet that suggests a high level of lay donations. By 1956, according to my informant, the number of residents had dropped to about 60. Lai-kuo died November 23, 1953: see *HTFH,* 1/54, p. 29.

76. *HTFH,* 9/55, p. 5.

77. *HTFH,* 9/55, p. 30.

78. *HTFH,* 5/54, pp. 25-26. I have simplified the story of what happened. There were five or six monks at this monastery, ranging from 50 to 80 years of age. Possibly the reason they put up the posters was to demonstrate that they were progressive and therefore qualified for livelihood subsidies from the State. They told worshipers that they would not refuse donations made to support them in their old age or to repair the monastery: they just wanted to discourage people from giving them money to repay a vow, burn effigies, and so on. It was the latter form of income that fell off 50 percent from the year before.

79. This was in Soochow where, with the establishment of the urban communes in 1958, the monks who had depended on rents were forced to go to work in light industrial enterprises, according to a refugee informant.

80. I have seen no reference in the press to this directive, which was recalled by a cadre of the Canton Religious Affairs Division. Other informants confirm that in 1958 donation boxes and divination slips disappeared from Shanghai temples.

81. *Tsu-kuo,* 26.7:18 (May 25, 1959).

82. *HTFH,* 10/59, p. 12.

83. *HTFH,* 1/60, p. 4.

84. In 1958 many monks had taken pledges that they would begin to support themselves by productive labor within one or two years. See, for example, *HTFH,* 7/58, pp. 18, 19; 11/58, pp. 3, 32.

85. *JMJP,* April 15, 1960. This important speech by Shirob, my own translations from which will often appear below, is translated in *CB,* 627:26-30 and JPRS 5635:196-201. It was reprinted in *HTFH,* 5/60, pp. 9-11 and incorporated parts of Shirob's article already printed in *HTFH,* 10/59, pp. 10-15. The latter is translated in URS 17:390-402.

86. In 1960-62 several different parties of Western visitors saw mortuary rites underway at the Yü-fo Ssu, Ching-an Ssu, and Fa-tsang Ssu, Shanghai. An overseas Chinese from Singapore made donations for the repair of monasteries on P'u-t'o Shan and found that monks in many other places, although they would not accept money with their own hands, were glad to have him put it in the donation box. Whereas one of the reasons for the arrest of Abbot Pen-huan in 1958 had been that he collected money from Hong Kong to repair the tile flooring of the Nan-hua Ssu, an overseas Chinese in Canada was able to send thousands of JMP to build a columbarium at the Yün-chü Ssu—the cadres permitted it because it meant foreign exchange. In 1960-62 several informants in Hong Kong were remitting money to their old masters on the Mainland just as easily as were the children of lay families. Donations from the faithful are also mentioned in the Mainland press. In 1962 the Ta-hsiang Ssu, Yao-hsien, Shensi, received over 10,000 JMP in donations from worshipers during just one of its two annual festivals for Kuan-yin: see *HTFH,* 5/62, p. 40 (October 1962).

87. *HTFH,* 10/59, p. 22.

88. Hong Kong *Ta-kung pao,* July 12, 1950. An informant who knew this monastery in the late 1940's said that it had about a hundred monks. The *Ta-kung pao* states merely that the number dropped from "several tens to several." Compare the drop at the Ching-an Ssu mentioned in note 34. Derk Bodde cites a similar report about a monastery near Wusih whose monks had been accused of being parasites on society. On August 3, 1949, the abbot "seeing that conditions in the new society are no longer favorable for Buddhist monks . . . proclaimed to all the monks the dissolution of the monastery and expressed the wish that they embrace the bosom of the new China and work for the New Democracy." On August 4 "all the monks

returned to lay life, collectively bought the revolutionary literature, and began to engage in study. On the eighth they furthermore registered at the school for the training of revolutionary cadres, desiring to act for the service of the people." See Derk Bodde, *Peking Diary* (New York, Henry Schuman, Inc. 1967), p. 245.

89. This was the purpose with which twenty young monks left one of the T'ien-chu monasteries in Hangchow: see *HTFH,* 3/52, p. 16.

90. By February 1950, 24 out of 40 students at the Ching-an Ssu Seminary in Shanghai had left to join the army or train for it: see Alfred Kiang, "A New Life," p. 173.

91. See Chapter I, note 135.

92. These were the motives ascribed, for example, to the seven or eight nuns who disrobed at the Kuan-yin An, Tung-t'ang, Kiangsu, leaving only one old sister to care for the buildings; see Hong Kong *Ta-kung pao,* May 13, 1951. The new Marriage Law made a much greater difference to nuns, since it gave them legal equality for the first time and hence made them readier than monks to disrobe. According to a former cadre of the Canton Religious Affairs Division, arrangements for their new life were often made by the Civil Affairs Bureau, and "success stories" were given wide publicity in order to encourage other nuns to follow suit.

93. Thirteen monks guilty of this kind of misconduct at the Ch'en-t'ien Ssu, Chüanchow, were finally expelled. The same kind of thing happened at the K'ai-yüan Ssu. See *HTFH*, 6/53, p. 40, and cf. 5/53, p. 3. In Kunming the Preparatory Committee of the local Buddhist association helped laicized monks to find regular jobs and insisted that those who remained in the robe should follow the code of rules. This represented a tightening up from the period just after Liberation: see *HTFH,* 6/53, p. 51. In Shansi in 1951 monks who had married and disrobed were still being allowed to stay on in the monastery: see *HTFH,* 12/51, p. 21.

94. *HTFH,* 12/51, p. 22. By 1959 readers of *Modern Buddhism* were told that they could return to lay life "simply by telling someone and then doing it": see *HTFH,* 7/59, p. 18. It did not violate tradition for a monk to renounce his vows in front of masters other than those who had ordained him, but before Liberation they would have insisted that there be a valid reason for his return to lay life.

95. According to a former cadre of the Religious Affairs Division in Canton, this kind of persuasion was used more often by cadres in the countryside than in the city, where popular support for the clergy weighed against a "simple" policy on religion.

96. For a description of the pseudo-family system in Chinese Buddhism, see Welch, *Practice,* pp. 276-285.

97. *HTFH,* 9/50, p. 29, in answer to a reader's question, explained: "When head monks are the representatives of monasteries with landed property and depend on land rents for their livelihood, naturally they belong

to the landlord class. You may refer to the G.A.C.'s recently promulgated 'Decisions Concerning the Differentiation of Class Status in the Countryside.' " These had been issued on August 4, 1950, and at the end of the section on landlords, they stated: "Any person who collects rent and manages the landed property for landlords and depends on the exploitation of peasants by the landlords as his main means of livelihood and whose living conditions are better than those of an ordinary middle peasant shall be treated in the same manner as a landlord." See *Agrarian Reform Law,* p. 19, and compare p. 46: "The management of landholdings of public bodies is an act of exploitation . . . By the management of landholdings of public bodies is meant management of landholdings and other properties belonging to all kinds of ancestral shrines, temples, associations and societies. There is no doubt that this system has been one of the forms of feudal exploitation of the countryside . . . The practice of managing such organizations, as are controlled by a few who make a large income through feudal exploitation, should be one of the factors in determining the class status of those who are engaged in management."

98. I failed to ascertain whether this informant was using the lunar or the Western calendar: what he said was "the twenty-second of the tenth month." I have interpreted it as referring to the lunar calendar, which is the one in terms of which Chinese Buddhist monks tend to think.

99. Descriptions of their duties may be found in Welch, *Practice,* pp. 10-29.

100. Beatings were the standard penalty for misbehavior in a Chinese monastery. They were considered part of the austerity that helped a monk make spiritual progress. See Welch, *Practice,* pp. 119-121.

101. He said the "fifth month."

102. *HTFH,* 3/52, p. 14. At Chiu-hua Shan it was said to be mostly the head monks who quit the monasteries after the donations from the laity were cut off. In fact, only one head monk, I-fang, was left on the whole mountain. See *Chüeh yu-ch'ing,* 12.3:24 (March 1951).

103. The monks of the Pao-shan Ssu in Antung were reported to have been the object of "struggle soon after Liberation," see *HTFH,* 3/51, p. 35. Another case involved six nuns in Shun-te (Shun-tak), Kwangtung. One of them disrobed soon after Liberation. Since some of her sisters refused to follow suit, she "used struggle tactics" (*yung tou-cheng-ti fang-shih*), saying: "The reason that you don't let your hair grow is that you belong to the landlord class with piles of silver and gold." Thereupon all the nuns in the district, old as well as young, let their hair grow. See *HTFH,* 9/53, p. 22. For the context of a general statement that some monks "were struck down by the peasantry in struggle," see this chapter at note 105.

104. Cf. note 97. *HTFH,* 9/50, p. 29 states that even the ordinary rank-and-file monks whose lives were full of hardships, also derived some benefit from land rents and, while not classifiable as feudal, were also not

proletarian. *HTFH,* 5/51, p. 26, tells its readers that whether or not a monastery belonged to the landlord class depended on how much land it had and on how much of this was cultivated by the monks themselves–a strong hint that they had better get to work.

105. *HTFH,* 3/52, p. 19. There is a very threatening tone in other statements, both before and after land reform. For example, a dispatch from Hangchow dated March 22, 1950, stated that "whereas monastery income before Liberation enabled monks to live like children of the Buddha in heaven, while the common people were in hell, all this has changed. The fields and property of the monasteries and nunneries used to be considered as something no one could encroach on. But now the awareness of the peasants has been raised, and monks and nuns who live off their rents must be classified as landlords." See Hong Kong *Ta-kung pao,* April 1, 1950. Compare the following statement made in 1953: "Buddhist monasteries, large and small, are mostly scattered in farming villages and mountain wastes. In the past most of them were monopolized by the tyrants and landlords that feudal society had created within Buddhism. They turned Buddhist communal property into their private possession for extravagant expenditure. In the large monastery buildings lived only a handful of their sons and grandsons [i.e., their disciples]. After Liberation, among these monopolizers, some who were cunning absconded; some who had clearly behaved like brigands were struck down by the peasantry in struggle. Therefore in the early days of Liberation, the property of many monasteries was affected to a certain extent. There were also some monasteries in the grip of die-hards. They did not flee nor were they struggled against. They did not want too many people living in their monastery. They kept dreaming about retaining control of Buddhist property and leading the typical old life of swindling donations from donors." See *HTFH,* 7/53, p. 17.

106. *Agrarian Reform Law,* pp. 40-41.

107. *Ibid.,* p. 50.

108. *HTFH,* 11/50, p. 21. This was reinforced by two directives in 1951, one applying to Tientsin and one to Peking. The Tientsin authorities had asked permission to convert run-down temples into schools. The GAC replied in August that they could do so on the following conditions. First, the temples had to be run down, without income, and to have no great influence among the masses. Second the people's representative conference of the district had to give its formal approval. Third, if monks and nuns were still living there, their consent had to be obtained and proper arrangements made for their livelihood. See *HTFH,* 11/51, p. 36. Also in August 1951 the GAC had approved a measure of the Peking Municipal Government stating that anyone wanting to use a temple with monks in residence had first to obtain their consent. See *HTFH,* 10/51, p. 3. Although these directives seemed to apply only to Tientsin and Peking, the first was distributed throughout the country in a series of reference materials on cultural objects and, as to the

second, all readers of *Modern Buddhism* were urged to cite it to cadres who laughed at their rites as superstitious. See *HTFH,* 12/51, p. 21. *Modern Buddhism* commented on the second as follows: "Some people will wonder why, when the government talks about the protection [of monasteries and temples], it is ready to have them used [by outsiders]. They should realize that in this period when intensive construction and Resist America Aid Korea are being pursued at the same time, the government needs a great deal of space and cannot put up new buildings quickly enough to get it. Hence the only solution is to borrow space from all kinds of social groups. Naturally Buddhist monasteries and temples cannot be an exception. Government authorities are deeply concerned lest this might arouse criticism, and that is why it has been specified that the consent of the head monk must first be obtained, as well as the approval of the Civil Affairs Bureau." See *HTFH,* 10/51, p. 10. The central authorities seem to have seriously intended to limit the occupation of monasteries, although their intention was not everywhere carried out at the local level.

109. See note 28 above. At the second national conference of the CBA in 1957 a Kiangsu delegate said that the problem of the utilization of monasteries and the right to their control had been solved in large cities but not in middle-size and smaller cities or in rural villages. "For example, some units are utilizing monastery buildings unilaterally, without having consulted [the head monks] and are hampering the religious activities of monks and nuns to the point where there are problems about where the monks and nuns are going to find living quarters." See *HTFH,* 5/57, p. 17.

110. On the PLA moving into the San-mei Ssu, see this chapter at note 88. Not only the land but the buildings of the T'ung-hsi Ssu, Changsha, were taken over during land reform: see *HTFH,* 3/51, p. 32. In 1951 a monk on an island in the mouth of the Yangtze wrote asking why his temple had been turned into a school: see *HTFH,* 11/51, p. 23. In Peking 219 families of servicemen killed in the Korean War were being lodged in local monasteries and temples in 1953: see *HTFH,* 6/53, p. 27. In 1958 the monks of a monastery in Chin-chiang, Fukien, were reported to have moved out of their quarters so that they could be used as barracks for troops: see *HTFH,* 11/58, p. 33. In 1962 one building at the K'ai-yüan Ssu in Fukien was being used as the Chüanchow Museum of the History of the Overseas Communication: see *China Pictorial,* 1/63, p. 13. According to an oral report the Pei-t'a Ssu, Soochow, was turned into the Industrial and Commercial School of T'ung-chi University.

No figures on the number of temples occupied were ever released. Yet such figures were collected in November, 1951, when *Modern Buddhism* asked Buddhists throughout the country to fill out a questionnaire on the condition of temples. One question was: "Are they being operated by some outside organs or have they been taken over for use by individuals? " See *HTFH,* 11/51, p. 36, and 3/52, pp. 35-36.

The history of the Communist occupation of temples goes back to 1927, when, after the failure of the Autumn Harvest Uprising in Hunan, Mao led his remnant forces to Chingkangshan on the Hunan-Kiangsi border. "All over the mountain there were Buddhist temples which could be used as hospitals, offices, and dormitories. The monks were ordered to leave." According to this source, images were used as clothes-drying racks and newspapers were printed on the back of Buddhist scrolls. See Robert Payne, *Mao Tse-tung, Ruler of Red China* (New York, 1950), p. 101.

111. Sunderlal, *China Today,* pp. 212, 360.

112. By 1960 it was said to have become a museum: see Wand B. Forman, *The Ancient Face of China* (London, 1960), p. 212. The many temples at Lo-fu Shan, not far from Canton, were permanently occupied by the army soon after Liberation.

113. The Ching-lien Ssu, Sung-chu Ssu, Ta-chung Ssu, Tz'u-hui Ssu, Ch'ang-ch'un Ssu, Pao-kuo Ssu, T'ien-ning Ssu, and Ta-fo Ssu became factories (on the last four see *Nagel's Encyclopedia-Guide: China* (Geneva, 1968), pp. 552, 553, 572, 586). The Ch'ung-hsiao Ssu and Wan-shou Ssu became schools and the Hsiang-chieh Ssu a rest home for primary school teachers (*ibid.,* p. 618). The Huang Ssu became a military barrack (*ibid.,* p. 576) and the Yen-shou Ssu was simply "out of use" (*ibid.,* p. 550). The Mo-ho An was a hospital. Information about the cases above that are not mentioned in *Nagel's Guide* came from foreigners resident in Peking who made a point of looking for ancient Buddhist landmarks. The Wan-shou Ssu had already been used as a school building under the Japanese and few of the other secularized temples had been places where Buddhism flourished before Liberation. Many temples in Shanghai must also have been secularized, but the only one I have heard about is the Kuo-en Ssu, which became a factory making radio parts in 1953.

114. See Welch, *Revival,* pp. 144-147.

115. On the prohibition of damage to monasteries, see Chapter I, notes 13-14. The destruction of monasteries in Shantung, Anhwei, and Kiangsu was reported soon after Liberation: see *HTFH,* 10/50, p. 24. In June 1950 Cheng Chen-to, head of the Monuments Office of the Cultural Bureau, in calling for an end to the destruction of ancient cultural momuments, cited as examples the Flower Pagoda at the Kuang-hui Ssu in Cheng-ting, Hopei; the Hall of the Three Great Men at the Kuang-chi Ssu, Pao-ch'ih, Hopei; and the Hai-hui Tien of the lower Hua-yen Ssu. The lumber from the last two buildings mentioned was used for bridge repair and an addition to a primary school. Cheng, who was friendly to Buddhism (see Appendix A, p. 402), stated that some provincial governments had already issued decrees to protect ancient monuments and culture, but that a lot of people did not understand their value and had demolished them in order to "utilize waste materials" so that many had been destroyed. "The examples cited above are merely the ones that we know about." See *Hsin-hua yüeh-pao,* 2.3:668 (July 1950).

116. *HTFH,* 10/50, p. 24.
117. See Chapter I at note 15.
118. *HTFH,* 5/57, p. 14.
119. *Chieh-fang jih-pao,* November 10, 1958, tr. in *SCMP,* 1943:10-11. Some small temples were used for mess-halls.
120. On the traditional system for entering the sangha and being trained in small temples, see Welch, *Practice,* pp. 132, 275, 282-283. Already in 1950 progressive Buddhist leaders in Peking had called for abolishing "the system of hereditary halls where young children are taken in and become monks." See Lan Kung-wu's remark in Appendix A, p. 401, and compare Chü-tsan's call on p. 402 for the elimination of the system of hereditary private ownership of temples.
121. The 500,000 monks in China before Liberation lived in 100,000 monasteries and temples (Welch, *Practice,* pp. 414, 419); simple arithmetic shows that the great majority of them had to live in tens of thousands of small temples. Closing the latter forced their residents to move into large public monasteries or, where these could not feed them, to disrobe. A few apparently tried to live as monks in people's houses. This probably explains an abbot's appeal in 1957 that more public monasteries be repaired so that "a number of Buddhist monks who are living scattered in various places can lead a collective Buddhist life": see *HTFH,* 5/57, p. 21-22.
122. On October 6, 1950, Ch'en Ch'i-yüan, head of the Social Affairs Department of the Ministry of Internal Affairs stated that, according to an incomplete survey, there were 500,000-600,000 monks and nuns living in 200,000-300,000 monasteries and nunneries: see *HTFH,* 11/50, p. 6. In November 1956 Chao P'u-ch'u presented a report to the Fourth Conference of the World Fellowship of Buddhists in which he stated that there were 500,000 monks and nuns and 100 million Buddhist followers: see *Report of the Fourth World Buddhist Conference* (Kathmandu, n.d.), p. 101. So far as I know, this was the first public commitment—before an international public at that—to figures that were frequently repeated thereafter, e.g., in NCNA, March 31, 1957 (*SCMP,* 1503:10). Cf. *HTFH,* 12/56, p. 13. In October 1957 Ho Ch'eng-hsiang told a Japanese visitor that there were about 500,000 members of the sangha, living in about 50,000 temples (*Chūgai nippō,* November 11, 1957). In 1958 the figure was given as 500,000 including lamas: see *Che-hsüeh yen-chiu,* 1/58, p. 39. The same figure was quoted late in 1961 by an official of the Chinese Buddhist Association. It can be argued that 500,000 is less than 500,000-600,000; and that 500,000 *including* lamas implies fewer Chinese monks than 500,000 *without* lamas; but the first sign of real hesitation about the round figure of "half a million" came in February 1963 when it was stated that "Buddhist monks and nuns number several hundreds of thousands in China": see *International Buddhist News Forum* (Rangoon), 2.12-3.2:12 (December 1962-February 1963); and *World Buddhism,* 12.4:6-7 (November 1963). Yet about 1964 an official of the

Religious Affairs Bureau in Peking told an Austrian visitor: "There are 400,000-500,000 Buddhist monks, nuns, and lamas in China": see Hugo Portisch, *Red China Today* (Chicago, 1966), pp. 284-285. The number of lamas in Inner Mongolia was 23,000 in 1958: see *JMJP,* May 21, 1958, tr. in *CB,* 509:37. The number of lamas in Tibet was 150,000 before the Tibetan rebellion in 1959 and 110,000 afterwards: see NCNA, April 9, 1960, tr. in *CB,* 626:15.

123. On the "more than 2,000" at the time of Liberation, see *HTFH,* 3/52, p. 14. On the 1,090 as of March 19, 1950, see Hong Kong *Ta-kung pao,* April 1, 1950. By October 1957 the number had dropped to 600: see Tsukamoto and Makita, p. 304.

124. See *HTFH,* 6/53, p. 46. Pao-sheng started the restoration of the K'ai-fu Ssu in 1922. Towards the end of the Republican period it had been occupied by Nationalist troops. See *HTFH,* 11/59, pp. 28-30. Monasteries like this where monks from other temples were concentrated often became the headquarters of the local Buddhist Association; or their historical importance enabled them to play a continuing role in people's diplomacy (like the Hsing-shan Ssu in Sian). Monasteries that served no such functions often lost most of their residents (e.g., Chin Shan and the Hua-t'ing Ssu). See Appendix C.

125. The policy was alluded to by Chü-tsan in 1950 when he spoke of "concentrating monks into groups to serve production." See Appendix A, p. 398. He repeated the point in 1952: "There are too few monks and nuns for the number of temples, so how can all the temples be maintained? Therefore the only thing to do is to select the important ones, preserving the famous mountains, the ancient monuments, and the large public monasteries." See *HTFH,* 1/52, p. 6. In 1952, answering a reader's inquiry, *Modern Buddhism* said that it was a good idea for monks from many different monasteries to move into one monastery, bringing their Buddha images with them. The monasteries vacated would provide space for government offices; and the move "would be advantageous to the protection of monasteries and spreading the dharma." See *HTFH,* 2/52, p. 26.

126. Ta-pei, then abbot of the Ling-yin Ssu, Hangchow, told the second plenary council meeting of the Chinese Buddhist Association in August 1955: "There are over 4,100 monasteries and nunneries, large and small and over 11,100 monks and nuns in our province of Chekiang." See *HTFH,* 9/55, p. 21. In the 1930's Chekiang had about 53,000 monasteries and nunneries and about 108,000 monks and nuns (Welch, *Practice,* pp. 412, 417). At the second national conference of the CBA in 1957 a Kiangsu delegate, Ming-shan, stated that Kiangsu had about 7,000 monasteries and nunneries and about 20,000 monks and nuns: see *HTFH,* 5/57, p. 17. That compares with about 79,000 monasteries and nunneries in the 1930's and 172,000 monks and nuns (Welch, *Practice,* pp. 412, 417). These figures may be tabulated as follows (in percent):

	Population reduced by	*Institutions reduced by*
Kiangsu (1957)	88	91
Chekiang (1955)	90	92

The greater drop for institutions is consistent with the idea that a higher proportion of small temples was closed down than of large monasteries.

We may assume that by 1957 the monastic population of Chekiang had gone down even further because of death and secularization, so that the overall decline in these two provinces during the first eight years after Liberation was closer to 90 percent than to 88 percent. On the importance of Kiangsu and Chekiang as the heart-land of modern Chinese Buddhism, see Welch, *Practice,* pp. 295-296; *Revival,* pp. 246-252.

The only other provincial figure I have seen is for Ninghsia, where, between 1949 and 1953, 34 out of the 112 monks and nuns in the region returned to lay life, about 14 to work in government departments, about 14 to engage in production labor, and 7 or 8 to attend school. See *HTFH,* 6/53, p. 32. This is a much lower rate of secularization than in Kiangsu and Chekiang but also much less significant because far fewer people were involved.

127. It could be argued that most of the 90 percent drop occurred *before* 1949 (since the base figures are for 1931). Yet this does not fit in with what we know about Buddhism in the two decades before Liberation. Large-scale annual ordinations were still held, and the reasons that had prompted people to become monks in the past continued to operate. Although there was economic hardship, I have heard of no cases where it caused monks to leave monasteries or the monasteries to close down. Before the Communist victory no major effort had been made by any Republican government to reduce the size of the sangha.

Furthermore *Modern Buddhism* sometimes hinted or openly admitted that a major drop in the number of monks and nuns had taken place *since* Liberation. For example, when a reader wrote to *Modern Buddhism* in 1951 asking how the sangha could be prevented from shrinking further, he was told that its size was no criterion of its prosperity. After all, in Hsuan-tsang's time there had been only 80,000 monks and nuns, whereas when the persecution came under Wu Tsung, there had been almost three million (*sic*), so "one can see that the prosperity of Buddhism and the number of monks and nuns bear an inverse relationship to each other." See *HTFH,* 8/51, p. 23. The same point–that Buddhism was most prosperous when the number of monks was reduced–was made again eight years later: see *HTFH,* 7/59, p. 19. The outright admission that the sangha had been greatly reduced came in the beginning of 1952, when Chü-tsan stated that "before Liberation there were about 800,000 monks and nuns, two or three living in each temple on the average. Since Liberation there has been a great reduction in the number of monks and nuns, and if those remaining were distributed evenly in the 300,000 monasteries and temples, I am afraid that each of the latter would have only one monk or nun." See *HTFH,* 1/52, p. 6. Since this amounts to saying that the sangha had been reduced to 300,000–a 62.5 percent drop–it is inconsistent with the figures published before and after (see note 122). It would appear that some time in 1952 or 1953 the decision was made to conceal the decline in monastic population, perhaps because of the plan to use Buddhism in people's diplomacy. See Chapter VI at note 23.

128. *HTFH,* 6/60, p. 34. Despite their fear, the nuns did join the coöperative and set up a factory for making sandpaper.

129. See *Nei-cheng nien-chien* (Internal affairs yearbook; Shanghai, 1936), IV, F126. The dénouement is there described as follows: "The Ministry of Internal Affairs accepted the points submitted by the Chinese Buddhist Association as not without merit, but for the country's Buddhist and Taoist monks to be so numerous, with all their food and clothing provided by others, was not compatible with the current economic tide. What was involved was the reform of religious life, and so it was proposed that as a first step the Buddhist and Taoist associations be directed to pay attention to the training of Buddhist and Taoist monks in vocational skills; and that, with due consideration for the circumstances, monasteries and temples also be instructed to start vocational [enterprises] in order that, besides performing rites for the dead, they might serve production, so that the innumerable members of the sangha would become self supporting."

130. For a more complete description of this work-study center, see Welch, *Revival,* p. 353. On earlier Buddhist plans to engage in production, see *ibid.*, p. 354. The Nationalists had had a land reform program on the books since 1942 but did not carry it out until after they moved to Taiwan, completing it in October 1953–only nine months after the completion of land reform on the Mainland. Landlords, including monasteries, were allowed to retain about 45 mou and got modest compensation for the land "compulsorily purchased." The result was to limit the number of monks that a single monastery could support from land rents alone; and, in fact, there are no large monasteries in Taiwan today like those that used to exist on the Mainland.

III. MAKING MONKS INTO GOOD CITIZENS

1. In the Pratimoksa the seventy-third of the ninety Patayantika rules forbids a *bhiksu* from digging the ground with his own hands or getting some one else to do it for him. See W. Pachow, *A Comparative Study of the Pratimoksa* (Santiniketan, Sino-Indian Cultural Society, 1955), p. 161. This is the tenth of these rules in the Pali version: see *The Patimokkha: 227 Fundamental Rules of a Bhikkhu* (Bangkok, Social Science Association Press of Thailand, 1966), p. 48. It is also the tenth in Chinese: see Samuel Beal, *A Catena of Buddhist Scriptures from the Chinese* (London, Trübner and Com-

pany, 1871), p. 221. Progressive Buddhists did not deny that some monastic rules interfered with production. Thus *Modern Buddhism* reported in 1958 that monks and nuns in Chin-chiang, Fukien, had "broken their regular rules" (*ta-p'o ch'ang-kuei*) and left the monastery to take part in productive labor: see *HTFH,* 11/58, p. 33.

2. The example of Pai-chang was often cited by progressive Buddhists after 1949. Sometimes they also pointed to Tao-an (312-385) and Fa-hsien (c.335-c.420) as being among the first people in feudal society other than peasants to engage in agricultural labor: see *HTFH,* 11/59, p. 28. Tao-an had indeed worked in the fields when he was a novice—because his master did not consider him good for anything better.

Partly because the existing editions of Pai-chang's Pure Rules do not specify that monks should support themselves by growing their own rice, these editions were declared to be forgeries compiled by successive feudal emperors and to have no connection with Pai-chang's original rules. See *HTFH,* 8/59, p. 21. Cf. Welch, *Practice,* pp. 105-107.

3. *HTFH,* 7/53, p. 18.

4. Informants who lived at Yün-chü Shan have testified to the genuine enthusiasm that monks there felt for the revival of "farming Ch'an" under the charismatic leadership of Hsü-yün. Cf. *HTFH,* 5/57, p. 25. Their enthusiasm dropped off only when the demands for labor and study seriously reduced their capacity to participate in meditation. At other monasteries, where charismatic leadership like Hsü-yün's was lacking, enthusiasm for "farming Ch'an" may always have been less.

5. *HTFH,* 9/50, p. 22. Cf. Appendix A.

6. *HTFH,* 10/50, p. 22.

7. *HTFH,* 3/56, p. 22. Cf. Chapter II at note 59.

8. *HTFH,* 3/56, p. 22, which cites the *P'u-hsien hsing-yüan p'in,* where I have been unable to locate it.

9. *HTFH,* 3/56, p. 21.

10. *HTFH*, 11/59, p. 29.

11. *HTFH,* 6/58, p. 24 and *HTFH,* 7/59, p. 34. This passage is especially interesting because it contrasts such labor with monastery chores. "In temples formerly we carried water and lugged firewood, burned incense and swept the floor, grew vegetables and planted trees, thinking that this kind of work assured our future happiness as individuals. Now we know that 'to purify the buddha land, beautify the land, and show kindness to living creatures' are even greater Buddhist services (*fo-shih*). Therefore we all look on labor as having the greatest merit of any kind of Buddhist service." More will be said in Chapter VIII about the reinterpretation of phrases like "beautifying the land."

12. *HTFH,* 6/53, p. 54. He had been in sealed confinement for eighteen years at the Kan-lu Ssu, Chiu-hua Shan. On sealed confinement (*pi-kuan*), see Welch, *Practice,* pp. 321-323. Other examples of a change in life style can be

cited. At the Asoka Monastery "one 55-year-old monk named Ch'an-ching, who had previously had the manner of a dignified old scholar, now took off his long monk's gown and played badminton. The masses reacted by saying, 'The New China and the new society can certainly transform people. The old become young and the stiff become lively.' " See *HTFH,* 5/53, p. 13.

13. In statements by Buddhist leaders after 1949 I have seen only one reference to idealism that was not hostile, and it was for foreign consumption: see chapter VIII, note 80.

14. *HTFH,* 5/56, p. 49, 6/58, p. 26, etc., quoted from p. 50 of the Northern Sung edition of the Platform Sutra. This is the Kōshōji edition cited by Philip Yampolsky (to whom I am indebted for this reference) in his *The Platform Sutra of the Sixth Patriarch* (New York, Columbia University Press, 1967), p. 191.

15. P'ang Yün, a lay disciple of Ma-tsu, wrote the famous lines (often quoted by progressive Buddhists after 1949),

> How wondrous it is! What a miracle!
> I draw water, I carry wood.

16. *HTFH,* 4/53, p. 15.

17. *HTFH,* 11/50, p. 20. This was the first report on study by Buddhists to be published in *Modern Buddhism.* A month earlier Chü-tsan had said: "If we continue in our old ways and give no thought to reform, the times will not put up with us." See *HTFH,* 10/50, p. 20.

18. Reports of study that have been utilized in making some of the generalizations that follow but that are not cited in the notes below include the following pages in *HTFH*: 9/50, p. 20 (Hangchow); 4/51, p. 32 (Wuhan); 5/52, p. 22 (Fukien); 12/51, p. 36, 2/53, p. 28, and 2/54, pp. 24-25 (Shensi); 6/53, p. 50 (Chungking); 9/53, p. 29 (T'ien-t'ai Shan); 2/55, p. 30 (Hunan); 1/56, p. 28 (P'u-t'o Shan); 8/58, p. 32 (Szechwan).

19. A notable exception was a number of study groups that met in Wuhan July-October 1950; they were led by comrades from the People's Court, the Justice Department, and a primary school: see *HTFH,* 12/50, p. 31.

20. Reports of study starting much later than this can perhaps be explained as referring to the resumption rather than the inauguration of classes. For example, in 1956 the CPPCC Kiangsu Provincial Committee set up a Buddhist Study Committee to make plans for starting patriotic study classes in Kiangsu (see *HTFH,* 5/57, p. 17, and *Hsin-hua jih-pao,* Sept. 2, 1956). It is hard to believe that no study had as yet been held in this, the province with the largest monastic population. Perhaps the classes held before then had not born the label "patriotic" or perhaps what we have here is merely the start of a new *series* of partriotic study classes. Study is mentioned in Shanghai as early as the spring of 1949: see Alfred Kiang, p. 174, and Hong Kong *Ta-kung pao,* July 12, 1950.

21. A good example of an early study program is the one published by the Changsha Buddhist Study Committee in *HTFH,* 11/50, pp. 23-25.

22. For examples, see *HTFH,* 4/51, p. 32; 4/52, p. 32; 4/53, p. 28; and *Chüeh yu-ch'ing,* 22.6-7:24 (July 1951). I have not heard of such "patriotic compacts" (*ai-kuo kung-yüeh*) being signed by the residents of any monastery before Liberation, but for centuries the larger monasteries had used codes of rules (*kuei-yüeh* rather than *kung-yüeh*) that served the leading monks as operating manuals. Sometimes programs for special occasions would be drawn up, in one case, for example, promising that on Amitabha's birthday in 1924 Buddhists would "pray for the people and the country": see James Bissett Pratt, *The Pilgrimage of Buddhism and a Buddhist Pilgrimage* (Macmillan, New York, 1928), p. 367.

23. Study in Canton began in the autumn of 1949 when Lo Hua, the head of United Front Work Department, decided to do something about the re-education of the city's monks and nuns. He started a training class for a small number of activists, who were afterwards to lead study on a larger scale. This was similar to what happened in Peking, where the three-month study class that started January 16, 1950, was not open to everyone. Over 70 monks and nuns were recommended by Peking temples, which filled out questionnaires and supplied biographies for each of them. They were then given written and oral examinations to ascertain their competence and the best 30 were admitted to the class. Social background played a major role in selection: less than a third of those admitted had gotten beyond primary school. See *HTFH,* 11/50, p. 20.

To return to Canton, the training of study leaders had to be suspended in spring of 1950 because the cadres in charge of it were re-assigned to the registration of social groups. Early in 1951 the Civil Affairs Bureau set up a Buddhist Patriotic Study Class, but a year later this too had to be suspended when responsibility for religious affairs was transferred from the Civil Affairs Bureau to the newly established Religious Affairs Division. The latter did not get around to organizing study for Buddhists, who were of less concern than Christians, until the summer of 1953. After a few months it was decided that greater efficiency would be achieved if the followers of different religions met in joint rather than separate classes. The Buddhist classes were suspended until this could be arranged, but, when it was arranged, it proved unsatisfactory because the followers of each religion responded best to a different approach. In 1954 separate classes resumed under a new organ, the Buddhist Patriotic Study Committee, which in 1956 became a department of the Preparatory Committee for the Canton Buddhist Association. This same on-again off-again pattern can be seen in reports of special study programs in other places, e.g., study of the general line by Peking monks and nuns in 1954 (*HTFH,* 3/54, p. 27), study of the first Five-Year Plan for the last quarter of 1955 (*HTFH,* 2/56, p. 30), and the *winter* study class in Shensi (*HTFH,* 2/55, p. 29).

From the outset in Canton the meeting place for classes was the Liu-jung Ssu, the principal monastery of the city. After 1952 attendance was compulsory for all monks and nuns, though not for lay devotees. Absence was noted, investigated, and, if no good excuse was forthcoming, the absentee could be criticized. In fact, however, attendance varied with the political climate. In 1954-55 it was running 180-200 (out of a total of about 300 monks and nuns); during the relaxation of 1956-57, it dropped to 70-80. This was partly because many had taken advantage of the chance to emigrate to Hong Kong and overseas but also because excuses for nonattendance were more readily accepted: one could plead business, devotions, visitors, and so on.

The usual schedule was to have one four-hour meeting a week. How it was conducted would depend on whether or not the religious affairs cadres had information of special importance to transmit. This did not necessarily relate to a campaign. In early 1955, for example, when the new currency was introduced, it had to be carefully explained to monks and nuns, just as to other elements of the population. On such occasions the cadre in charge might talk for the entire four hours. There would be no time for discussion. On other occasions, when he had less to say, questions and discussion would follow. These classes, at which all monks and nuns would sit together in one large hall, were called "plenary sessions" (*ta-k'o*). Usually they alternated every other week with small-group meetings, each of twenty persons or so, who would either discuss what the cadre had said in the last plenary session; or read newspapers and magazines. Most of the small groups were headed by nuns among whom it was easier to find activists, though their educational level was lower. (In Wuhan too nuns were said to be the ones who showed a special enthusiam for study: see *HTFH,* 12/50, p. 31).

There is little in the Mainland press that would confirm or contradict the above details on study given by the cadre from the Canton Religious Affairs Bureau. In late 1950 the monks of the Liu-jung Ssu were reported to be conducting group study every day: see Hong Kong *Hsing-tao jih-pao,* November 6, 1950. On the other hand in 1951 Buddhists from all over Canton were attending *ta-k'o* only once a week—every Monday: see *Chüeh-yu ch'ing,* 12.10:24 (October 1951).

24. These colloquia (*tso-t'an hui*) were sponsored by the CBA—its first such nationwide effort. The earliest of them started in January and the last ended in May. Each went on for about two months and they were attended in all by 1,100 monks, nuns and devotees (see *HTFH,* 5/62, p. 22). The themes studied are well illustrated by the following summary of the meeting for Buddhists in the north and northeast, held in Peking. "After studying for more than one month, an absolute majority of the participants clearly realized that Buddhists must join the rest of the people in the whole country in resolutely taking the road of socialism under the leadership of the Communist Party. Socialism is the great cause that affects the happiness of

six hundred million people, and Buddhists, since they belong to the people, must be fervently patriotic and love socialism, striving to raise their political awareness and actively participating in socialist construction. Buddhists definitely cannot put up their religious belief as a pretext for rejecting the leadership of the Communist Party, just as they cannot use their religious belief as a reason for rejecting patriotism. Religious belief is a question of ideological belief, a personal matter, whereas the refusal to accept the leadership of the Communist Party is a political question, a public matter of importance that affects the fate of the state and the people. Buddhists should coöperate with the people of the whole country politically. By accepting the leadership of the Communist Party, being patriotic and law-abiding, and taking the socialist road, Buddhists are laying a common foundation for political coöperation with the people of the whole country." (NCNA, March 11, 1958, tr. in *SCMP,* 1733:1).

These colloquia were considered important enough to be addressed by high-level cadres. In Wuhan, for example, where Chou Shu-chia arrived from Peking to chair the meetings, there were speeches by Chang Chih-i, the deputy director of the United Front Work Department, and Ch'en I-hsin, the vice-governor of Hupeh. The 182 participants came from Hupeh, Hunan, Honan, Kiangsi, and Kwangtung to attend the sessions, which lasted from March 2 through May 3. See *Hupeh jih-pao,* May 4, 1958, and *HTFH,* 6/58, p. 23. The participants then transmitted what they had learned to the Buddhists of their own localities; in some cases teams took the news about to individual monasteries. For example, from September 25 to October 3 representatives of the Buddhists of Shih-ch'eng hsien, Kiangsi, heard a report on the spring symposium in Wuhan. Then, after a week of study, they signed a patriotic compact promising to take the socialist road, surrender their hearts to the Party, cleanse Buddhism of reactionary elements, and so on. See *HTFH,* 11/58, p. 32. One gets the impression that on the local level the anti-rightist struggle was not so fierce as it had been in the regional symposia. On the symposium in Sian, see *HTFH,* 7/58, p. 18; in Chengtu *HTFH,* 6/58, p. 24; in Shanghai *HTFH,* 7/58, p. 17; in Peking NCNA March 11, 1958, tr. in *SCMP* 1733:1. On the local meetings for Fukien May 10-24, see *HTFH,* 9/58, p. 32, 10/58, p. 21; for Hunan June 20-July 9, see Peking *Kuang-ming jih-pao* August 8, 1958, tr. in *SCMP* 1837:39. Other local meetings are covered in *HTFH,* 6/58, pp. 24-25; 9/58, pp. 27, 28, 32; 11/58, p. 32; 12/58, p. 33; *Chi-lin jih-pao* June 20, 1958 (tr. in *SCMP,* 1834:10-11), and *Kuei-chou jih-pao* July 10, 1958 (tr. in JPRS, 1184N, pp. 25-26). In some cases these local meetings set up Buddhist associations for their areas (like the Canton Municipal Buddhist Association and the Fukien branch of the CBA).

25. *Hu-pei jih-pao,* May 4, 1958.

26. *HTFH,* 12/50, p. 31.

27. This information comes from a monk who was there at the time. On the evening meditation period see Welch, *Practice,* pp. 73, 436. For examples

of Hsü-yün's Explanations, see Lu K'uan Yü, *Ch'an and Zen teaching,* 1st ser. (London, Rider, 1960), pp. 49-109.

28. This compact was drawn up on July 21, 1958, after two months of intensive study (starting May 24). The monks then went to work making charcoal for the iron smelting campaign: see *HTFH,* 11/58, p. 34.

29. E.g., *HTFH,* 7/58, p. 18 (Sian) and see next note. Several have been translated into English. A good example is from Heilungkiang: see *HTFH,* 12/58, p. 33, tr. in JPRS, 1461-N:48-51. "Patriotic compacts" had long been a common device for mobilizing the masses. During the early 1950's they had been signed not only by monks, but by peasants promising to increase their crop production. Another device was the "patriotic competition," held in order to determine which monastery could show the greatest labor enthusiasm, frugality, cleanliness, etc. A good example was the ten-point challenge by the Buddhists of I-yang to those in three other places in Hunan: see *HTFH,* 8/58, p. 29, tr. in URS 13:75-77 and JPRS, 613D:45-46.

30. For examples of such clauses in patriotic compacts, see *HTFH,* 9/58, pp. 27, 28, 29; 11/58, pp. 32-33; 12/58, pp. 33, 34. Restrictions on accepting disciples and offering hospitality to wandering monks are dealt with in Chapter IV.

31. These two quotations come from *HTFH,* 6/58, pp. 25, 27. The article in which they appear is typical of many that were printed in 1958. On Buddhists handing over their hearts (minds) to the Party (*hsiang-tang chiao-hsin*), see *HTFH,* 7/58, p. 18; 9/58, p. 27; 12/58, pp. 32, 33. The campaign for people to surrender their hearts to the Party had been called for by Mao in his speech of February 27, 1957.

32. The last intensive study campaign for Buddhists seems to have been conducted in 1959. Its theme was the Tibetan rebellion taken in conjunction with the policy of freedom of religious belief: see *HTFH,* 10/59, p. 11.

33. *HTFH,* 3/52, p. 15. A similar account of the remolding of a monk at the Nan-ch'an Ssu is given in *HTFH,* 5/52, p. 22. I tend to discount the often perfunctory claims to success in study put forward in work reports.

34. *HTFH,* 5/53, p. 26; 11/58, p. 34.

35. *HTFH,* 10/57, p. 29, and *Chi-lin jih-pao,* June 20, 1958.

36. *HTFH,* 11/50, pp. 20-21. Poor attendance was also the reason study sessions were discontinued in Ningpo in the summer of 1950.

37. *HTFH,* 6/53, p. 53. The same was true at another sacred mountain, Chiu-hua Shan, and there only a third of the residents took part in the reading teams: see *HTFH,* 4/53, p. 27; 6/53, p. 55.

38. See, for example, *HTFH,* 8/58, p. 19.

39. *HTFH,* 5/53, pp. 12-15.

40. These dilemmas are reflected in the statement that "the inability of monks and nuns to unite [for remolding] is a universal phenomenon . . . In Wen-ling [Chekiang] the reason is perhaps because the most respected monks

are unwilling to play a leading role, while those who are willing to lead are backward feudal elements who are careless in their behavior and have not won the confidence of various quarters." See *HTFH,* 4/51, p. 30.

41. See, for example, *HTFH,* 12/51, p. 36 (Shensi); 2/53, p. 28 (Shensi); 4/53, p. 28 (Kwangsi). Sessions dealing with doctrine were presumably led by monks, not by cadres.

42. *HTFH,* 5/57, p. 4. Chao was admitting that the CBA had given little concrete help to the conduct of local study groups. He criticized the monks who opposed political study as having "forgotten that 'the dharma is in the world, there is no enlightenment apart from the world,' and 'bodhi belongs to all living creatures . . .' Forgettting this leads inevitably to 'scorching the bud or spoiling the seed' and it is incompatible with the rights and duties of citizens of the Chinese People's Republic." (Cf. the passage referenced in note 14.)

43. See the statement by Lung-yü in *HTFH,* 5/57, p. 24, and compare the statements by Ming-shan (p. 17), K'uan-neng (pp. 19-20), Miao-tzu, Hui-wen, and Ming-k'ai (p. 24), Ch'un-hsin, Pen-huan, Chüeh-ch'eng, and Chang Po-lin (p. 25). Several of these delegates suggested that *Modern Buddhism* should publish study materials on Buddhist doctrine.

44. Even more striking was the fact that when a reporter from a government news agency visited the monastery and asked to see the monks performing their morning devotions, the abbot politely declined permission, saying: "We people who live outside the secular world prefer to be alone and undisturbed when performing devotions and so we never allow anyone to look on." See *Chung-kuo hsin-wen,* June 22, 1957. If the abbot was motivated by caution (because of the anti-rightist movement, which had just begun), it is strange that he would speak of monks "living outside the secular world."

45. *HTFH,* 5/57, p. 4.

46. *HTFH,* 2/62, p. 21 (May 1962). Despite Chao's appeal for more political study, monks in many parts of China, after listening to reports on the Third National Conference, called for study of the doctrines and practice of the different schools of Buddhism: see *HTFH,* 6/62, p. 39 (December 1962).

47. On sangha officials under the Ch'ing see Welch, *Revival,* pp. 135-136. So far as I know, no monk ever held any public office during the Republican period.

48. See, for example, *HTFH,* 9/50, p. 31; 3/53, p. 29; 6/53, pp. 27, 29, 39, 49, 55; 7/53, p. 27; 8/54, p. 29; 5/61, p. 46; *Hōchū Nihon Bukkyō,* p. 15; *Chiang-hsi jih-pao,* May 3, 1957. Sometimes an appreciable portion of the sangha was involved. In 1957, for example, 5 of the 96 monks and nuns in Taiyüan were elected people's representatives at the provincial, municipal, or district level: see *HTFH,* 5/57, p. 23.

49. In 1954, for example, a Kansu monk reported on the local people's congress to the workers and businessmen of his district (*HTFH,* 8/54, p. 28), and a Kwangtung monk reported to his Muslim and Roman Catholic constitu-

ents (*ibid.*, p. 29). Monks were also eligible, like other representatives, for higher responsibilities. In Sining, for example, one was appointed to the Municipal Control Commission (*HTFH*, 6/53, p. 34).

50. In 1963 a Japanese delegation was told that there were seven "cadre monks" of the CBA and thirteen Buddhist lay believers who were delegates to the NPC and CPPCC: see *Ganjin wajō keisan hōchū Nihon Bukkyō daihyō-dan hokoku* (Tokyo, Zen Nihon Bukkyokai, 1963), p. 14. These figures may have included Tibetans and other members of minority nationalities.

51. For the Election Law, see *CB* 233:1. Counterrevolutionaries as well as landlords were disenfranchised under article 5. Cf. Chapter I at note 6.

52. For some examples of labor union membership, see *Chüeh yu-ch'ing*, 12.10:24 (October 1951), *HTFH*, 11/51, p. 23; on peasant association membership, see *HTFH*, 3/51, p. 32; 4/53, pp. 15-16; 5/57, p. 25; on the youth league, *HTFH*, 3/56, p. 32; 6/53, pp. 27, 29; 12/54, p. 27; 11/56, p. 36; 6/58, pp. 25-29; 11/59, p. 29; NCNA, June 11, 1953; on the women's federation, *HTFH*, 2/53, p. 28; 6/53, p. 27; 9/54, p. 22. The fact that *some* monks and nuns joined such groups in *some* places does not, of course, prove that many joined throughout the country. It seems logical to suppose that only progressive activists were involved and that they only joined groups controlled by cadres who were not strongly anti-clerical or who responded to pressure from the religious affairs organ of their area.

53. See, for example, the article "Communists Are Thoroughgoing Atheists" by Chu Ch'ing in *Min-tsu t'uan-chieh*, 3/59, pp. 17-18.

54. Edgar Faure, *The Serpent and the Tortoise* (London, 1958), p. 152. He was told this by officers of the CBA.

55. See Chapter I, notes 77 and 139.

56. *HTFH*, 2/53, p. 27.

57. Several such occasions are reported in early 1951 when pressure for monks to enlist was probably at its height. See *HTFH*, 2/51, p. 35, and cf. 4/51, pp. 32, 35.

58. Part of his story was published in *Hsin-sheng pao* (Taipei), January 1, 1966.

59. On these vows see Beal, *A Catena of Buddhist Scriptures*, pp. 209, 225-226; and cf. Pachow, *A Comparative Study of the Prātimoksa*, pp. 75, 144-145. Killing was also forbidden by the tenth vow of the *Fan-wang ching*: see J. J. M. De Groot, *Le Code du Mahayana en Chine* (Amsterdam, 1893), pp. 46-47. In Theravada countries monks have always been exempt from military service (as they were in China before 1933). One of the questions asked candidates for ordination is: "Are you exempt from military service?" See Henry Clarke Warren, *Buddhism in Translations* (New York, Atheneum, 1963), p. 399. This question means literally "Are you a servant of the king?" and could be interpreted to refer to any involvement with government.

60. See Welch, *Revival*, pp. 45, 127-128.

61. Monks called for the formation of ambulance units in 1950-1951 (*JMJP,* November 12, 1950, and *HTFH,* 4/51, p. 32), but I have found no evidence that they were ever set up.

62. *HTFH,* 12/53, p. 29.

63. At Omei Shan, for example, 30 monks had joined the army by 1953. This was 11 percent of the 264 monks then resident on the mountain, but 23 percent of those under 40 and 55 percent of those under 25 (assuming that the age distribution of the 28 resident nuns was the same as for the monks). See *HTFH,* 6/53, p. 56. On the other hand, there had apparently been a thousand monks and nuns residing there when the drive for enlistment was at its height (see Appendix C, note 80). If we use this figure as a base, only 5 percent of the monks had joined the army. At Chiu-hua Shan the number of monks rose from 96 to 104 between 1950 and 1953; during this period 6 monks had joined the army. See *HTFH,* 11/50, p. 32; 6/53, p. 54. At the Yü-wang Ssu, Ningpo, the 18 young monks who set up a militia unit in 1952 were 16 percent of the total number in residence, but 78 percent of those under 30. See *HTFH,* 4/53, p. 16.

No one was drafted into China's armed forces until experimental conscription began at the end of 1954. After the Military Service Law was approved in July 1955, all male citizens on reaching eighteen were required to serve three years in the army or up to five years in other branches of the service. See *CB,* 344:4-11. Before this the armed forces consisted of volunteers who had been recruited, in the words of one specialist, "through social pressures": see Ellis Joffe, *Party and Army: Professionalism and Political Control in the Chinese Officer Corps 1949-1964* (Cambridge, Mass., Harvard University Press, 1967), pp. 38-39. The recruitment of the monk from Szechwan provides a good example of the forms that such social pressures could take. I have seen no mention of monks being conscripted under the Military Service Law passed in 1955. Perhaps by this time there were almost no monks left who were fit for conscription.

64. *HTFH,* 4/51, p. 34.

65. *Buddhists in New China,* Chinese Buddhist Association, comp. (Peking, 1956), pp. 160-161, shows more than 20 monks and nuns holding paper cutouts of doves of peace during a parade before the T'ien-an Men, as well as placards reading "Protect world peace." The inside front cover of *HTFH,* 6/56, shows monks waving mock lotus fronds in a May Day parade before the T'ien-an Men. Although I have found no photograph of it, for at least one National Day monks organized a "war-drum corps," using drums and gongs from the altar to beat time for marching troops: see *HTFH,* 4/53, p. 16. This was so offensive to Buddhist principles that it may have been deliberately contrived to symbolize the end of monks' separation from the secular world.

66. The last three quotations come from *HTFH,* 3/52, p. 13. In 1952 an elder of the Asoka Monastery sang a song from Peking opera to celebrate the

31st anniversary of the Chinese Communist Party, and after the autumn harvest the monks there organized a spare-time drama troupe. See *HTFH,* 4/53, p. 16.

67. See Welch, *Practice,* p. 23. The only reference that I have seen to Buddhist afforestation work during the Republican period involved Ting-hu Shan, one of the largest monasteries in Kwangtung. Every monk who came there had to plant 500 seedling trees and look after them; only then was he free to live at peace in the monastery without further obligation. See *Tai Chi-tao hsien-sheng wen-ts'un,* ed. Ch'en T'ien-hsi, (Taipei, 1959), pp. 1240-1241.

68. *HTFH,* 6/51, p. 36. Cf. 9/54, p. 24 where the secular advantages of afforestation work were pointed out to monks: it would prevent floods, arrest the expansion of deserts, preserve the fertility of the soil, provide marketable timber, and attract tourists by making the environs of the mountain more beautiful. The trees recommended for planting were cedar, cyprus, elm, ash, and pine. In terms of its religious advantages, afforestation was justified by the fact that it would provide better surroundings in which to study and practice Buddhism, and monks would gain merit by purifying both their minds and their land at the same time. It also followed the Buddha's teaching that "if monks plant a tree for each of the Three Jewels, one bearing fruit, one flowers, and one leaves, the result will be boundless happiness." This quotation is from the *P'i-ni ching* (presumably *Taishō* 1489) chüan 5, *shang,* as cited by I-fang in *HTFH,* 6/56, p. 22.

69. See, for example, Chapter II at note 52. S. D. Richardson, a New Zealand silviculturalist who toured China widely in 1963, became skeptical of the high survival rates–70 to 90 percent–claimed by the Chinese foresters he talked to. He found that what some of them meant by 75 percent survival was that in 75 percent of the groups planted one or more trees had survived, yet the tree survival rate might be as low as 5 percent. In some places he observed "atrocious planting practices," but unfortunately he does not seem to have visited any of the plantations started by Buddhist monasteries. See S. D. Richardson, *Forestry in Communist China* (Baltimore, 1966), pp. 62-63.

70. *HTFH,* 6/53, p. 23. At the end of 1955, 23,592 of the trees planted on Wu-t'ai up to then were said to be still alive: see *HTFH,* 10/56, p. 31. In 1958 it was claimed that 750 mou of wasteland had been reforested. See *HTFH,* 6/58, p. 27.

71. *HTFH,* 1/55, p. 29.

72. On the 1956 activities see *HTFH,* 3/56, p. 6; 4/56, p. 5; 6/56, p. 22; 5/56, p. 52; and 10/56, p. 31; on the 1958-59 activities, see 5/58, p. 21; 7/58, p. 19; 11/58, p. 32; 12/58, p. 34; 10/59, p. 12. The last page cited states that 30 to 40 monks on Wu-t'ai Shan earned 6,000 JMP in 3 months by planting trees. Although the State Council issued its first directive on afforestation in 1953, little appears to have been done until after the national conference on

forestry was held in 1955. In each of the next two years about 4 million hectares were planted; then 26 million in 1958 and 19 million in 1959. Despite contradictory figures, it seems that 1958 was the year when claims, if not trees planted, were at their maximum. See Richardson, *Forestry,* pp. 55-62.

73. *HTFH,* 6/56, p. 22. The monk in charge of an afforestation team on P'u-t'o Shan in 1956 was elected to the CBA council the following year: see *HTFH,* 5/56, p. 52; 5/57, pp. 22, 28.

74. *HTFH,* 12/56, pp. 28-29. For examples of work on flood prevention, see *HTFH,* 11/54, p. 29; 7/59, p. 34; on anti-illiteracy work, see *HTFH,* 5/56, p. 52; on some model nuns, see *HTFH,* 6/53, p. 40; 5/60, p. 11.

75. *HTFH,* 6/58, p. 24. The 220 monks of Wu-tai Shan who harvested 1,800,000 catties of sweet potatoes (planted by the peasants) in twenty-three days of October 1958 were also said to be "taking part in a life of organized labor for the first time": see *HTFH,* 12/58, p. 27. This was not a demand made specially of Buddhists. Almost everyone in China, including Mao himself, took part in manual labor for the common weal in 1958-59.

76. For examples of the participation of Buddhist monks in the production of iron in 1958, see *HTFH,* 12/58, p. 34 (Chungking and Kiangsi); *Chieh-fang jih-pao,* Nov. 10, 1958, tr. in *SCMP,* 1943:11 (Shanghai); *HTFH,* 11/58, p. 29 (Nan-yüeh); *HTFH,* 11/58, p. 32 (Nan-hua Ssu), p. 34 (Yün-chü Shan). The most striking report was from Nanchang, published in *HTFH,* 12/58, pp. 30-32, tr. in JPRS, 1461-N:40-42.

77. Schools and orphanages were started by some monasteries between 1905 and 1949 partly in order to forestall confiscation of their property and partly in order to show that Buddhists were as capable of modern forms of social welfare as Christian missionaries: see Welch, *Revival,* pp. 10-15, 114, 121-131.

78. In 1950-51 all Christian missionary enterprises in China were taken over by the government. Universities and schools, hospitals and clinics, orphanages and foundling homes were all put in the charge of cadres; the missionaries who had formerly managed them were expelled; and no more subsidies were accepted from abroad. The ostensible purpose of this was to reduce foreign influence—especially American influence—during the Korean War; but it also helped to make the State the sole dispenser of education and social welfare.

79. *HTFH,* 10/58, p. 21.

80. *HTFH,* 6/53, p. 55. I-fang was an activist who enjoyed a rapid rise in Buddhist circles. See Chapter X, note 64.

81. On primary schools operated by monks or nuns see *HTFH,* 9/50, p. 31 (Hangchow); *HTFH,* 2/53, p. 30 (Shensi); *HTFH,* 7/53, p. 27 (Harbin); and Otani, *Shin Chūgoku,* p. 124 (Shanghai). As to the sangha's efforts in medicine, clinics are mentioned in Hangchow (*HTFH,* 9/50, p. 31) and Changchow, Fukien (*HTFH,* 5/53, p. 26). The latter, which had been

founded by a local monk, was taken over by the preparatory committee of the local Buddhist association and in the next 18 months (of 1952-53) treated 52,852 patients, charging them only for medicine, and another 12,000 persons entirely free of charge. The only private social welfare effort by the sangha that I have seen mentioned after 1953 was a hospital run by 13 monks and nuns in Taiyüan: see *HTFH,* 10/59, pp. 11-12.

82. *HTFH,* 3/52, pp. 8-9. The hollowness of this claim that the government did not discriminate is suggested by a letter from a monk in Changshu, who had done so well in helping with land reform work that he was made head of the peasant association of his village, then a member of the household registration committee, and was kept busy doing work that the cadres assigned to him. All this time he had not admitted to being a monk. Yet *Modern Buddhism* and *Chüeh yu-ch'ing* used to come addressed to him with his religious name and title. "The cadres happened to notice this and, after a big laugh at my expense, they investigated my thinking." Therefore he wrote asking that *Modern Buddhism* be sent to him under his lay name. This would not only make it easier for him with cadres, he said, but would also mean that he was better received by the masses and it would be in keeping with the changeover to the new era.

83. *HTFH,* 12/58, p. 34, differently translated in JPRS 1461-N:54-55. Other examples of the same kind of incredible enthusiasm are translated in *ibid.,* pp. 29-39. Along with so many rural residents during 1958 Buddhist monks promised astounding crop yields—like 20,000 catties a mou (instead of the usual 300-500): e.g., see *HTFH,* 12/58, p. 33. When reading their production claims—for example, at Chiu-hua Shan (*HTFH,* 12/58, p. 32)—we should remember that this was a year of widespread exaggeration, as the government itself eventually acknowledged.

84. *HTFH,* 6/53, pp. 30-31.

85. In 1930 there were about 460 monks and 30 nuns in Kansu, which then covered a larger area: see Welch, *Practice,* p. 413. Probably a sizable percentage disrobed soon after Liberation.

IV. THE REFORM OF MONASTIC LIFE

1. *HTFH,* 3/51, inside back cover.

2. *HTFH,* 6/53, p. 48. Italics added. On *uposatha,* see this chapter at note 59.

3. *HTFH,* 6/58, p. 26. In the past they had merely to walk across the courtyard to reach the shrine hall where devotions were held.

4. For reports of daily devotions continuing, see *HTFH,* 6/53, p. 42 (Nan p'u-t'o Ssu, Amoy); 12/54, p. 29 (Sung-yün Shan, Hunan); 7/54, p. 29 (Kuei-ch'ih, Anhwei); and *Chung-kuo hsin-wen,* June 22, 1957 (K'ai-yüan Ssu, Chaochow). As to continuing meditation, at Chin Shan it was still being conducted in 1952, both every day and in the special "meditation weeks" of

intensive practice, similar to Japanese *sesshin:* see *Chüeh yu-ch'ing,* 10/52, p. 19. By 1956 it had stopped there but continued at the Kao-min Ssu: see Chapter II at note 75. In 1953 two meditation weeks were held at the Jade Buddha Monastery in Shanghai, starting February 22: see Ts'en Hsüeh-lü, *Hsü-yün ho-shang nien-p'u,* 3rd ed. (Hong Kong, 1962), pp. 185-221. In 1955 meditation weeks were conducted at the Ta Mao-p'eng on Chung-nan Shan in Shensi, where, the year before, two monks were reported to have attained a transcendental state in their practice of the *po-chou* method of Tao-hsüan: see *HTFH,* 1/54, p. 29; 2/55, p. 27. As to the Pure Land practice of reciting buddha's name, there are a good many scattered reports of its continuing, particularly in the years of 1953-56. It was said to be carried on daily at the Pai-ma Ssu, Loyang (*HTFH,* 4/55, p. 30) and at the Fu-hsiu An, Shensi (*HTFH,* 6/53, p. 27). It was held twice a month starting in the winter of 1953-54 in Kuei-ch'ih, Anhwei (*HTFH,* 7/54, p. 29) and, starting in September 1955, in Lin-tse, Kansu (*HTFH,* 1/56, p. 28). Weeks of intensive recitation were held at the K'ai-fu Ssu, Changsha (*HTFH,* 6/53, p. 46), at the Ta Mao-p'eng, Shensi, and the P'u-tu Ssu, Anhwei (*HTFH,* 2/55, p. 29). Other reports of recitation of buddha's name are printed in *HTFH,* 6/53, p. 49 (the Lien-tsung Yüan, Chengtu); 10/54, p. 29 (the Ti-tsang Ssu, Kansu); 12/54, p. 29 (the Ching-yeh Ssu, Shensi); 1/55, p. 30 (P'u-t'o Shan, Chekiang).

The only published report that indicates a reduction of practice concerned the K'ai-fu Ssu in Changsha, where in 1952 morning devotions were reduced to half an hour and consisted of reciting the *Ta-pei chou* seven times and the *P'u-hsien hsing-yüan p'in* once: see *HTFH,* 6/53, p. 46. Before 1949 the liturgy had had many more parts and had lasted a full hour or more: see Welch, *Practice,* pp. 54-58, 71, *et passim.*

5. *China Reconstructs,* 1-2/54, pp. 42, 44.

6. The first edition (consisting of loose-leaf plates) was entitled *Buddhism in China.* The second edition was entitled *Buddhists in China;* and the third *Buddhists in New China.* The publication of two editions in one year probably reflects the high level of interest in foreign contacts, especially in connection with the 2,500th anniversary of the Buddha. The second of the two passages quoted comes from p. 5 of the second edition and p. 6 of the third, the only difference being the addition of the word "new" before "China."

7. The first foreign Buddhist to visit China, the Venerable Narawila of Ceylon, was told of daily devotions at the Kuang-chi Ssu in Peking and the Liu-jung Ssu in Canton. Raghu Vira saw them being performed in 1955, both at the Liu-jung Ssu and at the T'ung-chiao Ssu, Peking's principal nunnery. P. B. Bapat (1955) and the Venerable Amritananda (1959) had similar experiences. One member of a Japanese delegation that visited China in 1957 was told that devotions were normally held *three times* a day and that most temples had meditation halls with monks in them enthusiastically carrying on the practice of Ch'an: see *Chūgai nippō,* November 28, 1957. A Western diplomat who made it a point to visit many monasteries in 1962 was assured

at each of them that daily devotions were still being performed: at the T'ung-chiao Ssu they lasted an hour in the morning and again in the afternoon. So far as I know, it was not until 1966, just before the Cultural Revolution began, that a foreigner was told that devotions had been discontinued—by the lamas at the She-li-t'u Chao in Huhehot.

8. *HTFH,* 10/59, p. 14. The other two statements were made by Sheng-ch'uan and Sung-liu A-ch'ia-mu-ni-ya. Shirob said almost the same thing to the NPC the following spring and added: "Although monks are everywhere engaged in production, their self-cultivation and the morning and evening chanting of sutras are still carried on as usual." See *JMJP,* April 16, 1960. In an article published in the Hong Kong *Ta-kung pao,* October 1, 1961, the Protestant leader Wu Yao-tsung emphasized that although religious people took part in socialist construction, it did not impede their religious life.

9. This was reported by a monk who lived at the K'ai-yüan Ssu, Chüan-chow, from 1950 to 1957. He said that devotions there continued to be called *tsao-, wan-k'o,* but in actuality they consisted of merely reciting the Three Refuges for a couple of minutes. So far as he knew, this was the practice at all the monasteries in his area, since it left more time free for labor and study.

10. Here are some specific examples of the step-by-step reduction. At Yün-men Shan from 1951 to 1954 all the resident monks attended *morning* devotions which were held in the usual way. *Afternoon* devotions were performed too, but only by four monks who left the fields early in order to return to the monastery for this purpose. At Yün-chü Shan from 1954 to 1957 morning devotions were held every day, but evening devotions only when work permitted. In 1958 the daily schedule there was reorganized: devotions were held only on the first and fifteenth of the lunar month. Some confirmation of this is provided by the report on stepped-up productive labor at Yün-chü Shan during the Great Leap Forward. Certainly the sixty monks who pitched their tents in a nearby valley and worked day and night to make charcoal cannot have had time for religious exercises: see *HTFH,* 11/58, pp. 33-34, tr. in JPRS, 1347-N:17-18. A visitor in 1958 to Yün-men, Nan-hua, and Ting-hu Shan reported that none of them held daily devotions: "If they had held them, the cadres would have said they had nothing to do."

11. See *HTFH,* 6/53, p. 54. In 1955-56 seven meditation weeks—the traditional number—were held there annually: see *HTFH,* 3/56, p. 30. One reason why the practice of meditation continued so long at the Kuang-chi Mao-p'eng was probably the fact that its abbot was Neng-hai, an influential vice-president of the CBA.

12. As with devotions, this happened step by step. For example, at Yün-men Shan one period of meditation had been held after each meal in 1951-53. At Yün-chü Shan in 1953-57, the same had been true; and whereas the *evening* period had been compulsory for all monks, in the morning they had had the option of studying the *Surangama sutra* and were free to skip the

period after lunch entirely. In 1958 all three periods were replaced by labor and study. Because Hsü-yün, the eminent Ch'an monk, presided over both Yün-men and Yün-chü, the discontinuance of meditation there was particularly significant.

13. See Chapter I, n. 69.

14. C. K. Yang, citing no source, states that "a special tax is imposed on 'superstitious commodities' such as incense sticks, candles, and paper articles to be burned to the dead, with the obvious purpose of using financial pressure to reduce religious rites": see C. K. Yang, *Religion in Chinese Society* (Berkeley, 1961), p. 389. One of my informants recalls that the tax on incense began about 1953. Thereafter a small packet cost the equivalent of US20-25 cents. Another informant recalled that it cost 25-35 cents (which was still not much more than the cost of a packet of eighty sticks of high quality incense in Hong Kong). A third informant told of the fluctuation in the price and availability of tinfoil in Shanghai. In 1953-55 a hundred packages of 3 X 5 inch sheets cost the equivalent of US$24 (again not much more than in Hong Kong). After 1957 they were obtainable only in the black market at the equivalent of US$40-120. During the three hard years of 1960-62, they were sold only in shops where overseas remittances could be spent, again for US$24. Incense was usually easy to buy in Shanghai during the entire period before the Cultural Revolution, and the price did not rise as much as the price of tinfoil. Even when it was unobtainable, people could buy mosquito repellents that looked and burned like sticks of incense, although the scent was different. One of the few hints of all this to appear in the press was a question addressed to *Modern Buddhism* in 1951. A Honan monk asked what should be offered to the Buddha since proper incense was too expensive and extravagant. The answer was that if he picked wild flowers and offered them along with a glass of pure water, "the Buddha would certainly be pleased." See *HTFH,* 12/51, p. 21.

Paper, incense, and other materials employed in rites for the dead had traditionally been sold in paper shops. A cadre of the Religious Affairs Bureau in Canton recalled that in 1956 the paper shops there had changed to joint State-private ownership. This provided for tighter government control over the traffic in such merchandise, but it was never rationed. After 1958 it became scarce, he said, during specifically Buddhist festivals like the Buddha's birthday and the festival of the hungry ghosts, although not during general festivals like New Year's and Mid-autumn. At least through 1963 the supply and marketing coöperatives in some rural areas were still selling incense and paper, the production of which provided some communes with a sizable portion of their income. In 1964 they changed over to other products, and all supply and marketing coöperatives were discouraged from handling incense and paper at all. See *Ta-kung pao,* January 17, 1965, tr. in *SCMP,* 3389:11-14.

The cadre mentioned above denied that there had been any tax on the fees for Buddhist services in Canton. It may be that the tax was a local phenomenon. It was reported by only two informants, one from Shanghai and one from Wuhan. According to the former, all but 80 cents of the 9 JMP charged per day per monk was collected by the local Buddhist association and handed over to the government. Although there is no confirmation of this in the press (any more than there is for most of the changes discussed in this note), a tax on fees would have fitted in with the government's desire to discourage superstitious activities and it already had been imposed here and there under the Nationalists (see Welch, *Revival,* pp. 147, 151).

15. See Chapter II at notes 70-72 and below note 18.

16. *HTFH,* 5/54, p. 29. Cf. 9/51, p. 22.

17. Shanghai was the place where traditional rites continued to be held most frequently, but there are reports from other localities as well. For example, the Nan-t'ai Ssu on Nan-yüeh performed the elaborate Ten-thousand Buddhas Penance (*wan-fo pao-ch'an*) from January 17 to February 7, 1955: see *HTFH,* 3/55, p. 32. The same year Raghu Vira saw many small bronze images at the Liu-jung Ssu in Canton and was told that they were taken along by the monks when they went to people's houses to perform rites.

18. On the recrudescence of Buddhist services in 1960-62, see Chapter II at note 85. The anti-superstition campaign of 1958-59 found its clearest expression in patriotic compacts in which monks "guaranteed that they would not undertake illegal superstitious activities, manufacture rumors to deceive the masses, or extort money or goods from the masses": see *HTFH,* 9/58, p. 28. Compare the criticism in Changchun of "abuse of religious rites for the purpose of obtaining money by fraud from the Buddhist faithful" (*Chi-lin jih-pao,* June 20, 1958, tr. in *SCMP,* 1834:11); and the criticism in Kweiyang of monks "who, under the pretext of going out to chant scriptures for the people, swindled money from them" (*Kuei-chou jih-pao,* July 10, 1958, p. 1, tr. in JPRS 1184-N:26). Almost the same language is used in the Heilungkiang patriotic compact: see *HTFH,* 12/58, p. 33.

Not everyone will agree where to draw the line between a deserving clergy that accepts pious donations and an unscrupulous clergy that victimizes the gullible. Examples of the latter certainly existed in China as elsewhere. Yet what needs to be remembered is the way devout Chinese regarded their financial transactions with the sangha. The more they gave in donations or fees, the more merit was generated for them and, quite often, the more face they gained. Therefore, up to a point, which depended on their wealth, the more they were "cheated" the better they liked it.

19. *HTFH,* 9/53, p. 22. According to a monk in another part of the country, being busy with production and organizational work "meant that the time he could spend on religious practice was, of course, shortened": see *HTFH,* 11/51, p. 14. In 1957 Chao P'u-ch'u and Chü-tsan admitted to a Japanese visitor that sometimes the necessity for monks to take part in labor

meant that they could not continue to spread the dharma, perform rites for the dead, and keep up other forms of religious practice as they had in the past. See *Chūgai nippō,* October 10, 1958.

20. E.g., *HTFH,* 7/58, p. 18; 9/58, pp. 27, 28. Buddhists in Kweiyang agreed to work 7-9 hours a day, to spend less time on religious activities, and to put "production first": see *Kuei-chou jih-pao,* July 10, 1958, tr. in JPRS 1184-N:26. Compare the pledge to put production ahead of religion in the Shanghai *Chieh-fang jih-pao,* November 10, 1958, tr. in *SCMP,* 1943:11. This stated: "The interests of socialism and production must be taken care of first, and all kinds of religious activities disadvantageous to national construction and production must be reformed. In religious activity, the public interest must take precedence over private interests. National construction and production represent the public interest of the people as a whole, but religious belief is a matter that only concerns the individual." (*SCMP* translation slightly altered.)

21. See above notes 1-8.

22. *Min-tsu t'uan-chieh,* 3/59, pp. 17-18.

23. *HTFH,* 4/52, p. 5. The words that I translate "complete enlightenment" are *ta-ch'e ta-wu.*

24. The only case I have found in a documentary source involved the abbot of the Nan-hua Ssu, the Venerable Pen-huan, who was said to have taken 50 disciples: see *Nan-fang jih-pao,* June 11, 1958. The Nan-hua Ssu was a public monastery, where tonsure would not have been allowed before 1949: see Welch, *Practice,* pp. 128-129, 132. Three oral informants recollected cases of tonsure in Shanghai and Kwangtung before 1957. A foreign resident of Peking who visited the T'ung-chiao Ssu in 1962 was told that 20 of the 61 nuns there were young and had entered the sangha since Liberation. The fact that so few cases of tonsure are mentioned in the press is not necessarily significant. Because it was a personal matter, involving only two individuals, tonsure would not make news.

25. *HTFH,* 10/50, pp. 33-34. Cf. 4/52, p. 5.

26. *HTFH,* 12/50, p. 38.

27. The ordination at Yün-men was finally held from the 1st to the 19th of the sixth lunar month (July 15-August 2, 1951), according to one of the monks ordained. He himself had been waiting for three years, having been tonsured in Kunming in 1948. On the troubles at Yün-men in 1951, see Chapter VII.

28. In the question-and-answer column, just at the time of the trouble at Yün-men, there appeared the following item: "*Question:* the Buddha fixed twenty as the age that one had to be before one could be ordained as a bhiksu and there were many [other] limitations. The fact that today indiscriminate ordination and acceptance of disciples continue is a great obstacle to the future progress of Buddhism. What I mean is that people about to enter the sangha should go through an investigation and only those whose resolve is

firm and whose faith is sufficient should be allowed to become monks. Please tell me if I am right. *Answer:* the statement that monks should be investigated before ordination is completely correct, but it is a big question how actually to carry out this proposal. Fellow Buddhists must be asked to give it thoughtful consideration" (*HTFH,* 5/51, p. 27). The proposal that only those "whose faith was sufficient" should be ordained was in line with criticism of the motivation of monks that T'ai-hsü had begun to voice in 1908. Thus *Modern Buddhism* told its readers at the end of 1951: "Most of the monks and nuns in China today entered religious life to get a livelihood and not because of their faith. It is for this reason that temples have changed from 'houses of religion' to 'houses of charity.'" See *HTFH,* 12/51, p. 21, and compare the statement in *HTFH,* 8/51, p. 23, that the indiscriminate acceptance of disciples in the past "had amounted, if we are honest about it, to running a barber shop."

29. *HTFH,* 6/54, p. 25.

30. *HTFH,* 11/55, p. 4. This resolution was dated August 31, 1955.

31. *Buddhists in New China,* p. 126. The photograph reproduced there shows about 125 candidates for the full ordination and six women devotees (distinguishable by their long hair) who are receiving the lay ordination. Most appear to be in middle age or older. (A Japanese was told by Chao P'u ch'u in 1957 that fewer people were being ordained than before Liberation, but that a higher percentage of them were over 40: see *Chūgai nippō,* Oct. 10, 1958). The caption states that about 280 persons came to be ordained. Before 1949 this monastery, which was the most important ordination center in China, used to give the full ordination to about 300 monks twice a year and the lay ordination to several hundred devotees. An informant who left China in 1957 stated that he had heard about the ordination at Pao-hua Shan in 1955 and been told that the monastery had not been allowed to publicize it as had always been done before Liberation, when wall posters used to be pasted up in many cities of central China. Publicity was now restricted to word of mouth. Such a restriction would have anticipated the resolution of August 31, 1955, and would have made the large number of candidates even more surprising and disturbing to the cadres.

32. See Welch, *Practice,* pp. 294-296.

33. Edward C. Chan, "The Chinese Communist Approach to Religion: The Case of Kwangtung (1950-1958)" (M.A. thesis, Harvard University, 1969).

34. The original intention of Hsü-yün, the eminent monk who had restored Yün-chü and now headed it, was to ordain only a few dozen of the resident monks, some of whom were not completely ordained and some of whom wanted reordination (on the latter, see Welch, *Practice,* pp. 334-335). In order to avoid trouble he wrote to the CBA asking for permission to do this and told the monks not to talk about it, lest outsiders come asking to be ordained too. Nonetheless word leaked out and before long 300 applicants had arrived from different parts of the country, some from as far away as

Kansu. The monastery did not have enough rice to feed them or the space to house them. Moreover the political atmosphere was ominous. The Shanghai Buddhist Youth Society, some of whose members were supporters of Hsü-yün, had recently been exposed as a nest of hidden counterrevolutionaries and three of its leaders had been arrested (see Chapter VII at notes 30-41). Even more serious was the fact that the Kansu provincial authorities had sent a telegram informing their counterparts in Kiangsi that leaders of the outlawed syncretistic sects in the northwest had dressed up as Buddhist novices and gone to Yün-chü Shan to be ordained in order that they might conceal their past behind a new religious identity. After talking things over with the public security officials, Hsü-yün decided to employ an expedient provided for in the *Sutra of Brahma's Net:* self-ordination. For ten days he lectured the outside applicants on the meaning of the three sets of ordination vows. Then he gave them ordination certificates, completely filled in but with the dates lying in the future, and sent them back home with instructions to repeat the vows by themselves on those dates. However, about a hundred applicants, both resident monks and those outsiders about whom there was the least question, he kept at the monastery and gave the full ordination in the traditional way. It ended shortly before December 28, 1955, when the newly ordained monks joined in a week of intensive meditation. See Ts'en Hsüeh-lü, *Hsü-yün ho-shang nien-p'u,* pp. 268-269. An informant who officiated at the ordination recalled that, before it began, another hundred applicants had telegraphed from Fukien asking if they could be ordained too. He went to Nanchang to ask the Religious Affairs Division, which refused permission in accordance with the CBA resolution of August 31, 1955. According to him the ordination lasted about thirty days. Another informant, who later visited Yün-chü Shan, said that the authorities were annoyed by the large number of applicants and forbade Yün-chü to hold an ordination again, since it "interfered with public order."

35. *HTFH,* 5/57, p. 24. "Luckily the government gave a great deal of help and everything was completed smoothly." Contrast the accusation against Pen-huan on p. 241.

36. *HTFH,* 5/57, p. 22. The sponsors of this ordination, perhaps in order to be surer of getting permission for it, made plans to improve ordination procedures. Ordinands would be instructed: (1) in the Vinaya; (2) in the main points of doctrine; (3) in methods of cultivation; and (4) in the policy of freedom of religious belief. "This was an experiment in a new kind of ordination." Or was it? Only the instruction in religious policy was really new, and it may merely have been window dressing to cover up an ordination of the traditional type. In the passage cited, Ch'en-k'ung, the CBA delegate from P'u-t'o, admitted a failure to achieve all the improvements that had been hoped for. "We have to create an improved monastic system in the future—both not violating the Buddhist system and able to fit in with the new social system. A pure ordination is something that cannot solve the problem." By

"pure" he meant nonpolitical—not screening the candidates for political reliability and class background. In other words the ordination at P'u-t'o had still been "indiscriminate."

37. The ordination at Ku Shan began on March 16 and ended on May 7, 1957, that is, on the 8th of the fourth lunar month, which is celebrated in China as the Buddha's birthday. It is also the date on which spring ordinations traditionally come to an end. Before 1949, even at Pao-hua Shan, ordinations had lasted no more than 40 days: the 53 days at Ku Shan was a return to ancient norms. Whereas in most of the other reports of ordinations in 1956-57, it is not made clear what percentage of ordinands were devotees merely taking the lay vows, at Ku Shan 140 of the 154 received the full bhiksu ordination. A vegetarian feast for 200 monks and nuns was donated at the start of the proceedings by a prior who had returned from Malaya. All the proper offices were filled—ordination abbot, confessor, catechist, and a team of instructors. There was even a transmission of the dharma (*shou-chi*) to the ordinees. It almost seems as if Sheng-hui, the 80 year-old abbot, had decided to have one last fling. See *Chung-kuo hsin-wen,* May 16, 1957 (reprinted in *Sourcebook,* p. 198), and Hong Kong *Ta-kung pao,* April 15, 1957.

Perhaps something similar happened at the Hsing-chiao Ssu Sian, where the 79 year old abbot Miao-kua presided over the ordination of no fewer than 300 monks (*fa-shih*), concluded March 6, 1957: see *Chūgai nippō,* May 22, 1958.

38. Lang-chao proposed that indiscriminate ordination be prohibited. Chüeh-ch'eng (actually a conservative) proposed that the Chinese Buddhist Association take charge of ordinations. Tz'u-ch'ing and Neng-hai called for more study of the Vinaya. See *HTFH,* 5/57, pp. 24, 21, 12. Neng-hai's speech was particularly important because he was a vice president of the CBA and a link with Tibetan Buddhists. He proposed that a "Vinaya observances institute" (*lü-i yüan*) be set up in Peking for three purposes. First, it would call together various scholars who were well versed in doctrine and Vinaya observances. They would study the latter for a year or two and propose standards for ordination, which would afterwards be disseminated to the four famous mountains and to the famous monasteries of the Vinaya sect, so that these could start Vinaya halls and, if the right conditions existed, conduct ordinations. (On Vinaya halls, see Welch, *Revival,* pp. 103-104, 108.) Second, the institute would bring together student monks who wanted to specialize in Vinaya observances for a three-year period of study and, after their graduation, would send them out to be instructors in the Vinaya halls at various institutions. Third, it would admit student monks who were young or had just been ordained and give them five or six years of instruction in the Vinayapitaka so that they would devote themselves to its study and practice and take charge of ordinations. Neng-hai next said that all bhiksus, after they had been ordained, would have to make a careful study of the monastic rules under the auspices of the establishment that ordained them—this was a re-

sponsibility that ordaining monasteries had to assume. Otherwise—if the latter ordained with an irresponsible lack of discrimination and also took no responsibility for training disciples—it would be a "crime."

The institute proposed by Neng-hai never seems to have been established. Its tasks were partly assumed by the committee on ordination procedures referred to in the text.

39. These figures come from the ordination yearbook, a copy of which was made available to me through the kindness of Dr. Mary Edith Runyan. (On the nature of such yearbooks, see Welch, *Practice*, pp. 250-255.) It lists 373 monks and 430 nuns who received the full ordination; 115 female devotees who received the lay ordination; and seven young persons who were ordained as novices. The monks came from Kiangsu, Anhwei, Chekiang, Liaoning, Fukien, Hopei, Shansi, Hupeh, Kirin, Kiangsi, Kwangtung, Heilungkiang, Honan, Shantung, Inner Mongolia, Shensi, Szechwan, Kansu, and Peking (listed in the order of the number of monks from each). Many of them had had their heads shaved in third provinces (that is, neither their home province nor Kiangsu, where Pao-hua Shan was located). Thus they had been moving about the country. What was especially interesting was that more than half of those from Kiangsu (103 out of 200) came from what I have called the "cradle of monks" (Welch, *Practice*, pp. 6, 255-256). This was a strongly Buddhist area from which the most monks had come to be ordained at Pao-hua Shan in the decades before Liberation—an impressive example of old customs continuing in the new society. On the other hand, a far higher proportion of the total number of ordinands came from outside Kiangsu. There were other changes too. Although it made no mention of Chairman Mao or the Communist Party, the yearbook was printed in simplified characters and dates were given in the solar rather than lunar calendar. The ceremonies lasted 16 rather than the 35-40 days that were standard under the Republic. The ordination was not presided over by the resident abbot of Pao-hua Shan, as it would have been in the old days, but by Ying-ch'e, abbot of the P'i-lu Ssu, Nanking. Since he was re-elected to the CBA council in 1962, he does not seem to have offended the authorities by leading this, one of the largest ordinations held anywhere in China during the twentieth century.

40. *HTFH*, 11/58, p. 32 (Chin-chang, Fukien). Cf. 3/59, p. 34 (Hu-hsien, Shensi).

41. *HTFH*, 10/58, p. 21. Cf. 4/53, p. 15, and compare the notion that in the old society monks had been despised because they were "outside the world": see *HTFH*, 9/58, p. 32. In actuality, it was only when they were truly outside the world that they were respected—at any rate, by devout Buddhists.

42. In November 1961, I was told by a CBA leader that the committee on ordination procedures had "not yet completed its work" and, until it did so, ordinations of the normal type would not be permitted. In 1965 they were

still not being permitted, according to information given that year to Japanese visitors.

43. On the system of *kua-tan* and its importance in the training of monks, see Welch, *Practice,* pp. 305-310.

44. See *Chüeh yu-ch'ing,* 13.2:19 (October 1952). A monk who stopped at Chin Shan in 1956 told me that he stayed only one night and was informed that he could not have stayed for a much longer period as in the past. Regarding the past practice there, see Welch, *Practice,* pp. 10-18, 424.

45. The announcement read: "Since this factory was opened, a very large number of Buddhists from various places have come on their own to join in the work without consulting us first. A good many of them have been ignorant of the procedures for change of residence and have come surreptitiously without getting a change-of-residence permit from the local [authorities], adding very greatly to the difficulties of the factory. Therefore, notice is hereby given to all quarters that in the future anyone who wants to come to work here must first write us a letter about it. Only after receiving formal notification that we have considered and agreed to his request and after getting a change-of-residence permit from the local authorities will anyone be permitted to join in the work of the factory. Otherwise he will not even be able to stay here." See *HTFH,* 10/51, p. 11. On change of residence, see next note.

46. This is presumably why the Kuan-tsung Ssu, Ningpo, set up an "investigation team" (*chiu-ch'a tui*) to maintain a constant check on the arrival and departure of wandering monks: see *HTFH,* 3/52, p. 10. Under the Regulations on Household Registration an ordinary person could be away from his home up to three months without getting a change-of-residence permit. However, anyone belonging to one of the "five categories" of persons under control had to get police permission to be away for even one night and had to register wherever he stayed on his travels. The "five categories" were landlords, rich peasants, counterrevolutionaries, bad elements, and rightists. It would seem as if monks—even those not classified in one of these categories—were subject to some such restrictions. According to one informant rural monasteries were more often lax about registration of visitors than those in the city. When police checks revealed such laxity, the guest prefect would get a severe reprimand and be told that his "thinking was bad." Sometimes, however, the consequences were more serious. Unregistered visitors were one of the reasons for the arrest of Pen-huan (see Chapter VII, p. 242).

47. According to a cadre of the Religious Affairs Division in Canton, a wandering monk could stay at a local monastery there even if he did not have nationwide coupons (*ch'üan-kuo t'ung-yung liang-p'iao*). So long as he got permission from the Canton Public Security Bureau to stay in the city, the local rationing office would issue him the coupons he needed. Obviously, however, it was safer to get the nationwide coupons before one started on a trip—and more convenient too, if one were only staying in a place for a day

or two. In at least one place visitors did not have to surrender ration coupons in order to get their meals. This was Omei Shan, where a cadre at the foot of the mountain carefully registered all pilgrims and then issued printed forms for them to use during the several days that it would take them to go to the summit and back. At each monastery along the way the monk in charge would fill in the number of meals they had eaten there. Then, when that monastery wanted to replenish its supplies, it was eligible to receive as much grain as its registered guests had consumed. The informant who supplied this information visited all four of the Buddhist sacred mountains (see this chapter at note 52), but only at Omei—in August 1957—did he find the ration-free system that has just been described. This may be because Omei was the most popular place of pilgrimage.

48. The government, of course, was not ready to exempt Buddhists from their effect. When a reader wrote to *Modern Buddhism* in 1950 asking whether a monastery could get more land in order to provide food for wandering monks, he was told that since monasteries had never acquired additional land for this purpose in the past, they could not do so now. See *HTFH*, 12/50, p. 26. It is possible that things worked differently in urban monasteries, especially where visitors could get ration coupons easily, as in Canton. According to the cadre cited in note 47, monasteries in Canton eagerly welcomed wandering monks and tried to persuade them to become permanent residents, so as to fill up empty rooms and reduce the threat of confiscation. I have not heard of this eagerness elsewhere, and the cadre acknowledged that coupons were not the only problem: in order to buy food one had to have money as well. Therefore unless a wandering monk had money of his own (from lay supporters, for example) or unless he could earn it by productive labor, he would be more of a burden than an asset to a monastery that might otherwise consider inviting him to become a permanent resident.

49. *HTFH*, 11/55, p. 4. At the plenary meeting of the CBA Council that passed this resolution, most of the same things had been said in almost the same words by Ta-hsin, abbot of the San-fo Ssu, who had just been elected president of the Wuhan Municipal Buddhist Association: see *HTFH*, 9/55, p. 18.

50. Sheng-ch'üan, abbot of the Hsien-liang Ssu, Peking, and an old friend of Chü-tsan, called on the association to clarify what measures should be employed to provide hospitality for the monks who came to Peking: see *HTFH*, 5/57, p. 20.

51. *HTFH*, 6/58, pp. 23-24; 11/58, p. 31; 12/58, p. 33.

52. Among the places he stayed were the Kao-min Ssu (three nights), Chin Shan (one night), the Kuang-chi Mao-p'eng on Wu-t'ai Shan; the Wo-lung Ssu, Sian, and the Wen-shu Yüan in Chengtu. On each year's trip his ticket cost about one hundred JMP, which was given him by a lay devotee.

53. A Hong Kong nun who went to Yün-chü Shan in 1959 stated that she was still able to stay there as a guest but had to answer many more questions

than on a visit two years earlier. "Where do you live in Hong Kong? Whom have you come to see? Who are your relatives on the mainland? How old are you? Where have you just come from? How long will you be staying here? Where do you plan to go after you leave here? " A Chinese monk from Cambodia traveled about China quite freely in 1962 (see Appendix G) and one from Singapore did so in 1965.

54. *HTFH,* 5/53, p. 16. This controversy had already been alluded to in 1950 when it was reported that "the more conservative monks refuse to look at the changing world and are unwilling to reconsider their way of life. They regard the demand for progress by younger monks as an unforgivable rebellion against Buddhist tenets." See Alfred Kiang, "A New Life Begins," p. 173.

55. *HTFH,* 5/53, p. 3. The author of this article, entitled "A Few Tentative Ideas on the Reorganization of the Sangha System," is showing the excesses in preserving and discarding the traditional system. He goes on to say that these kinds of bad situation could be found not only in Hunan, Fukien, and Chekiang, but probably elsewhere as well. Cf. Chapter II, note 8.

56. *HTFH,* 6/53, p. 11. In the sentences I have omitted, Fa-tsun said that the first thing required to build the Buddhism of the future was to improve ordination procedures and training in the Vinaya. Thus he anticipated the stand taken by Neng-hai and others four years later (see above note 38). Another speaker at the inaugural conference–Po-ming, who gave the three-year work report for Changsha and was elected to the council of the CBA–emphasized that since the time monks had started productive labor, they had been following the Vinaya more closely than ever–reciting the sutras and buddha's name, performing the uposatha, and hearing lectures. He quoted the *Lotus sutra* and a Vinaya text in order to show that productive labor, which might seem to be a violation of certain rules, was actually in accordance with the principle of unselfishness. See *HTFH,* 6/53, p. 48.

57. In 1951 *Modern Buddhism* noted that many readers were dissatisfied with the Vinaya and asked them to submit their views on revising it. See *HTFH,* 4/51, p. 36.

58. See Chapter II, note 93.

59. *HTFH,* 1/55, p. 29. Members of the Study Committee assembled to perform the *uposatha* at the Pao-kuo Ssu on the 8th and 23rd of each lunar month; the rest performed it at their respective temples on the 1st and 15th. Those who broke the rules were not to be permitted to wear monastic dress or to live in the temples of Omei.

60. *HTFH,* 6/53, p. 48 (Changsha); 7/53, p. 27 (Mi-t'o Ssu, Harbin); 11/54, p. 30; 1/55, p. 29 (Omei Shan). A statement that the *uposatha* was being performed in Peking monasteries is made by Chü-tsan in *China Reconstructs,* January-February 1954, p. 42. On *uposatha* days before 1949, see Welch, *Practice,* pp. 110, 127, and 131. *Uposatha* was performed *four* times a month (as in Theravada countries) at the Nan P'u-t'o Ssu, Amoy, after Tz'u-chou, a Vinaya specialist, became abbot: *HTFH,* 6/53, p. 41-42. Another

Fukien monastery, the Nan-ch'an Ssu, is the only one from which I have seen a report of *uposatha* being stopped. In 1952 its monks were said to have "abolished *uposatha* in form, and in a lively, free, and informal *uposatha* spirit they are practicing the Sunday investigation system of criticism and self-criticism and helping each other to progress." See *HTFH,* 5/52, p. 22.

61. In March 1957 Wei-fang proposed to the CBA's second national conference that the daily liturgy in common use should be revised by the association "in order to eliminate old phrases that are tinged with feudalism; and a uniform version should be issued that will satisfy Buddhists' needs." So far as I know this was never formally approved. Even if it was, Wei-fang's proposal shows that it happened after 1957.

62. *HTFH,* 9/55, p. 3. Moderate though it is, this statement may be more radical than anything that Hsü-yün himself would have freely written. It uses some Marxist terminology and is very different in tone from a memorandum he wrote in 1953 when revision of the Vinaya was being discussed at the CBA inaugural conference. In this he sharply rejected any change in monastic dress—and even in the traditional Chinese Buddhist chronology, which makes the Buddha anterior to Confucius and Lao-tzu. See Ts'en Hsüeh-lü, *Hsü-yün ho-shang nien-p'u,* pp. 257-260. Hsü-yün's last words before his death were on the importance of preserving the monastic rules as symbolized by monastic dress: see *ibid.,* p. 426.

63. A monk near Mt. Omei complained in 1951 that traditional monastic dress was ridiculed as feudal by most of the population. In the question-and-answer column of *Modern Buddhism* he was told that it was not monks' dress, but their ideas and activities that were ridiculed as feudal. In Peking and Tientsin, when Buddhists were asked to attend some important meeting, "those concerned let the monks and nuns know that it is best for them to wear monastic dress, so there is no question about the latter in Peking and Tientsin." The column went on to say that any change in monastic dress must preserve the distinction between clergy and laity, although just how this would be done had to wait until a nationwide Buddhist organization was set up. See *HTFH,* 8/51, p. 23. This suggests that when the sangha was, so to speak, on display, the regime wanted it to look like the sangha—attesting to the policy of freedom of religious belief.

64. *HTFH,* 5/51, p. 28. The figure of 80 percent may be misleading, since it included not only those who were still in the sangha, but also those who had returned to lay life. *Modern Buddhism* emphasized that the switch to lay dress had taken place voluntarily in order to facilitate productive labor: it was "completely untrue to say that the authorities had *ordered* the elimination of monastic garb."

65. *HTFH,* 12/52, p. 11.

66. See Bapat, "A Glimpse," p. 392, and the plates in Chao P'u-ch'u, *Buddhism in China.* The lay collar worn by monks in the latter is not found, curiously enough, in any of the plates of *Buddhists in New China,* which show

either Chinese or Theravada robes (e.g., pp. 125, 127, 128). A Chinese monk from overseas who traveled widely in 1962 saw Sun Yat-sen uniforms (*Chung-shan chuang*) being worn only at the Yu-min Ssu in Nanchang and the Liu-jung Ssu in Canton. At the Ling-yin Ssu, Hangchow, and the Ling-yen Ssu, Soochow, traditional dress was still being worn by a few elderly monks. Elsewhere he found that the "T'ai-hsü suit" was commonest and, at the suggestion of the China Travel Bureau, he wore it himself (see Appendix G). It had a long grey jacket with a *Y* neck and a row of buttons straight down the middle. (For a forerunner, see Welch, *Revival,* p. 53.) Another monk from overseas who traveled widely in 1965 noted that all fifty monks at Ku Shan were still wearing traditional garb. This, of course, was not limited to long gowns but included short trousers and short jackets good for working in.

67. A Japanese Buddhist who visited the T'ung-chiao Ssu, Peking, in 1957 was told that the nuns there ate congee for breakfast, rice for lunch, but nothing in the evening: see Makita Tairyō, "Pekin no nisō tachi," *Kaihō* (Kyōto), No. 34, Oct. 10, 1959. Before Liberation some individuals had regularly fasted after twelve noon, but not (so far as I know) all the residents of any institution: see Welch, *Practice,* pp. 112-113.

68. According to the resident of a monastery in Fukien, the ritual character of meals was abandoned immediately after Liberation. One visitor observed square tables, seating four persons each, at the T'ung-chiao Ssu in 1962 (as in Fig. 16). Yet *Buddhists in New China* (1956), p. 132, shows the nuns of the T'ung-chiao Ssu seated at long tables in the traditional way, reciting grace, with everything as it should be. Makita took a similar photograph there in 1957: see Tsukamoto and Makita, p. 298. Perhaps long tables went out of use between 1957 and 1962, or perhaps even in 1957 they were only set up for the benefit of the photographers. The sole documentary reference I have seen to the etiquette of meals involved the Kuang-chi Mao-p'eng at Wu-t'ai Shan, where, in 1953, "meals were being conducted in the old way" and afterwards the monks marched in a serpentine procession reciting buddha's name: see *HTFH,* 6/53, p. 53. Even before Liberation this procession was exceptional.

69. Monks and nuns were living and working together at the K'ai-fu Ssu, Changsha, from as early as 1952 to as late as 1959: see *HTFH,* 6/53, p. 46; 11/59, pp. 28-30. During the winter of 1962 both monks and nuns were living at the Nan-t'ai Ssu, Nan-yüeh, and all year round at the Fo-yin Ssu: see Alley, *Amongst Hills and Streams,* pp. 17-18.

70. Representing the Hua-lin Ssu, this monk—Ch'i-shan by name—received the Japanese Buddhist delegation in 1957: see *Hōchū Nihon Bukkyō,* p. 35. In June 1958 he was identified as a member of the Preparatory Committee of the CBA branch, Canton: see *Nan-fang jih-pao,* June 12, 1958.

71. On the selection and authority of abbots before 1949, see Welch, *Practice,* pp. 143-177.

72. *HTFH,* 10/50, p. 21, and Appendix A.

73. For the exceptional control that the lay patrons called "mountain owners" (*shan-chu*) exercised over some monasteries in south China, see

Welch, *Practice,* pp. 134, 374, and cf. p. 515 note 27 for mention of lay devotees who hold monastic offices at some Buddhist monasteries in Taiwan. The power and privileges of *shan-chu* were specifically condemned after Liberation: see *HTFH,* 1/51, p. 27.

74. *HTFH,* 5/53, p. 3.

75. In 1952 the management committee of the Yü-wang Ssu, which claimed direct inspiration from Chü-tsan, organized teams for general business, personnel, production, religious exercises, and research. When it started a coöperative in September 1952 (see *HTFH,* 4/53, p. 12), three of its five teams were absorbed into the coöperative organization, as the following diagram shows:

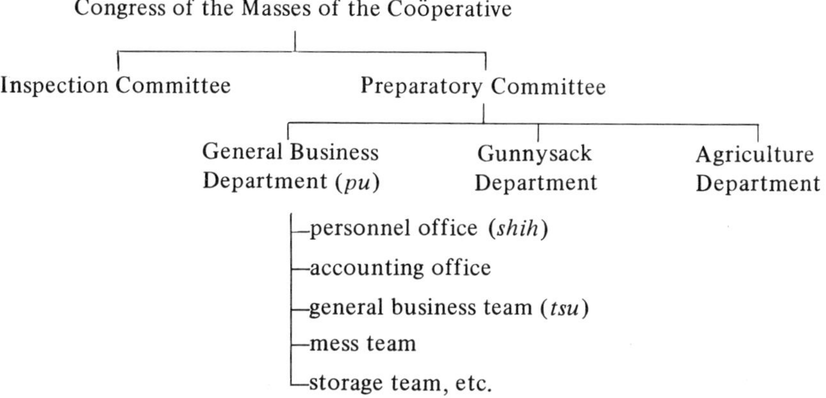

In 1952 the management committee set up to manage all the monasteries of T'ien-t'ai Shan had under it departments for general business, monastic administration, religious exercises, and productive labor. Department heads and deputy heads were elected by all the monks together: see Tsukamoto and Makita, p. 304.

Thus the committee-team structure could be found at two levels: at the higher level it had jurisdiction over all the temples of an area; at the lower level over an individual monastery. Sometimes only one level was to be found; sometimes both. For example, at Wu-t'ai Shan as at T'ien-t'ai all the temples came under a single management committee (*HTFH,* 11/50, p. 31); whereas the committee at the Yü-wang Ssu, Ningpo, had jurisdiction over that monastery alone. In Wuhan, on the other hand, there was *both* a higher-level committee for all the monasteries and lower-level committees for individual monasteries (*HTFH,* 9/50, p. 30).

76. At the Yü-wang Ssu the abbot continued to hold office "after the abbot system had been abolished." He retained his title of *fang-chang* and was put in charge of the religious exercises team, while another monk became head (*chu-jen*) of the Monastery Affairs Committee (*ssu-wu wei-yüan-hui*). See *HTFH,* 4/53, p. 10. It is possible that the abbot continued to serve "after

the abbot system had been abolished" at two other monasteries: the Yün-ch'i Ssu (or Hua-t'ing Ssu), Kunming (see *Chüeh yu-ch'ing* 12.1:24, January 1951) and the Chao-chüeh Ssu, Chengtu (see *HTFH,* 1/51, pp. 34-35). Although the tenses are not clear in the passages just cited, the meaning could be that the abbot and some of the senior officers continued to serve. In June 1951 managerial decisions were being made at the Liu-jung Ssu, Canton, by a "standing committee" (*HTFH,* 10/51, p. 24), yet there was an abbot in office there until at least as late as 1957: see *Hōchū Nihon Bukkyō,* p. 35. In 1950 at the 20 public monasteries in Wuhan only 5 of the 20 abbots "failed to get elected [to the reform committees] and 15 continued in office (*lien-jen*)." This could mean that they continued to serve, but in a new office, or that they continued to be abbots. The elections were "open and democratic" and were attended by all the monks in each monastery.

How were such elections conducted? In Canton, according to a cadre of the Religious Affairs Division there, the monks of a monastery would meet and elect both a new abbot and the officers to serve under him, while a cadre from the division looked on as an observer. If the choice was about to light on someone who was politically backward or who conspicuously lacked religious qualifications, the cadre would point out the disadvantages of such a step, but he would not veto it. What was, in effect, a veto came from the division after an inappropriate choice had been made and formally reported for approval. Then the division would suggest that the monks "think it over."

There were also other ways of filling the office of abbot. At one Canton monastery it rotated every other year between the two best qualified monks. The same thing happened at the Nan-ch'an Ssu, Changting, Fukien, where the office of head monk rotated (*lun-huan*) every half year, presumably among the most able of the eight monks left at the monastery: see *HTFH,* 5/52, p. 22. In some places a new abbot was apparently chosen by the local Buddhist association (after consultation, no doubt, with the religious affairs cadres). In 1963 a Japanese delegation was told that the CBA appointed abbots and that succession according to a monastery or dharma lineage was no longer considered suitable. See *Ganjin wajō,* p. 14. On the lineal succession of abbots, see Welch, *Practice,* pp. 156-176. For an example of lineages being canceled, see Chapter X at note 1.

What was commonest, perhaps, after Liberation was for the incumbent abbot to continue to serve, getting gradually older and feebler, but often retaining much of his traditional authority—at least until 1958. In that case, he continued to appoint the guest prefect, subprior, clerk, and so on, who, in monasteries where he had lost his power, were elected by the monks or appointed by the new prior or, where a management committee had been set up, replaced by heads of teams.

77. *HTFH,* 5/57, p. 19.

78. Tsukamoto and Makita, p. 304, and *Hōchū Nihon Bukkyō,* p. 15.

79. In 1958 it was stated that Buddhist rules and elements of the monastic system in the past that were disadvantageous to socialism and production

had been changed and should continue to be changed: see *Chieh-fang jih-pao,* Nov. 10, 1958, tr. in *SCMP,* 1943:10.

80. This report comes from an overseas Chinese monk who visited Yün-chü just before the change and heard about it on returning in 1959, at which time he saw the lay cadres there himself. Even before Hsü-yün took over Yün-chü, there had been a plan to make it a *"new ts'ung-lin"*: see *HTFH,* 7/53, p. 20. The plan was abandoned because of Hsü-yün's eminence and conservatism. (He had just been made honorary president of the CBA.)

81. This meant that it did not matter too much whether the abbot was progressive. He was a mere figurehead who led processions and greeted visitors. For him to be devout and old-fashioned did not necessarily hinder socialist transformation, and, when the time came, he might still be replaced by the same kind of man, useful in commanding the respect of the sangha and laity. Especially before 1958 political factors do not seem to have played a role in selecting new abbots or leaving old ones in office. K'uan-jun, who took over the T'ien-t'ung Ssu after the death of Yüan-ying, seems to have been no less of a conservative than his predecessor. Tz'u-chou, who was chosen abbot of Nan P'u-t'o, had long been an eminent authority on the Vinaya and had headed a seminary under Hsü-yün in 1934. Among the conservative abbots who were left in office after 1949 were Lai-kuo, who remained head of the Kao-min Ssu until he died in 1953; and Miao-hua, who remained acting head of Chin Shan at least until 1963. (He was elected to the CBA council in 1957: see *HTFH,* 8/57, p. 30.) On the other hand, two abbots who had been considered conservative before Liberation, became vocal supporters of the Communist Party after 1950. One was Wei-fang, who had been installed as abbot of the Jade Buddha Monastery just before the Communists came and who was in office as late as 1964 (NCNA, May 22, 1964). Another was Ta-pei, who had been abbot of the Liu-yün Ssu (Shanghai) and the T'ient-t'ung Ssu (Ningpo) under the Nationalists and who now headed two other important monasteries: the Ling-yin Ssu, Hangchow, and the Kuang-chi Ssu, Peking.

82. Article 2.2 of the Provisional Measures for the Management of Temples in Peking provided that all monasteries having monks and nuns in residence should come under the management (*kuan-li*) of the Civil Affairs Bureau. If they were of historical or cultural importance, they might alternatively come under the management of the Ministry of Culture. See *HTFH,* 10/51, p. 3. Later, management responsibility passed to the religious affairs organs. In the Republican period monks had successfully resisted government efforts to "manage" (*kuan-li*) the internal affairs of monasteries. See Welch, *Revival,* p. 303, note 37, and cf. pp. 137-142.

83. I have seen no credit given to T'ai-hsü in the domestic press, but Chao P'u-ch'u in his *Buddhism in China,* p. 23, praises T'ai-hsü as "a man who exerted his utmost efforts for the promotion of monks' education and was a learned Buddhist activist. His efforts in those dark days for Buddhism are worthy of our remembrance."

84. *JMJP* April 15, 1960. Shirob, a Tibetan, went on to illustrate the new mentality of monks by saying: "They have fully understood that the Tibetan rebellion was . . . a counterrevolutionary plot and have even more fully understood the spirit of the policy of freedom of religious belief." No doubt.

V. PRESERVING BUDDHIST CULTURE

1. For example, at the second conference of the CBA in 1957, a leading abbot, Ta-pei, spoke of the international importance of Buddhist culture and scholarship, which were "the legacy of our ancestors. Receiving them and putting them into good order would be of assistance to our nation's socialist construction . . . The problems of time, strength, and livelihood being encountered by the small number of Buddhist intellectuals must be taken care of, so as to give them peace of mind in their researches and religious studies." He went on to speak of the great accomplishments in Buddhist studies made by Japanese and Europeans. "Our capacities in this respect are extremely poor. At present we have barely begun to move ahead." See *HTFH,* 5/57, pp. 12-13.

Later that year Chao P'u-ch'u drew international attention to the Buddhist contributions to Chinese culture in *Buddhism in China,* pp. 23-31. A summary for domestic consumption was published in the *KMJP,* June 12, 1962, tr. in *SCMP,* 2815:5-6. See also the articles on the influence of Buddhism on Chinese literature and sculpture in *HTFH,* 9/58, pp. 12-18; 12/58, pp. 16-18 (tr. in JPRS 1184-N:1-24 and 1461-N:13-22). For an independent Western account, see K. K. S. Ch'en, *Buddhism in China: A Historical Survey* (Princeton, N.J., 1964), pp. 471-486.

2. The first reason was given in the Hong Kong *Wen-hui pao,* May 15, 1961. The second reason was given in Chao, *Buddhism in China,* p. 36.

3. *Ibid.* Similarly, the Hui-shan Ssu, Teng-feng, Honan, was repaired because it had the oldest octagonal pagoda in China and had been the abode of "great scientist monks" in the T'ang. See *Honan jih-pao,* January 11, 1958, in *SCMP,* 1732:30. Kuo Mo-jo told a Japanese Tendai delegation in 1965 that good care was being taken of the monasteries on T'ien-t'ai Shan because of Chih-i's great contribution to Buddhism and especially because I-hsing too had lived there and made great contributions to Chinese astronomy. When the delegation actually reached the mountain, they saw a notice posted near a Sui dynasty pagoda: "The Chinese people should carefully protect this national treasure." It was signed by the people's council. See Mibu, "Chūgoku Tendaisan," *Shūkyō kōron,* 9/65, p. 37.

4. See *Buddhists in New China,* p. 24. *Chinese Architecture* (Peking, Cultural Objects Press, 1958), p. 17, calls it "the oldest wooden structure now extant." This volume explains the importance, in the history of art and architecture, of many of the monasteries and pagodas that were restored in the 1950's.

5. The repair of the Flower Pagoda of the Liu-jung Ssu, Canton, was explained as follows: "The fact that the working people of China were capable of building such a large structure with a style all its own is indicative of the artistic capability of the working people and the long history of China's traditional architecture." See *Canton: The City, Economy, and March toward Socialism,* ed. Canton Branch of the Chinese People's Association for Foreign Cultural Relations (Canton, 1959), tr. JPRS 16369:43-44. In 1954 Otani Eijun was told that the first reason for the repair of monasteries was "to honor the great achievements of earlier generations of workers." See Otani, *Shin Chugoku,* p. 120. Cf. below note 71.

6. The Kuang-chi Ssu in Peking was headquarters of the national association. The Yü-fo Ssu in Shanghai, the K'ai-fu Ssu in Changsha, and the Liu-jung Ssu in Canton, after being repaired by the government, served as headquarters of the respective local associations. On museums, see below note 24.

7. NCNA English, May 12, 1958, in *SCMP,* 1773:34. Curiously enough, Ho Ch'eng-hsiang, the head of the Religious Affairs Bureau, had given a much higher figure (150 million yen, equivalent to US$420,000) to a Japanese visitor the previous October. He also told him that the restoration of the Kuang-chi Ssu, the CBA's headquarters in Peking, had cost the equivalent of US$700,000—the largest sum reported in connection with any Buddhist building project after 1949. See *Chūgai nippō,* May 18 and 27, 1958. Cf. Nitchū Yū-kō, p. 206.

8. *HTFH,* 10/59, p. 14, in JPRS 577:101a. Taking his cue from Hsüan-chung, perhaps, a delegate to the CBA's second national conference in 1957 called for government help in maintaining the T'ien-t'ung Ssu on the grounds that three famous Zen monks had come from Japan to study there: Eisai, Dogen, and Sesshū. See *HTFH,* 5/57, p. 19.

9. *Hōchū Nihon Bukkyō,* pp. 10-12. The figure on the cost of repairs was given to this delegation, which presented the monastery with portraits of Pure Land patriarchs, including T'an-luan, who had lived at Hsüan-chung. In 1960 the abbot of a Pure Land monastery in Tokyo sent its most precious meditation staff as a gift to convey his brethren's "very deep feelings about it [the Hsüan-chung Ssu] since they regarded it as the house of their patriarch": see *HTFH,* 7/60, p. 17 (November 1960).

10. *HTFH,* 4/61, p. 31 (October 1961). This article ended with the thought that "we should give the pagoda the same loving care and protection as we give the traditional friendship between China and Nepal." The issue of *Modern Buddhism* in which it appeared was published in the same month that the Sino-Nepalese Boundary Treaty was signed. See also Amritananda, *Buddhist Activities,* p. 27. Some Nepalese believe that Arniko's is another pagoda—one neglected by the Chinese.

11. On the cost, see *HTFH,* 7/60, p. 30 (November 1960). On the delegations, see Chapter II, note 18.

12. *Canton,* p. 43, which also explains its importance as an example of ancient architecture. A British visitor described the whole temple as a mu-

seum: see Wand B. Forman, *The Face of Ancient China,* tr. I. Urwin (London, Spring Books, 1960), p. 212. This temple also housed a drama school, whose cadres "by mistake" smashed the main Buddha images when they moved in (see below note 67); naturally this was not disclosed to visitors.

13. NCNA English, May 6, 1961, in *SCMP,* 2494:24.

14. *World Buddhism,* 11.11:7 (June 1963). [Aurel] Stein's interpretation of some Khotanese paintings was cited as an example.

15. *HTFH,* 10/59, p. 14. Cf. 6/53, p. 53. Four of the six institutions on which most of the money was spent were Chinese temples.

16. This was the Yung-ho Kung, one of the principal tourist attractions in Peking and the center there for Vajrayana Buddhism. Its repair was said to have cost the equivalent of US$336,000. See Peter Schmid, *The New Face of China,* pp. 56-57.

17. The figure of a hundred-odd was first given in 1957: "More than one hundred big monasteries have been repaired and renovated" (Chao, *Buddhism in China,* p. 36). This figure must have included pagodas because in 1959 Shirob reported that "to date one hundred monasteries and pagodas have been repaired in China": see *HTFH,* 10/59, p. 14. In 1964 still same figure was used: "more than one hundred big monasteries have been repaired." See *World Buddhism,* 12.4:6-7 (November 1963). This seems to indicate that not much additional restoration had been done between 1957 and 1964; and that is confirmed by the dates available in individual cases (see Appendix D).

18. These few were the Ling-yin Ssu in Hangchow, the K'ai-yüan Ssu in Chüanchow (where most of the money spent seems to have gone for conversion of its main hall into a museum of commerce), the Pai-ma Ssu (Loyang), the K'ai-fu Ssu (Changsha), the Ch'i-hsia Ssu (Nanking), the Hsüan-chung Ssu (Shansi), the Tz'u-en Ssu (Sian), the Hsien-t'ung Ssu (Wu-t'ai Shan), and the Kuang-chi Ssu and Yung-ho Kung (Peking). There is no reason for assuming that anything but minor repairs were made at other monasteries.

19. See Chapter I, note 14.

20. For example, in August 1951 the Government Administration Council informed the municipal government of Tientsin that if a temple had historical value, it could not be damaged and it could only be converted to another use after obtaining the consent of the Ministry of Culture in Peking: see *HTFH,* 11/51, p. 36. Also in August 1951 the GAC approved of a measure for the management of temples in Peking. It made their resident monks responsible for protecting their contents. A temple "with major historical or cultural value" could only be taken over for a school or some other use if the consent of the Monuments Bureau (Wen-wu Chü) of the Ministry of Culture in Peking had been obtained, and those who took it over became responsible for the protection of its buddha images, sacred texts, and cultural and religious objects. See *HTFH,* 10/51, p. 3. On November 7, 1951, the Central-South Military and Administrative Commission issued a directive signed by its chairman, Lin Piao, on the protection of cultural objects during agrarian reform

(thus reinforcing Article 21 of the Agrarian Reform Law). Cadres were told that they should protect ancient architecture and religious sculpture and that they would be punished if they failed to do so. See *Ch'ang-chiang jih-pao,* November 29, 1951, tr. in *SCMP,* 230:16. In 1954 the GAC sent another order to the Tientsin municipal authorities, pointing out that temples, pagodas, and other antiquities should be protected; their destruction was strictly forbidden; and no alterations could be made without the approval of the Municipal Bureau of Culture. Especially when old buildings had been made into schools (compare the earlier order), students had to be cautioned against doing any damage. See *HTFH,* 9/54, p. 30. The first of these orders was circulated by the Ministry of Culture to cadres in the rest of the country "for reference," and it is likely that all the orders were meant to have an effect that was more than local. Peking and other large cities often served as models for carrying out directives that later took effect nationwide (e.g., in the Five-Anti Campaign).

21. The directive of the Central-South Military and Administrative Commission of November 7, 1951 (see note 20), called on local authorities to make up lists of cultural objects, including temples and their contents, for submission to the Department of Culture. In the same month *Modern Buddhism* published two questionnaires addressed to its readers, the first on temples and second on cultural objects. One question on the second was: "What people or organs are looking after them [the cultural objects]? Have there been any losses or damage and what has been their real extent?" The purpose of the questionnaires was "to compile a report to the authorities concerned and then find means to extend protection." See *HTFH,* 11/51, p. 36; cf. 3/52, p. 33-36. It seems likely that the questionnaires and the MAC directive reflected some initiative in the autumn of 1951 by the Ministry of Culture. Again in 1953 *Modern Buddhism* printed an article calling on the head of each monastery to report all valuables to the local government, museum, and Buddhist association: see *HTFH,* 8/53, p. 16. Cf. Chapter I, note 96.

22. The full text of the regulations, together with the list of objects under national protection, was published in *KMJP,* April 2, 1961, tr. in *CB,* no. 654.

23. The principle of "keeping everything intact and restoring only the important parts" had been cited by Shirob in 1959: see *HTFH,* 10/59, p. 14. Already in 1951 Chü-tsan had called for setting priorities in conservation work, so that most of the money available would be used for putting one or two monasteries in each large city into good repair and leaving the rest "until Buddhist circles have the resources": see *HTFH,* 1/52, p. 6.

24. Many monasteries had already been converted into museums and institutions for the protection of cultural objects. For example the Pao-lin Ssu, Shun-te, Kwangtung, had been converted into a cultural institute: see *HTFH,* 9/53, p. 22. The Kuang-hsiao Ssu in Canton housed not only the Sino-Indian museum mentioned above, but also the Municipal Commission for the Protec-

tion of Cultural Property (Wen-wu Pao-kuan Wei-yüan-hui). The K'ai-yüan Ssu in Chüanchow housed a museum on overseas commerce; the Chieh-chuang Ssu, Soochow, housed a museum of Buddhist art (see Fig. 18e). Conversion to a museum did not exclude the continued residence of monks, who often acted as caretakers. For example, the Hai-ch'uang Ssu in Canton had been made into a public park after it was repaired (*Canton,* p. 47), but it still had an abbot in residence, who received foreign delegations and taught the art of miniature gardening: see *Hōchū Nihon Bukkyō,* p. 33, and Hong Kong *Wen-hui pao,* June 17, 1961. In other cases, as at the Pa-ta Ch'u outside Peking, the caretakers were laymen.

25. Until mid-1951 the supervision of all temples in Peking with major historical or cultural value had been in the hands of the Civil Affairs Bureau. Responsibility then shifted to one of the cultural organs. See *HTFH,* 10/51, p. 3. In the provinces it sometimes remained longer with the united front organs. For example, in December 1952 the United Front Department of Tzu-kuang, Szechwan, asked a local monk to draw up a report on monasteries and antiquities so that the most important could be repaired and protected. He got his fellow Buddhists together and they chose five monasteries. See *HTFH,* 2/53, p. 28. At about the same time the United Front Department of the Pei-chiang special district in Kwangtung called a meeting of local abbots to discuss restoration plans: see *ibid.* When repairs to the K'ai-yüan Ssu, Chüanchow turned out badly, it was the head of the United Front Department who asked the abbot to draw up a plan on how to set things right: see *HTFH,* 6/53, p. 37. In these cases a local division of religious affairs had probably not been set up yet.

26. In Changsha this was called the Commission for the Management of Cultural Property (Wen-wu Kuan-li Wei-yüan-hui): see *HTFH,* 11/59, p. 28. The Wo-fo Ssu in Peking was repaired in 1955 under the auspices of the "Park Commission" of the municipal government: see *Peking: A Tourist Guide* (Peking, Foreign Languages Press, 1960), p. 118. In Canton the Commission for the Protection of Cultural Property (see note 24) had a staff of about ten persons and came under the local Cultural Division. Its chief concern was monasteries and it often went for help in protecting them to the Religious Affairs Division, according to a former cadre thereof. Published reports of renovation often do not state which unit of the local government was responsible. They seldom mention Buddhist associations and almost never religious affairs organs.

27. On the Wu-t'ai Shan commission, see *HTFH,* 6/53, p. 53. On the Omei Shan Cultural Properties Renovation Commission (Wen-wu Cheng-hsiu Wei-yüan-hui), see *HTFH,* 6/53, p. 57. On the special commission set up in 1952 to handle the maintenance of the Yün-kang caves, see NCNA English, May 6, 1961, in *SCMP,* 2494:23 and NCNA English, June 9, 1961, in *SCMP,* 2517:24.

28. *China Reconstructs,* November 1961, p. 36. In 1950, even before this institute had been set up, an expert from the ministry had gone to Wu-t'ai Shan to advise the provincial authorities on the care of monasteries there.

29. See *HTFH,* 10/59, p. 14. Similarly the Pai-ma Ssu, which was repaired by the Loyang government in 1952 and 1955, had become a national responsibility by 1961. See *HTFH,* 1/55, p. 30, and *CB,* 654:15.

30. See *CB,* 654:12. Most of them had been repaired by 1961. The Lungmen caves in Ho-ch'in, Shansi, were also repaired by the central government: see *HTFH,* 11/56, p. 34.

31. The 8,000 cultural objects are mentioned in *CB,* 654:7.

32. See *HTFH,* 10/58, pp. 15-17, for the official report of the renovation committee. More information is contained in *World Buddhism,* February 1962, pp. 23, 25, and Mibu, "Jinmin Chūgoku," p. 10. The report of the renovation committee described several earlier altercations between the monks and Professor Teng as, for example, over the question of what material should be used. This was referred to the Chekiang Provincial People's Council and then to the State Council in Peking.

33. According to *The Buddha Tooth Relic in China* (Peking, 1961), p. 11, construction began in November 1957 and was completed in May 1960. The cornerstone, however, was laid on June 2, 1958: see NCNA English, June 2, 1958, in *SCMP,* 1786:37.

34. *HTFH,* 3/64, p. 57 (June 1964); 4/64, p. 45 (August 1964).

35. See Katsumata Shunkyō "Chūka Jinmin Kyōwakoku" in *Bukkyō Dainenkan* (Tokyo, 1969), p. 836.

36. More details on this will be given in Chapter VI. For references to the pagoda as proof of religious freedom in China, see Chapter VI, note 130.

37. The initiative for the construction of the Chien-chen Memorial Hall and for the visits by Japanese delegations had come from the Chinese, and it was their idea that the building should be modeled on the main hall of the Tōshodaiji in Nara (see *Ganjin wajō,* pp. 12-13). For a long article on the plans for the hall see *HTFH,* 1/64, pp. 12-14 (January 1964). On the religious services that preceded the laying of the cornerstone, in which first Chinese and then Japanese priests chanted sutras in front of the soul tablets of Chien-chen and his companions at the Fa-ching Ssu in Yangchow, see *Ganjin wajō,* pp. 21, 36, and NCNA English, October 15, 1963, in *SCMP,* 3084:18. The Japanese were told that they would be invited back to witness the opening of the hall, but they never heard anything more about it. In 1967 a Japanese visitor saw a wall poster accusing the Liu Shao-ch'i faction of being "proreligious" and having favored the construction of the Chien-chen Memorial Hall, which had now been canceled. See Tokuda Myōhon, "Bunkaku ka no Chūgoku Bukkyo o miru," *Asahi shimbun,* Oct. 22, 1967. On the memorial hall for Hsüan-tsang, to be erected at the Tz'u-en Ssu in Sian, see NCNA English, June 27, 1964, in *SCMP,* 3250:22.

38. On the seminaries in the Republican period, see Welch, *Revival,* pp. 107-120, 285-287.

39. Various English translations have been used by the Chinese themselves for Chung-kuo Fo-hsüeh-yüan: "Chinese Buddhist Academy" (1956), "Chinese College of Buddhism" (1957), "Institute of Buddhist Theology" (1960), and "Chinese Buddhist Theological Institute" (1965). I prefer to use the word "seminary" because it denotes more specifically a place for the training of the clergy and because it is consistent with the usage in the preceding volumes.

40. The inaugural ceremony was held September 28, 1956, and attended by 400 persons, including Buddhist delegates from seven Asian countries. The opening enrollment was 118 students. See *HTFH,* 11/56, pp. 3, 34.

41. The principal was Shirob Jaltso, and the deputy principals were Chao P'u-ch'u, Chü-tsan, Chou Shu-chia, and Fa-tsun.

42. See *HTFH,* 11/56, p. 4; Chao, *Buddhism in China,* p. 42; *Kuang-hui-ti pa-nien,* p. 176. The course for training administrators was originally to be of two years' duration and the first batch of students did indeed graduate in 1958 (*HTFH,* 9/58, p. 32). Then, however, it appears to have changed its name to "study class" (*hsüeh-hsi pan*) and its term to six months. At any rate the first study class graduated in September 1959 after half a year at the seminary, and its members were exhorted to "carry out the work in their posts under the local Party and government direction, unite the Buddhist community, and make positive contributions to socialist construction and the preservation of world peace." In the *second* "study class," which began the next month, 97 monks were enrolled: see *HTFH,* 11/59, p. 34. Graduation of the third and last study class, which ran one year, took place August 17, 1961: see *HTFH,* 4/61, p. 49 (October 1961).

43. The priority given to political study is clear from the speeches made when these classes began and ended: see *HTFH,* 11/59, p. 34, tr. in JPRS 6289:10-12. It may be, however, that politics were not so conspicuous at the seminary as at most educational institutions—in 1957, at least. Nogami reports seeing none of the wall posters there that he saw at other schools in Peking (Nogami, "Shin Chūgoku no tabi," *Chūgai nippō,* Aug. 23, 1957).

44. On the research department (*yen-chiu pu*) see *KMJP,* August 28, 1962, in *SCMP,* 2824:13-15. The changing organization of curriculum and departments is hard to trace. Successive reports do not employ the same terminology. For example, the second year of the "research class" (*yen-chiu pan*) began October 10, 1959: see *HTFH,* 11/59, p. 34. In August 1961, when this class graduated, most of its members had spent five years of study, including the basic course (*pen-k'o*). Some of them then entered the research department (*yen-chiu pu*): see *HTFH,* 4/61, pp. 49-50 (October 1961). The research department produced its first eleven graduates in 1964: see *Chung-kuo hsin-wen,* November 19, 1964. Apparently some students spent only the two years of 1956-58 in the four-year basic course, then transferred to the

research class for the three years of 1958-61, and finally entered the research department for another three years. Perhaps the research course was *replaced* by the research department.

45. On the curriculum after 1961 see *HTFH,* 6/51, p. 18 (December 1961); 2/62, pp. 22-27 (May 1962), and *Chung-kuo hsin-wen*, November 19, 1964.

46. See Chapter I at notes 39, 83, 84. In 1962 there was a Chinese from Peking studying at Vidyalankara, the Buddhist university outside Colombo. He reportedly kept very much to himself and refused to see visitors.

47. On the Tibetan department see *HTFH,* 6/62, p. 17 (December 1962).

48. Among the laymen Yü Yü gave a course in Buddhist logic; Yeh Ch'ün taught Pali and Theravada Buddhism; Chou Shu-chia taught Fa-hsiang philosophy. Tibetan Buddhism was taught by the Reverend Fa-tsun. *Nagel's Guide,* p. 556, states that there were "about ten teachers." A visitor in 1962 was told that there were eleven teachers and a "director of studies." Yeh Ch'ün may be identical with the monk Liao-ts'an, who went to Ceylon in 1946 to study Theravada, returned in the 1950's with the ashes from his master, Fa-fang, and then disrobed.

Oddly enough I have seen no mention of T'ang Yung-t'ung, China's leading scholar of Buddhism, in connection with the seminary. Over the years he only contributed three articles to *Modern Buddhism* (all in 1961-63). In 1962 it was announced that he had collected the materials to write a history of Buddhism in the Sui and T'ang (as a sequel to his masterful work on the Six Dynasties), but all that finally appeared was a collection of his old articles: see *KMJP* September 10, 1962, tr. in JPRS 15630, p. 12.

49. See *HTFH,* 2/64, pp. 36-37 (April 1964), for an impressive description of the operations and medical care given in 1962 to a monk from Wu-t'ai Shan who was enrolled at the seminary. As to the pocket money received by students there, the sums of 6 JMP for students in the basic course and 15 for those in the research department were mentioned to a foreign visitor. Other information about perquisites may be found in *HTFH,* 10/59, p. 13, and *Chung-kuo hsin-wen,* November 19, 1964. The cost of operating the seminary, including the salaries of faculty members, must have amounted to 15-20 thousand JMP per annum. It was never officially explained where the operating expenses came from, but anything on this scale can only have come from the government, probably via the CBA. In 1957 Chou Shu-chia, a deputy principal, said that the establishment of the seminary was "inseparable from the strong support and leadership of the People's Government": see *HTFH,* 7/57, p. 13. A former cadre of the Religious Affairs Division in Canton stated simply that the seminary was run by the Religious Affairs Bureau.

50. Nogami and Ogasawara were told in June 1957 that the 120 students of the seminary all sat for a certain number of hours each day in the meditation hall of the Fa-yüan Ssu (Nogami, "Shin Chūgoku no tabi," Aug. 23, 1957). There is no mention of this, however, in any of the articles about the

seminary published by the Chinese themselves, and a European visitor was told in 1962 that students were simply at liberty to meditate during their two and a half hours of free time per day.

51. *Chung-kuo hsin-wen,* January 10, 1966. There are many gaps and inconsistencies in the successive figures for how many students were enrolled in each course, how many graduated from each, and how many graduated in all. The most reasonable way of reconciling them may be to suppose that total enrollment ran from 115 to 120 in 1956-60 (of which about a hundred were in the "study course" that prepared them to be administrators and the rest either in the basic course or research course); and 50-70 in 1961-65 (of which about 15-20 were in the research department and the rest in the basic course). One visitor was told that in 1961 no new students had been accepted and hence the enrollment had dropped from 110 (in 1960) to 50 (in March 1962 at the time of the visit).

52. See Welch, *Revival,* p. 287.

53. In 1957 a delegate to the CBA's second national conference suggested that the number of students be increased and that one or two additional seminaries be set up in other parts of the country: see *HTFH,* 5/57, p. 17. A separate seminary for nuns had also been planned: see Chao, *Buddhism in China* (1957), pp. 42, 43 (omitted from the 1960 edition). In 1962 Chao said merely the preparations for the seminary for nuns should be made: see *HTFH,* 2/62, p. 36 (May 1962).

54. See *HTFH,* 12/54, pp. 20-23; 5/57, pp. 6, 17. Information about the 20,000 JMP provided by the municipal government was given to an Indian visitor in 1955. Only 47,420 blocks had been at Chin-ling before the process of centralization began. That the purpose of the centralization was not merely to keep scriptures in print is suggested by the transfer in 1957 of 22,600 blocks that formerly belonged to the Peking and Tientsin scriptural presses. These had closed down, but their blocks had continued to be used for printing by the San-shih Study Society: see *HTFH,* 1/54, p. 28; 10/54, p. 30.

55. The tax-free publication of Hsüan-tsang's works was announced in 1958: *Chung-kuo hsin-wen,* May 15, 1958, and Chao, *Buddhism in China* (1960), p. 39. However, the printing may have taken place earlier. A complete set of Hsüan-tsang's translations was presented by the Dalai Lama to Premier Nehru in December 1956: see *HTFH,* 5/57, p. 5. A mimeographed catalogue put out by the Chin-ling Press in 1956 (a copy of which is in the Harvard-Yenching Library) lists about 1,200 items, none of which appear to be new books or new editions. About 500 were printed with blocks collected from scriptural presses that had been closed down. The largest and most expensive item was the translation by Hsüan-tsang of the *Mahāprajñāpāramitā sutra* in 600 chüan, priced at 135.88 JMP. Most items were less than 1 JMP.

56. Hsü made this suggestion to the CBA's second national conference and it was echoed by other delegates: see *HTFH,* 5/57, pp. 17, 22, 24. It is almost certain that if the canon had been reprinted after 1949, the event

would have been given a lot of publicity. In 1956 it was announced that a Tripitaka would be printed from the 8,000 stone tablets in Fang-shan, but the next year the plan had been reduced to reproduction of rubbings for distribution as gifts to commemorate the Buddha's 2,500th anniversary. See NCNA English, February 22, 1956, in *SCMP,* 1235:15, and Chao, *Buddhism in China* (1957), p. 43. One of the best known sets of wood blocks of the canon, from which several printings were made under the Republic, was the Lung-tsang Tripitaka at the Po-lin Ssu. By 1961 its blocks had been moved to the National Library in Peking "where they could perform the function they ought to have"–apparently meaning to gather dust: see *JMJP,* July 23, 1961. Describing the work of the Chin-ling Press, Chao P'u-ch'u once said that its 110,000 blocks were "kept ready for printing Buddhist books to meet the needs of Buddhists in various places": see *Buddhism in China* (1960), p. 39. To keep them ready for printing was not the same as to print with them.

57. *HTFH,* 5/57, p. 17.

58. Mibu, "Jinmin Chūgoku," p. 9. This delegation, like others, was shown several workmen cutting blocks and binding books. They were told that the press operated on a government subsidy and received many orders from Theravada countries.

59. A photograph of the Shanghai Buddhist Bookshop appeared in *Buddhists in New China* (1956), p. 122. Cf. NCNA English, August 20, 1959, in *SCMP,* 2084:44.

60. On the announcement by the Central Scriptural Press, see *HTFH,* 12/50, p. 35. Its disposal sale may be what Wen Kuang-hsi referred to when he complained the next spring that scriptural presses were selling precious Buddhist books by the pound, like waste paper: see *HTFH,* 5/51, p. 24. By 1953 the Wen-ming Buddhist Library near Shanghai had given away all its books and asked Buddhists not to send in any more orders: see *HTFH,* 4/53, p. 27. It is not clear exactly what kind of financial pressure caused liquidations like this: it may have been higher rents or taxes. On the destruction of sutras, see Chapter IV at note 55. On an attempt to convert them into pulp, see below note 67.

61. In 1954 there were still four Buddhist bookshops in Shanghai: the Fo-hsüeh Shu-chü, Ta-fa-lun Shu-chü, Ta-hsiung Shu-chü, and Hung-hua She: see *HTFH,* 4/53, p. 27; 4/54, p. 21. Their amalgamation into the Shanghai Fo-chiao Shu-tien, reportedly a joint State-private enterprise, had taken place by 1956, the same year in which the *Hung-hua* monthly was taken over by the Shanghai Buddhist Association (see Chapter I, note 47). Already in 1952 the heads of the four Shanghai bookshops had gotten together to discuss how to screen books published before Liberation (which might contain reactionary materials): see *Chüeh yu-ch'ing,* 13.2:18-19 (October 1952). Ch'en Hai-lung, the head of the Ta-hsiung Bookshop, was arrested in 1955 for counterrevolutionary activities: see *HTFH,* 4/56, p. 5. In 1956 the only independent bookshop in Peking, the Keng-shen Fo-ching Liu-t'ung-ch'u in the Ta-fo Ssu

was still sending out new catalogues: see *HTFH,* 1/56, p. 28; cf. 7/53, p. 20. It had apparently ceased operating by 1962 when the CBA was about to set up a Buddhist bookshop to handle books and religious articles: see NCNA English, February 13, 1962, in *SCMP,* 2681:21.

62. See *China Pictorial,* 8/62, pp. 18-19. Cf. *HTFH,* 5/57, p. 15, *China Reconstructs,* 1-2/54, p. 43, and NCNA English, August 7, 1961, in *SCMP,* 2557:19.

63. See *Chung-kuo hsin-wen,* September 2, 1955, tr. in *SCMP,* 1128:10, and *HTFH,* 5/57, p. 6. By 1957 the copy of the Chi-sha Tripitaka that used to be in the Wo-lung Ssu, Sian, had been removed to the Shensi Provincial Library: see Tsukamoto and Makita, p. 301.

64. *HTFH,* 6/58, pp. 3-5. Translations into the vernacular would have offered an opportunity to reinterpret the sutras and "cleanse them of impurities," as Chü-tsan had called for in 1950 (*HTFH,* 10/50, p. 22); but the advantages of this were evidently outweighed by the difficulties of agreeing on *how* they should be reinterpreted and by what seems to have been the government's opposition to increasing the circulation of sutras in any form.

65. Chapter I at note 15; Chapter II, notes 115-116. Another case involved the tomb of a former abbot of the Hu-ch'iu in Soochow. It was destroyed by "a certain middle school that did not know how to cherish historical monuments" and then rebuilt at government expense: see *HTFH,* 5/53, p. 26. In 1956 there was a report of the demolition of old temples in Shensi by farmers who used the bricks to build conduits and wells. They were later prosecuted for destroying national cultural treasures: see *KMJP,* September 23, 1956, p. 1, cited in *CNA,* 221:6.

66. The only such case I have seen reported in the press involved nineteen large and small monasteries in Wuhan that were razed in 1956 to clear land for industrial construction. Their monks, after being consulted, were said to have "displayed an attitude of serving the general welfare and gladly accepting the demolition." See *HTFH,* 5/57, p. 19. According to oral reports, the Nan-ch'an Ssu in Soochow was torn down to make room for workers' housing; and the Twin Pagodas in Peking were demolished to widen the west end of Changan Street.

67. For example, in 1950 the three main bronze images of the Kuang-hsiao Ssu, Canton, were destroyed when a drama cadres' school took over the building. According to a former official of the Canton Religious Division, the cadres were criticized for this by the CCP Central Committee in 1953. Cf. *Nagel's Guide,* pp. 1179-1180. A more interesting case took place in An-tung, Liaoning. After the monks of the Pao-shan Ssu there were struggled against, all the monastery's bronze buddha images were allocated to machine factories for use as scrap metal; and all its sutras were allocated to paper factories for pulp. The abbot of the neighboring monastery then persuaded the authorities to let him ransom these articles by providing the equivalent weight in bronze and waste paper: see *HTFH,* 3/51, p. 35. Also in 1951, a reader wrote to

Modern Buddhism asking: "If the local government wants to confiscate Buddhist bells, chimes, and other liturgical instruments in order to make them into farm tools, does it contradict the GAC decreee that protects antiquities?" The reply was: " 'Wanting to confiscate' means having the plan to do so, but not yet having carried it out. It is all right to present one's views to the local government on the basis of the GAC's decree on the protection of antiquities, in order to prevent damage to ancient objects. When it comes to broken bronze and iron, we consider that it is all right to make them a contribution to the government." See *HTFH,* 9/51, p. 22. Other allusions to the destruction of images may be found in *HTFH,* 10/50, p. 24; 5/51, p. 25; 8/53, p. 17; *JMJP,* March 17, 1957 (quoted in *CNA,* 221:6); Hong Kong *Kung-shang jih-pao,* February 1 and 8, 1954. The Hong Kong *Hsing-tao jih-pao* of November 6, 1950, reported that the monks of the Liu-jung Ssu, Canton, had sold off gold and silver altar furnishings in order to buy food.

68. For example, temples in Shanghai contributed 200,000 catties of scrap iron and copper to the State: see *Chieh-fang pao,* November 10, 1958, tr. in *SCMP,* 1943:10. Buddhists in Shih-ch'eng *hsien,* Kiangsi, contributed 24,000 catties of bronze, iron, and pewter "scrap articles" in order to "answer the war maneuvers of the American imperialists": see *HTFH,* 11/58, p. 32. Cf. p. 33. With rare exceptions (e.g., see Chapter X at note 44) such reports do not state specifically that buddha images were taken off the altar to be melted down, but there is both oral and documentary evidence that they were. One informant, for example, recalled that the small temple where he was living in Wuhan had to contribute one bronze image, two bronze candlesticks weighing a hundred catties, and a bronze bell during the scrap metal campaign in 1958. As for documentary evidence, two years after the Great Leap Forward was over, the State Council passed the Provisional Regulations on the protection of cultural objects in 1961. Article 13 reads: "Departments concerned with the recovery of old and discarded materials and departments using such materials shall, jointly with the local cultural administration, be responsible for sorting out such cultural objects as may be present among the recovered materials of this kind. They shall also pay attention to the protection of cultural objects thus sorted out." See *KMJP,* April 2, 1961, in *CB,* 654:4. The easiest way to explain this provision is that the Ministry of Culture wanted to recover valuable images and other religious objects that had been contributed during the scrap metal drive. They were not necessarily returned to the Buddhists, however. After 1966 they began to be sold abroad. Antique dealers from Hong Kong could buy them in Canton.

69. The most important religious images destroyed in China were those of the Taoist temples at Wu-tang Shan: see *SCMP,* 1517:8-9.

70. *HTFH,* 5/51, pp. 26-27. Cf. Chapter I at notes 15, 29, 81.

71. *HTFH,* 10/53, p. 32 which reprints the decree of August 13, 1953, by the country government, ordering protection of the buddha images from the Five Dynasties, Sung, and Ming in the Thousand Buddha Caves, inside and

outside the Pao-kuo Ssu, and elsewhere in the area, as "artistic creations of the working people." Similarly, when Buddhist images and sutras were destroyed in Shun-te county, Kwangtung, it was blamed on the sangha, "who had not studied the government's religious policy and therefore were unable to do anything to correct the errors of the cadres": see *HTFH,* 9/53, p. 22.

72. *HTFH,* 10/50, p. 23. Although the Shang-feng Ssu was one of the principal temples on Nan-yüeh, it was still not in the first rank of importance among Chinese monasteries, like Chin Shan, Pao-hua Shan, Kao-min, T'ien-t'ung, Ling-yin, Ling-yen, and so on. (No such monastery, so far as I know, was touched before the Cultural Revolution.) It was important enough, however, so that its destruction was cited as one reason for the GAC directive of July 1950 on the protection of monasteries. See *ibid.* Possibly it was rebuilt, since in 1954 a third of the net profit from the pilgrim season went for subsidies to the Ta Miao and the Shang-feng Ssu: see *HTFH,* 2/55, p. 29.

73. For example, the Buddhists of Honan were reported in 1953 to be grateful for the government's restoration (*hsiu-fu*) of the Shao-lin Ssu (*HTFH,* 6/53, p. 43), but in 1958 it turned out that nothing had been done but "elementary repairs": see *Honan jih-pao,* January 11, 1958, tr. in *SCMP,* 1732:30. On the dilapidated condition of this monastery before Liberation, see Sekino Tei and Tokiwa Daijō, *Shina Bukkyō shiseki* (Tokyo, 1925-29), II, 118-138. The Ling-yin Ssu, Hangchow, was not "in ruins at the time of Liberation," as NCNA English claimed on May 12, 1958, (*SCMP,* 1773:34). The roof of the main shrine hall did not collapse until June 1949, two months after Liberation. Furthermore this hall had been built new in 1912 at a cost of 150 thousand taels provided by the Buddhists themselves—equivalent to somewhat more than the 500,000 JMP spent by the government in 1952-58. Nothing was said about this in reports of the new restoration. Nor was anything said about the fact that the Ch'i-hsia Ssu, repaired by 1954, had been rebuilt from the ground up in the 1920's by the Buddhists themselves; and was in excellent repair at the time of Liberation, as was the Kuang-chi Ssu in Peking.

Exaggeration can also be found in statements about the Chinese Buddhist Seminary. It was not true that "before Liberation seminaries had existed in name only and one can say that this is the first seminary in Chinese history" (*Chung-kuo hsin-wen*, January 10, 1966). Nor was it true that, as a visiting Sinhalese bhikkhu was told in 1958, the students enrolled there were being trained to go out into the villages and preach the dharma. That was indeed a goal that appealed to this particular visitor, but it was illegal in People's China for monks to preach in public places.

74. The 230,000 monasteries and temples that existed before Liberation had been maintained solely by the Buddhists themselves with no government assistance for forty years. In view of their great number it is not surprising (though seldom alluded to in the Mainland press) that many of them—including even important monasteries and pagodas—were *not* repaired after

Liberation, as, for example, the T'ien-ning pagoda in Peking (Fig. 26), the Pei-t'a Ssu in Soochow; the T'ien-ning Ssu, Yangchow, and the Kuang-hsiao Ssu, T'ai-chou (*HTFH,* 5/57, pp. 21-22); and six historic pagodas in Shansi in Hupeh (*ibid.,* p. 25). A visitor to Nanking in 1962 made a point of asking the vice-president of the Nanking Buddhist Association about six well-known Buddhist temples that were not on the tourist route. As to four of them, he replied that he was unsure whether they still existed; one definitely did not exist (the Hai-ch'ao Ssu) and the sixth (the Chin-ling Ssu) had been "destroyed by reactionaries."

Our information, however, is not complete enough to permit us to say that, because the repair of a temple has not been mentioned, it has not been repaired. We can only say that if up to a hundred temples were repaired in all, many thousands were not.

75. See Chapter II at note 66. In rare cases we hear of temples receiving enough donations to be able to make repairs on their own. For example, the Ta Hsiang-shan Ssu in Yao-hsien, Shensi, received over 10,000 JMP from worshipers during the Kuan-yin festival in 1962. It was to be used for redecorating the great shrine-hall and repairing the library. See *HTFH,* 5/62, p. 40 (October 1962). This would probably not have happened in years when the political atmosphere was less relaxed.

76. An example is the Nan-hua Ssu, which had been restored by Hsü-yün in the 1930's. At the time of Liberation it had 4.2 ounces of gold put aside to repair one of its buildings. This was kept hidden in Canton for nine years, but in 1958 it had to be contributed to support the iron-smelting campaign in order "to smash the US-Chiang bandits": see *HTFH,* 11/58, p. 31.

77. Thus a couple of monks on Omei Shan mended windows and propped up walls: see *HTFH,* 6/53, p. 57. Other monks there took part in major repairs made by the government but got wages for it "that helped to solve their livelihood problems." Some 35 monks and nuns were employed as technicians and workers by the Omei Cultural Property Renovation Commission. They worked side by side with the "labor reform squads" that also helped with restoration work (*ibid*). The only case in which monks did major construction themselves was the Yün-chü Ssu in Kiangsi, where twelve buildings were constructed between 1953 and 1958, all in traditional style. This was possible partly because of the inspiring leadership given by Hsü-yün and partly because the equivalent of more than US$50,000 was received from Buddhists abroad. See Ts'en Hsüeh-lü, *Hsü-yün ho-shang nien-p'u,* p. 394-395.

VI. BUDDHISM IN FOREIGN RELATIONS

1. Such reasoning was never publicly admitted, for that would have risked making foreign Buddhists feel they were being used. The closest thing to a public admission came in Chang Chih-i's "Discussion of the National Ques-

tion," where he stated: "Islam, Buddhism, Catholicism, and Protestantism all have a great many adherents throughout the world; in Eastern countries it is especially Islam and Buddhism that have large followings. *To deal correctly with the internal religious problem will thus have a bearing upon the peaceful international relations of our country and be beneficial to the unity and coöperation of the forces for international peace.* The adoption of a simple, crude attitude toward these religions would have international repercussions, causing certain people to become more distrustful of our country and adversely affecting efforts towards peace. Therefore the policy of freedom of religious belief is the fundamental policy of the Chinese Communist Party with respect to the religious question." See George Moseley, *The Party and the National Question in China* (Cambridge, M.I.T. Press, 1966), p. 116. Cf. Chapter I at note 17.

2. The cities most frequently visited by foreign Buddhists were Canton, Peking, Loyang, Shanghai, Hangchow, Soochow, Nanking, Sian, Taiyuan. Delegations on longer tours or with special interests visited Chen-chiang, Yangchow, Wuhan, Tientsin, Tatung, Shenyang, Anshan, Changchun, Sining, and Kunming. Appendix D does not list all these cities among those where monasteries were repaired at government expense. That is because it is based only on published information. Visitors were taken to monasteries in Soochow, Chen-chiang, Taiyüan, Tatung, Shenyang, and Changchun that were in such good repair that their maintenance seems likely to have been paid for by the government, although I have found no published statement to that effect. This is true of three monasteries in Soochow, for example: the Chieh-chuang Ssu, Han-shan Ssu, and Ling-yen Ssu.

3. Already in 1952 delegates to the Peace Conference of Asia and Pacific Region "during their tour of [Shanghai] monasteries and temples saw solemn religious rites underway in all of them—chanting and lecturing on the sutras with many monks taking part": see *HTFH,* 6/53, p. 37.

4. Among the Japanese delegations who joined in chanting were the Ōtani delegation in 1961, the Kongō delegation in 1963, and the Furukawa delegation in 1966. The Japanese would chant (often the same texts) after the Chinese had finished. The melodies and pronunciation had diverged too far for them to chant in unison.

5. For instances in which labor by monks was freely admitted to Japanese Buddhists (who, reading Chinese, would have learned about it anyway), see Tsukamoto and Makita, p. 301, and Mibu, "Jinmin Chūgoku," p. 8. Although most of the information about what Southeast Asian Buddhists were told comes orally from those I have interviewed, Amritananda wrote after his tour in 1959 that "Chinese Buddhist monks, as in any other country, live on charity. Some monasteries may have their own property. In China monastic property belongs to the monks and they are free of tax. In case of need, the government gives grant[s]to support the monks and temples." See Amritananda, *Buddhist Activities in Socialist Countries* (Peking, 1961), p. 18.

6. There is no photograph of productive labor or political study in *Buddhists in China; Buddhists in New China; The Friendship of Buddhism* (Peking, 1957); Chao, *Buddhism in China.* None was ever printed in *Modern Buddhism* (even though labor and study were often referred to in the Chinese text, which Southeast Asian Buddhists could not read); and none was among the photographs of Chinese Buddhist activities that were exhibited in Colombo, October 26-November 1, 1960.

7. This emphasis can also be seen in some of the illustrations in the first volume of this series (Welch, *Practice*). Those taken at the P'i-lu Ssu were supplied by the CBA to show foreigners what monastic life was like in China. Fig. 3 shows a wandering monk applying for admission–although in fact monks were being discouraged from the wandering life. Fig. 15 shows monks eating silently at long tables in the refectory–although in fact they seldom ate this way any more. Figs. 10 *et passim* show devotions and reciting buddha's name, both of which had also become less frequent than before Liberation. (All these changes have been described in Chapter IV.) What is particularly interesting is that the photographs of reciting buddha's name were labeled on the back: "meditation hall" (*ch'an-t'ang*). The last meditation hall had closed down several years before 1962, when these photographs were taken. Note that on the wall over the sitting mats are posted names and titles. Although it is the eastern wall, there are the names of three priors and three subpriors. The traditional practice was for the names of priors and subpriors to be posted in the west and simply entitled "secretaries" (their *rank*). It is odd to see *offices* posted here.

8. For a picture of the monks who greeted Sihanouk at the airport, see *The Friendship of Buddhism,* p. 29. The information about their collection by the truckload comes from a foreign diplomat who observed it several times during his eleven years in Peking. He said that there was a similar collection of mullahs to greet Muslim leaders. (An Arab diplomat recalled that he could always tell when there was a delegation in Peking from a Muslim country: the mosque, usually almost empty on Friday, would be full.)

9. One of my informants was among those who used to be collected in this way. An eminent Indian bhikkhu touring China in 1956 noticed that the monks he met often looked familiar. Then he realized that they were being taken from monastery to monastery in each city to greet his delegation.

10. See Chapter II, note 122.

11. For an early example of this, see *Chūgai nippō,* November 19, 1957.

12. See Chapter II, note 18.

13. See Chapter V at notes 8-13.

14. NCNA English, October 11, 1960. Since Fa-hsien's pilgrimage was 399-414 C.E., it is hard to see how this could have been its 1,500th anniversary. Perhaps it was a misprint for 1,550th–although 1,550th anniversaries are seldom celebrated.

15. *HTFH,* 1/61, p. 3 (April 1961). The Three Seals (*dharmoddāna*) are the criteria for distinguishing what is Buddhist from what is not.

16. On Shirob's speech in Colombo, see NCNA English, June 15, 1961, in *SCMP* 2521:30. My mimeographed copy of his address to the Sixth Council is dated April 28, 1955.

17. For example, all three Han monks in the delegation to the Sixth Council in 1955 wore Theravada rather than traditional Chinese robes. The 1956 delegation to Burma was led by Kupameng; the deputy head of the 1960-61 delegation to Burma was Sung-liu Achiamuniya. Another gesture was the celebration of the Buddha's birthday in 1956 according to the Theravada as well as the Chinese calendar. On Vesak day the 300 foreign Buddhist residents of Shanghai offered flowers to the Jade Buddha and were received by abbot Wei-fang. See *HTFH,* 7/56, p. 12. Some visitors report that they had to take off their shoes when they entered the Ten-thousand Buddhas Hall of the P'i-lu Ssu in Nanking—just as if they were in Burma.

18. In 1961 a Chinese who had returned from Ceylon in 1957 was polishing the translation he had made there of the *Visuddhimagga* and using it for the instruction of students in the Pali course: see *HTFH,* 2/61, p. 28 (July, 1961), which also states that the Chinese *Pratimoksa* was being translated into English at the request of the Burmese vice-minister of religion.

19. In 1955, after the government of Ceylon decided to sponsor an international encyclopedia of Buddhism, Prime Minister Kotelawala wrote Chou En-lai asking whether Chinese Buddhists would contribute a section on China. They not only accepted this responsibility, but decided to compile, within two years, a complete Buddhist encyclopedia of their own in Chinese. See *HTFH,* 4/56, p. 4. An editorial committee of fifteen members was set up with Chao P'u-Ch'u as head and Lü Ch'eng as his deputy: see NCNA English, February 22, 1956, in *SCMP* 1235:14. In 1957 its headquarters at the Chin-ling Press in Nanking were inspected by a Japanese delegation: see *Hōchū Nihon Bukkyō,* pp. 31, 34. By 1970 more than a dozen of the articles it prepared in English and sent to Ceylon had been published in successive fascicles of the international Buddhist encyclopedia. They were signed by men like Lü Ch'eng, Kao Kuan-ju, Lin Tzu-ch'ing, and Chou Shu-chia. (Curiously enough, none was by T'ang Yung-t'ung.) These articles, like the large monograph to be included on the history of Chinese Buddhism (which I glanced over at the encyclopedia headquarters in 1962), appeared to be devoid of any political slant. Kao Kuan-ju, for example, put nothing in his long piece on the *Avatamsaka Sūtra* that hinted at the attack on the Avatamsaka school that had taken place—or was soon to take place—in China at the time he wrote it (see Chapter XI, note 46).

As to the encyclopedia of Buddhism in Chinese, in 1957 there were reported to be 20-30 Buddhist scholars at work on it and its completion was not expected for five years: see *Kuang-hui-ti pa-nien,* p. 177. In April 1960

Shirob referred to its being compiled (*JMJP,* April 15, 1960), and this is the last mention of it I have seen. Presumably, like *Modern Buddhism,* it was a casualty of the socialist education movement.

20. I heard about this from the Sinhalese bhikkhu himself. Another Sinhalese present during their conversation told me that Chou had merely asked questions about the possibility of China's conversion and did not state it as a firm plan. The misunderstanding, if there was one, is reminiscent of the impression conveyed to Pannikar, the first Indian ambassador in Peking, that the Chinese Communist Party would make Buddhism the state religion. Whether or not Communist leaders actually said such things, they left a very favorable impression on the Asians who thought they had.

21. On the pagoda see, for example, *HTFH,* 4/64, p. 50 (August, 1964). On imperialist infiltration of the WFB, see this chapter at notes 80-82, and *HTFH,* 4/64, p. 40 (August 1964). The idea that it was the imperialists who had obstructed Buddhist contacts was mentioned by Ananda Kausalyayana in his speech at the inauguration of the Chinese Buddhist Seminary in September 1956: see *HTFH,* 11/56, p. 32. Chao P'u-ch'u, who may have suggested it to him, brought it up again at the Fourth WFB conference in Nepal the next month: see *HTFH,* 12/56, p. 14. He repeated it the next year: see *HTFH,* 5/57, p. 5.

22. *HTFH,* 1/61, p. 8 (April 1961). This account by Chao P'u-ch'u of the Chinese delegation's visit to Burma is a good example of the stress on friendship.

23. This information comes from a cadre of the Religious Affairs Division in Canton who himself took part in drawing up such a catechism for the visit of U Nu to the Liu-jung Ssu in 1954. The monk who had been chosen to talk to U Nu was not the abbot but Chüeh-ch'eng, who was better qualified because of his age and knowledge of the doctrine. The Religious Affairs Division warned him that the nation's reputation was at stake and that he had better not answer questions "carelessly." He was given the list of appropriate answers. U Nu, when introduced to him, kneeled down. This raised the possibility that the provincial governor, T'ao Chu, might also have to kneel—and it would be unthinkable for a Communist leader to kneel to a Buddhist monk. Chüeh-ch'eng nimbly stepped aside and knelt himself next to U Nu, so that both of them were paying homage to the Three Buddhas on the altar. T'ao Chu moved forward slightly and bowed. When the cadres discussed afterwards whether or not he had done the right thing, they decided that if he had not joined U Nu by removing his shoes and making a partial obeisance, the country's reputation and foreign relations would have suffered, since U Nu would have gotten a bad impression. His deference to the Buddha images had not shown a loss of Marxist awareness, for it had only been an external gesture. U Nu's visit to Liu-jung Ssu and his obeisance to the Buddha images there were briefly reported in *HTFH,* 1/55, p. 27.

24. This can be seen in *Hōchū Nihon Bukkyō,* pp. 30 ff.

25. This bhikkhu told me that he was particularly pleased by the three telephones. An equally good impression (perhaps for a more appropriate reason) was made on the International Buddhist Monks delegation in 1956 by the fact that at each hotel where they stayed, one room had been fitted out with a Buddhist altar.

26. See NCNA English, May 25, 1961, and May 29, 1961. Chinese gifts were sometimes exhibited abroad. For example, the Buddha image, Chinese scriptures, and relic pagoda presented to the Burmese delegates at the 1952 Peace Conference were put on display in Rangoon in July 1953: see NCNA English, July 19, 1953, in *SCMP* 613:13. The Buddha image presented to the Japanese Buddhist delegation in 1957 was unveiled for public worship in Tokyo in 1959: see NCNA English, May 23, 1959, in *SCMP* 2021:42.

27. Foreign Buddhists gave mementos like a sapling from the Bodhi Tree in Ceylon, an old meditation staff from a monastery in Japan, rosaries and towels for monks, and two small stone images from Angkor.

28. The donation of 300,000 JMP towards the construction of a Hsüan-tsang Memorial Hall at Nalanda was made by the Dalai Lama to Premier Nehru in December 1956 in connection with the visit of a Chinese Buddhist cultural delegation that came to India on pilgrimage to Buddhist holy places during the Buddha Jayanti Year. The Chinese government presented not only the money, but also a relic of Hsüan-tsang and a complete set of his translations. Chao P'u-ch'u, the head of the delegation, commented: "Thus Buddhism, which has made great contributions to the two thousand years of friendly history between our two countries, is again playing a positive role in our mutual collaboration." See *HTFH,* 5/57, p. 5. The Chinese delegation to the Fourth Conference of the WFB gave 10,000 rupees towards reconstruction of the Buddha's birthplace at Lumbini, while the Russian delegation only gave 3,300. On this and a gift of 2,000 rupees to the Japanese, see *HTFH,* 12/56, p. 32.

29. See NCNA English, October 28, 1960. On Amritananda's favorable comments, see notes 55, 56, 60. In 1970 Amritananda received 200,000 rupees for his school from a Soviet Buddhist delegation: see *World Buddhism,* 18.10:266-267 (May 1970). Again the Russians proved the less generous donors. Many smaller sums were also donated by the Chinese at different times. For example, a gift of 10,000 riels was made towards the Jayanti celebration in Cambodia in 1957; 1,000 rupees each went to the Buddhist Research Academy of Narawila Dhammawansa, the Maha Bodhi Society, and the Vajirarama in Ceylon (according to one of these beneficiaries).

30. See NCNA English, December 5, 1964, in *SCMP* 3353:27-28.

31. See Robert Fortune, *A Journey to the Tea Countries of China* (London, 1852), pp. 138-139, and C. F. Gordon Cumming, *Wanderings in China* (London, 1888), p. 186.

32. See Virgil C. Hart, *Western China* (Boston, 1888), pp. 204-205; and D. C. Graham, *Religion in Szechwan Province, China* (Smithsonian Miscellaneous Collections, Vol. 80, No. 4: Washington, D.C., 1928), plate 14. If, as Graham suggests, it was a fossil mammoth tooth, it must have been a mammoth mammoth.

33. Rachel Brooks in her unpublished ms. "The YMCA Government of China," p. 128, describes how she was taken to a large temple in the western quarter of Peking and shown the tooth, which "was a piece of rose quartz as large as my two fists." This was between 1920 and 1925.

34. I was told about this by the bhikkhu.

35. The information in this paragraph comes from one of the leaders of the Burmese delegation that fetched the tooth. Chou En-lai's offer to *give* it to Burma cannot be confirmed. According to Chinese sources, U Nu asked the Chinese ambassador, not Chou En-lai, for the "famous tooth relic"—mentioning that in the eleventh century Anuruddha had tried to "welcome it" to Burma: see *HTFH,* 1/56, p. 2. The fact that the gold reliquary was brought from the palace is confirmed by Katsumata, p. 836.

36. *HTFH,* 5/56, p. 9, tr. in JPRS 524:21-22 (slightly altered). Photographs of this scene appear in *Buddhists in New China,* p. 188. This volume as well as *The Friendship of Buddhism* has many other photographs of the first tour of the tooth relic.

37. On the CBA's presentation of a replica of the tooth to the Burmese Sasana Council, see NCNA English, November 5, 1958, in *SCMP,* 1892:43 and *HTFH,* 8/56, p. 6; 1/61, p. 3 (April 1961). The replica had been kept beside the original in Peking for several months, thus becoming a *menita* or "created" relic, sharing in the authenticity of the original. According to a Burmese Buddhist leader, most of his countrymen believed that the original *was* authentic, but even if it could not be proven so, it was their devotion to it that counted.

38. See Chapter V at note 33.

39. NCNA's English-language releases on the tour were dated May 26, 27, 28, 29, 31, June 1, 5, 6, 7, 8, 10, 11, 12, 15, 19, 20, 23, 27, July 3, August 5, 9, 10, 13, 19, 23, 1961. The delegation escorting the tooth received more coverage than was typical for Chinese Buddhist groups, since its activities were on a grander scale, but the *kinds* of activities are representative of what happened during most such exchanges of visits. On June 10 it left Kunming, apparently flying direct to Colombo, where the tooth was handed to Prime Minister Bandaranaike and went on display until June 23. On June 12 the delegation was received by the minister of Industry, Home, and Cultural Affairs, who presented it with a gift of sutras. On June 15 it was received by Governor-General Goonetilleke and visited Vidyalankara University, where it donated a set of the Tripitaka and monks robes and received a silver model of a Sinhalese dagoba. On June 15 it visited Vidyodaya University. On June 19

it gave alms to Sinhalese monks at the Young Men's Buddhist Association–and to two of its own members who were monks. On June 23 it visited the Sinhalese Tooth Relic in Kandy and conversed with the heads of the Siamese Nikaya. On June 24 it went in motorcade to Anuradhapura, where a crowd of ten thousand watched the rites performed for it at the Bodhi Tree. On June 30 Chao P'u-ch'u received an autographed copy of the first fascicle of the Buddhist Encyclopedia from Mme. Bandaranaike for presentation to Chou En-lai. On July 3 Shirob and Chao left for Peking by air, but the rest of the delegation stayed on to escort the tooth. After being received again by Mme. Bandaranaike on the eve of their departure, they returned to China on August 10. By that time the tooth had been venerated in Ceylon by 2,500,000 persons, according to the minister of Industry, Home, and Cultural Affairs.

40. NCNA English, May 29, 1961, in *SCMP* 2510:31.

41. These details on the negative side of the tour were supplied by Buddhists in Ceylon. The bhikkhus who went to China to escort the tooth back to Ceylon belonged to the Asgiri section of the Siamese Nikaya and to the Amarapura and Ramannya Nikayas. The Malwatte section of the Siamese Nikaya was unrepresented and its head is said to have made public statements expressing doubt about the authenticity of the Chinese tooth. According to one informant, these doubts were widely shared in Ceylon and the attitude of most of the people who came to see it was one of curiosity rather than veneration.

42. Kuo P'eng's article appeared in *JMJP,* August 22, 1961. It is interesting that he raises the number of people who saw the tooth to 3 million from the 2.5 million previously reported in NCNA English, August 10, 1961 (see note 39).

43. Of course no allusion to such feelings ever appeared in the press, but it is significant that although high-ranking Party members received and entertained the delegations that came to get the Buddha's tooth in 1955 and 1961, none was present on the occasion when it was actually handed over to them. On the Burmese delegation, which was given a banquet by Chou En-lai, see *HTFH,* 10/55, pp. 14, 17, 18, 20. In the case of the Ceylonese delegation, contrast NCNA English May 29 and 31 with June 7, and see *HTFH,* 3/61, pp. 18-20 (September 1961). It was one of the Burmese delegates who sadly pointed out to me the difference in rank between those who entertained them and those who had attended the ceremonies connected with the tooth itself.

44. Amritananda, *Buddhist Activities,* p. 20. In 1957 King Mahendra gave Chou En-lai fifty relics as a token of friendship. Sixteen were placed in the Tooth Relic Pagoda and thirty-four were kept at the CBA. By 1959 those at the CBA had spontaneously increased to forty-five.

45. In addition to his trips as a member of delegations, he went at least four times alone.

46. A photograph of the Chinese Buddhist art exhibition in Tokyo (May) and Kyoto (June) is printed in *The Friendship of Buddhism,* pp. 128-129. During the week-long photograph exhibition in Ceylon in November 1960 visitors were able to see the film "Buddhism in China," which had been commissioned by the CBA in 1957 (*HTFH,* 5/57, pp. 6, 24). It showed Chinese monks and devotees at worship. On the exhibition of Chinese Buddhist gifts, see note 26. A related phenomenon was the visit of a thousand monks, led by abbot Huot Tath, to a Chinese economic exhibition in Phnom Penh: see NCNA English, January 3, 1959, in *SCMP,* 1930:20.

47. Almost all these releases can be located in the *SCMP* Index. That is why fewer citations are provided in this chapter than in chapters on domestic developments, which depend so much on *Modern Buddhism.*

48. The first Japanese Buddhist visitors to China after Liberation appear to have been two priests, Nakayama Riri and Mibu Shojun, who went by boat in 1953, bringing with them 500 coffins with the bones of Chinese prisoners of war who had died working in the Kamioka mines. Although they were not considered to be a Buddhist delegation and did not see the headquarters of the CBA, they did meet Chao P'u-ch'u at a reception. Soon after their visit a committee was set up to return more bones and ashes of POWs. It was headed by the Reverend Ōtani Eijun, who went to China (on a cultural delegation) in 1954. By 1961 nine batches had been returned. Japanese Buddhist visitors usually paid for their travel up to the Hong Kong border, after which all their expenses were borne by their hosts, usually the CBA. Itineraries rapidly expanded and probably reached their maximum length in 1957.

49. These were the Japanese-Chinese Buddhist Exchange Society in Tokyo (Nitchū Bukkyō Kōryū Kondankai–leftist, headed by Ōtani Eijun); the Japanese-Chinese Buddhist Research Society in Kyōto (Nitchū Bukkyō Kenkyuka–nonpolitical, academically oriented, headed by Tsukamoto Zenryu); and the Japanese-Chinese Friendship Society in Okayama (Nitchū Bukkyō Kōryū Shinwakai–which was local and shortlived). In 1957-58 they jointly published three issues of a quarterly, *Nitchū Bukkyō* (Japanese-Chinese Buddhism), but collaboration among them and with the Chinese was impeded by disagreement about the degree to which they should be political. The Exchange Society eventually published its own journal, *Shūkon.* Its secretary, Nakano Kyōtoku, made arrangements for many of the Japanese Buddhist visits to China. He was a Nichiren priest and reportedly a member of the Japanese Communist Party. Other groups involved in arranging for exchanges included the Japan-China Friendship Association and the Japan Association of Religious Believers for Peace.

50. The periodicals included *World Buddhism,* which provided the best coverage of Buddhist news all over the world, and *The Buddhist.* The Buddhist Publications Society in Kandy distributed well-written booklets on Buddhist doctrines and practice. On the International Buddhist Encyclopedia, see note 19.

51. In 1957 Takashina Rosen and two other members of his delegation were taken to shake hands with Mao during the National Day parade. Chou En-lai received the Burmese in 1955, Narada (Ceylon) in 1957, the Cambodians in 1958, Malalasekera in 1959, and the Ōtani delegation in 1961.

52. *HTFH,* 6/61, p. 24 (December 1961–italics added). U Nu went on to support the Chinese government's domestic policy: "I wish to say a few words to Chinese Buddhists: since you have gained the great support of such a good government, you should follow the precept in the *Mangala Sūtra* that we should be grateful. You should not only coöperate with the Chinese government in religious affairs, but should also contribute your efforts in all the construction work called for by the government"–as if Chinese monks needed a reminder of what was expected of them. *Modern Buddhism* printed his speech under the headline "We Should Be Grateful."

53. Only from Japan and India do visitors appear to have come simply as private citizens. Delegations from Burma, Cambodia, Ceylon, and Nepal were usually invited through the Chinese embassy, which would approach the appropriate ministry of the government to which it was accredited. Most of the delegations from Burma and Ceylon were not merely chosen by their governments but included government officials. Even when the government had not chosen them, Buddhist visitors still had to get passports and exit permits: it was difficult for them to go to China without official approval.

54. NCNA English, July 26, 1958, in *SCMP,* 1822:39. Huot Tath repeated this to two thousand monks in Cambodia to whom he reported on his trip: see NCNA English, August 8, 1958, in *SCMP,* 1832:42-43. While still in China he said: "We see order and fairness everywhere in your country. After we return, we will make all this known to our own people in Cambodia." See *HTFH,* 12/58, p. 26.

55. NCNA English, July 25, 1959, in *SCMP,* 2066:37-38.

56. NCNA English, August 2, 1959, in *SCMP,* 2072:35; NCNA English, August 20, 1959, in *SCMP,* 2084:44-45. The next year while in Burma, Amritananda again spoke enthusiastically of the condition of Chinese Buddhism and called for more Asian monks to go there and to the Soviet Union: see NCNA English, January 19, 1960.

57. *Chung-kuo hsin-wen,* July 21, 1961. This group had been allowed to make a two-month tour of Buddhist centers in China and had been received by Chao P'u-ch'u and Chü-tsan. The latter gave them a talk on doctrine and practice that "greatly delighted them." On June 7 they attended the ceremony at the Kuang-chi Ssu where the Buddha's Tooth Relic was handed over for dispatch to Ceylon. See *HTFH,* 2/61, p. 28 (July 1961), and NCNA English, June 7, 1961, in *SCMP,* 2515:33.

58. Mainland sources are naturally selective, emphasizing visitors' praise and omitting criticism, but there has been no outright fabrication or distortion in the cases I have been able to check on. The closest thing to distortion was the statement that a group of foreign Buddhists who visited the Liu-jung

Ssu in 1952 "were all impressed by the greatness of Buddhist cultural monuments" (*HTFH,* 1/53, p. 24). A member of the group told me that the monastery was in poor repair and looked very shabby. The monk who received them apologized for being unable to provide a suitable meal: all he could offer was fried melon seeds. It left a very poor impression.

59. G. P. Malalasekera, "Nirvana or Fulfillment," in *Main Currents in Modern Thought* (New York) 16.3:51-52 (January, 1960), spellings corrected. Cf. *HTFH,* 6/59, p. 28.

60. NCNA English, August 20, 1959, in *SCMP,* 2084:44-45.

61. NCNA, August 9, 1959.

62. NCNA English, July 25, 1959, in *SCMP,* 2066:37-38. Amritananda had been met at the airport by a large crowd of monks and nuns, just as if he were a chief of state.

63. See note 29. Amritananda not only received large Chinese and Russian donations for his school, but four months of medical treatment for severe, chronic headaches at a Black Sea resort. From Western governments he never got a penny for his school—nor even an invitation to make the kind of lavish, expense-free tour he frequently made in Communist countries. The salary he received as a research assistant in Rome is said to have been anything but lavish. Few people can keep their political views unaffected by the way they have been treated. It is too harsh simply to say that they have been bought.

64. André Migot, "Le Bouddhisme en Chine," in René de Berval, *Présence du Bouddhisme* (Saigon, France-Asie, 1959), pp. 711-716.

65. *Hōchū Nihon Bukkyō,* pp. 1-2. Note how the last sentence attempts to take the sting out of the sentence beginning "Their protection of Buddhism . . ." (which it logically contradicts). There is a similar uneasiness in the statement made by Asaram Sakya, who was on the Nepalese delegation that was so favorably quoted by NCNA (see notes 60-62). He told reporters that China's incursions into India were the result of India's grant of asylum to the Dalai Lama. The Nepalese government should take a lesson from the Chinese treatment of India. "It is a most foolish policy either to appease or ignore China, which now aims at becoming the strongest power on earth." See *South China Morning Post,* December 4, 1959.

66. In 1966 a member of the last Japanese Buddhist delegation to visit China commented that the restoration of temples was important for tourism and the preservation of Chinese culture, "but it is very hard to see any religious significance in it." After noting how the Chinese Buddhist Seminary had been cut down in size, he concluded: "Since the situation is now like this, I feel there is really nothing to expect in the future for Buddhism in China." See Katsumata, pp. 836-837.

67. See *Shih-tai p'i-p'ing,* 13.8:12 (October 16, 1961). Something similar was said to me privately by an Asian ambassador in Peking: "Buddhism in China has no future . . . Buddhism and Marxism cannot coexist . . . Some Southeast Asian Buddhists are taken in by the show they see in China. This is

because they do not really understand Buddhism." This is particularly interesting because there had been many Buddhist contacts between his country and China and he had taken part in some of them. The author of one statement of praise of the Communist treatment of Buddhism told me privately that he knew he had only received a guided tour from which it was impossible to learn anything about how Buddhism was faring. Statements of praise cannot always be taken at face value.

68. See above note 43. A photograph in *The Friendship of Buddhism,* p. 82, hows the tooth relic on display in Burma. All the Burmese and four of the CBA representatives have their hands pressed together in reverence. Five of the CBA representatives do not. This too must have made a bad impression on the Burmese and is an illustration of the difficulties encountered by a Communist regime when it tries to act as a patron of religion.

69. Another member of the same delegation met a former student of his who could speak his language very well, but who refused to do so, and, again, would converse only through the interpreter.

70. A member of the Takashina delegation in 1957 told me that Yu Hsiang from the Religious Affairs Bureau in Peking seemed to stick with them twenty-four hours a day throughout their tour. Even when they went for a walk in the early morning, he or one of his assistants would turn up to accompany them. Ōtani Eijun noted that his discussions with Chinese monks were all monitored by expressionless, anonymous individuals, whom he took to be members of the secret police. See Ōtani Eijun, *Shin Chūgoku kenmonki,* p. 141.

In the only three cases I know of where visitors have talked to Chinese monks alone, the latter spoke as if an interpreter had still been present. For example, when André Migot visited the Kumbum Monastery in August 1957, he was able to converse alone with the head lama, who talked about nothing but how much better things were since Liberation: the monastery had more monks and novices and attracted more worshipers and donations. This was because the peasants were not so poor as they used to be—"a rather special viewpoint, but very significant." See André Migot, "Situation des religions en Chine populaire: Bouddhisme et Marxisme," *Le régime et les institutions de la république populaire chinoise* (Bruxelles, 1960), p. 46.

71. Another Indian was told by his hotel room boy that his father had become a monk and his mother a nun. When asked through the interpreter if he himself believed in Buddhism, "a startled look came into his face and he protested earnestly that he did not have anything to do with religion." The Indian concluded from this and other incidents (e.g., see note 9) that if the Communist regime lasted twenty years longer, there was no hope for the survival of Buddhism in China.

72. For example, some members of a Japanese delegation in 1957 wanted to see the Ch'ing-lung Ssu in Sian. They were told this was impossible because it lay too far away over bad roads. Actually it lay within the city. See *Hōchū*

Nihon Bukkyō, p. 8. The delegation was also refused permission to go to the Hua-ting Ssu when they were on T'ien-t'ai Shan (p. 15). At no time could diplomats and foreign correspondents in Peking go more than twelve miles from the city without a permit from the Ministry of Foreign Affairs. This meant that they could not visit the few large monasteries in the Peking area that had been alive before 1949, e.g., the T'an-che Ssu, Chieh-t'ai Ssu, and the temples at Miao-feng Shan. Even within the city many temples were closed to visitors without a permit.

73. This phrase is quoted from *The Buddha Tooth Relic,* p. 10.

74. I heard this story, like those in the preceding paragraphs, from the visitors involved.

75. On the roots of the WFB, see Welch, *Revival,* pp. 6-8, 63-64.

76. *HTFH,* 5/51, p. 32. This article cited three pieces of evidence for the fact that the meeting was "manipulated by the imperialists." First, among the flags displayed were a swastika flag and a Chinese Nationalist flag. Second, the meeting rejected a motion to appeal to the United Nations to prohibit atomic weapons. Third, delegates from colonies were described as coming from "nations," which seemed designed to offend movements for national independence.

The swastika (with the arms hooked in an opposite direction from the Hakenkreuz) was an ancient emblem of Buddhism in China as it was elsewhere. To cite it as evidence of imperialist control ("the Fascist Hitlerite German swastika flag") suggests that this article was written by someone who knew nothing about Buddhism in China or elsewhere—perhaps by a cadre in the Propaganda Department. The hostile tone of this 1951 article was entirely absent from the first report on the conference to appear in *HTFH* (9/50, p. 28), which was based on an account in a Ceylon Buddhist journal.

77. For Chü-tsan's statement that the WFB conference "was convened under the manipulation of American imperialists," see *HTFH,* 1/52, p. 4.

78. *JMJP,* December 5, 1954, tr. in *SCMP,* 941:33 (slightly altered).

79. The first allusion to the conference was in NCNA, November 23, 1961, which reported simply that the Chinese delegation was leaving for home. Nothing was said about the proceedings. It seems strange that the New China News Agency carried no items on the delegation's departure from Peking, its arrival in Phnom Penh, and its reception by Prince Sihanouk.

80. See *SCMP,* 2658:10-12, 2661:19.

81. NCNA English, January 16, 1962, in *SCMP,* 2664:12. This was the conclusion of a statement by Shirob Jaltso in which he said that the Kennedy administration was extending "its aggressive tentacles to every corner of the globe, even into the tranquility of a Buddhist gathering. He recalled that last November Kennedy dispatched a horde of his unholy pawns under the cloak of religion to the World Buddhist Conference held in Cambodia. Using a Buddhist rostrum, they tried to interject the shameless scheme of 'two Chinas,' in a vain attempt to turn the World Fellowship of Buddhists into a

tool of the policy of aggression. However, they were firmly rebuffed by all just-minded Buddhists" (NCNA paraphrase slightly altered). On February 13, 1962, at the third national conference of the CBA Chao P'u-ch'u "condemned the imperialist plots to penetrate Buddhist international organizations and split the international coöperation among Buddhists": see NCNA English, February 13, 1962. On December 25, 1963, *KMJP* published an article "Aggression under the Cloak of Religion" by Yang Feng-chu (*SCMP,* 3192:18) which said, in effect, that it was not China that was attempting to use religion for political purposes, but the United States. The attack focused on Christian missionaries, but mentioned that the United States had sent its "Buddhist monks to the Sixth World Buddhist Conference where they played the two Chinas trick."

82. NCNA English, January 8, 1964, in *SCMP,* 3137:35-36.

83. On October 23, 1964, the CBA issued a statement protesting, first, the invitation for Taiwan to attend the Seventh WFB Conference in India, and, second, the use of the words "Mainland China" on the invitation sent to the CBA. It said that these were part of a United States "two Chinas" plot, and that unlesss the invitation to the "Chiang Kai-shek clique" was withdrawn and the WFB's General Council was convened to discuss the site of the headquarters and the Seventh Conference, then "we absolutely will not send delegates to the conference . . . We appeal to our Buddhist brothers and sisters in Asia . . . to oppose U.S. imperialism in controlling the WFB." See NCNA English, October 23, 1964, in *SCMP,* 3326:31. On November 17, 1964, Chao P'u-ch'u, as a vice-president of the WFB, issued a personal statement repeating all these points (including the appeal to "Buddhist brothers and sisters") and announcing that he would refuse to attend the Seventh Conference. "The WFB must assume full responsibility for its illegal activities and for all the consequences arising therefrom. I reserve the right to speak in the future." See NCNA English, November 17, 1964, in *SCMP,* 3341:21-22. On December 3, 1964 (the next to last day of the Seventh Conference), the CBA issued a statement repeating the points of the three earlier protests, and using even stronger language. "We have of late learned that in defiance of the repeated protests lodged by the Buddhists of China and many other countries in Asia, the headquarters of the World Fellowship of Buddhists, which has illegally moved its site to Bangkok, has blatantly convened in India a seventh conference not approved in accordance with the procedure of the constitution, has flagrantly invited the 'Buddhist delegates' of the Chiang Kai-shek clique to attend as the delegation of a regional center, and has brazenly admitted to the conference the ringleader of the Tibetan rebel clique, Dalai, who has been openly carrying out activities of betrayal of his motherland under the wing of foreign countries for several years past." See NCNA English, December 3, 1964, in *SCMP,* 3352:34-35 (slightly altered). The reference to the protests lodged by "many other countries in Asia" probably

referred to the five-nations statement of July 6, 1964 (see below note 99). On November 14, 1964, Ray Lamouth had said that the Cambodian Buddhist Association "recognized only Rangoon as the site of the WFB headquarters." This is the closest thing to a protest that I know of originating outside the China Mainland.

84. In people's diplomacy too the Chinese had ignored the Buddhists of South Vietnam, only one of whom seems to have visited China before 1963. This was the Reverend Thich Minh Chau, who was selected by Ananda Kausalyayana to be one of the eleven members of the International Buddhist Monks delegation in 1956, when he was a student at Nalanda. He never became a member of the National Liberation Front nor sympathetic to Peking.

85. Buddhists in China were not allowed to hold parades on the Buddha's birthday or to carry an international Buddhist flag through the streets (see Chapter I, note 69).

86. NCNA English, June 3, 1961, in *SCMP,* 2995:34.

87. *HTFH,* 2/55, pp. 24-26.

88. NCNA English, June 21, 1963, in *SCMP,* 3007:38-39. The Yung-ho Kung was an odd place to hold the service, since the Vietnamese are not lamaists and this was the largest lamasery in Peking. Perhaps it was intended as a delicate riposte to criticism of the destruction of lamaseries in Tibet.

89. NCNA English, September 1, 1963, in *SCMP,* 3054:45.

90. The September 1 statement was an urgent appeal by the CBA, addressed to "Buddhists and kind-hearted people throughout the world," to support the Buddhists of Vietnam: see *HTFH,* 5/63, pp. 61-62 (October 1963). It mentioned a rally in Peking on August 30 by ten thousand people. Although this was not an exclusively Buddhist rally, it must have been the biggest political gathering since Liberation in which Buddhism played a conspicuous role. Individual statements on Vietnam by Chinese religious leaders had also been made at a meeting in July: see NCNA English, July 17, 1963, in *SCMP,* 3023:30.

91. The *Far Eastern Economic Review* of November 21, 1963, p. 381, states that the governments of Ceylon and Burma refused to allow their nationals to attend and attributes this to their fear of the spread of "fanatical notions about the place of Buddhism in modern Asia." I have seen no confirmation of this, but since Ceylon and Burma were the countries with which Chinese had had the longest history of successful Buddhist exchanges, it is safe to assume that invitations were issued; and we know that, in fact, no one came.

92. The North Vietnamese and North Korean delegates were obviously coöperative. The Laotian delegates came from the territory of the Pathet Lao and those from South Vietnam and Thailand seem also to have come from areas under Communist control, so that they were coöperative too. The gov-

ernments of both Pakistan and Indonesia were at that time working for better relations with Peking, and Peking must have expected this to be reflected in the voting.

93. The text of the eleven-national appeal is given in NCNA English October 19, 1963, in *SCMP*, 3086:31. The eleven nations (or regions) were Cambodia, China, Indonesia, Japan, Korea, Laos, Nepal, Pakistan, South Vietnam, Thailand, and North Vietnam. The head of the Japanese delegation was Kongō Shūichi, a former president of the Japan Buddhist Federation. The member who signed the appeal was Ōnishi Ryōkei, the 89-year-old chairman of the Japan Association of Religious Believers for Peace and abbot of Kiyomizu in Kyoto. Two members of the delegation have independently confirmed that the conference came as a complete surprise to the Japanese, although they did not mention this in their official report (see *Ganjin wajō*, pp. 39-40).

94. NCNA English, October 17, 1963, in *SCMP*, 3085:23. This is the only mention of nirvana that I can recall in any NCNA release.

95. It was announced at the beginning of 1961 that the opening ceremonies would be held that year: see *HTFH*, 1/61, p. 3 (April 1961). However, when a delegation from Ceylon visited it in May, they were told that the tooth would not be installed until the furnishing was complete: see NCNA English, May 30, 1961, in *SCMP*, 2510:32.

96. See *HTFH*, 3/64, pp. 61-63 (June 1964). The Japanese delegation had also attended memorial services for him in Sian and on T'ien-t'ai Shan.

97. On the installation of the tooth see NCNA English, June 25, 1964, in *SCMP*, 3249:17. On the commemoration of Hsüan-tsang, see NCNA English, June 27, 1964, in *SCMP*, 3250:21-22. Fuller accounts are given in *HTFH*, 4/64, pp. 43-65 (August 1964). The ceremonies provided the occasion for speeches referring to the imperialists' destruction of the original pagoda (see note 130) and contrasting the protection of religion in China with its persecution by the United States in Southeast Asia.

98. See NCNA English, July 4, 1964, in *SCMP*, 3253:29-30; *HTFH*, 4/64, pp. 41-42 (August 1964). There had been a harbinger of this the preceding month when an unnamed leader of the CBA issued a statement condemning U.S. air attacks on a monastery in Tra Vinh Province on May 1-2: see NCNA English, June 6, 1964, in *SCMP*, 3235; *HTFH*, 3/64, p. 55 (June 1964). It is noteworthy that the statement of July 1, 1964, was signed the day after departure of six of the nine Japanese delegates, including Rosen Takashina, the head of the Japan Buddhist Federation.

99. See NCNA English, July 13, 1964, in *SCMP*, 3260:29. The statement pointed out that the WFB was "being increasingly used to engage in various undemocratic, illegal, and autocratic practices" and called on Buddhists "to preserve the purity of Buddhism." It seems likely that this represents the watering down of a Chinese draft that condemned the United States for infiltrating and using the WFB. The countries whose Buddhist delegates signed this

statement were Ceylon, Indonesia, Laos, Pakistan, and Vietnam. Ray Lamouth, the head of the Cambodian delegation, seems still to have been in China, but, as a vice-president of the WFB, he may have felt it inappropriate to sign. However he paid tribute to freedom of religion in China when he returned home: see below note 128.

100. On January 30, 1965, the CBA issued a protest against "the bloody suppression" of some Buddhists who had been demonstrating in South Vietnam: see NCNA English, January 30, 1965, in *SCMP,* 3391:31-32. The next day a meeting of religious circles was held in Peking to repeat the protest. On February 11, 1965, the CBA sent a message to the Vietnamese Unified Buddhist Association hailing the victories of the North Vietnamese Army in repelling U.S. aggression: see NCNA English, February 11, 1965, in *SCMP,* 3398:26. Five months later five Chinese people's organizations sent messages to their counterparts in North Vietnam to condemn the bombing of Nam Dinh. They included trade unions, youth, and women; the absence of Buddhists is probably significant.

The fact that China made political use of the sufferings of South Vietnamese Buddhists does not make their sufferings any less real or the parties responsible any less reprehensible.

101. NCNA English, April 15, 1961, in *SCMP,* 2480:30. Probably this scene was as carefully staged as U Nu's visit to the Liu-jung Ssu.

102. On Madame Bandaranaike's visit to the Kuang-chi Ssu, at which she "prostrated herself in homage before the image of Buddha in the main hall, where incense was burned amidst the sound of the temple drum and the tinkling of temple bells," see NCNA English, January 1, 1963, in *SCMP,* 2892:31-32. On the memorial service in Shanghai, see NCNA English, January 8, 1963, in *SCMP,* 2896:23. Chinese political leaders had sometimes become involved in Buddhist ceremonials when traveling abroad. In 1966 Lin Hai-yün, the Acting Minister of Foreign Affairs, was conducted to Kandy's Temple of the Tooth Relic "in traditional manner in a procession": see *World Buddhism,* 15.6:175 (January 1967), which states that he went to Kandy "on pilgrimage." During Foreign Minister Ch'en Yi's visit to Ceylon in 1964, he did not go on pilgrimage, but did display considerable aplomb when it came to Buddhism. Confronted by a gigantic Sleeping Buddha, he said that it reminded him of two in his own country; and (combining a dig at an enemy with a compliment to his host) "he was happy to notice that although Buddhism had more or less disappeared from its mother country, India, Ceylon had become a Buddhist country with a preponderantly Buddhist population." See *World Buddhism,* 12.8:17 (April 1964). Cf. NCNA English, February 29, 1964, in *SCMP,* 3171:34.

103. For example, Chao P'u-ch'u was vice-president of the China-Burma Friendship Association and the China-Japan Friendship Association; Chou Shu-chia was vice-president of the China-Nepal Friendship Association; and Kuo P'eng was secretary-general of the China-Ceylon Friendship Association,

while Ngawang Jaltso was its vice-president. Conversely Amritananda was the president of the Nepal-China Cultural Association. (This may explain why a Chinese cultural delegation to Nepal in 1964 was given a tea party by the Nepal Buddhist Youth Association.) Nepal was not a predominantly Buddhist country, but, as in India under Nehru, Buddhism played a role in its relations with China.

104. NCNA English, August 2, 1958, in *SCMP,* 1828:45. Cf. Chapter VIII at note 45.

105. *HTFH,* 10/58, p. 28. Cf. *ibid.,* p. 29. A spate of meetings for the liberation of Taiwan had already been held in 1955, after the signing of the U.S.-Nationalist Mutual Defense Treaty, and more such meetings were held in June 1960 when Eisenhower visited Taiwan.

106. *HTFH,* 4/53, p. 15. I have seen mention of Buddhist chapters of the Sino-Soviet Friendship Association in Amoy, Wu-chou (Kwangsi), Haining (Chekiang), Chüanchow (Fukien), and Wu-t'ai Shan. There was also one for Kansu Province.

107. *HTFH,* 3/53, p. 2. In 1951 some young monks and nuns who belonged to the Ningpo Sino-Soviet Friendship Association were reported to be wearing Stalin badges as well as Mao badges and to "consider that nothing is more glorious": see *HTFH,* 3/52, p. 13.

108. For example, the nuns of the Mi-t'o Ssu, Harbin, held a memorial service for Stalin to climax forty-nine days of prayers for peace (see *HTFH,* 7/53, p. 27); and 260 Buddhists in Szechwan held a day-long memorial service "according to the Buddhist ritual" (see *HTFH,* 4/53, p. 28).

109. NCNA English, July 28, 1964, in *SCMP,* 3270:21 (slightly altered). Cf. *HTFH,* 5/64, pp. 40-45 (October 1964).

110. NCNA English, September 3, 1964, in *SCMP,* 3295:35.

111. *HTFH,* 6/51, p. 36. The phrase "take refuge in the Great Vehicle" presumably meant converting Theravada countries to Mahayana.

112. *HTFH,* 10/58, p. 28. Cf. Chapter I at note 17.

113. See *HTFH,* 4/61, pp. 45-49 (October 1961) tr. in *ECMM,* 294:9-15. I do not know whether this was ever used in Chinese propaganda to Latin America. A later article published in *Chung-kuo ch'ing-nien* seems reluctant to endorse the Buddhist claim: see *SCMP,* 2639:14.

114. An example is given in Welch, *Revival,* pp. 190-193. Several Mainland monasteries had branches in Hong Kong.

115. The only Chinese monks to go on foreign tours after 1949 visited Burma in 1955 and Cambodia in 1957 and 1961. None of them is reported to have lectured on the sutras to overseas Chinese.

116. An overseas nun who visited a certain monastery in 1957 reported that the cadres who kept an eye on it "were terribly polite, they invited me to have a meal with them, asked me if I needed clothing, and said: 'We in the government have not been good hosts. We very much welcome the visits of overseas Chinese like yourselves. Please give us your suggestions and tell us what is not being done right in the motherland. We shall certainly adopt your

esteemed ideas. Also please tell us if you had any difficulties on the way, if the PLA did not treat you in the right manner. Please instruct us in what we are doing wrong' . . . A-ya! They were terribly polite." When she returned in 1960 the atmosphere was stricter. The cadres supervised everything closely. They even followed her into the toilet (as they followed everyone else) to make sure that she did not hide anything there. It was natural for overseas monks and nuns to be more closely watched than devotees because they were more likely to receive confidences from the resident monks. Chinese devotees who went on pilgrimages have reported that they were sometimes allowed to spend the night in a monastery but found the monks too frightened to talk with them.

117. The only instance I know of in which the regime showed concern about their opinion of its treatment of Buddhism was in 1952, when an overseas Chinese delegation attended a symposium at the Nan P'u-t'o Ssu in Amoy and heard a report by monks and devotees on freedom of religious belief in China. The Nan P'u-t'o Ssu had just been repaired at government expense. The only overseas Chinese whose praise of the government's treatment of Buddhism was quoted in the Mainland press seems to have been the illiterate women devotees from Singapore who toured the Mainland in 1961. See above note 57.

118. One monk who left in 1948 returned for a three-month tour in 1962 (see Appendix G). Another, who left in 1957 (legally), returned in 1965 for a four-month tour during which he went to Lu Shan, Wuhan, Loyang, Sian, Peking, Tientsin, Nanking, Wusih, Soochow, Hangchow, Foochow, Chüan-chow and Canton. Other monks have returned too, but it has been easier and commoner for nuns to do so. Few monks were publicly criticized for remaining overseas, perhaps because it would have been a loss of face for the regime to admit that they did not wish to return. One of the few was Fa-fang, the disciple of T'ai-hsü, who got a teaching job at the University of Ceylon after fleeing the Mainland. A eulogy in *Modern Buddhism* replied to criticism by saying that before his death he had, in fact, been planning to return: see *HTFH,* 11/51, pp. 16, 35.

119. Two refugee monks in Hong Kong announced in 1952 that they would protest to the United Nations against the Communist Party's suppression of religion: see *Pan Asia* (Hong Kong), December 11, 1952. A letter of protest was actually sent by a later refugee in 1962: see *Hsiang-kang fo-chiao* (*Buddhism in Hong Kong*), 32:45 (January 1963). This monthly, *Buddhism in Hong Kong,* which had avoided any hostile reference to the Mainland in its first six years, finally printed a rebuttal to Jen Chi-yü's attack on Buddhist philosophical thought in the T'ang. This rebuttal appeared in No. 76, pp. 5-7 (September 1966), and used the word "bandit" for Communist, as was the custom in Taiwan (where the article had first appeared).

120. During the riots Buddhist monks were attacked in the Hong Kong Communist press and at least one temple was stoned. Afterwards officers of the Hong Kong Buddhist Sangha Association got word from local Communist

leaders that they had better mend their ways, because someday there would be a "reckoning of accounts." The story circulated that Erh-mai, a monk who had been sent to Hong Kong in 1958 to organize progressive Buddhists there, was recalled to Peking in September 1966 and executed. Whether or not the story was true, it made a deep impression on monks as far away as Singapore. I had several interviews with Erh-mai in 1961: he seemed sick with fright at contact with an American. (In 1952 Erh-mai had been a people's representative in Amoy and became chairman of the local Buddhist association: see *HTFH,* 6/53, p. 41. In 1953-57 he contributed 18 articles to *Modern Buddhism.* In 1958 he arrived in Hong Kong, where he changed his name to Miao-yin.) The effect of the Communist effort to intimidate the sangha could be seen at the Ninth Conference of the WFB in 1969, when, for the first time, no monks came from Hong Kong.

121. See Stephen FitzGerald "China and the Overseas Chinese: Perceptions and Policies," *China Quarterly,* 44:1-37 (October-December 1970).

122. In October 1963 Ōnishi Ryōkei (see above note 93) suggested to Chao P'u-ch'u that China take the lead in setting up an Asian Buddhist federation. Chao agreed, but never made an open attempt to do so, presumably because canvassing did not reveal enough support for it.

123. Jinaratana, a member of the 1956 International Buddhist Monks delegation, went to Taiwan in 1966; another Sinhalese monk soon followed suit. The Chinese Nationalists began to take an interest in using Buddhism themselves. In 1966 they dispatched Pai-sheng, president of the Chinese Buddhist Association in Taipei, to represent all Chinese religions at the Asian Conference for Peace and against Nuclear Weapons held in Japan "in order to protect Asian peace and counter the Japanese Socialist Party's slavish support of the nuclear tests of the Communist bandits." See *Chüeh-shih,* 322:1 (August 1, 1966).

124. *China Reconstructs,* 1-2/54. It is significant that Chü-tsan's refutation of foreign "slanders" was published in this journal, which was aimed at readers abroad. The next instance I have noted of Chinese sensitivity did not come for four years. In 1958 the new Buddha image at the Ling-yin Ssu, Hangchow, was said to "testify to the radiance of the religious policy of the Party" and to have convinced Buddhist visitors from Southeast Asia that the imperialists' slanders about freedom of religion in China were entirely groundless. See *HTFH,* 10/58, pp. 15-17.

125. On the destruction of temples, see Chapter I at note 15; Chapter II, notes 115-116; Chapter V, notes 65-66. On monks being driven out, see *HTFH,* 10/50, p. 26. Chü-tsan issued his denial just during the period when such "imprudently selected news reports" began to be kept out of *Modern Buddhism.* See Chapter I at notes 35-36.

126. They accused the Tibetan rebels of having "borrowed Buddhism as the banner under which they hoped to realize their evil plot of splitting the motherland and enslaving our Tibetan people." See *HTFH,* 10/59, p. 11.

127. Dr. Malalasekera, on behalf of Madame Bandaranaike and Premiers Nehru and U Nu, asked the Chinese to make a compromise settlement with the Tibetans. Chou said that there could be no compromise with rebels. Their meeting was reported in the press (*JMJP,* May 7, 1959), but nothing was said about the content of their conversation. Dr. Malalasekera was at this time Ceylon's ambassador to the Soviet Union.

128. See notes 55-56, 60-61. The earliest such statement that I have been able to find by a Buddhist visitor was made by the Venerable Ananda Kausalyayana on his return to India: "Some people say China is heaven, some people call it hell. I should say China is a country on its way from hell to heaven and, compared to many other countries today, it is already heaven." See *JMJP,* March 10, 1957, p. 4, and *HTFH,* 4/57, p. 2. The last such statement from a visitor came just before the effort to persuade foreign Buddhists was abandoned. After the Cambodian delegation returned from the inauguration of the Tooth Relic Pagoda, its head reported: "In China people enjoy complete freedom of worship, not only in Buddhism but in other religions . . . All propaganda contradicting this fact is nothing but foul imperialist slanders against China." See NCNA English, July 22, 1964, in *SCMP,* 3266:24.

129. The quotation comes from an article by Sheng-ch'üan, abbot of the Hsien-liang Ssu in Peking and an old friend of Chü-tsan, see *HTFH,* 10/59, pp. 22, 23. The similar statements in the same issue were by Shirob (pp. 11, 14) and Sung-liu Achiamuniya, a Thai nationality bhikkhu, who said: "In the past the imperialists and the KMT reactionaries have spread rumors, saying 'the Communists will destroy religion,' but the events that we ourselves have experienced have smashed these shameful rumors of the imperialists and the KMT reactionaries." See *ibid.,* p. 18.

130. After its June 1960 issue *Modern Buddhism* carried no further reports of labor by monks or of their participation in campaigns—although these phenomena continued. During the Buddhist Picture Exhibition in Colombo, October 1960, with its photographs of monks chanting sutras but not tilling fields, the following comments were written in the visitors' book by Sinhalese who had seen the exhibition: "The lying propaganda to the effect that Buddhism has no status in China is made bankrupt by this exhibition." "Those false scholars who complain that Marxism will destroy Buddhism should get their answer from this exhibition. I deeply believe that slanders will meet their end and that truth will become evident"—etc. See *HTFH,* 1/61, p. 30-31 (April 1961). In reporting on the tooth relic's tour of Ceylon the next year, Kuo P'eng wrote in the *People's Daily,* August 22, 1961: "The broad masses of the Sinhalese people not only venerated the Chinese Buddha's Tooth, but also gained an understanding of the religious policy of the new China. Not a few Sinhalese friends said to us: 'In the past we have heard the Western propaganda that there was no longer any religion in the New China because the Communist Party did not permit people to believe in

religion. Only now do we know that this is all a lie. Not only is there Buddhism in the New China, but religious belief in the New China receives the protection of the People's Government and the Communist Party.' Facts win the argument. Any rumor, in the face of facts, in the face of truth, will finally be exposed and go bankrupt." Cf. this chapter at note 54.

A perennial peg for the refutation of foreign criticism was the Tooth Relic Pagoda. The Chinese often pointed out that the original had been destroyed by allied gunfire during the Boxer rebellion in 1900. "That the imperialists destroyed the pagoda and the People's Government rebuilt it has forcefully exposed the slanders spread by the professional rumor mongers of the capitalist world against the Communist Party." *HTFH,* 10/59, p. 14. This was repeated by Hui-feng at the installation of the tooth in 1964 (HTFH, 4/64, p. 46 [August 1964]); and by guides to Buddhist visitors as late as 1966 (e.g., Katsumata, p. 836). According to a pre-Communist source, the pagoda was actually destroyed by Indian troops as a punishment for the fact that some Boxers had been harbored in the temple: see Arlington and Lewisohn, *In Search of Old Peking* (Peking, Henri Vetch, 1935), p. 301.

131. For mention of imperialist looting, see NCNA English, May 6, May 15, December 10, 1961; cf. *JMJP,* April 15, 1960, and Mibu, "Jinmin Chūgoku," p. 17. In a similar vein NCNA English, April 14, 1962, quoted the head of the Pathet Lao Buddhist Association as saying that Phoumi Nosovan under U.S. leadership "burned many monasteries and temples and abducted and killed many patriotic Buddhist monks," whereas "in the liberated areas . . . monasteries and temples are protected . . . Buddhist monks enjoy freedom" (*SCMP,* 2722:38, slightly altered). On Kuomintang abuse of monasteries, see NCNA English, August 9, 1961, and May 5, 1962. Cf. *HTFH,* 11/56, pp. 5-6. For articles about the conservation of Buddhist culture, see Chapter XII, note 15. Reports of Buddhist religious services are to be found in NCNA English releases for January 8, March 7, May 1, June 21, September 1, October 3, 14, 17, 27, and November 2, 1963; and during the first part of 1964 in the releases for March 18, April 7, May 19, 20, June 23, 25. Cf. *HTFH,* 3/64, pp. 63-64 (June 1964), and 4/64, p. 48 (August 1964). Some of these religious services were conducted jointly with foreign Buddhists, e.g., with the Japanese in 1963 to commemorate Chien-chen. They were told that it was the first time such a thing had happened since Liberation; and they recalled that in 1957, when the Takashina delegation had proposed joint services for Chinese and Japanese war dead, the Chinese had flatly refused (see *Chūgai nippō,* Oct. 4, 1957, and *Ganjin wajō,* p. 12). A big change had taken place–as could also be seen in the scale of the ceremonies. To commemorate Hsüan-tsang the celebrants made an offering to his tablet, then chanted the incense hymn, the *Heart Sutra,* the Maitreya Hymn and Maitreya Gatha, then performed a transfer of merit in the great shrine-hall, where there were incense, flowers, offerings, and a hundred oil lamps. See NCNA Chinese, March 18, 1964; cf. *HTFH,* 3/64, pp. 63-64; 4/64, p. 48 (August 1964).

132. After June 25, 1964, I have seen no further mention of Buddhist religious rites in NCNA English. Earlier that year came one of the last efforts to justify the regime's policy to Buddhists abroad. This was a long letter to the editor of *World Buddhism* in Ceylon. It defended Chinese actions in Tibet and on the Indian border; rejected criticism of productive labor and political study being carried on by Chinese monks; and accused Christmas Humphreys and other English Buddhists of acting like Devadatta, the schismatic who (so the story goes) tried to kill the Buddha. See *World Buddhism* 12.8:8-10 (March 1964).

133. See, for example, *Ta-kung pao,* January 17, 1965, tr. in *SCMP,* 3389:11, and *Nan-fang jih-pao,* December 18, 1964.

134. Hence it was four years before it gave up its over-hasty claim that the Dalai Lama had been abducted and was in India against his will.

135. For examples of the baffling reactions of some Asian Buddhists to the fate of Buddhism in China, see Appendix F.

VII. SUPPRESSING BUDDHIST OPPOSITION TO THE REGIME

1. See London *Times,* March 3, 1928, p. 11; March 9, 1928, p. 13b. Atrocities comparable to this, however, may well have been perpetrated in Tibet in and after the uprising of 1959.

2. Hong Kong *Hsin-wan pao,* Jan. 31, 1965.

3. See *HTFH,* 3/52, p. 10 (Ningpo), p. 15 (Hangchow); 4/53, p. 11 (Ningpo). This last report mentions the arrest of five counterrevolutionary monks who "had wormed their way" into the Asoka Monastery. This is the largest number arrested in any report I know of. Lay Buddhists too fell victim in the campaign. For example, Chang Tung-sun, who had been one of the founders of *Modern Buddhism,* was removed from all his posts in February 1952 as a "counterrevolutionary element."

4. *Chi-lin jih-pao,* June 20, 1958, tr. in *SCMP,* 1834:10-11, and JPRS 513:3. Even Nationalist propaganda booklets have been able to cite very few cases of execution. The Hong Kong *Kung-shang jih-pao* for June 18, 1954, was quoted in *Kung-fei pao-cheng chi-yao,* ed. Chung-yang Wei-yüan-hui Ti-liu-tsu (Taipei, 1961, p. 747), describing how twelve Buddhists were shot near Kükiang in May, 1954. It could be argued either that there has been a policy of strictly concealing the execution of monks (because it would cast doubt on the constitutional guarantee of freedom of religious belief) or that very few have, in fact, been executed. Perhaps both are true.

5. *HTFH,* 6/53, p. 37.

6. I prefer to break with convention and not to translate *hui-tao men* as "heterodox Taoist sects." They were heterodox only from the point of view of orthodox Buddhists and Taoists, who were, in turn, heterodox from the point of view of Confucians. They were Taoist only to the extent that "Tao-

ism" has come to be a catch-all for whatever is not Buddhist or Confucian. The etymology of the term *hui-tao men* is puzzling. What it seems to mean word for word is "sects" (*men*) of secret societies (*hui*) and Taoism. Cf. Chü-tsan's use of *hui-tao men* in *HTFH,* 2/51, p. 13. Although the *hui-tao men* were not so much sects as independent religions, I call them sects and their members "sectarians" to avoid clumsy compound terms and to follow the precedent of J. J. M. DeGroot in *Sectarianism and Religious Persecution in China* (Amsterdam, 1903).

7. Eighteen temples at Wu-t'ai Shan were said to have been occupied by syncretistic sects since the end of the Ch'ing dynasty: see *HTFH,* 11/50, p. 31. Cf. Welch, *Practice,* pp. 401-403.

8. See below notes 15-16.

9. Cf. Chapter XI, note 45. A useful guide to material on rebellions by religious sects and secret societies throughout Chinese history is provided by James P. Harrison, *The Communists and Chinese Peasant Rebellions* (New York, Atheneum, 1969), pp. 279-304. Cf. *ibid.,* pp. 165-189.

10. The first order for the suppression of the syncretistic sects appears to have been issued by the Peking Municipal Government on December 19, 1950 (see *HTFH,* 2/51, p. 13). Action against them, however, had already begun the preceding autumn: see *HTFH,* 11/50, p. 31.

11. See *HTFH,* 3/51, p. 27, 4/51, p. 30. The latter states that sectarians were permitted to listen to Buddhist sutras and to subscribe to Buddhist periodicals. It is indicative of the rigor of the campaign against them that a correction was issued in *HTFH,* 12/51, p. 36, stating that to permit this failed to distinguish between friends and enemies. The only sectarians exempted from registration were those who had withdrawn before the suppression of their sects had been ordered and who had, since the order, denounced some of their former brethren. See *HTFH,* 4/51, p. 31.

12. *HTFH,* 3/52, p. 19.

13. *HTFH,* 4/51, p. 31.

14. *HTFH,* 6/53, p. 41.

15. For example, when the Ta-ch'eng Chiao (see next note) was being suppressed in Kan-chou, Kiangsi, Buddhists held a meeting to approve of the government's "helping Buddhist circles to purify Buddhism": see *HTFH,* 5/58, p. 30.

16. Two Kiangsi delegates to the CBA's second national conference in 1957 called on the government to distinguish Buddhism from the Ta-ch'eng Chiao (the Mahayana religion or "Doctrine of the Great Vehicle") alias the Lo-tsu Chiao (the "Religion of the Patriarch Lo"—i.e., Lo Wei-ch'ün). Its principal scripture was called the *Lung ching* (Dragon sutra), and its rites were completely different from Buddhist rites—yet, they protested, it was pretending to be Buddhist. See *HTFH,* 5/57, p. 20-21. On Lo Wei-ch'ün, see 6/53, p. 32. The following year the Ta-ch'eng Chiao was suppressed in one district of Kiangsi (see preceding note) and five of its leaders were arrested in Hankow.

Under the Kuomintang these five leaders were said to have set up Buddhist temples everywhere, cheated the sick by quackery, collaborated with the I-kuan Tao (the most important of the sects), infiltrated Buddhist clubs, and "madly attacked the Communist Party": see *Ch'ang-chiang jih-pao,* September 27, 1958, tr. in JPRS 1454:5-7.

For a pledge to leave the sectarians no place to hide, see *HTFH,* 7/59, p. 34 (Hu *hsien,* Shensi). Cf. *HTFH,* 12/58, p. 33, which is especially interesting because it lists all the categories of people in Heilungkiang who were to be excluded and denounced by Buddhists: "landlords, counterrevolutionaries, persons under surveillance, member of syncretistic sects, and all anti-socialist elements." The last such pledge I have seen was passed by the Shansi Provincial Buddhist Association at its second conference in July 1962: members resolved "to purify the religious faith of Buddhists and draw a clear line of demarcation between themselves and the syncretistic sects." See *HTFH,* 6/62, p. 40 (December 1962).

17. Those arrested were Chen-ju, abbot of the Leng-yen Ssu near Tsamkong, and K'uan-chien, abbot of the Pao-feng Ssu in Kiangsi: see *HTFH,* 11/58, p. 34, tr. in *CB,* 550:9.

18. In some places Party and government organs were expected to select at least 5 percent of their members as targets during the campaign. See Ezra Vogel, *Canton under Communism: Programs and Politics in a Provincial Capital, 1949-1968* (Cambridge, Mass., 1969), p. 136.

19. *HTFH,* 9/55, pp. 15, 12. Lamas were also said to have hidden counterrevolutionaries and to have distorted government policy.

20. Ch'en Ming-shu and Liu Ya-hsiu were leaders of the Kuomintang Revolutionary Committee: on the accusations against them, see *SCMP,* 1604:11-12, and *CB,* 510:1-4. Fang Tzu-fan, one of the founders of *Modern Buddhism* along with Ch'en, was a member of the Shanghai Municipal Federation of Industry and Commerce and it was in this capacity that he had a seat on the Standing Committee of the First CPPCC Shanghai Municipal Committee, from which he was dismissed as a rightist: see *Chieh-fang jih-pao,* May 1, 1958. He was re-elected to the CBA council in 1962. Another rightist was Hsü Ying, who had long served as deputy director of the Religious Affairs Bureau in Peking. In September 1957 he was expelled from the Party and dismissed from all his posts.

21. *HTFH,* 10/58, p. 21. Care for the souls of counterrevolutionaries had long since been forbidden: see Chapter I at note 68.

22. *Chi-lin jih-pao,* June 20, 1958, tr. in *SCMP,* 1834:10-11, and in JPRS 513:2-4 (slightly altered: I have changed "peered" to "pierced").

23. In 1958 the abbot of the Yün-men Ssu, Kwangtung, was said to have been arrested because he had informed on the local cadres during the Hsü-yün case seven years earlier. Also in 1958 the leading officers of the Yün-chü Ssu, Kiangsi, where Hsü-yün then lived, were reportedly summoned to Peking and thereafter never heard from again. During struggle meetings that year at a

small temple in Hankow, the head monk was accused of living in luxury, riding on the heads of the people, and corruptly using the temple's money for private purposes. (For example, he had bought a watch to give to the child of one of the temple's lay supporters.) When he denied any wrongdoing, one of his own monks struck him in the face and told him he was not being sincere. Soon afterwards he drowned himself in the Yangtze. Buddhist suicides were also said to have occurred during earlier campaigns. A case of self-immolation by fire seems to have taken place in 1948 (see Welch, *Practice,* p. 327); and the publication of an article in 1955, ridiculing self-immolation by fire, suggests that at least one more case may have occurred about that time: see *HTFH,* 2/55, p. 25.

24. See this chapter at note 56. Parallel cases of rehabilitation are reported from central China.

25. For a clear instance of this, see Chapter X at note 1.

26. It is not clear whether the Shanghai Buddhist Youth Society (Shanghai-shih Fo-chiao Ch'ing-nien Hui) was identical with the Buddhist Youth Group formed by one thousand monks and two hundred nuns in January 1950 (see Alfred Kiang, p. 173); or whether it went back to a group sometimes referred to in English as the Young Men's Buddhist Association, which was set up in 1946. The reference in 1955 to "six or seven years" of its counterrevolutionary activities makes the latter seem more likely: see *HTFH,* 9/55, p. 11. Late in 1951 it moved into new quarters: see *HTFH,* 3/52, p. 34.

27. *HTFH,* 11/55, p. 5.

28. *HTFH,* 9/55, p. 30.

29. *Ibid.,* p. 31 and cf. p. 11.

30. *Ibid.,* p. 29, and cf. p. 23. The work report submitted to the enlarged council at the opening session spoke simply of local Buddhist organizations that had fallen under the influence of "bad elements" without mentioning by name the Shanghai Buddhist Youth Society.

31. *Ibid.,* p. 14.

32. *Ibid.,* p. 30.

33. See Chapter II at note 21 and Table 1, note d.

34. *HTFH,* 11/55, p. 5. This summary of the charges makes it clear that it was not a group of ordinary members of the society, but its leaders themselves who were under fire as counterrevolutionaries.

35. *HTFH,* 9/55, p. 16.

36. Suffering (*duḥkha*), emptiness (*śūnyatā*), impermanence (*anitya*), and illusion (*māya*) are among the most basic concepts of Buddhism. Lü Ch'eng had himself specialized in the study of the Dharmalaksana school, which holds the physical world to be a mental projection. The only phrase in the passage quoted to which an orthodox Chinese Buddhist might take exception is that "wordly things and Buddhism are separated by an unbridgeable gap." Chinese Buddhists consider that a person's mode of daily life should precisely reflect his knowledge that its preoccupations are empty and impermanent.

The traditional "negativity" and "escapism" of Buddhist doctrine (here denied by Lü Ch'eng) are elsewhere frequently attested to by other Buddhists, e.g., in Shirob's saying that Buddhism's "negative attitude of rejecting the world has been handed down from the past." See *JMJP,* April 15, 1960.

37. *HTFH,* 9/55, p. 26.

38. *Ibid.,* p. 11.

39. *Ibid., p. 32.*

40. *HTFH,* 4/56, p. 5. The Vajra Shrine (Chin-kang Tao-ch'ang) still had 35 practicing lamas when visited by a Japanese delegation in 1957: see *Chūgai nippō,* May 27, 1958. Ch'ing-ting seems to have been an elderly Han monk who was also active in the Pure Karma Society: see Ōtani, p. 123.

41. *Ibid.*

42. See Chapter IX, n. 66.

43. On the restoration of the Nan-hua Ssu, see Welch, *Revival,* pp. 92-93.

44. He had been trained in meditation at the Kao-min Ssu, one of the two best centers of Ch'an practice in China, where Hsü-yün himself had been trained. Starting about 1940 he had served as prior of the Kuang-chi Mao-p'ing, "the model public monastery" of Wu-t'ai Shan, admired for its "strict enforcement of the rules" (*HTFH,* 11/50, p. 31). Neng-hai, a vice-president of the Chinese Buddhist Association, was its abbot.

45. Hong Kong *Wen-hui pao,* Jan. 30, 1955.

46. NCNA Sept. 2, 1955, tr. in *SCMP,* 1128:12.

47. *HTFH,* 5/57, p. 24.

48. *Nan-fang jih-pao,* May 13, 1957.

49. Hong Kong *Ta-kung pao,* June 7, 1957. This was published on the day before free criticism was declared to have gone too far. Pen-huan began his interview by pointing out that food rations for the sangha were higher than those for peasants.

50. *Nan-fang jih-pao,* June 11, 1958, reprinted in *HTFH,* 8/58, pp. 30-31. Except for occasional corrections necessitated by the original text, I have used a composite of the three translations available: *CB,* 510:21-23; URS 13:82-85; and JPRS 613:48-51.

51. Some monks must have showed special enthusiasm because they felt that they were themselves vulnerable. Ch'i-shan, for example, the abbot of the Hua-lin Ssu, was vulnerable because of his affair with a nun.

52. *HTFH,* 8/58, p. 31.

53. *Ibid.*

54. The monks of the Great Temple in Manas sent a statement to *Modern Buddhism* enthusiastically supporting the arrest of Pen-huan. *Inter alia,* it said: "We Buddhists should not forget the intrigues of the enemy because we are supposed to be compassionate . . . We are determined to wage a ruthless struggle against bad people and bad deeds. Our abbot, Jung-t'ung, has said: 'Such false Buddhists as Pen-huan are the black sheep of Buddhism and they should receive severe punishment from the government. Arresting counter-

revolutionary elements can definitely enhance freedom of religion and the internal purity of Buddhism." See *HTFH,* 10/58, p. 34.

55. See *HTFH,* 8/58, p. 31 and 11/58, p. 32.

56. This information comes from a single informant and I have not seen it confirmed by anything in the Mainland press.

57. For more information on Hsü-yün, see Welch, *Practice,* esp. pp. 69-70, 82-83, 307, 313, 317-318, 324-325, 385, 404-405; and *Revival,* esp. pp. 34, 90-96, 123, 154-155, 191-192, 218-219.

58. See A. K. Seidel, *La divinisation de Lao tseu dans le Taoïsme des Han* (Paris, Ecole française d'Extrême-Orient, 1969), p. 16.

59. See Hong Kong *Ta-kung pao,* May 23, 1950, and Ts'en Hsüeh-lü, *Hsü-yün ho-shang nien-p'u,* pp. 162-163.

60. See Ezra Vogel, "Land Reform in Kwangtung 1951-1953: Central Control and Localism," *China Quarterly,* 38:46 (April-June 1969).

61. I here summarize a portion of the text omitted in my translation. Hsü-yün's visit to the Tusita Heaven is like the visit of T'an-hsü to hell: see Welch, *Practice,* p. 266.

62. This sentence is no more than partly true. Many sections of *Hsü-yün ho-shang nien-p'u,* first published in 1953, are virtually identical with the text of *Hsü-yün lao-ho-shang shih-chi,* first published in 1944 by Hsü-yün's disciples at the Nan-hua Ssu. (I have not seen the original edition of this, but only Lin Yüan-fan, ed. *Hsü-yün lao-ho-shang shih-chi* [Hong Kong, 1951] which, according to Lin's preface, was re-edited [*ch'ung-p'ien*] from the 1944 edition.)

The main differences between the 1944 *shih-chi* and the 1953 *nien-p'u* are that Hsü-yün is referred to in the third person in the earlier work but in the first person in the identical passages of the later one; and the date of his birth has been moved back from 1846 to 1840. Hsü-yün, while still gravely ill from his beating in April 1951, can scarcely have dictated his memoirs word for word as they had already been recorded seven years earlier. It is only the events since 1943 that he can have dictated in 1951 for inclusion in his so-called autobiography. Nonetheless, when I questioned the compiler of the autobiography, Ts'en Hsüeh-lü, his associates, and some of Hsü-yün's other disciples, they have insisted that the whole of it was dictated by Hsü-yün himself in 1951. More research is needed.

Another vexing problem is Hsü-yün's age. Every one whom I have questioned agreed that Hsü-yün was usually silent about his age. There is reason to think that he was not six but more than twenty years younger than stated in the autobiography: see Welch, *Practice,* p. 510,note 43. The 1939 ordination year book of Ku Shan gives the age of every ordination master except Hsü-yün, who, as the ordaining abbot, controlled the text of the entries. Yet the highest age claimed by his disciples was endorsed by the Communists: see Chao, *Buddhism in China,* p. 40.

As to the reliability of the autobiography as a whole, in a letter photographically reproduced in the third edition (1962) Hsü-yün wrote that in September 1956 he had looked over the text as it then stood and asked his acolytes to record the mistakes he had found and forward them to Ts'en. However, he immediately went on to say that his sight and hearing were impaired and that he had been unable to read the text carefully. This letter therefore cannot be considered a blanket endorsement of the autobiography. Yet I tend to believe that most of its contents did originate with what Hsü-yün told his followers at one time or another.

63. Ts'en Hsüeh-lü, *Hsü-yün ho-shang nien-p'u,* pp. 183-186.

64. I was told the story about Chu Teh and Hsü-yün by Ts'en Hsüeh-lü (although he does not appear to have included it in the autobiography that he edited) and by several other disciples of Hsü-yün. They have not agreed about the date or the details, but on the basis of Chu's biography in Boorman, I, 460, and *CB,* 822, I would think that the likeliest time for the episode was the autumn of 1921 when Chu had to flee from Yünnan after it was retaken by T'ang Chi-yao. Eventually he went to Europe. A former cadre of the Religious Affairs Division in Canton recalled that he had read the story of Chu Teh and Hsü-yün in a file of "Reference Materials for the Study of Party History." According to his recollection, however, the episode took place sometime in 1927 after Chu Teh's defeat in the Nanchang Uprising. In this version too Chu Teh asked to be made a monk and Hsü-yün refused. (In 1927 Hsü-yün was not yet connected with any monastery in Kwangtung that lay in the area through which Chu retreated.) Chu's brother is said to have become a Refuges disciple of Hsü-yün; and Chu's own interest in Buddhism is suggested by the fact that he received the delegates of the CBA's second national conference and allowed himself to be photographed with them, smiling and waving: see *HTFH,* 5/57, p. 32, and the foldout group picture.

65. Another high-ranking Communist is reported to have been hidden by Hsü-yün at the Nan-hua Ssu in the winter of 1948-49 when the American Buddhist woman devotee, Ananda Jennings, was taking part in meditation there. The former cadre of the Canton Religious Affairs Division recalled hearing that Hsü-yün had once given asylum to T'ao Chu, who was a leading Party official in South China at the time of the beating.

66. Miao-yün came from Changsha and was born about 1911. After graduating in economics from the University of Hunan, he worked as an auditor for the Ministry of Finance, latterly in Shanghai. There he grew so disgusted with the corruption he saw that he decided to become a monk. He was unmarried and already several years earlier he had become a Refuges disciple of Hsü-yün. Now in 1948 he was tonsured by him and in 1949 he was ordained by him at the Nan-hua Ssu. (The ordination year book states that he was tonsured in 1944; perhaps that was when he took the Five Vows. The abbot of Nan-hua and other informants have insisted that there was less than a year between his

tonsure and ordination.) Immediately after he was ordained, Hsü-yün transmitted to him the dharma of the Yün-men lineage, which had become extinct centuries earlier (see Welch, *Practice*, p. 278). That was why he had given him the religious name Miao-yün and the style Shao-men: they were an anagram for Yün-men. See Ts'en Hsüeh-lü, *Hsü-yün ho-shang nien-p'u*, p. 184. Miao-yün was at first quite clever in handling the cadres: in 1950 he was quoted as saying that "monks who have engaged in reclamation work no longer feel like leading a lazy life of chanting scriptures and sitting in meditation" (Hong Kong *Ta-kung pao*, May 23, 1950)—a statement that certainly would not reflect the real feelings of a disciple of the great meditation master.

67. See Vogel, *Canton under Communism*, p. 64.

68. A monk then living at the Yün-men Ssu recalled that the old man walked very slowly because of the pain that he still felt from the rib that had been broken by a heavy blow with the mallet of a large "wooden fish."

69. Ts'en Hsüeh-lü, *Hsü-yün ho-shang nien-p'u*, p. 187.

70. Hsü-yün's name is listed first among those who took part in the preparatory meeting: see NCNA English, November 15, 1952, in *SCMP*, 453:25.

71. Ts'en Hsüeh-lü, *Hsü-yün ho-shang nien-p'u*, p. 191.

72. On Hsü-yün's role in 1912, see Welch, *Revival*, p. 34, and p. 300 note 15.

73. The story is told that, when he was staying in Peking, Chu Teh came to call on him and jocularly asked if he would accept him as a disciple *this* time. Hsü-yün answered: "If you were far away from it before, you are even further now."

74. This story comes from one of Hsü-yün's disciples from overseas who used to visit him at Yün-chü Shan in the late 1950's. According to this informant, Mao had treated him with deference and a cousin of Mao's was a Refuges disciple of Hsü-yün. Hsü-yün's reluctance to complain is similar to that of the Dalai Lama in his interview with Mao in 1954: see Dalai Lama, *My Land and My People* (London, 1962), p. 99.

Most of my informants have maintained that because Hsü-yün would not lodge a complaint, the cadres responsible for beating him were merely censured and never punished. However, a former cadre of the Religious Affairs Division in Canton recalled that the person immediately in charge of the case (an official of the Shaokuan Civil Affairs Section) was demoted. Overall responsibility, he said, was held by the Shaokuan Public Security Office, since a religious affairs section had not yet been set up for Shaokuan, so that religious affairs cadres, he emphasized, were in no wise responsible for what happened. Anyway, he went on, Hsü-yün *had* been guilty: a radio transmitter *was* concealed at the Yün-men Ssu; and two of its monks *were* Kuomintang agents.

75. On the ceremonies, see below note 90 and Chapter IX at note 5. In the Republican period Yüan-ying and T'ai-hsü had also been invited to serve

as abbots of monasteries where it was believed that their influence would help prevent government encroachment.

76. He never attended any of the CBA's meetings, and for its second national conference he was the only one of the four honorary presidents who did not send greetings—a fairly conspicuous omission. The CBA, however, sometimes used his name. In February 1955, for example, he was elected one of the sixty-five members of its committee to collect signatures against the use of atomic weapons: see NCNA, February 12, 1955. In 1954 he was elected to the Second National Committee of the CPPCC (Hong Kong *Ta-kung pao,* December 12, 1954), but its meetings too he did not attend.

77. Ts'en Hsüeh-lü, *Hsü-yün ho-shang nien-p'u,* p. 398. A variation of the story has it that he was accused of keeping women in a secret chamber behind his bedroom and of never having been properly ordained. According to one informant, among those denouncing him was Tz'u-ts'ang, who was himself in trouble as a rightist and hoped thereby to "get rid of his rightist hat." A year before, Tz'u-ts'ang had reported to the CBA second national conference on how well religious life was being kept up at Yün-chü Shan under the leadership of Hsü-yün, who, he said, was being solicitously cared for by the local government, "for which we feel deep gratitude": see *HTFH,* 5/57, p. 25. Cf. *ibid.,* p. 20 where Chi-kuang spoke on behalf of the five Kiangsi delegates to the conference and "reported on the life of the Venerable Hsü-yün, about whom Buddhists in our country feel concern. The Venerable Hsü-yün is now in good health and he is leading his disciples in the restoration of Yün-chü Shan . . . The Religious Affairs Division of Kiangsi Province and of the Ch'ü-chiang Special District both feel very special concern for all aspects of the Venerable Hsü-yün's life and health." The tone is certainly different from what it became a year later.

78. One of those arrested was Fo-yüan, who had been chosen the abbot of Yün-men when Hsü-yün was in Peking. According to one informant his arrest was partly to pay off an old score—having complained to Peking about Hsü-yün's beating by the local cadres seven years earlier. Others arrested in 1958 included Yin-k'ai, the prior of Yün-chü, and Ch'uan-shih, a guest prefect. The proctor of the monastery was said to have been beaten to death for "stubbornness."

Another reason these monks may have been in trouble was the publication of the second edition of Hsü-yün's autobiography in 1957, with its detailed account of how the local cadres had behaved. This had been sent to Hong Kong in progressively detailed versions, written on the blank inner pages of thread-bound sutras. To this day the most detailed version has not been published, since those who received copies of it, including myself, were cautioned that publication might result in further difficulties for monks still in the Mainland. Yet no refutation of the published account, so far as I know, has ever come from the Communists, perhaps because they consider it irrefutable or perhaps because they realize that atrocity stories of this sort tend to be discounted as anti-Communist propaganda.

79. This story is close to Ts'en Hsüeh-lü, *Hsü-yün ho-shang nien-p'u,* p. 399. The informant from whom it came added that someone he knew later went to Peking and told Chü-tsan that he wanted to write a tribute to Hsü-yün. Chü-tsan said: "Do you still admire that old fellow? I'll show you something that I have in a room here." He then produced the dossier which Mao had refused to have brought up at the NPC.

80. NCNA English, October 17, 1959.

81. See *P'u-t'i shu,* 4/62, p. 48. Hsü-yün was evidently the only person who knew about the gold at the time he was beaten. His followers told the truth when they claimed ignorance of it.

The Kuang-hsiao Ssu was famous as the monastery where the Sixth Patriarch had his head shaved and became a monk. This was probably the reason why Hsü-yün defended so tenaciously the money he had collected for its repair. It had been converted into a judicial school under the Nationalists (see Welch, *Revival,* p. 146) and into the headquarters of a drama troupe just after Liberation. By 1960 part or all of it had become a museum. See Chapter V at notes 12, 24.

82. Parts of the following section first appeared in Welch, "Facades of Religion in China," *Asian Survey,* 10.7:614-626 (July 1970).

83. *HTFH,* 10/50, pp. 31-33. The thirty-one sponsors comprised eight monks and nuns, sixteen lay devotees, and seven lamas. They included Chü-tsan, Fa-tsun, Neng-hai, Li Chi-shen, Yeh Kung-cho, Chou Shu-chia, and other influential Buddhists. On the last day an audience of over six hundred monks, nuns, lamas, and lay devotees heard an address by Ch'en Ch'i-yüan.

84. It seems strange that men like Chü-tsan and Li Chi-shen would endorse "subduing by the power of exorcism" (*i chiang-mo-ti li-liang shih-chih chiang-fu*–see *HTFH,* 10/50, p. 32). Of course it could have been meant metaphorically, but that is not consistent with the hair-splitting way in which the term "prayer" (*ch'i-tao*), which the sponsors originally wanted to apply to the services, was rejected in favor of a term that might best be translated as "self-dedication" (*chu-yüan*). "After everyone studied [the question], it was felt that to use the term prayer would imply that there was an object of prayer like God or divinities. This would be suitable in other religions, but the worship of the Buddha by Buddhists is worship of his great and perfect character and means simply a resolve to follow his example and not an expectation that he will do something for us. Besides, Buddhist teachings emphasize karmic causation and karma is what each man creates himself. Prayer was therefore not a suitable word" (*ibid.,* p. 33). The explanation may be that the word prayer, being in the title of the meetings, attracted the notice of the cadres, while exorcism, buried in the text, did not.

85. The person who lectured on the *Heart Sutra* was Chü-tsan. Perhaps he introduced progressive political themes into his lecture, but there is no indica-

tion of this in the published report. Another service inspired by the appeal of the thirty-one Buddhists in Peking was held in Wuhan to bring about permanent world peace and to dispel disasters: see *HTFH,* 12/50, p. 31. The following summer, when a Kuan-yin service was held at Chung-nan Shan, the equivalent of about US$130 was donated by worshipers. The monks gave the entire sum to the Resist America Aid Korea Campaign "in order to show their fervent patriotism." It must have been fervent indeed, for they needed the money to buy food. They were then living on corn and potatoes and "life had been rather hard for the past year or so": see *Chüeh yu-ch'ing,* 13.2:20 (October 1952).

86. *HTFH,* 5/57, p. 4. "To do Buddhist things" is *tso fo-shih.*

87. *HTFH,* 8/53, pp. 24-25. Cf. *JMJP,* Nov. 2, 1958.

88. For a report of this at the Mi-t'o Ssu, Harbin, see *HTFH,* 7/53, p. 27; at the Ching-yeh Ssu, Shensi, 1/51, p. 30; at the Pai-ma Ssu, Loyang, 4/54, p. 30; at the Fu-hsiu An, Shensi, 8/53, p. 27. This last speaks of "missing none of the four," the additional element being "patriotism" (*ai-kuo*).

89. The peace service at the Ta-chien Ssu, Shaokuan, was held November 17, 1952: see *HTFH,* 2/53, p. 29. Cf. 3/53, p. 28 (Kweilin). A peace service at the Hsing-fu Ssu in Changshu (Kiangsu) January 4-10, 1953, was sponsored by the municipal Buddhist association and on the average more than five hundred persons took part each day. During the service the secretary-general of the United Front Department and a cadre from the Propaganda Department gave addresses on the policy of freedom of religious belief and the struggle for world peace. Small group meetings were held and a summary was drawn up of their achievements and shortcomings. In the report on this peace service in *Modern Buddhism,* nothing is said about the religious activities carried on: see *HTFH,* 3/53, p. 28. Presumably, however, the activities were much the same as at other services of "self-dedication to world peace" held at this time, like the one in Shanghai next to be described in the text.

90. See *Chüeh yu-ch'ing,* 14.1:7-9 (January 1953) and Ts'en Hsüeh-lü, *Hsü-yün ho-shang nien-p'u,* p. 192. On this type of forty-nine day service, termed in Chinese *shui-lu fa-hui,* see Welch, *Practice,* pp. 190-191. The future council members of the CBA who took part in the rites for the dead were Wei-fang and Miao-chen. As to the charges for soul tablets, 2,000,000 JMP (old currency) entitled a layman to two specially decorated tablets installed for both sessions of the "inner altar" (*nei-t'an*), one tablet to help the dead towards a better rebirth and the other to prolong the life of the living; and he himself could enter the *nei-t'an,* from which ordinary lay people were excluded. For 500,000 JMP he could have a single undecorated tablet for one session. The lowest rate, 20,000 JMP, entitled him to a very small tablet in the hall of longevity or the hall of rebirth (on a nature of which see Welch, *Practice,* pp. 203-204). All the traditional features of *shui-lu fa-hui* seem to have been present, including the dispatch of messengers to heaven (*ch'ing-sheng, sung-sheng*)–that is, burning paper horses so that they could go up to

heaven and invite the Jade Emperor to attend; and then escort him back afterwards. A vegetarian feast was given for all the monks. The dates of the various activities were published according to the lunar calendar.

91. Other peace services were held as late as May: see *HTFH,* 8/53, pp. 24-25.

92. *HTFH,* 12/54, p. 29 (Chung-nan Shan, Chin-yang, both in Shensi); 2/55, p. 29 (P'u-tu Ssu, Anhwei); and 4/55, p. 29 (P'ing-lo *hsien,* Kansu). This type of recitation was not a mechanical exercise, but a means of focusing the mind on Amitabha. The Chinese term *nien-fo* means both. In Anhwei the name recited was not that of the Buddha Amitabha, but of the Bodhisattva Samantabhadra, who is the patron of religious practice. Recitation went on for fifty-three days—an unusually long period. At Chung-nan Shan it went on even longer—from the 1st of the tenth month to the 8th of the twelfth, for a total of nine recitation weeks, the longest I have ever heard of before or after Liberation. It is not made clear how many hours a day recitation was carried on. The fifty-five monks taking part in it were reported to be studying China's new Constitution at the same time, but they may have done this for only a few hours a week as a "license" for their intensive religious practice.

93. *HTFH,* 12/54, p. 29 (Shih-yün Ssu, Shensi). Cf. 12/54, p. 27. The week of buddha recitation at the Shih-yün Ssu was held to liberate Taiwan and "to commemorate the Venerable Yin-kuang on the fifteenth anniversary of his death." Yin-kuang had been the greatest advocate of buddha recitation during the Republican period and was regarded as the twelfth patriarch of the Pure Land school: see Welch, *Practice,* pp. 90-100. Since he had been a conservative, there is a certain irony in the use of the "liberation" of Taiwan as a pretext for commemorating his death.

94. *HTFH,* 7/55, p. 30 (Lin-tse, Kansu; An-k'ang, Shensi). I cannot explain why so many of the reports cited in these notes come from Shensi and Kansu.

95. *HTFH,* 7/55, p. 30 (Chung-nan Shan). The celebration of the Buddha's birthday lasted seven days and was also intended to speed up the "liberation" of Taiwan.

96. See *HTFH,* 6/55, p. 30 (Ch'ing-shan Ssu, Shensi). This names the martyrs as "Shih Chung-ang and others." The crash of their Air India plane off North Borneo on April 11, 1954, was attributed by Peking to the explosion of a "time bomb placed in the plane by U.S.-Chiang agents in Hong Kong." See *Handbook on People's China,* p. 210. All aboard lost their lives and the real cause of the accident was never ascertained.

97. It was a service (*fa-hui*) for self-dedication to world peace, but it was held on Amitabha's birthday, December 15, 1951, on the significance of which the 242 people who attended heard an address by a local monk. They also heard addresses by a comrade from the China Democratic League on preserving world peace; by a member of the CPPCC Committee on the Korean Comfort Mission; and by a comrade from the United Front Department

on the Chinese People's Volunteers in Korea. At the end they signed a "patriotic religious compact in which they promised: (1) to make an effort in productive labor, to learn the spirit of Pai-chang's 'no work, no eating', to practice strict economy, to make early payment of the grain tax, to strengthen Resist American Aid Korea,' and to welcome the great construction of the motherland; (2) to step up study of Marxism-Leninism and Chairman Mao's thinking, thoroughly to reform feudal superstitious thinking and, in the service of the people, to spread the Mahayana Buddhist doctrines of 'no self, no gods . . . '; (3) in addition to making sure that neither production, study, nor religious exercises would go by the board, to help the government investigate and expose the secret activities of reactionary syncretistic sects and to prevent such sects from borrowing the good name of Buddhism in order to carry out acts that harm the people and corrupt Buddhism." See *HTFH,* 4/53, p. 28.

In this report, sent to *Modern Buddhism,* it was natural to emphasize political more than religious activities even though most participants may have cared more for the religious than the political. The same is true for reports of the celebration of Kuan-yin's birthdays. For example, when a temple in Peking held a service on her birthday in 1953, the news in *Modern Buddhism* was headlined: "An-yang Ching-she Holds Self-Dedication to World Peace" and ended: "The seven-day service made Buddhists even more aware of the positive Buddhist spirit of entering the world": see *HTFH,* 12/53, p. 30. In 1954 a three-day celebration of Kuan-yin's birthday was held in a Kwangtung nunnery as an act of self-dedication to world peace and in order to bring about the early "liberation" of Taiwan: see *HTFH,* 12/54, p. 27. A few days later her birthday was celebrated for the same purposes at the newly renovated Tz'u-en Ssu in Sian; see *ibid.,* p. 29. (Kuan-yin has three "birthdays": on the 19th of the second, sixth, and ninth months, to celebrate her birth, enlightenment, and death. The ceremonies at the Tz'u-en Ssu were held from the 1st to the 7th of the tenth month, perhaps because its renovation had not been completed early enough to hold them at the usual time two weeks earlier.) On the 19th of the second month in 1955 the nuns of the Hsiang-shan Ssu on Nan-yüeh recited Kuan-yin's name as an act of self-dedication to world peace and the happiness of the people: see *HTFH,* 5/55, p. 30.

98. For example, when Tz'u-chou was invested as abbot of the Nan-p'u-to Ssu on October 12, 1952, five thousand Buddhists attended the ceremony. Such large public gatherings drew attention to popular support for Buddhism and were therefore discouraged (though not prohibited) by the religious affairs organs. Probably for that reason Erh-mai gave a speech during the ceremony in which he reported on the topics discussed at the second session of the People's Representative Conference of Amoy, which he had attended. See *HTFH,* 6/53, p. 41. In May 1953, to celebrate the founding of the CBA, four hundred of the sangha and laity in Ch'ang-ning, Fukien, recited Amitabha's name for two days: see *HTFH,* 8/53, p. 25.

99. *HTFH,* 10/54, p. 29.

100. *HTFH,* 5/57, p. 16. Cf. Chao P'u-ch'u, *Buddhism in China* (1957), pp. 34-35.

101. *Nan-fang jih-pao,* May 13, 1957.

102. *HTFH,* 5/53, p. 26.

103. *HTFH,* 11/58, p. 34. This case has already been mentioned in Chapter III at note 34.

104. *HTFH,* 5/54, p. 28.

105. *HTFH,* 5/54, p. 29.

106. *HTFH,* 4/56, p. 5. The earliest example I have seen of this kind of turnabout comes from Changsha. On March 31, 1949, fourteen nuns formed the Changsha First Sewing and Weaving Production Coöperative, located in the Tzu-tsai An. One might suppose this showed how progressive they were—and how farsighted, since Changsha was not "liberated" until the following August. Actually their coöperative turned out to be a screen behind which "remnant feudal elements" hoped to perpetuate their "feudal dictatorship" of the Tzu-tsai An. Struggle against them began in April 1950 and continued until December, by which time one had fled and the rest were isolated. On December 18, 1950, the coöperative was reorganized, political study was started, and production began to soar. A year later its members consisted of 124 nuns—90 percent of the nuns in Changsha—who operated 56 looms and eight sewing machines. See *HTFH,* 7/52, pp. 18-20.

107. During the campaign to collect signatures for the world peace petition, religious services were held under its protective umbrella in at least nine localities, one in Hunan, two in Chekiang, six in Shensi (*HTFH,* 4/55, pp. 26, 29; 5/55, pp. 29, 30; 7/55, p. 30). See also notes 86, 89. The cadres may also have been made suspicious by occasional cases of sycophancy. In 1952, for example, Buddhists reported that the monkeys of Omei Shan, who had fled into the woods before Liberation, had returned "as if they realized that the friendly and peaceful co-existence of men and monkeys was only possible under the radiance of the five-starred Red Flag." See *HTFH,* 6/53, p. 56.

108. A large number of religious rites were held for the benefit of foreign Buddhist visitors in 1963-64 (see Chapter VI, 94, 96, 102, 131). They do not belong to the same category, however, as the rites before 1957, since they directly served people's diplomacy and presumably were endorsed by the Foreign Ministry.

109. On Buddhists' efforts to combine the study of doctrine with political study, see Chapter III at notes 41-43. On their effort to combine devotions and labor into a package, see this chapter at notes 87-88. For an example of their exploitation of the regime's desire for good relations with overseas Chinese and foreign Buddhists, see this chapter at note 101.

At the CBA conference in 1957 one delegate suggested that the association compile a history of the intercourse between Buddhists in Southeast Asian countries and Buddhists in China (*HTFH,* 5/57, p. 24). The suggestion sounds constructive, but does not appear to have been carried out. Could this be because the cadres felt there was danger in giving too much credit to the role of Buddhism in foreign relations?

110. See Welch, *Revival,* p. 351, note 72. Early Buddhist missionaries in north China offered their magical powers to help rulers win battles.

111. *HTFH,* 3/55, p. 32.

112. See Welch, *Revival,* p. 179.

113. *HTFH,* 5/57, p. 21. Something similar comes from Chungking, where hundreds of Buddhists were gathering to recite buddha's name each month. "In deep appreciation for the great kindness shown them by the Communist Party and the People's Government, after each time that they hold daily devotions or a religious service, they transfer all the merit therefrom to repay the kindness of the State and of all living creatures, and they offer prayers for world peace." See *HTFH,* 5/57, p. 16. This seems exactly like the transfer of merit that used to be made for the benefit of the emperor.

114. FBIS, August 30, 1966, DDD3 (Harbin). Ching-kuan had been elected to the council and standing committee of the CBA in 1957.

VIII. INTERPRETING BUDDHIST DOCTRINE

1. This comes from "On the New Democracy": see Mao, *Selected Works,* III, 155.

2. *HTFH,* 2/51, p. 29. Cf. Ch'en Ming-shu's article on May Day tasks for Buddhists, which included the distribution of land directly to the people: see *HTFH,* 6/51, p. 36. Perhaps it was at this time that the Nan P'u-t'o Ssu "conscientiously contributed" (*tzu-chüeh-ti hsien-ch'u*) its 80 mou of farmland: see *HTFH,* 6/53, p. 41.

3. *HTFH,* 12/51, p. 36.

4. This information comes from a former cadre of the Religious Affairs Division in Canton. He said that the directive ordered that the doctrines of each major religion be sorted into three categories: first, those doctrines that were completely idealistic and reactionary (like going to Heaven); second, those that were more or less realistic and could be utilized (like commandments against lying and stealing); and third, those that were ambivalent and could be utilized only by bringing out their positive content. For example, the ideal of compassion was negative insofar as it interfered with the liquidation of class enemies but positive insofar as it justified "killing bad people to help good people."

According to the former cadre the Religious Affairs Bureau did not do this work of scriptural analysis on a centralized basis in Peking. It expected its local personnel to go through the scriptures of the religions for which each was responsible, selecting usable passages. This prepared them better to make speeches at study meetings. Selection was easy to do, he said, with the Bible but difficult with the Tripitaka, which was so full of technical Buddhist terms and repellently idealistic concepts.

5. According to the same informant, since no real compromise with religious doctrines was desirable, it was best for the cadres to avoid going into details and not to answer questions like "What is the ultimate goal of Buddhism?" "Were Sakyamuni and his teaching good for mankind?" Their job was simply to utilize religious sayings "in a crude way."

6. This is from chüan 40 of the *Avatamsaka Sūtra* in 40 chüan. See T. 293, vol. 10, p. 846a. It was partly quoted in *HTFH*, 3/56, p. 21, and fully quoted two months later in an article on the four main points to be studied in Buddhism. The second point was "bringing benefits and joy to sentient beings. This means serving the people. The Buddha taught us that we should 'resolve to become buddhas in order to benefit sentient beings.' This is because our purpose in becoming buddhas is to bring benefits and joy to sentient beings, and also it is only by doing so that we can become buddhas. Therefore the chapter on Samantabhadra's vows in the *Avatamsaka Sūtra* says . . . [here is quoted the passage I have translated in the text]. . . The Buddha also told us that in our activities for the benefit of all living creatures we must act courageously, 'not seeking happiness for ourselves but resolving that all living creatures may get deliverance from their suffering.' As Buddhists of the New China we must follow the Buddha's words and do whatever the people require of us, 'hastening to provide for all living creatures.' " See *HTFH*, 5/56, pp. 49-50. Other passages from the chapter on Samantabhadra's vows (*P'u-hsien hsing-yüan p'in*) of the *Avatamsaka Sūtra* were quoted too—like the following, which was meant to show that Buddhists should take part in socialist construction: "Be a good physician to those who are sick and suffer; show the right path to those who have gone astray; and be a bright light for those who are in darkness . . . Whoever brings happiness to living creatures brings happiness also to all the buddhas. The bodhisattva's greatest wish is to dwell with living creatures [i.e., the masses] and never be separated from them." See *HTFH*, 3/56, p. 22.

7. See *HTFH*, 1/56, p. 6. I have been unable to locate the second passage in the *Avatamsaka Sūtra*, from which Chao said it came. When Chao P'u-ch'u again used the first passage in his address to the CBA's second national conference in March 1957, he drew from it the lesson that "the interests of Buddhism coincide with those of all living creatures. If Buddhists will put their greatest effort into activities that benefit all living creatures, then, in Buddhist terms, they can create greatest merit." See *HTFH*, 5/57, p. 8.

8. On the definition of "living creatures" as "the masses," see Chapter III at note 9.

9. *HTFH*, 1/55, p. 6.

10. *HTFH,* 11/59, p. 29. On the same page Buddhists are said to consider that "productive labor is inseparable from the exemplification of the bodhisattva ideal." Cf. *HTFH,* 6/53, p. 48, and Chapter III, note 11.

11. The entire passage reads: "To subscribe to [National Economic Construction] Bonds is to carry out the *paramitā* [perfection] of *dana* [charity], which is among the four ways of leading sentient beings to liberation (*ssu-she*) and six kinds of practice by which bodhisattvas attain enlightenment themselves (*liu-tu*); and it also realizes Samantabhadra's vow 'to beautify the land and do good to sentient beings.' " See *HTFH,* 3/54, p. 24. Cf. Chapter III at note 74. Previously a reader had written to *Chüeh-hsün* suggesting that what the Buddha had meant by his injunction to "amass wealth as if it were the dharma" (which I have been unable to locate in the canon) was nothing other than increasing production and practicing thrift. Therefore Buddhists ought to buy National Construction Bonds: see *HTFH,* 2/54, p. 29.

12. *HTFH,* 12/50, p. 3. A pamphlet of speeches by leading monks published in Fukien "identified the goals of Buddhism with patriotism": see *HTFH,* 6/53, p. 39. There were frequent references to "the patriotic thinking of Buddhism," as in 1959 when Shirob said that such thinking had been enhanced by the suppression of the Tibetan rebellion: see *HTFH,* 10/59, p. 11.

13. In 1960 Shirob Jaltso told the NPC: "There is no religion that does not hold to the principle of doing good to other creatures. We consider that the Communist Party's policy of protecting the minority, not the majority, of protecting the weak, not the strong, of protecting the poor, not the rich, runs along the same lines as the Buddha's idea of 'feeling as much compassion for others as for oneself.' For this reason we must resolutely support the Party." See *JMJP,* April 15, 1960.

14. This phrase can be found, for example, in the *Mahāprajñāpāramitopadeśa,* chüan 18: see T. 1509, vol. 25, p. 192b. Cf. T. 310, vol. 11, p. 288b. Compare the passage from the *Vimalakirti-nirdeśa Sūtra* referenced in note 84.

15. See *World Buddhism,* 12.8:9 (March 1964). In 1958 an editorial in *Modern Buddhism* stated: "To overcome selfish thoughts of personal gain and to set one's heart on the welfare of the masses of the people–this may be called one way to realize the ideal of 'purifying one's own thoughts' (*tzu-ching ch'i-i*)." See *HTFH,* 1/58, p. 4. In 1964 rule 31 of the *P'u-sa chieh-pen* was cited apparently as an attempt to show that Buddhists would be guilty of "the offense of noncoöperation" if they refused to join agricultural coöperatives: see *World Buddhism* 12.8:9 (March 1964) and T. 1500, vol. 24, p. 209b.

16. *HTFH,* 11/58, p. 32. See Chapter III, note 31.

17. For an example, see this chapter at note 88.

18. According to an article by Wan-chün in *HTFH,* 3/59, pp. 19-22, Buddhist dialecticians included Nagasena, Buddhaghosa, Vasumitra, Dharmatrata,

Vasubandhu, Kumāralabhda, and Bhadanta. Even Nagarjuna and Asanga, he says, were dialecticians, although, like Hegel, they were also idealists. Nagasena, Vasumitra, and Buddhaghosa "by their rigid logic wiped out all the mysticism of the Brahmanical philosophy that had dominated India for centuries." Part of this article is translated in JPRS 828:8-9. What should be especially noted is that Wan-chün bases it on a history of Indian philosophy by Monoronjon Roy (?), translated into Russian and published in 1958 by the Foreign Books Publishing Association in Moscow—surely impeccable credentials. Early Buddhist dialecticism is also discussed in *HTFH,* 3/60, p. 30 (March 1960).

Somewhat different was the idea of reinterpreting Buddhism by applying *modern* dialectical methods. When Ch'en Ming-shu came under attack as a rightist in 1957, it was revealed that in July 1950 the *Hung-hua Monthly* in Shanghai had published a small pamphlet of his entitled "The New Meaning of Buddhist Doctrine," in which he proposed that "a new meaning for Buddhist doctrine . . . can be found simply by approaching the dharma from a materialist viewpoint and with dialectical methods." Some excerpts were quoted in *HTFH,* 10/57, p. 28, which cites *Wen-hui pao,* July 13, 1957.

19. See the article by Chin-hui, "Atheistic Thought in Buddhist Scriptures," in *HTFH,* 5/60, pp. 25-26 (May 1960), tr. in JPRS 4240:1-8. Again foreign authorities are invoked (Rahula and Stcherbatsky).

It is true that primitive Buddhism rejected the notion of a supreme God who had created the universe, as well as the notion of a permanent soul. On the other hand it acknowledged the existence of innumerable gods (devas), of many varieties and degrees of power, as occupants of the highest of the six planes of existence in the Indian cosmology; and it placed great stress on the transmigration of something very like a soul through these six planes. In China the soul was far more openly accepted as a basic feature of Buddhism. In 1951 a reader asked *Modern Buddhism:* "Do the new Buddhists accept the operation of karma through successive lives in the six planes of existence?" The editor of the correspondence column answered that if by "the new Buddhists" was meant those who were really trying to fit the spirit of Buddhism into the new era, then they did indeed "correctly accept the operation of karma through successive lives in the six planes of existence." See *HTFH,* 11/51, p. 22.

20. Ch'en Ming-shu explained in April 1951 that in the New China a person should not have individual feelings but only collective feelings. This was why no one should feel sympathy with the landlords. See *HTFH,* 4/51, p. 28.

21. In 1955 *Modern Buddhism* published an article mentioning how the Buddha said: "When you are ill, get medical treatment and do not pray to the gods": see *HTFH,* 2/55, p. 26. The quotation attributed here to the Buddha appears to come from one of the Chinese versions of the *Dhammapada:* see T.

Two comments are needed on the translation in the text. The phrase that I have rather loosely translated as "bring down upon them Heaven's displeasure" is *shang yin-chih,* which means literally to act to the detriment of the secret blessings by which Heaven, which never speaks, expresses itself in rewarding good men. This was a pre-Buddhist analogue of karma. For monks and nuns to have asserted that participating in the suppression of counterrevolutionaries would create bad karma might have been taken as criticism of the government. It was safer to invoke the more obscure concept of "secret blessings."

I have italicized "attending . . . public trials" in order to support the parenthetical suggestion in the next sentence. I believe it was for the same reason that, when the Kansu Buddhist Association organized a counterespionage team to ferret out Kuomintang agents, it had its members to attend the public trials and executions of counterrevolutionaries. These provided another of the object lessons that raised class-consciousness. See *HTFH,* 6/53, pp. 30-31.

35. *HTFH,* 3/52, p. 15.

36. *Hsin-wan pao* (Shanghai), May 19, 1951. I have been unable to locate the source of the words quoted by Wei-fang, "unless you crush heterodoxy, you cannot make the orthodox shine forth." However, "smashing heterodoxy and making the orthodox shine forth" was an important concept of the Madhyamika school in China: see T. 1852, vol. 45, p. 1.

37. See, for example, *HTFH,* 9/55, p. 30, and below note 76. A sentence in the *Lotus Sūtra* about "the Tathagata and all the elect fighting demons" was invoked to mobilize Buddhists against the Hu Feng clique in 1955: see *HTFH,* 7/55, p. 2.

38. A Buddhist saying that was cited to exhort people to struggle against United States was "subdue a demon and become a buddha": see *HTFH,* 4/55, p. 28. This saying can be found in T. 130, vol. 2, p. 846b and T. 156, vol. 3, p. 165c. Cf. "to subdue demons and achieve the Way" in the *Avatamsaka Sūtra,* T. 278, vol. 9, p. 705b.

39. *HTFH,* 2/51, p. 34.

40. *HTFH,* 4/51, p. 35. Since Americans were demons and demons were heretics, the Korean War—from the progressive Buddhist point of view—became like a Jehad or a crusade.

41. *HTFH,* 4/53, p. 16. This argument is said to have persuaded three quarters of the young monks at the Asoka Monastery to join the militia. I have been unable to locate in the Buddhist canon the "ancient precept" about killing people being a good resolve. However the second sentence of the passage translated in the text recalls the well-known aphorism of Confucius who, when asked about returning good for evil, said that one should return good for good, but justice for evil (*Analects* 14.36). The Chinese Communists' insistence on moral dualism owes much to Confucius.

42. *HTFH,* 3/52, pp. 10-11. Cf. 4/53, p. 15. In 1958 Inner Mongolian lamas were presenting war plays during religious festivals. See *Nei-meng-ku jih-pao,* November 16, 1958.

43. See *HTFH,* 12/51, pp. 16, 21; 2/53, p. 28. Cf. *Chüeh yu-ch'ing,* 12.9:24 (September 1951), which reported that a hundred odd Buddhist monks in Canton had raised the equivalent of US$145 to be used for the purchase of arms and ammunition for the People's Volunteers in Korea.

44. *HTFH,* 1/52, pp. 6-7. For the passage in the *Nirvana Sūtra,* see note 61.

45. NCNA English, July 22, 1958, in *SCMP,* 1820:32. Cf. Chapter VI, note 104.

46. *HTFH,* 9/58, p. 27.

47. See this chapter at notes 33, 35, 40 and 41. In 1957 the Buddhists of Kirin held a meeting to discuss the anti-rightist movement and concluded: "In order to provide the most fundamental benefits for the motherland, for all living creatures, and for Buddhism, and on the basis of Sakyamuni's teaching that one should suppress the heterodox and make the orthodox shine forth, we Buddhists will certainly carry on a ruthless struggle against the heterodox views of you bourgeois rightists." See *HTFH,* 10/57, p. 29.

48. The former cadre admitted that Buddhists were not always convinced by his interpretation of compassion and he sometimes made concessions to their feelings. For example, after a jail was set up in the Hai-t'ung Ssu, Canton, he urged the Public Security Bureau to move it elsewhere, since some of the more pious devotees considered it inappropriate in monastic premises. Other space could not be found, however, and finally a wall was built to separate it from the rest of the monastery.

49. Parts of this section first appeared in the *World Buddhism Vesak Annual* (Colombo, 1971), pp. 17-19.

50. Paul Demiéville, "Le Bouddhisme et la guerre," *Mélanges* (Institut des Hautes Études Chinoises, Paris), I, 347-385 (1957). A much slighter treatment of the same subject is given in Ohrui Jun, "A View of War in Buddhism," *Tōyō University Studies,* II, 51-64 (1964).

51. *Mahaprajñāparamitopadeśa,* tr. E. Lamotte, *Le Traité de la grande vertu de sagesse* (Louvain, Bureaux du Muséon, 1949), p. 790, cited by Demiéville, p. 348. I have not checked the original text of many of the passages that Demiéville cites, nor have I included all his related citations, for which the reader should consult his article. In this case the passage cited appears to be T. 1509, vol. 25, p. 155, where Nagarjuna states that "killing [or murder] is the gravest of all offenses and not to kill is the highest of all virtues." For a monk to kill another human being intentionally was the third *pārājika,* or cause for automatic expulsion from the sangha.

52. *Abhidharmakośa-śāstra,* tr. by L. de La Vallée Poussin, Chap. 4, p. 152, cited by Demiéville, p. 349. Cf. Chapter III, note 59.

53. *Fan-wang Ching,* T. 1484, vol. 24, 1005c, 1007b, cited by Demiéville, p. 353.

54. Rahula Walpola, *History of Buddhism in Ceylon* (Colombo, M. D. Gunasena & Co., 1956), pp. 79-80.

55. Tsukamoto Zenryu, *Shina Bukkyōshi kenkyu: Hoku-gi hen* (Tokyo, 1942), pp. 247-285, cited by Demiéville, p. 358. Fa-ch'ing also attacked the established sangha as demons, saying "a new buddha has appeared in the world, away with the old demons!"

56. Demiéville, pp. 361-363, cites many sources for this episode.

57. *Sung-shih,* 455:25a, cited by Demiéville, p. 367.

58. Ch'en Mao-heng, "Ming-tai wo-k'ou k'ao-liu," *Yenching Journal of Chinese Studies,* Monograph Series No. 6 (Peking, 1934), p. 152, cited by Demiéville, p. 367.

59. See G. Renondeau, "Histoire des moines guerriers du Japon," *Mélanges,* pp. 159-341, to which Demiéville's article is a "postscript"; and see Demiéville, pp. 369-375.

60. *Mahāparinirvāna Sutra,* T. 374, vol. 12, 459a-460b, cited by Demiéville, p. 378.

61. *Ibid.,* 383b-384a, cited by Demiéville, p. 378. Cf. this chapter at note 44. As Ohrui, p. 56, points out, defense of the dharma was so important because those who threatened it threatened the seed of buddhahood in everyone. Without the dharma no one had any hope of achieving enlightenment and release from suffering.

62. *Ibid.,* cited by Demiéville, p. 379. To protect the Buddha, dharma, and sangha was the eighth *paramita* of the path of salvation.

63. *Ta fang-pien fo-pao-en ching,* T. 156, vol. 7, 161b-162a. The *Fan-wang ching* enjoined the bodhisattva to take evil upon himself for the good of all living creatures. Expedient killing (*fang-pien sha-sheng*) was discussed by Fa-tsang (alias Hsien-shou), the founder of the Avatamsaka or Hsien-shou school, who quoted Asanga in his *T'an-hsüan chi,* chüan 19, to the effect that expedient killing was permissible for a great bodhisattva, and, although he would have to suffer in hell for it, it would take him to the highest stage of bodhisattvahood. See T. 1733, vol. 35, p. 467b. Cf. William Edward Soothill and Lewis Hodous, *A Dictionary of Chinese Buddhist Terms* (London, Kegan, Paul, Trench Trubner & Co., 1937), p. 154: "*Fang-pien sha-sheng* The right of great Bodhisattvas, knowing everyone's karma, to kill without sinning, e.g., in order to prevent a person from committing sin involving unintermitted suffering, or to aid him in reaching one of the higher incarnations."

64. *Yogācārābhūmi,* T. 1579, vol. 29, 517b, cited by Demiéville, p. 379.

65. *Ratnakūta Sutra,* T. 310, vol. 11, 590b-c, cited by Demiéville, p. 381.

66. Hui-yüan, *Ming pao-ying lun* in T. 2103, 33b-34b, cited by Demiéville, p. 381.

67. Demiéville seems to follow Suzuki in interpreting this famous episode as a lesson in nonduality, but other interpretations are possible. The text reads: "Because the monks of the Eastern and Western Halls were quarreling over [which hall owned] a cat, the Venerable Nan-ch'üan picked up the cat and said: 'If you can find the right word, the cat is saved; if you can't, I am going to cut it in two.' The monks found nothing to say to this and Nan-ch'üan cut the cat in two. That evening when Ch'ao-chou came back, Nan-ch'üan asked him what he would have done. Ch'ao-chou took off his sandals, put them on his head, and walked out of the room. Nan-ch'üan said: 'If you had been here you would have saved the cat.' " See T. 2005, vol. 48, p. 294c. Rather than interpreting this as a lesson in nonduality, it might be simpler to take it as a lesson in the evil consequences of attachment—including Nan-ch'üan's attachment to his own words, which seemed to have made it necessary to violate the first precept.

68. Demiéville, p. 353.

69. To be fair to them I should add that they justified "compassionate killing" *only* in cases where the killer was *really* a bodhisattva—a being far advanced along the bodhisattva path. They said that if an ordinary human being, who was not far advanced, used this kind of reasoning as an excuse for killing, he would commit a grave offense, since he would be prostituting and desecrating the highest principle. The *Sūrangama Sūtra,* chüan 6, they added, said that a pauper who called himself a king was taking the path of destruction—how much more so was the progressive Chinese Buddhist who killed "bad elements" and then called himself a king of the dharma!

70. The only warrior monk I have seen mentioned in *Modern Buddhism* is Chen-pao, discussed by Demiéville, p. 366. See *HTFH,* 1/55, p. 26.

71. See notes 57, 61, 64.

72. See note 76.

73. *HTFH,* 12/56, p. 27. The original Chinese for "made killing into a divine service" is *i sha-sheng erh tso-fo-shih*—more literally "performed Buddhist services (in the sense of holy rites or serving the Buddha) by killing living creatures." After suggesting that punishment caused the wicked to reform, the article in *Modern Buddhism* went on: "We must follow the spirit of King Anala and fully understand that 'the Buddha and demons cannot co-exist,' which means that the people and the enemies of the people cannot co-exist." This article was entitled "Our Models" and dealt with five inspiring figures in the *Gandavyūha.*

74. Jan Fontein, *The Pilgrimage of Sudhana: A Study of Gandavyūha Illustrations in China, Japan, and Java* (The Hague, 1967), p. 9. Sudhana was a young boy born under auspicious circumstances who was singled out of a crowd by Mañjuśrī and sent on a pilgrimage to get instruction in the bodhisattva's conduct from fifty-three "Good Friends," whom he visited one after the other. King Anala was the eighteenth. At the end of his pilgrimage he achieved final samadhi when Samantabhadra touched his head. The text of

the Gandavyūha is included in the two complete Chinese translations of the *Avatamsaka Sūtra.*

75. Fontein, p. 28. A later picture book said that with King Anala's methods it was possible to "make the masses put an end to their false views by cutting them with swords, boiling them in water, by roasting them in blazing fire" (*ibid.*, pp. 136-137).

76. *Jñānottara-bodhisattva-pariprcchā Sūtra,* translated into Chinese as *Hui-shang p'u-sa wen ta-shan-ch'üan ching,* chüan 2, T. 345, XII, 163c-164a. This translation was made in the third century. A somewhat different but more comprehensible translation of the tenth century is given in the *Ta-fang kuang-shan ch'iao-fang-pien ching* T. 346, vol. 12, 175-176. I am indebted to Mr. N. Aramaki for collaborating on the translation into English that I have offered.

I never found a Chinese informant who had read or heard of this particular exposition of "expedient killing." For references to it in the Mainland press, see above at notes 31, 36, 40. It is also mentioned in the following passage, from *HTFH,* 5/56, pp. 50-51, which is important for combining so many of the justifications for killing that have been mentioned so far.

> The Buddha was certainly not indiscriminately compassionate in a way that failed to distinguish between good and evil. He felt warm love for the people (*jen-min*) but with "evil demons" he fought things out mercilessly. From many of the stories of the Buddha in his earlier incarnations we can see that he made an extremely clear distinction between "good" and "evil," "love" and "hate" (*tseng*). For example, when he was still sowing the seeds of his future enlightenment, in order to save five hundred merchants who had gone to sea to gather treasure, he killed a pirate who was secretly planning to do them in. In another of his previous incarnations he was a lion and, in order to save the whole people of a certain country, he bit to death a poisonous dragon who was insatiably devouring them. The night before he became a Buddha, he subdued the incomparably wicked "Pāpīyān, King of Demons," his "demon women" with their ten thousand enticements, and the great "demon army" that he had under his command. The Buddha, by means of his upright and radiant compassionate mind, routed the demons and made them admit their defeat: only then did he attain supreme enlightenment. After he had become a Buddha, he once subdued a *samjñeya mahayaksa* in order to save the son of a rich and virtuous man; and he converted this creature who was so bad that even his own mother wanted to kill him. Again there was the time that he subdued a *vaiśravana* in order to save the lives of many children. From these vivid stories we can clearly see the Buddha's compassion and love for the people and his refusal to tolerate the existence of "evil demons" who harmed people. We can also see that we can beautify the land, benefit sentient

> beings, and study all the branches of knowledge only if we are struggling against the "evil demons" who threaten the people . . .
>
> At present, together with the people of the entire country, our confidence raised a hundred-fold, we are advancing towards the wonderful happiness of socialism, bubbling over with enthusiasm. However, the counterrevolutionary elements, who are even more sinister and vicious than Pāpīyān and the *vaiśravana,* resent our efforts in construction, resent our wonderful and happy future. They are in fact just like demons and play all kinds of sly tricks, even donning a mask of bogus virtue and wrapping themselves up in a cloak of religion so that they can worm their way into the ranks of us, the people, in order to carry on their evil activities that threaten the people and Buddhism in China. Therefore we must heighten our vigilance, brush the cobwebs from our eyes, learn the spirit in which the Buddha subdued the demons' malice, and conduct a merciless struggle against all the "evil demons" in human form who threaten the welfare of the people of our country.

On how the Buddha subdued the demon army on the eve of his enlightenment, see *Hsü-tsang-ching* (Taipei, 1967), ts'e 130, pp. 172-173; on how he subdued the *vaiśravana,* see *ibid.* pp. 190-191. *Samjñeya mahayaksa* and *vaiśravana* are usually beneficient spirits who subdue demons themselves. A footnote to the passage translated above in this note refers to *HTFH,* 1/54, pp. 21-23, for two of the stories about the Buddha's activities in previous lives–saving the five hundred merchants and killing the dragon. Yet the first story, curiously enough, is not given there. The second story is told in detail–how the Buddha, born as a lion, joined forces with an elephant (Maitreya) to kill a dragon who was devouring the people, young and old, of a certain country. The elephant had doubts whether they should try, but the lion pointed to the great amount of bad karma which the dragon was creating by his misdeeds and which he would have to expiate by suffering. They killed him at the cost of their own lives. Similar birth stories were printed in *HTFH,* 12/58, pp. 26-27, tr. in JPRS 1461-N:26-27.

77. *Ch'ing-hai jih-pao,* November 24, 1957, tr. in *SCMP,* 1698:19 (slightly altered). Shirob also made the following long statement about suppressing counterrevolutionaries in his speech to the NPC in 1960.

> As the saying goes "unless the weeds are removed, the crop will not grow well," and so "unless the enemies of Buddhism are exterminated, those Buddhists on whom the *sasana* depends will not be able to reach buddhahood." In our country every clean Buddhist and clean monastery are protected by the laws of the land. For believing in Buddhism no good monks or nuns have ever been discriminated against and no good monasteries have ever been damaged. It is only when Buddhists are utilized by counterrevolutionaries and engage in counterrevolutionary activities against the Party, the people, and socialism so frantically that it puts them

> beyond hope of remedy,–it is only then that the People's Government will, in consideration of the interests of the people, be forced to take suppressive measures against them and to eliminate the evil-doers in order to give peace to the good. It does not allow public enemies of the people to enjoy immunity from the law. Besides, the measures taken to eliminate evil-doers in order to give peace to the good are taken in the interest not only of the people in general but also of Buddhism and Buddhists. Since those who borrow the name of Buddhism to engage in counterrevolution are not genuine Buddhists but are abscesses on Buddhism, therefore to show them mercy would mean giving abscesses the nutriment to grow.

This passage, was directed in the first instance against rebel lamas in Tibet, but was obviously meant as a warning to all Buddhists. See *JMJP,* April 15, 1960, tr. in *CB,* 627:27 (slightly altered).

78. I have only seen one such report. In 1958 the Buddhists of I-yang issued a "patriotic challenge" to their brethren in other parts of Hunan. The tenth clause was: "To participate actively in patriotic hygiene work, every single person will do his part in achieving the eight no's (no flies, no sparrows, no rats, no bed bugs, no mosquitoes, no cockroaches, no snails, and no schistosomiasis)." See *HTFH,* 8/58, p. 29.

In 1953 the editors of *Modern Buddhism* suggested that at the Asoka Monastery, where an animal husbandry department had been set up and pigs were being slaughtered, it would be better to keep the latter as "long life pigs"; or to excuse monks from working in that particular department; or simply to close down the department and use the same manpower for afforestation work. See *HTFH,* 4/53, p. 10, and on "long life pigs" see Welch, *Practice,* p. 378. On the other hand, monks at the Asoka Monastery did light lamps that would attract moths–and, presumably, kill them: see *HTFH,* 4/53, p. 15.

One reason for special compunction about campaigns to eliminate pests could be found in works like Chu-hung's *Tzu-chih lu,* according to which it was meritorious to save the lives even of animals that could kill. "To save the life of rats and snakes and other beings which inflict injury, one good [i.e., one unit of merit is given] for each life saved. Note: if a snake has not yet bitten a man, it does not merit the death punishment. However great the injury inflicted by a rat, it never commits a deed sufficient to merit capital punishment." See S. H. Wainwright, "The Kokwa Jichiroku, or a Buddhist Parallel to Poor Richard's Almanack" in *Transactions of the Asiatic Society of Japan,* 42.2:744-745 (1914). An Indian visitor reported in 1955 that the only place in China where he heard the chirping of birds was at the Ch'i-hsia Ssu near Nanking.

79. *HTFH,* 5/51, pp. 34-35.

80. The only nonderogatory reference that I have seen to Buddhist idealism was made for the benefit of Buddhists abroad. In 1957 Chao P'u-

ch'u summarized the goal of the San-lun sect as "to disclose the unreality of all Dharmas of the five Skandhas through the realization of true voidness, and to destroy completely the delusions of the 'three evils,' so as to establish the right conception of the Middle Path in which everything is non-existent." See Chao, *Buddhism in China*, p. 18.

I have also seen only one attempt since 1949 to justify the First Noble Truth (that life is inextricable from suffering), on which Buddhist otherworldliness is largely based. In 1960 an article on the social factors in the spread of Buddhism in India explained that the Buddha's view of life as suffering was caused by the exploitation and oppression of the masses, whose sole means to avoid suffering was to withdraw from the world: see *HTFH*, 3/60, p. 30. (Presumably if the Buddha had lived in the New China, he would not have formulated the Four Noble Truths but found the solution to suffering in revolution rather than withdrawal.)

81. *HTFH*, 6/53, p. 39. Cf. Chapter III at notes 7, 13-14, Chapter IV at notes 23, 84, Chapter VII at notes 35-37.

82. This is quoted from the *Avatamsaka Sūtra*, T. 279, vol. 14, p. 72b.

83. *HTFH*, 5/56, p. 49. The words omitted in my translation (represented by elipsis dots) consist largely of reiteration of the importance of beautifying the land (*chuang-yen kuo-t'u*).

84. This appears to be a slight misquotation of the lines in the *Vimalakirti-nirdeśa Sūtra:* "If you wish to reach the Pure Land, you must make your mind pure. Once the mind is pure, then the buddha-land becomes pure." See T. 475, vol. 14, p. 538c. Cf. 520c, 559c.

85. *HTFH*, 5/51, pp. 29-30. The last sentence could also, perhaps, mean "Rise up with your hearts set on *creating* a Western Paradise," but I think the point is that only by helping to create its analog here on earth during his lifetime could the Buddhist hope to be reborn in it after he died. This passage is taken from a reader's letter published in the correspondence column and is the earliest reference I have seen to the Western Paradise on earth being built by the Communist Party. Prior to this *Modern Buddhism* had apparently published statements critical of Pure Land doctrine. To the complaint of one reader, it answered: "*Modern Buddhism* treats all sects equally and impartially. Individual writers have censured the deviations of Buddhist circles who are divorced from reality and have criticized those who specialize in Pure Land, but this cannot be regarded as disparagement by this journal." See *HTFH*, 11/51, p. 22.

86. *HTFH*, 8/55, p. 2. Cf. *CB*, 355:10. An editorial the month before had declared: "In the not too distant future, we will completely wipe out exploitation and poverty and set up a happy, prosperous socialist society. This is the great enterprise of establishing 'the Western Paradise on earth' in order that all men may be released from suffering and win happiness." See *HTFH*, 7/55, p. 2. Cf. Chao P'u-ch'u's article "All the Country's Buddhists Must Struggle to Fulfill the Five-Year Plan" in *HTFH*, 8/55, pp. 3-4, first printed in the *KMJP*, July 21, 1955 (see *SCMP*, 1094:9).

87. *KMJP,* February 8, 1956, p. 5; *HTFH,* 4/56, p. 4; 5/56, p. 49. Yu Yu-wei told a Japanese Buddhist visitor in December 1956 that the Pure Land was not separate from this world but created by gradually transforming this world, which was what the Communist Party planned to do. See Hayashi, p. 121.

88. *HTFH,* 11/59, p. 34. I have restored the first person singular in my translation since I believe that this is a direct quote. For stylistic reasons I translate *jen-chien* sometimes as "on earth" and sometimes as "in this world." So far as I know, Ho is the highest ranking member of the Party to employ this Buddho-Marxist simile.

89. Ku-chia-sai, a Living Buddha from Tsinghai, told the CBA's second national conference that "we regard him [Mao] as a buddha, a bodhisattva." See *HTFH,* 5/57, p. 19. Two years earlier he had spoken of Mao's "great compassion" and said that Buddhists should prostrate themselves in gratitude for the blessing he had conferred: see *HTFH,* 9/55, p. 18. Cf. Chapter VI at note 57.

90. On this cult see Welch, "The Deification of Mao," *Saturday Review* (Sept. 19, 1970), pp. 25, 50. Mao would not have been the first Chinese ruler to be considered a buddha. T'ai-tsu, the Northern Wei ruler at the end of the fourth century, was declared to be "the Tathagata in person." This enabled the head of the sangha to kowtow before him, which he was not supposed to do before an earthly ruler. See Ch'en, *Buddhism in China,* p. 146. The cult of Mao was gradually discontinued in 1970-71.

91. See above note 1.

92. Some of the more conservative Buddhists were also opposed to Buddho-Marxist syncreticism. Thus *Modern Buddhism* told its readers in 1954: "There are points where religious doctrines and Marxism-Leninism coincide, but they are basically different . . . If you force the interpretation of religious belief so as to make it into Marxism-Leninism, not only will you become a general laughing stock, but devout religious believers will not be pleased.": see *HTFH,* 7/54, p. 24.

93. *Che-hsüeh yen-chiu,* 1/58, p. 46, tr. in *CB,* 510:18 (slightly altered).

94. *Min-tsu t'uan-chieh,* 3/59, p. 18.

95. Shirob said in April 1960: "Naturally between the political and the religious there are also points of difference, but these differences certainly should not obstruct the service of the people. When solving the problems that arise from these points of difference, if the points on which [Buddhism] differs are contrary to Party policy and are not important for Buddhism, then one must 'rely on the Party, not on Buddhism,' resolutely abandon the tenet of Buddhism involved, and absolutely follow the Party policy. If the point of difference has no bearing at all on Party policy, but is very important for the religion, then consideration must be given to religious belief. Our government has been doing just this." See *JMJP,* April 15, 1960.

96. *Che-hsüeh yen-chiu,* 1/61, pp. 13-21 (Jan. 20, 1961), tr. in URS 24:6. More will be said about this article in Chapter XI.

97. See above notes 6-7.

98. *KMJP,* Jan. 23, 1963, tr. in *SCMP,* 2924:1-6 (slightly altered).

99. The article "Buddhism Today" by A. N. Kochetov was published in *Science and Religion* (June 1960) and summarized in *Asian Analyst,* (November 1960), pp. 19-20. I have not seen the original text, but there is ample evidence of the Soviet government's hostility and suspicion towards any attempts on the part of religious organizations "to adapt to modern-day conditions" or maintain that there is "no conflict between Communism and religion." See Chapter XI, note 56, and articles published in 1956, 1959, and 1961 cited by Rensselaer W. Lee III in "General Aspects of Chinese Communist Religious Policy, with Soviet Comparisons," *China Quarterly* 19:171 (July-September 1964).

100. *Wen-i pao,* Dec. 11, 1963, tr. in *SCMM,* 402:39-41; cf. above note 4.

101. Colin MacKerras and Neale Hunter, *China Observed* (New York, 1967), p. 87.

102. E. Sarkisyanz, *Buddhist Backgrounds to the Burmese Revolution* (The Hague, 1965), pp. 168-172, 199-200. Here and below I have not distinguished among the different schools of Burmese Buddho-Marxism but have selected parallels to Chinese developments wherever I found them.

103. The foregoing elements of Buddho-Marxism, all of which had parallels in China, are discussed in Sarkisyanz, pp. 175, 196, 212, 220, 217-218, 199, and 153-154. Another reason the Burmese gave for why the elimination of capitalism would help people reach nirvana was that the economic distress caused by capitalism deprived people of the leisure to meditate; and the economic prosperity promised by socialism would enable them to make larger donations to the sangha and thus to increase their store of merit (*ibid.,* pp. 171-172). This reasoning had no parallels in China, where meditation and donations to the sangha were both discouraged.

104. *Ibid.,* pp. 193-194. Cf. note 19. One of the most striking presentations of Gautama as a rationalist and social reformer was made by a Sinhalese, D. C. Vijayavardhana in his *Dharma-Vijāya or the Revolt in the Temple* (Colombo, Sinha Publications, 1953). For him Marxism was "a leaf taken from the book of Buddhism—a leaf torn out and misread" (p. 595). He was as harsh a critic of the sangha as the most radical Buddhist in China.

B. R. Ambedkar, the framer of India's Constitution, who led three million of his fellow untouchables towards conversion to Buddhism, also considered the Buddha to be a social revolutionary who preached a purely rational religion of liberty, equality, and fraternity. Through conversion to Buddhism the untouchables achieved not political power or economic gain but a "psychological liberation" that was even more important for their well-being. See Adele M. Fiske, "Buddhistische Bewegungen in Indien," in Heinrich Dumoulin, ed. *Buddhismus der Gegenwart* (Freiburg, Herder, 1970), pp. 84-85.

105. See Sarkisyanz, pp. 196-199, 204-205.

106. See Welch, *Revival,* pp. 65-66.

107. See Sarkisyanz, pp. 210-212.

108. *Ibid.*, p. 220. By the time U Nu formally rejected the noneconomic aspects of Marxism in 1958, Burmese Buddho-Marxism had come a long way from its position in the 1930's, when U Ba Swe called Stalin "a builder of Lokka Nibban": see *ibid.*, p. 170.

109. The most enthusiastic reaction that I have seen to the modernization of Buddhist doctrine by Chinese progressives was written, curiously enough, by a European, André Migot, in a book on religion in China, based on a visit there in 1957. He argued that the Buddha's teachings were parallel to those of Heraclitus, Marx, and Engels. The Buddha substituted reason for faith, eliminated a Creator, considered all to be in flux, rejected the existence of the ego, saw the mind as a function of matter (just as Marx did), and advocated verification by practice rather than acceptance of dogmas. "Buddhism and Marxism have a common aim: the struggle against evil and social injustice. Buddhism and Marxism have a common means of attaining this aim: the liberation of man from all alienations . . . We should recall the struggle carried on by the Buddha against man's social alienation when he rejected the authority of the Brahmins and the caste system; against man's philosophical alienation when he propounded his materialist and dialectical doctrine and the dialectic of the world and of beings; against man's religious alienation when he denied the existence of a transcendent creator God" (p. 50). "Buddhists, like the great majority of the Chinese people, took an active role in the overthrow of the Chiang Kai-shek regime and the establishment of a people's democracy; there are many Buddhists in the bosom of the government and even in the key posts of the regime" (p. 44). "On its part the People's Government in Peking would never have committed the political error of alienating itself from a religion that represents a considerable force among the people" (p. 44). These quotations come from André Migot, "Situation des religions en Chine populaire: Bouddhisme et Marxisme," in *Le Regime et les institutions de la république populaire chinoise,* which repeats passages from his earlier article (see Chapter VI, note 64).

Much that was said about Buddhism by its modernizers, in China and elsewhere, was partly or wholly true, and at the same time partly or wholly untrue. The Buddhist tradition, its doctrines, practice, and canon, are so vast and varied that it is a misleading oversimplification to say, for example, that the Buddha substituted reason for faith, saw the mind as a function of matter, and so on.

110. Until 1963 the closest thing I had seen to a justification of violence was in a 100-page book by Leuke, *Gautama the Buddha and Karl Marx* (Vijaya Publishing House, Colombo, March 1, 1943), which is in the pamphlet collection of the Buddhist Society, London. Leuke attempts to show that Buddhism and Marxism can be reconciled and maintains that while the use of force creates bad karma, this can be outweighed by the merit created by the good results that it may lead to (pp. 98-100).

The Southeast Asian Buddhists with whom I have brought up the story of the Buddha killing a heretic (note 76) had never heard of it. Unintentional killing was blameless, they said, as in the case of Chakupala Thera, whereas intentional killing—although sometimes inevitable, as for soldiers and police—could never be considered good or giving rise to a net balance of karma in favor of the killer. It was simply a necessary evil. See the *World Fellowship of Buddhists News Bulletin,* 7.6:47-48 (November-December 1970).

On November 20, 1963, an Indonesian Buddhist delegation declared in Peking: "In accordance with the teachings of Buddhism we may use violence to resist external calamities so long as we do not nurse rancour in our heart. It is the duty of peace-loving Buddhists to resist those people who have brought calamity to mankind." See NCNA English, October 20, 1963, in *SCMP,* 3087:20. This suggests that the Chinese Buddhist theory of compassionate killing had begun to have an appeal abroad.

111. See Appendix F. The most complete treatment of the problem of the modernization of Buddhism in Theravada countries is given in Heinz Bechert, *Buddhismus: Staat und Gesellschaft in den Ländern des Theravada-Buddhismus,* (Frankfurt, Institut für Asienkunde, 1966, and Wiesbaden, 1967), 2 vols. A less reliable source is Ernst Benz, *Buddhism or Communism: Which Holds the Future for Asia*? tr. Richard and Clara Winston (New York, Doubleday, 1965).

112. Cf. Chapter VI, note 6. Even when foreign Buddhists knew Chinese, they were not necessarily discouraged by what they could read in the Mainland press. After a tour of China in 1965 (by which time the official rejection of Buddho-Marxist syncretism was clear), one eminent Japanese buddhologist still felt that "perhaps Buddhism and Marxism will somehow combine to create a new and different Chinese religion." See Nitchū Yū-kō Daihyōdan, ed., *Shin Chūgoku annai* (Kyoto, 1966), p. 213.

113. Once when the usurper, Chi K'ang, was questioning Confucius about how to govern, he asked whether he should not "kill the bad people in order to encourage the good people." Confucius replied: "You're trying to govern people. Why kill them? If your desires are good, the people will become good too. The character of the effective ruler is like the wind, and his subjects' is like the grass. When the wind blows over it, the grass must bend" *Analects,* 12.19 (very freely translated).

114. Arthur F. Wright, "The Formation of Sui Ideology, 581-604," in John K. Fairbank, ed., *Chinese Thought and Institutions* (Chicago, University of Chicago Press, 1957), p. 97.

IX. THE LAITY

1. Chou En-lai told a foreign visitor in 1956 that there were fifty-five million Buddhists in China who belonged to Buddhist organizations or contributed money to temples. In 1959 Shirob stated: "At present people of more than ten nationalities believe in Buddhism, with more than a hundred

million Buddhist monks, nuns, and devotees." See *HTFH,* 10/59, p. 10. This figure was repeated in articles sent to Buddhist journals abroad: *World Buddhism* 12.4:6-7 (November 1963) and *International Buddhist News Forum* (Rangoon), 2.12-3.1-2:12 (December 1962-January-February 1963). Cf. *Ganjin wajō,* p. 26. The next year Ch'en Yi told people in Ceylon that there were ten million Buddhists in China: see *World Buddhism,* 12.8:17 (April 1964). The truth is that the number of Buddhists depended on how they were defined: see Welch, *Practice,* pp. 357-358, 393.

2. This was stated by a former cadre of the Canton Religious Affairs Division, and it is to some extent confirmed in the press. For example, *Modern Buddhism* told its readers in 1951: "It is superstitious to worship Buddha images, do reverence to the Buddha, and study Buddhism if one's purpose is to get help from buddhas and bodhisattvas in making money or having a son; whereas it is not superstitious to worship Buddha images or study Buddhism if one's purpose is to revere and study the sublime greatness of the Buddha." See *HTFH,* 9/51, p. 22. The ordinary worshiper in China, as elsewhere, went to temples not merely to do reverence, but to get help.

3. Wu Yao-tsung, the Protestant leader, complained in 1957 that "during agrarian reform local cadres received instructions from the higher level to stop religious congregations for the time being. This measure, designed to avoid possible complications during agrarian reform, was well-intentioned at the time." See *JMJP,* March 9, 1957, tr. in *CB,* 449:2 (slightly altered). A former cadre of the Canton Religious Affairs Bureau recalled this measure and said that it applied to Buddhists as well as Protestants. It is interesting that no Buddhist during the Hundred Flowers seems to have made complaints like those of Wu Yao-tsung, who went on to say that even after land reform some cadres prohibited worship on the grounds that it interfered with production and also prohibited donations, new buildings, recruitment, and travel. Probably such prohibitions affected some Buddhists, who were, however, too cautious to complain.

4. *HTFH,* 6/53, p. 41.

5. *HTFH,* 5/53, p. 26. Hsü-yün is here stated to have been the person who called for the repair of the tomb, which held the remains of the Venerable Shao-lung. It had been dismantled by "a certain middle school that did not know how to give loving care to historical monuments." On the scale of the Buddhist ceremonies that had just been performed in Shanghai, see Chapter VII at note 90.

6. Although he was a reliable informant who kept a meticulous diary, I am inclined to think that his failure to see lay worshipers was due partly to chance and partly to the fact that his itinerary lay mostly in the north: Canton, Peking, Tatung, Huhehot, Peking, Tun-huang, Sining, Lanchow, Sian, Loyang, Peking, Mukden, Anshan, Peking, Nanking, Shanghai, Hangchow, Canton. There are dependable reports of lay gatherings early and late in 1955. See Chapter VII, notes 94, 95, 107.

7. On the plenary mass at the Yü-fo Ssu, Shanghai, in 1956, see below note 23.

8. On the factors that chronically tended to reduce public worship, see Chapter IV at notes 13-15. All were intensified in 1958. In some places pledges were taken against the use of paper money. In Amoy, for example, Buddhists resolved in 1958 that within two years or so orthodox Buddhist families there would not burn paper money at New Year or tinfoil ingots at rites for the dead and, in general, would avoid wasteful practices at weddings and funerals, thus "following the Buddhist rule." See *HTFH,* 9/58, p. 26.

One informant recalled that in a Kwangtung commune during 1958 all temples were converted to other uses, and their images were destroyed or removed. Candles, incense, paper money, etc., became too expensive to buy. People no longer professed to being Christians, Buddhists, or Taoists and, if they worshiped, it was in secret.

9. See Chapter XI at notes 41-42.

10. I have found little in the press to confirm this anomalous pattern and wonder whether it may not have been a local phenomenon or observable chiefly in Christian churches, where my informant admitted it was more common. He said, for example, that Protestant church membership rose markedly during the Three-Anti, Five-Anti, suppression of counterrevolutionaries, and anti-rightist movement. The Religious Affairs Division kept close track of the number of new parishioners and sent its agents to observe church attendance: there was no doubt of the increase during each campaign of suppression. A Shanghai informant (different from the one cited above) also said that during such campaigns more people went to temples to pray for help with their political problems.

11. See Katsumata, p. 836. Cf. Nitchū Yū-kō, pp. 207-208.

12. Eskelund, who saw busy temple worship in Shanghai (see this chapter at note 20), writes that in Peking temples were empty or converted to other uses. "People are careful–if you burn incense to the gods, you risk being considered superstitious or reactionary." See Karl Eskelund, *The Red Mandarins* (London, L. Redman, 1959), p. 135. Many other Mainland visitors noticed the contrast between Peking and Shanghai.

13. See Welch, *Revival,* pp. 246-252.

14. A Shanghai woman reported seeing many young men among the people who thronged the Yü-fo Ssu in 1961-62. For photographic evidence of the same thing at the Ling-yin Ssu, see Fig. 49. In August 1960 a European visitor to the Kuei-yüan Ssu, Wuhan, saw ten or fifteen lay women lighting incense and praying: most seemed to be in their thirties and had their children with them. See also this chapter at notes 17-19.

15. *HTFH,* 5/57, p. 23. He made this statement in a speech to the CBA's second national conference.

16. See Welch, *Revival,* pp. 208-216, and "Facades of Religion in China," *Asian Survey,* 10.7:615-617 (July 1970).

17. See the photographic section by Henri Cartier-Bresson following p. 131 in Welch, *Revival.*

18. *Mibu,* "Jinmin Chūgoku," p. 10. Mibu visited the Ling-yin Ssu on June 11, 1961. He was told that during the slack farming season in winter, the number of worshipers was particularly large—just as it had been before Liberation. Also in 1961 it was reported that many visitors were going by car from Foochow to the Yung-ch'üan Ssu, the famous monastery outside the city. Since Liberation a road had been built up Ku Shan on which it was located. See Hong Kong *Wen-hui pao,* June 6, 1961, which says that people went there "to see all the sights." Probably some of them also went to worship.

19. This informant visited Ling-yin in October 1960. At another Hangchow temple she saw a group of pilgrims change into red robes. At Ch'i-hsia Shan near Nanking she saw a storyteller telling stories in the garden below the monastery. In several cities she observed old women offering incense and praying in a loud voice in front of the altar.

20. Karl Eskelund, *The Red Mandarins* (London, 1959), pp. 135-136.

21. In China the 8th of the fourth lunar month is celebrated as the day the Buddha was born. In Theravada countries the first full-moon day in May is celebrated as the anniversary of the days on which he was born, enlightened, and died. In China his enlightenment and death are considered to have fallen on other days of the year.

22. Celebrations of the Buddha's birthday at the Kuang-chi Ssu and one or two other temples in Peking are reported in the Mainland press from 1953 to 1964, but no figures are given on the number of lay people who attended—in contrast to Shanghai (see next note).

23. In 1961 20,000 were said to be coming each year to the Buddha's birthday celebration at the Ling-yin Ssu in Hangchow: see Mibu, "Jinmin Chūgoku," p. 10. In Shanghai the figure for all the city's hundred temples was given as 200,000 in 1956: see *JMJP,* March 16, 1956, tr. in JPRS 524:27. In 1959 200,000 reportedly visited the Ching-an Ssu alone during the three days of the Buddha's birthday celebration there; one thousand kept vigil all night: see *HTFH,* 10/59, p. 13. In 1962 100 monks and nuns and 1,200 devotees were said to have taken part in a seven-day ceremony at the Yü-fo Ssu: see NCNA English, May 5, 1962, in *SCMP,* 2735:21. In 1963 there was a seven-day ceremony at the Yü-fo Ssu and a three-day ceremony at the Ching-an Ssu. Several hundred monks and devotees were at the Yü-fo Ssu on the last day. See NCNA English, May 1, 1963, in *SCMP,* 2973:14. The same thing happened in 1964, when ceremonies were also held at four other monasteries: see NCNA English, May 19, 1964, in *SCMP,* 3225:8. In 1965 a Japanese Tendai delegation attended: see Fig. 50 and NCNA English, May 8, 1965, in *SCMP,* 3455:19.

The above indicates that while attendance was large even during periods of political tension, it tended to decline over the years, as did the elaborateness of the rites performed by the monks. These were probably most elaborate in 1956, when a two week plenary mass was held at the Yü-fo Ssu. Lectures were given by eminent monks on five sutras; ten more sutras were chanted at the different altars of the plenary mass. Tibetan services (both "yellow hat" and "red hat") as well as other Tantric rites were performed at their respective altars. There was even Ch'an practice in a meditation hall. Ying-tz'u and Ching-ch'üan bathed the image of the infant Sakyamuni on the 8th of the fourth lunar month; and on the 15th three hundred Theravada laymen living in Shanghai (natives of Ceylon and India) gathered in the abbot's quarters to offer flowers and food to the Buddha image and hear an address by Abbot Wei-fang. See *HTFH,* 7/56, p. 12.

An idea of the large scale and attendance is given in the photo facing p. 17 of *HTFH,* 8/56. It shows a procession winding back and forth in the courtyard despite falling rain. Four monks playing pipes lead dozens of others while hundreds of laymen look on. On the facade of one hall can be seen a sign reading " . . .world peace."

On some celebrations of the Buddha's birthday elsewhere, see Chapter VII, notes 94-96.

24. Photographs of the fair at the Ching-an Ssu on the Buddha's birthday in 1955 were printed in *Buddhists in New China,* pp. 136-137. They showed not only the bustle around the stalls, but old women worshiping. A Western visitor to the fair held at the Lung-hua Ssu, April 19-21, 1962, saw "immense crowds of peasants and city dwellers," many of whom entered the temple, but very few of whom made offerings or worshiped. See *South China Morning Post,* April 30, 1962.

In Peking most of the temple fairs appear to have been discontinued (perhaps because there were no longer enough hawkers and small tradesmen to keep them going). In 1962, however, a "market day" was being held twice a month at the Miao-ying Ssu where one could buy shoelaces and such, according to a foreign resident. In 1965 a fair was still being held at the Taoist Po-yüan Kuan: see *Nagel's Guide,* p. 569. Cf. Chapter XI, note 35.

25. See *HTFH,* 8/54, p. 28; 3/56, p. 30, NCNA English, January 27, 1958, in *SCMP,* 1703:2.

26. On the celebration of Kuan-yin's birthday see *HTFH,* 5/54, pp. 25-26; 8/54, p. 28; 1/58, p. 27. One photograph at the Buddhist Photographic Exhibition in Colombo, October 1960, showed the celebration of Kuan-yin's birthday at the Yü-fo Ssu, Shanghai. On Amitabha's birthday, see Chapter VII, note 97.

27. *Canton,* p. 82.

28. *Yang-ch'eng wan-pao,* September 1, 1960, tr. in *SCMP,* 2355:10 (slightly altered). Already in 1958 Amoy Buddhists had resolved "not to follow the popular custom of making offerings to the ghosts during the Hungry Ghosts Festival": see *HTFH,* 9/58, p. 26.

29. The People's Government was not the first to discourage popular festivals. Lewis Hodous quotes a Sui dynasty memorial and a Ch'ing proclamation calling for an end to the Lantern Festival, since it wasted materials and imperiled social order: see *Folkways in China* (London, Probsthain, 1929), pp. 46-47.

Nothing came of Chueh-ch'eng's proposal to the CBA's second national conference in 1957 that the Buddha's birthday be made a national holiday (as it is in most Buddhist countries): see *HTFH,* 5/57, p. 24.

30. *HTFH,* 5/57, p. 16. The average stay of three or four days is calculated from the fact that the 37,000 visitors consumed 123,000 catties of rice. In 1952 three thousand Tibetans came to Omei from Sikang alone: HTFH, 6/53, p. 57.

31. Casual estimates of crowds, many of which appear in this chapter, are, of course, unreliable. For example, Dryden L. Phelps heard that two *million* pilgrims a year used to come to Omei, whereas a monk who spent his life there told me that the number seldom reached a thousand a day—and only in summer, because in winter the trails were deep in snow.

32. *JMJP,* April 15, 1960. In this speech Shirob said that male and female devotees could be seen regularly coming to the "four famous mountians" (Wu-t'ai, P'u-t'o, Chiu-hua, and Omei Shan). In the summer of 1962, 1,500 monks, nuns, lamas, and lay devotees were said to have visited Wu-t'ai, the largest number in many years: see NCNA English, August 17, 1962, in *SCMP,* 2805:18.

33. *HTFH,* 6/62, p. 41 (December 1962).

34. Alley, *Amongst Hills and Streams,* p. 11. Alley's figure of 7,000-10,000 a day fits well with the report that in the autumn of 1953 the net profit made on pilgrims by three temples at Nan-yüeh was equivalent to US$17,600: see *HTFH,* 1/54, p. 28. The next autumn the net profit (apparently on all the temples of the whole mountain, or possibly excluding two of the three temples just mentioned) was equivalent to US$11,000: see *HTFH,* 2/55, p. 29. These sums suggest that the number of pilgrims was indeed in the tens of thousands. In 1924 "huge pilgrim traffic" was seen by a Western traveler, who was told that it totaled 100,000 a year: see Harry A. Franck, *Roving Through Southern China* (New York, 1925), pp. 636-638.

35. At Wu-t'ai they came for a festival held in the sixth lunar month. The patron bodhisattva of P'u-t'o Shan was Kuan-yin, and it was for her birthday, also in the sixth lunar month, that the crowds came. At Nan-yüeh the peak season was the ten days around the Mid-Autumn Festival (the 15th of the eighth lunar month). At T'ien-t'ai Shan the large traffic in the fifth lunar month arose partially from the belief that, if devotees went there then, they might have a helpful dream. It is interesting that, although progressive Buddhists referred to the lunar calendar less than had been common among Buddhists before 1949, there was no attempt to shift the dates of festivals to

the solar calendar (as has been done in Japan). For information on lay pilgrimages before 1949, see Welch, *Practice,* pp. 370-375.

36. The informant who visited Omei in the summer of 1957 reported that lay pilgrims there were charged the equivalent of US$0.08 per meal of four dishes and a soup. Imposing a fixed charge was a subtle secularization of the ancient tradition of monastic hospitality. See Welch, *Practice,* pp. 213-215; *Revival,* pp. 184-185.

37. Alley, *Amongst Hills and Streams,* pp. 11-12.

38. Although more temples here were Taoist than Buddhist (see *Nagel's Guide,* pp. 948-949), the description would probably hold good for Buddhist festivals in such places. Four years earlier at Chung-nan Shan, a little to the south of Sian, over 10,000 men and women pilgrims came to the Kuan-yin service that started on the 1st of the sixth lunar month at Nan Wu-t'ai. A special feature was the ten-piece Buddhist orchestra that played during the day for worship and at night for entertainment. All through the night worship continued "amidst the blaze of candles, the glowing clouds of incense, and a bustle and excitement that is seldom seen." See *HTFH,* 5/62, p. 40 (October 1962).

39. At the Lung-men caves near Loyang in 1965 she saw incense being stuck into a low metal tray on a stone table in front of an image in the first cave to which visitors were led. Among other worshipers there she saw an old woman with bound feet, accompanied by what were evidently her grandchildren, who kneeled in front of the image as she offered incense and fruit. At the entrance to the caves at Kung-hsien to the east of Loyang, the same informant saw offerings of flowers placed in front of the Buddha images outside the entrance. Near Yenan itself during the spring festival in 1966 she saw incense burning in one of the Thousand-Buddha Caves.

40. A week of buddha recitation was held at the Ch'eng-t'ien Ssu, Chüanchow, in March 1952, attended by 500 persons. Lectures given during the week emphasized the link between Buddhism and patriotism. See *HTFH,* 6/53, p. 39. In 1953 dozens of laymen were coming to take part in buddha recitation held on the 1st and 15th of every lunar month at a temple in Chengtu. They were organized into groups of ten so that they might know each other better and thus prevent infiltration by members of the outlawed syncretistic sects. See *HTFH,* 6/53, p. 49. In 1954 fifty-odd devotees were coming daily to a monastery in Shenyang where, together with the twenty-odd resident monks, they chanted the *Lotus Sutra* from 4:00 to 6:00 P.M. Some of them also attended morning devotions at 4:30 A.M.: see *HTFH,* 10/54, p. 29. Cf. Chapter VII, notes 91-93.

41. See Ts'en Hsüeh-lü, *Hsü-yün ho-sheng nien-p'u,* pp. 16 ff, tr. in Lu K'uan-yü, *Ch'an and Zen Teaching, First Series* (London, Rider, 1960), pp. 49-109, and Chang Chen-chi, *The Practice of Zen* (London, Rider, 1960), pp. 61-70.

42. See Welch, *Practice,* p. 385; *Revival,* pp. 82-85. Joint practice by monks and laymen has been a significant success at certain Zen monasteries in Japan.

43. See Appendix A, pp. 137, 399.

44. Regarding the lay women who worked on the same jute-stranding team as the monks at the Yü-wang Ssu, see *HTFH,* 4/53, pp. 10, 14. Regarding the several dozen laymen who lived with the twenty-odd monks of the Ling-shan Ssu, Kwangtung, "studying and laboring together," see *HTFH,* 5/53, p. 26. Cf. Welch, *Revival,* p. 313, n. 33.

45. See Welch, *Practice,* pp. 310, 314.

46. On September 10, 1950, the Fa-ming Hsüeh-hui in Shanghai, which had suspended its activities for over a year, decided to hold lectures by monks every Sunday. It was described as "the only Buddhist research organization in this country." See *Chüeh yu-ch'ing,* 9.10:30 (October 1950).

47. The lectures began December 2, 1952, and continued through January 19, 1953. Seven monks expounded texts and four more lectured on practice or doctrine seriatim, each for a period of from two to ten days, sometimes overlapping one another. See *Chüeh yu-ch'ing,* 14.1:7-9 (January 1953).

48. In 1954 Chü-tsan mentioned lectures on the *Avatamsaka Sūtra* being given in Peking temples: see *China Reconstructs,* 1-2/54, p. 42. In the autumn of 1955 the Shanghai Buddhist Association sponsored two series of lectures: October 7-22 Ying-tz'u lectured on the *P'u-hsien hsing-yüan p'in* from the *Avatamsaka Sūtra* and from October 22 onwards Ching-ch'üan lectured on the *Yao-shih ching.*

49. See note 23.

50. See Chapter X after note 47.

51. In 1919 he had expounded the *Sūtra on Perfect Enlightenment* (T. 842) to an audience of three hundred at the T'ien-t'ung Ssu: see *Hai-ch'ao-yin wen-k'u,* 3:119-120. In *HTFH,* 7/56, p. 17, there is a photograph of him expounding the *Lotus Sūtra.*

52. In 1957 up to seven hundred people, mostly lay, were attending monthly lectures and buddha recitation held at a subtemple in Chungking: see *HTFH,* 5/57, p. 16. In 1958 Neng-hai lectured for the three months of the summer retreat at Wu-t'ai Shan: see *HTFH,* 8/58, p. 32. In 1960 Shirob emphasized that lectures continued to be frequent at three places (Wu-t'ai Shan, T'ien-t'ai Shan, and the Yü-wang Ssu near Ningpo). See *JMJP,* April 15, 1960. This was a far cry from the dozens of monasteries in which lectures used to be held before Liberation. A Japanese who visited the Kuo-ch'ing Ssu, T'ien-t'ai Shan, in 1965 was told that the elegant lecture hall there was used twice a month, but no lecture was held while his delegation was at the monastery.

53. On October 30, 1955, he had begun to expound the *Lotus Sutra* at the Liu-jung Ssu every Tuesday and Saturday "for the prosperity of the state

and world peace." See *HTFH,* 12/55, p. 30. According to the cadre, he gave a special lecture series in connection with the Hungry Ghosts Festival.

54. *HTFH,* 9/58, p. 28.

55. *HTFH,* 10/58, p. 32. The photograph that goes with the article shows Neng-hai sitting comfortably on a chair while those who are resting from labor stand. Neng-hai himself seems never to have taken part in productive labor despite his use of the word "we." Another example of a Buddho-Marxist inspirational talk is given in *HTFH,* 6/53, p. 39.

56. See Welch, *Revival,* pp. 72-81.

57. Kiangsu and Chekiang were the two provinces with the largest number of devotees in the early 1930's. Fukien stood fifth (after Szechwan and Hupeh). See Welch, *Practice,* pp. 412-413.

58. All four of the groups mentioned in Amoy by *Chüeh yu-ch'ing,* 11.11:24 (November 1950) had Pure Land names like "the Society for Reciting Buddha's Name," "the Pure Karma Society," "the Lotus Society," and "the Lien-ch'ih Group for Help in Recitation," named after Lien-ch'ih, i.e., Chu-hung, the great Ming advocate of Pure Land and Ch'an combined. Cf. *HTFH,* 6/53, p. 40. There were also thirty-one *chai-t'ang* in Amoy—"vegetarian halls" in which 159 unmarried and elderly women who had taken the Five Vows lived a semi-monastic life: see *ibid.* and cf. *Chüeh yu-ch'ing,* 11.11:24 (November 1950).

59. See *HTFH,* 2/53, p. 29. Every time there was a recitation of buddha's name or a Buddhist festival, the society's newspaper reading team led study of the latest issues of *Modern Buddhism* and *Hung-hua.* Twelve members were servicemen's dependents (presumably wives and mothers), which made them less vulnerable to criticism for superstitious activities than they would otherwise have been.

60. See *HTFH,* 10/51, p. 28.

61. Before August 1954 members of the Pei-ching Chü-shih-lin were performing penance services (*li-ch'an*), reciting buddha's name, and studying religious doctrine and politics every Sunday and on the two days that fell at the middle and the end of the lunar month. On this and their research program see *HTFH,* 3/55, p. 28. Their elimination of certain festivals is reminiscent of measures taken by local government authorities under the Nationalists to eliminate the temples of divinities "without historical basis or present value": see Welch, *Revival,* p. 327, note 37. In 1956 the club apparently celebrated the Buddha's birthday according to the Chinese calendar on the 8th of the fourth month and then again on the 15th according to the Theravada calendar. See *HTFH*, 6/56, p. 25.

62. See *HTFH,* 1/54, p. 28, which states that Chao P'u-ch'u became president of the society in 1952. Other members included Lin Tzu-ch'ing, Kao Kuan-ju, Shih Ming-k'o, Yü Yü, and Li Jung-hsi. There were also at least two women members: Chu Tsun-hui and Li Jen-p'ing. In 1959 the society published an English translation of the travels of Hsüan-tsang.

63. See Hayashi, p. 121. He was told that all members believed in the Pure Land. The previous year, when Ōtani Eijun visited the society on October 20, 1954, he thought the buildings looked shabby. He was told that it had 57 monks in residence and was supported by 1,700 devotees. See Ōtani, p. 123.

64. See Welch, *Revival,* pp. 76-77. Another change was the discontinuance of the Buddhist radio station, XMHB.

65. See *HTFH,* 5/51, p. 36. On July 1, 1954, it changed its name from "World Lay Buddhist Club" (Shih-chieh Fo-chiao Chü-shih-lin) to "Shanghai Buddhist Club" (Shang-hai Fo-chiao Chü-shih-lin) because it no longer hoped to develop relations with Buddhists abroad. See *HTFH,* 7/54, p. 30, and cf. Welch, *Revival,* p. 311, note 18. The club had been revived on March 4, 1951 (apparently after two years of inactivity), by a reorganization committee. A new constitution was adopted and officers were elected. Recitation of buddha's name was held every Tuesday, Thursday, Saturday, and Sunday at 2:00 P.M.; and one chapter of the *Lotus Sutra* was chanted every Sunday at 9:00 A.M., while at 2:00 P.M. Miao-chen came to lecture. The club was housed in some buildings in T'ung-jen Street, since its original headquarters had burned down during the Japanese attack "a decade earlier." See *HTFH,* 5/51, p. 36. When Ōtani visited it in 1954, he was told that it had 800 members and that non-members could use its library of Buddhist books. See Ōtani, p. 124.

66. On October 13, 1957, the Takashina delegation visited the "Pure Karma Lay Buddhist Club" (Ching-yeh Chü-shih-lin): see *Hōchū Nihon Bukkyō,* p. 31. In June 1962 an overseas Chinese monk (see Appendix G) was told that the Religious Believers Society (Hsin-tsung Hui) was a center for lay Buddhist youth and had formerly been named the "Shanghai Buddhist Youth Association" (Shang-hai Fo-chiao Ch'ing-nien Hui). It had over two thousand members, all lay Buddhists. It held morning and evening devotions every day (except October 1), which were usually attended by about a hundred members. Every Tuesday, Thursday, and Saturday there was recitation of buddha's name and every Sunday a monk came to expound the sutras. It was housed in a fine two-story building and had a library with six sets of the Tripitaka. Many Buddhists—especially elderly ones—did research there during the day. Formerly it had had only seven hundred members—so that membership was rising. The similarities with the Lay Buddhist Club are striking.

67. See Welch, *Practice,* pp. 378, 382; *Revival,* p. 311.

X. THE INDIVIDUAL BUDDHIST

1. After the meeting at which Ju-ying submitted his written confession to the eleven kinds of criminal conduct of which he had been accused, although he "had sly plans to pick his own successor, the power of the masses was much greater" and in the end he was expelled. The preparatory committee for the Nanking Buddhist Reform Committee then elected the Venerable Yün-kuang as the next abbot and he formally took office on August 8, 1951.

"He fixed a new code of rules in twenty articles that provided for democratic methods of leading the masses (now only nine persons), for planting vegetables and gluing up wooden crates by day and holding study meetings in the evening. This is the way in which a public monastery has really become publicly supported. Its residents labor peacefully and no longer suffer the oppression that is summed up in the saying 'There are mountains of rice in monasteries everywhere, but only the toadies can get it.' From now on the P'i-lu Ssu is not going to be a base for corrupt and rotten dynasties of monks, but a great training camp for the reform of Buddhism in Nanking." See *HTFH,* 10/51, p. 26.

By 1962 none of these four monks (Ju-ying, Yün-kuang, Yin-t'an, Yung-p'ei) appears still to have been at the P'i-lu Ssu. Its abbot was Chüeh-yüan, who may be identical with the monk of that name who was sent to Thailand in 1936 to study Theravada Buddhism. See Welch, *Revival,* p. 181. Chüeh-yüan's photograph appears in Welch, *Practice,* p. 146.

The P'i-lu Ssu used to be controlled by the followers of T'ai-hsü and had served as the national headquarters of the old Chinese Buddhist Association after they took it over in 1947. Perhaps Ju-ying was one of them.

2. See Welch, *Practice,* pp. 147-152.

3. Occasionally we find reference to the "onerous procedures and hard life" that abbots now faced: see *Chüeh yu-ch'ing,* 15.2:19 (October 1952). On the selection of abbots, see Chapter IV, note 76.

4. Hsü-yün took his meals in his room, eating only gruel soup, *hsi-fan t'ang,* because of his great age. Such was the food shortage that everyone else also had gruel soup for lunch, but perhaps something more substantial was served to them in the evening as they sat in the meditation hall.

5. Aside from Yün-chü Shan, I have seen allusions to extensive meditation at the Kao-min Ssu, Kuang-chi Mao-p'eng, and Yün-men Shan. An informant who lived at Yün-men Shan in 1952-54 reported the following schedule:

A.M.	3:30	Up
	4:00	Morning devotions
	5:00	Breakfast congee
	6:00	One period of meditation for those who wanted to attend
	7:00	Farm work (with a half hour's walk each way to and from the fields)
	11:30	Noon rice
	12:00	One period of meditation for those who wanted to attend
P.M.	1:30	More farm work (four monks returned early to hold afternoon devotions)
	6:30	Supper (usually potatoes)
	7:00	One long period of meditation, attended by most of the resident monks
	9:00	Retire

In March 1963, during the period of political relaxation, Ōtani Eijun visited Chin Shan and was informed that the monks there arose at 4 A.M., recited buddha's name (*sic*), attended devotions, breakfasted at 6, from 8 to 10 engaged in *gongyō* (which might conceivably have referred to meditation), then worked until lunch at noon, after which they worked again until 4, recited buddha's name, held devotions at 6, and retired for the night at 8. This information, which I received from the Reverend Ōtani on April 3, 1963, does not fit in with Chin Shan's tradition and may reflect either what the cadres wanted him to think or what he chose to understand as a leader of the Shinshu sect. Nor is it consistent with another point he was quite sure about: monks there under seventy ordinarily worked eight hours a day in the fields. On the schedule before 1949, see Welch, *Practice,* pp. 426-441.

6. *HTFH,* 10/54, p. 29. This is the only monastery for which I have seen anything approaching a daily schedule published in *Modern Buddhism.* The monks rose at 4 A.M. and at 4:30 attended devotions. After breakfast, from 7 to 9, they had their class in Pure Land doctrine. From 9 to 4 they went out to earn their living, each on his own. One was an acupuncturist, others included an electrician, a carpenter, and a cobbler. At 4:00 they returned to the monastery and were joined by some fifty devotees in two hours of chanting the *Lotus Sutra* for the sake of world peace. Then the monks (no mention of supper) had an hour of political study before going to bed.

They were reported to be "extraordinarily happy" about this life. They declared: "We could not go back to being dead wood as in the old society. Because the nation has given us true freedom of religious belief and because the atmosphere has completely changed and become happy and friendly, we monks can truly realize the six harmonies advocated by the Buddha [for monastic life—harmony of body, speech, ideas, morals, views, and economic arrangements] ."

The abbot of the monastery at this time was Hsing-ju, who had received the T'ien-t'ai dharma from T'an-hsü and founded the Ta-ch'eng Ssu in Heilungkiang in 1929. As a T'ien-t'ai monk he would naturally make a special effort to have his followers engage in doctrinal study.

7. See *Chung-kuo hsin-wen,* June 22, 1957, which states that the monks there held devotions from 4 A.M. until dawn and from 7 to 9 P.M.—periods almost twice as long as was traditional. In 1954 the Kuang-chi Mao-p'eng solicited the donation of a hundred copies of the *Avatamsaka Sūtra:* perhaps they were for use as a classroom text: see *HTFH,* 9/54, p. 30. In 1962 the monks of the Kuo-ch'ing Ssu on T'ien-t'ai Shan asked that a time be fixed for them to conduct regular study of T'ien-t'ai doctrines (which indicates, of course, that they had *not* been studying them regularly): see *HTFH,* 6/62, p. 39 (December 1962). Cf. Chapter III, note 41.

8. On the monk in Hupeh see *HTFH,* 6/54, p. 24. On hermits before Liberation, see Welch, *Practice,* pp. 318-319. A good example of a pre-Liberation hermit was Ch'an-hsiu, whom Hsü-yün met when wandering through Yunnan in 1904. Ch'an-hsiu had spent years improving a rough stretch of

mountain road–so rough that he had taken pity on the men and pack animals who had to use it. He had formed a compassionate resolve (not in response to a government appeal) that he would work on it with pick and hoe until it was repaired or he died. See Ts'en Hsüeh-lü, *Hsü-yün ho-shang nien-p'u,* p. 37.

9. The head of this temple was the master's master of the monk whose travel memoir is given in Appendix G. The disciple who stayed with him was actually his own son, born before he entered the sangha. (I know of no other case of a Chinese master and disciple being father and son, as is so common in Japan.)

10. In 1952 one of my informants, then living at Yün-men Shan, burned a Buddhist swastika on his chest. In 1955 an Indian visitor was shown a nun at the T'ung-chiao Ssu in Peking who was writing out five pages of scripture a day, two hundred characters to a page, with blood from her tongue. She would cut her tongue and then used the blood to wet a very small brush. She had been at it for the preceding five years, that is, since Liberation. On such practices before 1949 see Welch, *Practice,* pp. 320-328.

11. For the year 1952 members of the Yü-wang APC were paid less than 14 JMP apiece in wages, but there was a much larger item in the budget to cover the food grown or purchased by the monastery to feed them. See *HTFH,* 5/53, p. 13.

12. One of the points on which I have contradictory information is how ration coupons were issued to monks and used. Either each monastery was regarded as a household and received a single ration book for all its inmates; or each inmate had his own book and gave his coupons to the prior, who pooled them to purchase the food eaten by the inmates together. Apparently the practice varied from place to place. One reliable informant reported that in the monasteries where he had stayed, the individual monk was only served as much food as he had paid for and covered with ration coupons, but that food was prepared in bulk for all.

13. On monks' personal income and expenses before Liberation, see Welch, *Practice,* pp. 328-334. Cf. 199-201.

14. *HTFH,* 11/59, p. 29.

15. One Shenyang nun did so well with the practice of Chinese medicine that from her earnings she built and defrayed all the expenses of a nunnery with seven resident nuns, who were thus "enabled to keep up their religious practice without worry." See *HTFH,* 5/57, p. 14.

16. *HTFH,* 10/59, p. 12. A little arithmetic shows that with the total of 6,000 JMP and thirty-five participants, the average monk earned less than 1.5 JMP per day (US$0.67).

17. See *HTFH,* 6/53, p. 52. The figure of 185,000,000 yuan (old currency) apparently also included the cost of the padded robes given to each of 359 residents in November, "when it was snowing heavily and officials of the United Front Department and the Bureau of Culture and Education conducted an investigation in person." (Clothing had already been distributed in

October.) The relief grain was given in three categories: 169 monks were on total relief, getting 2.5 catties per day in January-March 1953; 53 were on partial relief, getting 2 catties per day; and 92 got 1.5 catties. Thus out of the 374 residents, at least 359 got clothing and 314 got food. Yet only the 46 who were in a home for the aged and the 56 who were feeble enough to be on permanent subsidy were getting more than temporary relief. The rest had to depend on donations and what they could grow on the land allocated to them in land reform, which was only enough to support a hundred of them. See Chapter II, table 1, note g. In this respect less was being done than in 1950, when *all* members of the sangha, residents and pilgrims, at Wu-t'ai Shan received 20 catties of grain per month from the Wu-t'ai Shan management committee. See *HTFH,* 11/50, p. 31.

18. The government also "took care of" eighteen monks and lamas there by giving them the equivalent of 20 JMP for the whole year. See *HTFH,* 6/53, p. 31.

19. In early 1953 the Kweilin municipal government gave the equivalent of 5 JMP to each of six monks and three devotees (who "really needed help"). Five of them also received one cotton garment apiece. See *HTFH,* 3/53, p. 28. Compare the money and clothes that the United Front Department gave to a few monks and nuns in Shansi (*HTFH,* 6/53, p. 29) and the money distributed to the elderly and disabled monks of two monasteries in Chiu-ch'üan, Shensi (*HTFH,* 3/53, p. 29).

20. *HTFH,* 1/54, p. 29.

21. In December 1952 five Wusih monks were each receiving a monthly food allowance of 90,000 yuan (old currency) equivalent to US$3.85 and a clothing allowance of 30,000 yuan: see *HTFH,* 12/52, p. 14. In 1954 nuns at the K'ai-fu Ssu, Changsha, were also receiving 90,000 yuan per month: see *HTFH,* 3/54, p. 24. Three Shansi monks and nuns started to get permanent relief in February 1953, apparently amounting to only 50,000 yuan per month: see *HTFH,* 6/53, p. 29. Some forty elderly and disabled monks and nuns on Chiu-hua Shan (more than a fifth of the monastic population) began to get an annual subsidy (the amount unstated) in 1953: see *HTFH,* 6/53, p. 54. An overseas monk who visited many monasteries in 1962 (see Appendix G) reported that 10 JMP a month was the usual sum then being given to those elderly or disabled monks who qualified for an allowance.

22. There is one report of living allowances at a higher level. In Changsha twenty-nine monks and nuns wholly incapable of labor were getting 90 catties of rice per month in 1953; and sixteen with partial labor capacity were getting 60-75 catties. Since each could eat no more than about 30 catties, they presumably sold the surplus to get cash for other living expenses: see HTFH, 6/53, p. 47. This seems to have been double the allowance they had received, on the average, in the three years from March 1950 to March 1953, during which time the total they had received was 77,320 catties: *ibid.,* p. 46.

23. In 1954, for example, some of the disabled nuns at the K'ai-fu Ssu, Changsha, pledged 50,000 JMP for the purchase of National Construction Bonds, although it was pointed out to them that their monthly living allowance for everything including food was only 90,000 and that they should probably limit their pledges to 10,000-20,000, so as to be able to redeem them in five months. Some other nuns, who worked at a textile coöperative where they had already subscribed to bonds, subscribed to more at the monastery–up to 100,000 on top of the 150,000 they had already pledged. (Their wages ran 160,000-320,000 per month.) See *HTFH*, 3/54, pp. 24-25. This report is interesting in that it uses the old term for allowance (*i-tan*, see Welch, *Practice*, p. 330) as well as the usual new one (*sheng-huo fei*). Cf. *HTFH*, 2/55, p. 30 (Canton).

24. *HTFH*, 10/59, p. 12.

25. The money was distributed from the Religious Affairs Bureau in Peking directly to its municipal organs and by its provincial organs to religious affairs sections at the county level. Any unused balance was returned to Peking at the end of the year. On other sources of money for allowances, see below note 29.

26. An overseas monk (Appendix G) was told that everyone over sixty years old who had no labor power *and had not been a landlord* received an allowance of 10 JMP per month. This could have been interpreted so as to exclude a good many elder monks, but it is not the same as a policy of making allowances contingent on current political activism. No allusion to such a policy, so far as I know, has ever appeared in the Mainland press, but this would be natural, since one purpose of allowances was to demonstrate the magnanimity of the government's religious policy. However, it is significant that a Japanese visitor was told in 1957 that Hui-wen, abbot of the Ta-pei Ssu, Tientsin, was getting a subsidy *because* he served on a peace committee (*Chūgai nippō*, September 8, 1957); and in at least one area we have a good indication that far fewer persons received allowances than should have been qualified for them by age and infirmity. In Chekiang, 1953 was stated to be the "post-Liberation year when monks and nuns had the greatest difficulties with their livelihood. The government appropriated a large sum of money, enough to buy 100,000 catties of rice, to be distributed to monks and nuns individually who were suffering from hardship in the various places." See *HTFH*, 9/55, p. 21. An amount of 100,000 catties was enough to feed 275 persons for one year–less than 2.5 percent of the sangha in Chekiang. The number of elderly and disabled monks and nuns ran 30-40 percent–or even higher. In places like P'u-t'o Shan more than half the monks were aged or ill: see *Chüeh yu-ch'ing*, 13.2:20 (October 1952). Cf. Chapter II, note 20.

27. The size of the sangha declined, hence the large spread in percentage. According to the former cadre, most of them got 12-15 JMP per month–less than Chüeh-ch'eng, but more than what the press reports for Buddhists elsewhere.

28. Monks at Nan-hua may have been getting an allowance after 1954, when the Shao-kuan religious affairs section was set up, but they were not in 1952, when the monastery's eight remaining monks were described as "old and enfeebled and unable to labor well enough to support themselves. Their livelihood constitutes quite a problem." See *Chüeh yu-ch'ing,* 13.2:20 (October 1952).

29. One informant reported that in Soochow, where allowances ran 12-13 JMP per month until 1958, they came from the Soochow Buddhist Association. In 1953 relief funds (*chen-k'uan*) were being distributed to poor monks, nuns, and lamas by the Kansu Buddhist Association: see *HTFH,* 6/53, p. 31. In 1959 allowances to residents of the K'ai-fu Ssu (cf. note 23) were being distributed by the Changsha Buddhist Association: see *HTFH,* 11/59, p. 28. In these cases the funds distributed may still have come from the government. At Nan-yüeh in Hunan, however, funds came mainly from the profits of the temples of the area ("profits" meaning pilgrims' donations minus operating expenses). See *HTFH,* 11/53, p. 32. In 1954 living allowances from this source amounted to 1,000 JMP: see *HTFH,* 2/55, p. 29. Cf. 11/58, p. 28, and Alley, *Amongst Hills and Streams,* p. 13.

30. For mention of such a home at Wu-t'ai Shan see *HTFH,* 6/53, p. 52. On one in Paotow, see *JMJP,* April 13, 1960. In 1958 elderly monks in one area of Inner Mongolia set up a "Lamas' Garden of Happiness" with the help of the local coöperative. Its inmates, who were up to eighty-seven years old, raised beans and hogs and watched peoples' houses while they were away at work. See *HTFH,* 11/58, p. 30.

31. See Welch, *Practice,* pp. 276, 282. Cf. pp. 335-340.

32. *HTFH,* 2/55, p. 30. He was said to be doing all this to express his self-dedication to world peace. In 1965 a Western visitor to the Ling-yen Ssu, Soochow, came across a shrine at the foot of the hill, inside which he saw a little old monk prostrating himself and rising again as he offered food and incense to a mural of Kuan-yin.

33. *HTFH,* 4/53, p. 11. Cf. 5/53, p. 13, and compare the case of the former abbot of the Hua-yen Ssu near Chungking, who lived in a wooden shed and lugged thirty gallons of water a day up the hill to the monastery kitchen. Because of his advanced age the other monks implored him to stop, but he insisted on continuing, apparently so as to share their hardships. See *Chüeh yu-ch'ing,* 13.2:19 (October 1952).

34. See for example *HTFH,* 5/57, p. 23; 5/58, p. 21; 6/58, p. 24.

35. Peasants near Wu-t'ai Shan were said to be "moved to tears" by the sight of the monks at work: see *HTFH,* 12/58, p. 28. Already five years earlier 43 percent of the monks there were over sixty years old: see *HTFH,* 6/53, p. 52.

36. *HTFH,* 6/53, p. 47. "Buddhist association" refers here to the preparatory committee for the Buddhist Work Committee of Changsha. It is not clear whether burial included cremation, but this had been the standard practice for Buddhist monks and was also now favored by the regime.

37. On the increase in temple patronage towards the end of political movements, see Chapter IX, before note 10.

38. See *HTFH,* 9/50, p. 31 (italics added). On the lay initiation, see Welch, *Practice,* pp. 359-366.

39. Forty thousand people are said to have come to Shanghai at the end of 1952 and taken the Refuges under Hsü-yün: see Ts'en Hsüeh-lü, *Hsü-yün ho-shang nien-p'u,* p. 192. In Hangchow in February 1953 he administered the Refuges to a thousand persons (*ibid.,* p. 253) and in Soochow and other places to thousands more (*ibid.,* p. 256). Oral informants who had no connection with Hsü-yün confirm the magnitude of these figures.

40. In the winter of 1952-53 twenty-two members of the Mu-kuang Lotus Society, Nantung, Kiangsu, took the Refuges on Amitabha's birthday: see *HTFH,* 2/53, p. 29. One hundred persons took them on August 25, 1953, in Soochow: see *HTFH,* 10/53, p. 31. In Kiangsu the Refuges were administered to 34 persons in Ch'i-tung at the end of a week's Ullambana service (for the hungry ghosts): see *ibid.* In October 1954 three hundred believers in Chekiang took the Three Refuges and Five Vows on Kuan-yin's birthday: see *HTFH,* 11/54, p. 30. More took the Five Vows at the ordinations that were held in 1955-57 (see Chapter IV).

41. See Welch, *Practice,* p. 388.

42. The only later initiation I know of was given to seventy devotees in Amoy in October 1957. It was cited to refute "the rightists' slander . . . that in the New China religious belief is not so free": see *HTFH,* 1/58, p. 27. Oral informants state that after 1957 monks were reluctant to initiate lay people and lay people were reluctant to be initiated. The monks had been told that it would be better not to perform the ceremony but that, if they did so, they had to report the names of those who had been initiated. Naturally lay people preferred to avoid the trouble that this could lead to.

43. *HTFH,* 8/51, pp. 23-24.

44. *JMJP,* September 4, 1958, tr. in *SCMP,* 1859:9 (slightly altered).

45. I have referred to this woman in "Buddhism since the Cultural Revolution," *China Quarterly,* 40:134 (October-December 1969) as an illustration of the effect of the Cultural Revolution. I should have made it clear that she had started her imperceptible devotions before the Cultural Revolution began and continued them while it was underway. By then her images had been hidden away.

46. On Eight Fingers, see Welch, *Revival,* pp. 34-38.

47. See Welch, *Practice,* p. 160, and *Revival,* p. 203. The latter is misleading on one point. Although Ying-tz'u refused to become abbot of T'ien-ning, he repeatedly served as abbot of the Hsing-fu Ssu in Changshu, to which his elder dharma brother, Yüeh-hsia, had brought the T'ien-ning dharma when he became its abbot shortly before he died. A brief biography of Ying-tz'u appears in *Chüeh-shih,* 314:2.

48. *Buddhists in China,* pp. 132-133, reprinted in *Buddhists in New China,* pp. 134-135. Counting heads in the photograph, I find a total of

fourteen monks, eight nuns, and about eighty lay people, mostly elderly women.

49. *Chieh-fang-chün pao,* July 14, 1962.

50. See "The Wishes of the Buddhists," *Chieh-fang jih-pao,* November 10, 1958, tr. in *SCMP,* 1943:10. The article shows a satisfactory degree of political awareness, but it seems likely that this was supplied by another of its four authors, perhaps Wei-fang.

51. His name alone is given as translator of the version that appears in the *Bilingual Buddhist Series Volume One: Sutras and Scriptures* (Taipei, 1962), pp. 239-269, but W. Liebenthal in his translation, *Sutra of the Lord of Healing: Bhaisajyaguru Vaidūryaprabhāsa* (Peking, 1936), 32 pp., thanks Chou Shu-chia in the preface for help in making the translation, which appeared as the first number in the Buddhist scripture series of which Chou Shu-chia was editor and which was being published by the "Society of Chinese Buddhists" at the Nien-hua Ssu, Peking.

Since I have only seen Liebenthal's translation in the pamphlet collection of the London Buddhist Society, I have not had an opportunity to compare the texts and see whether they are the same. Chou's translation was published in Taiwan without consulting him. If he had been consulted, he might well have wanted to share the credit with Liebenthal. The fact that it was published over his name in Taiwan is an interesting indication of the degree to which he had succeeded in avoiding politics. When T'ang Yung-t'ung's history was reprinted there, his name was everywhere deleted. See *Han Wei liang-Chin nan-pei-ch'ao fo-chiao-shih* (History of Buddhism in the Han, Wei, Chin, and Six Dynasties; Taipei, Commercial Press, 1962).

52. For example, he helped to restore and maintain the Mi-le Yüan: see Welch, *Revival,* pp. 82-84.

Some of the information given here about Chou Shu-chia comes from Hashikawa Tokio, *Chūgoku bunkakai jimbutsu sōkan* (Peking, 1940), pp. 227-228. Chou came from Chih-te, Anhwei, and was born in 1898. He held the post of lecturer in several institutions, including Fujen, Peking, and China universities and the Chinese University of Law.

53. To a Japanese delegation in 1957 he was introduced as head of the Lay Devotees' Club (Chü-shih-lin) and vice-president of the CBA. See *Hōchū Nihon Bukkyō,* p. 32.

54. See NCNA English, July 24, 1959, in *SCMP,* 2066:37 and NCNA English, August 2, 1959, in *SCMP,* 2072:35. The two sides to his life made a neat contrast when in the morning of May 3, 1960 he attended the celebration of the Buddha's birthday at the Kuang-chi Ssu and in the afternoon presided at a reception for the Nepalese table-tennis team.

55. The fourteen articles he contributed to *Modern Buddhism* over the years were all on Tun-huang, the printing of the Tripitaka, and similar academic subjects. On one occasion his name was signed to a political manifesto (against the U.S.-Japanese security treaty—see *HTFH,* 7/60, p. 9), but it appeared there *ex-officio* as a vice-president of the CBA. A European who

knew him well recalls that at their last meeting (in Peking after Liberation) he had asked Chou about the Communists, and Chou had said that regimes would always be changing but the Buddha would remain the Buddha. The alternation of rise and decay was nothing to bewail.

56. In 1925, when Hsü Sen-yü was librarian at the National Library in Peking, he attended the East Asian Buddhist Conference in Tokyo (see Welch, *Revival,* pp. 166-168). He was a council member of the CBA from its foundation in 1953 and served on the standing committee of the Shanghai Municipal Buddhist Association. He was on the Municipal Commission for the Management of Cultural Property, becoming head of it in 1961 (at about the same time he became head of the Shanghai Municipal Museum). He was elected to the NPC in 1959 and re-elected in 1964. Thus he was an important link between Buddhism and the government, particularly in cultural matters. As such he was sometimes chosen to help entertain Buddhist visitors. Yet he never appears to have become a political activist in Buddhism. His only contribution to *Modern Buddhism* was to sign his name, along with fourteen others, including several strong conservatives, to an article denouncing the sabotage conducted by the Roman Catholic Church in China: see *HTFH,* 8/53, p. 24.

57. *HTFH,* 5/59, p. 31. Soon afterwards he condemned the "Indian expansionists' interference in China's internal affairs": see NCNA, May 2, 1959.

58. NCNA, August 11, 1964.

59. E.g., see Boorman, *Biographical Dictionary of Republican China,* I, 213-217.

60. In 1928 Ch'en, then governor of Kwangtung, asked Hsü-yün to become abbot of the Nan-hua Ssu (an invitation that Hsü-yün only accepted in 1934): see Ts'en Hsüeh-lü, *Hsü-yün ho-shang nien-p'u,* p. 90. During the war he reportedly studied with Ou-yang Ching-wu in Chungking. Some of the men he dealt with in political life were also Buddhists (like T'ang Sheng-chih and Chang Chi) and it would be interesting to know what effect this had on their dealings. When Buddhist leaders met in Peking after Liberation, Li Chi-shen and T'ang Sheng-chih were across the table from Ch'en Ming-shu.

61. See Chapter I, note 1.

62. In 1950-53 thirty-four items authored by Ch'en appeared in *Modern Buddhism,* some of them political. After a gap of three years one article and six poems appeared in the first three months of 1957: thereafter nothing. On the accusations against him see *HTFH,* 12/57, p. 28, tr. in *CB,* 510:1-2. Li Chi-shen called Ch'en a "reactionary filled with venom from head to toe," who had obstructed the Fukien revolt against Chiang (actually he had led it). Chü-tsan denied that Ch'en was a real Buddhist, but admitted that if it had not been for the anti-rightist movement, "we would still be under his spell." Ch'en himself said: "I confess to the crime of possessing a complete set of reactionary, anti-communist and anti-socialist principles; to the crime of organizing cliques in Peking, Shanghai, and Shantung; to the crime of writing a

'Ten-thousand-word anti-Communist Letter'; and to the crime of carrying out secret anti-Communist activities by means of Buddhism . . . I will go on and submit a written account of what my crimes concretely were. I wish to repent them and start a new life." See *HTFH,* 12/57, p. 28, tr. in *CB,* 510:1-2 (slightly altered); cf. *ibid.,* pp. 3-4.

63. E.g., Ming-chen, Li Jung-hsi, Shih Ming-k'o, Wei-fang, Chü-tsan.

64. Another progressive Buddhist who died prematurely was I-fang. He was the only head monk to stay at Chiu-hua Shan when conditions became difficult after Liberation. Perhaps because of his activism in starting schools (see Chapter III at note 80), he was elected to the Anhwei People's Conference in 1952, then to the CBA council in 1953. In 1955 he was chosen for the signal honor of going to Burma on the Chinese Buddhist delegation that attended the Sixth Council. Dressed in Theravada robes, his picture appears in *Buddhists in New China,* p. 180.

In 1957 he was elevated to the standing committee of the CBA and became a deputy secretary-general. By then he had moved to Peking, where he also served as head of the research section of the Chinese Buddhist Seminary. He died on September 20, 1959, of stomach cancer at the age of 45.

XI. THE CULTURAL REVOLUTION AND AFTER

1. Parts of the following section first appeared in Welch, "Buddhism since the Cultural Revolution," *China Quarterly,* 40:127-136 (October-December 1969).

2. NCNA English, Aug. 3, Aug. 4, 1966, in *SCMP,* 3756:31-32. On the tour of this delegation (July 24-Aug. 20, 1966) see Katsumata, pp. 835-837.

3. Checks of biographical files in Hong Kong (U.S. Consulate General, Union Research Institute, etc.) revealed that the last dates on which important Buddists were mentioned as Buddhists were as follows. Ngawang Jaltso (Aug. 3, 1966); Chou Shu-chia (Aug. 3, 1966); Chü-tsan (June 16, 1966); Chao P'u-ch'u (March 1, 1966); Kuo P'eng (Aug. 23, 1965); Li I-ping (Aug. 6, 1965); Ch'ih-sung (May 8, 1965); Lü Ch'eng (Dec. 13, 1964); Wei-fang (Sept. 15, 1964); Shih Ming-k'o (Aug. 11, 1964); Ming-chen (Aug. 11, 1964); Shirob Jaltso (June 27, 1964); Ying-tz'u (July 14, 1962). Many of the other directors of the CBA were mentioned for the last time in connection with its third national conference in February 1962.

4. See *ECMM,* 566:16-20.

5. See *SCMP,* 3778:7, and *Yang-ch'eng wan-pao,* Aug. 24, 1966, tr. in *SCMP,* 3774:13. The *Yang-ch'eng wan-pao* for Aug. 31, 1966, called for getting rid of altars, ancestor tablets, geomantic compasses, and trigram divination—as well as birthday parties, neckties, and pointed shoes (*SCMP,* 3778:7). Many of the articles published at this time attacked tailors and

barbers (for making tight pants and cutting hair short); none that I have seen attacked monks.

6. See Mackerras and Hunter, pp. 82-83, and compare the observations of some Japanese and English visitors in the autumn of 1966 and the spring and summer of 1967 as summarized in *China Notes,* 5.3:2 (July 1967), 5.4:4 (October 1967), and 6.1:4 (January 1968). The closure of temples in the Cultural Revolution may have begun before August 18, 1966. A foreigner who visited Hangchow at the end of July found that all three T'ien-chu monasteries were closed and locked. At the Shang T'ien-chu, which appeared to have been closed quite recently, "no entry" signs were posted at the outer gate, and, looking through the windows of the main shrine-halls, one could see that the images and religious paraphernalia had been removed. Yet the same visitor a few days earlier had seen scaffolding around the pagoda of the Pei-t'a Ssu, Soochow, which was evidently being repaired.

Monasteries were not the only Buddhist institutions to feel the advance tremors of the Cultural Revolution. When a Japanese delegation visited the Chinese Buddhist Seminary at the end of July 1966, it found that there were only 37 students (down from 70 the year before) and three teachers (down from 11). The delegation asked to be shown the classrooms and library, "but our request was refused." After trying in vain to discuss with their hosts how Buddhism coöperated with Communism in theoretical matters, they concluded that "perhaps Chinese Buddhists did not want to talk about this"—although Buddho-Marxist syncretism had previously been a welcome topic. See Katsumata, pp. 336-337. Already in June the Rinzai delegation saw students and workers parading through the streets of Peking, carrying red flags and striking drums and cymbals. Kuo Mo-jo told them that the parade was part of the Cultural Revolution, which was designed to bring urban facilities to the countryside and to educate the children of workers and peasants as well as bureaucrats and intellectuals.

7. An interesting photograph appeared in *P'u-t'i shu,* 169:6 (December 8, 1966). Presumably taken in August or September, it showed slogans posted over the doors of the Kuei-yüan Ssu, the principal Buddhist monastery in Hankow. The slogans read: "Smash the old, establish the new; smash greatly, establish greatly." The doors were sealed with strips of paper, so that they could not be secretly opened.

8. Known cases include the Neng-jen Ssu in Chiu-chiang, Kiangsi, where foreign visitors observed that all the images had been removed; and the Liu-jung Ssu, Canton, on which information is provided in the Mainland press (Canton *Hung-wei pao,* Sept. 1, 1966, tr. in *SCMP,* 3781:15). Cf. *World Buddhism,* 15.10:291 (May 1967) and below note 55.

9. The Wo-fo Ssu near Peking was occupied by Red Guards according to the Tokyo *Shimbun,* Sept. 29, 1967. The Liu-jung Ssu may have been converted into a cardboard box factory: see *China Notes,* 5.2:4 (April 1967).

Refugees reported the conversion into factories of the San-yüan Kung (Canton's principal Taoist temple) and the Hung Miao in Shanghai, a center of the popular religion.

10. AP dispatch by Cecile Nichols printed in the *Boston Globe,* Aug. 28, 1966.

11. A Shanghai resident also heard that the Jade Buddha had been removed (perhaps to a place of safety).

12. Richard C. Bush writes: "It is noted in several publications that the famous Temple of the Bubbling Well [the Ching-an Ssu] in Shanghai was razed" and cites as his source *Église Vivante* 19:185 (May-August 1967). See Richard C. Bush, *Religion in Communist China* (Nashville, 1970), p. 344.

13. Tokuda Myohon, "Bunkaku ka no Chūgoku Bukkyō o miru," *Asahi Shimbun,* Oct. 22, 1967, p. 18. When Tokuda asked about seeing the Kuang-chi Ssu, his interpreter was evasive, so he went there on his own. He found the main gate closed, but a side gate open. When Tokuda asked the gatekeeper (a layman) if he could talk with the monks, he was told: "They are not here." When he asked if he could worship at the ordination platform (since he belonged to the Vinaya sect), he was told that he could not because he had no introduction from the "Religious Department" (*tsung-chiao pu*).

14. The abbot in question had been a member of the council of the CBA since 1957 and vice-president of its Fukien branch since 1962. He had also been elected to the Fukien People's Representative Conference.

15. *Far Eastern Economic Review,* 61.29:148 (July 18, 1968). The only other statement about religion that I have seen attributed to Chiang Ch'ing was in her talk to literary circles on the Cultural Revolution. "To put aside the old and bring forth the new is a new phenomenon with mass content . . . What the masses like includes much that does not fit this slogan, like gods, ghosts, and religion. How can we judiciously accept such things? I think we cannot. For we are atheists, we are Communists, and basically we do not believe there are such things in the world as ghosts and gods." See *JMJP,* Dec. 4, 1966.

16. *Life,* Oct. 7, 1966, pp. 40-41, printed photographs of the images, altars, and other furnishings of the San-yüan Kung blazing away before a crowd of spectators.

17. NCNA, Aug. 25, 1966, quoted by *Hsiang-kang fo-chiao* (Buddhism in Hong Kong), 77:3 (Oct. 1, 1966).

18. *New York Times,* Dec. 25, 1966. Cf. Mackerras and Hunter, p. 83. Hunter heard that soldiers had been sent to protect the Lung-men Caves from vandalism.

19. See Anne-Marie Carmentrez, "J'ai vu les bouddhas éclater sous les masses des gardes rouges," *Paris-Match,* Sept. 1966, p. 64.

20. In Chang-te, Hunan, old people who had always believed in the gods "spontaneously" handed over their buddha images to the Red Guards. The latter smashed to bits a little temple in the public park and put in its place a

brand new statue of Chairman Mao, flanked by the couplet "Obey Chairman Mao; follow the Party." See BBC Summary of World Broadcasts, FE2265/B/7, Sept. 15, 1966 (Changsha, Sept. 5, 1966).

In Hsiang-chen, Kwangsi, Red Guards went to "feudal temples" and "burned images of the Buddha and many other superstitious objects, replacing them with Chairman Mao's portraits and quotations from his works." Within a few days all the ancestor tablets and buddha images in twenty-nine villages had been burned, and Mao's portraits and quotations had been hung up in temples and homes. See BBC Summary of World Broadcasts, FE/2271/B/14, Sept. 22, 1966 (Nanning, Sept. 6, 1966). Similar episodes were reported in broadcasts from Kwangtung, Kiangsi, and Yunnan. Cf. Mackerras and Hunter, p. 90, which reports that Mao had replaced the Buddha in many temples and that "today pasted up in almost every house in the country, there is a 'holy picture' of the Chairman, usually consisting of his portrait flanked by political slogans or a couplet from his poems." (See Figs. 17, 35o.) On the cult of Mao, see Welch, "The Deification of Mao." It is important to distinguish the installation of Mao's effigy in places of worship and its presence elsewhere. Already in 1963 visitors noted that Mao's picture was hung in the reception rooms of many temples (see *Ganjin wajō,* p. 14). The last Japanese Buddhist delegation to come before the Cultural Revolution broke out found this to be so in every temple it visited, and one of its members remarked: "Without studying Chairman Mao's thought under the leadership of Chairman Mao, no temple could survive." See Katsumata, p. 836.

In spite of the large number of reports of iconoclasm, there is none that concerns an important buddha image in a well-known temple.

21. *Chung-yang jih-pao* (Taipei), April 14, 1967. A similar report (of unstated origin) was published in *World Buddhism,* 15.6:175 (January 1967) which described how an overseas Chinese woman had had to pay "bail" to some Red Guards who had "gaoled" her two buddha images "as a hindrance to the Cultural Revolution."

22. See FBIS, Aug. 30, 1966, DDD3. Ching-kuan had been in good standing until then, having served on the council of the CBA since 1957: see HTFH, 5/57, p. 21.

23. A report apparently brought by a refugee to Hong Kong tells of three elderly monks living in a village between Hong Kong and Canton. When Red Guards from Peking arrived there (as part of the influx that began in November 1966, like the influx of northern cadres during land reform in the spring of 1951), they beat the monks with leather whips and searched the temple, then announced that they had discovered gold and banknotes to a value of several hundred dollars. This showed that the monks had been "bad elements" or possibly even enemy agents. The Red Guards demolished the temple and replaced all ancestor tablets in the village with portraits of Chairman Mao as part of the campaign against the Four Olds. The monks disappeared.

A similar episode is reported from Jukao in northern Kiangsu, where three nuns still lived in a thatched hut they had built behind their former nunnery, which now served as a commune storehouse. The Red Guards struggled against the two younger nuns as "freaks and monsters" and demanded that they confess to spreading "superstitious thinking" and carrying on "superstitious activities." The nuns only wept. Then the younger one was accused of having had relations with a 70-year-old man, who had often praised her calligraphy. It was announced that she and the man would be tied together and paraded through the streets. The nun fainted, was taken home, and that night hanged herself on a tree behind her house. This caused the eldest nun to die from shock and only one was left, partly demented. See *Chung-yang jih-pao,* April 14, 1967. (Although this can be discounted as Nationalist propaganda, it is no more outré than some of the stories printed in the Red Guards' own newspapers.)

24. BBC Summary of World Broadcasts, SE2265/B/18, Sept. 15, 1966 (Kunming, Sept. 3, 1966).

25. This statement is based on the biographical checks mentioned in note 3.

26. Among those attacked or arrested during the Cultural Revolution was Liu Ying "former director of the Religious Affairs Section of the United Front Work Department": see Canton *Yeh-chan pao,* No. 12-13 (March 1958), tr. in *SCMP,* 4158:11. In 1957 Liu had been introduced to a Japanese Buddhist delegation in Peking as a "division chief" (*ch'u-chang*) of the Religious Affairs Bureau under the State Council (*Hōchū Nihon,* p. 32). He is the only casualty whose name I have seen mentioned in the press.

27. See *China Notes,* 6.3:4 (July 1968) and 7.2:13-15 (Spring 1969). I tend to discount the report in the Hong Kong *Hsing-tao jih-pao* for June 11, 1967, quoted in *CNA,* 682:4, that on April 8, 1967, one Red Guard faction in Peking claimed support, *inter alia,* from the "cabinet's commission for religious affairs and the research institute for the religions of the world."

28. See Wolfgang Appel, "Chinesische Impressionen in Jahre 20 nach Mao," *Neue Württembergische Zeitung* (Göppingen), April 10, 1969. The Corban Festival was celebrated at the Peking mosque in 1967 as usual: see NCNA English, March 22, 1967, in *SCMP,* 3907:28.

29. See *JMJP,* Aug. 8, 1962, tr. in *SCMP,* 3048:1-10. In saying that this article equated religious and superstitious activities, I do not do justice to its dialectical approach. "All religious activities are superstitious activities," writes Ya Han-chang, "but not all superstitious activities are religious activities." He distinguishes between primitive "spontaneous religion" and "man-made religion" (e.g., Buddhism or Christianity). He criticizes the former as foolish, but the latter as vicious. The reason why artificial religions explain the suffering of the masses in terms of karma or God's will is in order to defend the interests of the exploiting class. Nonetheless, among the masses, especially the peasants, ideas about the existence of gods and an afterlife are "still quite widespread" and cause "spontaneous superstitious activities." Un-

like the activities of geomancers, fortune tellers, etc., these cannot be combatted by administrative orders. "In other words, when we conduct atheist propaganda and oppose religious superstition, we must absolutely not interfere with worship by other people or tamper with the proper religious activities of believers" (*SCMP* translation slightly altered). Ya Han-chang's many pages of twisting and turning all come down to a plea for the continuation of the then liberal policy on religious activities.

30. See *Kung-jen jih-pao,* Aug. 10, 1963, tr. in JPRS 22444:51-56 and *SCMP,* 3061:13-15 (italics added). The same issue contained an attack on fortune telling (*ibid.,* pp. 9-12).

31. Needless to say, this was not the first time that such activities had come under attack. For example, one of the topics discussed before the CBA's inaugural meeting in 1953 was "how to help the People's Government get rid of charlatans who practice exorcism, sorcery, and other harmful superstitions under the guise of religion": see NCNA Jan. 2, 1954. More recently, an attack on geomancy had appeared in the *Nan-fang jih-pao,* July 26, 1962, tr. in *SCMP,* 2838:7-10, and the *Kung-jen jih-pao,* Sept. 22, 1962, tr. in JPRS 16813:94. There had been a broader target in "Have You Ever Been a Victim of Superstition? " *Honan jih-pao,* March 13, 1963; and in the article that mentions the latter, "I No Longer Believe in the Gods," *JMJP,* April 4, 1963, tr. in *SCMP,* 2973:11 and *Communist China Digest,* 108:44. The socialist education campaign is usually considered to have begun in the second half of 1962, but frequent attacks on "old customs" did not begin until the summer of 1963.

Some later articles criticizing "old customs" are translated in *SCMP,* 3060:15-16 (witch doctors); 3230:12-13 (visiting clan tombs); 3217:7-10 and 3260:18-20 (weddings and funerals); JPRS 21792:18-14 and 22752:42-50 (plays about ghosts); JPRS 29480:117-119 (weddings). Some articles attacked a wide variety of old customs: see *SCMP,* 3237:17-20; 3346:15-16; 3379:12-13; JPRS 28286:32-38. In Kwangtung, probably at the end of 1963, the People's Publishing House and the Kwangtung Scientists Association jointly published a 30,000-word booklet entitled "Do Gods and Fate Exist? " which included exposés of the arts of physiognomy, palmistry, geomancy, spiritualism, and divination with bamboo slips. Such superstitious practices, it said, had been created by the exploiting classes in order to cheat the people. See Hong Kong *Hsing-tao jih-pao,* Jan. 11, 1964, which comments that the booklet shows that superstititous activities still persisted, since the government "would not shoot an arrow if there was no target."

32. See the article "Be a Vanguard to Change Old Customs and Practices," *Nan-fang jih-pao,* Nov. 16, 1963, tr. in *SCMP,* 3141:4-7.

33. See Chapter V at note 68 and Chapter X at note 44.

34. Shanghai *Wen-hui pao,* Feb. 11, 1962, tr. in URS 34.26:435-436. This number of the Union Research Service contains seven articles from national and local newspapers on the reform of the Spring Festival. People were urged

not to burn incense, not to waste money, not to prostrate themselves to the elders in their families. Rather than pasting up couplets beside their doors with the traditional invocation of good luck for themselves, their couplets should be about the General Line of Socialist Construction; and rather than resting until the seventh day after New Year, they should start work again on the fourth.

In 1967 the State Council decreed that the Spring Festival would not be held. This was supposedly done in response to a call by 57 revolutionary organizations to abolish the festival and all its old customs: "To hell with the worship of gods, exchange of visits on the lunar New Year's Day, giving dinner parties, making gifts, eating, drinking, and having a good time! " See *SCMP,* 3875:1-3. The partial return of the Spring Festival was a measure of the waning of the Cultural Revolution. Cf. *SCMP,* 4112:26-27; *CNA,* 744-745, p. 2, etc.

35. *JMJP,* Aug. 25, 1964, tr. in *SCMP,* 3299:17. The *People's Daily* also called for reform of popular festivals, funerals, weddings, and the construction of houses (for which the site should not be chosen by a geomancer). The reform of the Double Ninth temple fair in Chieh-chou, Shansi, is described in the Peking *Ta-kung pao,* Dec. 3, 1964, tr. in URS 38.2:19-20. The creation of new operas on proletarian themes was an important feature of the socialist education campaign.

36. See Shanghai *Hsin-min wan-pao,* Aug. 16, 1964, tr. in URS 58.1:2 and *KMJP,* Dec. 6, 1964, tr. in *SCMP,* 3361:11-14. Renaming resumed with the outbreak of the Cultural Revolution, e.g., in the case of Kuan-yin Street in Foochow. "In socialist Foochow we resolutely refuse to allow existence of such a feudal streetname." See BBC Summary of World Broadcasts, FE2253/B/8, Sept. 1, 1966 (Foochow, Aug. 26, 1966).

37. *Nan-fang jih-pao,* Dec. 18, 1964, tr. in *SCMP,* 3379:13-14. A few weeks later *Time* reported that when the Lantern Festival was celebrated in Shanghai on February 16, girl cadres were sent to stop worshipers from entering the temple of the Goddess of Mercy, while shop windows displayed posters calling on people to end superstitious practices: see *Time,* Feb. 26, 1965, p. 27.

38. See *Ta-kung pao,* Jan. 17, 1965, tr. in *SCMP,* 3389:11-14. The proprietors of paper shops in Hong Kong have told me that they continued to import incense and paper from the Mainland until about the time of the Cultural Revolution, when their manufacture ceased. In early 1967 a Chinese resident of Hong Kong who went to visit relatives in Canton told a reporter on his return: "People in the Mainland today, regardless of what festival or whose anniversary it is, although they can shut the front door and make offerings in the dark, still have no way of buying incense and paper ingots. But everybody has a copy of Mao's quotations." See Hong Kong *Ming Pao,* March 16, 1967.

39. *Jen-min shou-ts'e,* 1965, p. 143.

40. An article in the *Nan-fang jih-pao,* May 3, 1962 stated that "in a number of areas in the countryside recently, temples and ancestral halls were repaired on a large scale, involving the use of a great deal of money, materials, and manpower, and affecting agricultural production." Such temples, said the article, should not be looked on as cultural monuments and preserved at great expense. See *SCMP,* 2742:19-20.

41. Kuo-fang-pu Ch'ing-pao Chü (Intelligence Bureau of the Ministry of Defense), ed. *Fan-kung yu-chi-tui t'u-chi Fu-chien Lien-chiang hsien lu-huo fei-fang wen-chien hui-pien* (Compilation of Communist documents captured by anti-Communist guerrilla forces raiding Lien-chiang county, Fukien; Taipei, 1964), p. 54. This is translated, with slight differences, in C. S. Chen and Charles Price Ridley, *Rural People's Communes in Lien-chiang: Documents Concerning Communes in Lien-chiang County, Fukien Province, 1962-1963* (Stanford, 1969), p. 110. The original documents are on microfilms in several libraries (e.g., Harvard-Yenching F1019) and are regarded as authentic: see *China Quarterly,* 45:171 (January-March 1971). The remainder of the passage I have quoted was water-soaked or lost.

42. See Chen and Ridley, pp. 97-98. Early in 1963 a conference of local Party secretaries in this area was told that things had improved since the year before. "Fewer persons now engage in feudalistic superstitious practices. Some cadre members and members of the masses have even voluntarily removed and destroyed the images of the bodhisattvas . . . Little temple construction is now going on and in some places . . . the temples have been transformed into storage houses." Nevertheless, it was admitted that some people still had bad attitudes and wanted to "worship bodhisattvas and stage idolatrous processions. At present . . . religious swindlers and gambling have returned." *Ibid.,* pp. 200, 203. Lien-chiang is thirty kilometers northeast of Foochow.

43. See Chapter I at note 5. The ineffectiveness of the 1958 campaign against religion may have made Mao all the more impatient.

44. In July 1959 an authoritative article by Ya Han-chang in *Hung-ch'i* explained how religion would become extinct as class oppression was elimianted and as natural forces were brought under control. Immediately followed the sentence: "The policy of freedom of religious belief has been formulated on the basis of the aforementioned knowledge of the law of development of religion on the part of Marxism-Leninism." See *Hung-ch'i,* 14/50, p. 31 (Aug. 16, 1959), tr. in *ECMM,* 183:3. In other words, it was conceived as a policy of freedom for religious belief to disappear, and when the latter did not disappear, there was no longer any justification for the policy.

45. For a translation of the article "Tentative Views on the Relationship between Peasant Wars and Rebellion in China," *JMJP,* Oct. 17, 1960, see *China News Digest,* 31:77-84. It admitted that exploiting the masses' hopes for the next world could backfire if they began to think of getting equality

and happiness in *this* world. Reviewing the history of rebellions in China, the authors saw religion as a factor in six and as no factor in nine.

46. See Jen Chi-yü, "A Brief Treatise on the Thought of the Hua-yen School," *Che-hsüeh yen-chiu,* 1/61, pp. 13-31 (February 1961), tr. in URS 24:59-91. Jen writes that Avatamsaka doctrines were intended "to lay a theoretical foundation for the corrupt, reactionary, and cruel exploiting system of the T'ang" (*ibid.,* p. 88).

47. An example is the article on the contributions of Buddhism to Chinese culture in *KMJP,* June 12, 1962, tr. in *SCMP,* 2815:5-6. After describing the contributions the article ends: "Buddhist philosophy had a great influence on the people of China. There are, however, two different opinions on this question. One of them is that the reactionary rulers of the past used the passive and pessimistic philosophy of Buddhism as a tool to obtain their selfish ends. However, according to another opinion, there were also many outstanding personalities in history who carried on struggles against feudal despotism with the Buddhist spirit of equality and peace. Some progressive thinkers such as Li Cho-wu of the Ming dynasty and T'an Ssu-t'ung of the Ch'ing dynasty challenged feudal ethics with the anti-oppression thinking of Buddhism . . . and finally lost their lives." The last two sentences probably would not have been printed a year or so later.

In February 1963 Jen Chi-yü, who wrote the attack on the Avatamsaka school cited in note 46, published "The Diffusion and Development of Buddhist Philosophical Thinking in China from the Han through the T'ang." Not a word in it is hostile to Buddhism: it is an apolitical description of how Buddhist thought developed in terms of its Indian origins, the influence of Taoism, Chinese social conditions, etc., and how it had exercised a great influence, so that one had to understand it in order to understand the development of Chinese thought as a whole. See *KMJP,* Feb. 15, 1963.

48. Winfried Glüer, "Religion in the People's Republic of China: A Survey of the Official Chinese Press, 1964-1967" in *Ching Feng: Quarterly Notes on Christianity and Chinese Religion and Culture* (Hong Kong), 10.3:34-57 (1967). Cf. *China Notes,* 3.4:1-7 (October 1965) and *CNA,* 593:1-5. Those who wish to know more about the details of the debate should read the articles listed in Appendix H.

49. Yu Hsiang was a section chief in the Religious Affairs Bureau in Peking. He and Liu had already received the support of Chou Chien-jen, the borther of Lu Hsün and one of China's leading scientist-politicians, but not a Party member. In 1964 Chou had written an article stating that religion was part of superstition and that "we cannot wait for [superstition] to destroy itself." See *KMJP,* April 2, 1964, tr. in *SCMP,* 3326:15-17.

50. See *Hsin chien-she,* Vol. 10, No. 33, pp. 29-34 (Oct. 20, 1965). This foreword was summarized in *JMJP,* Dec. 7, 1965, tr. in *SCMP,* 3599:15-17. An equally crude attack on Buddhism had already been published at the local level in the Atheists Column of the Canton *Yang-ch'eng wan-pao,* March 8,

1965: "Of what use is Buddhism" by Wan Hui-tsao, whose main point was that Buddhism served to perpetuate human slavery.

Only in 1964 a Western observer had written that "unlike their Russian comrades . . . the Chinese Communists do not consider religion so dangerous a force that an intensive atheist propaganda struggle must be waged against it." See Rennsselaer W. Lee III, "General Aspects of Chinese Communist Religious Policy, with Soviet Comparisons," *China Quarterly* 19:163 (July-September 1964). This article illustrates well the magnitude of the reversal of religious policy that took place in China between 1963 and 1965.

51. Chi Hsien-lin's "Problems Regarding the Historical Origins of Primitive Buddhism," *Li-shih yen-chiu* 3/65, pp. 78-83, echoed many of the interpretations favorable to Buddhism that had appeared in *HTFH,* 3/60, pp. 28-30 (March 1960). He said, for example, that the pessimism of Buddhism reflected the deplorable condition of the masses. Its class connections had been mainly with the Vaisya caste of farmers and merchants. The Buddha had been able to understand the religious needs of the masses because he came from the same race.

Two exceptions might be seen to my statement that after December 1965 no more voices were raised sympathetic to Buddhism. One is Feng Yu-lan's article "More on Some Problems Relating To Research in the History of Chinese Philosophy," published in *Hsin chien-she,* Feb. 20, 1966, in which Feng tried to show that some Buddhist philosophers were materialists and that Buddhist idealism provided a stimulus for the development of materialist ideas (*SCMM,* 541:13-20). However, by this time the publication of Feng's articles were evidence not so much of the acceptability of his views as of the regime's desire to give him more rope on which to hang himself.

Chung-kuo ch'ing-nien, 1/66, tr. in *SCMM,* 513:11-12, urged YCL members to be patient in persuading older people to give up superstitious practices and not to follow the "simple methods" of the child who tore up a pack of paper money that his mother was going to burn for the dead. It was conservatism like this that caused the Youth League to be inactivated during the Cultural Revolution.

52. *Ganjin wājo,* p. 18. In 1964 another Japanese delegation was told that they were the first foreigners since Liberation to visit the T'ien-lung Shan caves. See Shigenoi Satoru, "Chūgoku nikki sho," *Ōtani Daigaku shigaku,* vol. 11, p. 12 (November 1965).

53. When Ngawang Jaltso's death was announced two years earlier, he had been identified as an NPC deputy and a member of the CPPCC Standing Committee, but not as a vice-president of the CBA.

54. In August 1967 the Chinese embassy in Colombo had protested against Ceylon's intercourse with Taiwan, including the permission for "Chiang bandit gang elements to participate in . . . the World Mahasangha Conference": see *SCMP,* 4011:38. When the tenth WFB conference was finally held in May 1972, the Sinhalese hosts saw to it that no one from Taiwan was invited and again made serious efforts to have a delegation come

from Peking. The fact that none came could be interpreted to mean that the Communist leadership had definitely decided against any further use of Buddhism in people's diplomacy; or it could be seen as merely another effect of the policy of "suspension" (see p. 362).

55. The following is based on information collected from foreigners who visited China in July-December 1971. The Liu-jung Ssu, Canton, had been converted into a wool-processing plant and a second-hand shop selling old clothes, radios, tools, bicycle parts, and the like. All images and religious decoration had been removed. They had also been removed at the Ling-yen Ssu, Soochow, which had become a public park. On the other hand, at the Chieh-chuang Ssu, Soochow, and the Ling-yin Ssu, Hangchow, images, incense burners, and decoration remained in place, as in a museum. The Kuang-chi Ssu, Peking, was closed to the public and occupied by soldiers. Some other monasteries were closed, apparently unused, but kept in good repair: the Yung-ho Kung and Fa-yüan Ssu, Peking, and the Yü-fo Ssu, Shanghai.

No worship or burning incense was seen at any of these temples (or elsewhere in China). No monks were seen either—and in most cases local people said that there were no longer any monks in residence. (At the Yü-fo Ssu, Shanghai, the residence of monks was denied to one visitor, affirmed to another.) In most cases the sign bearing the name of the monastery had been removed. In all cases posters with political slogans were conspicuous. One visitor was told that the Chinese Buddhist Seminary had been moved into the Institute for Islamic Studies, but that teachers and students were still off working on farms.

Over all, the picture seemed to be that some Buddhist institutions continued to be in a state of "suspension" but that many had already been converted to non-religious uses, perhaps irrevocably.

56. Evidence of the Mongolian intention to continue if not to expand its use of Buddhism may be seen in the Asian Buddhists Meeting held in Ulan Bator, June 11-13, 1970. It was attended by about fifty representatives from ten Buddhist countries (Mongolia, USSR, North Vietnam, South Vietnam, Nepal, India, Ceylon, Singapore, Malaysia, and Japan—but not by anyone from China). Although the Mongolian Buddhist Center issued the invitations and played host, the conference obviously had the backing of the Soviet as well as the Mongolian governments. The delegates entered Mongolia from the Soviet Union and visited the Soviet Buddhist headquarters near Ulan-Ude afterwards. Officials of both countries were solicitous in making the expense-free tour as pleasant and instructive as possible. For example, in Ulan Bator, where some delegates noted the small size and advanced age of the sangha, they were told that a seminary was to be opened in September 1970 at which the thirty young lamas enrolled would take a six-year course covering Buddhist philosophy and ritual, the Mongolian Constitution, Sanskrit, English, and Russian (or Mongolian in the case of the lamas who came to study there from the Soviet Union).

The immediate purpose of the conference, however, was not to show off the prosperity of Buddhism in Russia and Mongolia, but to protest the activities of the "imperialists" in Vietnam. Two resolutions were passed condemning the United States and calling for its acceptance of the National Liberation Front's ten-point formula. The resolutions were described as unanimous, which was technically correct, since the delegates from Japan, Malaysia, and Singapore had absented themselves from the session that passed them. Thus the meeting was a kind of replay of the Eleven-Nation Conference held in Peking at the end of October 1963. In one respect, however, it was more successful: it set up a permanent "Committee for Promoting the Coöperation of Asian Buddhists for Peace" with the following officers: president, S. Gombojav (the Mongolian Hambo Lama or hierarch); vice-presidents, Venerable Jinaratana (Maha Bodhi Society, Calcutta) and Venerable M. Sumanatissa (Ceylon); secretary general, Ch. Jugder. The latter was the Mongolian counterpart of Chao P'u-ch'u in China and S. D. Dylykov in the Soviet Union. Like Dylykov he was an academician, whose approach to Buddhism was probably not devotional. As one delegate wrote, "At present the general interest of Soviet Buddhist scholars lies in the field of archaeological and bibliographical researches." See Bandō Shōjun, "Travels in Mongolia," *Eastern Buddhist* (new series), 3.2:127 (October 1970). For other materials on this little known conference, see *ibid.*, pp. 119-126, and *World Buddhism* 18.12:325 (July 1970).

The Soviet intention to make further use of Buddhism in people's diplomacy became dramatically clear with the publication of the third edition of the *Great Soviet Encyclopedia* in 1971—clear if we compare it with the earlier editions. The first (1927) was hostile to Buddhism, but not inordinately so, considering the Marxist viewpoint from which it was written. For example: "One can say without exaggeration that the whole philosophical edifice of Buddhist doctrine was based on the ideology of the merchant class"; "Every monk was an instrument used to extract the fuse and obscure the issues of class struggle"—and so on. On the other hand, Buddhism got good marks for being "without the slightest theistic ingredient and, in some respects, despite its peculiar idealism, it is even very materialistically oriented . . . The doctrine of dependent origination of the dharmas resembles the theory of evolution with its dialectical characteristics." When it came to the Mahayana, the article was almost enthusiastic. "Cold and complacent *metta* was transformed into a burning love for all human beings and non-resistance to evil was replaced by heroic self-sacrifice."

In contrast, the second edition in 1951 had not one kind word. It took as "irrefutably proven" that Sakyamuni was merely a "myth" invented by the exploiting class to tighten its grip on the exploited. (The 1927 edition had not denied the existence of the Buddha; it merely suggested that Buddhism was "a rich collective creation that perhaps has little to do with the doctrine of the historical Gautama.") Now, far from being "materialistically oriented,"

Buddhism was called "the most backward mysticism. The materialist doctrines of ancient India originated in the struggle *against* the Buddhists" (italics added). "The ideologists of the exploiting class have tried to dress up Buddhism. They have declared it to be an 'atheistic religion' or a 'purely philosophical system.' In the colonialist era, bourgeois manipulators attempted to utilize Buddhism in the service of a perfidious fideism. Not only did they support Buddhism in the colonial and dependent areas of the East, but they propagated it even in Europe and America. [So much for the Maha Bodhi Society!] Soviet scholarship alone has succeeded in laying bare the roots, the historical path, and the reactionary nature of Buddhism and in pointing out its true role in the exploitation of the working masses." Reincarnation, for example, was "invented to stifle the protests of the workers." The place in Buddhism of figures like Sakyamuni, Maitreya, and Amitabha showed "the untenability of the thesis of bourgeois scholars that Buddhism is atheistic." As if all this were not enough of a slap in the face of Buddhist intellectuals in Ceylon and Burma (who lay stress on the atheistic character of Buddhism), the article went on to say that "after the Second World War the Anglo-American imperialists enlisted the reactionary clique of the Buddhist church to serve the goals of their aggressive policies in the East Asia. The mystical idealism of Buddhist doctrines is being used by the Anglo-American philosophical lackeys of imperialism in the struggle against materialism and for the 'reinforcement' and 'underpinning' of an idealism that represents the most varied and sinister ideological manipulations." Lest any uncertainty be left about what this meant inside Russia, the article declared that "a predominant majority of the followers of Buddhism in the Soviet Union have liberated themselves from their religious prejudices."

Fortunately for the Soviet government, this authoritative statement of its attitude towards Buddhism, which remained official from 1951 to 1971, was published only in the Russian language and hence (one assumes) escaped the notice of men like Dr. G. P. Malalasekera who made a special point of looking into the condition of Buddhism when he was Ceylon's ambassador to Moscow and wrote in 1960, "It may be said with justice that in that country [the Soviet Union] Buddhism is a living force" (see Chapter VI, note 59).

Soviet representatives were permitted to join the WFB in 1956, and since then they have been welcomed at all world Buddhist conferences. Almost every year Southeast Asian Buddhists have toured the Soviet Union to see the bright future of Buddhism there. In 1965 German translations of both the 1927 and 1951 articles were printed in *Ostprobleme,* no. 14/15, pp. 448-458 (July 30, 1965); and in May 1970 a few pungent excerpts came out in *World Buddhism.* It is not surprising, then, that when the third edition of the encyclopedia began to appear the following year, it included a wholly new article on Buddhism—one that could be posted on the main street of Kandy without raising an eyebrow. "The Indian prince Siddhartha Gautama," it began, "is considered the founder of Buddhism." It went on to describe in a neutral tone and at considerable length the doctrines and history of Buddhism, which was characterized as individualistic and asocial, so that it had stood aside from struggles for social and political reform. Nonetheless "in many parts of Asia . . . Buddhist religious leadership is participating in social and political life. Thus in South Vietnam Buddhists are included in the struggle for national liberation . . ." In the race to win Buddhist friends abroad the Chinese appeared at least to have been left far behind.

I am indebted to Daniel T. Orlovsky for a partial translation of the article in the third edition.

XII. THE FUTURE OF BUDDHISM IN CHINA

1. See, for example, Wilfred Cantwell Smith, *The Meaning and End of Religion* (New York, Mentor, 1964), Chapters II and V.

2. See Welch, *Revival,* pp. 203-206. Cf. Chapter VIII at note 104.

3. "Obliged to submit to natural forces, and capable of using only simple tools, primitive man could not explain the surrounding phenomena and hence sought help from spirits. This is the origin of religion and idealism." See Mao's 1938 essay, *Dialectical Materialism,* tr. by Stuart Schram, *The Political Thought of Mao Tse-tung,* rev. ed. (New York, 1969), p. 184.

4. "So long as classes exist there will be as many doctrines as there are classes . . . the Buddhists [have their] Buddhism." See Mao's 1940 "On New Democracy," tr. in *Selected Works* II, p. 361. I have not found a passage in which Mao states that religion was deliberately created by the exploiting classes as a tool of oppression (a view that was often voiced during the debate on religion).

5. See Mao, "On the Correct Handling of Contradictions among the People", NCNA English, June 18, 1957, in *CB,* 458:4. Other translations have "problems relative to the spiritual world" instead of "distinctions of right and wrong."

Engels, after scoffing at the Blanquist attempt to use a decree to "obliterate God," stated: "First, a flood of decrees can be issued, but how futile they are. Second, persecution is the best way to boost an unpopular belief." He added that such a method of prohibiting religion meant rendering a service to God. This passage was quoted by Chang Chih-i in *Che-hsüeh yen-chiu,* 1/58, tr. in *CB,* 510:16. Similar passages from the writings of Lenin are quoted in *SCMP,* 3048:9. In the 1919 program of the CPSU he called for anti-religious propaganda but added that "at the same time it is necessary carefully to avoid giving such offense to the religious sentiments of believers as only leads to the strengthening of religious fanaticism." Under certain circumstances even anti-religious propaganda would, Lenin wrote, "only be playing into the hands of the church and the priests." See V. I. Lenin, *Religion* (New York, Little Lenin Library, Vol. VII, 1933), pp. 6, 16.

At the start of the debate on religion, Ya Han-chang was essentially echoing Mao's 1957 speech when he wrote: "Using administrative orders to compel people to discard belief in gods will inevitably drive religion underground . . . It will only strengthen the faith of the believers and religious followers, who will then become more unwilling than ever to give up their beliefs . . . If we limit ourselves to the use of mass media—books, newspapers, magazines, academic forums, radio broadcasts, and stage plays—to propagate atheism, then anyone can make his own choice as to whether or not he wants to read, see, or hear them." The conclusion he drew from this was that, since people had free choice, the quality of atheist propaganda had to be improved if it was to succeed. See *JMJP,* October 30, 1962, tr. in *SCMP,* 2862:4 (slightly altered).

6. See Chapter I at note 5.

7. For example *Modern Buddhism* told its readers in 1951 that "freedom of religious belief does cover religious ceremonies." See *HTFH,* 9/51, p. 22. Some Buddhists hoped to benefit from the freedom of speech, assembly, procession, and demonstration, guaranteed by Article 87, which they hoped would eventually result in the toleration of religious activities *outside* their temples.

8. A monk in Kaifeng said: "Article 88 specifically provides that citizens have freedom of religious belief. I never get tired of reading it, even after a hundred times. I keep gazing at every word and cannot bear to put it down." See *HTFH,* 8/54, p. 28. Buddhists in Kweichow called Article 88 " a weapon that assures religious believers of being able to believe and to *practice* their religion. Prompted by what we feel as Buddhists, we will support our Constitution to our last breath—like the Three Jewels in which we take Refuge." See *HTFH,* 9/54, p. 30 (italics added). Study and enthusiasm in many other localities is reported in these and the adjacent pages.

9. See Chapter I, note 69. In general, what the policy of religious belief really meant has to be deduced from events and reading between the lines. For example Chang Chih-i warned that Buddhists were not permitted to "utilize religious belief to conduct activities jeopardizing the socialist cause" (*CB,* 510:17). Compare Sheng-ch'üan's statement the next year: "We religious followers must not read this sentence [Article 88] in isolation . . . People who have not done a good job of studying the Constitution and the whole of our policies and laws are apt to talk up freedom of religious belief and forget the Constitution's basic spirit." See *HTFH,* 10/59, p. 22. In the same issue Shirob reminded readers that religious belief belonged in the category of thinking and that religious practice was something for monks to carry on "in the time left over from labor." See *HTFH,* 10/59, p. 12.

10. See Wu Yao-tsung's speech to the CPPCC on March 8, 1957, in *JMJP,* March 9, 1957, tr. in *CB,* 449:3. The number of pamphlets is mentioned in *CB,* 449:8. Wu Yao-tsung's complaint seems to have been taken seriously.

According to one source, the Religious Affairs Bureau in Peking immediately sent out specialists to make a detailed investigation; and issued an order for local cadres to stop vilifying religion as "an opiate of the masses": see *Hōchū Nihon Bukkyō,* p. 17.

11. A delegation from the Religious Affairs Bureau, headed by Hsiao Hsien-fa, visited the Soviet Union, East Germany, Czechoslovakia, and Hungary. See NCNA, July 25, 1958, in *SCMP,* 1822:49.

12. See *JMJP,* Sept. 4, 1958, tr. in *SCMP,* 1859:10 and cf. *JMJP,* Dec. 10, 1958, and FBIS Dec. 8, 1959, BBB8.

13. *HTFH,* 6/62, p. 41 (December 1962). This report emphasized the continuation of religious practice and the solemn services held on P'u-t'o Shan during Buddhist festivals.

14. See *HTFH,* 6/62, pp. 39-41 (December 1962). Cf. 3/63, pp. 48-49 (June 1963).

15. On the increase in worship see Chapter IX at notes 9, 17-19. On the increase in attention to Buddhist culture, see the following articles in NCNA English for 1961 (each followed by an *SCMP* reference): April 1 (2471:16); May 6 (2494:23); May 15 (2500:23); June 9 (2517:24); June 30 (2531:33); Aug. 7 (2557:19); Aug. 9 (2558:22); Aug. 15 (2562:17); Oct. 21 (2562:17); Dec. 10 (2640:18). For 1962 July 8 (2777:18); March 31 (2593:9). See also *JMJP,* July 18, 1961 (woodblock printing in the T'ang); July 23, 1961 (Lung-tsang Tripitaka); *KMJP,* June 12, 1962, in *SCMP,* 2815:5-6; *China Reconstructs,* 1/62, pp. 20-27; 7/62, pp. 18-23, 10/62, pp. 12-13; 12/62, pp. 18-23; 5/63, pp. 23-31; *China Pictorial,* 8/62, pp. 18-19. Already in 1959 *Modern Buddhism* was publishing a series of articles entitled "Questions and Answers on What Everyone Should Know about Buddhism," which were at many points a reassertion of tradition: only by entering the sangha could one become an arahat; the Buddha had urged people to become monks; in primitive Buddhism monks had not taken part in production (this was a "fine development in China"); reaching decisions by the silent assent of all the monks in the area was "the oldest form of public meeting in the world and can be called one of Buddhism's important inventions." See *HTFH,* 8/69, pp. 7-16.

16. Nitchū Yu-kō, p. 213.

17. In 1913 Li Ta-chao, disillusioned by the turn of political events, appears "to have considered retreating into the Buddhist 'Pure Land' sect . . . In his brief autobiographical sketch he noted, 'During my stay in Peking [in the summer of 1913] I envied the life of a pure society in a fit of misanthropic thought. In the nick of time my friend[s] wanted me to come to Tokyo to continue our studying with them." See Maurice Meisner, *Li Ta-chao and the Origins of Chinese Marxism* (Cambridge, Mass., Harvard University Press, 1967), pp. 14-15. Meisner considers that Li's influential theory of national rebirth (China went through a continuous dynastic cycle of birth and death)

came mainly from Emerson, but also from Chuang-tzu and the Buddhist doctrine of reincarnation. (*Ibid.*, p. 28).

Ch'ü Ch'iu-pai wrote of himself about 1917, when he was enrolled in the Russian Language College: "A bright path gradually revealed itself out of my studies in Buddhism: I believed that the world was to be saved through the practice of Bodhisattvahood and that everything was impermanent, including the social system. But such a philosophy could not hold long when the May 4 Movement sucked me in like a whirlpool." See *Journey to the Land of Hunger*, tr. by T. A. Hsia, *China Quarterly*, 25:186-187.

Lu Hsün once made a donation to the Chin-ling Scriptural Press to support the printing of the *Sutra of One Hundred Parables* (*Pai-yü ching*?): see Chao, *Buddhism in China*, p. 24. Lu Hsün's story "Morning Flowers Collected in Evening" deals with his childhood reminiscences, especially of local superstitions, which he rejects but for which he feels nostalgia.

18. In October 1963, according to one of the assembled Buddhist delegates from eleven nations, Chou said at a reception for them that there was no conflict between Marxism-Leninism and Buddhism because both Communists and Buddhists loved their great country, China, and got along very well with each other. "For example, my mother was a Buddhist, but I am a Communist." According to another delegate he said that both his parents were Buddhists. See *Ganjin wajō*, pp. 26-27, 30. For Ch'en Yi's reference to his mother's continuing Buddhist devotions, see *Chūgai nippō*, Oct. 12, 1957.

19. See David Roy, *Kuo Mo-jo: The Early Years* (Cambridge, Mass., Harvard University Press, 1971), pp. 58, 60.

20. See Chapter VII, n. 64.

21. Edgar Snow, *Red Star over China* (New York, Grove Press, 1961), pp. 128-129.

22. Robert Payne, *Mao Tse-tung* (New York, 1950), pp. 25-26.

23. *Ibid.*, pp. 31-32. Han Yü's famous essay recommended that the emperor, instead of welcoming the holy relic to the palace, should have the filthy thing thrown away or burned, since the Buddha was a barbarian and his doctrines had only brought disaster to those who believed them. See Ch'en, *Buddhism in China*, pp. 225-226.

24. Snow, *Red Star*, p. 131.

25. Schram, *Political Thought*, p. 156. During a walking trip through Hunan in the summer of 1917 Mao visited a large Buddhist monastery, talked philosophy with the abbot, and learned something about monastic life and organization. He does not seem to have received a bad impression. See Siao Yu, *Mao Tse-tung and I Were Beggars* (London, Hutchinson, 1961), pp. 107-119.

26. See Chapter I at notes 3-5. It was in the same essay that Mao wrote: "The gods and goddesses are indeed pitiful; worshiped for hundreds of years,

they have not knocked down for you [the peasants of Hunan] a single local bully or one of the bad gentry." See Mao, *Selected Works,* I, 48.

27. Schram, *Political Thought,* p. 188. It was in this essay that Mao attributed the origin of religion to primitive man's need to explain and control the natural forces around him (p. 184).

28. For example, he twice used the phrase "lay down the butcher's knife and become a buddha" (*Selected Works,* I, 280, and II, 428). He was reported to have told Anna Louise Strong that "thanks to the Cultural Revolution I did not become a buddha," that is, an idol to be put up on a shelf and then ignored: see *Shūkan posuto* (Tokyo), April 1, 1971, p. 86. In 1971 he told Edgar Snow that he was not a complicated man, but really very simple. He was, he said, only a lone monk walking through the world with a leaky umbrella: see *Life* 70.16:48 (April 30, 1971).

An interesting study could be made of the fairly widespread use by the Chinese Communists of metaphors from religion, mythology, and folklore, for example "meetings of the immortals," "cow-headed monsters," "Chou Yang, the number 1 demon in the kingdom of hell," "Eisenhower, the god of plague," etc. Mao's love of earthy language led him to use figures of speech that were, in Marxist terms, meaningless, e.g., "Chiang Kai-shek has lost his soul, he is merely a corpse."

29. The Dalai Lama, *My Land and My People* (London, 1962), pp. 101-102.

30. See Chapter VII at notes 74, 79.

31. Except in figures of speech, as pointed out in note 28. No direct quotes are available from his discussions of religion with Edgar Snow. For a casual, but ill-informed reference to the Tripitaka, see *CB,* 891:42.

32. Mackerras and Hunter, p. 83. Cf. Katsumata, p. 337.

33. See J. J. M. DeGroot, *Sectarianism and Religious Persecution in China* (Amsterdam, 1903), I, 108, 110, 115. On p. 114 he cites a regulation placing wandering monks under the jurisdiction of sangha officials. On pp. 139-140 he quotes a law prescribing banishment to the frontiers for the heads of Buddhist and Taoist monasteries who, without inquiring about their past, offered hospitality to ten or more members of heterodox Taoist sects—exactly the same people against whom Buddhist monks were so often warned after 1949.

34. On the Ch'ing handling of Buddhism, see Welch, *Revival,* pp. 132-137. There was nothing new in Ch'ing efforts to control and limit the sangha. Already under the T'ang dynasty, Hsuan-tsung had prohibited private construction of new temples, limited temple landholdings, forbidden monks and nuns to wander about the countryside preaching and selling scriptures, and instituted a system of examining applicants and issuing ordination certificates that was intended to restrict entry into the sangha. However, whereas his and most other dynasties had been ready to tolerate a sangha with a hundred thousand members or more, the goal of the Communist regime seems to have

been a few hundred—just enough to greet foreign Buddhist visitors and to belie any claim that freedom of religious belief, as guaranteed by the Constitution, was being violated.

35. *Ta-Ch'ing lü-li hsin-tseng t'ung-tsuan chi-ch'eng* (Newly enlarged comprehensive edition of the Ch'ing legal code; Shao-chou, 1898), 8:24. On the use of this phrase after 1949, see Chapter IV, notes 30, 38.

36. For information on the enforcement of the laws on the sangha under the late Ch'ing, see Welch, *Revival,* pp. 132-137, 324-325.

37. On the government's handling of Buddhism during the Republican period, see Welch, *Practice,* pp. 137-156.

38. On May 12, 1931, the National People's Convention, meeting in Nanking, passed the Provisional Constitution of the period of political tutelage. The section on "Rights and Duties of the People" did not include a clause on freedom of religion. In the draft of the permanent constitution, released March 8, 1934, between the clauses on privacy of correspondence and freedom of assembly and association, which were already in the tutelage constitution, a new clause (Article 15) had been added: "All persons shall have freedom of religious belief: such freedom shall not be restricted except in accordance with the law." See *The China Year Book, 1934* (Shanghai, 1934), pp. 466-467, 471.

39. On confiscation, see Chapter II, note 130. As to conscription, monks in Taiwan now have to do regular military service just as on the Mainland and in Japan. The Buddhist Association there has made no effort to get them assigned to ambulance work, as it did during the Sino-Japanese War. In 1967 its head received a citation for the services he had rendered to the armed forces: see *P'u-t'i shu*, 183:36 (February 1968).

As to the prohibition of religious activities outside temple premises, according to a 1950 regulation of the Taiwan Provincial Police Bureau, temples were allowed to conduct rites and propagate the doctrine inside temple premises without interference, and "inside" was explained as including the wide yard in front of the temple. Meetings held outside the premises to propagate the doctrine required permission (as on the Mainland) from the local authorities or the police. See *Chüeh-shih,* 407:1 (Sept. 1, 1968).

There is one more parallel that is beginning, perhaps, to be important. When land reform dispossessed the large landowning monasteries of Taiwan in 1953—the same year that reform was completed on the Mainland—the trend for monks to become self-sufficient through labor, which had started under the Nationalists in the 1930's, resumed. In 1968 three monasteries near Kaohsiung in southern Taiwan established a "religious affairs committee" (*tsung-wu wei-yuan-hui*) to undertake "educational, cultural, and charitable activities . . . since these offer the only safe haven for the future of Buddhism." In one of the three monasteries a production team was set up "to grow various kinds of trees and fruit and create a new life of farming Ch'an." This phrase, "farming Ch'an," is the same one repeatedly invoked on the

Mainland to justify monks participating in labor. See *Chüeh-shih,* 416:1, 4 (Dec. 1, 1968).

40. This is similar to the idea expressed by a Tendai priest after he visited the Kuo-ch'ing Ssu in 1965: "The people's commune reflects the standpoint of the Tendai's *samatha vipasyanā* (*chih-kuan*), samadhi through no special practice or meditation (life itself being practice and meditation)." See Mibu Shōjun, "Chūgoku Tendai-san," 9/65, 33.

41. Schram, *Political Thought,* pp. 252-253.

42. This point was made by Chü-tsan in 1950 when he addressed the first study class in Peking. Asked about the future of Buddhism, he answered: "If Buddhism is not the Truth, then there is no point in asking about its future. But if Buddhism is the Truth, the Truth cannot be struck down, and so there is still no point in asking about its future." See *HTFH,* 10/50, p. 23.

43. Schuyler Camman writes that "when (the Chinese) finally expelled the Mongols, together with most of the foreigners whom the latter had in their employ, these [annual festivals] took on a special patriotic significance; in celebrating them the Ming Chinese felt that they were reinforcing their national culture." See A. F. Wright, ed. *Studies in Chinese Thought,* (Chicago, Chicago University Press, 1953), p. 219. Such a revival of national culture ought logically to take place in China some day, but at present it is hard to see when or how.

44. K. S. S. Ch'en, in discussing the closing of monasteries, notes that Buddhists and Taoists have been accustomed to religious cultivation in private and wonders "if it is not possible that in the future the 'home congregation' will be the most widespread form of religious life." He points out that in Christian circles, when churches were closed down, "underground" congregations still existed. (See the original version of his Ditchley Conference Paper—p. 29—later printed in *China Quarterly,* 22:14-30 [April-June 1965].)

The transformation of the underground Christian church in Japan illustrates the difficulty, I think, of maintaining a tradition without temples, clergy, or publications. Elsewhere, Ch'en points out that in India, when the last monasteries were finally destroyed, Buddhism was wiped out (*Buddhism in China,* p. 400). In 1954 *Modern Buddhism* told a worried reader that religion would cease to exist in China only if there were no more believers, and so the question of the future of religion would be freely decided by the believers themselves (*HTFH,* 7/54, p. 24).

45. See Carl G. Jung, *Man and His Symbols* (London, Aldus Books in association with W. H. Allen, 1964), p. 93. The next two paragraphs are worth quoting here.

> Our times have demonstrated what it means for the gates of the underworld to be opened. Things whose enormity nobody could have imagined in the idyllic harmlessness of the first decade of our century have happened and have turned our world upside down. Ever since, the world has remained in a state of schizophrenia. Not only has civilized Germany

> disgorged its terrible primitivity, but Russia is also ruled by it, and Africa has been set on fire. No wonder that the Western world feels uneasy.
>
> Modern man does not understand how much his "rationalism" (which has destroyed his capacity to respond to numinous symbols and ideas) has put him at the mercy of the psychic "underworld." He has freed himself from "superstition" (or so he believes), but in the process he has lost his spiritual values to a positively dangerous degree. His moral and spiritual tradition has disintegrated, and he is now paying the price for this break-up in world-wide disorientation and dissociation.

These were Jung's last words on an important theme.

APPENDIX A

1. The original Chinese text appeared in *HTFH,* 9/50, pp. 22-25; 10/50, pp. 20-24.

2. Chü-tsan came from a Kiangsu family and was born about 1909 (since he was twenty-three sui in 1931—see below). On his Kiangsu origin, see Hong Kong *Hsin-wan pao,* Jan. 10, 1963, which states that he spent many years in Japan studying Buddhism. He makes no mention of this in the present account of his life.

3. See Chapter X at notes 46-50.

4. T'ai-hsü was the leading reformer of the Republican period. See Welch, *Revival,* pp. 15-18, 28-33, 41-71, et passim.

5. One of the most famous anthologies, including poems from the third century B.C. to the sixth century A.D.

6. It was not uncommon for people to want to become Buddhist monks before they knew anything about Buddhist doctrine.

7. See Welch, *Revival,* pp. 110-114.

8. On Ou-yang and the Metaphysical Institute, see Welch, *Revival,* pp. 117-120.

9. On this seminary established by T'ai-hsü, see Welch, *Revival,* pp. 199, 318.

10. Yin-kuang was the leading exponent of Pure Land practice in the Republican period.

11. According to oral informants, Chü-tsan considered that the monasteries on Nan-yüeh were backward and set up the Buddhist Research Center in or near the Fo-yen Ssu to provide young monks with a more modern education. They flocked in, partly because they could sing, play tennis, and live more comfortably. This angered the elderly conservatives, one of whom, after losing a disciple to Chü-tsan, concealed a knife in his sleeve and went to kill him. Chü-tsan was forewarned and fled from the mountain. In Kweilin one of my informants told him about Ying-huang, a late Ming monk from Chekiang who had had to flee Nan-yüeh because his ideas were too progressive. Chü-tsan cried: "Exactly the same thing happened to me."

12. This untranslatable phrase refers to almost everything in Buddhism that is not purely religious: the system of administration, finances, training, personnel, and so on.

13. Several sources state that at this time Chü-tsan headed the Wa-lin Seminary in Wusih and divided his time between Wusih and Hangchow: see, for example, Hong Kong *Hsin-wan pao,* Jan. 10, 1963.

14. This is one of the few references to T'ai-hsü after 1949.

15. His flight to Hong Kong is all the more surprising because he had just told Wing-tsit Chan that the Communists would restrict temple land, suppress superstitious practices, reduce the number of people entering the sangha, make monks do productive labor, and serve the people. If that was all they did, then Chinese Buddhists would "welcome them with open arms." See Chan, *Religious Trends,* p. 92. Perhaps Chü-tsan feared they would do more than this. According to one report, his fears were soon quieted by reading Hewlett Johnson's *Soviet Russia since the War* (New York, Boni and Gaer, 1947), which was given him by "progressive friends." Presumably he had kept up his English since 1937.

16. Hung-i was a talented actor and artist who became a monk specializing in study of the rules of discipline. Hsü-yün and Chi-yün were eminent monks of the Ch'an sect.

17. Li Chi-shen, whom Chü-tsan had gotten to know in Kweilin, was already slated to receive a high post in the new regime. He was head of the Kuomintang Revolutionary Committee, which he had formed in Hong Kong in 1948 and of which Lü Chi-i was a central committee member.

18. Ch'iao Mu (Ch'iao Kuan-hua) was, like Chü-tsan, from Kiangsu and about the same age. Presumably they had met in Hong Kong, where Ch'iao headed the New China News Agency's South China Bureau 1946-49. He was now chief of the International News Bureau in the GAC Press Administration and was to play an important role as adviser to Chou En-lai on foreign missions. He was married to Chou's former aide, Kung P'eng.

19. This indicates that a new and probably shorter form was being planned.

20. Pu Hua-jen was active in relief and welfare work and a member of the second CPPCC National Committee. I cannot explain why he was at a meeting of the Religious Affairs Team of the first National Committee.

21. It is not clear who said this: presumably it was Ch'en Ch'i-yüan. I have also not confirmed that September 23 here refers to 1949, but Chü-tsan's report is dated September 26, 1950, and it seems unlikely that he was referring to an event that had taken place only three days earlier.

22. Hsieh Pang-ting was a CPPCC delegate representing the Chinese National Students' Federation.

23. The hosts were all Buddhists and all but two (Fang and Chou) were in the CPPCC (then or later). At least five of the guests were Buddhists (Yeh, Li

Ming-yang, Li Ken-yüan, Shirob Jaltso, and Sha Yung-ts'ang) and nine of them were in the CPPCC. The names of most of these men appear elsewhere in the book and can be found through the index.

APPENDIX C

1. *HTFH,* 11/50, p. 32.
2. *HTFH,* 6/53, p. 54.
3. See Chapter II, note 126.
4. *HTFH,* 3/52, p. 14.
5. Hong Kong *Ta-kung pao,* April 1, 1950.
6. *HTFH,* 2/54, p. 23.
7. Tsukamoto and Makita, p. 304.
8. Mibu, "Jinmin Chūgoku," p. 9.
9. In 1965 a Japanese visitor was told at the Ling-yin Ssu that Hangchow had over 360 monks and over 200 nuns, living in 200 temples. See Nitchū Yū-ko, p. 206.
10. Ch'en Hui-chu, *Chung-kuo hsien-kuang jih-chi* (Diary of China's present glories; Singapore, 1957), p. 39.
11. Nitchū Yu-kō, p. 206. An overseas Chinese monk who visited Ling-yin that year said that there were about ten monks there.
12. Makita Tairyō, *Chūgoku kinsei Bukkyōshi kenkyū* (Kyoto, 1957), pp. 254-255.
13. Letter from Mrs. F. R. Millican of June 12, 1929 (Pratt Collection, Williams College). Monks who lived there in the 1930's and 1940's reported that the population reached 500.
14. *HTFH,* 5/57, p. 19.
15. *HTFH,* 4/53, p. 10.
16. *HTFH,* 5/57, p. 24.
17. Welch, *Revival,* p. 289.
18. *HTFH,* 6/62, p. 41.
19. *Chüeh yu-ch'ing,* 13.2:20 (October 1952).
20. *HTFH,* 9/54, p. 29.
21. *Hochū Nihon,* pp. 13-15.
22. *HTFH,* 10/58, p. 33.
23. Mibu, "Jinmin Chūgoku," p. 8.
24. *HTFH,* 6/53, p. 40.
25. Tokiwa Daijō, *Shina Bukkyō shiseki kinen-shū* (Tokyo, 1931), p. 253. Residents from that period report that the number was maintained or increased until the Japanese invasion.
26. *HTFH,* 6/54, p. 30.
27. Hong Kong *Ta-kung pao,* April 15, 1957.
28. Raghu Vira entered this figure in his well-kept travel journal.

29. Amritananda, *Buddhist Activities,* p. 15.

30. The abbot told a British visitor in May 1960 that there were 15 residents: he told a British visitor in August that there were 17.

31. Nitchū Yu-kō, p. 54. An Australian visitor in 1965 was given the figure of 16; an overseas Chinese that year reported 2; and in 1966 another Australian visitor reported 5-6. At a showpiece monastery like this one ("the oldest monastery in China") many factors could distort the numbers reported. Pai-ma had been virtually in ruins before it was restored in 1934-36 under the patronage of Tai Chi-t'ao and the former CBA. The repairs made by the Loyang authorities in 1954 (*HTFH,* 1/55, p. 30) were renovation, not restoration.

32. Pratt Notebooks, Williams College Library, mention 40-45 monks at a monastery that is most probably the K'ai-fu Ssu.

33. *HTFH,* 3/54, p. 24. Cf. *Buddhists in the New China,* p. 139.

34. *HTFH,* 11/59, p. 28.

35. Alley, *Amongst Hills and Streams,* pp. 11-13. Cf. *Nagel's Guide,* p. 1151.

36. *HTFH,* 7/53, pp. 17-20.

37. *HTFH,* 5/57, p. 25.

38. *HTFH,* 11/58, p. 30.

39. See Welch, *Practice,* p. 425.

40. *Chüeh yu-ch'ing,* 13.2:19 (October 1952).

41. Prip-Moller, p. 356.

42. *Chüeh yu-ch'ing,* 12.5:20 (May 1951).

43. *HTFH,* 10/51, p. 26.

44. Makita Tairyō, "Gendai Chūgoku Bukkyō no seikatsu kihan," in *Bukkyō Daigaku kenkyū kiyō,* no. 35 (Oct. 23, 1958).

45. *Chüeh yu-ch'ing,* 13.2:20 (October 1952).

46. Amritananda, *Buddhist Activities in Socialist Countries,* p. 38.

47. Nitchū yu-kō, p. 58.

48. *Chüeh yu-ch'ing,* 13.2:20 (October 1952).

49. William C. Hunter, *Bits of Old China* (London, Paul Trench, 1885), pp. 166-176; Mrs. C. F. Gordon Cumming, *Wanderings in China* (Edinburg, 1888), p. 62. I include this figure as an example of the big drop that sometimes came *before* Liberation.

50. Hong Kong *Hsing-tao jih-pao,* Nov. 6, 1950.

51. *Ibid.,* Sept. 26, 1950.

52. *Chüeh yu-ch'ing,* 12.2:24 (October 1951).

53. Hong Kong *Ta-kung pao,* May 23, 1950.

54. *Chüeh yu-ch'ing,* 13.2:20 (October 1952).

55. *Ibid.,* 14.1:25 (January 1953).

56. *HTFH,* 8/58, p. 31.

57. *HTFH,* 11/58, p. 32.

58. Hong Kong *Ta-kung pao,* May 23, 1950; *Chüeh yu-ch'ing,* 12.10-12:32 (December 1951).

59. *Chüeh yu-ch'ing,* 13.2:20 (October 1952); 14.1:25 (January 1953).

60. *HTFH,* 6/53, p. 28.

61. *HTFH,* 5/57, p. 23.

62. *HTFH,* 11/50, p. 31.

63. *HTFH,* 6/53, p. 52: 263 of these were Chinese monks, the rest lamas and nuns.

64. *HTFH,* 5/57, p. 23.

65. *NCNA,* Aug. 17, 1962.

66. *HTFH,* 1/54, p. 30.

67. *HTFH,* 12/54, p. 29.

68. *Tsu-kuo* 65.8:29.

69. Hong Kong *Ta-kung pao,* Oct. 1, 1961. The dramatic increase in the population of this monastery is probably a good illustration of the policy of concentrating monks from temples that had been closed down. The Hsing-shan Ssu had been completely renovated in 1956 because of its importance in the history of Sino-Indian relations and was therefore a natural concentration point.

70. *Hochū Nihon,* pp. 8-9.

71. *Ganjin wajō,* p. 22.

72. Nitchū yu-kō, p. 52.

73. *HTFH,* 1/51, pp. 34-35.

74. *HTFH,* 6/53, p. 49.

75. *Chüeh yu-ch'ing,* 12.3:24 (March 1951).

76. *HTFH,* 6/53, p. 49.

77. *HTFH,* 6/53, p. 50.

78. Prip-Møller, "Buddhist Meditation Ritual," *Chinese Recorder,* 66.12: 714 (December 1935).

79. *HTFH,* 6/53, p. 49.

80. *HTFH,* 4/51, p. 35. The date for this figure of "over 1,000" is February 22, 1951; this is significant because in winter the population was usually much less at Omei than in summer. In the 1940's the winter population was reported to be 4,000 by a monk who lived there, but who was not a reliable source. The figure of "over 1,000" appears to be directly contradicted by a statement that Omei Shan had 300 monks (plus some nuns) just after Liberation. Several dozen of them soon joined the army. See *HTFH,* 8/51, p. 23.

81. *HTFH,* 6/53, p. 56.

82. *Ssu-ch'uan jih-pao,* Feb. 24, 1955.

83. *HTFH,* 5/57, p. 16.

84. *Chüeh yu-ch'ing,* 12.1:24 (January 1951), which states that within a year the number of monks was reduced from about 200 to 63 "because of the prevailing circumstances." This was "the foremost monastery in Yün-

nan," restored by Hsü-yün in 1922. He changed its name from Hua-t'ing Ssu to Yün-ch'i Ssu, but the earlier name was resumed under the Communists.

85. *HTFH,* 6/53, p. 51.

86. Welch, *Practice,* p. 414. (In the 1967 edition of *Practice* the cities in this table were printed out of order. Tsingtao should be last, not second.)

87. *HTFH,* 3/54, p. 27. This is not stated to be the total of the sangha in Peking at this time, but the total of those who took part in study of the General Line. It would have been natural to claim that nearly everyone did.

88. *NCNA,* June 8, 1961. This was the total number of the sangha who saw off the tooth relic at Peking airport. Again, this probably included all the monks and nuns who could be trucked there from the temples of the capital.

89. Amritananda, *Buddhist Activities,* p. 16.

90. This is what I was told by a monk then resident in the monastery. A European diplomat was given the same figure when he visited it in 1962.

91. This figure was given to a European teacher then resident in Peking.

92. Hong Kong *Hsin-wan pao,* Jan. 30 and May 24, 1965. The figure of 300-500 "usually in residence" is higher than what was remembered by residents of Peking who used to visit the temple.

93. Mrs. C. F. Gordon Cumming, *Wanderings in China,* p. 392.

94. Peter Schmid, *The New Face of China,* pp. 56-57. Bapat and Fernand Gigon were given the same figures in 1956. Schmid's figure of 300 "before Liberation" fits in with the recollection of Peking residents.

95. Amritananda, *Buddhist Activities,* p. 22.

96. Shigenoi, p. 6.

97. Welch, *Practice,* p. 414.

98. *HTFH,* 6/53, p. 36.

99. Alfred Kiang, p. 173, which also mentions 2,000 at the time of Liberation.

100. An Indian visitor was given the figure of 2,400 monks and 800 nuns.

101. *HTFH,* 4/57, p. 11. The big fluctuation in the monastic population of Shanghai fits in with the fact that some monks moved to Shanghai in order to avoid labor or difficulties at their own monasteries in other areas.

102. Bapat, "A Glimpse," p. 391. In 1955 the same figure had been given to another Indian visitor.

103. Shigenoi, p. 5.

APPENDIX E

1. In retrospect I think it was because he realized that his failure at the conference would jeopardize the survival of the Chinese Buddhist Association—and here was one of the overseas Chinese—a Chinese, mind you—who had helped to cause the failure.

2. This was the author.

3. This was the author, whom the chief delegate from H asked to act in his place and so informed U Chan Htoon. The a directed by the remaining members of the Hong Kong deleg: against the expulsion of the Taiwan Regional Center).

Bibliography

The Agrarian Reform Law of the People's Republic of China and Other Relevant Documents. 4th ed. Peking, 1953; 85 pp.

Alley, Rewi. *Amongst Hills and Streams of Hunan in the Fall of 1962.* Peking, 1963; 130 pp.

Amritananda. *Buddhist Activities in Socialist Countries.* Peking, 1961; 89 pp.

Bapat, P. V. "A Glimpse of Buddhist China Today," *Maha Bodhi* 64.8:388–392 (August 1956).

BBC, *Summary of World Broadcasts,* London, 1960–

Biographical Dictionary of Republican China. Howard L. Boorman, ed. New York, Columbia University Press, 1967–

The Buddha Tooth Relic in China. Chinese Buddhist Association, comp. and pub. Peking, 1961; 10 pp. + plates.

Buddhism in China. Chinese Buddhist Association, comp. Peking, Nationalities Publishing House, 1955; consists of 24 loose plates with captions.

Buddhism in China, see Chao P'u-ch'u.

Buddhism in China, see Ch'en, Kenneth K. S.

Buddhism in China, see Yang I-fan.

Buddhists in China. Chinese Buddhist Association, comp. Peking, Nationalities Publishing House, 1956; 177 pp.

Buddhists in New China. Chinese Buddhist Association, comp. Peking, Nationalities Publishing House, 1956; 189 pp.

Bush, Richard C., Jr. *Religion in Communist China.* Nashville, Abingdon Press, 1970; 432 pp.

Canton: The City, Economy, and March toward Socialism. Canton Branch of the Chinese People's Association for Foreign Cultural Relations. Canton, Kuang-chou Library Press, 1959, 122 pp., tr. in *JPRS,* 16369.

Chan Wing-tsit. *Religious Trends in Modern China.* New York, Columbia University Press, 1953; 327 pp.

Chao Kuo-chün. *Agrarian Policy of the Chinese Communist Party, 1921-1959.* New Delhi, Asia Publishing House, 1960; 399 pp.

Chao P'u-ch'u. *Buddhism in China.* Peking, 1957; 56 pp. Also 2nd ed., Peking, 1960; 52 pp.

Che-hsüeh yen-chiu 哲學研究 (Philosophical studies). Peking, 1955–

Chen, C. S., ed., and Charles Price Ridley, tr. *Rural People's Communes in Lien-chiang: Documents Concerning Communes in Lien-chiang County, Fukien Province, 1962-1963.* Stanford, Hoover Institution Press, 1969; 243 pp.

Ch'en, Kenneth K. S. *Buddhism in China: A Historical Survey.* Princeton, Princeton University Press, 1964; 560 pp.

China Notes. New York, 1962–

China Pictorial. Peking, 1951–

China Reconstructs. Peking, 1952–

China Quarterly. London, 1960–

Ch'iu Shih-chih 邱實之. "Chung-kuo ta-lu-ti seng-ni sheng-huo" 中國大陸的僧尼生活 (The life of monks and nuns in Mainland China). *Tsu-kou chou-k'an* 8.17:28–33 (Aug. 1, 1965).

Chūgai nippō 中外日報. Kyoto, 1957–

Chung-kuo hsin-wen 中國新聞 (The China news service). Canton, 1954–

Chung-kuo ta-lu fo-chiao tzu-liao hui-pien 中國大陸佛教資料彙編 (Sourcebook on Buddhism in Mainland China, 1949–1967). Hong Kong, Union Research Institute, 1968; 541 + 21 + 75 pp.

Chung-yang jih-pao 中央日報. Taipei, 1950–

Chüeh-hsün 覺訊. Shanghai, 1950–1955.

Chüeh-shih 覺世. Kaohsiung, Taiwan, 1957–

Chüeh yu-ch'ing 覺有情. Shanghai, 1950–1953.

Dalai Lama. *My Land and My People.* London, Weidenfeld and Nicolson, 1962; 255 pp.

Demiéville, Paul. "Le Bouddhisme et la guerre," *Mélanges* 1:347–385. Paris, Institut des Hautes Etudes Chinoises, 1957.

Fan-kung yu-chi-tui t'u-chi Fu-chien Lien-chiang hsien lu-huo fei-fang wen-chien hui-pien 反共游擊隊突擊福建連江縣擄獲匪方文件彙編 (Compilation of Communist documents captured by anti-Communist guerrilla forces in Lien-chiang hsien, Fukien). Kuo-fang-pu Ch'ing-pao Chü 國防部情報局 (Intelligence office of the Ministry of Defense), ed. Taipei, 1964; 278 pp.

Far Eastern Economic Review. Hong Kong, 1946–

Fontein, Jan. *The Pilgrimage of Sudhana: A Study of Gandavyūha Illustrations in China, Japan, and Java.* The Hague, Mouton and Co., 1967; 229 pp.

Franck, Harry A. *Roving through Southern China.* New York, 1925; 649 pp.

The Friendship of Buddhism. Chinese Buddhist Association, comp. Peking, Nationalities Publishing House, 1957; 160 pp.

Ganjin wajō keisan hōchū Nihon Bukkyō daihyōdan hōkoku 鑑眞和上慶讃訪中日本佛教代表團報告 (Report of the Japanese Buddhist delegation that visited China for the commemoration of Chien-chen). Tokyo, Zen Nihon Bukkyōkai, 1963; 44 pp.

Gendai Chūgoku jimmei jiten 現代中國人名辭典 (Biographical dictionary of contemporary China). Tokyo, 1966; 1209 + 22 pp.

DeGroot, J. J. M. *Sectarianism and Religious Persecution in China*. Amsterdam, Johannes Müller, vol. 1, 1903; vol. 2, 1904; 595 pp.

Handbook on People's China. Peking, Foreign Languages Press, 1957; 236 pp.

Hashikawa Tokio 橋川時雄. *Chūgoku bunkakai jimbutsu sōkan* 中國文化界人物總鑑 (Comprehensive dictionary of Chinese cultural personages). Peking, 1940; 815 + 28 + 12 + 8 pp.

Hayashi Reihō 林靈法. *Shin Chūgoku kikō* 新中國紀行 (A tour of the new China). Nagoya, 1957; 243 pp.

"Hōchū Nihon Bukkyō shinzen shi-dan hōkokusho" 訪中日本佛教親善使團報告書 (Report of a visit to China by the Japanese Buddhist Friendship Delegation), *Nitchū Bukkyō* 日中佛教 (Buddhism in Japan and China) 1.3:1–36 (May 20, 1958).

Hsiang-kang fo-chiao 香港佛教 (Buddhism in Hong Kong). 1960–

Hsien-tai fo-hsüeh 現代佛學 (Modern Buddhism). Peking, 1950–1964.

Hsin chien-she 新建設 (New construction). Peking, 1949–

Hsin-hua yüeh-pao 新華月報 (New China monthly). Peking, 1949–1955.

Hsin-wan pao 新晚報. Hong Kong, 1949–

Hsing-tao jih-pao 星島日報. Hong Kong, 1949–

Hsüeh-hsi 學習 (Study). Peking, 1949–1958.

Hung-hua yüeh-k'an 弘化月刊. Shanghai, 1950–1957.

International Buddhist News Forum. Rangoon, 1961–1963.

Jen-min jih-pao 人民日報 (People's daily). Peking, 1949–

Jen-min shou-ts'e 人民手册 (People's handbook). Peking, 1963, 1965.

Katsumata Shunkyō 勝又俊教. "Chūka Jimmin Kyōwakoku" 中華人民共和國 (The Chinese People's Republic), in *Bukkyō dainenkan* 佛教大年鑑. Tokyo, 1969; 1220 pp.

Kiang, Alfred. "A New Life Begins in the Temples," *China Weekly Review* 116.11:173–174 (Shanghai, Feb. 11, 1950).

Kuang-hui-ti pa-nien 光輝的八年 (Eight glorious years). Hong Kong, 1958.

Kuang-ming jih-pao 光明日報 (Kuang-ming daily). Peking, 1949.

Kung-fei pao-cheng chi-yao 共匪暴政紀要 (The facts on the cruel rule of the Communist bandits). Chung-yang Wei-yüan-hui Ti-liu Tsu 中央委員會第六組 (Kuomintang Central Committee Sixth Section), ed. Taipei, 1961; 820 pp.

Kung-shang jih-pao 工商日報. Hong Kong.

Li-shih yen-chiu 歷史研究 (Historical studies). Peking, 1954–

Mackerras, Colin and Neale Hunter. *China Observed*. New York, Frederick A. Praeger, Inc., 1967. 194 pp.

Makita Tairyō 牧田諦亮. *Chūgoku kinsei Bukkyōshi kenkyū* 中國近世佛教史

研究 (Studies in the recent history of Chinese Buddhism). Kyoto, 1957; 311 + 27 pp.

———"Gendai Chūgoku Bukkyō no seikatsu kihan" 現代中國佛教の生活規範 (The norms of Buddhist life in contemporary China), *Bukkyō Daigaku kenkyū kiyō,* no. 35, pp. 238–270, (Oct. 23, 1958).

———"Pekin no nisō tachi" 北京の尼僧たち, *Kaihō* 會報 no. 34 (March 10, 1959). Nishū Gakkō Kōyūkai 尼衆學校校友會, Kyoto, pub.

———"Rozan sampai ki" 廬山参拜記, *Shūkon* 宗懇 3:13–15 (January 1968).

Mao Tse-tung. *Selected Works of Mao Tse-tung*. Vols. I-IV. New York, International Publishers, 1954–1962.

Mibu Shōjun 壬生照順. "Jimmin Chūgoku no Bukkyō-o miru" 人民中國の佛教を觀る (A look at Buddhism in People's China), *Shinri* 眞理 27.9:6–10 (Tokyo, September 1961).

———"Chūgoku Tendai-san junreiki" 中國天臺山巡禮記 (Record of a pilgrimage to Mt. T'ien-t'ai), *Shūkyō kōron* 宗教公論 (Review of religions). Tokyo, 7/65, pp. 31–37; 8/65, pp. 42–47; 9/65, pp. 32–37.

Migot, André. "Situation des religions en Chine populaire: Bouddhisme et Marxisme," *Le régime et les institutions de la république populaire chinoise.* Bruxelles, Institut de Sociologie Solvay, 1960.

Min-tsu t'uan-chieh 民族團結 (Solidarity of national minorities). Peking, 1957–

Modern Buddhism, see *Hsien-tai fo-hsüeh.*

Nagel's Encyclopedia-Guide: China. Geneva, Nagel Publishers, 1968; 1504 pp. + plates.

Nitchū Yū-kō Daihyōdan 日中友好代表團 (Japanese-Chinese Friendship Delegation), ed., *Shin Chūgoku annai* 新中國あんない (Guide to the new China). Kyoto, 1966; 215 pp.

Nogami Shunjō 野上俊靜. "Shin Chūgoku no tabi" 新中國の旅 (A trip to the new China), *Chūgai nippō* 中外日報 (Kyoto, Aug. 21–23, 1957).

Ogasawara Senshū 小笠原宣秀. "'Kono mede mita' Chūgoku ikkagetsu no inshō" 'この眼で見た' 中國一月の印象("What I saw with my own eyes": Impressions of a month in China), *Chūgai nippō* (Kyoto, July 23, 1957).

Ohrui Jun. "A View of War in Buddhism," *Tōyō University Asian Studies,* no. 2:51–64 (Tokyo, 1964).

Ōtani Eijun 大谷瑩潤. *Shin Chūgoku kenmonki* 新中國見聞記 (What I saw and heard in the new China). Tokyo, 1955; 143 pp.

Payne, Robert. *Mao Tse-tung, Ruler of Red China.* New York, Henry Schumann, Inc. 1950; 303 pp.

Portisch, Hugo. *Red China Today,* Heinz von Koschembahr tr. Chicago, Quadrangle Books, 1966; 383 pp.

P'u-t'i shu 菩提樹 ("Bodhedrum"). Taichung, 1958–

Religion in Communist Dominated Areas. New York, 1962–

Richardson, S. D. *Forestry in Communist China.* Baltimore, Johns Hopkins Press, 1966; 237 pp.

Sarkisyanz, E. *Buddhist Backgrounds of the Burmese Revolution*. The Hague, Martinus Nijhoff, 1965; 250 pp.

Schmid, Peter. *The New Face of China*. London, G. G. Harrap, 1958; 167 pp.

Schram, Stuart. *The Political Thought of Mao Tse-tung*. New York, Frederick A. Praeger, Inc., 1969, 2nd rev. ed.

Sekino Tei 關野貞 and Tokiwa Daijō 常盤大定. *Shina Bukkyō shiseki* 支那佛教史蹟 (Buddhist monuments in China). Tokyo, 1925–29.

Shigenoi Satoru 滋野井恬. "Chūgoku nikki shō" 中國日記抄 (Diary excerpts on China). *Ōtani Daigaku shigaku* 大谷大學史學 (Ōtani University historical studies), Vol. 11 (November 1965).

Sourcebook, see *Chung-kuo ta-lu fo-chiao tzu-liao hui-pien.*

South China Morning Post. Hong Kong. 1949–

Sunderlal, Pandit. *China Today*. Allahabad, Hindustani Cultural Society, n.d.; 145 pp.

Ta-kung pao 大公報. Hong Kong, 1949–

Tai Chi-t'ao hsien-sheng wen-ts'un 戴季陶先生文存 (Writings of Tai Chi-t'ao). Ch'en T'ien-hsi, ed. 陳天錫. Taipei, 1959; 82, 16, 1776 pp.

Taishō shinshū daizōkyō 大正新修大藏經 (Taishō Tripitaka), ed. Takakusu Junjirō 高楠順次郎 and Watanabe Kaigyoku 渡邊海旭. Tokyo, 1924–1929; 55 vols.

Tokiwa Daijō 常盤大定. *Shina Bukkyō shiseki kinen-shū* 支那佛教史蹟記念集 (Buddhist monuments in China, memorial collection). Tokyo, 1931; 282 pp.

Tokuda Myōhon 德田明本. "Bunkaku ka no Chūgoku Bukkyō o miru" 文革下の中國佛教を見る (Seeing Chinese Buddhism under the Cultural Revolution), *Asahi shimbun* 朝日新聞 (Osaka, Oct. 22, 1967).

Ts'en Hsüeh-lü 岑學呂. *Hsü-yün ho-shang nien-p'u* 虛雲和尚年譜 (Chronological biography of the Venerable Hsü-yün), 3rd ed. Hong Kong, 1962; 427 pp.

Tsu-kuo chou-k'an 祖國週刊. Hong Kong, 1953–1964.

Tsukamoto Zenryū 塚本善隆 and Makita Tairyō 牧田諦亮. "Chūgoku hōmon-ki" 中國訪問記 (A visit to China), *Tōhō gakuhō* 東方學報 28:297–304 (March 1958).

Vogel, Ezra. *Canton under Communism: Programs and Politics in a Provincial Capital, 1949-1968*. Cambridge, Mass., Harvard University Press, 1969. 430 pp.

Welch, Holmes. "Buddhism under the Communists," *China Quarterly* 6:1–14 (April-June 1961).

———"An Interview with the Hambo Lama," Royal Central Asian Journal 49.2:172–182 (April 1962).

———"Buddhism in Crisis," *Life* (International Edition) 36.2 (Jan. 27, 1964).

———"Buddhism after the Seventh," *Far Eastern Economic Review* 47.10:433–435 (March 12, 1965).

———"The Reinterpretation of Chinese Buddhism," *China Quarterly* 22:143–153 (April-June 1965).

———"Changing Attitudes towards Religion in Modern China," in *China in Perspective*. Wellesley, Mass. 1967.

———*The Practice of Chinese Buddhism, 1900-1950*. Cambridge, Mass., Harvard University Press, 1967; 568 pp.

———*The Buddhist Revival in China*. Cambridge, Mass., Harvard University Press, 1968; 385 pp.

———"The Chinese Art of Make-Believe," *Encounter* 30.5:8–13 (May 1968).

———"Buddhism since the Cultural Revolution," *China Quarterly* 40:127–136 (October–December 1969).

———"Facades of Religion in China," *Asian Survey* 10.7:614–626 (July 1970).

———"The Deification of Mao," *Saturday Review* (Sept. 19, 1970), pp. 25, 50.

———"May Buddhists Kill?" *World Buddhism,* Vesak Annual (1971).

Wen-hui pao 文滙報. Hong Kong, 1948–

World Buddhism. Ceylon, 1950–

Yamada Mumon 山田無文. "Nanaoku no bosatsu" 七億の菩薩 (Seven hundred million bodhisattvas) *Shūkon* 宗懇, no. 1:1–2 (Tokyo, July 7, 1967).

Yang-ch'eng wan-pao 羊城晩報. Canton, 1950–

Yang, C. K. *Religion in Chinese Society*. Berkeley, 1961; 473 pp.

Yang, I-fan. *Buddhism in China*. Hong Kong, Union Press, 1956; 98 pp.

Glossary

This glossary includes only the more important names mentioned in the text.

ai-kuo kung-yüeh 愛國公約
an ko-jen ch'eng-fen, fen-p'ei t'u-ti 按个人成份, 分配土地
Andō Kōsei 安藤更生

Ch'a An-sun 查安蓀
chai-hsin 齋信
chai-t'ang 齋堂
Chang Chih-i 張執一
Chang Tung-sun 張東蓀
ch'ang-wu li-shih 常務理事
chao-p'ai ssu-yüan 招牌寺院
Chao P'u-ch'u 趙朴初
chen-k'uan 賑款
Ch'en Ch'i-yüan 陳其瑗
Ch'en Hai-liang 陳海量
Ch'en-k'ung 塵空
Ch'en Ming-shu 陳銘樞
Cheng Chen-to 鄭振鐸
Cheng-kuo 正果
cheng-shou 征收
Cheng Sung-ying 鄭頌英
cheng-ts'e yen-chiu-shih 政策研究室
Chi-kuang 濟廣
chi-t'i nung-ch'ang 集體農場
Ch'i-shan 琦山
ch'i-tao 祈禱
ch'iang-ling 强令
chiao-hui 教會
chiao-wu 教務
chiao-wu kai-ke 教務改革
chiao-ya pai-chung 焦芽敗種
chiao yang ping-chung 教養並重
chiao-yen shih 教研室
chieh-tai k'o 接待科
chien-ch'üan 健全
Chien-hsing 見性
chien-hsing t'ang 見性堂
chien-t'ao shu 檢討書
chih-hui 支會
Ch'ih-sung 持松
ch'ih-tan je-lieh, yüan-li chuang-yen 赤怛熱烈, 願力莊嚴
chin-kang nu-mu 金剛努目
Chin-kang Tao-ch'ang 金剛道場
Ching-ch'üan 靜權
Ching-kuan 靜觀
Ching-t'u shih-i lun 淨土釋疑論
ch'ing-chung 清衆
ch'ing-fei fan-pa 清匪反覇
ch'ing-sheng, sung-sheng 請聖送聖
chiu-ch'a tui 糾察隊
Chou Shu-chia 周叔迦
Chou T'ai-hsüan 周太玄
Chou Yüeh-ch'ing 周月卿
chu-p'o ts'ai 猪筐菜
chu-yüan 祝願
ch'u 處

ch'u-chang 處長
chuang-yen 莊嚴
chuang-yen kuo-t'u 莊嚴國土
Chung-kuo Fo-chiao Hsüeh-hui 中國佛教學會
Chung-shan chuang 中山裝
chung-sheng 衆生
ch'ung-pien 重編
Chü-tsan 巨贊
chüan-shui 捐稅
Chüeh-ch'eng 覺澄
Ch'üan-kuo Tsung-chiao Kung-tso Hui-i 全國宗教工作會議
ch'üan-kuo t'ung-yung liang-p'iao 全國通用糧票
ch'ün-chung 群衆

Erh-mai 二埋

Fa-fang 法舫
fa-hui 法會
Fa-tsun 法尊
Fan Wen-lan 范文瀾
fang-chang 方丈
fang-pien sha-sheng 方便殺生
Fang Tzu-fan 方子藩
fen-hui 分會
fo-chiao chiao-wu 佛教教務
fo-chiao chieh 佛教界
fo-chiao hsieh-hui 佛教協會
fo-chiao t'u 佛教徒
fo-hsüeh 佛學
fo-shih 佛事

Gelatsang 噶喇藏
gongyō 勤行

Ho Ch'eng-hsiang 何成湘
hsi-fan t'ang 稀飯湯
hsia-fang 下放
hsiang-mo 降魔
hsiang-tang chiao-hsin 向黨交心
hsiang-yu 香油
Hsiao Hsien-fa 蕭賢法
hsiao-tao 小道
hsiao-tsai 消災
hsieh-ming 邪命
hsieh-shang 協商
hsien-kung hou-ssu 先公後私
Hsin-ch'eng 新成
hsin, chieh, hsing, cheng 信, 解, 行, 證
hsiu-ch'ih tsu 修持組
hsiu-fu 修復
Hsü P'ing-hsüan 徐平軒
Hsü Ying 徐盈
Hsü-yün 虛雲
Hsüan-ch'ung 玄沖
hsüeh-hsi pan 學習班
hui-tao men 會道門
Hung-miao 弘妙
hung-yang fo-fa 弘揚佛法
huo-tien 火鈿

i chiang-mo-ti li-liang shih chih chiang-fu 以降魔的力量使之降伏
I-fang 義方
i-pan 一盤
i sha-sheng erh tso-fo-shih 以殺生而作佛事
i-tan 衣單

jen-chien 人間
jen-min fo-chiao hui 人民佛教會
jen-min pi 人民幣
jen-min tai-piao hui-i 人民代表會議

kai-ko fo-chiao 改革佛教
kan ching-ch'an 趕經懺
Kao Shan 高山
k'o 科
K'uan-chien 寬鑑
K'uan-neng 寬能
ko-hsin wei-yüan-hui 革新委員會
Kongō Shūichi 金剛秀一
kua-tan 掛單
kuan-ch'an 官產
kuan-li 管理
Kuang-chi Ssu 廣濟寺

kuei-yüeh 規約
kung-ch'an 公產
kung-hsing yin-cheng 功行印證
kung-yang 供養
kung-yu 公有
Kuo P'eng 郭朋

Lai-kuo 來果
lan shou-t'u 濫受徒
lang 浪
Lang-chao 朗照
li-ch'an 禮懺
Li Chi-shen 李濟深
Li Ching-wei 李經緯
li-hsing 理性
Li I-p'ing 李一平
Li Jung-hsi 李榮熙
Li Ming-yang 李明揚
li-shih hui 理事會
Liao-ts'an 了參
lien-ho hui 聯合會
lien-i hui 聯誼會
lien-jen 連任
Lin Chih-chün 林志鈞
lin-shin hu-k'ou pu 臨時戶口簿
ling-huo hsing 靈活性
Ling-yen Ssu 靈巖寺
Ling-yin Ssu 靈隱寺
Liu Chün-wang 劉俊望
Liu-jung Ssu 六榕寺
liu-tu 六度
Liu Ya-hsiu 劉亞休
luan 亂
lun-huan 輪換
Lung-lien 隆蓮
Lü Ch'eng 呂澂
lü-i yüan 律儀院

Mao-jan 貿然
mi-hsin ying-yeh 迷信營業
mi-shu k'o 祕書科
Miao-chen 妙眞
Miao-hua 妙華
Miao-yin 妙因
Ming-chen 明眞
mo shou 沒收
Nakano Kyōtoku 中濃教篤
nei-t'an 內壇
Neng-hai 能海
Neng-pen 能本
Ngawang Jaltso 阿旺嘉措
nien-fo 念佛
Nitchū Bukkyō Kenkyūkai 日中佛教研究會
Nitchū Bukkyō Kōryū Kondankai 日中佛教交流懇談會
Nitchū Bukkyō Kōryū Shinwakai 日中佛教交流親和會
nung-ch'an 農禪

O-mei-hsien ti-san-ch'ü t'e-pien-ts'un kung-so 峨嵋縣第三區特編村公所

pa chen-hsin chiao-kei tang 把眞心交給黨
pan-shih ch'u 辦事處
p'an-t'u 叛徒
Pen-huan 本煥
pen-k'o 本科
po-chou 般舟
pu-chu fei 補助費
pu-fei tien-t'ang 不廢殿堂
pu-shao k'un-nan 不少困難
pu-shih 布施
pu t'o-tang 不妥當
pu-tui 部隊

san pu-wu 三不誤
seng-lü 僧侶
Sesshū 雪舟
Sha Yung-ts'ang 沙詠滄
shan-chu 山主
Shang-hai-shih Fo-chiao Ch'ing-nien Hui 上海市佛教青年會
shang yin chih 傷陰隲
shen-ch'a tsu 審查組
shen-ch'üan 神權
shen-kun 神棍
shen-miao 神廟

sheng-ch'an tsu 生產組
Sheng-ch'üan 聖泉
sheng-huo fei 生活費
shih-chien wu-wo 實踐無我
shih-fang san-pao 十方三寶
shih-kung 師公
Shih Ming-k'o 石鳴珂
shih-wu wei-yüan-hui 事務委員會
Shirob Jaltso 喜饒嘉措
shou-chi 授記
shui-lu fa-hui 水陸法會
Shūkon 宗懇
Sōsei 荣西
ssu-an so-yu 寺庵所有
ssu-nien 私念
ssu-she 四攝
ssu-wu wei-yüan-hui 寺務委員會

ta-ch'e ta-wu 大澈大悟
ta-k'o 大課
Ta-pei 大悲
ta-p'o ch'ang-kuei 打破常規
ta-tao chieh-chi 打倒階級
t'ai-chi ch'üan 太極拳
T'ai-hsü 太虛
tan-chan hsin-ching 膽戰心驚
Tan-yün 澹雲
T'an-hsü 倓虛
t'an-yu 炭油
T'ang Sheng-chih 唐生智
T'ang Yung-t'ung 湯用彤
tiao-ch'a teng-chi tsu 調查登記組
t'iao-cheng 調整
tsai-chiao yen-chiao 在教言教
tsai yin-wei chih chung 在因位之中
ts'an-hsüeh 參學
ts'an-kan-che 參幹者
tsao, wan-k'o 早晚課
tseng 憎
tso 坐 (sit)
tso 作 (do)
tso fo-shih 作佛事
tso-t'an hui 作談會
tsung-chiao pu 宗教部
Tsung-chiao Shih-wu Tsu 宗教事務組
tsung-wu tsu 總務組
tsung-wu wei-yuan-hui 宗務委員會
ts'ung-lin 叢林
Tung Lu-an 董魯安
tzu-ching ch'i-i 自淨其意
tzu-chüeh-ti hsien-ch'u 自覺地獻出
tzu-liao shih 資料室
Tz'u-chou 慈舟
tz'u-pei 慈悲
Tz'u-tsang 慈藏

wan-fo pao-ch'an 萬佛寶懺
wan-wu 萬物
Wei-fang 葦舫
wei-jao-ti shui-lu fa-hui 圍繞的水陸法會
Wen-chiao She 文教社
wo-chih 我執
wu-ch'ing-ti 無情的
wu-shen 無神
wu-wei 無爲

Ya Han-chang 牙含章
Yang Ch'eng-sen 楊成森
Yang Shu-chi 楊叔吉
Yao Yü-p'ing 姚雨平
Yeh Ch'ün 葉均
Yeh Chung-t'ing 葉中亭
Yeh Kung-cho 葉恭綽
yen-chiu pan 研究班
yen-chiu pu 研究部
yen-chiu tsu 研究組
yen-su 嚴肅
Yin-kuang 印光
Ying-ch'e 映徹
Ying-tz'u 應慈
Yu Hsia 游俠
Yu Hsiang 游驤
Yu Yu-wei 游有維
yung tou-cheng-ti fang-shih 用鬭爭的方式
Yü Yü 虞愚
Yü Ch'eng 餘崢
Yüan-ying 圓瑛
Yüeh-t'ao 月濤

Index

This index covers only the text, not the appendices and notes.

Harvard East Asian Series

1. *China's Early Industrialization: Sheng Hsuan-huai (1884-1916) and Mandarin Enterprise.* By Albert Feuerwerker.
2. *Intellectual Trends in the Ch'ing Period.* By Liang Ch'i-ch'ao. Translated by Immanuel C. Y. Hsü.
3. *Reform in Sung China: Wang An-shih (1021-1086) and His New Policies.* By James T. C. Liu.
4. *Studies on the Population of China, 1368-1953.* By Ping-ti Ho.
5. *China's Entrance into the Family of Nations: The Diplomatic Phase, 1858-1880.* By Immanuel C. Y. Hsü.
6. *The May Fourth Movement: Intellectual Revolution in Modern China.* By Chow Tse-tsung.
7. *Ch'ing Administrative Terms: A Translation of the Terminology of the Six Boards with Explanatory Notes.* Translated and edited by E-tu Zen Sun.
8. *Anglo-American Steamship Rivalry in China, 1862-1874.* By Kwang-Ching Liu.
9. *Local Government in China under the Ch'ing.* By T'ung-tsu Ch'ü
10. *Communist China, 1955-1959: Policy Documents with Analysis.* With a foreword by Robert R. Bowie and John K. Fairbank. (Prepared at Harvard University under the joint auspices of the Center for International Affairs and the East Asian Research Center.)
11. *China and Christianity: The Missionary Movement and the Growth of Chinese Antiforeignism, 1860-1870.* By Paul A. Cohen.
12. *China and the Helping Hand, 1937-1945.* By Arthur N. Young.
13. *Research Guide to the May Fourth Movement: Intellectual Revolution in Modern China, 1915-1924.* By Chow Tse-tsung.
14. *The United States and the Far Eastern Crises of 1933-1938: From the Manchurian Incident through the Initial Stage of the Undeclared Sino-Japanese War.* By Dorothy Borg.

15. *China and the West, 1858-1861: The Origins of the Tsungli Yamen.* By Masataka Banno.
16. *In Search of Wealth and Power: Yen Fu and the West.* By Benjamin Schwartz.
17. *The Origins of Entrepreneurship in Meiji Japan.* By Johannes Hirschmeier, S. V. D.
18. *Commissioner Lin and the Opium War.* By Hsin-pao Chang.
19. *Money and Monetary Policy in China, 1845-1895.* By Frank H. H. King.
20. *China's Wartime Finance and Inflation, 1937-1945.* By Arthur N. Young.
21. *Foreign Investment and Economic Development in China, 1840-1937.* By Chi-ming Hou.
22. *After Imperialism: The Search for a New Order in the Far East, 1921-1931.* By Akira Iriye.
23. *Foundations of Constitutional Government in Modern Japan, 1868-1900.* By George Akita.
24. *Political Thought in Early Meiji Japan, 1868-1889.* By Joseph Pittau, S. J.
25. *China's Struggle for Naval Development, 1839-1895.* By John L. Rawlinson.
26. *The Practice of Buddhism in China, 1900-1950. By Holmes Welch.*
27. *Li Ta-chao and the Origins of Chinese Marxism.* By Maurice Meisner.
28. *Pa Chin and His Writings: Chinese Youth Between the Two Revolutions.* By Olga Lang.
29. *Literary Dissent in Communist China.* By Merle Goldman.
30. *Politics in the Tokugawa Bakufu, 1600-1843.* By Conrad Totman.
31. *Hara Kei in the Politics of Compromise, 1905-1915.* By Tetsuo Najita.
32. *The Chinese World Order: Traditional China's Foreign Relations.* Edited by John K. Fairbank.
33. *The Buddhist Revival in China.* By Holmes Welch.
34. *Traditional Medicine in Modern China: Science, Nationalism, and the Tensions of Cultural Change.* By Ralph C. Croizier.
35. *Party Rivalry and Political Change in Taishō Japan.* By Peter Duus.
36. *The Rhetoric of Empire: American China Policy, 1895-1901.* By Marilyn B. Young.
37. *Radical Nationalist in Japan: Kita Ikki, 1883-1937.* By George M. Wilson.
38. *While China Faced West: American Reformers in Nationalist China, 1928-1937.* By James C. Thomson Jr.
39. *The Failure of Freedom: A Portrait of Modern Japanese Intellectuals.* By Tatsuo Arima.
40. *Asian Ideas of East and West: Tagore and His Critics in Japan, China, and India.* By Stephen N. Hay.
41. *Canton under Communism: Programs and Politics in a Provincial Capital, 1949-1968.* By Ezra F. Vogel.
42. *Ting Wen-chiang: Science and China's New Culture.* By Charlotte Furth.
43. *The Manchurian Frontier in Ch'ing History.* By Robert H. G. Lee.

44. *Motoori Norinaga, 1730-1801.* By Shigeru Matsumoto.
45. *The Comprador in Nineteenth Century China: Bridge between East and West.* By Yen-p'ing Hao.
46. *Hu Shih and the Chinese Renaissance: Liberalism in the Chinese Revolution, 1917-1937.* By Jerome B. Grieder.
47. *The Chinese Peasant Economy: Agricultural Development in Hopei and Shantung, 1890-1949.* By Ramon H. Myers.
48. *Japanese Tradition and Western Law: Emperor, State, and Law in the Thought of Hozumi Yatsuka.* By Richard H. Minear.
49. *Rebellion and Its Enemies in Late Imperial China: Militarization and Social Structure, 1796-1864.* By Philip A. Kuhn.
50. *Early Chinese Revolutionaries: Radical Intellectuals in Shanghai and Chekiang, 1902-1911.* By Mary Backus Rankin.
51. *Communication and Imperial Control in China: Evolution of the Palace Memorial System, 1693-1735.* By Silas H. L. Wu.
52. *Vietnam and the Chinese Model: A Comparative Study of Nguyễn and Ch'ing Civil Government in the First Half of the Nineteenth Century.* By Alexander Barton Woodside.
53. *The Modernization of the Chinese Salt Administration, 1900-1920.* By S. A. M. Adshead.
54. *Chang Chih-tung and Educational Reform in China.* By William Ayers.
55. *Kuo Mo-jo: The Early Years.* By David Tod Roy.
56. *Social Reformers in Urban China: The Chinese Y.M.C.A., 1895-1926.* By Shirley S. Garrett.
57. *Biographic Dictionary of Chinese Communism, 1921-1965.* By Donald W. Klein and Anne B. Clark.
58. *Imperialism and Chinese Nationalism: Germany in Shantung.* By John E. Schrecker.
59. *Monarchy in the Emperor's Eyes: Image and Reality in the Ch'ien-lung Reign.* By Harold L. Kahn.
60. *Yamagata Aritomo in the Rise of Modern Japan, 1838-1922.* By Roger F. Hackett.
61. *Russia and China: Their Diplomatic Relations to 1728.* By Mark Mancall.
62. *The Yenan Way in Revolutionary China.* By Mark Selden.
63. *The Mississippi Chinese: Between Black and White.* By James W. Loewen.
64. *Liang Ch'i-ch'ao and Intellectual Transition in China, 1890-1907.* By Hao Chang.
65. *A Korean Village: Between Farm and Sea.* By Vincent S. R. Brandt.
66. *Agricultural Change and the Peasant Economy of South China.* By Evelyn S. Rawski.
67. *The Peace Conspiracy: Wang Ching-wei and the China War, 1937-1941.* By Gerald Bunker.
68. *Mori Arinori.* By Ivan Hall.
69. *Buddhism under Mao.* By Holmes Welch.

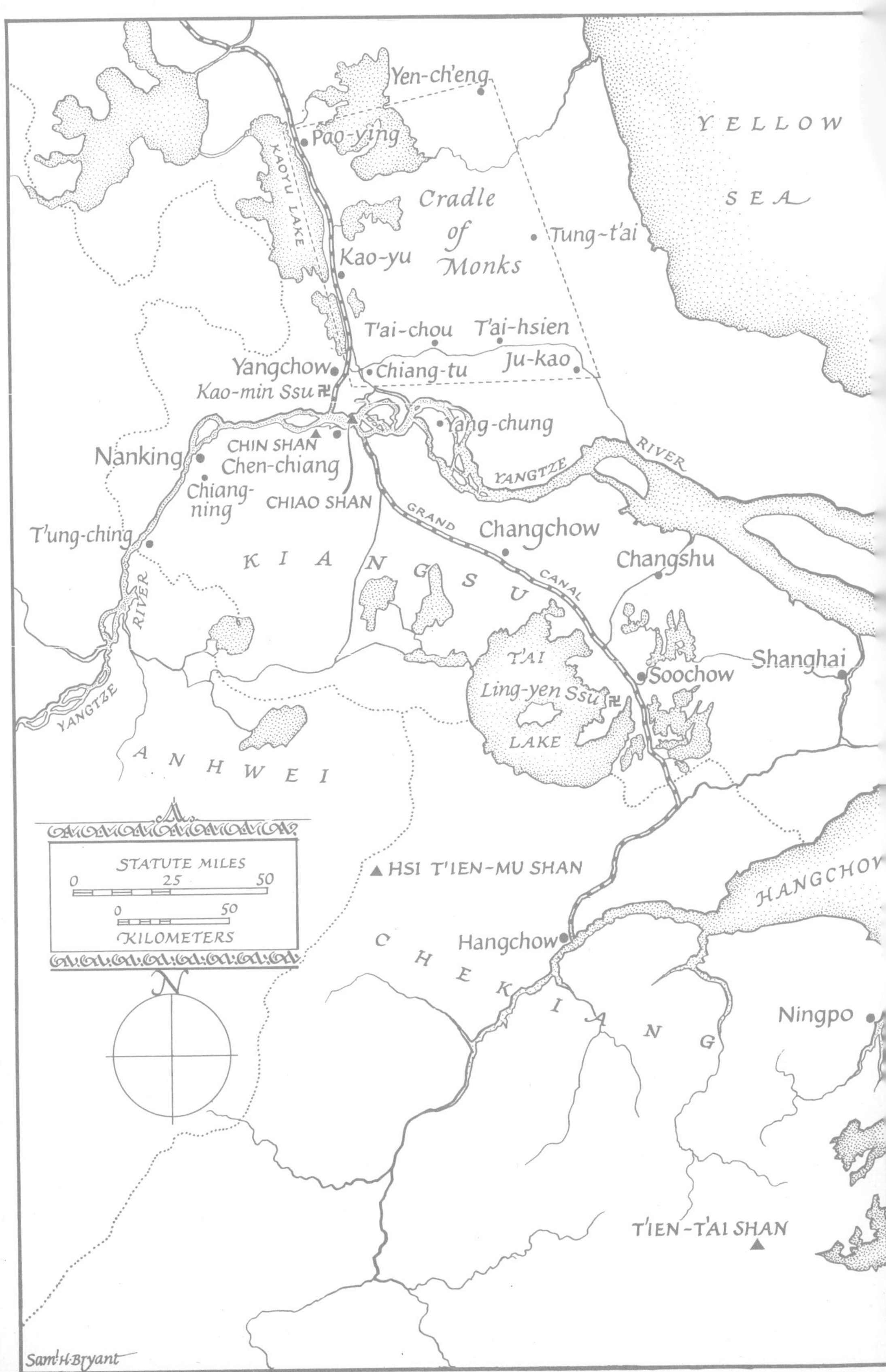
Yen-ch'eng
YELLOW
SEA
Pao-ying
KAOYU LAKE
Cradle of Monks
Tung-t'ai
Kao-yu
T'ai-chou
T'ai-hsien
Yangchow
Chiang-tu
Ju-kao
Kao-min Ssu
Yang-chung
CHIN SHAN
Nanking
Chen-chiang
RIVER
YANGTZE
Chiang-ning
CHIAO SHAN
GRAND
T'ung-ching
Changchow
KIANGSU
CANAL
Changshu
RIVER
T'AI
Shanghai
Soochow
Ling-yen Ssu
LAKE
YANGTZE
ANHWEI
STATUTE MILES
0
25
50
0
50
KILOMETERS
HSI T'IEN-MU SHAN
HANGCHOW
Hangchow
CHEKIANG
N
Ningpo
T'IEN-T'AI SHAN
Sam! H. Bryant